Understanding
World Religions

Understanding World Religions

A Road Map for Justice and Peace

Second Edition

David Whitten Smith
and
Elizabeth Geraldine Burr

ROWMAN & LITTLEFIELD
Lanham • Boulder • New York • London

Published by Rowman & Littlefield
A wholly owned subsidiary of The Rowman & Littlefield Publishing Group, Inc.
4501 Forbes Boulevard, Suite 200, Lanham, Maryland 20706
www.rowman.com

16 Carlisle Street, London W1D 3BT, United Kingdom

British Library Cataloguing in Publication Information Available

Library of Congress Cataloging-in-Publication Data

Smith, David Whitten, 1937–
  Understanding world religions : a road map for justice and peace / David Whitten Smith and Elizabeth Geraldine Burr.—Second Edition.
    pages cm
  Includes bibliographical references and index.
  ISBN 978-1-4422-2642-5 (cloth : alk. paper)—ISBN 978-1-4422-2643-2 (pbk. : alk. paper)—ISBN 978-1-4422-2644-9 (electronic) 1. Religions. 2. Religion and justice. 3. Peace—Religious aspects. 4. Church and social problems. I. Burr, Elizabeth Geraldine, 1950– II. Title.
  BL80.3.S65 2015
  201'.7—dc23
                                                              2014015014

Printed in the United States of America

Brief Contents

Detailed Contents

Preface

In 1987, the University of St. Thomas inaugurated a minor in justice and peace studies. We decided that it would be important to study how people's worldviews affect the choices they make that promote or inhibit justice and peace. At the time, our program was unusual. Not many people in this country understood why it would be not only useful but even essential to understand other people's worldviews. After the September 11, 2001, attacks on the World Trade Center and the Pentagon, the country started coming around to our point of view. In 1987, there was no textbook available to introduce what we wanted to talk about, so David Smith started to write one and shared it with his students in duplicated form over his twenty years of teaching the courses. Elizabeth Burr became the book's secondary coauthor for the first Rowman & Littlefield edition (2007), and together we have co-revised the text for the second edition (2015). Many other people have helped along the way. This book, now in its second edition, is the result.

In the course Theologies of Justice and Peace, for which this book was originally designed, in addition to reading and discussing this book, each student was asked to research one worldview that differs from her own, using a series of steps to organize her study. At the end of the semester, students read and discussed each other's projects. When we duplicated this book in its earlier forms for their use, we included in the book extensive instructions and other aids for that study project. Since we could not predict how many people would be interested both in the content of this book and in the instructions for such a project, we decided to put the instructions on the World Wide Web at http://courseweb.stthomas.edu/justpeace/Rowman .html. Here we will briefly describe what is available there.

DETAILED PROJECT INSTRUCTIONS
FOR STUDENTS AND FACULTY

Students are instructed how to study a worldview according to the following eleven steps:

1. Describe your own worldview and presuppositions by answering the nine sets of questions given. (Those steps are summarized in the introduction to this book.) This step will help you (a) to think about many things you have taken for granted, (b) to become aware of the variety in our own class, and (c) to accept and value our differences. The step is graded pass-fail.

2. Describe what you know as you begin your study: the worldview you have chosen to study, what you know or don't know about it as you start, what you want to find out.

3. Select a local resource to help you with your study, preferably someone who lives the worldview you are studying.

4. Experience the worldview through a vicarious experience—a narrative such as a novel, memoir, autobiography, film, play, interview, or foreign travel. We are looking here for stories, not yet for academic information or analysis.

5. From academic research, describe the main ideas and practices of the worldview, especially with regard to justice, peace, prosperity, and security.

6. List and describe briefly the main sacred books, classics, and traditions (including oral traditions) of the worldview. Read parts meditatively and report on the experience.

7. Describe how some real person has been influenced by the worldview in their work on behalf of justice and peace, or how some community living the worldview has responded in some real conflict. This step will consider what happens when one person or a group attempts to live out the worldview's ideals in the actual, messy world.

8. Rewrite your responses to the questions of step one as if you personally held the worldview you have been studying.

9. Write a utopia that would make sense to someone holding the worldview. What would a perfect world be like, why isn't the world like that, what is the best situation we might hope for in the real world (a "possi-topia"), and how might we move toward that better future?

10. Reflect on your study. Compare what you know and believe now with what you did in step 2 when you started. Did your study confirm your expectations, challenge, or surprise you? How helpful was your local resource of step 3? How could this course be improved?

11. Give us a list of the resources you used with comments for future studies indicating how useful each item was, and for what steps it was useful.

Extensive resource lists for the project: For the last twenty years, we have been assembling the annotated resource lists that our *students* have produced (step 11 above)—you can see *their* comments on books, periodical articles, websites, and more.

OTHER TREASURES ON OUR WEBSITE

Space limitations have prevented us from publishing everything we would like to share. Some of what didn't fit is already or will be available at our website.

- Two sets of maps showing Native American and Palestinian loss of land.
- Footnote lists for each chapter and a bibliography list, all with active hotlinks, so that one can read the book in front of the computer or notepad and jump quickly to materials mentioned in the footnotes and bibliography with a click of the mouse or a tap on the screen.
- Overflow topics that didn't fit and are mentioned in the text as available on our website.
- Expanded suggestions for further reading.
- Additional spokespersons for each worldview.
- An article David wrote that applies many of the things we talk about in the book; it is called "Inspired Authors and Saintly Interpreters in Conflict: The New Testament on War and Peace."
- An article Elizabeth wrote about Palestinian Christians, which supplements the content of chapter 8; it is called "Out of Palestine: Solidarity with a Displaced People."
- Further web links, study questions, additional diagrams and tables, photographs, and maybe even a PowerPoint presentation or two.

We will continue updating the second edition on the website.

WHAT IS NEW IN THIS EDITION?

As we revised the book for its second edition, we considered feedback from reviews submitted to the publisher plus other sources. We wanted to broaden the framework where possible, for example, in chapter 9, which is no longer strictly limited to a Christian perspective. In the introduction, we expanded treatment of nonreligious moral norms, and added a section on the counterfeit traditions deceitfully advocated by psychopaths. In chapter 5, we added sections on modernism and Islamophobia. In chapter 6, we discuss how indigenous cultures react to colonial evangelization, with special attention to the Lakota, Black Elk, who became a Roman Catholic catechist, and to Yoruba slaves in the Americas who combined their African beliefs with Roman Catholicism to create the syncretistic religions of Santería, Umbanda, Candomblé, and Vodou. In chapter 7, we added material on how Chinese religion has adapted to Marxism and survived. In chapter 8, we brought the Israeli-Palestinian struggle up to date. We added more Jewish and Muslim material to chapters 9 through 12. In particular, in chapter 12 we clarified how Judaism and Islam relate to the ten principles of communal force. Apart from these specific additions, the book has been thoroughly revised throughout.

A FEW ADMISSIONS

This book is not neutral; it does not treat war, peace, injustice, and justice "impartially." As Johan Galtung points out,[1] peace studies are similar to health studies—both go beyond impartial understanding. Doctors don't study medicine just because they find diseases intriguing; they want to cure people. We don't study worldviews just because they interest us; we hope that understanding them will help us further our work for justice and peace. Finally, we have tried to make the book interesting rather than comprehensive. We sincerely hope that you will find our work (even the second time) compelling but incomplete, so that you will be moved to explore on your own some of the areas we introduce.

The two of us come from different backgrounds with somewhat different perspectives, although we share significant common ground. David is a Roman Catholic priest with a doctorate in theology and a licentiate in sacred scripture. A covenant member of Servant Branch of the People of Praise (a Christian ecumenical charismatic community), he has studied in Rome and Jerusalem, and has traveled extensively to research sacred scriptures, religions, and movements for justice and peace through Europe, the Middle East, South Asia, Africa, the Caribbean, and Central and South America. He has served on a peace team in the occupied territories of Gaza and the West Bank. Elizabeth's formal religious background is Protestant Episcopal. Her doctorate is in the study of religion. In addition to introductory university courses in Christianity, especially the New Testament, she has taught "The World of Islam" numerous times, as well as several justice and peace courses. Since 1970, she has visited Israel-Palestine a number of times and is involved with others in seeking a just resolution to this conflict. She is also a trained Jungian analyst. Further background information for both will be available on our website.

ACKNOWLEDGMENTS

Many people have helped this book take its current shape. We express sincere gratitude to Tatha Wiley, who originally introduced us to Rowman & Littlefield. We are also especially grateful to Anne King, who wrote a large part of chapter 7 on Marxist worldviews, to Jack Nelson-Pallmeyer for his contribution to chapter 4 on Christian worldviews, and then in preparation for the book's second edition, to Edward (Ted) Ulrich for reviewing chapters 1–2, Susan Stabile for reviewing chapter 2, David Penchansky for reviewing chapters 3–4, and Samir Saikali for reviewing chapter 5. We are equally grateful to Ross Miller, our first edition editor at Rowman & Littlefield, for his editorial guidance, and now to Sarah Stanton for her expert oversight and patience during the process of revising the book as well as to Jehanne Schweitzer for her fine work as production editor. We appreciate the helpful comments of reviewers of the first edition: Prathiba Nagabhushan for the *International Journal on World Peace*, Carlo Filice for the *Journal for Peace and Justice Studies*, and Andrea Wisler and Bethany Haworth for the *Journal of Religion, Conflict, and Peace*. Others who have read and offered helpful comments on various chapters, who have taught the course the book was designed for, who have helped David out with his various study trips, or who in other ways have helped us gather significant material and experience contained in this book, include Zev Aeloni, D. C. Ahir, Fr. Antonio d'Agostino, A. T. Ariyaratne, Rev. Naim Ateek and others at Sabeel in Jerusalem,

Mubarak Awad, Kedar Bahadur Basnet, Fr. Tissa Balasuriya, Jeff Carlson, Dennis Carroll, Soraya Castro, William Cavanaugh, Michael Cullen, the late David Dellinger, Lorna Dewaraja, Rev. Noel Dias, Fr. Peter Dougherty, Rabbi Amy Eilberg, Jay Erstling, H. R. H. Chief Fonkem Achankeng I, Arun Gandhi, Giselle Garcia Castro, the late Fr. Rafael García-Herreros, the late Ira Gordon, the late Ned Hanauer, Linda Hulbert, the late Abp. Dennis Hurley, Fr. Diego Jaramillo, James Jennings, Michael Klein, Jonathan Kuttab, Carol Schersten LaHurd, John Landgraf, Martha Larsen, Ramu Manivannan, Orlando Marquez, Patrick Mawaya, Ashok Mehrotra, José Míguez Bonino, Fr. Hugo Montero, Fred Nairn, Michael Naughton, Leuben Njinya-Mujinya, Michael Novak, the late Arsham Ohanessian, Adil Ozdemir, Rev. George Palackapilly, Agapitos Papagapitos, Santiago Pérez Benitez, Fr. Aloysius Pieris, Vivek Pinto, Calvin Roetzel, the late Fr. Greg Schaeffer, Gerald Schlabach, Sylvia Schwarz, Juan Luis Segundo, Dr. Suniti Solomon, Padre Dagoberto Sotelo, Sr. Florence Steichen, Ahmed Tharwat, Cris Toffolo, Heidi Tousignant, Dr. Solomon Victor, Gerald Vizenor, Sr. Liz Walters, Ira Weiss, Susan Windley-Daoust, Fr. Alex Zanotelli, and Fred Zimmerman. We are grateful to colleagues in the American Academy of Religion, the Catholic Biblical Association, the International Peace Research Association, the Peace and Justice Studies Association, and the Society of Biblical Literature at the University of St. Thomas, the other University of St. Thomas in Rome (the "Angelicum"), the Catholic University of America, the École Biblique et Archéologique Française (Jerusalem), and the European Peace University (Stadtschlaining, Austria).

Elizabeth expresses sincere thanks to the Theology Department and the Justice and Peace Studies Department at the University of St. Thomas for a grant that enabled her to devote significant time to preparing the book's second edition.

And now the book is in your hands. We pray that God will help you to understand, appreciate, and put into practice whatever we have said that is true and helpful, and to overlook or ignore whatever we have said that is not.

David Whitten Smith
Elizabeth Geraldine Burr

Introduction

The Study of Worldviews

[Humans] expect from the various religions answers to the unsolved riddles of the human condition, which today, even as in former times, deeply stir [human] hearts: What is [a human]? What is the meaning, the aim of our life? What is moral good, what sin? Whence suffering and what purpose does it serve? Which is the road to true happiness? What are death, judgment and retribution after death? What, finally, is that ultimate inexpressible mystery which encompasses our existence: whence do we come, and where are we going?

—*Nostra Aetate*[1]

Talk about justice and peace can be frustrating when my worldview (set of presuppositions) differs radically from yours. Your comments may not even make sense to me. This is especially true for people from different parts of the world or from groups holding radically different religious or ideological beliefs. But many of the most difficult world conflicts seem to take place between such groups: Jews, Muslims, Christians, and Marxists in Israel-Palestine; Hindus, Muslims, and Sikhs in India and Pakistan; Hindus and Buddhists in Sri Lanka; Marxists and Christians in North Korea and Cuba; and so forth. Conflicts also occur between subgroups within a major worldview, for example, Protestants and Catholics in Northern Ireland, or Sunni and Shia Muslims in Iraq.

A *worldview* is an overall way of seeing and relating to the world we live in and any larger world that may be beyond our world. It asks about the meaning of what we experience and how we should respond to the people, forces, and things that surround us. This book seeks (a) to help you decide whether it is true that understanding other worldviews promotes justice and peace, (b) to help you learn the most basic elements of some worldviews you are likely to encounter as you pursue justice and peace, and (c) to teach you how to study other worldviews in a sympathetic way so that you can understand why others think, feel, and act the way they do, anticipate their actions, and perhaps enrich your own worldview.

1

We hope this book will reduce your fear of people whose views of the world differ from yours. We also hope it will encourage you to examine your own worldview more deeply so as to embrace those of its dynamics that promote justice and peace, and to resist or reshape those that promote self-interested privilege and violence. You may find that much of what you have presumed to be common sense held by all reasonable people is rather part of your own particular worldview and open to critical challenge. In multicultural societies, people disagree about what constitutes "common sense."

None of the worldviews featured here will be presented completely, but you can become aware of how worldviews influence other people's vision and judgment so that you will be less surprised by how they react. You will learn what needs to be investigated to clarify positions: what implicit claims and questions lie concealed beneath the surface of an argument, and what values are at stake in the answers to those questions.

This book will briefly explain seven influential worldviews: Hinduism, Buddhism, Judaism, Christianity, Islam, indigenous (mostly Native American with some attention to the Yoruba) religions, and Marxism (with some attention to Chinese religions). In chapter 8 we present the Israeli-Palestinian issue as a case study of worldviews in conflict. We also give special attention to Christian and other religious social teaching, liberation theologies, active nonviolence, and just war theories because they illustrate how religious beliefs influence attitudes and actions toward justice and peace.

TRADITIONS: GREAT, LITTLE, COUNTERFEIT, HIDDEN

What influences one's attitudes and actions is not necessarily the worldview that one *claims* to hold, but rather the worldview that one *actually* holds. People are often unaware of the difference between their alleged worldview and the actual principles that govern their actions. In addition, some people deliberately lie about their worldview and principles.

The **great tradition** denotes the way a particular tradition is *taught* by its most enthusiastic leaders and practitioners, *developed* by major writers and apologists (propagandists), and *expressed* in its sacred and classic texts. In contrast, the **little tradition** denotes the way many people—often only vaguely committed to the principles of a classic tradition—are *actually living out* the worldview. Little traditions tend to focus on immediate, short-term, individual desires and pleasures; great traditions encourage people to sacrifice those desires and pleasures in favor of deferred, long-term, socially shared goals.

In this book, the **counterfeit tradition** denotes the deceptive values and principles *falsely* claimed by some people to justify their actions—they don't actually believe in them or act on them; and the **hidden tradition** denotes the *actual* values, principles, and goals that motivate these deceptive actors. The last two terms are not commonly used, but their reality is enormously important for understanding world injustice.

Psychological research has challenged the popular notion that all humans have a conscience—a basic understanding of right and wrong—despite the different forms it might take in different people.[2] But just as some humans are born physically crippled or become crippled through an accident, some humans are born without *any* capacity to sense or understand what other people are feeling; others lose this capacity through accident, disease, or early traumatic life experience. They are as incapable of understanding what other people mean by "compassion" or "empathy" as a colorblind person is incapable of understanding what other people mean by "red" or "green." Normal people are usually unaware of these people's hidden tradition: the latter experience no doubts, no regrets, and no shame for anything they do. They lie constantly with no restraint and no emotion. They believe that they are exceptionally talented, although they seldom are. They still make choices on the basis of their (hidden) worldview, but that worldview takes no account of other people's feelings. Like a newborn infant, they simply seek whatever feels good to them with no attention to anyone else except insofar as others can meet their desires. Early in their lives, they become aware that most people are different, and they become adept at *pretending* to have compassion. But the contrast between what they say and what they do eventually reveals to perceptive people that they not only don't *have* compassion, they don't even know what compassion *means*. The most dangerous of these handicapped people are called *psychopaths*.

Some psychopaths become serial killers or other types of criminals. However, many succeed in hiding their handicap and gaining positions that promise wealth or power—especially in politics and business. They hide their handicap by using the moral language of accepted worldviews, but they distort the meaning of the words they use—words like *freedom* or *democracy*—creating a counterfeit tradition, and they do not act according to the values they claim to hold. Rather, they act according to their hidden tradition to gain what they want without regard for anyone else.

It would be comforting to think that these people are rare, but research reveals that 0.5 percent to 1 percent of humans are "essential psychopaths" by heredity, and about another 5 percent lose their capacity for conscience through brain injury, disease, toxic pharmaceuticals, or early childhood trauma.[3]

Sometimes these people succeed in taking control of a nation or culture, as happened in Nazi Germany and Stalinist Russia.[4] Their counterfeit appeals to widely held values can confuse ordinary people and lead them to cooperate with disastrous and criminal policies—aggressive war, repression, genocide. Another 12 percent of people can *suppress* their conscience (at least for a time) and cooperate with the psychopaths, believing that this is the only way to "get ahead" or have an influence on the actual world.[5] Once a culture has been captured by this 18 percent, a large share of the remaining population is likely to go along with the leadership because they accept as true the counterfeit tradition preached by the leaders, are confused by the distorted way that tradition is presented, and lack the self-confidence to resist the leaders. A famous series of psychological experiments by Stanley Milgram in the

United States in the early 1960s shows that most people will defer to people in authority, even against their own conscience, to an astonishing and frightening degree.[6] Likewise, the book *They Thought They Were Free* documents how Germans under Nazi rule failed to confront their leaders, whom they saw as "big people," whereas even the professionals among them saw themselves as "little people" who were not qualified to get involved in politics.[7]

Moral outrage at the true psychopaths is counterproductive, since they *really are incapable* of understanding how their actions affect other people. What a society needs to do is to *recognize* the situation (the falsity of the counterfeit tradition these leaders appeal to, and the influence of the hidden tradition that explains what is actually happening) and *refuse to cooperate* with their plans.

Full-blown psychopaths cannot be treated psychologically, since they don't believe that there is anything wrong with them. Treatment efforts just teach them new ways to manipulate ordinary people.

Fortunately most people still have a functioning conscience. Eventually, often after great suffering, they realize what is going on. Some then refuse to cooperate with the corrupted leadership, or even oppose it actively—at great personal cost. Others find safer ways to act inefficiently or interfere secretly, thus weakening the power of psychopathic evil.

While this book will make some reference to counterfeit and hidden traditions, it will primarily seek to understand the great traditions of major worldviews and to encourage people to act "creatively, compassionately, and nonviolently"[8] in line with the most positive characteristics of these traditions.

When one believes in a great tradition, one trusts the doctrinal teachings of that religion or worldview and acts on them. But many members of a religion, even some of those who carefully think through its implications, are not so sure that the great tradition is right. They act on what they think is *really* true—their little tradition—rather than on what they *are supposed to* think is true. *Psychopaths* cannot understand the rules at all—the rules seem like naïve nonsense to them—but they may appeal to the rules deceitfully to gain the support of ordinary people while violating those rules by their own actions.

RELIGIONS AND WORLDVIEWS

Some worldviews are called *religions*. Others, like Marxism and secular humanism, are not. Still, secular worldviews act like religions in many ways.

Most Westerners presume that they know what a religion is: it is something like Christianity, or Judaism, or Islam; it believes in something beyond the "ordinary"—in God or gods, some unseen Power or powers, something beyond common, everyday experience. Yet when Western scholars began studying "world religions," they found that many peoples don't even have a word for religion.

How much does a worldview like Hinduism have to be "like" Christianity to qualify as a "religion"? Is there any single "thing" that we might call Hinduism?

(Even the word "Hindu*ism*" was invented by Westerners.) For that matter, is there a single thing we can call Christianity? Rather than decide these questions, we will study "worldviews" as a more generic reality. We will consider several "dimensions" that are widely, if not universally, shared by worldviews, and we will presume that everyone in the world has (1) *at least some experience of something,* (2) *at least a shadowy sense of what they are experiencing,* and (3) *a preferred or habitual way of understanding and relating to whatever that is.*

As we carry out this study, we will keep in mind several questions that help focus our attention on how our worldviews affect how we act for justice and peace. More detail regarding the questions is available on our website.[9] Worldviews disagree over how to answer these questions:

1. Is there something about humanity as it actually exists that might help *explain* the persistence of war, oppression, torture, criminal activity, corruption, quarrels, and broken relationships? If so, what is it about humanity that has these effects, and what is the cause of this situation?
2. Depending on your answer to question 1, *what might be done* to respond to the real situation of humans? Can we make these changes for ourselves without outside aid? What kind of aid might we need?
3. Does an *invisible world* interact with our world of experience? Do spiritual powers care about us or answer prayers? Do we survive death?
4. How do we *decide what actions are good?* Through "secular" experience and study, divine command, the example of a religious leader, a personal relationship with God or other spiritual power, our own intuition, or "common sense"?
5. Why does *suffering* exist? Does it have any positive purpose? What should we do about it?
6. What is the *purpose of human life?* What is success? What brings happiness? How does this life relate to a possible future life?
7. What does *justice* mean? Equality? The freedom to keep what one has earned? Is justice for others as important as justice for oneself?
8. What can we be *secure* about or confidently control? How do we handle feelings of insecurity or powerlessness? Is it all right to maintain our security at the cost of someone else's well-being?
9. Are we primarily promoting or defending *goodness, justice, peace, freedom, security,* or *prosperity? For whom?* What should we be defending? *Can* we do so effectively, without causing more harm than good? Can *force or violence* be justified in their defense? Can *nonviolence* be equally or more effective?

THE SEVEN "DIMENSIONS"

In his book *The World's Religions,*[10] Ninian Smart proposes seven dimensions that are common to all or most religions.[11] They are not "pieces" of a religion or worldview as much as "viewpoints" or "aspects." As a material object has three "dimensions," and all three are dimensions of the same thing, so a religion or worldview has seven "dimensions." Rearranging Smart's order to make them easier to remember and to show connections between them, these seven dimensions are:

1. *Experiential and emotional*—people gain experience of life; some people have life-changing experiences.
2. *Social and institutional*—they seek out others with similar experiences and form groups for support; gradually these groups grow in size and complexity.
3. *Narrative or mythic*—within the group, they pass on their experiences in the form of stories.
4. *Doctrinal and philosophical*—as people ask questions about the experiences and the stories, they explain them rationally as best they can—some of the meaning cannot be expressed rationally, but must remain as expressed in the stories themselves.
5. *Practical and ritual*—if they understand their experiences to relate to powers or beings beyond visible, everyday experience, they work out concrete ways of relating to those powers or beings (for example, through liturgy or worship); they also work out formalized ways of relating to ordinary people and things (for example, social etiquette).
6. *Ethical and legal*—they decide what actions and way of life are appropriate to their experiences and their understanding of those experiences; they also develop laws to govern the communities they have formed.
7. *Material and artistic*—in living out the preceding six dimensions, they produce material things (buildings like temples, songs like hymns, visual arts, literature like drama and poems) that are appropriate to their experiences and their understanding.

In brief, people *have experiences* (1); *come together* with others (2); *try to share and understand* their experiences in story (3) and reasoned discourse (4); and seek to *live out* their experiences in solemn or sacred acts (5), ordinary acts (6), and the material facilities they create (7).

This order has a certain logical attractiveness and was probably the order in which the founders of the worldview and early converts to the worldview experienced these dimensions, but it is not the order in which many later followers experience them. Most people are "born into" a particular religion or worldview—socialized into it within their family. While they begin life with individual experiences, these are not the experiences most central to their parents' worldview. Perhaps the first dimension they experience is (6): "Johnny, don't do that!" When they ask why not, they are more likely to get a narrative (3) than doctrine (4), since they are too young for doctrine. They also experience the social (2), ritual (5), and material (7) dimensions before they understand the reasons for them. As they grow older, they may get a good dose of the doctrinal dimension (4) through some form of religious education before they finally (if ever) share the core experiences (1) that are the basis for all the rest.

When people who were born into a worldview do finally share the core experiences that underlie it, they find that everything has deeper meaning than they had realized—the rest "comes to life." Often they have to rethink it all. This is called "adult conversion"—not conversion from one worldview to another, but conversion of a person from a merely theoretical knowledge of a worldview to a deeply personal relationship with it.

Now let us look at each dimension in more detail.

EXPERIENTIAL AND EMOTIONAL DIMENSION

Many Westerners first encounter "mysticism" in a context of Far Eastern religious thought, perhaps through the New Age Movement, Hare Krishna, or Transcendental Meditation. Concepts like yogis, reincarnation, the illusory nature of everyday reality, "mind over matter," and astral projection are foreign ideas to the Western mind. Some are then surprised to hear that there is a long-standing and widely developed *Christian* mystical tradition[12] that *describes* experiences often similar to those recounted in Far Eastern traditions, while it *understands and explains* them differently. You can read about a variety of mystical experiences from many different traditions in *The Varieties of Religious Experience* by the American psychologist and philosopher William James.

Sociological Support

Impressed by James's book, the American sociologist-priest Andrew Greeley, in a national survey of 1,500 average Americans, added a few questions looking for mystics. He asked, "Have you ever had the feeling of being very close to a powerful spiritual force that seemed to lift you out of yourself?" He was astonished to find that 40 percent of his sample said "yes, at least once"; 20 percent said "several times"; and 5 percent said "often." He asked them how intense the experience was. Two-thirds of them put it at the top of a seven-point scale. He gave them a simple psychological test to see whether they were all "crazy." They came out healthier psychologically than any other group who had ever taken that test.

He was disappointed when some of his colleagues dismissed his results without discussion and he couldn't attract money for further research. He thought that a group showing superior psychological health who reported having mystical experiences was worth investigating. *Other* colleagues—professional sociologists—approached him quietly to ask whether he might be interested in *their* mystical experiences.[13]

Mystical Experience

Mystical experiences are hard to put into categories, but there are some characteristic types.

Numinous Experiences

One type has been called **numinous** experiences. The name comes from the Latin word *numen*, which refers to a local spirit believed to inhabit a brook, grove of trees, mountain, or other natural feature. Experiences of this sort bring us into contact with *a presence that (a) attracts us while, at the same time, (b) sending a thrill of awe or fear down our spines.* Picture yourself walking through a graveyard at two o'clock in the morning just as a shadowy shape rises from the ground. A number of Jewish prophets describe their visions in ways that seem to fit this type. Seeing God, Isaiah falls flat on his face crying, "Woe is me" (Isaiah 6:5). Paul falls to the ground when he sees a bright light and hears the voice of the risen Jesus, his expectations of arresting Christians in Damascus shattered (Acts 9:4; 22:7; 26:13f). Fear is not always the dominant element. Some numinous experiences are dominated by the feeling of love and joy. Still, there is a sense of contact with someone or something "different" or "Other"—something powerful that we don't control.

Pan-en-henic Experiences

Quite different is a mystical experience more typical of Hinduism, though not unknown among Christians.[14] In this experience, technically termed **pan-en-henic** (literally: "all-in-one"), the mystic feels herself united with all of reality. Far from feeling fear or awe in the presence of an *Other*, the mystic feels almost a loss of the sense of *self*, which can also be frightening. Many yogic exercises are designed to lead a person into a pan-en-henic experience. The yogis believe that such an experience shows us what the world is really like.

Shamanic Experiences

A third type of mystical experience is common among **shamans**. These are religious leaders who, either without willing it or through a deliberate vision quest, pass from this world to another, have experiences there that endow them with power, and then return to this world—often carrying the marks of the journey in chronic illness or woundedness. Having made that journey, they can use their power to help others. You will find accounts of shamans' visions in Native American literature, for example, the classic book *Black Elk Speaks*.[15]

"Born Again" Experiences

A fourth type is the "born again" experience of adult religious conversion, either into one's own religion or worldview, now seen in a new way, or into a completely new worldview. Typically, a surrender of faith leads to intense experiences of conviction and joy and to a new clarity about the meaning of doctrines that were previously "accepted on faith" without understanding. There are numerous Christian accounts of the "born again" experience, especially in Evangelical and Pentecostal literature. An example of the "born again" type outside of confessional church contexts is the Alcoholics Anonymous experience of surrender followed by group exploration of the "twelve steps," which suddenly take on new life and new power.

More Subtle Experiences

Many mystical experiences don't fit neatly into any of these categories. Even the 60 percent of people who answered "no" to Andrew Greeley's question may well experience feelings of a more subtle intensity that give meaning and justification to the worldviews they hold. Our deep convictions can be supported by emotions felt at the birth of a child, at the death of a friend, while walking in nature, during a religious ritual such as Communion at Mass or the singing of hymns, or when sitting quietly in prayer, perhaps in a holy place. Even such a simple feeling as the thrill of hearing our national anthem played during the Olympic Games grows out of and gives support to our commitment to each other as citizens of our nation.

If one has such experiences, and if—as is sometimes the case—they don't follow the usual rules of time and space, they may be difficult to describe to others. One usually begins by telling a narrative or myth, our third category below. But first, one may seek out others who have had similar experiences, leading them to create societies and institutions of like-minded people. This brings us to the social dimension.

SOCIAL AND INSTITUTIONAL DIMENSION

When people share a life-changing experience, they come together to support, encourage, and discuss it with one another. Their association eventually takes on concrete, institutional forms. Different worldviews produce different types of communities. Islam has been particularly well organized socially. It gives central importance to the *umma*, or religious community. Since for Muslims every aspect of life should be marked by submission to Allah, they see no reason to separate religion and state.

Institutional Forms within a Religion or Worldview

Religious groups organize themselves socially in a self-conscious way, since their sense of being in contact with a spiritual reality gives them a deep awareness of shared experience and moves them to come together for common worship. Different religious groups prefer different institutional forms. Many Protestant churches have a fairly democratic structure. The Roman Catholic Church has a monarchical international structure, although it is becoming more democratic at the local, parish level. But these are broad generalizations. Major churches change their structures over time, adapting them to local conditions.

Institutional leadership is not the only, or perhaps even the most important, kind of leadership in churches. There is also the leadership of sanctity and spiritual experience. Sufis, prophets, and saints may elicit more reverence than caliphs, chief rabbis, and bishops. Respected local churchgoers and activists may be more influential than imams, preachers, and pastors. Reflect on the social structures in whatever church or analogous group you belong to. What sorts of things are done in common? Who makes the *decisions*? Do the decision makers represent one particular group, age, sex, or race to the exclusion of others? Who has the most *influence* on others? In what ways do members depend on each other and relate to each other?

Relation between Religion and Society

Typically, in primitive societies the entire tribe shares the same worldview. No one asks how the tribal society relates to the larger society, because there is no larger society other than external tribes, which are seen as foreign.

More complex societies may have an official religion, albeit challenged by alternative worldviews; the society may see itself as religious but not committed to a particular religion; or it may think of itself as indifferent to religion—leaving religion to the "private sphere." But societies are never indifferent to worldviews as such: even societies that treasure separation of church and state have widely accepted principles or ideals that derive from a worldview, although that worldview may be unexpressed and unconscious. The conviction that separation of church and state is valuable and necessary is itself a value judgment deriving from a particular way of seeing the world. So is the conviction that citizens should be ready to fight to defend the state.

A worldview or religion may see itself as the dominant faith in one geographic area, as one among many in another area, and as an embattled outsider in a third. Islam is dominant in Muslim-majority countries such as Egypt and Saudi Arabia, influential in India, and marginal in the United States, though less marginal than it used to be. Some religions or groups are not large enough to be dominant or even major actors anywhere. These are groups such as the Amish, often called "sects" or (by those who are hostile to them) "cults." They relate to society defensively, doubt that they can have much influence on the larger society, and fear the influence the larger society may have on them. Major religions are so extensive that they dominate large areas of the world. These are the so-called world religions, most of which we are studying in this book. Liberal Protestants are an example of a subgroup within a major religion that actively tries to influence the larger society without fearing that the society will overwhelm them.

In general, religions and other voluntary associations (such as Alcoholics Anonymous, the Freemasons, Marxist parties, justice and peace groups) both influence the larger society and are influenced by it. The question of whether such groups are more "democratic" or more "monarchical" illustrates how church structures are influenced by secular structures. Reflect on your own experience and consider to what extent your church or similar group has felt self-confident or threatened in relation to the larger society. Does your church try to *conform* to the larger society—

"to fit in"? Does it try to *influence* or change the larger society? Does it prefer to *separate* from the larger society?

Influence of Religious Structure on Members

Religious and analogous groups aim *consciously* to encourage and influence their members. They also influence their members *unconsciously* by the structures they adopt. Sometimes these structures act against their conscious efforts: exhortations to love can be ineffective in a structure of dominance and special privilege, as was true of colonial churches in Africa. It is important to examine whether the *structures* of a particular group reflect and encourage the *ideals* preached by that group.

NARRATIVE OR MYTHIC DIMENSION

Narrative of an Experience

After a mystical experience, how does one describe what happened? In his book *Life after Life*, Raymond A. Moody tells about a woman who became frustrated because she had only "three-dimensional words" with which to describe her near-death experience even though the experience was more than three-dimensional.[16] In *I Have Met Him: God Exists*, André Frossard writes, "All these impressions which I find it so hard to translate into the deficient language of ideas and images occurred simultaneously and were so telescoped the one into the other that after many years I have not yet been able to digest all they contained."[17] After his final vision, Thomas Aquinas quit writing entirely. Still, people narrate as well as they can. People's stumbling narratives are understood best by those who have had similar experiences.

Myth

Beyond describing the *experiences*, people want to describe the *kind of world that might explain* such experiences. Often narrative and poetry are better suited to describe the indescribable than academic discourse is.

Modern Westerners tend to use "myth" to mean "false," for example, the "six myths" of good health, or the "five myths" of weight loss. In this book we are using the term in a different sense. Theologically, myths intend to express truth. Some myths succeed and some fail, just as some scientific theories succeed and some fail. In *Worldviews*, Ninian Smart defines a "myth" as "a story of divine or sacred significance."[18] Scholars of religion like Ernst Cassirer or Mircea Eliade point out that myths are not just *literary* products, although we often meet myths, like those of Greece and Rome, in written form from the past. Native American tribal societies *act out* myths in sacred poetry, song, and drama. Through the Mass or the Lord's Supper, Christians act out, in sacred readings, song, and drama, the myth of the death and resurrection of Jesus, a myth that they believe is grounded in history and yet transcends history.

Committed participants believe they come into contact with sacred power through the ritual celebration of a myth. They overcome the normal limitations of time and space to encounter personally the primal energy of an ancient event, or of a reality that can only be expressed by nonhistorical narratives. Thus Christians encounter the power of Jesus' resurrection at the Lord's Supper, the power of creation in the Easter vigil, the power of God to transform humans in baptism. Other myths try to explain how the physical and spiritual reality we live in came to be (creation), where human sin and evil came from ("original sin"), and how history as we know it will end (eschatology).

In his book *Myths and Realities*, John McKenzie discusses myths in relation to biblical narratives such as the creation and flood stories. Speaking of myths and mythmaking in general, he points out that *myth intends to express truth, but through symbolic forms of expression*. It tries to represent an insight into a reality that cannot be expressed logically. Myth deals with basic questions of importance to all humans that lie deeper than the things we can touch and see: questions like the nature of God or spiritual forces; the purpose, direction, and goal of human existence; the origins of the world, of humans, of sin and evil, of human institutions; how humans relate to spiritual being, to physical nature, to each other. Myth does not "solve" these problems. Rather it suggests to humans what *attitude* they should take in the presence of such mysteries.

Four Characteristics of Myth

McKenzie outlines four characteristics of mythic language and thought:

1. Myth does not expect to *understand* what is unknowable. Instead it expresses the unknowable in symbols taken from experience. What is expressed is an intuition rather than a "fact."
2. Myth believes that the events we see are controlled and energized by a divine or spiritual background that is personal. Believers in the myth do not see it as a "personification" of natural forces. That is, they do not speak of it *as if it were* personal because the events we see *look* personal; rather they believe that the events we see *are* the way they are *because the background is* personal.
3. Myth does not deal with normal historical events (events that happen in a certain time and place), but rather with timeless realities in the "eternal Now" of the spirit world, which is the source of the recurrent events we observe. Even the death and resurrection of Jesus, which in one respect can be fixed in history, in another respect is seen by Christians as timeless and eternally effective because it is an action of God, who is outside time.
4. Sometimes different myths seem contradictory, not because one of them is wrong, but because no single myth can express the full reality. Several myths are used to try to embrace the reality. They may contradict each other on the surface level of signifier, but not on the underlying level of what is being signified.[19]

Modern American Secular Examples

All of this may seem remote to secular people who don't believe in a spirit world. But before such people decide they are superior to "primitive" mythmakers, they might ask themselves what stories they tell each other, and what those stories mean to them. Why do Americans repeat stories about George Washington "unable to tell a lie," "honest Abe" Lincoln, and victorious General Eisenhower? Do these stories express what Americans are like? And by what sort of "causality" might Americans share in the abilities and virtues of their heroes?

Similarly, when we speak of success and the purpose of life, what message do we give and receive from the programs we watch on television—dramas like police and spy shows, "reality" shows, and confrontational talk shows? What attitude do we take in the face of opposition? That evil is a temporary mistake caused by a few stupid or evil people, and that strength and cunning will enable us to restore good by destroying those evil people? If so, we are illustrating what the theologian Walter Wink calls the "myth of redemptive violence."[20]

In short, narratives and myths are one way a community passes on its combined experience to the next generation and reinforces its common understanding of what reality is like. If a person gives no attention or authority to the myths and narratives of her tradition (in psychological terms, to the unconscious), she reduces her understanding of reality to the narrow range of experience that she herself can have. At the same time, we need to be critical of the myths of our own society and culture, recognizing that they are but one set of myths, different from those of other peoples though sharing archetypal features, and equally likely to mislead if taken literally. Prophets challenge myths of their own societies in the name of what seems to them to be a higher authority.

Ritual Enactment of Myths

Finally, how do we act out our myths? Think of public events marking national holidays, major political demonstrations, memorial remembrances of national figures like Martin Luther King Jr., ticker-tape parades for triumphant generals, postage stamps showing national symbols like the Statue of Liberty, anniversaries of historically significant events, and Olympic victories that reinforce our sense of superiority. The acting out can go beyond mere ceremony. It can bring us into contact with a power capable of blessing us or saving us from danger. This aspect of myth leads us to the practical and ritual dimension, which we will discuss shortly. But first, consider another response to religious experience. Such experience gives rise to many questions, to which people seek rational answers as far as possible. The response to that quest is the doctrinal dimension.

DOCTRINAL AND PHILOSOPHICAL DIMENSION

Doctrine is a shorthand way of expressing the meaning of religious experiences and narratives. It has several functions: (a) it attempts to explain as clearly as possible what our experiences and our narratives mean; (b) by expressing the worldview in as brief and clear a form as possible, it helps us to articulate and pass on to others our new vision of the world; (c) it helps us to see how the different parts of our worldview relate to each other and tries to resolve apparent inconsistencies; (d) it helps us to judge which new ideas and which new explanations of the worldview succeed in expressing, or at least do not do violence to, the central experiences and insights of the worldview; (e) it helps us to relate the worldview to new questions and new ideas in the larger society around us; (f) it helps us to know who is a member of the community and who is not.

When one understands the doctrine of a particular worldview, one is in a position to understand why its members act in the ways they do. That is, doctrine influences ritual, ethics, and the social and material shape of the culture that the worldview generates. There is a classic saying in medieval theology: *lex orandi, lex credendi*. It means that the way we pray (ritual) reveals what we believe (doctrine). This is true even of psychopaths, if one realizes that they are acting on the doctrines of their *hidden* tradition rather than on those of the counterfeit tradition which they purport to follow. So let us consider how doctrine shapes ritual.

PRACTICAL AND RITUAL DIMENSION

Ritual deals with actions that are in some way particular to a worldview; they are not just generic human actions like sleeping, waking, eating, and so on. They are generic human actions that are done *in a particular way* as a result of a particular worldview. For example, the Zen Buddhist tea ceremony, which differs from a suburban career woman's microwaved morning tea, assumes the character of a ritual. The meaning of a particular ritual depends on the worldview within which it is performed. When we think of rituals, we are most likely to think of prayer or public liturgical worship, which are forms of ritual common to Jewish, Christian, and Muslim worldviews. In these religions, prayer and liturgical rituals enact conversations with God or other spiritual beings.

Sacrifice

Animal and vegetable sacrifice is—or was—a widespread ritual practice among humans. Since it seems foreign to many of us today, it is useful to examine its meaning. Sacrifice is usually considered to be a gift given to God or other spiritual beings. The primitive view is that valuable things can be transferred over from this world to the spirit world in a variety of ways. Fire seems a divine medium for such exchange, since it is capable of turning solid, material things into spiritual substance. Killing an animal is another way to transfer value over to the spirit world, since death frees the soul, considered to be the most valuable part of the animal, from matter.

Worshipers transfer gifts to the spirit world in order to develop and maintain a relationship with God and spiritual beings. While to some people such gift giving may look like bribery, at its best it is an attempt to build a relationship of caring and trust: I show my good disposition to God by offering things of value in the confidence that God, now well disposed to me and by nature good, will meet my needs or desires. To create such a relationship, I must not be cheap or deceitful in my gifts. The offerings must be "spotless," of good quality, such as I might offer to people of influence in human affairs. "First" things are especially valuable (first-born animals, the first armful of harvested grain) because the first symbolizes and stands for the whole. When I offer the "first," I am symbolically offering everything to God. More generally, rituals within many worldviews also offer God *nonmaterial* gifts: praise, obedience, service, time, and attention in prayer.

Festivals and Sacred Times

Rituals also celebrate sacred times: annual or recurrent celebrations commemorating key events whose power continues to reverberate in the community. Examples include Jews celebrating their rescue from bondage in Egypt at Passover and their reception of the Law of Moses at *Shavuot* (Jewish Pentecost); Christians celebrating the birth of Jesus at Christmas, his resurrection at Easter, and the descent of the Holy Spirit at Christian Pentecost; Muslims celebrating the initial revelation to Muhammad during Ramadan, etc.

The significance of an event depends on the particular meaning that event has for the community celebrating it. The original historical event takes on a mythical aura, which carries its symbolic power down into the present time. For example, Jews celebrate the establishment of the state of Israel in 1948; Palestinians recall the same event as *al-Nakba*—the catastrophe—because for at least 750,000 Palestinians it meant the loss of their homes, farmlands, and country. Similarly, Protestants of Northern Ireland annually celebrate their victory in the Battle of the Boyne (1690) by marching through Catholic neighborhoods; the Catholics experience these victory parades as humiliating.

Rituals and Power

If rituals can reenact historical events, they can also act out ahistorical myths. Native American tribal societies act out myths in sacred poetry, song, and drama. Through the Mass or the Lord's Supper, Christians act out, in sacred readings, song, and drama, the myth of the death and resurrection of Jesus, a myth that they believe is grounded in history and yet transcends history.

Committed participants believe they come into contact with *sacred power* capable of blessing them or saving them from danger when they celebrate a myth. Through ritual, they overcome the normal limitations of time and space to encounter personally the primal energy of a historically ancient event, or of a reality that can only be expressed through nonhistorical narratives. Thus Christians believe they encounter the power of *Jesus' resurrection* at the Lord's Supper, the power of *creation* in the Easter vigil, the power of God to *transform humans* in baptism.

ETHICAL AND LEGAL DIMENSION

How we choose to act depends on what we think the world is like, that is, on our doctrine. We understand that our actions have consequences. If we think, as some spiritual Hindus do, that the world is an illusion that perpetuates suffering, we choose actions that separate us from the world. If we think, as some monotheists do, that a punitive God is watching our every move and comparing it with a list of rules, we choose to follow the rules. Religious people think through the implications of their beliefs for action and express the results in moral judgments and laws.

Some religions base their laws and moral judgments closely on the original mystical experiences of the group. They speak of "divinely revealed laws." Muslims make this claim for the Quran, Jews make it for the Law of Moses (especially the core of the law as expressed in the "Ten Commandments"), and Christians make it for the teachings of Jesus of Nazareth as represented in the New Testament Gospels.

"Divinely revealed" laws may or may not seem reasonable. If we act against the law of gravity by stepping out of a skyscraper window, there are rapid and obvious consequences. If we act against the arbitrary rules of someone bigger than we are, the consequences depend on whether that person is watching. Yet the divinity that is revealing the laws may be warning us of natural consequences that we cannot see with our limited vision.

In general, we are more likely to follow laws willingly if they make sense to us. If all we perceive is the law and the authority that punishes lawbreakers, we may follow the law but do so resentfully. In the former case, our motivation is **intrinsic**; in the latter case, it is **extrinsic**. Social research shows that extrinsic motivation *reduces* a person's eagerness to do what the motivator is encouraging, even when that action is intrinsically attractive. Low grades and ridicule discourage students, but high grades and gold stars *also reduce* students' eagerness to read, question, and learn in comparison with those who are not being *extrinsically* motivated—extrinsically motivated students forget the excitement of learning and instead study mainly for grades. Young children are always asking, "Why?" By the time they are in college, they ask, "Will that be on the test?"[21] Religious founders, leaders, and sacred texts often say we will be rewarded and punished for our actions, but the founders themselves and their immediate followers weren't primarily motivated by rewards and punishments. They just fell in love with God, goodness, beauty, compassion, and truth for their own sake. Saint Augustine expressed his conviction that God's commands make sense when he said, "Love God, and do what you want." He did not mean that by loving God you can get away with anything, but that when you love God you end up wanting what God wants.

Nonreligious Moral Norms

Trying to avoid the sense that our laws are just the arbitrary whims of some God, and trying to avoid moral arguments between people of different religions, secular thinkers have proposed nonreligious moral norms based on their own worldviews. Thus these "secular" norms, too, depend on the worldviews of those who developed them. Still, it is useful to consider some of the norms they suggested.

Kant's Categorical Imperative

The German philosopher Immanuel Kant (d. 1804) judged acts to be morally good when they are *motivated by a sense of duty*. He developed a principle that he called the "**categorical imperative**." It has two parts: (1) we must act in such a way that our action could be a universal law for everyone; and (2) we must treat other human beings as ends in themselves, never as a means to something else.

Utilitarianism: Bentham and Mill

Liberal social reformers Jeremy Bentham (d. 1832) initiated and John Stuart Mill (d. 1873) further developed a system that Mill named "**utilitarianism**." Actions are good because they are useful, as judged by their consequences ("consequentialism"), principally because they *promote happiness and prevent pain. So the norm for good actions is whatever brings the greatest good to the greatest number of sentient beings—humans and animals.* From these principles, Bentham and Mill argued for separation of church and state, and against limitations on individual and economic freedoms (especially freedom of expression—free speech and press), against slavery, the death penalty, physical punishment of children and adults, the subordination of women, and cruelty to animals. They accepted humans' use of animals for food and for medical experimentation so long as pain to the animal was avoided as much as possible.

In his "calculus" for determining what pleasures and pains cause happiness and unhappiness, respectively, Bentham took account of how intense the pleasures or pains were, how long they lasted, how many people they affected, and—if they were expected in the future—how certain they were, and how soon they might appear. Bentham refused to value some types of pleasures above others, but Mill ranked pleasures by their quality and category: physical or mental—for example, the taste of good beer or the delight of intellectual discovery. Only those people who were capable of experiencing both types of pleasure—such as good beer and intellectual discovery—could rank them. For this reason, some critics accused Mill of class prejudice.

To apply utilitarianism, we need to predict what will cause happiness and pain. Do actions that increase one's possessions cause happiness? Possessions by themselves are neutral. It is how they are used that determines whether they increase

human happiness. Furthermore, the amount of human pain or happiness contributed by an object or action is difficult to predict. Recent research shows that humans
are not very good at predicting what will make them happy. We regularly exaggerate
the *degree* of happiness or sadness that various imagined situations will produce,
and the *length of time* that those feelings will last. The bad news is that we will not
be as happy as we imagine if we actually win the lottery, buy that new product, or
get married, nor will our happiness last as long as we expect it to. The good news is
that we won't be as devastated as we expect to be if we actually get fired, fail that
test, or experience the death of a family member or close friend, nor will our grief
last as long as we expect it to.[22] Advertisers try to convince us that what they are
selling will make us happy. A quick look at what we have abandoned in our closets,
attics, or garages may leave us wondering.

It is also difficult to *compare* the relative happiness we will experience from different situations. Which causes more human happiness: material, social, artistic, intellectual, or spiritual goods? Who causes more human happiness, a volunteer at a
food shelter or a tutor who helps children? In order to answer these questions, one
has to consider societal values and moral ideals, both of which vary from person to
person and from group to group. For these reasons, utilitarian principles may need
to be supplemented by other social and religious criteria.[23]

A final, serious problem is how to judge a case in which some people benefit at
the expense of other people. Is it right to torture people, knowing that some of them
are probably innocent, in order to save a large group of people? This is not a fair
criticism of Bentham and Mill, who explicitly condemn slavery, but rather of the
way their principles could be applied. Note that Kant would say "no": torturing a
few innocent people to bring good to others is using them as the means to an end,
not as ends in themselves. This is not an abstract question, since many governments
routinely use torture to combat what they describe as rebellions that threaten the
"common good," even though torture is illegal in almost all countries of the world.
After the terrorist attacks of September 11, 2001, the "Patriot Act" expanded the
power of the U.S. government to arrest and hold suspects without charge. Supporters argue that these limitations on basic human rights are necessary to combat terrorism. Critics may see this stance as a "counterfeit tradition" hiding the true,
hidden aims of supporters, and they may point out that such arguments led to the
abuses at Abu Ghraib in Iraq and Guantanamo in Cuba.

John Rawls's Thought Exercise

Concerns like these led the American philosopher John Rawls (d. 2002) to take a
different approach. Although Mill was confident that utilitarianism would condemn
slavery, Rawls was not convinced that it would. He proposed that justice should
guarantee fairness for everyone. Noting that human wealth is produced through
cooperation, and that much poverty and suffering is caused not by direct attacks
but by the flawed collective structures under which we live—our constitutions,
institutions, laws, and traditions—he asked how people of different worldviews

might agree on structures that all could live under. It is unreasonable and ineffective to force people to change their worldview, or to live under structures that violate their deepest-held beliefs. To be sustainable, the basic structures of a society should be seen as fair by those living under them.

Rawls suggested a moral thought exercise that can help us create structures that are more just and that satisfy people of differing worldviews. To ensure impartiality, *imagine* that you are part of a group designing a new society from an "original position." That is, you are not now a member of that society, but you will become a member of it—only you don't know in advance who you will be in that society: you are working behind a "veil of ignorance." You don't know whether you will be religious (and if so of what religion) or atheist, white or black, male or female, highly talented or marginally competent, rich or poor, healthy or ill, young or old, employed or unemployed. Now, what kind of political, economic, educational, and health care systems would you design?

Rawls maintained that, under such conditions, reasonable people would design systems that would assure them of a decent life no matter where they ended up in the new society. Thus among various "candidates" for a system, they would choose the one that gives the best possible life to people on the bottom. One might imagine that an equal sharing of wealth would be the top choice, but experience shows that people work harder, and highly talented people are more willing to accept difficult and challenging positions, when they get some personal return for their work, so a system that rewards hard work and responsibility produces more wealth to share. It can be designed to provide more even for those on the bottom who can't work.

Rawls concluded that reasonable people would develop these two "principles of justice": (1) everyone should have extensive basic rights as long as those rights do not deny the same rights to others, and (2) certain positions and offices should be allowed to offer social or economic advantages over other people (inequality) as long as (a) those positions are equally available to all who are equally qualified, and (b) allowing those advantages will provide the best results for "the least advantaged members of society."[24]

Human Rights

Both Bentham and Mill rejected "natural rights" on the grounds that no one can agree on what they are. Bentham and Mill also argued that such supposed rights are based on utilitarian principles anyway. Recent social thought in the West has emphasized "human rights" especially because these rights were so flagrantly violated during the Second World War. Eleanor Roosevelt, wife of the wartime U.S. president, spearheaded the 1948 Universal Declaration of Human Rights[25] of the then new United Nations. Its thirty articles were later supplemented by international covenants on "Civil and Political Rights"[26] and on "Intellectual, Social, and Cultural Rights."[27] Western capitalist governments emphasized civil and political rights (like free speech), which *forbid* governments to do certain things (like torture), while communist governments emphasized intellectual, social, and cultural rights (like elimination of poverty), which *obligate* governments to promote or provide certain things (like social safety nets). Communist China signed but did not ratify the former, political covenant, while the United States signed but did not ratify the latter, social covenant. Along with two optional protocols, the whole set of documents was signed and ratified by enough nations by 1976—in fact, by most countries in the world—to become international law.

Some have criticized the Western emphasis on human rights for being based too exclusively on individualism, the belief that the individual is prior to and more important than society. In contrast, *Marxism* thinks that society is prior to and more important than the individual. The difference is important because rules are necessary to make a society work. Do we choose our morality simply on the basis that "if no one is hurt, it must be okay"? Or do we establish rules that will help create a cohesive society in which individual humans can be supported and brought to maturity?

MATERIAL AND ARTISTIC DIMENSION

People build and decorate material objects to help them live out in community the insights they have gained from their mystical experiences, which they celebrate in myth and understand according to their doctrine. For example, the ancient Greeks thought that the gods lived in their temples, so the focal point of the temple was the central room, at the far end of which a cult statue of the god was placed. Because worshipers did not gather as a body *inside* the temple, their temples could be small compared with later Christian churches. The *Jewish* temple in Jerusalem followed this general pattern, although it did not have an image of God in its central room. When Jews gathered for worship, they did so in the courtyard *in front of* the temple. In contrast, *Christians* believe that God is present in the midst of their *assembly*. Their churches are places where the assembly gathers, so they have large interior spaces for that purpose. Muslims, like Christians, concentrate on the assembled faithful, so their mosques provide large indoor spaces for the faithful to gather and pray, along with courtyards and other facilities.

Decorations on religious buildings do more than just make the building beautiful. They are designed to put worshipers in a prayerful state or to affect them in other ways. Medieval Gothic architecture draws the eyes of worshipers skyward, encouraging them to think of God and heavenly things. Stained glass windows move the feelings of worshipers with the play of light and color while offering pictures of basic biblical narratives—"the Bible for the illiterate." In contrast, the bare meeting rooms of New England Congregational churches avoid distractions and concentrate the worshipers' attention on the preacher (or on God). Jewish and Islamic religious buildings avoid images of God and, in most cases, even of human beings. Muslim sacred art employs geometric and floral designs as well as Arabic calligraphy for their decorative effects.

Eastern Orthodox Christians have a particularly mystical understanding of religious art. They consider their paintings of religious figures, called icons, to be more than just reminders of holy people or illustrations of sacred stories. They are windows on the spirit world, windows through which a person can gain a spiritual experience. A painter needs a long period of apprenticeship painting secular subjects before he is allowed to paint an icon. When the apprenticeship is over, the painter fasts and prays before producing his first icon. After the icon is finished, it is shown to the congregation. Only if the congregation senses that the icon has the appropriate spiritual power is the painter allowed to exercise this ministry. Once he has entered into the ministry of painting icons, he no longer paints secular subjects.

Objects used in sacred worship—chalices, candlesticks, scrolls and books, altars, vestments (sacred clothing)—are beautifully made to reflect the value of the spiritual realities which they reflect and serve. The material dimension is closely linked with the ritual dimension. Rituals make use of physical places, buildings, objects, sights, sounds, actions, and smells (like incense).

Music, Dance, Drama, and Recitation

Another material dimension is sound, alone or in combination with movement. Hymns, processions, dances, sacred drama, and sacred poetry are frequently used by religions to dispose worshipers to prayer and to inspire them to action. Native Americans and Africans make extensive use of dance as a religious act. Muslim Sufi "whirling dervishes" use dance to experience the presence of God. Secular nations, too, make use of parades, national anthems, and patriotic songs to inspire citizens to sacrifice for the "common good." Even silence can be a material dimension, for example, in a Quaker meeting.

Holy Places

Besides objects produced by humans, the material dimension includes sacred *places*. Worshipers seek contact with the power of key events by visiting the places where they happened. *Jews* are attached to the land of Israel. Many of the narratives in their sacred books took place there, and their laws presuppose that Jews are living there along with other peoples. *Christians* also value holy places, encouraging pilgrimage to the "holy land" and to other sacred sites, although their theology proclaims that God has overcome limitations of place and time. *Muslims* make the hajj to Mecca because the events that took place there in the time of Muhammad are central to Muslim identity. They venerate Jerusalem because Muhammad ascended to heaven from Jerusalem during his mystical visionary experience called the "night journey." For the Dakota, Mount Rushmore in the Black Hills is sacred: the carvings of four U.S. presidents on the side of the mountain are worse than a mere insult—they desecrate a sacred place.

We will draw attention to these seven dimensions throughout the coming chapters on worldviews. But first, a few general cautions should be noted about this study.

TWO DANGERS

There are two dangers associated with studying other people's worldviews: (1) Failing to be *objective:* failing to understand the other's worldview because we never see it in its own right, but only as an "error" in comparison with our own. If we fail to understand someone else's worldview, we will probably not understand why he thinks, feels, and acts the way he does. As a result, we may miscalculate his likely responses to our actions. (2) Failing to be *serious:* failing to understand that worldviews make claims on us and want to be received as truth. Some people become so confused by the diversity of worldviews that they end up doubting that *any* worldview can be true—*without noticing that they are still living by a worldview:* a worldview that says the world is too complex to understand *and that it doesn't matter whether they understand it.* They still implicitly make choices on the basis of what they consider to be most valuable. They just don't *examine* their values.

1. Can We Be Objective?

In the past, scholars were confident that they could be "objective." Today it is widely acknowledged that we are all influenced by unconscious presuppositions based on our experiences and learning as well as our human inheritance. The best we can do is to acknowledge our starting point as clearly as possible, make *an effort* to "set it aside" or "bracket it out," and try for a period of time to comprehend another's worldview as if it were our own. *Is it possible* for us to "set aside" our own presuppositions long enough to understand someone else's viewpoint? Most of us know people who don't do this very well; they are constantly judging everything piece-by-piece on the basis of what they already "know to be true." You can be quite critical of an airplane if you compare it piece-by-piece with an automobile without comprehending the airplane as a whole or understanding its purpose: you will note that the wings are too wide to go under a highway bridge, the wheels don't steer well, and so on. Other people seem able to *approximate* the ideal: to listen carefully to others long enough to see their point of view as a whole. In the end, they may or may not agree with it, but they will *understand* it better.

A number of Muslim peace activists and scholars have been urging Westerners to try to understand Islam *as a whole* in relation to issues like just war, violence, and nonviolence. See chapter 5 on Muslim worldviews for a discussion of Chandra Muzaffar from Malaysia, president of JUST: the International Movement for a Just World. We need to understand not only *faraway* worldviews that we learn about from books, but also *"far-out"* worldviews held by friends and coworkers.

2. Can We Be Serious?

Although we may "bracket out" our own presuppositions long enough to understand someone else's, we should not leave our own convictions "set aside" forever. This book deals with some of the most important questions people ever ask. We encourage you to make the pursuit of these questions and their implications a personal quest. You may not be sure *what* you believe at the beginning of this study. Such a state of mind is common in the late teens and early twenties. We predict that, by the end of this book, the consideration of other people's worldviews will have helped you to clarify your own.

IS STUDYING OTHER RELIGIONS HARMFUL TO ONE'S OWN FAITH?

Some more conservative people worry about whether it is safe or morally right to study alien worldviews; they fear that reading about other religions might lead them to be unfaithful to their own religion. Some Christian churches teach that other religions are misguided human creations, or worse, demonic. Historically, the Catholic Church considered itself to be the "one true Church" and the only way to salvation. Both of these attitudes affected the way colonial powers treated indigenous people and their traditions in the areas that they colonized. Certain groups within Islam have strongly resisted postcolonial Western cultural and religious domination, calling the United States "the Great Satan." Within the Catholic Church, parochial attitudes began to change under the influence of its worldwide missionary experience interpreted in light of new theological insights. These new insights were published in documents of the Second Vatican Council, especially the *Declaration on the Relation of the Church to Non-Christian Religions (Nostra Aetate)*[28] and the *Dogmatic Constitution on the Church (Lumen Gentium)*,[29] which make positive comments on many of the worldviews we will be studying.

COMPLEXITIES

With only passing reference to several Chinese and Japanese worldviews, we will be studying together the classical religious patterns of the majority of the earth's peoples. But the picture is complicated by at least three factors:

1. The major classical worldviews interpenetrate each other: India is heavily Hindu, but many Muslims and Christians live there too. The United States is thought of as Christian, but many other classical worldviews are strongly represented there, and their influence is growing.
2. All major worldviews exist in a multitude of forms. Expect to be frustrated in your attempt to determine the "*real, or one true, form*" of any worldview you examine.
3. Religious leaders, scholars, and saints don't speak for all their members. Indeed some leaders, while *claiming* to accept the classic formulations of their religion's worldview, often base their concrete actions on quite different principles. An early Christian writer reflects that pagans are impressed when they

read that Christians love their enemies. Then they observe the lives of Christians they know and find that they don't even love their friends—and they laugh at us.[30] So don't presume that what you read in books is what people really believe and live out. Test the ideals against real lives.

When comparing worldviews, it is important to compare the great tradition of one with the great tradition of the other, and the little tradition of one with the little tradition of the other. We have heard students exclaim, "Hindus are *so* impressive! They apply their worldview to every aspect of life, not like Christians who go to church now and then and ignore their religion in the rest of their lives." In fact, many members of *all* worldviews are lax about their religion's core beliefs, while the "saints" in *all* religions or worldviews, even Christianity, apply their worldview to every aspect of life. We learn about our own worldview mostly from everyday, common folk, whereas we learn about other worldviews mostly from books written by or about the most committed members of those worldviews.

Be careful not to confuse "great tradition" with "important, educated people," and "little tradition" with "ordinary, everyday people." Some people who appear to be very "pious" may actually be living lives of self-centered hypocrisy, seeking human approval and admiration. Some may even be psychopaths, living lives based on their "hidden tradition" while loudly proclaiming a "counterfeit tradition." Many scholars and religious leaders live their lives based on the "little tradition" (what they consider "practical"), while some very ordinary people—laborers, peasants, office workers, unemployed—live their lives totally committed to and shaped by the "great tradition." Some even live the deep insights of the great tradition while suffering lives marked by inequities, discrimination, oppression, injustice, and violence.

DO RELIGIONS CAUSE VIOLENCE? CAN THEY PROMOTE PEACE?

Many people assert that religion is more problem than solution, that religious convictions cause or intensify communal violence, that the major danger today is "fundamentalist" religious nationalism, especially the Islamic variety.[31] Here are some examples of religion being used to justify violence:

> I will always be a warrior, this is the nature of a real Jew—the soldier is always under the skin. . . . Our goal is simple and absolute, it is set out in our scriptures, we must possess the land and conquer it. . . . There can be no debate about the word of God, [for God] defines the land as ours, His gift to us.[32]

> Violence is our only means of safeguarding the Protestant heritage. . . . The [Roman Catholic] Church sanctions terrorism, gunmen are given the last rights [*sic*], murderers are not excommunicated. . . . There is no such thing as an ordinary Catholic: because

of their religion they are in league with the republican movement . . . if you scratch any Catholic you'll find a terrorist sympathizer under the surface.[33]

The evil in the modern world is a result of weakness and the love of luxury. It is not a part of true Islam; it has spread from the outside world and tainted our leaders, who in turn lead the people into corrupt ways. . . . I will kill my own brother with the same force as I would any nonbeliever who opposes the war against evil.[34]

But we also find *peacemakers* who are motivated by religion: Mohandas Gandhi, Khan Abdul Ghaffar Khan, Martin Buber, Mother Teresa, Martin Luther King Jr., Dorothy Day, Thomas Merton, Marc Ellis, Farid Esack, and numerous others.

Douglas Johnston and Cynthia Sampson, in their book *Religion, the Missing Dimension of Statecraft*, argue that secular prejudices have prevented international relations experts and practitioners from noticing the key role that religious individuals and groups have played in international crises. Influenced by their belief in the separation of church and state, U.S. scholars and practitioners of international relations have been embarrassed to talk about the place of religion in *public* affairs. Restricting religion to *personal* affairs, they don't appreciate the degree to which people in other parts of the world integrate religion and politics. The blind spot imposed by their own worldview leads to uninformed policy decisions: diplomats fail to grasp what is really at stake.

Johnston and Sampson's book presents seven case studies.[35] Three involve non-violent struggles that would have turned violent without church influence:

1. Cardinal Sin and the Catholic Church mediated in the Philippines in 1986, when President Marcos lost power to Corazon Aquino.
2. Lutheran and other Christian churches mediated in East Germany in 1989, as Communist rule was challenged and then collapsed.
3. Christian churches mediated the end of apartheid in South Africa and the election of Nelson Mandela in 1994. The Dutch Reformed Church had originally justified apartheid and helped to develop and implement its policies. The English-speaking churches, with a few notable exceptions, resisted *verbally*, but accepted apartheid *in practice*. At a 1990 interdenominational church meeting, the Dutch Reformed spokesman said, "Apartheid is a sin; my church has been guilty of distorting scripture to defend it; we ask your forgiveness." His confession began a process of confession and forgiveness, although a sizable black faction called it "cheap grace" and asked, "Where's the restitution?"

Three involve ending wars that were already in progress:

4. The Moravian Church mediated an end to the war in the 1980s between the Sandinista government of Nicaragua and the East Coast Miskito Indians.
5. Quakers mediated an end to the Nigerian civil war of 1963–1967, when the eastern part of Nigeria tried to secede and form an independent state called Biafra.

6. The Catholic Church, Quakers, and Moral Rearmament mediated an end to the Rhodesian Civil War of 1975–1980. Moral Rearmament had put together a "cabinet of conscience." The day before the government was to pass from Ian Smith to Robert Mugabe, Ian Smith was poised to initiate a white coup. A nephew of Mugabe in the inner circle suggested that the two leaders meet. Ian Smith's son was also a member of the group. He persuaded his father to meet Mugabe that night. The atmosphere was highly charged, but Mugabe was a gracious host. Smith shared his concerns; Mugabe accepted some of them, and the coup was averted.[36]

The seventh case study concerns reconciliation after a major conflict had ended, namely the reconciliation of France and Germany at the end of the Second World War:

7. Moral Rearmament held meetings between French and German leaders following World War II in Caux, Switzerland. Starting in 1946, they brought two thousand French together with three thousand Germans over a three-year period. The meetings also deliberately brought together union leaders and industrialists to mediate *class* resentments. The participants shared personal stories, cooked and washed dishes together (the hotel where they were meeting had no staff), and came to know each other as human beings. Konrad Adenauer and Robert Schumann, who met there, later developed the European Coal and Steel Community—the forerunner of the European Common Market, and eventually of the European Union.

Finally, note that religious worldviews are not the only ones that justify violence. Both Adolf Hitler and Josef Stalin appealed to antireligious or secular worldviews to justify their oppressive government policies and major wars. President George H. W. Bush justified the first war in the Persian Gulf by appeals to secular concepts of "human rights" and to free market economics (the control of oil supplies and their impact on Western economies). So as we study worldviews, religious and secular, be attentive both to the characteristics that may promote violent conflict and to those that may promote reconciliation.

WHAT LIES AHEAD

In the chapters that follow, you will encounter doctrinal descriptions of the major worldviews, along with some indication of how doctrine motivates action. Doctrine is the fastest way to encapsulate the meaning contained in a worldview. As you read, try to imagine what experiences lie behind those doctrines—what experiences they have grown out of. Then ask whether *your* worldview has been influenced by similar experiences, and what meaning *your* worldview may have given to those experiences. Such an exercise can keep the worldviews you study from being reduced to mere words. We will pay special attention to the way doctrines influence actions toward justice and peace.

SUMMARY

Although all people live their lives on the basis of a particular worldview, some worldviews are not religious, some people have not thought their worldview through very well, and some people lie about their worldview. The seven dimensions can help us understand worldviews—our own, and others that differ from ours. In order to understand other worldviews, we need to set aside our own worldview long enough to see the world through someone else's eyes. We can never be completely objective, but we can seriously consider other worldviews without fear. Worldviews interact with each other and appear in various forms. The worldview that actually determines how one acts (the "little tradition" or perhaps the "hidden tradition") may be quite different from the "official" worldview that one claims to espouse (the "great tradition" or perhaps the "counterfeit tradition"). Worldviews are sometimes used to encourage violence. At other times, they can provide positive energy and insight to promote justice and peace. Many seemingly intractable conflicts have been resolved with the help of religious people committed to compassion and justice. Our study hopes to encourage the multiplication of such results.

KEY TERMS

categorical imperative	little tradition
counterfeit tradition	numinous
extrinsic motivation	pan-en-henic
great tradition	shaman
hidden tradition	utilitarianism
intrinsic motivation	

DISCUSSION QUESTIONS

1. How do the seven dimensions of worldviews apply to the worldview your parents taught you as you were growing up? How did that worldview relate to the larger society—was it dominant, influential, or marginal?
2. How do the seven dimensions relate to the *official* worldview you currently hold (its great tradition)? How do they relate to the *actual* worldview you currently hold (its little tradition), including all the qualifications you make or disagreements you may have with the official worldview that you are associated with?

3. What is your attitude toward "mystical experiences"? Do you know someone well who claims to have had one? Include "near death" experiences and "born again" experiences. Do you trust what they say? Have *you* had a mystical experience yourself? If so, what did it mean to you?

4. Would you find John Stuart Mill's "utilitarian ethic" helpful in deciding how to act? Kant's "categorical imperative"? How about John Rawls's "thought exercise"? What other criteria do you use to determine your actions?

5. Do you know of instances where religion has been harmful, or helpful, in contexts where people were working for justice and peace? Can you explain why it had one or the other effect?

SUGGESTIONS FOR FURTHER READING

Babiak and Hare. *Snakes in Suits.*

Cannon. *Six Ways of Being Religious: A Framework for Comparative Studies of Religion.*

Cleckley. *The Mask of Sanity.*

Ferguson. *War and Peace in the World's Religions.*

Fischer-Schreiber. *The Encyclopedia of Eastern Philosophy and Religion.*

Frossard. *I Have Met Him: God Exists.*

Gertner. "The Futile Pursuit of Happiness."

Greeley. *Death and Beyond.*

Hare, Robert. *Without Conscience.*

Hinde and Watson, eds. *War: A Cruel Necessity?*

James. *The Varieties of Religious Experience: A Study in Human Nature.*

Johnston, ed. *Faith-Based Diplomacy: Trumping Realpolitik.*

Johnston and Sampson, eds. *Religion, the Missing Dimension of Statecraft.*

Juergensmeyer. *The New Cold War? Religious Nationalism Confronts the Secular State.*

Kohn. *Punished by Rewards: The Trouble with Gold Stars, Incentive Plans, A's, Praise, and Other Bribes.*

Lobaczewski. *Political Ponerology: A Science on the Nature of Evil Adjusted for Political Purposes.*

McKenzie. *Myths and Realities.*

Mill. *Utilitarianism.*

Moody. *Life after Life: The Investigation of a Phenomenon—Survival of Bodily Death.*

Neihardt, ed. *Black Elk Speaks.*

Rawls. *Justice as Fairness: A Restatement.*

Second Vatican Council. *Lumen Gentium: Dogmatic Constitution on the Church.*

———. *Nostra Aetate: Declaration on the Relationship of the Church to Non-Christian Religions.*

Shaw, William H. *Business Ethics.*

Smart. *Worldviews: Crosscultural Explorations of Human Beliefs.*

———. *The World's Religions.* 2nd ed.

Wink. *Engaging the Powers: Discernment and Resistance in a World of Domination.*

1

Hindu Worldviews

The Spirit is neither born nor does it die at any time. It does not come into being, or cease to exist. It is unborn, eternal, permanent, and primeval. The Spirit is not destroyed when the body is destroyed.

—Bhagavad Gita 2:20

Just as a person puts on new garments after discarding the old ones, similarly, the living entity or the individual soul acquires new bodies after casting away the old bodies.

—Bhagavad Gita 2:22[1]

EXPERIENTIAL AND EMOTIONAL DIMENSION

As we mentioned in the introduction, Hinduism is familiar with the *pan-en-henic* experience in which the mystic feels united with all reality. Many yogic exercises are designed to produce such an experience. Rather than fear or awe in the presence of an Other, the mystic loses the sense of a "self" that is distinct from the rest of creation and from God. Yogis believe this shows what the world is really like. Here is an experiential account from Yogananda's *Autobiography of a Yogi:*

The flesh was as though dead; yet in my intense awareness I knew that never before had I been fully alive. My sense of identity was no longer narrowly confined to a body but embraced the circumambient atoms. People on distant streets seemed to be moving gently over my own remote periphery. The roots of plants and trees appeared through a dim transparency of the soil; I discerned the inward flow of their sap.

The whole vicinity lay bare before me. My ordinary frontal vision was now changed to a vast spherical sight, simultaneously all-perceptive. Through the back of my head I saw men strolling far down Rai Ghat Lane, and noticed also a white cow that was leisurely approaching. . . .

All objects within my panoramic gaze trembled and vibrated like quick motion pictures. . . . An oceanic joy broke upon calm endless shores of my soul. The Spirit of God, I realized, is exhaustless Bliss; His body is countless tissues of light. A swelling glory within me began to envelop towns, continents, the earth, solar and stellar systems, tenuous nebulae, and floating universes. The entire cosmos, gently luminous, like a city seen afar at night, glimmered within the infinitude of my being.[2]

HISTORICAL PERIODS

Diversity of Hindu Thought

Western writers invented the term "Hinduism" to denote a religion. Its practitioners prefer the designation "Sanatana Dharma" ("eternal religion"). The adjective "Hindu" simply refers to the Indian subcontinent—the area East from the Indus River valley. Hinduism encompasses the highly diverse beliefs of the majority of the people who live there. Despite this diversity, certain concepts and viewpoints are widely held. In the nineteenth century, Ramakrishna (1836–1886) and his disciple Vivekananda (1863–1902)[3] developed a synthesis of Hindu thought that more closely resembles Western ideas of a "religion."

The Early Vedic Period (3000–1000 BCE)[4]

The earliest stages of religion in India are not well known. The first stage for which we have much evidence is the indigenous Dravidian culture of the third and second millennia BCE, supplemented by the urbanized Harappan civilization from ca. 2500 to 1500 BCE. The "Aryan invasion theory," formerly widely accepted in the West but now seriously debated, held that Aryans from the Northwest invaded the Indus Valley and elsewhere in the second millennium BCE, gaining control over the local inhabitants. The Aryans were thought to have composed the earliest written Hindu scriptures, the **Vedas.** Aryan priests, the Brahmins, offered sacrifices and guarded the secret, inspired revelations called **Shruti.**[5]

Originally the Brahmins worshiped and sacrificed to many gods—traditionally 330 million. The Brahmins were the religious specialists who could, by their sacrifices, wield power (brahman) on behalf of those who employed them. Among key early gods were Indra, god of war; Varuna, god of cosmic order and judgment; Agni, god of fire (who transformed sacrifices so that they could pass over from our world to the world of spirits); and Soma, god of an intoxicating drink used in rituals.

The Pre-Classical Period (1000 BCE–100 CE)

In the first millennium BCE, the key gods were three: *Brahma,* the creator god; *Vishnu,* the protector—a kindly deity who appears on earth in diverse forms (such as *Krishna* and *Rama*); and *Shiva,* the destroyer, who is also associated with storms. The three relate to the natural cycle of life, namely birth, living, and dying. All living things not only decay but also pass on their elements as the eternal source for the regeneration of life. These three gods form a sort of trinity called the Trimurti or *trivarga*.

Gradually in the pre-classical period, under the influence of *sramanas*, or wandering ascetics, religious thinkers began to believe in one God who appeared in a multitude of forms. Thinking of this God as the foundation of everything, they named him *Brahman* (Power). This theological shift illustrates how *doctrine*, which explains *narrative or myth*, can change over time. It also illustrates the difference between the "great tradition" as taught by the sramanas and the "little tradition" that survives among many common people today. The situation is complicated: beliefs vary widely from place to place and among different peoples.

Terms Clarified

There are five terms that are easily confused because their spellings are similar and their meanings may overlap:

Brahma: creator god, early period (capital B);

Brahman: Power (capital B, capital P), the one source or ground of being in the universe, which manifests itself in the many gods of tradition;

brahman: spiritual power (small b, small p), for example, the ability of a Brahmin to make sacrifices and prayers that would effectively control spiritual reality on behalf of those who ask for his help;

Brahmana: either (1) Brahmin, a Hindu priest; or (2) a part of the Shruti containing inspired traditions used by the Brahmins to regulate their rituals;

Brahmin: a Hindu priest = a Western form for the term Brahmana in its first meaning, an attempt by Westerners to avoid confusion.

Later Historical Developments

In the *classical period* of Hindu development (100–1000 CE), *Buddhism* (the subject of chapter 2) challenged the views of the Brahmins, initially flourished in India, moved out to other countries, and finally withered in India where it had begun. In part Indian Buddhism became too formalistic, and in part the Brahmins took over many of its elements in a new period of Hindu creativity. Thus in India Buddhist insights were absorbed into the larger Hindu worldview.

In the *medieval period* (1000–1750 CE), *Islam* (the subject of chapter 5) entered India and became very influential, first in the north but eventually under the Moghul Empire (1520–1857) over much of the subcontinent. The Moghul emperor Akbar (d. 1605) encouraged Hindu-Muslim integration as well as interfaith dialogue in his House of Worship.

In the *modern period* (from about 1750 to the present) Great Britain gained first economic and then political control over India, and Christian missionaries made strong efforts to convert Indians to Christianity (the subject of chapter 4). In the twentieth century, Mohandas Gandhi developed **satyagraha**, or "truth-force," as an active nonviolent way of life that overcame British rule and led to Indian independence and the creation of Pakistan in 1947.

NARRATIVE OR MYTHIC DIMENSION INCLUDING SACRED WRITINGS

After a mystical experience, *myth* attempts to *describe* what happened. The *doctrinal* dimension comes later as theologians try to *explain* that mystical literature. The *narrative or mythic* dimension gave rise in Hinduism to secret, inspired literature, the Shruti, and to more public, noninspired, but still sacred writings, the **Smriti.**[6]

The Shruti were for centuries handed down orally. They included the *Vedas*, inspired hymns to various gods (in the *Rgveda*, collected about 1000 BCE); hymns for ritual reenactments of cosmic events (in the *Yajurveda*), for example, rituals designed to ensure the authority and power of the king; chants to accompany sacrifices in which Soma, an intoxicating sacred drink, was poured out to various deities (in the *Samaveda*); and practical charms and prayers used by the Brahmins to exercise spiritual power on behalf of those who sought their help (in the *Atharvaveda*).

Early in the first millennium, the second part of the Vedas, the *Brahmanas* (prose instructions for the ritual use of the hymns, rather like Catholic "rubrics" for the liturgy, but also containing legends) were produced. Much later, between about 700 and 400 BCE, the third and fourth parts of the Vedas were composed through cross-fertilization with developing Buddhist and Jain thought, radically reinterpreting the Vedas. These were the *Aranyakas* ("Wilderness" or "Forest" Books reinterpreting the sacrificial texts for meditation by recluses outside of sacrificial contexts) and the **Upanishads,** also known as the **Vedanta** ("End of the Vedas"—esoteric teaching). Much of what we think of today as Hindu doctrine is based on the Upanishads.

Of the noninspired Smriti, the most important are the great national epic poems the **Ramayana** and the **Mahabharata,** which recount the lives and exploits of gods and heroic humans. The **Bhagavad Gita**, probably the most widely read Hindu scripture, is part of the *Mahabharata*.

DOCTRINAL AND PHILOSOPHICAL DIMENSION: BASIC DOCTRINAL POSITIONS

When we ask how Hindus *explain* their mystical experiences and the mythical narratives of the reality behind these experiences, we are moving into the area of doctrine and philosophy: the Upanishads and modern commentaries, for example, commentaries on the Bhagavad Gita. These *explanations* change and develop over time even as the *experiences* and their mythical representations remain the same. In the Christian tradition, these changes are called the *development of doctrine*.

In the pre-classical period, a number of concepts important to modern Hinduism developed, including **reincarnation**, or the **transmigration of souls**, **karma**, **maya**, **samsara**, **moksha**, and the unity of Brahman and **atman**. With Buddhism and Jainism originating in the sixth century BCE, it is likely that Hinduism and the two "new" religions developed these new concepts through mutual interaction.

Reincarnation and Transmigration

A key concept very widely held in India is the transmigration of souls, often called reincarnation. This is the belief that when a person dies her soul enters another body and is reborn as a baby. *Reincarnation* refers to the transition from one *human* body to another. *Transmigration* more generally refers to the transition from one *physical form* to another, where the forms may be human, animal, vegetable, or even mineral (what Westerners would consider "nonliving," or inanimate). The Hindu word for this cycle of transmigration through many lives—in fact, millions of lives—is *samsara*. One is not always reincarnated immediately after death. There are heavens of varying degrees of happiness and hells of varying horror. But one cannot remain forever in any of them. One's "merit" (or "demerit," negative karma) gets gradually used up, and we need to be reincarnated to earn more merit, or to escape the cycle of merit and demerit entirely through the liberation called *moksha*.

Karma

The "merit" or "demerit" that we accumulate as the result of our good or bad actions in life is called *karma*. More generally, karma consists of our actions and the results they cause in us. Good actions produce good results, and bad actions produce bad results. These results stay with us and continue to affect our present and future lives. What form we are transmigrated into, or what heaven or hell we spend time in, is determined by our karma at the moment of death.

Maya, Samsara, and Moksha

According to the Hindu "great tradition," the world of our sense experience, despite its apparent solidity and reality, is an illusion in comparison with the reality of God. *Maya*, or "playful illusion," deceives us into thinking that what we see is ultimate reality. The goal of human life, then, is not an infinite series of reincarnations, not even progressively more desirable reincarnations, but escape from the depressing round of births and deaths (*samsara*). This escape is called *moksha*. It leads to a permanent union with God, as a result of which one will no longer be reincarnated. What will that union be like? Hindu doctrines differ on that point. A major tendency today, which probably developed under the influence of Buddhism, is called **Advaita Vedanta**.

Advaita Vedanta[7]

Although it is only one of several possible Hindu ways to understand reality, Advaita Vedanta has had a major influence on modern Hindu theology. Advaita Vedanta argues that (a) all humans share one soul or Self (called **atman**: the eternal and imperishable part of each human), (b) all gods are appearances of one God (this one God behind all gods is called *Brahman*), and (c) God (Brahman) and Self (atman) are identical. The name of this group indicates its key belief: *A-dvaita* ("undivided," or nondualistic) *Veda-anta* (end and explanation of the Vedas). (Note that Sanskrit and English, as "Indo-European" languages, share common roots, with "d" and "t" often interchanged: *dvaita*/divided and *anta*/end.) "Nondualistic" means that there is no distinction between my atman and Brahman. Those who hold this doctrinal position express their insight by saying that Brahman is identical with atman.

Historically the most famous proponent of Advaita Vedanta and of the concept of maya was Shankara, who lived around 800 CE.[8] In the nineteenth century, under pressure from Christian missionaries, the Ramakrishna movement promoted an updated version of Advaita Vedanta. Swami Vivekananda (d. 1902), speaking at the 1893 Parliament of the World's Religions in Chicago, popularized Advaita Vedanta as "the definitive . . . form of Hinduism."[9] For many Hindus this remains true today. Yet not all Hindus hold this view of reality: there are also adherents of Dvaita (dualistic) Vedanta, who maintain that there is an eternal and real distinction between Brahman, the cosmos, and the individual atman. A. C. Bhaktivedanta Swami Prabhupada, the founder of the Hare Krishna movement (International Society for Krishna Consciousness), seems to hold this position.[10] There are also other, more complex, positions on this relationship.

The Advaita identification of Brahman and atman offers an argument in favor of absolute **ahimsa**, or nonharm to sentient beings: if my deepest reality (atman) is identical with yours and with the ground of all being, then when I injure you I injure myself as well. But the argument is weakened by the observation that nothing I do to you can truly injure your atman because the atman is the eternal soul that is unaffected by the death and destruction of the physical body. In the Bhagavad Gita, this is one reason Krishna tells Arjuna not to shrink from killing in battle.

PRACTICAL AND RITUAL DIMENSION

Many common people consider the escape of moksha to be beyond their grasp in their current state; therefore, they concentrate on gaining merit so that they will be reincarnated in a more desirable state, such as that of a rich male. Others use their religious prayers and rituals primarily to improve their fortunes and guard against misfortune in this present incarnation, as in the charm quoted below, to secure the love of a woman. Numerous prayers in the Atharvaveda speak to these intermediate goals, while the later philosophical explanations of the Upanishads tend toward moksha as a goal. "The rituals enjoined in the Vedas are applicable to the realm of **dharma** [the material realm in which we are governed by our caste duties], but the one who seeks liberation does not merely desire a place in heaven; he is in search of ultimate Reality itself."[11]

Brahmins and Brahman

Brahmins use sacrifices and incantations to wield spiritual power on behalf of their clients. This power can assure success in business, gain the attention of a lover, or protect one from attack. Here is an example from the Atharvaveda:

Book VI, Hymn 8. Charm to secure the love of a woman.

1. As the creeper embraces the tree on all sides, thus do thou embrace me, so that thou, woman, shalt love me, so that thou shalt not be averse to me!
2. As the eagle when he flies forth presses his wings against the earth, thus do I fasten down thy mind, so that thou, woman, shalt love me, so that thou shalt not be averse to me.
3. As the sun day by day goes about this heaven and earth, thus do I go about thy mind, so that thou, woman, shalt love me, so that thou shalt not be averse to me.[12]

Figure 1.1.   Hindu Temple of Shiva Mylapore, near Chennai (Madras), India.
Courtesy David Whitten Smith, 26 January 1998.

The success or failure of these prayers and rituals is part of the experiential or mystical dimension, which leads followers to gain or lose confidence in their god or gods.

How to Gain Moksha

Deeply spiritual Hindus are more concerned to attain moksha than to gain advantage in this life. The search for God and union with God is called **yoga**, and the person who undertakes this search is called a **yogi**. An aspiring yogi needs the help of a more experienced elder yogi (similar to a Christian "spiritual director") called a *guru*. The mystical experience of Yogi Paramahansa Yogananda described above began when his guru Sri Yukteswar "struck gently on [his] chest above the heart."[13]

There are as many types of yoga as there are theories about the nature of reality and the ways to attain moksha. This diversity illustrates the connection between *doctrine* on the one hand, and *practice and ritual* on the other. In general, Hindus believe that moksha can be attained through devotion (**bhakti**), works (karma), and/or knowledge (**jnana**).

Gaining Moksha through Bhakti

Bhakti refers to fervent *devotion* and surrender (in faith and trust) to God (seen as personal) or to a particular god, who then saves the devotee by grace. The path of bhakti, combined with the pursuit of good karma and the avoidance of bad karma, is the path followed by most devout Hindus. Many Hindu rituals and feasts, in the temple and at home, are expressions of bhakti to particular gods, and most Hindus center their spiritual practice around these traditional rituals and feasts. "Worship of the Personal God is recommended as the easier way open to all, the weak and the lowly, the illiterate and the ignorant. The sacrifice of love is not so difficult as the tuning of the will to the Divine purpose or ascetic discipline or the strenuous effort of thinking."[14]

"The weak and the lowly, the illiterate and the ignorant" are not the only people who make use of Hindu rituals. When I (David) visited Nepal, my host—a practicing lawyer—knelt down before a niche in a temple we were visiting. When I asked him to explain the significance of his action, he replied that he was kneeling at the shrine of a god associated with skill in speech and argument, and he was asking the god to share that skill with him so that he could more effectively defend his poor clients.

Gaining Moksha through Karma

One attains moksha through *works* (karma) when one learns how to act well in service to other humans but without "holding on to the fruits" of that action. That is, one acts well without attempting to manipulate or control other people or circumstances, and without being anxious about what the results of the action will be.

One *cares* about what the results will be, but one *does not fret* about it. One is not *attached* to the action or its results, so one does not develop either good or bad karma as a result of that action. This is a key insight of the Bhagavad Gita, and we will see Gandhi reflecting on this insight below.

Note that *good* karma, when we *do* hold on to the fruits of our action, prevents moksha by sending one to a heaven or a better incarnation, just as *bad* karma prevents moksha by sending one to a hell or a worse incarnation. It is our "attachment" to the ego-centered attractions and desires of this life that keeps our atman from uniting with Brahman.

Gaining Moksha through Jnana

For those who follow Advaita Vedanta, moksha can be attained by jnana when one realizes through a *personal experience* that her atman (as well as everyone else's atman) is identical with Brahman. One actively seeks such an experience through the practice of meditation best learned with the guidance of a guru (a sort of "spiritual director"). This insight is not evident to sense perception. Having come to an experiential realization of this truth, the person will no longer be reincarnated at death.

Note that the attainment of this state of moksha can only occur through our actions in a *life on earth*, as opposed to our actions in one of the many temporary heavens or hells. If moksha has not been attained by the time of death, one will eventually need to be reincarnated to continue one's progress toward moksha. Periods spent in any of the various heavens or hells gradually *use up* good karma (in heaven) or bad karma (in hell). Only in the human stage on earth is one capable of *overcoming* the formation of karma through disinterested action according to one's dharma (duty of one's **caste** and state in life) or of gaining the required knowledge (jnana) to enter moksha.

SOCIAL AND INSTITUTIONAL DIMENSION

The Caste System

According to the "Aryan invasion theory" described above, when the Aryans conquered the earlier population of India, the Dravidians, they introduced or intensified a division of society into four distinct classes, which reinforced the new power structure. These classes are called *varna*, translated as "caste" in English. But the English word "caste" is also used of a later and much more complex division. Here we are using the word in the earlier sense. The root meaning of the word *varna* is "colors." It seems to refer to differences between the light-skinned Aryan invaders and the dark-skinned Dravidian earlier inhabitants. This connection relates caste divisions to race divisions as found in other societies like that of the United States.

The Brahmin priests were the highest caste of the new society. Under them were the **Kshatriya**, or warrior caste (which included politicians and civil authorities), and the **Vaishya,** or merchant, artisan, and farmer caste. Members of these three castes became "twice-born" by an initiation at adolescence. The fourth caste was the **Shudra,** or servant caste. Under all four castes were the **outcastes,** or **untouchables.**

The name *untouchable* developed from the fear of caste members that they would be polluted by contact with the outcastes—in some cases even by contact with their shadows. In reaction to this notion, and in resistance to the oppression that it caused, Gandhi devised the name **Harijan,** meaning "Friends of God." The late colonial British and postcolonial Indian secular governments coined the term **scheduled castes** (pronounced in the British fashion as "sheduwuld") as a neutral name that carries no opprobrium and indicates that its members are eligible through affirmative action to receive certain benefits. The government similarly uses **scheduled tribes** to refer to indigenous tribes that continue to follow their animist hunter-gatherer way of life. About 17 percent of Indians are members of the "scheduled castes"; another 9 percent belong to "scheduled tribes."[15]

The members of the scheduled castes have themselves decided that none of these terms accurately describes them. Even Gandhi's attempt to raise their dignity with the term Harijan seemed to them to be patronizing. They refer to themselves as **Dalit**—a word that means "oppressed, ground down"—to emphasize that their condition is the result of unjust actions by others. We will most often refer to them by the name they themselves prefer.

Members of scheduled tribes call themselves *adivasi,* which means "original dwellers" and is roughly equivalent to the term *indigenous.* (Note that Ojibwa Native Americans call themselves *Anishinaabeg,* meaning "original people.") The *adivasi* are proud of their native cultures and do not consider themselves to be second-class. Some wealthy, upper-class conservatives say the so-called *adivasi* are only *vanavasi* ("forest dwellers"), thus denying their claim to be "original dwellers" with the rights that claim might imply.

According to the Aryan invasion theory, it was the successful Aryan invaders who established and became members of the Brahmin, Kshatriya, and Vaishya castes. The conquered population provided the Shudra caste and the outcastes. Some conservative critics contest this history, maintaining that the light-skinned Aryans were the original inhabitants of India and the darker Dravidians were outside immigrants. They also maintain that the system of varna, or caste, is of divine origin and thus unchangeable. Therefore light-skinned Indians should have a higher status because they are the "real" or "original" Indians. This dispute illustrates how theology and history can be used or abused to support one party's claim to status and power.

The Four Stages of Life

One tradition in India supposes that the *male* members of the "twice-born castes" (namely, the Brahmin, Kshatriya, or Vaishya castes, but not the Shudra or Dalit) go through four ideal stages of life. The first stage is youth as a student, where one is under the direction of others. The second stage is marriage, where the procreation and rearing of children and participation in society, including the attainment of comfortable affluence, is the center of attention. The third stage is withdrawal to the forest for study of the Vedas and meditation—a sort of retirement that allows younger people to take over active control of society. The fourth stage is that of the detached pilgrim or *sannyasin* (a sort of end-of-life *sramana*), who wanders as an ascetic seeking God or moksha.

The *female* members of society, in contrast, pass through *three different* stages of life: The first stage is as a child under the direction of her father; girls were not given formal education. The second stage is as a wife, mother, and homemaker under the direction of her husband. The third stage is as a widow (whose husband has died or withdrawn to become a *sannyasin*) under the direction of her eldest son.[16]

ISSUES FOR JUSTICE AND PEACE

Caste

Many Hindus explain the serious inequalities of opportunity and fortune that we observe in the world by relating caste to karma—one's caste and one's good or bad experiences in the present life are the results of karma from previous lives. (Note the relation between experience and doctrine.) This belief tends to support the status quo, favoring those in positions of power and privilege. If I can convince myself and others that the poor are only working out their bad karma from misdeeds in previous lives, I have little incentive to share my wealth and power with them. Such sharing might even reduce their ability to "use up" bad karma by suffering, and thus deny them a better reincarnation.

Marxist thinkers, judging Hinduism externally through their own worldview, might well argue that the concept of karma was invented by Aryan elites to justify their control and to suppress resistance by the lower classes.

Some Hindus assert that the only reason Christians help poor Hindus is to convert them to Christianity, exploiting the poverty and the social discrimination of the caste system to serve their own agenda of expanding their religious base in India. Christians could challenge Hindus with the following considerations: we earn good karma from good acts, and helping suffering people is a good act. Ignoring or oppressing suffering people is a bad act. People who oppress the poor could well develop bad karma, which could then lead them to share the ill fortune of the poor when they are reincarnated.

Some worldviews, such as that of Burmese Buddhism, which we will study in the next chapter, believe that helping others earns good karma *only if those we help are good people.* Such a belief leads laypeople to help allegedly holy monks but not poor people, who presumably are to blame for their own suffering.[17] Yet Vivekananda said that God can be honored and served by *any* human, *especially* by the poor:

I should see God in the poor, and it is for my salvation that I go and worship them. The poor and the miserable are for our salvation, so that we may serve the Lord, coming in the shape of the diseased, coming in the shape of the lunatic, the leper, and the sinner![18]

Mohandas Gandhi and Vinoba Bhave (see below) also appealed to Hindu principles to reinforce their commitment to the poor. Nevertheless, Gandhi supported the caste system, which put him at odds with Bhim Rao Ambedkar, a Dalit who converted to Buddhism. Gandhi also supported Indian laws of "reservation," which assigned a certain quota of school and government positions to depressed classes (a form of affirmative action). Ambedkar wanted to abolish the caste system altogether—he was one of Gandhi's most vocal and articulate critics.[19]

Despite these theological advances and its political repudiation, caste remains a challenge for Hindu theologians. Anantanand Rambachan cites caste as the primary challenge for a Hindu theology of liberation. Promoting "open-source Hinduism," he argues that in India today Hinduism can be freed of caste and gender discrimination, offering an alternative to the market-driven, competitive pursuit of money and pleasure, which uses religion to divide people.[20]

Women

The status and evaluation of women were higher in the Vedic period than around the turn of the Common Era. In the Vedas, women function as poets, religious seekers, philosophers, and mothers instructing their sons.[21] The epic *Ramayana* (400 BCE to 200 CE) tells the story of Rama and Sita, husband and wife, whose marriage is one of mutual love. Sita is both a faithful wife and a strong woman who finally chooses to defend her integrity at the cost of her marriage.[22] By the time the Brahmin code of conduct for the four castes appeared in written form as *The Laws of Manu* (200 BCE–200 CE), women's status had declined. In this text women are considered "not fit for independence" yet to be "treated with due reverence."[23] Many centuries later, the Hindu reformer Ram Mohan Roy (d. 1833) opposed female infanticide, child marriages, and *sati* (live widows dying by fire on their husbands' funeral pyres).[24]

Since Indian independence from Great Britain in 1947, social, political, and economic conditions have improved for women, and more roles have been opened to them. Better health care is available, and more Indian women pursue higher education, with some entering fields traditionally closed to women, including politics and in rare cases religious leadership.[25]

Serious problems remain. Because families arranging a marriage for their daughters must pay a significant dowry to the groom's family, girls may still be regarded as an "economic burden," promoting female infanticide and the abortion of female fetuses.[26] Husbands disappointed with the size of the dowry they received (which confers status), or otherwise dissatisfied with their wives, have thrown acid in their faces to disfigure them or arranged "accidental" death by fire in the kitchen (with the aid of a little kerosene): an estimated 2,500 "bride burnings" occur each year in India.[27] Recent headlines have underscored the frequent occurrence of rape in India, even in public settings, which thus remains a pressing social issue. Yet Hindu texts and traditions uphold "the view that the human being [whether male or female] embodies the real and infinite divine spirit (*Brahman*)." The "cardinal ethical principle" of ahimsa prohibits such practices as the abortion of female fetuses, the dowry system and dowry deaths, and of course rape; it requires justice for women as much as for men.[28]

War

The Vedic worldview accepted war as the responsibility or duty (dharma) of the Kshatriya or warrior class and as essential to good order. Killing in animal sacrifice and in war were not regarded as violating ahimsa (nonharm to living things). In fact, the Bhagavad Gita seems on the surface to justify war in the face of various pacifist arguments.

The Bhagavad Gita is, for many Hindus, the most influential of their holy books. Technically it is part of the Smriti, or noninspired traditions complementing the Shruti, or inspired books. As noted earlier, among the Smriti are two great national epics, the *Ramayana* and the *Mahabharata*. The Bhagavad Gita (often abbreviated as "The Gita," literally "The Song") is one section of the *Mahabharata*. It has been the basis for many commentaries that explain Hindu beliefs.

In the Gita, Arjuna the hero is contemplating a battlefield just before the battle begins. He tells his chariot driver, Krishna (who happens to be an *avatar*, or earthly manifestation, of the god Vishnu), that he will not fight because he does not want to harm his kin even though they are attacking him. In response, Krishna instructs Arjuna that it is right for him to fight, using the following arguments among others: (a) You are Kshatriya, and so it is your dharma or duty to fight. If you disobey your dharma, you will suffer bad karma. (b) The soldiers you kill today will not really die. Only their bodies will die—their atman will survive untouched and be reincarnated. You cannot pierce, hack, burn, or in any way harm the atman. (c) Even if you hold back and refuse to fight, the soldiers you would have killed will still die in some other way, because it is their fate (decreed by Vishnu) to die today. So they will still die, but you will fail to perform your dharma.

As the Gita continues, we do find there are rules about war that are similar to Western just war principles but differently justified. If the soldiers are fighting to carry out their dharma, they must do it correctly. So, for example, cavalry may attack other cavalry, but they must not attack foot soldiers. Most Hindus have thought that the Gita and other Hindu traditions allow and even urge war in certain circumstances, as is demonstrated by the history of Hindu civilization. Most Hindu rulers have used war to achieve their aims, and most of their citizens have supported it. But some Hindus believe that ahimsa is absolute and forbids both war and animal sacrifice under any circumstances. These Hindus base their conviction on the ascetic (or *sramanic*) traditions, especially those influenced by Buddhist or Jain thought.

The best known of these antiwar Hindus was Mohandas Gandhi. (See our discussion below, under spokespersons for justice and peace, explaining how he interpreted the Bhagavad Gita on war.) Another was Vinoba Bhave, the most famous of Gandhi's followers and successors. Note that in general, discussion of "just war" (the use of war to end a war or injustice, as advocated by Krishna to Arjuna) implies that "the ends justify the means." Gandhi reversed the causal order, asserting that "the means justify (or shape) the end." As an example, he gave the relationship between the seed and the tree.

Relations with Other Religions: Communalism

Religious differences are often blamed for conflict, for example, in India, Northern Ireland, and the Middle East. In India, *communalism* refers to "blind loyalty to one's own religious group,"[29] leading to legal and illegal discrimination, and frequently to homicidal riots.

Communalism in India, especially between Hindu and Muslim, has ebbed and flowed. In 1998, the nationalist Bharatiya Janata Party (BJP) swept to power and responded to Hindu feelings of disadvantage by declaring that "India is for Hindus," implying that Muslims and other non-Hindu Indians were not welcome. Its party platform promised nuclear tests. Soon after gaining power it kept that promise, to the surprise of most of the world. Pakistan followed suit, not to be outclassed by its neighbor nation. Early in 2002 in the western state of Gujarat, alleged Muslim arsonists set fire to a train, killing fifty-eight Hindu religious pilgrims. Hindu mobs retaliated by carrying out a "pogrom"[30] that killed at least two thousand Muslims and deprived thousands more of their homes, with the apparent complicity of some police and BJP government officials. Since then, economic inequality popularly linked to economic globalization has escalated tensions by increasing both Hindu and Muslim poverty, setting the two groups against each other.

In 2004 the Congress Party, supported by India's rural poor, regained control nationally from the BJP. Recent polling suggests that the pro-Western provincial leader of the BJP, Narendra Darmodaras Modi, who though accused of complicity in the Gujarat massacres was cleared by a controversial court decision, is likely to win the office of prime minister of Gujarat in the spring 2014 elections.[31]

Some suggest that inter-communal violence would greatly diminish if we could just put religion aside. In situations of conflict, though, we should first ask whether religion is relevant to the conflict and then, if so, to what extent religion is a *cause* of the conflict, to what extent it is the *organizing principle* that helps people in a conflict "choose sides" and establish identity, and to what extent its teachings and practices actually *shape* the course of the conflict and the actions of the participants. Without religion would conflicts cease, or would they just organize themselves differently?[32] Beth Roy describes an interesting case in Bangladesh, the former East Pakistan.

Some Trouble with Cows

In *Some Trouble with Cows*, the sociologist Beth Roy describes a village conflict in Bangladesh between Hindus and Muslims. The trouble began when a Muslim's cow got loose and ate some of the lentils in the field of a Hindu neighbor. When the Hindu complained, the Muslim tied his cow carelessly in the same field the next day. It got loose again and ate more Hindu lentils. The Hindu then took the Muslim's cow home and held it. When the Muslim came to retrieve it, the Hindu would not give it back. As he left without his cow, the Muslim insulted the Hindu by asking in anger, "Why do you want to keep the cow? Do you want to eat it?"

This deliberately offensive remark to his Hindu neighbor is one of the few actions in the whole adventure that can be directly related to either worldview. Nevertheless, the village was divided between its low-caste Hindus and its Muslims. Note that the quarrel could well have divided the village differently, for example, between peasants (low-caste Hindus and poor Muslims) on the one hand, and landowners and political leaders (high-caste Hindus and wealthy Muslims) on the other. The result was three days of tension, with tens of thousands of people from miles around sitting on the ground in a face-off; scattered "raids" from one side to the other resulting mostly in cuts, bruises, and a burned building; and finally shots fired by the regional police that killed two Hindus and two Muslims.

Religious convictions mainly gave people a sense of identity; they identified friends and enemies. Yet Roy questions why it was *religion* that was chosen as the identifying factor. She suggests three reasons: (1) religion provided a powerful sense of community as over against the secular, political community, which villagers saw as "outsiders"; (2) religion had played a key role in the 1947 political turmoil—religious identities had been used to determine privilege or oppression—when Pakistan (majority Muslim, including what later became Bangladesh) separated from India (majority Hindu);[33] and (3) the particular daily religious practices of the two groups set up certain cultural differences: Hindu practices centered on the home and thus reinforced family ties, whereas Muslim practices centered on the public mosque, reinforcing ties within the Muslim community.

Another interesting division that cut across the religious divide was between the men and the women. In general, the women refused to support the disturbance, declining for example to prepare food for the men while the conflict was underway. Roy comments:

> Men meet more in public spaces, in marketplaces and fields, for instance, where sources of competition and conflict are common. Women meet more on domestic and ritual grounds [visiting neighbors on holiday and other occasions, and attending to births, marriages, illnesses, and deaths], where they have voluntarily sought each other out and therefore approach with a more assured sense of friendliness.[34]

Great Tradition, Little Tradition

As illustrated by the problems above, many people claim membership in religious groups without being very reflective about their religious traditions, and often without those traditions having much effect on their lives. Their lives *are* shaped by their deepest convictions, but often those convictions are more societal or self-centered than religious. Now let us consider some people unusual in the degree to which their expressed religious ideals shaped the way they lived their everyday lives in every detail: Mahatma Gandhi, Vinoba Bhave, and Swami Agnivesh.

SPOKESPERSONS FOR JUSTICE AND PEACE

Mohandas (Mahatma) Gandhi

Gandhi is remembered especially for his highly successful campaign of active non-violence to free India from British rule. As his success and fame grew, he came to be called "Mahatma," a term of respect which means "great soul."

He grew up in a Hindu family in close contact with Muslims and in an area where Jains were also influential. (*Jains* are followers of Jainism, which has a strong commitment to nonviolence similar to that of Buddhism.) He studied law in England, where he had to confront Christianity and Western ideas. It was also here that he read the Bhagavad Gita for the first time—in English translation. After his studies he returned as a lawyer to India, where he had very little success in law. He then went to South Africa to defend Indian citizens who were being mistreated. There he came to see the injustices of the South African laws, discovered how powerfully ahimsa could confront those laws, and directed a successful resistance movement against them.

Gandhi interpreted ahimsa in a broad sense to rule out killing in war. In so doing, he had to deal with the Bhagavad Gita because it seemed to demand war.

1. First, he interpreted the Gita as a *spiritual* message dealing with the inner need to overcome our resistance to internal struggle and our reluctance to "put to death" habits and tendencies that are so familiar to us that they seem to be "family" or "relatives." Gandhi shares this interpretation with many other interpreters.[35]
2. Second, the *Mahabharata as a whole*, in dealing at length and in detail with the historical Mahabharata war, illustrates the futility of war as a means of solving problems and bringing justice because, at the end of the war after much death and suffering, the situation is worse than it was at the beginning. Thus it illustrates the reality that resorting to violence, by the bad karma it produces, outbalances the good karma that one is attempting to produce.[36]
3. Third, Gandhi notes that Arjuna is not opposed to killing other humans *in general*, since he has willingly fought in other wars. He is just opposed to killing *his relatives*. This is selfish favoritism. If war is acceptable, then it must be acceptable even if our family members and relatives are among those killed.[37]

To those who objected that Gandhi had no qualifications for interpreting the Gita, he agreed in terms of scholarship, but maintained that the more important qualifications for interpretation are not scholarship but personal commitment to *live* the message of the Gita and one's experience in attempting to do so. He said,

"I have something far more powerful than argument, namely, experience . . . an effort to enforce the meaning [of the Gita] in my own conduct for an unbroken period of forty years" and, "It is a misuse of our intellectual energy and a waste of time to go on reading what we cannot put into practice."[38]

Gandhi's justification raises the interesting question of which is more important for understanding religious traditions and convictions: meticulous scholarship or personal spiritual commitment. Modern Western scholars seek knowledge that is dependent only on careful study, not on the holiness or personal life of the scholar, and that can thus be repeated by any scholar using the same scholarly methods. Others maintain that you can't really understand what the words mean unless you have personally experienced the reality they are talking about. We maintain that both careful scholarship and personal spiritual engagement are essential to understanding spiritual realities. We have experienced the weakness of people who have one without the other; perhaps you have too. At the same time, everyone has something valuable to teach others.

Gandhi held that the eternal truths contained in the Gita, like those contained in all sacred writings, are filtered through two imperfect media: (1) human prophets, and (2) the interpreters who attempt to explain the prophets.

So Gandhi felt justified in reinterpreting the prophets based on his own experience. He went so far as to say, "I believe that the teaching of the *Gita* does not justify war, even if the author of the *Gita* intended otherwise," and:

> Let it be granted, that according to the letter of the *Gita* it is possible to say that warfare is consistent with renunciation of fruit. [In other words, the *Gita* claims that one can engage in warfare while remaining detached from emotions like greed, hatred, rage, and fear; and from concern for victory or defeat.] But after 40 years of unremitting endeavor fully to enforce the teaching of the *Gita* in my own life, I have, in all humility, felt that perfect renunciation is impossible without perfect observance of ahimsa in every shape and form.[39]

Positively, Gandhi believed that the essence of the Gita was contained in the last twenty stanzas of chapter 2. This section describes how one gains perfect control over self along with inner peace *by learning how to remain detached* from what is pleasing and what is displeasing. Thus we can act without the influence of self-centered desire or fear. If we can. As Gandhi might say, it is simple but not easy.

To those who believed that the historical Krishna was an avatar or incarnation of the god Vishnu and therefore was perfect in all respects, Gandhi responded that *every* human is potentially an incarnation of the Absolute God because every atman is God. Krishna was not "ontologically" different from any other human, just more developed. The *literary* Krishna is perfect, but this literary figure is imaginative. The *historical* Krishna, like any human, despite his immense merit and consequent state of moksha or near-moksha, was still only in the final stages of being "on the way" to perfection. Thus, the literary Krishna urges *inner, spiritual* battle against evil, and this advice is perfect. The historical Krishna urged *outer, physical* battle, and this advice was flawed, as is evident from the long-term effects of the war.

Gandhi's interpretation of the Gita is unusual, and few Hindu scholars have followed him so far as to delegitimize war. But his theory and practice of nonviolence have been much more effective and influential.

Returning to India with these new ideas and considerable fame, he began to use the techniques of ahimsa assertively to challenge the British colonial rule of India. For Gandhi, ahimsa was more than a technique; it was a way of life. He learned how to use provocative actions to force a confrontation, and how to make imprisonment and fasting work in his favor. It was in prison that Gandhi had the time to study the Gita at length. As a result of Gandhi's nonviolent campaigns, conducted for more than twenty-five years, the British left India by their own choice in 1947 and on good terms with the Indians. Unfortunately, the internal power struggle in India was not yet resolved. Hindu and Muslim tensions led to widespread rioting, the transfer of ten to twenty million people, and hundreds of thousands of deaths over the partition of the former colony into Hindu India and Muslim Pakistan. Gandhi went on a "fast to death" or until the violence stopped. His fast did end the violence. But then, on January 30, 1948, a right-wing Hindu who thought that Gandhi favored Muslims assassinated him.

Once the government in India passed over into the hands of those who had cooperated with Gandhi, the new rulers did not maintain a consistently nonviolent approach to power. For many of them, ahimsa had been a tactic for the circumstances of British colonial rule, not a consistent way of life. In Gandhi's terms, they had been using a "**nonviolence of the weak**" rather than a "**nonviolence of the strong**." *Nonviolence of the strong* is practiced even when one has the power to enforce one's position violently, because it is based on a way of life and the conviction that the means we choose shape the ends we achieve. It requires courage and strength of character to accept suffering. *Nonviolence of the weak* is merely a prudent tactic adopted by those who have insufficient power to use violence effectively. When they develop enough power to use violence, they use it. This nonviolence reveals cowardice and weakness of character.

Gandhi urged nonviolence of the strong and made ahimsa a way of life, but for many of his followers ahimsa was just a tactic to be used in certain circumstances. To be fair to them, there must be a great temptation to use violence when one inherits an existing government and army.

Satyagraha

To explain the power that ahimsa can yield when used correctly, Gandhi coined the new word **satyagraha**. It is often translated as "truth-force" or "soul-force" (the translation Martin Luther King Jr. preferred) to emphasize its power. More literally it is *satya*/"truth" plus *graha*/"holding." Thus it refers to the powerful impact that honesty and integrity have when they are courageously maintained and expressed in the face of threats and violence without retaliation.

Satyagraha combined with ahimsa—holding courageously to truth in threatening situations without harming the opponent—acts powerfully to transform oppressive situations. When an opponent realizes that I am not going to hurt him but that I will accept torture and death rather than comply with a line of action I consider unjust, his conscience is deeply touched. If on the other hand I threaten him with harm, he will feel justified when attacking me in self-defense.

Key Principles of Satyagraha

We must not force others to accept our view, because we can never be sure that our view is wholly right. We must respect the humanity of our opponents and offer them an honorable solution that does not shame them. In even the most desperate situation we always have good choices. We can always (a) refuse to cooperate with actions we consider evil, and (b) suffer. Innocent suffering has the power to touch hearts and convert people.

Violence is better than cowardice. Satyagraha requires bravery. Cowardly people give in to threats of violence and cooperate with what they know is wrong. Thus they fail to practice satyagraha because they do not act in truth, and they fail to practice ahimsa because they cooperate in harming their neighbor, at least by failing to confront those who cause harm.

Rules for a Satyagraha Campaign

Gandhi proposed the following rules for a campaign of satyagraha:

1. *Self-reliance.* The practitioners must not depend on outsiders; they must maintain their independence of action. As a result, they must be modest in their goals.
2. *Initiative.* The resisters must keep the initiative in the struggle by constantly analyzing the situation and beginning new actions that keep the opponent off guard.
3. *Communication.* The resisters must communicate clearly to educate their followers, mobilize outsiders in their support, and speak their demands clearly to the opponent.
4. *Reasonableness.* The resisters must demand no more than truth and integrity require. They must be ready for reasonable negotiation. Even if they have the power to force excessive concessions, they should not use it.
5. *Advance by stages.* The resisters must understand the progress of the campaign so that they can choose the steps toward their goal.
6. *Self-examination.* Morale and discipline require that the resisters keep examining their own strengths and weaknesses and acting to purify themselves.
7. *Respect for opponent.* The opponent must be able to see that the resisters seek a solution that respects both sides and does not seek to humiliate the opponent.

8. *Holding on to essentials.* Despite the willingness to negotiate fairly taught in step four, there must be no compromise of the essentials demanded by truth and integrity.

Gandhi's "Constructive Program"

Besides his program of provocative nonviolence to make it impossible for the British to govern India, Gandhi also promoted a "**constructive program**" designed to teach Indians how to rule themselves. He wanted to help the poor masses of India overcome their sense of powerlessness. This program centered on small-scale technology and a village-based economy, symbolized by village health, cleanliness (sanitation and hygiene), education, and industry. Gandhi led a campaign to encourage all Indians to spin cotton, weave cloth, and wear clothing made by themselves or by local artisans (from khadi, or homespun cloth) rather than to buy factory-made clothes imported from England.

Gandhi considered it bad economics to have millions of Indians out of work while British workers made clothing for Indians to wear. An economy that fails to use local resources and wastes the talents and energies of local people is not a good economy. Many of his ideas continue to influence those who urge "sustainable development." In India, they continued to be applied especially in the famous land reform campaigns of his follower Vinoba Bhave.

Vinoba Bhave

The most famous of Gandhi's followers was Vinoba Bhave. He first joined Gandhi when he was twenty-one, just after he graduated from college. A multilingual scholar of Sanskrit and Indian religious and philosophical literature, he was very active in Gandhi's constructive program. After Gandhi was assassinated, Vinoba became the leader of his movement.

Bhoodan and Gramdan (Land Distribution)

In 1951 Vinoba met a group of Dalits who wanted him to help them purchase eighty acres of land. He called a public meeting and presented the problem. A rich landowner offered to donate one hundred of his five hundred acres. Inspired by this act of generosity, Vinoba began a national campaign to encourage voluntary donations of land (**Bhoodan**), and later of villages (**Gramdan**), money, time, and other contributions. Vinoba traveled around India organizing public gatherings at which the wealthy were invited to make such donations. In addition to meeting the needs of the poor and teaching the poor how to "stand on their own feet" to meet their own needs, this campaign was designed to heal owners of their "slavery to money" and to promote a unity of hearts between all classes. By the time of his death, over four million acres of land, and all the property in over one hundred seventy thousand villages, had been donated to the poor or the public good.

Vinoba related these activities of Gramdan and Bhoodan to the Gita by noting that the Gita emphasizes the importance of *bhakti*, or worship of God. But *if God is in all of creation, especially in every human, then worship of God includes service to other humans, especially those in need.* The Gita says that we pay our debt (a) to the universe that sustains us by practicing sacrifice *(yajna)*, (b) to the society of humans that we depend on by giving alms *(dana)*, and (c) to our own bodies by spiritual discipline *(tapas)*. By donating excess land or resources, we (a) express our devotion to God through service, (b) sacrifice to the universe in service, (c) give alms to society through service, and (d) exercise spiritual discipline through service.

Vinoba also connects the concept of action without desire for personal results (fruits) with service. One lets go of control over the results of one's actions and dedicates the action and its effects to the Lord. Thus it is easier to let go of land, resources, money, time, and use of talents if one is not hoping to gain something from the loss. One should not act generously in hopes of getting something in return, not even fame or prestige.[40]

Swami Agnivesh

Born in 1939, Agnivesh studied law and economics at the University of Calcutta. In 1970 he started a political party inspired by the reformist Arya Samaj movement. As a political activist, Agnivesh has focused his efforts on achieving economic and gender justice. In *Vedic Socialism*, Agnivesh calls for nationalizing "the means of production," free public education, guaranteed employment, free health care and legal aid, and a universal pension system. As a Hindu, he opposes inter-religious "communalism" as well as spirituality that is "individualistic or escapist." Religion must "address social needs," and "positive elements from all religions should be integrated into mainstream politics." Thus he sees religion and politics as inseparable.[41]

SUMMARY

Hindus believe that the world of sense experience is illusory compared with the spirit world of their atman. They pray and sacrifice to many gods, seeking advantage in this world of sense experience, but see these gods as various manifestations of the one Brahman. They explain suffering as a natural result of a person's own past bad actions. Understanding that humans are caught in an endless cycle of reincarnation, they seek to escape this dreary round by choosing to act well, but without anxiety about the results of their actions, hoping thus to enter moksha. They attempt not to harm life in general, but Gandhi and his followers were unusual in applying the principle of ahimsa to every form of life, including violent opponents. By contrast, most Hindus see warfare and violence as a normal part of life, especially for kshatriyas.

KEY TERMS

Advaita Vedanta   maya
ahimsa   moksha
atman   nonviolence of the strong
Bhagavad Gita   nonviolence of the weak
bhakti   outcastes
Bhoodan   *Ramayana*
Brahma   reincarnation
Brahman   samsara
brahman   satyagraha
Brahmana   scheduled castes
Brahmin   scheduled tribes
caste   Shruti
constructive program   Shudra
Dalit   Smriti
dharma   transmigration of souls
Gramdan   untouchables
Harijan   Upanishads
jnana   Vaishya
karma   Vedanta
Kshatriya   Vedas
Mahabharata   yoga, yogi

DISCUSSION QUESTIONS

1. If we were to apply the four Hindu castes to our own society in the United States, which caste would you and your family fall into? In which caste would your future plans (profession or work appropriate to your major field of study) place you?

2. Which of Gandhi's *principles* of satyagraha do you agree with? Which do you disagree with? Explain your reasons. (Or which do you find most convincing? Least convincing?)

3. Think of a campaign or struggle that is important to you (violent or nonviolent). Indicate which of Gandhi's *rules* for a satyagraha campaign are being observed in that campaign. Would the struggle be more or less successful if it followed his principles more closely? How so?

4. How important do you think a "constructive program" is when a group is struggling for freedom or self-determination? If you think it is important, identify a struggle that is important to you and suggest a constructive program for that struggle.

5. Identify a current conflict that is thought to be based on religious differences. Then ask yourself to what extent religion is a *cause* of the conflict, to what

extent religion is the *organizing principle* that helps people "choose sides" and establish identity, and to what extent the teachings and practices of religions actually *shape* the course of the conflict and the actions of its participants. Alternatively, do you think the conflict is essentially unrelated to religion? Could religion point toward a solution?

6. Mohandas Gandhi and Vinoba Bhave strongly opposed war and embraced simple lives of poverty in order to help the poor. These are not typical Hindu reactions to the world's suffering. Can you name some members of *your own* worldview who interpret your worldview in such striking and unusual ways? Are such people impractical dreamers, dangerous crackpots, or helpful models for the rest of us?

SUGGESTIONS FOR FURTHER READING

The Bhagavadgita, with an Introductory Essay, Sanskrit Text [Transliterated], English Translation and Notes by S. Radhakrishnan.

Bhave. *Revolutionary Sarvodaya.*

———. *Talks on the Gita.*

Bondurant. *Conquest of Violence: The Gandhian Philosophy of Conflict.*

Coward, Harold, ed. *Indian Critiques of Gandhi.*

Erikson. *Gandhi's Truth: On the Origins of Militant Nonviolence.*

Fisher. *Living Religions,* 5th ed.

Gandhi. *An Autobiography: The Story of My Experiments with Truth.*

———. *The Bhagvadgita.*

———. *Non-Violence in Peace and War.*

———. *Non-Violent Resistance (Satyagraha).*

Griffiths, ed. *Christianity Through Non-Christian Eyes.*

Jordens. "Gandhi and the *Bhagavadgita.*"

Matthews. *World Religions,* 4th ed.

Minor, ed. *Modern Indian Interpreters of the Bhagavadgita.*

Nanda. *Mahatma Gandhi: A Biography.*

Oxtoby, ed. *World Religions: Eastern Traditions,* 2nd ed.

Oxtoby and Segal, eds. *A Concise Introduction to World Religions.*

Prabhupada. *Bhagavad-Gita as It Is.*

Radhakrishnan. *Indian Philosophy.*

Rambachan. *The Advaita Worldview.*

———. "A Hindu Perspective."

Roy. *Some Trouble with Cows: Making Sense of Social Conflict.*

Sharp. *Gandhi as a Political Strategist: With Essays on Ethics and Politics.*

Spiro. *Anthropological Other or Burmese Brother?*

———. *Buddhism and Society: A Great Tradition and Its Burmese Vicissitudes.*

Vasto. *Gandhi to Vinoba: The New Pilgrimage.*

Weber. *Gandhi's Peace Army: The Shanti Sena and Unarmed Peacekeeping.*

Wilson. "Vinoba Bhave's Talks on the *Gita.*"

Yogananda. *Autobiography of a Yogi.*

Zaehner. *Hinduism.*

2

Buddhist Worldviews

Now, this, O bhikkhus, is the noble truth concerning suffering: Birth is attended with pain, decay is painful, disease is painful, death is painful. Union with the unpleasant is painful, painful is separation from the pleasant; and any craving that is unsatisfied, that too is painful. In brief, bodily conditions which spring from attachment are painful.

Now this, O bhikkhus, is the noble truth concerning the origin of suffering: Verily, it is that craving which causes the renewal of existence, accompanied by sensual delight, seeking satisfaction now here, now there, the craving for the gratification of the passions, the craving for a future life, and the craving for happiness in this life.

—Buddha, "The Sermon at Benares"[1]

EXPERIENTIAL AND EMOTIONAL DIMENSION

When Siddhartha Gautama, who had been raised in a privileged and highly protected environment, first encountered an old man, a sick man, a corpse, and an ascetic, he was deeply shaken. When traditional Hindu doctrine, asceticism, and meditation failed to explain the problem to his satisfaction, he committed himself to meditating under a single tree until he arrived at a satisfactory answer. After forty-nine days, he was suddenly *enlightened*. We will outline the intellectual understanding of that **enlightenment** below under the doctrinal dimension; the meditative search for the experience of enlightenment itself, and the peace and joy that enlightenment brings, are the experiential and emotional center of the Buddhist faith. Buddhist writings discuss meditation techniques at length, but Buddhists generally believe that nothing can take the place of experience: one's own, and for some Buddhists that of a guide or *guru* who has already achieved enlightenment.

HISTORICAL PERIODS[2]

1. The initial period of Buddhism, including the life and teaching of Siddhartha Gautama, extended from about 550 to 450 BCE. During much of that period, the **Buddha** taught his new insights and organized his disciples into monastic communities.
2. From about 450 BCE to the first century CE, various Buddhist schools of thought argued over the correct interpretation of the **dharma** (Buddhist teaching).
3. From the first to the seventh centuries CE, a new form of Buddhism called **Mahayana** developed, even as the earlier **Theravada** form was being more completely developed. This period is considered the classical period.
4. Beginning in the seventh century, the form of Buddhism called **Vajrayana** emerged and evolved, especially in Nepal and Tibet.
5. From the thirteenth century, Buddhism essentially died in India—or rather was absorbed by a Hindu renewal that adapted many of its ideas—although it maintained a strong presence in Sri Lanka just off-shore, and continued to grow in Nepal and Tibet to the North, and to the east as far as China and Japan. Ninian Smart calls 4 and 5 the "Medieval Period."[3]
6. Finally, from the eighteenth century CE to the present, Buddhist societies experienced the impact and aftermath of Western colonization. Most recently, Buddhist centers have been founded in the West.[4]

For further discussion of the three major forms of Buddhism, see the doctrinal and philosophical dimension below.

SACRED WRITINGS

Buddhism does not claim that any of its sacred literature has been inspired by a god, since it sets aside the question whether a god or gods even exist. It offers the experience and insights of Siddhartha Gautama and later Buddhists; then it encourages people to try out those ideas and see for themselves. Learning from what other people have said is useless unless one validates it with one's own experience. Nevertheless, the classical Buddhist writings are highly valued. The *Tripitaka* (or "Three Baskets") represents the Buddhist canon of scripture. The first basket (*pitaka*) gives a history of the Buddhist **sangha**, or community of monks, and the rules it follows; the second is thought to recount the Buddha's teaching sessions; and the third is a collection of Buddhist philosophy and psychology. The ***Jataka Tales***, while not considered part of the canon, narrate stories of the Buddha in his earlier lives before his incarnation as Siddhartha Gautama. The Tripitaka tends to relate to the doctrinal and practical dimensions, the *Jataka Tales* to the narrative dimension, although there is considerable overlap in types of content.

NARRATIVE OR MYTHIC DIMENSION

Life of Siddhartha Gautama

Tradition holds that Siddhartha Gautama was born in 563 BCE:[5] the last rebirth of the one who was to become the Buddha—the "Enlightened One." The *Jataka Tales* describe many edifying experiences he had in previous lives, human and otherwise, that prepared him for this last round of samsara, in which he was to attain **nirvana** (nibbana[6])—the cessation of all suffering—and leave us the *dharma* (dhamma)— the "teaching of the Buddha"[7]—which can help us follow him into nirvana.

Siddhartha was born a member of the Sakyas, so he is also remembered as Sakyamuni: sage of the Sakyas. Early in his marriage he was moved by four striking experiences to abandon his family and join a small group of *sramanas*, or wandering ascetics, in search of truth. After many adventures, including near collapse from excessive fasting and other disciplines, he realized the importance of moderation, which he called the "middle way" or "middle path." Eventually he attained enlightenment (**bodhi**) while meditating for forty-nine days under a particular tree, afterward called the Bodhi Tree.

Filled with this new enlightenment and with a zeal to teach the truths it revealed, the Buddha returned to his companions, instructed them in the "four noble truths"—his revolutionary discovery—and founded the *sangha*, or community of disciples who would pass on knowledge of the true way to nirvana. He lived for forty-five more years, during which he traveled and taught. Finally he attained **parinirvana**, a mysterious state from which he would never be reborn into this world, but in which it is neither correct to say that he exists, nor to say that he does not exist, nor both, nor neither. His followers cremated his body.

Siddhartha was not the only Buddha, just the most recent. All the schools of Buddhism recognize earlier Buddhas. In Mahayana belief, a new Buddha appears after a period of decay to restore true faith. With the death of the Buddha and the passage of time, decay sets in again; as things hit rock bottom, another Buddha appears, again restoring truth faith, and so on. Buddhist scripture also speaks briefly of a future time when the tradition will be almost totally forgotten. Then a Buddha named Maitreya will restore the lost Buddhist teachings.

DOCTRINAL AND PHILOSOPHICAL DIMENSION

Buddhism's Challenge to Hinduism

The core of the Buddhist message was a new view of the nature of life and reality which challenged traditional Hindu doctrinal views and the authority of the Hindu Brahmins. It claimed that enlightenment came from personal discovery and that the ancient tradition of the Vedas and the authority of the Brahmins was comparatively unhelpful. Buddhism also denied the reality of a self-subsisting, eternal human personality, of an imperishable atman or soul that could come into personal relationship with a god after death.

The Four Noble Truths

The key experience that Buddhist doctrine attempts to explain is the experience of enlightenment, which the Buddha and his followers discovered by meditating on the tragic and unsatisfying experience of life itself. Enlightenment gave the Buddha these insights:

1. *The truth of suffering. All life is suffering* (**dukkha:** *ultimately dissatisfying because nothing is permanent*). This insight can be explained as follows: What we *dislike* causes suffering because (a) we hate it when we have it, and (b) we fear it when we don't have it. But what we *like* causes suffering, too, because (c) we want it when we don't have it, and (d) we fear losing it when we do have it.
2. *The cause of suffering. Suffering is caused by our "attachment": yearning, desiring, and attempting to hold on to things* both *material* and *spiritual—even to existence itself.* Although *everything* is impermanent, we suffer not because things *are* impermanent, but because we cling to an *imagined* permanence that does not exist and dissolves in our hands. Even when we seem to have a firm grasp on good things, we realize that everything, even life itself, even our "personality," is impermanent and we will eventually have to let everything go.
3. *The cessation of suffering.* Since suffering is caused by yearning and desire, *we could overcome suffering if we could overcome yearning and desire.*
4. *How to overcome yearning and desire. We overcome yearning and desire by following the eightfold path.* This path leads us eventually to nirvana (see below).

Table 2.1.

Things, material and spiritual		
	We have them	*We don't have them*
Things we like	fear losing them	want them
Things we dislike	want to get rid of them	fear getting them

The Eightfold Path

The eightfold path divides into three groups:

Group A. *Relating to wisdom (panna or prajna)*
1. *Perfect understanding* about the four noble truths, the reality of impermanence and suffering, and the fact that there is no human soul or atman.

2. *Perfect resolve* to trust and follow the perfect understanding by renouncing desire, loving all beings, and harming none.

GROUP B. *Relating to morality (sila) in daily life (ethical and legal dimension)*
3. *Perfect speech.* Don't lie, slander, gossip.
4. *Perfect conduct.* Follow the right ethical observances. (There are various opinions on what constitutes right observances, expressed in different lists.)
5. *Perfect livelihood.* Avoid professions like butcher, hunter, or bomb maker that conflict with Buddhist values because they cause harm or injustice to sentient beings.

GROUP C. *Relating to concentration (samadhi), meditation, yoga (practical and ritual dimension)*
6. *Perfect effort.* Do what will help your karma, avoid what will hurt it. Keep out new evil, throw out old evil; bring in new good, cultivate old good. The purpose is self-perfection.
7. *Perfect mindfulness.* Meditative practice that centers attention in turn on body, emotions, mind, and ideas produced by the mind (mental objects). The purpose is to be aware of our inner states.
8. *Perfect concentration.* Meditative practice of concentration on a single physical or mental object, realizing that all is impermanent, unsatisfying, without substance. The purpose is to lead the mind through four stages of progressively deeper absorption and detachment into enlightenment.

While this is the traditional order for arranging the eightfold path, one is not likely to pass successively along each path in this order on the way to enlightenment. Actual progress will be circular. Although one may first be impressed by the vision (path 1) and make an initial commitment to try it out (path 2), it is not likely that one will understand that insight very well if one is living a corrupt life (paths 3 and 4) thoughtlessly (paths 6–8) in a wretched job (path 5). As one works to reform one's moral life (paths 3–5), meditation becomes easier (paths 6–8) and wisdom becomes less frightening and threatening (paths 1–2). Meditation helps one experience the truth of Buddhist wisdom (paths 1–2). Deeper insight into that wisdom strengthens one's practice of morality and meditation, and the circle goes on.

Analogues in Other Traditions

Without too easily claiming agreement, it is useful to consider whether the experiences and traditions of other religions express similar ideas. For example, Christian tradition says we should be detached from disordered desire for material things, should trust in God's will rather than our own, and should love even our enemies. Similarly, Islam urges self-surrender to God's will. In your own experience, have you felt relief when you let go of some desire or goal that you could not attain? When you let go of resentment and forgave someone who had hurt you, did your feelings toward that person change?

Here are two Christian examples of detachment:

1. A Russian Christian staretz, or spiritual director, Staretz Silouan (d. 1938), quotes Paissey the Great, who was trying to overcome anger. God spoke to this holy man in his prayer: "Paissey, if thou dost not wish to get angry, desire nothing, neither criticize nor hate any man, and thou wilt have no anger."[8]
2. An American Jesuit priest in prison in Moscow during World War II, Walter Ciszek, had a deep experience of frustration that tempted him to commit suicide: he was unable to convince his interrogator that he was telling the truth. Then he realized he didn't need to be so frustrated. The interrogator was not frustrating God's will—the interrogation itself was at this moment God's will for him. God wanted him to let go of all attempts to control the situation, then to speak naturally and honestly what felt right at the moment: what happened next was God's responsibility. This realization freed him from his agony and radically changed the situation.[9]

These Christian examples are not encouraging us to be cowards. When we truly hold on to nothing but God, we are freed to risk ourselves totally for God, justice, and peace.

Anatman and Nirvana

Buddhist doctrine teaches that the individual ego or soul is just as impermanent as the rest of the reality we experience, although the Buddha never affirmed this clearly. This impermanence of the ego is indicated by the term **anatman**, combining the negative "a" with the word "atman." The doctrine of anatman complicates Buddhist teaching about karma and rebirth (see below).

Nirvana is escape from all suffering, which is attained when we overcome desire, hatred, and delusion. It frees us from the effects of karma, the constant progression of birth, growth, decay, and death—"arising, subsisting, changing, and passing away."[10]

Those who achieve the state of nirvana by the time they die escape from the round of births and deaths called samsara. According to the great tradition, nirvana means "extinction of *suffering*"; it does *not* mean "annihilation," but rather "entry into another mode of existence." The true nature of nirvana is beyond our capacity to understand; it cannot be described adequately in human words. It is not located in space, yet the person who attains nirvana does not "cease to exist." The Buddha thought that efforts to *describe* it would be a distraction from the spiritual practice that can lead one to *attain* it—it should be enough to know that nirvana extinguishes all suffering.[11]

Since for Buddhists there is no atman or individual, independent, eternal soul to survive death, nirvana differs from Hindu moksha. Buddhists believe there is a human *ego*, but it is dependent on and arises out of five impermanent and constantly changing human "aggregates"—form (our body and the physical world that surrounds it), sensation (pleasant, unpleasant, or indifferent sights, sounds, tastes, smells, and touches, and the emotions they give rise to), perception (understanding what we are sensing), mental formations (habits and willful choices), and consciousness. There is also no Brahman or universal soul (in the Hindu sense) with whom the atman of Hindu nondualistic theology could merge.[12]

Students—and scholars—sometimes ask, If there is no soul, how can there be rebirth? What is born again? What we experience as our ego is just a combination of energies of various types—the "aggregates" mentioned above. These energies arise from the desires that trap us in the round of samsara. It is this impermanent collection of energies that produces the new birth. Some Buddhists insist that the term "rebirth" is more accurate than the term "reincarnation," since there is no "eternal soul" to be "en-fleshed" or "em-bodied" (the meaning of "in-carnation"). But many Buddhists use the term "reincarnation" anyway.

To put it another way, every present moment is caused by the immediately preceding moment. We like to think that there is some permanent "thing" that connects the present with the past. But in reality the only connection is the karmic causation of the present collection of energies by the immediately preceding collection of energies. Because this process has been going on forever, every new moment is causally connected with every past moment, since the immediately preceding arrangement of energies was shaped by what preceded it, and so on back down the line. When a person dies, the process continues without interruption. In other words, there is no more discontinuity between the moment before death and the moment after death than there is between any two moments in one's current life. So the "shape" of the collected energies just before death determines what happens at the moment of death and then in the next moment, and the process continues.

Through karma, our actions based on desire produce good or bad effects in this life or a future life. In your own life, if you experience pain that you connect consciously with past bad choices that "you" made (although the Buddhists claim there is no unchanging "you" to connect "your" past to "your" present), the same will be true on the other side of death, with the exception that your memory of the past before your new birth may be dulled. You can decide whether it is safe to amass bad karma on the gamble that the consequences won't strike you in this life, and it won't be "you" who suffer the consequences when "your energies" cause a new birth. Was it not "you" who made the bad choices earlier in "your" life which you are suffering from now? If you get drunk and kill a pedestrian, will it be "someone else" who goes to jail?

Note that in Christian theology, the human being—body and soul—is a *creature*. At every moment we are dependent on God for every aspect of our existence. Yet God lives within the *redeemed* human, by God's grace. So the Christian, like the Buddhist, does not believe in a human atman that is a "piece" or "spark" of God, eternal in the same sense that God is eternal, but the Christian *does* believe that the eternal God lives in intimate union with everyone who has surrendered to God's will.[13]

Moving from the great tradition to the little tradition, it is doubtful that many Buddhists have internalized the concept of "no atman." To judge from sociological studies conducted by Melford Spiro in Burma, most Burmese Buddhists concentrate on gaining merit so that they will experience a better rebirth—as rich males.[14] Either they lack confidence that their spiritual progress is sufficient to make the passage to nirvana likely at the end of this lifetime, or they are not attracted to nirvana, which they perceive as annihilation. According to Spiro, "The average Burmese villager . . . desires . . . to remain in the wheel of life [samsara] and to experience pleasure, luxury, and enjoyment."[15]

Three Forms of Buddhism

Theravada

Originally Buddhism concentrated on liberating the *individual* through meditation and the monastic life. Non-monks could gain good karma through their actions, in the hopes of being reborn with enough merit to become monks. Among the actions that promoted good karma was material or financial support of monks and their monasteries. This individualistic emphasis continues in the *Theravada* Buddhism that is dominant today in Southeast Asia: Sri Lanka, Burma, Thailand, and Indochina, with the exception of Vietnam.

Mahayana

Another emphasis developed in the *Mahayana* school, dominant in China and Japan. Zen is derived from the Mahayana school. "Mahayana" means "great vehicle." The followers of this school called the older school of Theravada Buddhism "**Hinayana**," or "lesser vehicle." Mahayana sees Theravada as self-centered in its individualism. Instead, Mahayana proposes to liberate the whole world. One who achieves enlightenment should have the compassion to wait and reach out to others, as Siddhartha did, before entering nirvana. This new insight is expressed in the figure of the **Bodhisattva**: a person who has the enlightenment to pass into nirvana but postpones doing so in order to teach the dharma and bring others into nirvana as well. As the Mahayana tradition developed, these Bodhisattvas were thought to exist in a state between this world and nirvana, and to be capable of helping those who were still in this world. People began to offer devotion to the Bodhisattvas, hoping to gain merit that would move them toward nirvana. The possible danger in this position is thinking that one can attain nirvana by the merit of others without going to the trouble and discipline of seeking enlightenment oneself, although some schools of Buddhism endorse this position.

Today both Theravada and Mahayana propose that people in the world can attain nirvana without becoming monks, thus making enlightenment more widely available. If the world is ultimately empty, they argue, there is no need to leave it and enter monastic life.

The validity of the four noble truths and the emptiness of the world are not simply *intellectual* affirmations. They have to be *realized in a true mystical experience* before they will have the power to transform us and lead us to nirvana. This shows the connection between the *ritual, experiential,* and *doctrinal* dimensions: the *ritual* leads one to *experience the reality* described by the *doctrine*; it is the mystical experience that enlightens one and brings one to nirvana.

Vajrayana

In Tibet, Mahayana Buddhism incorporated "magical" practices: pronouncing mantras and using rituals to put the worshiper into contact with spiritual powers. This form of Buddhism is called *Vajrayana*, or "diamond vehicle."

By visualizing oneself as various Buddha-emanations (gods and goddesses who embody different energies), practitioners overcome obstacles on the path to enlightenment. The Dalai Lama is thought to be the most recent incarnation of Chenrezig (Avalokiteshvara), the Buddha of Compassion. The various Buddha-emanations act as "patron saints" to preserve the community. After Buddhism declined in India, many of the early Indian Buddhist texts were translated into Tibetan and preserved there, along with later Vajrayana texts. When the Maoist Chinese invaded and occupied Tibet and began to suppress Tibetan worship, many Vajrayana Buddhists fled to the West, taking their literature and practices with them.

PRACTICAL AND RITUAL DIMENSION

Buddhist ritual as shaped by Buddhist doctrine is quite different from Jewish, Christian, and Muslim ritual. Most religions use rituals to develop a relationship with God and spiritual beings. What, then, can ritual mean within a worldview like that of early Buddhism, which has little or no relationship with a god or spiritual beings? Theravada Buddhists do not depend on a god for their future, but rather on their own enlightenment. Thus their rituals are designed to incline them toward enlightenment, weaning them from dependence on and preoccupation with whatever might distract them from reality. Their prayer is designed to still their desires, to concentrate their attention, and so to open them to enlightenment. Sacrificial ritual would only attach them more closely to material appearances.

A Japanese Zen tea ceremony, for example, can last four hours in a garden and an adjoining simple room with tatami mat flooring. Each action is carried out slowly, with attention to what is being done and to the simple objects being used. Rather than acting from habit, one concentrates on the present moment—on each movement and on the sights, sounds, and feelings of simple material objects like charcoal fire, light, poured water, lacquered bowls, pottery, crafted wood, flower arrangements, poetry, and calligraphy. Even the simplest object receives attention, since there is no clutter to distract attention. The host concentrates on each guest, seeking to help all enter into a state of tranquility.[16]

In short, most Buddhist rituals are designed to transform a person without reference to his or her relationship with a god or spiritual being. However, Vajrayana Buddhism and some forms of Mahayana Buddhism (such as the Pure Land sect) do use rituals designed to connect practitioners with spiritual beings who can help them gain enlightenment. In fact, many Buddhists pray to the Buddha, regarding him as a great being who is able to respond to their needs. Spiro writes that ordinary Burmese Buddhists see the Buddha as "a personal redeemer who, by forgiving their sins, can assure them of a happy rebirth."[17]

The "Little Tradition" in Ritual

The situation becomes more complex when we look at the "little tradition." Despite the Buddhist conviction that our fate is determined by karma, the effects of which cannot be avoided as long as one's actions are motivated by desire, Spiro[18] found that Burmese Theravadan Buddhists practiced rituals designed to protect them from dangers, and that these rituals were based on a *paritta* or prayer-spell *composed by the Buddha himself*, as preserved in the Buddhist canon. There is a spell to protect one from snakebite—a prayer designed to "let one's love flow out over the four royal breeds of serpents." Unfortunately, the spell will not work if it is one's karma to die, or if one is living an immoral life without faith. But if one's karma leaves the question open, the spell will keep snakes from biting, robbers from striking, elephants from charging, and so on. Numerous other parittas, taken from early Buddhist writings, are used in such rituals.

It is not clear how these spells work, according to Buddhist teaching. Spiro found that most of the Burmese whom he questioned were vague and uncertain on the subject. They used the spells regularly without questioning how they worked until he asked them. Then their answers were confused and varied. One lay group gave the "correct" response that the Buddha was dead. When he asked who would then respond to the ritual offering they were preparing for the next day, they carried on quite a discussion among themselves, concluding that, since it was the Buddha who answered the prayers, he must be alive after all. Other responses Spiro received were that the prayers are answered because the words have power, because the Buddha is "alive in his message," by the power of the Buddha's relics, because the person who built the pagoda had great faith, because there is power in the Buddha image, because the worshiper's faith or confidence has increased, because the worship is a meritorious act that improves not only future karma but present karma, or because the person is helped by one or another of the **devas**, or minor gods.[19]

ETHICAL AND LEGAL DIMENSION

Table 2.2 offers a common list of ethical observances that exemplify "perfect conduct"—the fourth element of the eightfold path. Although there are variations among different lists, the first five points are fairly consistent. For comparison, the

Figure 2.1. Biggest Buddhist stupa in Nepal: Kathmandu. Note (all-seeing) eyes between dome and pitched roof tower. Courtesy David Whitten Smith, 16 February 1998.

ten biblical commandments (in their Roman Catholic division) have been listed in a parallel column. The Christian love command has also been stated in its negative form: "you shall not hate." There are more than ten Buddhist observances because three lists have been combined. The Buddhist and Christian lists are traditionally arranged in a different order—here the order has been varied to show parallels between the two columns.

Buddhists leave open the question whether gods exist, so they have no parallel to the Christian (and Jewish) commands, "You shall not (1) worship other gods, (2) blaspheme, (3) dishonor the Sabbath."

The "Little Tradition" in Ethical Life

In his sociological study of Burmese Theravadan Buddhists, Spiro[20] found three rather different attitudes:

1. The "orthodox" Theravada emphasis on overcoming karma (bad *and* good karma) in order to enter nirvana at the end of one's current life: for this goal, both good and bad karma are barriers, since each leads to rebirth. Even rebirth as a *deva* (minor god or good spirit) prevents one from entering nirvana by causing one to be reborn in a temporary heaven. People who hold this view

Table 2.2.

Buddhist: I undertake to abstain from	Christian: You shall not
harming living beings	kill
taking the not given	steal
sexual misconduct	commit adultery
false speech	lie in law court
use of intoxicating drink or drugs	—
harsh speech	insult
useless speech	—
slanderous speech	lie in law court
covetousness	covet other's spouse
covetousness	covet other's goods
—	dishonor parents
animosity	hate
false views	believe heresy
And from a list for monks: *I undertake to abstain from*	*Christian monks and nuns also live simpler lives than laity do. They vow themselves to*
solid food after noon	poverty
music, dance, etc.	chastity
perfume, jewelry	obedience
high, soft beds	
money, valuables	

try to live in a manner that is "indifferent" to merit, to act with detachment. According to Spiro's research, this position was held by very few.

2. An emphasis on overcoming the effects of bad karma and increasing good karma by gaining merit, especially by making donations to monks and other holy people. The degree of merit was in proportion to the holiness of the recipient—donations to "unworthy" needy people had little or no value. The goal was to be reborn in a more pleasant state: perhaps as a *deva*, or at least as a rich male. In contrast to the first attitude, some believed that eventually lots of good karma would lead one to nirvana.

3. An emphasis on gaining worldly goods and avoiding worldly sufferings in the *present* life, with the help of spells and incantations, without worrying about rebirth and the next life.

SOCIAL AND INSTITUTIONAL DIMENSION

The Sangha

The Buddhist community is called the *sangha*. In a narrower sense, the term refers to its communities of monks, nuns, and novices; in a wider sense, it includes all Buddhists. The *Vinaya-Pitaka* ("discipline basket") contains instructions and rules for these groups as well as "stories about how [the Buddha] came to institute each rule."[21] In heavily Buddhist societies such as Sri Lanka, monks and nuns exercise strong political influence.

Political Stability

For many Buddhists, the doctrine of karma encourages passivity in the presence of "fate." Yet this doctrine may also encourage a political coup d'état, as Spiro found in Burma. When one's good or bad karma has been "used up," one's fate can change abruptly even in this life. So a person whose karma was leading him to be ambitious might attempt to seize control of the government, reasoning that, if the coup were successful, it would mean that his or her own karma had led to his or her new good fortune and the deposed ruler's karma had led to his or her fall from power. The general public, accepting this explanation, would quickly switch its allegiance to the new ruler. So the doctrine can produce general stability punctuated by sudden instabilities. It also produces lots of new pagodas built by leaders who hope that the merit derived from these gifts will make up for the bad karma they accumulated by the lies they told and the people they killed. This last ploy depends on the belief that good karma blots out bad karma. Unfortunately, there is an alternative belief that bad karma must be overcome by suffering, no matter how much good karma one has—even saints have to spend time in hell to overcome the bad karma accrued from their sins.

ISSUES FOR JUSTICE AND PEACE

Women

Early Buddhist texts express both positive and negative views of women, perhaps reflective of the Buddha's stance. He allowed a sangha (monastic order) to be established for nuns and declared women to be men's spiritual equals, "as capable as men of achieving enlightenment,"[22] yet he made the male and female sanghas unequal in status and did not permit nuns to teach monks.[23] As in Hinduism, women were largely excluded from religious leadership. This is changing, though, with more Asian Buddhist women assuming leadership roles.[24] In the U.S., "many Buddhist centers . . . are led by women."[25] Historically with the development of Mahayana Buddhism and later developments in Theravada Buddhism, women's spirituality received greater recognition.[26] The Buddhist "ethic of nonviolence" tended to protect women from male violence.[27] Buddhist men are reported to have a more positive attitude toward nuns or women without children than toward mothers' fertility,[28] since mothers bring new humans into this world of suffering.

War

Buddhism in its origins was pacifist. War and political power were seen as dangerous to one's spiritual progress: the attachment to this world that power, wealth, and violence express and promote yields bad karma and inhibits enlightenment. Worse, political and economic power is often the result of trampling on the rights of others.

There is an incident in the life of the Buddha that illustrates this pacifism. Two peoples, the Sakyans and the Koliyans, lived on opposite sides of the river Rohini. They shared the river as a source of water for their crops. One year there was a drought: there was not enough water in the river for both groups. In this situation of emergency, each laid claim to *all* of the water. Competition led to insults, then to anger, and both groups prepared for war.

The Buddha was the son of a Sakyan father and a Koliyan mother. He happened to be in the area at the time. When he heard of the dispute, he placed himself between the two armies. Both armies saluted him. He then began a discussion to clarify the issue being disputed, which by this time had been lost in mutual insults. When he realized what the dispute was about, he asked the two sides which was more valuable: water or warriors. They agreed that warriors had more value than water. So why were they about to sacrifice the more valuable to get the less valuable? As a result of this intervention, the war was averted and the Sakyans committed themselves to nonviolence.

Some years later the Sakyans were attacked by the king of Kosala. (Note: this is a *third* group, not the Koliyans.) The Sakyans maintained their nonviolent commitment and were slaughtered. Does that prove that nonviolence is impractical? In Buddhist terms (if you believe in karma, rebirth, and nirvana), which is worse: to be slaughtered or to slaughter? Note also that in order to resolve the original Sakyan-Koliyan conflict, the Buddha had to place himself between the two hostile armies, which is normally an uncomfortable position to be in. But if you are truly detached from this world . . .

Warrior Buddhists

With this background, it is surprising to find that some later Buddhists were warriors. There were even professional Buddhist soldiers who claimed that true detachment would free one to be a warrior without anxiety either for oneself or for the enemy. Since this life is impermanent, ending it cannot cause bad karma. And why fear death?

Before and during World War II, such attitudes produced widespread Buddhist support in Japan for the war with China, England, and the United States, including even the "Rape of Nanking," in which between 250,000 and 300,000 Chinese were massacred after the surrender of the city. Zen Master Harada Daiun Sogaku wrote in 1939: "[If ordered to] march: tramp, tramp, or shoot: bang, bang. This is the manifestation of the highest Wisdom [of Enlightenment]. The unity of Zen and war . . . extends to the farthest reaches of the holy war [now under way]."[29] And Lieutenant Colonel Sugimoto Goro wrote: "Warriors who sacrifice their lives for the emperor will not die. They will live forever. Truly they should be called gods and Buddhas for whom there is no life or death. . . . Where there is absolute loyalty, there is no life or death."[30] Such assertions could well be examples of the "counterfeit tradition" created by psychopaths to obscure the "hidden tradition" of their self-centered, imperialist motives.

From 1983 to 2009, a civil war was fought in Sri Lanka between the Buddhist government and a Hindu minority group, the Tamils. When I (David) asked a Tamil refugee how the Buddhists justify warfare according to their worldview, he replied that Sri Lankan Buddhists appeal to an ancient chronicle of how Buddhism came to Sri Lanka. According to the chronicle, the first Buddhist monks entered Sri Lanka in the very hour that the Buddha was dying. The Buddha had had a vision that the Buddhist settlement in Sri Lanka would be the one guarantee of the future purity of Buddhism. Therefore, they feel it is essential for Sri Lanka to remain an explicitly Buddhist society with an explicitly Buddhist government in order to ensure the survival and purity of Buddhism.[31]

How Buddhism can retain its original purity if its followers torture and kill Tamil dissidents is a disturbing question. Buddhists whom I (David) questioned in Sri Lanka in 1998 responded by saying, "You have to defend yourself when others attack you," which didn't sound to me like a Buddhist principle. After I had asked three or four Buddhists, my Buddhist hostess complained, "Why do you keep asking that question? You can't expect us to live our *whole* life according to Buddhist principles." This is an example of the little tradition and the great tradition not coinciding—a reality experienced in all major religions.

Relations with Other Religions

As with Hinduism, serious Buddhist reflection on Christianity does not occur until the nineteenth century. At odds with theism, whether Hindu, Muslim, or Christian,

Buddhists have also focused on ethics, especially saving compassion and love. *Colonialist and missionary* Christianity evoked a *polemical* response, whereas *Communist Chinese aggression in Tibet* led Buddhists to see Christians as *allies.*[32] Even in its own missionary aspect, Buddhism is regarded in general as having cooperated peacefully with Hinduism, Taoism, Shinto, Christianity, and other religions.[33] For low-caste Hindus or untouchables, especially since the mid-twentieth century, Buddhism has offered a no-caste alternative religion that feels familiar, since it also was born in India and shares certain major features with Hinduism. Hindu scholars today admire the Buddha as "a social reformer who advocated equal opportunity for all, regardless of caste and class."[34]

INDIVIDUAL INNER PEACE

A Metta Bhavana Meditation

There is an important relationship between large-scale peace among groups and inner peace within individuals. One way of promoting inner peace is through a Theravada meditation practice called **metta bhavana.** *Metta* means kindness; *bhavana* is meditation. The kindness meditation proceeds in a series of steps as follows:

1. Concentrate on *yourself.* Think kind thoughts toward yourself, concentrating on your good qualities and on times when you felt best about yourself. Let yourself feel appreciated and valued. This basis is important if you are to have the energy to love anyone else.
2. Develop similar positive feelings toward *somebody you like* and feel close to but not in a self-interested way (not, for example, a family member or lover).
3. Now let your good will go out toward *someone you feel neutral toward.*
4. Now do so for *someone you don't like,* someone you feel negative toward.
5. Finally, let your good will expand so that it includes not only the previous individuals but gradually *all humans, everything in the world, and all being throughout all space and time.*

Other Peace Meditations

Joanna Macy writes and offers workshops teaching spiritual exercises and meditations for aspiring peacemakers.[35] Two of these exercises are called "Breathing through the World's Pain" and "The Great Ball of Merit."

Breathing through the World's Pain

We tend to block out the pain of the world, to numb ourselves, because we don't have solutions. But pain is part of the web of life. If we block pain out, we block out our connection with the world. If we can let it through, we become more resilient.

Relax, breathe. Imagine we are breathing in the world's pain in concrete images. Imagine it coming in through mouth and nose, passing through us, and out through a hole in the bottom of our heart back into the web of life. Observe the painful images without fear, and without feeling we have to do anything special about them at this moment beyond recognizing them. Let sorrow ripen and our hearts expand. We don't need to rush off and inflict the world's pain on others who are not so involved at this moment. They will observe and respond in due time.[36]

The Great Ball of Merit

The previous meditation helps us deal with the *pain* of others. This one helps us deal with their *good fortune* without resentment or envy. We learn to take joy in others' joy (Buddhist *muditha*). We begin by opening ourselves to a power beyond ourselves. Buddhists speak of a "ball of merit," roughly similar to Christian concepts of "grace," the "cloud of witnesses," and the "treasury of merit." The idea is that the good fortune of others is not loss to us, but gain.

Meditate on the merit of all humans, past, present, and future. All have some. We imagine that we are heaping it into a huge ball. Rejoice in it; roll it back into the world for healing. We look at the person across from us—perhaps someone in conflict with us. What does this person add to our ball of merit? stubborn endurance? imagination? love? kindness? courage? healing? Inhale awareness of that person; experience gratitude. Observing the good in others, without jealousy, we take pleasure in their goodness, aware that it adds something to us. We imagine ourselves to be detectives spying out riches. When we find some, we congratulate ourselves on our insight. As others begin to sense our visions for them, they tend to respond by acting out those positive visions.[37]

SPOKESPERSONS FOR JUSTICE AND PEACE

Nagarjuna (Second Century CE, India)

Nagarjuna, advisor to the Satavahana king Yajnasiri Satakarni, wrote the *Jewel Garland of Royal Counsels* for the king. His recommendations show how Buddhist principles could influence social and political life. He begins by inviting the king to resign, since perfecting oneself is more important than anything else.[38] He points out that key Buddhist virtues are not individualistic: they have specific *social* expressions:

1. *Individual transcendence or enlightenment:* This is at the base of all social activism, since everyone's final goal is to enter nirvana, and people do that one by one. Further, once the king and others are liberated and compassionate, they won't need *detailed* instructions for social policies—right policies and actions will come naturally.[39]

2. *Tolerance, detachment, and pacifism:* Overcome lust by meditating on ugliness, the filthy body. Don't hunt; animals don't like it, and you won't like what it does to you.[40] Judges should be compassionate to criminals, especially murderers. Judges should imprison humanely, with compassion, or they should banish criminals.[41] Nagarjuna mentions several reasons why Buddhists should not practice capital punishment:

   a. Buddhists should be compassionate, especially to those who don't deserve it.
   b. Capital punishment would suggest that sometimes killing is permissible.
   c. Because nothing is permanent, a criminal's mind can always change.
   d. Because there is no "self," and everyone's actions are conditioned by circumstances, any person is reformable.
   e. Every life is precious, especially a human life, because it is so rare to be born as a human, and it is only in the context of human existence that one can come to enlightenment.[42]

3. *Universal education:* Educate to create Buddhas; support sound teaching (dharma) and the monastic community (sangha).[43] People should be educated to attain enlightenment and liberation, not to prepare them to provide services for selfish rich and powerful people. (Here it is worthwhile thinking about modern higher education. How many of our "professions" are designed to service wealthy people?) Fear of being exposed by the teachings of Buddhist education should motivate self-centered rulers to reform. This education should be free for all, no matter what the cost to the society.[44] Teachers must be examples in their own lives of what they teach.[45]

4. *Compassionate socialism:* The king must provide for every member of society, making specific provisions especially for the needs of the poor, such as special shelters for beggars and cripples. The instructions become very detailed: "Provide water fountains on arid roadways . . . At the fountains, place shoes, umbrellas, water filters, tweezers for removing thorns, needles, thread, and fans."[46] The king should keep taxes low. Police should counter thieves and bandits.[47]

People are afraid that there isn't enough wealth to go around. But experience shows that generosity creates abundance. A main source of wealth is the rulers' gifts of resources to their people. If the wealthy clutch their wealth, then love, optimistic confidence, and the creativity of people will all be destroyed.[48] Once basic needs are met, humans are free to contemplate higher needs.

Did these teachings make any difference? Ideals of this sort need to be checked against history: fine ideals are often ignored in practice. Based on the accounts of contemporary Chinese pilgrims, however, the program of Nagarjuna does seem to have been effective.

Contemporary Counsels[49]

The modern scholar Robert Thurman draws some contemporary counsels from Nagarjuna's writing. He says most Americans don't want to hear that:

We are being waited on and served by people in or from developing countries. We shouldn't consume so much.

The ill, the poor, and death itself should be *visible*, so we can see that life is impermanent and impure.

All beings are of as much value as are we ourselves and those dear to us.

There is no absolute self, no absolute property, no absolute right.[50]

We must face our obligations to other peoples, other species, and nature itself.

The wealth of nations today has come from:

1. the work and invention of former generations;
2. the exploitation of peaceful nations in Asia, Africa, and Latin America; and
3. the generosity of the earth, sun, ocean, and wind.

If we are not generous, we will lose our wealth. *We must* limit economic growth and restrain consumption in order to invest in the future for future generations, to restore resources to the exploited, and to heal our environment—*or we will face disaster!*[51]

Thich Nhat Hanh (1926–, Vietnam, in Exile in France)

The Buddhist monk Thich Nhat Hanh founded the Tiep Hien order in 1964 in Vietnam to "study, experiment and apply Buddhism in an intelligent and effective way to modern life, both individual and societal,"[52] that is, to practice **Engaged Buddhism**, and to resist the Vietnam War. The order started with six persons. It organized demonstrations, wrote and distributed literature, offered social services, organized an underground for draft resisters, and cared for victims of the war.

Under very difficult circumstances the Tiep Hien order practiced social action based on these Buddhist principles: (a) emptiness and nonego in action, (b) the impermanence and insubstantiality of reality, (c) the lack of real separation between myself and my opponents, (d) remaining aware and in a state of compassion, (e) having the courage to see the nature of suffering in its concrete reality, and (f) working to liberate all beings.[53] Members experimented first with themselves, seeking to develop understanding and compassion in ways that could be verified by experience.[54]

The order began with four foundational principles. Note the relationship of these principles to the war in Vietnam, which was underway at the time:

1. *Nonattachment to views* in a time when everyone around them was killing in order to force their views on others.
2. *Direct practice-realization* rather than intellectual speculation, whereas the warring parties were using speculative ideologies to justify the war.
3. *Appropriateness* in meeting the "needs of people and reality of society" rather than the desires of the elite, yet in conformity with the basic tenets of Buddhism.

4. *Skillful means*, or the importance of choosing means that are effective, in contrast to the ineffective means chosen by the warring parties.

The Fourteen Tiep Hien Precepts

The order maintained its spiritual core in the midst of its social service by meeting about every two weeks and publicly and meditatively reciting the following fourteen precepts, which illustrate well the connections between one Buddhist worldview and social action.[55] As you read the precepts, consider how they would have applied in the midst of the war in Vietnam, as well as how they might apply to our own situation today.

1. Do not be idolatrous about or bound to any doctrine, theory, or ideology, even Buddhist ones. All systems of thought are guiding means; they are not absolute truth.
2. Do not think the knowledge you presently possess is changeless, absolute truth. Avoid being narrow-minded and bound to present views. Learn and practice nonattachment from views in order to be open to receive others' viewpoints. Truth is found in life and not merely in conceptual knowledge. Be ready to learn throughout your entire life and to observe reality in yourself and in the world at all times.
3. Do not force others, including children, by any means whatsoever, to adopt your views, whether by authority, threat, money, propaganda, or even education. However, through compassionate dialogue, help others renounce fanaticism and narrowness.
4. Do not avoid contact with suffering or close your eyes before suffering. Do not lose awareness of the existence of suffering in the life of the world. Find ways to be with those who are suffering by all means, including personal contact and visits, images, sound. By such means, awaken yourself and others to the reality of suffering in the world.
5. Do not accumulate wealth while millions are hungry. Do not take as the aim of your life fame, profit, wealth, or sensual pleasure. Live simply and share time, energy, and material resources with those who are in need.
6. Do not maintain anger or hatred. As soon as anger and hatred arise, practice the meditation on compassion in order to deeply understand the persons who have caused anger and hatred. Learn to look at other beings with the eyes of compassion.
7. Do not lose yourself in dispersion and in your surroundings. Learn to practice breathing in order to regain composure of body and mind, to practice mindfulness, and to develop concentration and understanding. (This seventh precept is the heart of Tiep Hien life. It deals with delusion = **avidya.**)
8. Do not utter words that can create discord and cause the community to break. Make every effort to reconcile and resolve all conflicts, however small.

9. Do not say untruthful things for the sake of personal interest or to impress people. Do not utter words that cause division and hatred. Do not spread news that you do not know to be certain. Do not criticize or condemn things that you are not sure of. Always speak truthfully and constructively. Have the courage to speak out about situations of injustice, even when doing so may threaten your own safety.

10. Do not use the Buddhist community for personal gain or profit, or transform your community into a political party. A religious community, however, should take a clear stand against oppression and injustice and should strive to change the situation without engaging in partisan conflicts.

11. Do not live with a vocation that is harmful to humans and nature. Do not invest in companies that deprive others of their chance to live. Select a vocation which helps realize your ideal of compassion.

12. Do not kill. Do not let others kill. Find whatever means possible to protect life and to prevent war.

13. Possess nothing that should belong to others. Respect the property of others, but prevent others from enriching themselves from human suffering or the suffering of other beings.

14. Do not mistreat your body. Learn to handle it with respect. Do not look on your body as only an instrument. Preserve vital energies (sexual, breath, spirit) for the realization of the Way. Sexual expression should not happen without love and commitment. In sexual relationships, be aware of future suffering that may be caused. To preserve the happiness of others, respect the rights and commitments of others. Be fully aware of the responsibility of bringing new lives into the world. Meditate on the world into which you are bringing new beings.[56]

In 1973, after traveling to the United States, Thich Nhat Hanh was denied reentry to Vietnam. In 1982, he established a community dedicated to the practice of mindfulness in southern France called Plum Village, where he lives and teaches. He has written numerous books.[57]

The Dalai Lama (1935–, Tibet, in Exile in India)[58]

Tenzin Gyatso is the fourteenth Dalai Lama (meaning "Ocean of Wisdom"), or rebirth of the Buddhist Bodhisattva of Compassion. Tibetans call him the "wish-fulfilling gem" or "the presence." He was born in the village of Takster in Tibet, into a peasant family. After he was discovered to be the successor of the thirteenth Dalai Lama,[59] he was taken to Llasa, the capital of Tibet, to begin his education. In 1950, while still a teenager, the Dalai Lama assumed the political office of Head of State and Government for Tibet. Four years later, he met with Chinese leaders regarding the status of Tibet, which China had invaded in 1949–1950. Before being awarded a Doctorate of Buddhist Philosophy, he was examined by numerous scholarly monks in logic, the "middle path," monastic discipline, and metaphysics.

As a result of China's military occupation of Tibet in 1959, he moved from Tibet to India, where Dharamsala ("Little Lhasa") has served as the capital-in-exile of the Tibetan government. The Dalai Lama's work on behalf of Tibetan independence has taken the form of (among others) representing the cause of Tibet at the UN, which then issued three Security Council resolutions (1959, 1961, 1965); proposing a Five-Point Peace Plan (1987–1988), according to which an autonomous, democratic Tibet would be established "in association with the People's Republic of China"; and drafting a 1963 constitution that led to the democratic Charter of Tibetans in Exile and in 1992 to the outline of a constitution for a free Tibet.

In 1989 the Dalai Lama received the Nobel Peace Prize. Much traveled in the West as well as the East, he has met with Catholic, Anglican, Jewish, and other religious leaders. For example, in February 2006, he spoke with an ecumenical Korean women's group and went to Israel to promote Israeli-Palestinian dialogue. In May 2011 he resigned as political head of Tibet, retaining his role as Tibet's spiritual leader. A strict advocate of nonviolence in the struggle for Tibetan autonomy and a prolific author, the Dalai Lama also promotes environmental justice and engages in dialogue with world-renowned scientists. He supports religious pluralism in a multi-religious world, or even a world based on compassion apart from religion, and stresses the importance of feeling the suffering of others.[60]

A. T. Ariyaratne (1931–, Sri Lanka)

This Sri Lankan Buddhist layman began a movement of Buddhist social and spiritual development called *Sarvodaya Shramadana* ("the awakening of all through labor donated for the common good") which has helped to mobilize people in over eleven thousand villages in Sri Lanka. He seeks to develop a "no poverty, no affluence society." That may not seem attractive to the affluent—unless they reflect on how poorly their affluence satisfies them—but imagine how it sounds to the poor.

Ariyaratne calls the current world system a "vicious, power-oriented political system" in which affluence is an addiction. He explains that consumerism is against the Buddhist middle way, because it makes everyone want to join the small, affluent elite. The free-market economy provides nonessential but tempting goods. As a result, malnutrition, crime, bribery, and corruption go up; teenagers loot; and other social ills proliferate. People see the consumer society, but find themselves unable to take part in it.[61] Quoting Gandhi, to be nonviolent requires us to desire nothing that the poorest can't have. We need to resist the "hypnotic dazzle" coming with "violent force from the West."[62]

In contrast, Ariyaratne uses the traditional Buddhist "four sublime abodes" to explain how his program leads people to live happier lives:

1. *Metta* (loving kindness) gives one respect and compassion for all lives, especially the lives of the very poor.

2. *Karuna* (compassionate action) leads one to change those things that cause others to suffer; to help those in great need by shared labor; and to fight evil— not the evil-doer. As a result, one experiences
3. *Muditha* (altruistic joy), which is the joy of service; one rejoices in the happiness of those one helps, and as one makes such actions habitual, one comes gradually to experience
4. *Upekka* (equanimity).

He also promotes four principles of *group* behavior:

1. Sharing resources with all to overcome selfishness and craving (*thanha*);
2. Pleasant speech;
3. Constructive activity, material and spiritual—activities conducted together for everyone's benefit; and
4. Equality.[63]

He relates social action to the four noble truths as follows:

1. All life involves the suffering of egoism: "possession, competition, hatred, harsh speech, destructive action, inequality."
2. This suffering has causes such as *avidya* (ignorance), *thanha* (grasping and greed), "disunity, oppression, disease, poverty, and stagnation."
3. The causes can be removed by "awareness building and awakening" through common effort and action for the common good.
4. One should work out a path or concrete plan for doing so.[64]

With regard to appropriate development, he speaks of ten basic human needs:

1. "a clean and beautiful environment,"
2. "a safe and adequate supply of water,"
3. "basic . . . clothing,"
4. "a regular balanced diet,"
5. "a simple abode,"
6. "basic health care services,"
7. "transport and communication facilities,"
8. "fuel,"
9. "continuing education for all" through the whole human cycle of births and deaths, and
10. "cultural and spiritual development."[65]

Note that employment and income are not on the list. They are *only means* to the attainment of these ten human needs. In different circumstances there may be alternative means to attain them.

Finally, Ariyaratne lists four essential components of a good economic system:

1. efficiency in production;
2. protection of what is produced, for example, preservation of food;
3. a healthy "social environment in which production takes place"; and
4. balanced consumption patterns.[66]

Throughout his teaching, he emphasizes the key Buddhist concepts of overcoming one's ego-centeredness (*anatman*) and one's craving (*thanha*) for impermanent, unsatisfying things. We need to overcome our preoccupation with "I, me, and mine," which leads to anger, hatred, and greed. Ariyaratne's writings have been compiled in eight volumes of Collected Works.

During the Sri Lankan civil war (1983–2009) between Sinhalese Buddhists and Tamil Hindus, Ariyaratne was very active in peacemaking endeavors. One of his most successful efforts was a program to bring together Sinhalese and Tamil youth—fifty of each—for a common workshop in which the youth were matched up in pairs. After the workshop they lived together for two months and worked together in their respective communities: one month in the home of the Sinhalese youth, the next month in the home of the Tamil youth. By the time of my (David's) visit with him in Sri Lanka in 1998, he had suspended the follow-up to the workshop because life in the Tamil area had become too dangerous. But he continued the seminars themselves. At the end of a seminar, one of the Tamil youth stood up and said, "My father was killed by Sinhalese. I vowed that in retaliation I would kill seven Sinhalese. But this weekend I have come to know a Sinhalese boy, and I publicly renounce my vow."

Ariyaratne relates the experience of a Buddhist monk who was captured by terrorists, beaten, and abducted. The monk thought to himself:

> Owing to some wrong information I am being beaten and questioned by these foolish people. Perhaps some past karma of mine might even lead to my death. Therefore, there is no point in my hating these people or even generating self-pity toward myself. Rather, I should have loving-kindness for them. Perhaps loving-kindness will bring them to their true senses. At the same time I might be strengthened to bear my suffering with equanimity like a true disciple of the Buddha, and die with loving-kindness in my heart.[67]

During his ordeal, he concentrated on the teachings of the Buddha and on metta. The group that had abducted him came to realize their mistake. They asked him to forgive them, treated his wounds, and released him.

Ariyaratne's work has been quite dangerous at times, and he himself has faced death. Once a Sri Lankan president gave orders to have him assassinated. While praying his Buddhist devotions one evening, he felt a strong force push him forward—a sort of spiritual energy. He went out of his house into the garden and found himself facing a man who was pointing a gun at him. He said, "Go ahead. Shoot. But tell whoever sent you that I die with no hatred in my heart." The man dropped his arm and said, "I can't shoot you. Please go hide."[68]

Aung San Suu Kyi (1945–, Burma)

Suu Kyi was born in Rangoon, Burma. Her father, General Aung San, led Burma's struggle for independence from Britain; he was assassinated in 1947, when Suu Kyi was two years old. Her mother, Khin Kyi, served as the Burmese ambassador to India from 1960 to 1967.

After studying in India and at Oxford University, Suu Kyi worked as assistant secretary of the Advisory Committee on Administration and Budgetary Questions of the UN Secretariat in New York from 1969 to 1971. In the same period she volunteered as a reader and companion to poor hospitalized patients. At the beginning of 1972, she married Michael Aris (who died in 1999) and had two sons with him. She continued her scholarly work at Kyoto (Japan), Simla (northern India), Oxford, and London.

In the spring of 1988 Suu Kyi left England and returned to Burma to care for her mother, who had suffered a stroke. She has remained in Burma since then, dedicating herself to the nonviolent transformation of Burma's government from military dictatorship to popular democracy.[69] When the National League for Democracy won the general elections called by the military junta in 1990, although she was already under house arrest, Suu Kyi should have become prime minister, but the junta did not allow this to happen. In 1990 she was awarded the Sakharov Prize, and in 1991 the Nobel Peace Prize. Released from house arrest in November 2010, Suu Kyi was elected to Burma's parliament in April 2012. The author of several books, including *Freedom from Fear* (1991) and *Letters from Burma* (1997), she is extensively interviewed in *The Voice of Hope: Aung San Suu Kyi* (1997; second edition, 2012).[70] Delivering the opening keynote address to the 1995 NGO Forum on Women in Beijing, China, she said: "It is not the prerogative of men alone to bring light to the world: women with their capacity for compassion and self-sacrifice, their courage and perseverance, have done much to dissipate the darkness of intolerance and hate, suffering and despair."[71]

SUMMARY

The doctrinal core of Buddhism is expressed in the four noble truths, all of which relate to human suffering. Buddhists concentrate on overcoming suffering by letting go of the desire to hang on to impermanent material and spiritual things, including existence itself, through meditation and appropriate, or right, living. If we fail to do so, we will continue to experience rebirth and re-death. Clinging to one's ego produces the main barrier to enlightenment. In practice, few Buddhists pursue nirvana single-heartedly or love other humans unselfishly, but those who do have been very effective in promoting justice and peace. The ultimate authority validating Buddhist teaching is one's own experience as one meditates on and then enacts what one has learned.

KEY TERMS

anatman	Hinayana
avidya	*Jataka Tales*
bodhi	Mahayana
Bodhisattva	metta
Buddha	metta bhavana
deva	nirvana
dharma	parinirvana
dukkha	sangha
Engaged Buddhism	Theravada
enlightenment	Vajrayana

DISCUSSION QUESTIONS

1. Do you agree with the first noble truth, that all life is suffering—or perhaps, that there is an element of dissatisfaction in every aspect of life? Do you agree that suffering comes when we try to hold on to impermanent things? Have you ever experienced relief when you let go of something you had been trying unsuccessfully to hang on to?
2. "Perfect livelihood" is one component of the "eightfold path." How well does your present or anticipated occupation meet its criteria?
3. This chapter shared some ideas of five Buddhist workers for justice and peace: Nagarjuna, Thich Nhat Hanh, the Dalai Lama, A. T. Ariyaratne, and Aung San Suu Kyi. If you had the time and opportunity to read about the life of one of them, or to read his or her writings, which would you be likely to choose first? Why might you choose that one? Was there something in the textbook description that particularly caught your attention and interest? Was there something you especially agreed with? Something you especially disagreed with?
4. If you had to choose one of their lives as your own, whose life would you most like to have led? Whose life would you most like *not* to have led? Why? Do their lives suggest any activities or insights that you would like to incorporate into your own life? If so, which activities or insights, and how?
5. The modern scholar Robert Thurman draws some contemporary counsels from Nagarjuna's writing. Which of his observations and counsels seem right to you? Which do not? What should we do about them?

SUGGESTIONS FOR FURTHER READING

Ariyaratne. *Buddhism and Sarvodaya.*
Aung San Suu Kyi. *Letters from Burma.*

Chappel, ed. *Buddhist Peacework.*
Ciszek. *He Leadeth Me.*
Clements. *The Voice of Hope, Aung San Suu Kyi*
Dalai Lama. *The Buddhism of Tibet.*
Diamond. *Collapse.*
Eppsteiner, ed. *The Path of Compassion: Writings on Socially Engaged Buddhism.*
Fischer-Schreiber. *Encyclopedia of Eastern Philosophy and Religion.*
Fisher, *Living Religions,* 5th ed.
Galtung. *Buddhism: A Quest for Unity and Peace.*
Griffiths, ed. *Christianity through Non-Christian Eyes.*
Heinberg. *The Party's Over.*
———. *Power Down.*
Macy. *Despair and Personal Power in the Nuclear Age.*
Matthews. *World Religions,* 4th ed.
Nhat Hanh. *Being Peace.*
———. *Interbeing: Commentaries on the Tiep Hien Precepts.*
———. *Vietnam: Lotus in a Sea of Fire.*
Oxtoby, ed. *World Religions: Eastern Traditions,* 2nd ed.
Pieris. *Love Meets Wisdom*
Queen, ed. *Engaged Buddhism in the West.*
Queen and King, eds. *Engaged Buddhism.*
Rinpoche. *Selected Writings and Speeches.*
Silouan and Sofronii. Wisdom from Mount Athos.
Sivaraksa. *Conflict, Culture, Change: Engaged Buddhism in a Globalizing World.*
———. *Socially Engaged Buddhism for the New Millennium.*
Spiro. *Anthropological Other or Burmese Brother?*
———. *Buddhism and Society: A Great Tradition and Its Burmese Vicissitudes.*
Thurman. "Nagarjuna's Guidelines for Buddhist Social Action."
Victoria. *Zen at War.*
———. *Zen War Stories.*

3

Jewish Worldviews

Hear, O Israel! The LORD is our God, the LORD alone! Therefore, you shall love the LORD, your God, with your whole heart, and with your whole being, and with your whole strength.

—Deuteronomy 6:4–5

Justice, justice alone shall you pursue, so that you may live and possess the land the Lord, your God, is giving you.

—Deuteronomy 16:20

You have been told, O mortal, what is good, and what the LORD requires of you: Only to do justice, and to love goodness, and to walk humbly with your God.

—Micah 6:8

Whoever destroys a single life is as guilty as though he had destroyed the entire world, and whoever rescues a single life earns as much merit as though he had rescued the entire world.

—Mishnah Sanhedrin

EXPERIENTIAL AND EMOTIONAL DIMENSION

The central experience giving rise to the Jewish worldview is rooted in history far more than were the two previous worldviews. Not only have Jewish experience and beliefs varied *throughout* history, as is the case for all religions; Jews also experienced God *through God's acts in* history. Jews believe that their ancestors escaped slavery in Egypt and entered the land called Canaan at the eastern end of the Mediterranean through a powerful act of God, who chose them to be his own people and enabled them to settle the land in the face of its indigenous inhabitants. God established a unique covenant with them, calling them to be faithful to God alone (in a world that worshiped a multitude of gods), to live justly, and to be a light to the nations. God accomplished this remarkable act through key leaders—prophets, judges, and kings—who would speak and act for God. When the people accepted and kept the words that God spoke through the prophets, they prospered; when they turned away to worship other gods, they experienced disaster. God's instructions eventually included sacrifice exclusively at one temple in Jerusalem.

Yet for long periods of Jewish history, they lived outside the land they believed God had promised them, the temple in Jerusalem destroyed. As they tried to understand the meaning of this disaster, they maintained their sense of being a separate people and gradually developed alternative ways of worshiping God and following his directions. For the most part, they lived as culturally distinct communities within the various countries where they found themselves. Previously, their contact with God had been mediated through prophets and through the Law that the prophet Moses had received from God. But prophecy waned, and they centered their devotion on the Law itself, written and oral. Eventually, this was supplemented by a form of mystical union with God called **Kabbalah**. Some Jews never entirely gave up their expectation that God would restore their own kingdom in their ancestral land through a messiah—an anointed king—sometime in the future.

As they entered the modern period and began to be accepted in modern nation-states as full-fledged citizens, yet with worrisome episodes of persecution, they were torn between their sense of separateness and their desire to belong to the larger society. Toward the end of the nineteenth century, some Jews concluded that they should return to their ancient land and reestablish a Jewish society there without waiting for God to anoint a messiah; others thought such a move was premature, and even a rejection of God's will. In the middle of the twentieth century, the Holocaust shook their confidence that they understood their relationship with God, with non-Jews, and with their own community. This crisis accelerated the establishment of the state of Israel and continues to haunt its domestic and foreign policy, especially in relation to the Palestinians, hundreds of thousands of whom were driven from their homes when the state was established in 1948. The majority of Jews choose to remain outside Israel, where they discuss and practice various ways of being Jewish in their varied circumstances and of relating to the state of Israel, which claims all self-identified Jews throughout the world as potential citizens.

HISTORICAL PERIODS[1]

The history of Judaism can be divided into four main periods:

1. The Biblical Period (from the "beginning" to the Babylonian Exile, which destroyed the kingdom of Judah and the first temple in 587 BCE and lasted about fifty years). Depending on when you think this period "began," it could

be divided into two or three sub-periods: (a) from Abraham (ca. 1800 BCE) to the exodus (ca. 1300 BCE)—during which Abraham, his extended family, and his descendants lived as foreigners in Canaan or Egypt, (b) from the exodus to the kingship of Saul (ca. 1000 BCE)—the entry into Canaan of twelve tribes called Israelite and their occasional common defense against enemies, and (c) the period of the kings of Israel and Judah. During this biblical period, much of the Hebrew Bible (roughly equal to the Christian "Old Testament") was written. The term "Jews" in this period refers only to those who lived in the kingdom of Judah, not the larger number who lived in the kingdom of Israel. Although the Hebrew Bible "great tradition" insistently demanded that the people worship only one God, its own text shows that many of them were polytheists. The community later attributed the tragedy of the exile to this fact.

2. The Second Temple Period (from the restoration after the exile through the Roman destruction of the second temple in 70 CE). For all but a brief period, the community had limited autonomy under foreign rule. Ritual centered on animal sacrifice exclusively at the second temple in Jerusalem. During this period, the community became more exclusive and began to develop the detailed observance of the Law, which characterized later Judaism, although different parties disputed the proper interpretation of the Law.

3. The Period of Rabbinic Judaism from the destruction of the second temple to the beginning of the "Modern Period"; the modern period began at widely different dates in different countries: by about 1800 in the United States and France, as late as the 1950s in Yemen. The Roman destruction scattered many Jews outside their homeland in the **Diaspora**; the scattered communities maintained their cohesion because they were allowed limited autonomy exercised through local rabbis. As they lost hope that they could come home to restore political freedom and animal sacrifice, they centered their Jewish identity on detailed observance of the Law. During this period, the Jews also developed a complex mysticism called Kabbalah.

4. The Modern Period. Starting around 1800, some nations began to accept Jews as full citizens rather than as a foreign subculture. As a result, the authority of their rabbinic leaders declined. At the same time, some Jews sought to adapt their traditional Law to modern conditions. The tensions that developed within the Jewish community and with the larger world outside will be discussed in this chapter and in the case study of chapter 8.

SACRED WRITINGS

Jews refer to the inspired scriptures of the Second Temple Period as the **Tanakh**. They also call them the *Bible* or the *Hebrew Bible*—meaning, approximately, what the Christians call the *Old Testament*. The word *Tanakh* is the acronym made up from the first letters of the words for the three major sections of that collection: (1)

Torah *("Law" or, better, "Teaching")*: Genesis through Deuteronomy—the Pentateuch, (2) **Nevi'im**: the Former and Latter Prophets (the Former Prophets are listed
by Christians as "historical books"—for example the Books of Kings), and (3) **Ket-
uvim**: the "Writings"—everything that doesn't fit under the first two categories. In
a broader sense, *Torah* can mean the whole *Tanakh*, or even the whole of Jewish
moral teaching.

In addition to the Tanakh, Jews have many other sacred traditions. In the time
of Jesus, a major group of exclusively oral traditions promoted especially by the
Pharisees discussed how to live the Torah in every aspect of daily life. Traditional
rabbis claim that these traditions are as old and as authoritative as the Torah itself,
that Moses received both the written Torah and the oral Torah from God himself
on Mount Sinai. After several centuries, these oral traditions were written down in
several collections. The first collection was called the **Mishnah**. A later and much
expanded version, a sort of commentary on the Mishnah, is the **Talmud**, which
exists in two quite different forms, the Jerusalem and Babylonian Talmuds. In form,
each page of the Talmud contains several blocks of text: the Mishnah in one block
surrounded by several different blocks of commentary. Those commentaries taken
altogether are called the **Gemara**, so it is commonly said that Mishnah plus Gemara
makes Talmud.

Regarding content, the Talmud distinguishes **halakhah** from **haggadah**. Halakhah refers to the specifically *legal* materials: ritual, ethical, and civil rules, including
both biblical rules and post-biblical rules added by the rabbis from the oral tradition; the word is derived from the verb "to walk" and means "how you walk." Haggadah refers to *all the rest*, consisting largely of narrative materials like stories,
legends, folklore, anecdotes, short sayings, and homilies on biblical passages.

Study of the Talmud has accustomed Jews to divergent interpretations of their
sacred texts: the very form of the Talmud—a collection of abbreviated rabbinic discussions—and the way it is taught develop in them a flexibility and openness to
contrasting interpretations. Other traditions include the **Targums**, which are rather
free translations of the Tanakh from Hebrew into Aramaic. In the time of Jesus,
Hebrew had become a religious and classical language, like Latin in our day, and
Aramaic was the everyday language of most Jews in Palestine. The Targums at first
were exclusively oral; later some Targums were written down. Another type of literature was called *midrashim* (plural of **midrash**)—expansions and explanations that
functioned as commentaries on the Tanakh (including the Nevi'im and the Ketu-
vim, which are largely absent from the Talmud). Besides these more or less authoritative writings, there are also many Jewish stories, such as the Hasidic tales collected
by Martin Buber, Elie Wiesel, and others.

NARRATIVE OR MYTHIC DIMENSION

As the Jewish community passes on its history, in which God reveals himself and
through which Jews believe God has entered into a special relationship with them,
several themes stand out.

Covenant and Chosen People

Pronounced among Jews is the idea of a *covenant* or solemn agreement between themselves and God, who has revealed himself to them and formed them into a community. This conviction gives Jews a strong sense of being a special or "chosen" people, which has been very important to them, because historically Jews have been a small group and often threatened by more powerful neighbors. Influenced by their theology of election, Jews historically disputed among themselves whether to cooperate with non-Jews or separate from them. Their sense of being a chosen people should not lead to arrogance: it is not for their personal glory that God chose Jews, but to be the bearers of God's revelation, God's glory and holiness, and the suffering that the world visits on God's followers. This sense of being chosen also explains why Judaism cannot be understood apart from its history. The Holocaust and the state of Israel have become a central challenge to Jewish self-understanding.

Promised Land

In the thirteenth century BCE, Hebrew tribes identifying themselves as the twelve tribes of Israel moved into Canaan, later called Palestine after the Philistines. They believed that God had promised this land to Abraham, their ancestor, and to his descendants. At first the Israelites lived on the margins of the urban society—most of the largest cities remained Canaanite (Judges 1:1–2:5). Over a two-hundred-year period, the Israelites gradually gained control over the country: King David captured Jerusalem about 1000 BCE. From that time until 587 BCE, Israelite kings (of the kingdoms of Israel and Judah) controlled significant parts of the Near East. From 587 until about 140 BCE the Israelites were under foreign control (Babylonian, Persian, Greek, Syrian), but at first the majority of them still lived in Palestine-Israel-Judah. As time went on, a larger percentage lived outside of that area. The people came eventually to be called Jews after the place name Judea. One prominent attitude, represented especially in the book of Deuteronomy and the Prophets, attributed their earlier successes to God's help and their later failures to their failure to obey God's commands. But another attitude, exemplified by the book of Job, challenged this understanding as too simplistic.

In the second century BCE the Seleucid king Antiochus IV Epiphanes of Syria tried to force all his subject peoples to conform to the religious, philosophical, and scientific ideas of Greece. Among his Jewish subjects, he prohibited Sabbath observance, circumcision, use of the Torah, and worship of the God of Israel. Antiochus rededicated the (second) temple in Jerusalem to the head of the Greek pantheon, Zeus. He destroyed all copies of the Law of Moses that he could find, killed women whose children had been circumcised, and hung their babies from their necks, according to Maccabees 1:60ff.

A revolt against these measures began in 167 BCE in a village near Jerusalem, where a Jewish priest, Mattathias, refused to obey the orders of Seleucid officers. He and his sons—the Maccabees (or, in Greek, Hasmons)—then led a guerrilla operation to end Seleucid control of Palestine. In 164 BCE they reclaimed the temple for

Jewish worship. The festival of **Hanukkah** celebrates the rededication of the temple. Eventually the Maccabees (Hasmons) established the (Jewish) Hasmonean kingdom, which endured until 63 BCE, when quarreling factions invited Roman intervention. As a result, the Romans incorporated Palestine into their empire, effectively ending its independence.

Christian readers are familiar with Pharisees and Sadducees from the Gospels, where they are presented in a generally hostile light. The Sadducees were wealthy priests with political standing who controlled sacrificial worship, which was restricted to the temple in Jerusalem. They tended to collaborate with the Roman occupiers. The Pharisees were lay people who accused Sadducees of laxity, and sought to apply the Jewish law (Torah) to all areas of life. They promoted and led worship conducted in local prayer meeting halls called synagogues, based on a Greek word meaning "assembly" or "gathering." Both of these groups had their scribes, or professional intellectuals. Two more marginal groups were the Essenes and the Zealots. Regarding the Sadducees, who controlled temple worship, as wholly corrupt, the Essenes had separated and formed an alternative community in the desert near Jericho. The Zealots were radical revolutionaries pressing their fellow Jews to revolt against Rome. First-century Christians could be considered a fifth Jewish group. Most Jewish inhabitants of the Roman province of Palestine did not belong to any of these groups, although they might have been sympathetic to one or another of them. It has been estimated that the "people of the land," including farmers and artisans, the unclean, and the homeless, comprised 90 percent of the Jewish population at that time.

The Jewish leaders, mainly Sadducees, were generally moderate, cooperating with the Roman occupiers. When a spontaneous Jewish rebellion against Roman rule broke out in 66 CE, the Zealots assassinated all the leaders who opposed the revolt. After initial Jewish success, Rome crushed the revolt by 73 CE. They crucified Zealots wherever they found them, considering them to be terrorists and the main instigators of the revolt. The Sadducees lost their political power, since they had been the Jewish political leaders at the time of the revolt. Roman troops destroyed the Essene community at Qumran, as its location threatened their supply lines and the Essenes had allied themselves with the rebels. The Christians had refused to join the revolt, but they were not yet numerous enough to be much noticed by the Romans. Of the dominant Jewish groups, the Pharisees were the least implicated in the revolt.

The main center of the Sadducees' power had been the temple with its sacrificial priesthood, which they lost when Rome destroyed the temple and suppressed Jewish sacrificial worship. The Pharisees, in contrast, had already developed an alternative form of piety centered on prayer worship in synagogues, which had first appeared in Babylonia during the Babylonian exile after 587 BCE. The exiles were far from Jerusalem and the *first* Jerusalem temple had been destroyed, so they had developed another form of worship requiring only a congregation of ten Jewish men to study the Torah, pray, and sing hymns. Now that Rome had destroyed the *second* temple, the Pharisees expanded this piety into what became rabbinic Judaism. Rabbis thought out ways to preserve Judaism without the temple and its animal sacrifice.

In their place, they put the *written* Torah, the *oral* traditions (which they believed also went back to the Sinai revelation), scriptural commentary, and a calendar of sacred festivals.

Over the course of time, more and more Jews moved out of Palestine to other areas of the Greco-Roman world. Yet there never was a time when all Palestinian Jews had left the country: centers like Safed, Tiberias, and Jerusalem maintained Jewish populations down to the modern period.

The communities of Jews scattered throughout the world outside Palestine made up the Diaspora. Most of the earliest Christian missionary activity was carried on among these Diaspora Jews. These Diaspora communities kept the memory of the "holy land" alive, praying at each **Passover**, "Next year in Jerusalem." For the drama in our day of how the majority Zionist understanding and application of the ideology of national restoration has impacted the indigenous Palestinian population, which has lived for centuries in that same land, see chapter 8 on the Israeli-Palestinian Conflict.

A Holy People

Given their historical experience, Jews needed a sense of identity to survive as a community. With the destruction of the temple and exile from Jerusalem, which was rebuilt as a Roman city, Jews could no longer sense God's presence in the *temple* and the *city*. Instead, Jews developed a sense of God present among the *people*, reflected in their holiness expressed in a special way of life. Study of the Torah and the living out of that study in daily life, ritual, and ceremony became a safeguard of Jewish identity and a guarantee that Judaism would endure.

Premodern Jewish Experience in Europe and Russia

In medieval Christian Europe under feudalism, Jews were not allowed to own land. In Italian and German cities from the mid-sixteenth century on, Jewish inhabitants had to live in urban *ghettos*—quarters assigned exclusively to Jews, since Jews were not allowed to live anywhere else. Jewish rabbis were allowed to regulate these ghettos internally in accordance with rather authoritarian Talmudic law, but they were not pleasant places to live. For their part, medieval Jews on the whole avoided social relations with Christians or Muslims. The Jews were protected by the local rulers, who often employed them as agents or buffers between themselves and the peasants—as tax collectors, merchants, artisans, and moneylenders. Some rulers sought out Jewish moneylenders to finance their schemes, since Christians were not allowed to charge interest and so had little incentive to lend money. The Jews often found themselves to be convenient targets of peasants' resentment toward their lords. Elsewhere in the Diaspora, especially under Muslim rule, Jews were much more integrated into the larger culture and sometimes attained high position, as we will see in chapter 5.

Figure 3.1. "Western Wall" with Temple Mount—alleged site of destroyed Second Temple—in background. Note Muslim Dome of the Rock on the Temple Mount (Haram al-Sharif). Courtesy David Whitten Smith, about 1975.

Persecution by Christians

For centuries Jews in Europe learned to stay indoors and out of sight on Christian holy days, because at those times it was not unusual for mobs of Christians to beat up Jews and burn their homes. This kind of active persecution is sometimes called a **pogrom**: a late-nineteenth-century Russian word. Christians felt threatened by Jews because they kept the ancient faith rather than becoming Christians, thus challenging the Christian faith. Christian mobs accused Jews of being "Christ-killers." Martin Luther, in 1543, wrote a famous tract entitled *Against the Jews and Their Lies*.

Besides this unofficial, popular persecution, there were also official persecutions of Jews. As cultural and moral habits changed and *Christians* began to finance at interest, Jews no longer filled that vital societal function. Therefore they were expelled from a number of countries between 1290 and 1569. Christians remember 1492 as the year that Ferdinand and Isabella of Spain sponsored Christopher Columbus's voyage seeking an alternate route to India—a voyage that accidentally led him to the "New World," previously unknown to Europeans. Jews and Muslims remember it as the year that Ferdinand and Isabella, having conquered the last Muslim resistance in Spain, expelled all Jews from Spain. Especially in Spain and Portugal, the *Inquisition* used torture to seek out "heretics" (including not Jews as such, but those Jews who had publicly converted to Christianity while secretly retaining their Jewish practices), expel or execute them, and expropriate their property. Some of these Jews had been baptized and "converted" to Christianity by force. Many of the Jews driven from Spain in 1492 went to North Africa or Turkey, both under Muslim government. Besides expulsions, there were a number of massacres, pogroms, and forced conversions to Christianity.

The expulsions led to a major population shift of Jews from Western to Eastern Europe, in particular Poland. There they lived *without* ghettos, and often with few or no non-Jews in their midst. These Yiddish-speaking Jews enjoyed freedom of religious expression. (Yiddish is a combination of German and Hebrew.) However, in the mid-seventeenth century, rebelling Russian Orthodox Cossacks targeted Jews as well as Roman Catholics; huge numbers of Jews were massacred.

From the Jewish standpoint, then, the *Holocaust* (**Shoah** in Hebrew, meaning "catastrophe")—Nazi Germany's program to exterminate all Jews and thus eliminate the need to relate to them—was the action of a Christian country and just the most murderous example of a common Christian attitude. Hitler was not a practicing Christian, but most of the people who voted him into office and who continued to support him were; and many Christians, especially in Eastern Europe, cooperated with Hitler's persecution of Jews. Yet there were German and other Christians, like Corrie Ten Boom of the Netherlands and her father, who risked or lost their lives to save Jewish lives. Israel honors them as "righteous Gentiles." Others adamantly opposed Hitler and the entire Nazi agenda; Sophie Scholl and Dietrich Bonhoeffer are two examples. University student Sophie Scholl (1921–1943) was executed in Munich for distributing anti-Nazi literature as a member of the White Rose nonviolent resistance movement. The theologian Dietrich Bonhoeffer (1906–1945) was executed at Flossenburg for his participation in a failed plot to assassinate Hitler. Bonhoeffer saw his Christian identity and commitment, in Nazi-ruled Germany, as inevitably leading to martyrdom.

DOCTRINAL AND PHILOSOPHICAL DIMENSION

Religious Jews believe that there is only one God—personal, loving, and just—who created the physical and spiritual worlds and demands that his creatures act justly. This God has full power, and intervenes in behalf of those who love him. He chooses whomever he wills to receive his blessings, but has special love for the small, the weak, and the oppressed. He chose Abraham and formed from his descendants a chosen people. He rescued this chosen people from slavery in Egypt, revealed his law to them through Moses at Sinai, empowered them to take possession of the "promised land," and protected them so long as they acted justly and worshiped God alone. But he allowed them to be defeated by their enemies when they strayed away from the path he had pointed out to them. He sent prophets to speak his word to them so that they would be recalled to the proper path. Note that this cycle of idolatry-injustice-disaster-repentance-rescue was not clear to the Israelites at the time. It was strongly argued by some Israelites, or Jews, centuries later as they looked back on their history. Others resisted the implication that, if one is suffering, one must have sinned. See, for example, the Book of Job. Because the non-Jewish world did not know God or understand his will, it persecuted his people, but they were called to withstand the persecution, trusting God to be their protection and bring justice.

Orthodox Judaism believes in a spiritual survival of the soul after death, a later resurrection of the body, and a judgment involving punishment or reward according to one's deeds in life. Reform Judaism has raised questions about some of those beliefs. Jews in general spend much less time thinking and talking about personal survival after death than Christians do: it is not at the center of Jewish self-consciousness. **Ashkenazic** (Central and Eastern European) Jews, for example, think of the afterlife more in terms of memory. They will name a child after someone who has died in order to maintain her memory. They recount her life to the one who bears her name. On the anniversary of her death, if religious, they affirm their belief in God.

In reflecting on human sin, a Jewish tradition speaks of two inclinations in every human: the **yetzer ha tov**, or good inclination, and the **yetzer ha ra'**, or evil inclination. Humans are born morally neutral. As they grow and face moral choices, their good and evil inclinations come into play. This understanding is very different from the Christian doctrine of original sin. The Jewish notion of sin is communal as well as individualistic, which is illustrated by the communal confession of proscribed sins at the ceremonies of **Yom Kippur**.

The Thirteen Articles of Maimonides

Moses Maimonides (d. 1204) was a Spanish physician and Jewish religious philosopher who lived and worked in Muslim Spain (called "Andalusia") seeking to combine Aristotelian philosophical reasoning with religious revelation. Persecution by the newly empowered Almohad Muslim leadership forced him to flee to Islamic Egypt. His best-known work is *The Guide for the Perplexed*.

In his commentary on the Torah, he spelled out thirteen articles of Jewish faith that by the fourteenth century were incorporated into Jewish liturgy at morning prayer: (1) the existence of God as the perfect creator and primary cause of all that exists, (2) the absolute unity of God, (3) God's nonphysicality, (4) God's eternity, (5) the exclusive worship of God, (6) God's communication with humans through prophecy, (7) the priority of Moses's prophecy, (8) the divine origin and (9) immutability of the Torah, (10) divine omniscience (all-knowledge) and providence, (11) divine reward and retribution, (12) the arrival of the messiah and the messianic era, and (13) the resurrection of the dead.[2]

PRACTICAL AND RITUAL DIMENSION

The Jewish faith expresses itself in a rich life of festival and ritual and a strong sense of community. Its feasts embody the main Jewish themes we have seen, especially trust in God in the face of suffering and insecurity.

The Sabbath

The central Jewish celebration is the weekly **Sabbath**. According to Exodus 16:23–29, it was demanded of the Israelites in their desert flight from Egypt, when they were ordered to gather manna on only six days and to rest on the seventh, even before they received the Torah at Mount Sinai. It is the only celebration explicitly commanded by the Ten Commandments—the leading covenant rules, which Moses received from God on Mount Sinai (Exodus 20:8–11 and 31:12–17; Deuteronomy 5:12–15). Violation of the Sabbath was to be punished by death (Numbers 15:32–36). Motivations for Sabbath observance include the following: God rested from creation on the seventh day; it makes the people holy as God is holy; and it shows compassion for those who work (including children, slaves, aliens, and even animals), since the Israelites were slaves in Egypt. The land, too, is given a Sabbath: no sowing or tending every seventh year, when the people may eat only what grows naturally (Leviticus 25:1–7). When the Israelites failed to give the land its Sabbaths, God sent them into exile, allowing the land to make up for its lost Sabbaths during their absence (Leviticus 26:34–35; Second Chronicles 36:21; Nehemiah 10:32).

As clarified by rabbinic tradition, no work can be done on the Sabbath, from sundown Friday to sundown Saturday—that time is dedicated to God.[3] Special foods, prepared the day before, are eaten. Special attention is given to family and guests. The rest from work is an anticipation of paradise, as well as a sign of trust in God to meet the needs of his faithful people. Special prayers and ceremonies are carried out at home, and services are held in the local synagogue.

Daily Prayer

The Jewish prayer book provides morning, afternoon, and evening prayers to sanctify the day. All males thirteen and older are supposed to pray them, facing Jerusalem, preferably in groups of ten or more. During morning prayer, except on the Sabbath and during festivals, adult males wear tefillin (phylacteries)—leather boxes containing brief biblical passages that are attached to head and arm with leather straps.

Pesach (Passover)

Celebrated on Nisan 15, the full moon of the first month of the Jewish religious calendar, **Pesach** commemorates God's rescue of the Israelites from slavery in Egypt under Pharaoh. On the night of their rescue, the destroying angel *passed over* the Israelite houses, which had been marked with the blood of the lambs sacrificed to God. It is a reminder that they depend on *God* for their freedom, not on their own virtue or power. Jews today celebrate a *seder* ("order of service") at home on the first night. Participants eat unleavened bread and bitter herbs; they drink four cups of wine and recite prayers, perform rituals, sing songs, and read from their sacred traditions. They reflect on and discuss the meanings the exodus story has for those present. The Passover commemoration reminds Jews that life is fragile in this world of power politics, and invites them to be grateful to God for their rescue. Unleavened bread called *matza* (plural *matzot*) is eaten for a week. Jewish tradition recalls that the Israelites fled from Egypt so abruptly that they did not have time to leaven the bread they were making. Since ancient leaven was a kind of sourdough that easily symbolized corruption, leaven was a sign of sin in our life and unleavened bread was a sign of a fresh start.

Shavuot

Shavuot (Pentecost) comes fifty days (seven weeks and a day) after Pesach. This feast was associated with receiving the Torah (Law of Moses) from God at Mount Sinai, after the rescue from Egypt and before the conquest of the "promised land"; thus, it commemorates their special relationship as God's chosen people and the Law as their grateful response. Jews decorate their synagogues with greenery to celebrate this feast, and read the Ten Commandments and passages from the Book of Ruth.

The High Holy Days: Rosh Hashanah (The New Year) and Yom Kippur (the Day of Atonement)

The *High Holy Days* are celebrated as the new moon starts the seventh month of the *religious* calendar (Tishri): ten days of self-examination leading to repentance so as to start the *civil* new year with a renewed spirit. They begin with **Rosh Hashanah** (literally, the "head of the year") and end with *Yom Kippur* (the **Day of Atonement**)—a day of fasting and repentance for sin. In modern Judaism, Yom Kippur is the most important holiday of the year. Jews abstain on this day from all food, drink, work, washing, and sexual intercourse. In synagogue readings and prayers, they celebrate a humble awareness of God's glory, their own fragility, and their need for God's mercy. Since the Mishnah says that the rituals of this day atone only for one's sins before *God* and not for one's sins against other *human beings*, participants supplement those rituals on this day by seeking reconciliation with each other. Rosh Hashanah and Yom Kippur take place a few days before Sukkoth (the seven-day Feast of **Tabernacles**), forming with them an extended period of ritual activity called the *Days of Awe*.

Sukkoth (Tabernacles, or Tents)

Sukkoth falls exactly half a (lunar) year after Pesach, beginning in the fall at the full moon of the seventh month (Tishri). Agriculturally, Sukkoth represented the fall harvest; the feast is also called the *Ingathering*. During the weeklong celebration people live in fragile huts (*sukkot*) made of branches, commemorating the period of their wandering in the desert before they entered the "promised land." Religiously, the fragility of these huts reminds participants of the fragility of life on earth, and memories of the desert wanderings remind them that it is often in the desert of loss and poverty that we find God. The festival runs seven days, followed by an eighth day for solemn assembly and a ninth day called *Simhat Torah*—a day to "rejoice in the Teaching."

Hanukkah (Festival of Lights)

Hanukkah originated in the second century BCE to commemorate the victory of the Maccabees over the Seleucids. When the Jews purified the desecrated temple, they set up the sacred menorah (lampstand), but found only enough un-desecrated oil to fuel the lamps for one day. They lit the fire anyway, and were astonished to see it burn for the entire eight days of the dedication, even growing brighter each day. In memory of that miraculous event, on each night of Hanukkah Jews light one more candle in their nine-branch candlestick (the ninth is used to light the other candles). There are also special games played, foods eaten, and gifts exchanged.

Purim

Purim commemorates the story recounted in the Book of Esther, almost certainly fictional in its present form, in which the Jewish communities in Persia, threatened with extinction by a wicked king's advisor, manage to turn the tables on their tormenter and kill, not only him, but tens of thousands of other Gentiles. Jews value the story as celebrating victory over persecution. Gifts are exchanged, the drama may be reenacted, and children dress up in costumes, making the feast a sort of Jewish *Carnevale* or *Mardi Gras*.[4] The story and its festival raise serious questions about celebrating a massacre of Gentiles who had nothing to do with the original conspiracy:

> For as long as I can remember, I never liked the holiday of Purim, with its story of the massacre of the gentiles and its message of revenge and rejoicing at the downfall of others. . . . And so every year all that's left for me to do is to grit my teeth during the synagogue reading of the Megillah, taking comfort in the fact that historically, at least, the veracity of this story is very much in doubt.[5]

ETHICAL AND LEGAL DIMENSION

Some religions connect their laws and moral judgments closely or directly to the mystical experiences that were the origins of the group. Thus, they speak of "divinely revealed laws." Muslims make this claim for the Quran, as do Jews for the Law of Moses, especially the core of the law expressed in the Ten Commandments. Judaism, like Islam, is especially marked by its attention to how we *act* as opposed to what we *believe*. While Christians have strongly emphasized "ortho*doxy*" or right *doctrine*, Jews have emphasized "ortho*praxy*" or right *action*.

Central to all Jewish laws is the conviction that they are not just rules; they are the desire of a God who has chosen and blessed the Jewish community. Jews keep the laws not to avoid God's anger, but to conform to God in holiness and to show gratitude for what God has done for them. God has initiated a special relationship with the Jewish community: their faithfulness to the Torah is their grateful response.

The character of rabbinic teaching is illustrated by a story about the famous first-century CE rabbi Hillel, in contrast with the more conservative rabbi, Shammai. A man asked Shammai to teach him the whole law while he stood on one leg. Shammai drove him out. The unbeliever went to Hillel. Hillel made him a convert by telling him: "What you hate, don't do to your neighbor. That is the whole law; the rest is commentary. Now, go study!" Thus, social justice is a key component of Jewish law and the vast commentary on it. Nevertheless, women could not then participate in formal study of the Torah.

In the period of rabbinic Judaism, the institution of the synagogue meant that Jews could live in any cultural context and yet be distinguished as Jews by such aspects of their lives as diet and Sabbath observance, which helped them maintain their communal identity, prevent assimilation, and avoid being dissolved into the larger culture.

Medieval and Post-Medieval Judaism

Babylon, Baghdad, Andalusia

Jews had lived in Babylon since the exile; many exiles had made new lives for themselves there and did not return to Judah at the end of the exile. Babylon was a major Jewish intellectual center until the tenth century—the Islamic conquest did not alter that status. Two renowned *yeshivot* (rabbinic academies) of Babylon oversaw the completion of the Babylonian Talmud in the sixth century CE. Their leaders also wrote responses to questions from Jews who lived in distant places; these answers took the form of legal opinions.

Baghdad, founded by the new Muslim Abbasid dynasty after 750, was another center of Jewish life. There Jews functioned as scholars and other professionals (for example, doctors), as merchants and tradespeople, and as artisans. Jews and Christians contributed to the Islamic renaissance under the Abbasids. Overall in Muslim-controlled areas, Jews experienced relatively good treatment, despite occasional examples of oppression and intolerance; Jews and Christians lived as "People of the Book," enjoying local autonomy and exemption from military service in exchange for payment of a tax. Speaking Arabic, Jewish scholars produced religious and philosophical works, scientific works, and Hebrew poetry.

In Andalusia (Muslim Spain), Jews also held political office. As noted earlier, the great Jewish thinker Maimonides flourished in Andalusia.

Kabbalah and the Zohar

The roots of Jewish mysticism are found in the Hebrew Bible, extra-biblical literature, and the Talmud. Medieval Jewish mysticism is known as *Kabbalah*, and the foremost textual expression of Kabbalah is the **Zohar** ("Way of Splendor"), thought to have been written by Moses de Leon (d. 1305). The Zohar is a compendium of stories, visionary accounts, and esoteric (secret) commentary on the Torah. In the Zohar the hidden, transcendent God is connected to the immanent creator God by ten emanations (recalling ancient Gnosticism). The world of sense perception is seen as an inferior reflection of the spiritual world, and the divine life is likewise paralleled in the life of humanity, whose acts influence the cosmos. Through the Kabbalah, Jewish mystics sought union with God and the restoration of divine unity. Jewish critics alleged that these speculations threatened the unity of God.

Isaac Luria (1534–1572) and Tikkun

An important sixteenth-century Spanish Kabbalist, *Isaac Luria*, taught that the cataclysmic process of creation had shattered God's unity, sending divine sparks into the world that have penetrated all objects and actions. The human task is to collect these divine sparks to help repair the chaotic, evil state of the world, which will not be fully repaired (**tikkun** means "repair") until the messiah comes. The practices Luria taught included obeying the Torah, asceticism, prayer, and chanting of religious formulas.

Hasidism and the Baal Shem Tov (1700–1760)

The term **Hasidism** can be traced back to the second century BCE and the oppressive reign of the Seleucid ruler Antiochus IV, who attempted to eradicate Judaism in Palestine in order to unify his kingdom through a common Greek religion and culture. The Hasidim were the "pious ones" who stood up to him and preferred martyrdom to apostasy.

Modern Hasidism began as an expression of ecstatic piety originating in the eighteenth century. Founded in Poland by the **Baal Shem Tov** (d. 1760), it represented a populist devotional and mystical revolt against the learned scholars of the Talmud. The Baal Shem Tov ("Master of the Good Name," abbreviated BeSHT or **Besht**) taught that personal piety as expressed in prayer is more important than intellectual study of the Torah and literal Torah obedience. Since God is omnipresent, we have less need for a messiah. He encouraged ecstatic worship of God, including music and dance, and a joyful consciousness of God in day-to-day life. Thus the soul aspires to *devekut* (cleaving to God).

A Hasidic teacher named Dov Ber contributed to the phenomenal growth of Hasidism among the Jews of Eastern Europe. He supported the special status of the **tzaddik**, or holy man, as distinguished from ordinary Hasidim. This distinction was opposed by those who supported the spiritual equality of Hasidim. Nevertheless, the tzaddik as charismatic leader has remained a key component of Hasidism up to the present. Modern Hasidism is a continuation of the original movement. Its values include humility and universal love. The Jewish philosopher Martin Buber (d. 1965) was a student and interpreter of Hasidism.

SOCIAL AND INSTITUTIONAL DIMENSION

Varieties of Judaism

In one sense, Christianity and modern Judaism represent two lines of development from first-century Judaism down through the past two thousand years of history to the present. Although the two communities sometimes quarreled intensely, their *formal* separation into two religions is dated to "the second century at the earliest" by Calvin Roetzel, and possibly as late as the early fourth century by Daniel Boyarin.[6]

Western Varieties and the Enlightenment

Most Americans are familiar with the division into **Orthodox, Reform,** and **Conservative Judaism.** The division began in Western Europe, where the eighteenth-century Enlightenment ushered in positive change for Jews with its emphasis on reason and tolerance rather than religious and political authority and tradition. The *égalité* (equality) of the French revolution naturally included Jews and set a precedent for Europe more generally. Western European Jews no longer had to live in ghettos; they were given previously unheard-of opportunities for advancement. In certain countries of Western Europe they even received citizenship. Thus began the modern period of Judaism.

Moses Mendelssohn and the Jewish Enlightenment

A German Jew named Moses Mendelssohn (d. 1786) sought freedom of religion; separation of church and state; and Jewish integration into European culture through language, dress, and outward appearance. Envisioning a society in which the shared humanity of Christians and Jews would transcend their religious differences, he established a movement called the Jewish Enlightenment.

Reform Judaism

As part of this movement toward "modernity," Reform Judaism developed first in Germany in the mid-nineteenth century, attempting to bring Jewish life and belief more in line with modern thought. It reinterpreted doctrines such as messiah and resurrection. The Jewish liturgy was modernized or Westernized so that returning to the land, or building a third temple in Jerusalem, was no longer mentioned, and the liturgical language shifted from Hebrew to the vernacular. In some synagogues, men and women could sit together. Jews were told to excel as citizens in the countries where they resided. In 1845, also in Germany, Rabbi Zecharias Frankel broke away from Reform Judaism to create Positive-Historical Judaism, which attempted to "conserve" Jewish tradition in a modified form rather than rejecting it. Frankel wished to retain kosher food regulations (kashrut) and the use of Hebrew in official prayers. He taught that Jewish law was not static, but had always adapted to new situations.

Jewish Immigration to the United States from the Mid-Nineteenth Century

Jews began immigrating to the United States in significant numbers in the middle of the nineteenth century—first German-speaking, mostly Reform Jews; then Eastern European and Russian working-class Jews, some Orthodox and some secular socialist. Today more Jews live in the United States than in any other country except Israel. One of the strongest world centers of Hasidism is Brooklyn, New York. The number of American Jews may now be approximately equal to, or slightly less than, the number of American Muslims.

American Reform Judaism developed in the late nineteenth century. This denomination of Judaism founded Hebrew Union College (HUC) in Cincinnati in 1875. The first graduating class of rabbis, in 1883, expressed its rejection of kosher laws by serving shellfish at its graduation banquet. The Pittsburgh Platform of 1885 officially dispensed with the dietary regulations of the Torah (kosher laws), as well as purity and dress laws, retaining only the ethical commandments. The emphasis was on Jewish faith in the God of justice and love.[7] In contrast, Orthodox Judaism, vigorously supported today by Hasidic Jews, sought to maintain all the historical Jewish traditions and beliefs.

Conservative Judaism

In the United States in 1886, two **Sephardic** rabbis founded the Jewish Theological Seminary (JTS) in New York City as an alternative to Reform Judaism's Hebrew Union College in Cincinnati. JTS helped to develop modern Conservative Judaism, adopting modern scholarly methods in an effort to conserve Jewish traditions in a modified form, similar to the German movement of Positive-Historical Judaism. Conservative Judaism was for some time the largest Jewish denomination in the United States. More recently, as some Conservative synagogues split off to form **Reconstructionist Judaism**, it has been superseded by Reform as the largest U.S. denomination.[8]

Reconstructionist Judaism

The most recent branch of American Judaism is Reconstructionist Judaism, based on the theology of Rabbi Mordecai Kaplan (1881–1983), who began as an Orthodox rabbi but taught—with considerable controversy—at the (Conservative) Jewish Theological Seminary from 1909 until 1963. He presented Judaism as a civilization rather than a religion, rejected the traditional view of the Torah as supernatural revelation along with the exclusivist doctrine that Jews are the only chosen people of God, revised the prayer book to eliminate pejorative comments about women

and Gentiles, and performed the first bat mitzvah for his daughter. Women participate equally in Reconstructionist synagogue worship. In 1934, he expressed his
vision in *Judaism as a Civilization: Toward a Reconstitution of American-Jewish Life*.
In 1968, his son-in-law Ira Eisenstein founded the Reconstructionist Rabbinical
College (RRC) near Philadelphia as an alternative to the Conservative JTS. Kaplan
died in 1983 at the age of 102.

Numbers for these various denominations are hard to determine. It depends on
whether you survey *all* Jews or only *synagogue* members. If you ask *all American
Jews* what group they identify with, you get 10–12 percent Orthodox, 26–29 percent
Conservative, 35–41 percent Reform, and 18–29 percent other, which includes
about 2 percent Reconstructionist. If you ask *synagogue members* which group they
affiliate with, you get 21 percent Orthodox, 33 percent Conservative, 39 percent
Reform, 3 percent Reconstructionist, and 4 percent other.

Within Israel, affiliations are different. Only Orthodox rabbis are officially recognized. Israelis group themselves as 8 percent Haredim (very orthodox), 12 percent
religious, 13 percent "religious traditionalist," 25 percent "non-religious traditionalist," and 42 percent "secular."[9]

Ashkenazim, Sephardim, and Mizrahim

As is true of most major worldviews, Jews have been influenced by the diverse cultures surrounding them. A major *cultural* split is that between the three Jewish
groups of Ashkenazim, Sephardim, and Mizrahim. Ashkenazim represent a basically
Germanic culture, Sephardim a basically Spanish-Arabic culture, and Mizrahim
(often counted with the Sephardim) an Arabic–Middle Eastern culture.

From a German base, Ashkenazim spread through Eastern Europe and Russia;
then, under nineteenth-century persecution in those countries, they moved back to
Western Europe and on to the United States. They spoke Yiddish, a dialect of German with Hebrew and Aramaic additions. Before the Nazi Holocaust, about 90 percent of Jews worldwide were Ashkenazim. Since the Holocaust, the percentage has
dropped to about 83 percent.

From a Spanish base, Sephardim moved beyond Spain after Ferdinand and Isabella expelled all Jews from the country. Since Spain had been for centuries a multicultural Muslim-ruled civilization and the Muslims had given Jews more freedom
than Christians had, many Sephardim moved to North Africa and the Middle East.
Others moved to the Balkan states. They spoke Ladino, a Romance-based language.
Today, many Sephardim have been strongly influenced by Arabic culture.

From a Middle Eastern base, Mizrahim (Oriental Jews) inhabited Iraq, Iran,
Yemen, and the various Central Asian Soviet provinces surrounding Afghanistan.
Rather than a specific language of their own, most Mizrahim spoke the language of
their host country. Today, most Mizrahim live in Israel or the United States.

About half of the Jews in the state of Israel are Ashkenazim, and about half are
Sephardim or Mizrahim. Ashkenazim are much more widely represented in the

Israeli government and in positions of power than are Sephardim or Mizrahim. Sephardim and Mizrahim complain that they are discriminated against.

ISSUES FOR JUSTICE AND PEACE

Women

In biblical and rabbinic Judaism, women were generally regarded as inferior to men and men were socially dominant. In one traditional Jewish prayer, a man thanked God that he had been created male rather than female. However, there are striking examples of noteworthy women in the Tanakh, for example, Sarah, Rebekah, Rahab, Ruth, the Queen of Sheba, and Esther. The Bible uses feminine as well as masculine imagery to portray God, and the Shekinah was revered as God's feminine presence. The Mishnah makes a woman subordinate to her father before marriage, and to her husband after marriage. It also lists her mandatory household tasks such as cooking and washing clothes. Rabbinic Judaism did not allow women to participate in "formal Torah study."[10] In modern times women can be ordained as rabbis in all branches of Judaism except Orthodox Judaism. Today Jewish feminist scholars are engaged in ground-breaking reinterpretation of the Hebrew Bible and in historical research on prominent Jewish women of the past; they are also working for gender justice in the state of Israel and elsewhere.

War

In the Tanakh, there is frequent mention of war, and God is seen as a warrior. But there is also an urgent call for justice on the grounds that God is just and calls his people to be just. There is an equally urgent call for peace, found especially in the prophetic books and symbolized by Isaiah's vision of a future in which "the nations" will "beat their swords into plowshares and their spears into pruning hooks" and "the wolf shall be a guest of the lamb" (Isaiah 2:4; 11:6). Jewish daily worship includes a petition for peace in both the morning and evening prayers.

Talmudic Attitudes toward War

Leonard Grob surveys the Talmud and concludes that it supports the priority of peace and urges peacemaking, although it does not rule out war. Thus, he notes, it does not take a definitively pacifist position, but it does state that a person may not kill another person in order to save his or her own life,[11] although it is often said that self-defense is obligatory for Jews, and for that reason suicide is forbidden. Referring to two groups that intermarried with each other despite their differing views, the Talmud says, "[They put] into practice the injunction, 'Love truth and peace' (Zechariah 8:19)."[12]

Note that the Hebrew word **shalom**, often translated "peace," actually has a broader, more diverse set of meanings. In grammatical origin, it means wholeness or completeness. In the Tanakh it is used to denote a variety of things, including physical health, safety, long life, prosperity, and (strangely) military victory.

When it deals with organized war, the Talmud is reflecting on the past, when the Israelite nation engaged in war. Jewish tradition distinguished two kinds of *"obligatory* war" (*milhemet mitzvah*): (1) war *commanded by God*, such as the wars by which the Israelite tribes occupied Canaan, and (2) *"defensive* war," responding to external aggression. (3) A third legitimate kind of war was *"discretionary* war" (*milhemet reshut*), undertaken to gain territory beyond that assigned to Israel by the Torah, which could only be waged with the permission of the Sanhedrin.

Wars commanded by God were limited to the wars against **Amalek**, the desert tribe that had attacked Israel in its exodus from Egypt to Canaan, and against the six nations (peoples) that inhabited Canaan when the Israelite tribes invaded. Most Jewish interpreters conclude that these nations no longer exist, so that there can be no more wars commanded by God. In those wars, the Torah ordered the Israelites to kill all men, women, children, and animals of these Canaanite nations, lest the survivors lead the Israelites to violate the Torah by imitating their religious practices. This command is called **herem**. It was practiced also by some of Israel's neighbors. The king of Moab, Mesha, bragged on a stele that he "devoted to destruction" the 7,000 inhabitants of Nebo on behalf of his god.[13] Historically, the command was not effectively carried out. The descriptions in the Book of Joshua suggest that it was, but Judges 1:1–2:5 indicates that many local peoples survived. Pre-Christian rabbis were already uncomfortable with this command. They sought ways to question it without directly attacking the Torah, which they considered God's word. The Talmud suggests that the Canaanites were given the chance to leave their homeland to make room for the Israelites, but refused to do so.

Modern commentators are even more uncomfortable that some religious Zionists equate Palestinians or neighboring Arab nations with Amalekites and still think in terms of herem. Questions to think about when researching this issue might include: (a) Does it answer the problem to note that God has ultimate authority over human life and death? (b) Does it answer the problem to speak of moral development in the Sacred Scripture, implying that herem might have been understandable in the ancient period but not later? (Jewish scholars do speak of "development" in scriptural understanding as they interpret the meaning of herem.) (c) Is there any modern analogy to herem? Most Jews think there is not. (d) For those who think there is, how could a modern government determine that God is calling for it?[14]

Defensive wars were also obligatory to protect the community, but they did not require wholesale slaughter of the enemy population.

The concept of *discretionary war* was originally developed to explain the wars for territory or plunder fought by the kings of ancient Israel and Judah. With regard to wars against nations outside of the "promised land," regulations were derived from Deuteronomy 20:1–20 and rabbinic commentary on that chapter. Only those who were courageous and unencumbered with family responsibilities were authorized to fight. Israel was first obligated to "offer peace," on the condition that the foreign nation agreed to accept Jewish control, provide forced labor, and pay taxes. If the nation refused, Israel had to allow civilians to flee if they wished to, then it could execute the males, take the women and children captive, and plunder the city. After Israel signed a peace treaty, it was bound to honor the agreement even if it could be advantageous to violate it.

During a siege, the army should avoid cutting down trees. If it needed to use a battering ram or build siege works, it should not make them from the wood of fruit trees. It should leave one side of the siege open so that civilians could flee, and when a battle had ended, the soldiers should not rejoice at the death of the enemy.[15]

Since discretionary wars had to be ordered by the king and ratified by the Sanhedrin, and modern Israel has neither king nor Sanhedrin, many Jewish commentators conclude that there can be no discretionary wars today. If so, that leaves defensive wars as the only type still open to modern Israel.

The Shoah ("Catastrophe," Specifically the Holocaust)

Many Western Jews since the Enlightenment tried to enter into the modern European culture and distance themselves from their Jewish roots. The Nazi Holocaust was unique in that it refused to accept such choices as valid. Hitler intended to kill every Jew no matter what his or her personal convictions or actions were. Even a single Jewish grandparent was enough to identify a person as a Jew.

It is hard to imagine the horror of the situation. In other persecutions, one could escape by denying one's faith, by complying with the oppressor, or by deception. Those who died felt that they were at least witnessing to their convictions. In the Holocaust, in contrast, there was no escape. An entire quasi-ethnic group (defined by religion, history, and—allegedly—genetics) was threatened with complete annihilation. The psychological effects on those who survived are hard for outsiders to appreciate. That is the significance of Holocaust literature.

Also of great importance was the Jewish experience of often (though not always) being abandoned by their Christian friends and neighbors (who were, admittedly, living under a totalitarian police state). While the full extent of the Holocaust was kept secret for a long time, it was no secret that Jews were being systematically and cruelly persecuted. Many proposals were made to relieve the situation, but other countries did little to help. At an international conference before the Holocaust had been set in motion, Hitler offered to let all the Jews under German control emigrate. But the other countries at the conference, including the United States, refused to expand their immigration quotas adequately to accept these Jews.

"Nobody wants them" claimed the German newspaper *Völkischer Beobachter* after the Evian Conference in July 1938, and Hitler gloated, saying, "It is a shameful spectacle to see how the whole democratic world is oozing sympathy for the poor tormented Jewish people, but remains hard hearted and obdurate when it comes to helping them."[16]

And while the defeat of Germany in the war finally ended the slaughter of Jews (and other groups, such as homosexuals, who were deemed undesirable), there was no effort by the Allies to direct the war effort in a way that would free Jews from the concentration camps quickly. Even after clear photographs showed the purpose of the camps, proposals to bomb the ovens and gas chambers were rejected. Many Jews concluded from these experiences that they could not trust non-Jews, and so Jews must have a country of their own that they could control without depending on anyone else. They must remain a majority in that country and hold uncontested political power.

Jews consider the lessons of the Holocaust to be vital to their survival. They exert great effort to pass on the memory of their experiences to the next generation, which did not live through them. An example of an author who has engaged in this process of remembrance is Elie Wiesel. See especially his book *Night*, which is an autobiographical account of his experiences in the death camp where his father died. On seeing a young child hanged, Wiesel recalls,

> Behind me, I heard the same man asking: "Where is God now?" And I heard a voice within me answer him: "Where is He? Here He is—HE is hanging here on this gallows. . . ." That night the soup tasted of corpses.[17]

In Jerusalem and in Washington, D.C., there are deeply moving museums of the Holocaust. The Jerusalem museum is called *Yad Vashem* ("a memorial and a name," quoting from Isaiah 56:5).[18]

Responses to the Holocaust

This section summarizes a small-group interview that I (David) had with Marc Silverman in 1988 at the Holocaust museum *Yad Vashem* in Jerusalem regarding Jewish theologies of the Holocaust under three aspects. He described a wide range of influential Jewish positions, although some are held by small numbers of Jews.

Theological Explanations   Some ultra-orthodox Jews believe that the Holocaust was a punishment for Jewish failure to live the Law of Moses, and that the state of Israel is a blasphemous attempt to bring in the messianic era without the messiah. The appropriate response to the Holocaust, then, would be to return to meticulous observance of the covenant law as they interpret it. There is also a claim, very controversial among Jews, that the Jewish community has a special vocation to suffer.

At the other extreme, some secular Zionists, such as the socialist pioneers of the kibbutzim and moshavim, believe that the Holocaust was the natural result of trusting God to protect you when what was needed was human strength. For them, sin is unwillingness to take your history into your own hands.

Some modern Orthodox religious Zionists, represented by groups like the National Religious Party and *Gush Emunim* (the "Block of the Faithful"), see the Holocaust as the first stage of a process of dying and rising. For these Jews the dying was necessary, and the rising has begun with the state of Israel, which is a sort of human first step toward the messianic kingdom that God will eventually establish.

It is the "first fruits" of God's kingdom. Jews of this persuasion sometimes advocate the expansion of Israel to include Jordan and parts of Syria: all the territory contained under ancient Israel and Judah at the time of its greatest extent. They promote this expansion concretely by building and moving into Jewish settlements in the (illegally) occupied Palestinian territories.

Silverman strongly rejected any suggestion that the Holocaust was punishment for sin, or somehow necessary to produce God's kingdom, pointing out that no sin could be great enough to justify the Holocaust and asserting that "six million Jews are not the cost of this country." He called such theories "beneath contempt."

Social-Cultural Aspects   The dominant reaction of Israeli Jews who visit the Holocaust museum *Yad Vashem* is, "We must do all in our power to ensure that Jews are no longer powerless." Jews born in Israel, when visiting the Holocaust museum, feel not so much *pity* for the Jews pictured there, as *disgust*: "Why didn't they do something to help themselves? I must not be like that." They insist that the Holocaust must be constantly relived in memory so that it will not be relived in fact. (Some Jews insist that the Holocaust must not be relived by *anybody*, whether Jew or non-Jew.)

Political Aspects   Some take the attitude that all Gentiles are guilty of allowing the Holocaust to happen. Since the Gentile nations failed to prevent it, they all stand accused of moral failure and have no right to criticize the state of Israel. Israel, then, has no need to listen to any criticism from Gentiles regardless of its actions.

Enemies who are perceived to threaten the state of Israel are sometimes compared with the Old Testament neighboring tribe Amalek. God called the Israelites to destroy Amalek totally because they had opposed God's people—a key instance of herem. When local Palestinians, or neighboring states like Jordan, Syria, or Iraq, are equated with "Amalek," no pity need be shown and no rules of war need apply. Note that these symbols can operate on an unconscious level, with little analysis to moderate their impact.

Traumatic Results

Hajo Meyer, a Dutch Jewish survivor of the Auschwitz extermination camp, writes of how the Holocaust has traumatized the worldwide Jewish community, especially within the Jewish tradition of continually reliving traumatic historical experiences. This reliving seeks to prevent traumatic events from being repeated, but in fact it reenergizes the trauma and passes it on to future generations. Survivors' children and grandchildren can easily come to believe that the Holocaust reflects a permanent Gentile hatred of Jews, and that the Jewish community or nation stands in constant danger of annihilation. Psychopathic leaders encourage such paranoia in order to undergird their own drive for power, and to deflect any criticism of their self-serving, highly destructive policies. Meyer applies these principles to the Israel-Palestine situation in part by pointing out similarities between Nazi German dehumanization of Jews leading up to—but not including—the actual mass slaughter in the death camps, and Israel's dehumanization of Palestinians today.[19]

Zionism

Zionism in general is an international movement aiming to bring Jews from European and other nations to live together in Palestine, which they regard as their ancient homeland. Jewish Zionism in its modern form dates from the late nineteenth century. It was preceded by a mostly British and American *Christian* Zionism (originally called "restorationism") from the early nineteenth century with even earlier roots in British and American Puritanism. As we will see in chapter 4 on Christianity, modern *Christian* Zionism is of a very different character from the *Jewish* form, although politically it strongly supports Jewish Zionism. In its earliest form, Jewish Zionism spoke simply of living together *in one place*, but Palestine soon became the only place seriously considered. Not all Zionist thinkers were planning to create a Jewish *state*. But *some* were, even from as early as Theodor Herzl in the late nineteenth century.

Throughout the nineteenth century, many Jews in Western Europe were moving out of the ghettos into the wider society, gaining education, and being accepted into areas of life that had formerly been closed to them. For these Jews, integration into the larger culture was more important than maintaining their Jewish identity and traditions. Surprisingly, this integration was accompanied by renewed discrimination. Both secular and religious Jews had hoped that their "enlightened neighbors" would support them. Assimilated Jews (those who were not practicing the Jewish religion or who had converted to Christianity, atheism, or agnosticism) wondered why their neighbors still considered them to be "Jews" and discriminated against them. If being Jewish is not a religion, some thought, perhaps it is a nationality, like being French or British. It was a time when Italians and Germans were developing a national character and forming modern nation-states. But Jews, like Kurds and Armenians, had no nation-state. So Zionists began to think that Jews should gather themselves into a single homeland to gain security and develop their potential national character.

Forms of Zionism[20]

Political Zionists thought that the best way to gain Jewish security was to get authorization from the international community or from one or more powerful states to emigrate from their European homes and colonize a Jewish state somewhere else. Theodor Herzl tried to convince the Ottoman Empire, and later Britain, that it should support Jewish colonization in Palestine, despite the fact that the land was already inhabited.

Socialist Zionists thought that waiting for great powers to grant Jews a state would be useless. Jews should simply move into Palestine and begin developing the society that would eventually become a state. Influenced by Marxist theories of class struggle (see chapter 7 on Marxist Worldviews), they thought Jews needed to reform their national character. For centuries they had been forbidden to own land or to farm, so they had become small merchants and moneylenders, and eventually with European enlightenment, professionals and financiers. They needed to develop a strong agricultural and manufacturing working class.

Cultural Zionists were not so concerned with creating a Jewish *state*, but rather with restoring and renewing Jewish *cultural and religious life in Palestine*, where history, geography, climate, and other natural factors were most suitable to that project. Some cultural Zionists supported a *bi-national state*—Jewish and Arab—with equal rights for all its citizens, open to the development of Jewish, Muslim, and Christian cultures. The famous Jewish philosopher Hannah Arendt was a cultural Zionist who wanted a "Jewish presence," but not a Jewish state, in Palestine.[21]

Originally most *Orthodox* Jews resisted Zionism, claiming it was blasphemous to ask politics to accomplish what God intended the messiah to do. More recently, however, some have supported Zionism despite its secular roots. This is the origin of **religious Zionism**. Rabbi Abraham Isaac Kook, a leading religious Zionist, argues that

> Zionism was not merely a political movement by secular Jews. It was actually a tool of God to promote his divine scheme and to initiate the return of the Jews to their homeland—the land he promised to Abraham, Isaac and Jacob. God wants the children of Israel . . . to establish a Jewish sovereign state in which Jews could live according to the laws of Torah. . . . Therefore, settling Israel is an obligation of the religious Jews and helping Zionism is actually following God's will.[22]

Religious Zionists are the most tenacious Israeli settlers on Palestinian land in East Jerusalem, the West Bank, and the Golan Heights. They insist that to give back a square centimeter of the "promised land" to *goyim* (non-Jews) would be rebellion against God.

The Origins of Jewish Statehood

Early movement toward an organized Jewish community or state began in the middle of the nineteenth century. A wealthy Jew, Baron Edmond de Rothschild, financed two agricultural settlements in (Ottoman) Palestine in 1882–1884. The Austrian journalist Theodor Herzl (d. 1904) was responsible for establishing Jewish Zionism as an international *political* movement. In France in 1894, a popular Jewish army officer, Alfred Dreyfus, was falsely accused and convicted of treason for allegedly selling military secrets to Germany. "Enlightened" Gentiles failed to defend Dreyfus. Some Jews concluded that emancipation might be *increasing* anti-Jewish feelings rather than diminishing them, by increasing contact between Jews and Gentiles. Herzl argued that Jews needed a homeland of their own. Perhaps enlightened European Gentiles would support a wholly Jewish state on the enlightenment model somewhere *outside* Europe in order to get rid of the Jews in their midst.

Herzl regarded Zionism's triumph as inevitable, not only because life in Europe was ever more untenable for the Jews, but also because it was in Europe's interests to be rid of the Jews and relieved of anti-Semitism: The European political establishments would eventually be persuaded to promote Zionism.[23]

He began to urge European political leaders to sponsor such a homeland. He did not describe it as "a state" to the political leaders he was approaching.

Herzl presented his proposal to the Grand Vizier: the Jews would pay the Turkish foreign debt and attempt to help regulate Turkish finances if they were given Palestine as a Jewish homeland *under Turkish rule* [emphasis added].[24]

Herzl convened the first Zionist Congress in 1897 in Basel, Switzerland. He considered several possible locations for a Jewish state: Argentina, where Baron Hirsh was already settling East European Jews; the Sinai Peninsula, proposed by Britain as a temporary measure (but Egypt objected); or another British offer of some "unoccupied" land in Uganda. But most Jews insisted the settlement had to be "a publicly recognized, legally secure homeland in Palestine," and the Zionist conference formally agreed.[25] The conference also created the World Zionist Organization to further these aims.

A compromise formula proposed by Herzl [which came to be known as the "Basel Program"] was eventually adopted: "Zionism seeks to establish a home for the Jewish people in Eretz Israel [or Palestine] secured under public law."[26]

At the 1919 Paris Peace Conference, speaking for the World Zionist Organization and quoting the Basel Program of 1897, Nahum Sokolow said:

The object of Zionism is to establish for the Jewish people a home in Palestine secured by public law. . . . It has been said . . . by anti-Zionists . . . that Zionism aims at the creation of an independent "Jewish State." But this is wholly fallacious. The "Jewish State" was never part of the Zionist programme. The Jewish State was the title of Herzl's first pamphlet, which had the supreme merit of forcing people to think. This pamphlet was followed by the first Zionist Congress, which accepted the Basle programme—the only programme in existence.[27]

According to Florence Steichen, at the Paris Peace Conference the World Zionist Organization presented a map of the Jewish homeland it envisioned, with boundaries that encompassed not only Palestine but also parts of Egypt, Jordan, Lebanon, Syria, and even Saudi Arabia.[28]

Many Jews rejected Zionism. Reform Jews, inspired by the Enlightenment, thought that Jews should live as full citizens among non-Jews. Orthodox Jews thought that only God could return the Jews to Palestine if and when God chose to do that. The Nazi Holocaust drastically changed the balance of Jewish opinion on Zionism. Suddenly Zionism seemed to be a matter of survival.

Kibbutzim and Moshavim

At first, the largest groups of Jews who *did* support Zionism and moved to Palestine were socialists or Marxists, not religiously observant Jews. They set up cooperative communities called *kibbutzim* (plural of **kibbutz**) and partial-cooperative communities called *moshavim* (plural of **moshav**). In a kibbutz, the more fully communal of these institutions, *all* property was held in common. Children were raised communally, splitting their time between common dormitories and their parents' homes. Members ate in common dining halls and cultivated fields in common. The first kibbutz was founded on the south shore of the Sea of Galilee in 1910.[29]

Kibbutzim and moshavim at first represented pioneers willing to accept hardship to create a new Jewish state. They provided the most committed soldiers and politicians to the development of Israel. As they have grown more affluent, they have lost much of their original egalitarianism, and their influence on Israeli society has waned.

To continue the story of how Zionism produced the state of Israel and the conflict that resulted, turn to chapter 8 on the Israeli-Palestinian conflict.

Judaism in Relation to Other Religions

Because of the theological emphasis on their covenant relationship with God along with election as God's "chosen people," and their history of persecution, Jews have tended to be separate and not to seek interfaith dialogue. Although neither Christianity nor Islam is seen as invalid, the Christian doctrines of incarnation and Trinity,[30] and the Muslim belief that Muhammad was the final prophet, are considered mistaken, as is Hindu polytheism. Historically Jewish relations with Christianity and Islam have been mixed, including times of positive coexistence[31] (for example, in Muslim-ruled Andalusia and in the United States today, although American Jewish-Muslim relations have been affected by Islamophobia) and times of oppression under Christian rule, as in medieval Europe during the Inquisition. Since the end of World War II, Jewish-Christian dialogue has contributed to improved relations between Jews and Christians. The Roman Catholic Second Vatican Council devoted the largest part of its declaration *Nostra Aetate* (on "the relation of the Church to non-Christian religions") to Judaism, stating explicitly that

> God holds the Jews most dear for the sake of their Fathers; He does not repent of the gifts He makes or of the calls He issues. . . . The Jews should not be presented as rejected or accursed by God. . . . The Church . . . decries hatred, persecutions, displays of anti-Semitism, directed against Jews at any time and by anyone.[32]

The Jewish theologian Marc Ellis cautions, however, that the Christian desire for dialogue with Judaism must not prevent Christian churches from criticizing Israel's oppression of Palestinians, a tendency which he calls a destructive "ecumenical deal."[33]

Judaism as a small community of about 14 million, among 2 billion Christians and 1.7 billion Muslims, is concerned about losing its identity through assimilation or conversion. Jews resent groups like Jews for Jesus and remain ambivalent about Christian Zionists. Israeli Jews express concern that American Jews may lose their identity especially as a result of intermarriage, which is running at about 50 percent in the United States.[34]

In his book *Jesus of Nazareth: Holy Week*, Pope Benedict XVI wrote that the Catholic Church should not try to convert Jews to Christianity. Although he still believes that Jesus came to save all humans, including Jews, he "approvingly quotes Cistercian abbess and biblical writer Hildegard Brem: 'The church must not concern herself with the conversion of the Jews, since she must wait for the time fixed for this by God.'"[35]

SPOKESPERSONS FOR JUSTICE AND PEACE

Ahad Ha'am (Asher Ginsburg, 1852–1927, Russia)

In the early history of Zionism, Ahad Ha'am represented *cultural Zionism* as distinct from Theodor Herzl's *political Zionism*. Russian-born, with a Hasidic background, he believed that Zionism and a Jewish state could culturally and spiritually renew the Jews of both Western and Eastern Europe. In 1890 Ahad Ha'am traveled to Palestine, where he wrote "Thoughts from the Land of Israel." Noting that Palestine was by no means empty and that its Arab-owned land was entirely cultivated except for "sand dunes or stony mountains," he deplored the Jewish "use of violence and humiliation" against the Arab residents. In 1912 he spoke out against the Jewish "boycott of Arab labor as a strategy to conquer the land," fearing that future "power in Eretz Israel" would bring worse: "If this be the 'Messiah,'" he wrote, "I do not wish to see his coming." Before he died in 1927 in Tel Aviv, he asked, "Is this the dream of our return to Zion, that we come to Zion and stain its soil with innocent blood?" Thus, in his view, was the Jewish prophetic tradition being destroyed.[36]

Martin Buber (1878–1965, Austria)

Martin Buber was a philosopher and religious thinker; two of his most famous books are *I and Thou* and *Between Man and Man*. A cultural Zionist, Buber believed that Jews returning to Palestine must relate to the indigenous Arabs as equals, inhabiting a shared Palestine. In his view "modern political Zionism" was "intensified," but not caused, by anti-Semitism. Zionism had been produced by the "unique connection of a people and a country." The Jews had been called to found a just community in Palestine, and from there to spread justice around the world at the behest of their prophets.[37]

Buber recognized three legitimate demands of Zionism: for land, for Jewish immigrants to settle the land, and for Jewish self-determination in the land. He envisioned peaceful coexistence with the Palestinian Arabs and joint development of the land; such cooperation was essential for the successful "redemption of [the] land." He imagined the two peoples as sharing some "spheres of interest and activity" and not others. For Buber, "national rebirth" did not mean "becoming a normal nation." After 1948, he protested consistently against "Israeli nationalism." Supporting confederation, bi-nationalism, and religious socialism, and advocating connection over domination, he ended up living as an internal exile in the state he had helped to build.[38]

Etty Hillesum (1914–1943, Holland)

After earning a law degree at the University of Amsterdam, Hillesum studied Slavic languages and eventually psychology. The Germans occupied Holland in 1940. She had worked for two weeks as a typist for the Jewish Council in Amsterdam when she decided to be among the "first group of Jews" to go to the transit camp Westerbork in the eastern part of the country, en route to Auschwitz in Poland. For over a year she worked in a hospital in the camp. Despite having the opportunity, she chose not to try to escape. With most of her family she was sent to Auschwitz in 1943, where she and three others died. Marc Ellis calls Etty Hillesum's spirituality, expressed in her diaries, "eclectic and beautiful, though in some ways disturbing." She wrote of being "without the least bitterness and so full of strength and love"; of living in continuous dialogue with God with "tears of gratitude" running down her face; of the Jews helping God even if God could not help them; of safeguarding "that little piece of You, God, in ourselves"; of not exempting herself from "what so many others have to suffer." Far from "empowerment," Hillesum urged "witness" and forgiveness, refusing to hate the enemy yet recognizing the "monstrous conditions" created by humans.[39]

In his first general audience after his resignation from the papacy, Benedict XVI spoke these words:

> I am also thinking of Etty Hillesum, a young Dutch girl of Jewish origin who died in Auschwitz. At first far from God, she discovered him looking deep within her and she wrote: "There is a really deep well inside me. And in it dwells God. Sometimes I am there, too. But more often stones and grit block the well, and God is buried beneath. Then he must be dug out again" (*Diaries*, 97). In her disrupted, restless life she found God in the very midst of the great tragedy of the 20th century: the Shoah. This frail and dissatisfied young woman, transfigured by faith, became a woman full of love and inner peace who was able to declare: "I live in constant intimacy with God."[40]

SUMMARY

Through their historical experience as a people, Jews came to believe that the one true God had chosen them for a covenant relationship with Himself and promised them a land where they could live securely and independently in conformity to His will. That belief has been sharply tested throughout history. Prophets, claiming to speak for God, declared that it was the people's own infidelity to God which destroyed their security and exiled them from the land. In their exile, they developed a strong tradition of fidelity to the Torah, along with a rich Jewish mysticism, through which they maintained their distinctive identity. In modern times, an outside world open to Jewish assimilation has drawn many Jews away from their ancient faith, and the Holocaust threatened to end the community's very existence. In reaction, many Jews turned to their own resources (with British, French, U.S., and South African support) to establish the state of Israel, bringing to fruition a Zionist project launched decades before the Holocaust. Some Jews have denounced this move as showing a lack of faith that God will fulfill his promise of a messiah. Jews are engaged in a vigorous search for a theology that could explain why God allowed the Holocaust to happen and what the community should do now.

KEY TERMS

Amalek	pogrom
Ashkenazic	political Zionism
Baal Shem Tov	Purim
Besht	Reconstructionist Judaism
Conservative Judaism	Reform Judaism
cultural Zionism	religious Zionism
Day of Atonement	Rosh Hashanah
Diaspora	Sabbath
Gemara	Sephardic
haggadah	shalom
halakhah	Shavuot (Pentecost)
Hanukkah	Shoah
Hasidism	socialist Zionism
herem	Tabernacles
Kabbalah	Talmud
Ketuvim	Tanakh
kibbutz	Targums
midrashim	tikkun
Mishnah	Torah
moshav	tzaddik
Nevi'im	yetzer ha ra'
Orthodox Judaism	yetzer ha tov
Passover	Yom Kippur
Pesach (Passover)	Zohar

DISCUSSION QUESTIONS

1. Which of the theological responses to the Holocaust do you find most convincing? Which do you find most problematic, or even repellent? If you don't like any of those described, what theological response would you propose?
2. How might non-Jews have responded to Hitler's program so as to prevent the Holocaust without war? Why didn't they? Would their responses have been effective?
3. Some Jews believe that there ought to be one nation in the world—Israel—where one's Jewish faith can shape one's entire life, and where Jews can be safe from attack, and from diminution through assimilation. Such a nation ought to have a government based on Jewish law, they maintain. They also claim that such a government would allow other faiths to practice their beliefs without interference. Do you agree? If not, what *should* be the basis of Israeli law? How *should* Jews and Judaism be protected? What if their nation contains a substantial or equal number of non-Jews? How should these non-Jews be treated?
4. This chapter introduced three Jewish voices for peace: Ahad Ha'am, Martin Buber, and Etty Hillesum. Which one of them would you be most interested in reading about further? What caught your attention and interest? With which of their ideas did you agree or disagree?

SUGGESTIONS FOR FURTHER READING

Arendt. *Eichmann in Jerusalem.*
Buber. *Between Man and Man.*
———. *I and Thou.*
Ellis. *Toward a Jewish Theology of Liberation.*
Fisher. *Living Religions,* 5th ed.
Gordon and Grob. *Education for Peace.*
Griffiths, ed. *Christianity through Non-Christian Eyes.*
Hillesum. *Etty: The Letters and Diaries of Etty Hillesum.*
Matthews. *World Religions,* 4th ed.
Meyer. *The End of Judaism.*
Morris. *Righteous Victims.*
Potok. *The Chosen.*
Rubenstein. *After Auschwitz.*
Rubenstein and Roth. *Approaches to Auschwitz.*
Schmidt et al. *Patterns of Religion,* 3rd ed.
Shahak and Mezvinksy. *Jewish Fundamentalism.*
Sokolow. *History of Zionism (1600–1918),* vol. 1.
Vorspan and Saperstein. *Tough Choices: Jewish Perspectives on Social Justice.*
Watterson. *Not by the Sword: How the Love of a Cantor and His Family Transformed a Klansman.*
Wegner. *Chattel or Person? The Status of Women in the Mishnah.*
Wiesel. *Night.*
Wigoder. *Everyman's Judaica.*

4

Christian Worldviews

Love your enemies, and pray for those who persecute you, that you may be children of your heavenly Father.

—Matthew 5:44–45a

Jesus answered, "You say I am a king. For this I was born and for this I came into the world, to testify to the truth. Everyone who belongs to the truth listens to my voice." Pilate said to him, "What is truth?"

—John 18:37–38

For I am convinced that neither death, nor life, nor angels, nor principalities, nor present things, nor future things, nor powers, nor height, nor depth, nor any other creature will be able to separate us from the love of God in Christ Jesus our Lord.

—Romans 8:38–39

Yet we do speak a wisdom to those who are mature, but not a wisdom of this age, nor of the rulers of this age who are passing away. Rather, we speak God's wisdom, mysterious, hidden . . . which none of the rulers of this age knew, for if they had known it, they would not have crucified the Lord of glory.

—1 Corinthians 2:6–8

EXPERIENTIAL AND EMOTIONAL DIMENSION

The basic Christian experience is the life and ministry of Jesus of Nazareth combined with his followers' experience of the new life that he brings. His followers saw him heal and exorcise (drive evil spirits out of afflicted people), and heard him preach with astonishing authority. They came to believe that Jesus was the one whom God had promised to send to the Jewish people. Although the religious and political leaders had Jesus condemned to a shameful death, his followers reported that he appeared alive to them afterward—raised from the dead by God, who thus vindicated his ministry and preaching. They came to believe that God would raise *them* from the dead, too—at the end of their lives or when Jesus returned in glory.

Early Christians experienced extraordinary power, enabling them to do many of the things that Jesus had done. They understood this power to come from God's own Spirit—a Spirit somehow linked with the risen, living Jesus Christ, who now was authorized to act for God. Christians also understood themselves to be in conscious, personal relationship with the risen Jesus, with God the Father, and with other Christians who had died—especially those who, like Jesus, had been killed because of their faithful lives. In the Catholic and Orthodox traditions, this understanding has continued in ongoing relations through prayer with "saints" who have died.

In all Christian traditions, some people have performed acts of spiritual power in the name of Jesus and have undergone mystical experiences. Many Christians today have modest spiritual experiences such as unexpected joy and peace, for example, at individual or community prayer.

The central point of Christian experience is an awareness of one's own sinfulness combined with a powerful sense of being forgiven by God. This forgiveness, which creates or restores a sense of connection to God, is called "justification" in New Testament writings. Ultimately, it leads to final "salvation" from all that threatens humans.

HISTORICAL PERIODS

1. *Apostolic*—the first century after the death of Jesus in approximately 30 CE. Most of the books that became the New Testament were composed during this period.

2. *Church of the Martyrs*—from the early second century until the early fourth century. During this time Christians were periodically attacked, exiled, had their property confiscated, or were killed by local authorities or the Roman state. "Martyr" means "witness." The Christian martyrs witnessed to the fact that their Christian faith (commitment to Jesus and to God) was more important than their lives and possessions. People often joined the church despite the danger of martyrdom because of what they observed in the extraordinary lives of their Christian neighbors.

3. *Roman Empire after Constantine*—the fourth and fifth centuries. The Roman emperor Constantine (d. 337) made the Christian faith legal and moved the capital of the empire from Rome to Byzantium, which was renamed Constantinople. Soon it became advantageous to be Christian, especially after Theodosius I made Christianity the state religion ca. 380, resulting in many weakly committed Christian converts. Some of the more committed tried to recover

the earlier vigor by becoming hermits or monks. The main doctrinal explanations of the nature of God, Jesus, and the **Holy Spirit** were developed in this period.

4. *Fall of Rome; local control and monasticism*—from the late fourth century to the eleventh century. An overextended Roman Empire in the West was destroyed by non-Roman tribes, beginning in the late fourth century. Christianity continued to be the state religion in the Eastern Roman empire, ruled from Constantinople, and flourished as far east as India, but gradually came under the political sovereignty of expanding Islam. Western societies were more locally organized. Christian monasteries preserved books and literacy.

5. *High Middle Ages and the* **Crusades**—the twelfth and thirteenth centuries. This period saw the rise of universities, scholastic theology, and Gothic cathedrals. During the Crusades, European Christians invaded Palestine to set up short-lived Christian kingdoms. Christianity was enriched by interaction with the more advanced Islamic culture.

6. *Protestant Reformation*—the sixteenth century. Beginning with Martin Luther in 1517, divergent theologies responding to various church abuses found support from local rulers, producing rival churches to the Roman Catholic Church.

7. **Enlightenment** *and post-Enlightenment*—the eighteenth and nineteenth centuries. In the wake of global missionary activity and scientific advances, the Enlightenment brought with it the growth of large nation-states, liberal notions of human freedom, and scientific challenges to traditional Christian doctrines. Churches responded defensively (fundamentalist movements) or adaptively (liberal movements).

8. *Postmodernism*—from the 1970s to the present. The previous search for a neutral standpoint from which one could judge all beliefs is regarded as a delusion; each person is affected by her or his own background and experiences. The best one can do is first to be open about one's own starting-point and then to engage in honest dialogue. During this period, ecumenical movements (seeking unity among Christian churches) and interfaith movements (seeking cooperation between all religions) developed.

SACRED WRITINGS

Unusual among major worldviews, Christians actively read (privately and in liturgical worship) and study the sacred writings—the Tanakh—of the worldview that gave it birth; they call these writings the "Old Testament" to show their chronological relation to the books written by first- and early second-century mostly Jewish Christian authors. Christians do not generally read the Mishnah or the Talmud, which developed *after* the Jewish Christian movement had split from the Rabbinic Jewish movement.

The earliest Christians wrote books about Jesus and his teachings (the **Gospels**), occasional letters to new Christian communities (the **Epistles**), an account of how the new faith was spread from Jerusalem to Rome by the apostles Peter and Paul (Acts of the Apostles), and a theological vision (claiming to be based on visionary experience) proposing how Christians should respond to the Roman Empire (the Revelation of John). These books—the "New Testament"—were considered to have authority at least equal to that of the Tanakh (Hebrew Bible), based on the belief that both were "inspired" by God so that, in some sense, God could be said to be their ultimate author.

Christians revere and study many later Christian writings—decisions of ecumenical (church-wide) and local councils (for example, Nicea to Vatican II, Baltimore, Medellín); expositions of Christian doctrine (creeds and catechisms); theological investigations (Origen, Augustine, Thomas Aquinas, Martin Luther, Karl Barth, Karl Rahner, Hans Küng); prayers and liturgies; mystical writings (the Philokalia, Julian of Norwich, John of the Cross, Teresa of Avila); summaries and interpretations of earlier writings (manuals of theology); histories (Eusebius); poetry and fiction (Dante's *Divine Comedy*, Milton's *Paradise Lost* and *Paradise Regained*), and more.

NARRATIVE OR MYTHIC DIMENSION

Jesus in the New Testament

The New Testament presents Jesus as the **messiah** (promised in the Hebrew Bible) and **Son of God** sent to introduce the Kingdom of God (indicating that God is the real ruler of the world). In the hybrid Jewish-Hellenistic context of the New Testament, readers would be familiar with the Hebrew Scripture's use of "Son of God" with reference to (1) someone, like an angel, from the heavenly realm, and (2) a human individual or group in a close relationship with God (like Israel in covenant with God, a king anointed by God, or a devout Israelite). They would also be familiar with the Hellenistic and Roman meaning of (3) a human person of power, like the emperor, and (4) "someone of divine descent," or a "divine man." The New Testament applies the term to Jesus in a special sense, to indicate his unique relationship with God the Father, shown by his **resurrection** and sending of the Spirit.[1] According to the Gospels, Jesus gathered and trained twelve intimate followers. He preached with unusual authority (as though he knew from personal experience what he was talking about); prophetically judged his society, its leaders, and the "common sense" of ordinary people; healed people of physical disease with spiritual power; drove out evil spirits that were "possessing" (inhabiting and tormenting) people; and urged people to trust in God and in God's forgiveness. Religious and political leaders sought to kill him; succeeding with the help of one of his inner circle who betrayed him, they had him executed in Roman fashion on a cross. Although guards protected the tomb, Jesus rose from the dead "on the third day" and appeared to his followers. Later, Jesus sent the "Holy Spirit" to "baptize" his followers "with the Holy Spirit and fire" (Matthew 3:11; Luke 3:16)—as a result, they overcame their fears and preached the "good news" boldly despite murderous opposition. The Holy Spirit made the risen Jesus present in power within his followers; they continued to do what he had started. The new worldview spread rapidly far beyond the reaches of its Jewish origins in Palestine, as Christians spoke the word and baptized new believers.

The Kerygma (First Announcement, Mission Preaching)

Early Christians developed a common way of announcing what they had experienced and what it meant. In Acts of the Apostles 3:1–11, Peter and John first cure a cripple. Then when they have everyone's attention, Peter gives a speech—a typical first message for people who don't know what God has recently accomplished in Jesus and why it is important. This is "good news"—a mission speech, technically called **kerygma**. Note that, according to Acts 3:1–11, the apostles are *not just telling about what Jesus did*; they are *demonstrating it by doing it themselves*. The healing (act of God's power) provides the occasion for Peter to proclaim the *kerygma* to the crowd by explaining the significance of the healing that has just taken place.

Six key elements, or steps, turn up over and over again in these speeches. Steps 1 to 4 have happened already when the apostles are preaching. They expect step 5 to happen very soon, so step 6 had better happen soon, too. (1) God's promise of a messiah has been fulfilled (2) by the life, death, resurrection, and ascension of Jesus of Nazareth (3) and by his exaltation at the right hand of God the Father. (4) From heaven, Jesus has sent the Holy Spirit upon us to transform us. (5) Jesus will soon return to judge the living and the dead. (6) Therefore repent right now while you have the chance.

DOCTRINAL AND PHILOSOPHICAL DIMENSION

Christianity began as a renewal movement within first-century Judaism. It shared all the basic Jewish beliefs. Into these beliefs, early Christians had to fit their experience of Jesus (who seemed to have a unique relationship with God), of the Holy Spirit (that Jesus sent upon them), and of the resulting transformation that they experienced in their own lives. Starting in the first century CE as the New Testament was being written, Christian thinkers began to develop three key themes: (1) what God saves us from, and how God does so (redemption), (2) how divine and human are present and united in Jesus (Christology), and (3) how God the Father, the divine element in Jesus, and the Holy Spirit are one God (Trinity).

Jesus' followers, even up to the moment of his execution, expected that he would save them from oppression by the Roman occupiers and their local collaborators. Jesus insisted that he had come to save people from their *sins* (Matthew 1:21; 9:2, 6; and especially 26:28). After Jesus was seen risen from the dead, as his followers asserted, they came to understand who he really was, what he was doing, and how they should respond.

Salvation from Original Sin

Humans generally observe that there is something wrong with the world: war, crime, corruption, torture, extreme poverty next to extreme affluence. Presuming that *someone else* is at fault, they determine to find out who is at fault, and then to capture or kill them. Walter Wink calls this the "myth of redemptive violence."[2]

Christianity asserts, however, that we are *all* sinners. President Obama, speaking at Notre Dame University in May of 2009, expressed this common *Christian* understanding:

> Part of the problem, of course, lies in the imperfections of man—our selfishness, our pride, our stubbornness, our acquisitiveness, our insecurities, our egos: all the cruelties large and small that those of us in the Christian tradition understand to be rooted in original sin.[3]

In explaining this belief, Christians refer to the narrative or mythic passage in Genesis, chapter 3: God commanded the first humans—Adam and Eve—not to eat the fruit of a certain tree, warning them that they would die if they did. A serpent enticed them to eat it, explaining that it would not kill them but would give them knowledge of good and evil and make them like gods. They trusted the serpent rather than God, ate the fruit, and became "mortal" (subject to death). God then threw them out of paradise; all their descendants (the human race) thereby also lost access to paradise and became subject to death.

In the New Testament, Paul expands on this story:

> I take delight in the law of God, in my inner self, but I see in my members another principle at war with the law of my mind, making me captive to the law of sin that dwells in my members. Miserable one that I am! Who will deliver me from this mortal body? Thanks be to God through Jesus Christ our Lord! (Romans 7:22–25)

> Just as through one person sin entered the world, and through sin, death, and thus death came to all, inasmuch as all sinned . . . just as through one transgression condemnation came upon all, so through one righteous act acquittal and life came to all. (Romans 5:12, 18)

Doctrinal and philosophical reasoning tries to explain the meaning of these biblical passages. Starting with Augustine in the fifth century, there has been general agreement that **original sin** affects *all* humans (with the exception of Jesus and, some believe, Mary his mother). Augustine and Calvin thought that the *guilt* of Adam and Eve are passed on to all humans, but most Christians believe that it is only a *wounded human nature* that is passed on—although they differ on how deeply wounded humans are. Our wounded human natures cause us to hurt each other as we try anxiously to gain security, power, and comfort. We also create distorted societies: systems of government, education, business, and so forth. Some Christian groups believe that our distorted human nature is passed on by physical inheritance. Others say that we pick it up by imitating our sinful ancestors and by living in a sinful society. Both causes may be active.

The Challenge of the Enlightenment

The European "Enlightenment" and post-Enlightenment of the eighteenth and nineteenth centuries required Christians to rethink their theology. Before that period, theologians could count the ages of the patriarchs listed in Genesis, add in the life-spans or terms of office of succeeding leaders of Israel correlated with other ancient records, and estimate when creation had occurred. In the seventeenth century CE, James Ussher, the Archbishop of Armagh, dated creation to the year 4004 BCE.[4] Subsequently geologists produced evidence that the earth was millions of years old; anthropologists discovered human skeletons (buried with tools) hundreds of thousands of years old; Charles Darwin found evidence suggesting that humans, like other plants and animals, had evolved from earlier life forms, raising the question of whether the first humans could have lived in a perfect Garden of Eden; and Sigmund Freud explored the influence of the human unconscious on human thought and behavior. These scientific discoveries forced theologians to consider new ways to understand biblical narratives.

How we understand human nature affects how we live our private and public lives. If humans are *by nature* self-serving, maybe moral judgment is inappropriate in politics ("political realism" or "realpolitik") and what we need is to increase our power to protect ourselves. If original sin is a *distortion* of human nature, which can be progressively healed by God's unearned grace and forgiveness working through us, maybe moral judgment is appropriate in politics, since humans can respond to conscience and are not doomed to be self-serving.

In the nineteenth century, growing democracy and the effects of the Enlightenment led many people to embrace optimism. Perhaps we could overcome evil by means of our own progress. The twentieth century shattered that optimism with World Wars I and II, the Depression, and a Cold War that threatened nuclear annihilation. Theologians like Karl Barth, Reinhold Niebuhr, and Paul Tillich began to reexamine original sin.[5]

Contemporary Explanations

The Philippine liberation theologian Vitaliano Gorospe explains the case well: "We do not inherit Adam's personal sin, but rather the sinful condition in the world and our own weakened human nature resulting from Adam's sin."[6] Our *disordered desires and passions*, especially our self-centered pride, anxiety, and lust for power drive us to sin, to make bad choices; the choices we make strengthen our disordered desires and passions and feed our pride. *Bad human choices* create, strengthen, and support distorted *structures* of the world (economic, military, political, and social institutions; laws; habitual ways of acting), which encourage and enforce injustice. The structures make it easy for us to sin, and our sin reinforces the structures. Sin is contagious, both through personal example and through the influence of social structures with their commonly accepted values. When we try to correct these situations, we find that both the world around us and our own inner selves are surprisingly resistant to correction. Without God's help, we are so conditioned by our disordered inner desires, and by the way the world around us has affected us, that our very efforts to undo the problem, such as war against "bad people and nations" (as in the "war on terror"), are themselves flawed and ineffective.

The good news, say Christians, is that through Jesus Christ, through his **incarnation**, death, and resurrection, we can resist the disintegrative and destructive tendencies of the world around us and of our own inner selves. "Through God's redeeming grace we are strengthened to overcome this disorder within us. . . . Baptism 'takes away original sin' by bringing to the baptized the gift of the Holy Spirit, God's saving, sanctifying, presence."[7] God endows even infants, says Gorospe, with the Holy Spirit and (through baptism) initiates the infant into a Christian community where he or she will find the Christian atmosphere needed to grow up as a disciple of Christ. The local church is intended to be "a less sinful and more favorable Christian environment."[8] Original sin is only half of the story—God's grace is the other half.

We are not responsible for having been born with a wounded nature and into a world whose laws, institutions, and habitual ways of acting are so flawed that they systematically mis-educate us and mis-develop us, *but we are responsible* for ways we may have reinforced or taken advantage of the injustice. We also have a responsibility to cooperate with God to *change* the situation. Once we realize the power that God is giving us to transform ourselves and the world around us, we have a responsibility to act.

Humans need a double liberation: (1) *personal* conversion and (2) transformation of *structures*. Structures are transformed only through cooperative community action. There is no *permanent* solution: struggle against sin is continuous.

> The Christian doctrine of original sin is a realistic reminder that there is no perfect society and we should distrust absolutes and ideologies that promise a perfectly just society. Any concrete proposal for a more just society must seriously take into account not only human greed but the sinfulness of the human situation. . . . We would be totally subject to the power of sin and death if it were not for the liberating, healing grace of Jesus Christ.[9]

Three Types of Social Sin   To clarify what he means by "**social sin**," or "**structural sin**," Gorospe distinguishes three types: (1) "Structures which systematically oppress human dignity and violate human rights, stifle human freedom and impose gross inequality between the rich and the poor." Possible examples include military dictatorships, slavery, oppressed groups like the Dalits in India (the class of people who fall below the traditional four Hindu castes),[10] and poverty in the midst of affluence in the United States and globally. (2) "Situations which promote and facilitate greed and human selfishness," for example, corruption, war for national advantage, and an exaggerated consumer society. (3) "The complicity of persons who do not take responsibility for evil being done or who silently allow oppression and injustice," for example, those who fail to testify as witnesses in law courts from fear of retaliation, and those who fail to resist injustice from fear, laziness, or concern about what others might think.[11] Overcoming social sin requires personal "conversion"—that is, real inner change—of two types: (1) "**conversion of the head**"—coming to *see* things as God sees them, and (2) "**conversion of the heart**"—coming to *love* people and things as God loves them. Two obstacles to conversion of the head are (a) "unexamined ideological presuppositions, assumptions, [and] values," especially unwillingness to question the status quo that privileges us; and (b) "isolation from the pain and suffering of others."[12] Conversion of the heart requires (a) "a radical change in lifestyle, vocation, or way of life" and (b) a willingness to "subvert unjust structures."[13]

How Does God Do It?   If original sin (their sinful condition which separates them from God) is what humans need to be saved from, theologians of most Christian churches agree that there are two key events that make this salvation possible: the *birth* (or more properly, the *conception and incarnation*) of Jesus, and his *death and resurrection*. It is Christian belief that *something radical changed in the nature of creation* through these two events.

Different Christian churches have had various ways of explaining how this salvation works. For most, it depends on how the human and divine interact in Jesus. If Jesus is truly human, he can represent the human race. If he is also truly divine, his actions can have infinite value. Thus, according to one explanation, when Jesus accepted the death that humans deserved, he "paid the price" of human sin, and "bought us back" (redeemed us) from the powers of evil that had dominated us.[14]

Incarnation and Indwelling: Christology and Trinity   Christian theology teaches that the *human conception or incarnation* of Jesus *connected* humans to God in a new way: God united himself to *one* human, Jesus, in a mysterious and powerful way that potentially gave *all other* humans a new capacity to share in God's nature. Humans could receive this capacity by uniting themselves in faith, trust, and confidence to Jesus. When they did, he began to *live within them* and to act through them. They became so intimately related to him that they could be thought of as part of his "body." But what does it mean for God to unite himself to one human? And can God still be "one" if God is thus united?

It took several centuries to work out acceptable formulas, and Christian groups divided over the issue. A council at Chalcedon in 451 CE, speaking mostly for the Christian churches in the Roman Empire, developed a simple verbal formula: God is three "persons" in one "nature"; Jesus is two "natures" in one "person." Unfortunately, the modern word *person* doesn't mean what the fifth-century Greek word

Figure 4.1.   Church of the Nativity in Bethlehem on the West Bank. Courtesy David Whitten Smith, about 1975.

that it translates meant. For Chalcedon, Jesus has two centers of knowing and two centers of willing—one divine, the other human. God has only one center of knowing and one center of willing—the same for all three "persons." If this sounds confusing, it is because we are trying to apply human concepts to God, and God doesn't fit human concepts very well.[15]

Christian groups (including the Roman Church) that adopted the language and theology of Chalcedon were called "Orthodox." Other Eastern Christian churches (in Egypt, Syria, Iraq, Iran, and farther east) developed similar but somewhat different formulas.[16] It was those other Christian churches that were primarily in contact with Islam as it developed. Initially, they were as large and significant as the Orthodox churches; we often forget about them because they are not included in the narratives of the Acts of the Apostles. Over time they diminished as many of their members converted to Islam.

Rabbinic Jews concluded that belief in the divinity of Jesus and a Trinitarian God violated the unity of God; Muslims later agreed with this judgment.

Death and Resurrection   The church came to understand that it was Jesus' willingness to die, trusting God the Father beyond what Jesus could control, that somehow transformed the rebellious state in which humans found themselves in relation to God. It was Jesus' commitment to truth, goodness, justice, nonviolence, forgiveness, and love of enemies—his insistence on speaking the truth fearlessly to those in power, even when they threatened to kill him if he didn't shut up—that led to his death. Christians believe that Jesus' trusting, loving, faithful death transformed creation itself at its roots, making possible a relationship between humans and God that had not previously been possible. Before three days had passed, Jesus rose or was raised from the dead (the New Testament uses both expressions) no longer subject to death. Thus the Christian great tradition maintains that Jesus did far more than *teach* good ideas to humans; Jesus *acted in power to transform radically the nature of reality—to defeat powers of evil that had held humans in bondage to hatred, fear, and death.* This understanding of the effect of Jesus' death is well expressed in the Letter to the Hebrews in the New Testament:

> Now since the children [whom God has given to Jesus] share in blood and flesh, he likewise shared in them, that *through death he might destroy the one who has the power of death, that is, the devil, and free those who through fear of death had been subject to slavery all their life.* (Hebrews 2:14–15, emphasis added)

Christian Reception of Salvation: The Coming of the Holy Spirit Christians believe that Jesus has broken the power of sin. But to take part in that victory, they need to be united to Jesus through baptism, to surrender their life to him through faith, and to cooperate with the Holy Spirit, which they receive through baptism. Then God can begin to undo the damage caused by human mistrust, symbolized by Adam's failure to trust God. Christians have to trust God in the face of death, as Jesus and his followers did, living and responding as Jesus did: loving their enemies, doing good to those who hate them, praying for those who persecute them. But they are only able to live this way when they freely choose to trust God in everything. When they do that, they believe that God acts through his Spirit, in mysterious connection with the resurrection of Jesus, to unite them with the risen Jesus, empowering them to live as Jesus did; God gives them this power as a free and unearned gift that no one deserves. Christians continue to struggle against the effects of original sin, but with God's grace they progressively experience a radical change in their lives—loss of fear, new confidence, and the ability to love seemingly unlovable people.

Christians of the first few centuries experienced periodic, deadly persecutions. Under persecution, they came to associate their own suffering with that of Jesus. If Jesus had not escaped death at the hands of God's enemies, and if they had become part of his "body," then they should not expect to escape death either. At the same time, as "members of his body," they experienced the power and guidance of the Holy Spirit, and could confidently expect to share in his resurrection. Struggle against "the world" did not end when the empire became Christian; it continues to the present day.

Nontraditional Views of Jesus in His Palestinian Context

In addition to the new understandings of original sin discussed above, recently discovered ancient documents and recent advances in archaeology, history, and especially sociology have greatly increased our understanding of first-century Palestinian society. Many popular traditional views of Jesus have presumed that he was living in a society more or less like ours. Marcus Borg, in contrast, explains that first-century Palestine was colonial (under Roman occupation), cosmopolitan (with much Aramaic-Greek bilingualism), peasant (with the ruling 10 percent of the population monopolizing 90 percent of the product), patriarchal, and deeply concerned about purity.[17] This new understanding of the culture in which Jesus lived and worked helps to explain more fully many of his words and actions reflected in the New Testament, and can revolutionize our understanding of the political, social, and spiritual significance of his life. Scholars continue to dispute how to characterize Jesus: "restoration eschatology prophet, Hellenistic-type Cynic sage, egalitarian wisdom prophet, social prophet, spirit person (healer), Jewish Cynic peasant,"[18] movement founder, tax resister, advocate of debt release, one who restored honor to the marginalized.[19] Some scholars, for example, have concluded that Jesus was an apocalyptic prophet who expected the Kingdom of God to arrive soon, replacing Roman rule over Palestine and indeed all earthly kingdoms, reversing people's status in the final judgment, and ushering in a new age of justice and peace, truth and love. To prepare for God's judgment and kingdom, Jesus called for repentance (see Mark 1:15).

Starting in 1985, a group of scholars called the "**Jesus Seminar**" has been searching for the "**historical Jesus**." Given the fact that the Gospels were composed decades after the death of Jesus and to some extent reflect the theologies of the communities within which they were formed, scholars need a process for distinguishing between authentic Jesus content and content pertaining to the communities in which the Gospel writers lived and worked. Thus Jesus scholars apply "criteria of authenticity" to the Gospel texts (the four canonical Gospels in addition to the Gospel of Thomas) in an effort to determine what Jesus of Nazareth actually said and did. Two of these criteria are (1) "dissimilarity" from a post-Jesus, early Jewish-Christian perspective; and (2) "contextual credibility," that is, congruence with an early first-century Jewish-Palestinian context.[20] Using these criteria, historical Jesus scholars conclude, for example, that Jesus did tell parables about the Kingdom of God (contrasted with the Roman Empire), did teach love of enemies, and did perform a symbolic action in the Jerusalem temple. Jesus' crucifixion is certainly historical. Advancing a political view of Jesus, in *The Political Aims of Jesus* (2012), Douglas Oakman writes, "Jesus' opposition to Mammon, his advocacy of tax and debt forgiveness, under God's eminent domain, led to his political execution on a Roman cross."[21]

These nontraditional views of Jesus relate closely to issues of justice and peace. For a fuller exposition, see our companion website.[22]

PRACTICAL AND RITUAL DIMENSION

Baptism and Eucharist

To the two key doctrines of incarnation/**indwelling** and death/resurrection correspond two key rituals: **baptism**, designed to "incorporate" the recipients into the "body of Christ" so that they are reconciled to God, share something of his divine nature, and are empowered to resist the effects of original sin; and the **Eucharist** (or *Lord's Supper*), which reenacts or symbolizes the final meal that Jesus shared with his disciples before his crucifixion, death, and resurrection. With regard to baptism, Paul writes of being united with Christ "in a death like his" as the prelude to being united with Christ "in a resurrection like his" (Romans 6:3–11). Acts of the Apostles represents Paul as expecting that people will receive the Holy Spirit when they are baptized (Acts 19:1–7). With regard to the Eucharist, the first three Gospels (reflected also by Paul in 1 Corinthians 11:24–26) give the words of Jesus in variant forms: (for the bread) "Take and eat; this is my body"; (for the wine) "Drink from it, all of you, for this is my blood of the covenant, which will be shed on behalf of many for the forgiveness of sins" (Matthew 26:26–28). They also include commands like "Do this in remembrance of me" (Luke and Paul) and "Proclaim the death of the Lord until he comes" (Paul), and a promise that Jesus when he returns will drink the cup anew with his disciples in God's kingdom (Matthew, Mark, Luke). Thus the Eucharist is a memorial meal, a present union with the risen Jesus, and an anticipation of Jesus' return.

Different Christian churches vary in the ways they celebrate and explain the meaning of these rituals. Some baptize infants, and others wait until a person is capable of making a personal commitment to God. Some believe that the risen, glorified Jesus is physically present in what appear to be bread and wine at the Eucharist, whereas others think that Jesus is spiritually but not physically present, or even just remembered.

Sunday and Saints' Days

Almost all Christian churches reserve Sunday of each week as a special day for community and individual prayer, similar to but generally less intensive than Jewish observance of the Sabbath. Christians justify the shift from Saturday to Sunday on the grounds that Jesus rose from the dead on a Sunday. Many churches celebrate the Eucharist every Sunday; most advise members to abstain from work on Sunday, although few require it.

Catholic and Orthodox churches celebrate those of their deceased members who lived holy lives (saints) by assigning one or more saints to each day of the year and encouraging living members to pray to them for wisdom and God's help. Some Protestant churches object that this "devotion" to saints is a form of idolatry.

Christmas, Easter, and Pentecost

Most Christian churches also celebrate three annual ritual festivals: **Christmas**, celebrating the incarnation and birth of Jesus; **Easter** with Good Friday, commemorating the death and resurrection of Jesus; and **Pentecost**, recalling the Holy Spirit descending upon the apostles (as it had upon Jesus at his baptism) and empowering them to continue what Jesus had started. For Catholic, Orthodox, and some Protestant churches, forty days of preparation, called *Lent*, precede Easter. The Lenten preparation used to require significant fasting, but very little of that discipline remains obligatory for Catholics. Celebration of Christmas reminds Christians that they are united with Jesus as Jesus was with God (although not in the same way), that God was willing to become vulnerable as we are, and that God is present among poor and simple people. Good Friday and Easter remind them that God, incarnate in Jesus, loved them (and still loves them) enough to die for them, and that they need not fear suffering or death, since they can depend on resurrection with Jesus. Pentecost reminds them that Jesus lives and acts in and through them by the power of the Holy Spirit, enabling them to do things that their own human power cannot do.

ETHICAL AND LEGAL DIMENSION

Jesus' Sermon on the Mount (Matthew 5–7)

Emphatically pacifist statements are found in the **Sermon on the Mount** in Matthew's Gospel (Matthew chapters 5–7). What Jesus says there makes people nervous because it seems extreme, especially in comparison to our common practice. His demands seem impossible to meet as described unless the Holy Spirit were to empower one to overcome the effects of original sin:

> Blessed are the meek, for they will inherit the land. (5:5)

> You have heard that it was said, "An eye for an eye and a tooth for a tooth." But I say to you, offer no [violent] resistance to one who is evil. When someone strikes you on (your) right cheek, turn the other one to him as well. If anyone wants to go to law with you over your tunic, hand him your cloak as well. Should anyone press you into service for one mile, go with him for two miles. Give to the one who asks of you, and do not turn your back on one who wants to borrow. (5:38–42)

> You have heard that it was said, "You shall love your neighbor and hate your enemy." But I say to you, love your enemies, and pray for those who persecute you. (5:43–44)

These passages have been discussed for centuries, and there are various ways to understand them. Here are the major ways people have understood Jesus' Sermon on the Mount:

1. Absolute. *Take Jesus' sayings as they stand and try to live by them.* Francis of Assisi interpreted the Sermon this way. He said, in effect, "Scholars may know some special way to explain these sayings. But I am just a simple man. I hope you'll excuse me if I just live the sayings as they stand." And he did most of the time. But even he couldn't do so all the time. Mohandas Gandhi was

another who tried to live the Sermon literally. The Sermon on the Mount was the part of Jesus' teaching that appealed most to him as a Hindu.

Note, however, that "as they stand"—a "literal" interpretation—requires us to study the world in which Jesus' sayings were spoken so as to understand what they would have meant to their original audience. According to the interpretation of Walter Wink, a first-century Galilean would most likely have been "struck on the cheek" by a person of "importance" who wished to humiliate him with a backhanded slap. Turning the other cheek, and so requiring the forehanded slap reserved for equals, would reject the humiliation, indicating a refusal to grovel; and it would do so nonviolently, refusing as well to attack or insult the striker. Giving a debtor one's *underwear, too,* when he demanded only one's outerwear, would highlight the debtor's injustice with humor, as Francis of Assisi demonstrated when his father challenged his religious commitment to poverty.[23]

In contrast, the next three interpretations reduce the intensity of Jesus' commands:

2. Rhetorical exaggeration. *Preachers exaggerate to make a point. The sayings are challenging enough without being rigid about it.* Here we might put two subheadings: (a) General principles. *The sayings deal with* types *of acts, not* specific *acts.* The saying, "If he slaps you on the right cheek, turn the other cheek" does not leave one free to respond violently to kicks or punches. On the other hand, when Jesus was slapped at his trial, he didn't literally "turn the other cheek." He nonviolently challenged his attacker, saying, "If I have spoken wrongly, testify to the wrong; but if I have spoken rightly, why did you strike me?" (John 18:23). Yet he remained vulnerable to further blows, and in fact got them later. (b) Attitudes, not acts. *The internal attitude is more important than the external act.* Augustine urged this second view. Still, if our external act is never the one that Jesus suggests, we might wonder whether our internal attitude is any better.

3. Reach for perfection. *Jesus knows we can't really accomplish what he says, but if we try very hard we'll do better than we would have otherwise.* However, if we think this is what he meant, we may not even try very hard.

4. Impossible demands break pride. *Jesus knows we can't keep his commands, but wants us to try so that we will see how sinful we are. Then we won't be able to look down on other sinners.* This explanation has been popular with Lutherans. It avoids the danger of justification by works. But there is nothing in the Sermon on the Mount itself to suggest that Jesus wasn't asking people to do what he said.

The next three interpretations limit the area that the commands apply to:

5. Distinguish precept from counsel. *Some people are called to keep all the demands of the Sermon on the Mount, others only to keep the more basic Christian demands. Hermits, monks, nuns, and similar especially committed people are*

called to keep them all. The commands that all Christians must keep are called "precepts"; those that only special people must keep are called "counsels of perfection." This explanation has been traditional with Roman Catholics. There are some weak hints in the New Testament that support this view (Matthew 19:16–30, 10–12; 1 Corinthians 7:38). But it can lead to clericalism and a sense that the laity is second-rate. And there's nothing in the Sermon itself to suggest that any listeners are being left out of the demands.

6. Two realms. *The demands apply to the spiritual realm and to the life of the* individual, *but not to the* temporal, or secular, *realm and the life of the* community. *To learn how to live in the secular realm, ask your secular leader. Christians in their* individual *relationships should turn the other cheek, but Christian* nations *should not.* This distinction was urged by Martin Luther. It has lost much of its attraction because it led many German Christians to support Hitler.

7. Dispensational. *The Sermon on the Mount was intended to be the new Law for Jews who accepted Jesus as their Messiah. Its high standards convicted them all of sin. When the Jews rejected Jesus, God put a different plan into action and saved Gentiles through faith. At the end of time when the Jews are finally saved,* they *will follow the Sermon on the Mount, but in the meantime it doesn't apply to Gentiles.* This position is held by some dispensational Protestants, but not by all of them. Dispensational Protestants believe that God deals differently with different historical periods or "dispensations."[24]

The last two interpretations invalidate the demands of the Sermon:

8. **Interim ethic**. *Jesus believed that the world would come to an end very soon. He thought that in this urgent, apocalyptic age people could keep the demands of the Sermon for the short time necessary until the end. If he had known how long the interim period would be, he would not have made such difficult demands.* This modern theory arose as biblical scholarship asked how much Jesus actually knew. It is risky to decide what Jesus would have done if circumstances had been different. There is nothing in the Sermon itself to suggest either that Jesus regarded the end as near or would have spoken differently if he had known it wasn't.

9. Harmful. *The demands of the Sermon turn Christians into weak cowards. Strong men would act with power.* Friedrich Nietzsche proposed this view. Unfortunately his attitudes were influential with Nazis, making many others hesitant to embrace them with enthusiasm. Also, it would be hard to describe Jesus, Francis of Assisi, Gandhi, and others who embraced the Sermon as weak cowards.[25]

The Sermon on the Mount looks a lot more impractical to affluent people than it does to the poor. Perhaps a large part of one's discomfort comes from one's attachment to wealth and comfort. Wealth and comfort bought at the price of anger and resentment are costly. Psychosomatic medicine teaches that unexamined, unprocessed anger and resentment cause physical and emotional illness. So if we don't want to be ill, perhaps we should take seriously Jesus' call to forgive, as implied in Matthew 5:44 and as stated explicitly in the Lord's Prayer (Matthew 6:12–15 and parallels) and elsewhere in the New Testament.[26]

SOCIAL AND INSTITUTIONAL DIMENSION

The Protestant Reformation: Martin Luther

Martin Luther was an Augustinian monk when he began the Protestant Reformation in Germany in 1517 by calling for a public discussion of ninety-five theses which challenged points of Catholic faith and practice connected to indulgences and spiritual pardons.[27] Luther's doctrine of justification by "faith alone" was popularly contrasted with the Catholic doctrine of salvation by faith in combination with the good works that faith produces. Actually, both believe that justification is by faith alone, and both agree that justification leads one to live a life of good works—if there are no good works in evidence, one can suspect that there is no faith either. Note that justification and salvation are not identical. "Justification" is the first act that puts a Christian in right relationship with God: we experience it *now*. "Salvation" is the final rescue from all danger, pain, and death as we pass through death to life: we experience it *in the end times or when we die*. "How much more then, since we are now justified by his blood, will we be saved through him from the wrath of God. . . . Our salvation is nearer now than when we first believed" (Romans 5:9, 13:11).[28] Recent Catholic-Lutheran dialogue shows that the modern Catholic and Lutheran positions are not very far apart. But conditions in the sixteenth century made that convergence difficult to see.[29]

Luther spoke of "two realms"—church and state—and maintained that the state, not the church, had authority in the political arena. The fact that state power sometimes supported him against the pope may have influenced his judgment.

In the lead-up to the "Peasants' Revolt" of 1524–1525 against the socioeconomic oppression they were experiencing under secular authorities, the peasants found inspiration in some of Luther's reformist writings. In fact, Luther strongly agreed with the lower classes that princes, lords, clergy, and other elites were treating them unjustly. But when, encouraged by his language, the peasants actually revolted, Luther denounced their violence and rebellion against the established order. Although their demands were just, social order must be maintained. Christians must obey "even unjust and cruel rulers" as "ordained by God" unless "the gospel [was] in jeopardy." When the peasants continued their armed rebellion, Luther encouraged the princes to slaughter the rebels wholesale, as they were already doing:[30]

> It is better that all the peasants be killed than that the princes and magistrates perish, because the rustics took the sword without divine authority. . . . Even if the princes abuse their power, yet they have it of God, and *under their rule the kingdom of God at*

least has a chance to exist. Wherefore no pity, no tolerance should be shown to the peasants, but the fury and wrath of God should be visited upon those men who did not heed warning nor yield when just terms were offered them, but continued with satanic fury to confound everything (emphasis added).[31]

In his earlier *Treatise on Christian Liberty*, Luther wrote that Christians should act in a Christ-like way toward their neighbors, becoming "Christs to one another." Such neighborliness would include financial assistance to those in need. Attention to the needs of others was later emphasized by seventeenth-century German Pietists. In the United States today, the Lutheran Social Services (LSS) exemplifies that teaching, as does the Lutheran World Federation (LWF) globally. Minnesota's LSS offers adoption; financial and psychological counseling; and disability, employment, homelessness, refugee, and many other services to the general population.[32]

The Reformer John Calvin

Another Reformer, John Calvin (1509–1564), placed church power above state power; in Geneva, Switzerland, he established a theocracy based on laws derived from the Bible. According to Calvin, original sin made humans "totally depraved." God is the all-powerful creator, and God's world order is to be maintained. To that end, humans, once they have been justified by God's free grace, must practice the virtues of "thrift, hard work, sobriety, responsibility, and self-reliance."[33] The sociologist Max Weber proposed that the virtues promoted by this Calvinist doctrine made European capitalism possible.[34]

Peace Churches

Some Protestant denominations, especially the **Anabaptist** churches (Christians who insisted that people baptized as infants had to be baptized again as adults),[35] advocated following the Sermon on the Mount literally with regard to nonviolence, thus refusing any participation in war. This movement was called the "**Radical Reformation**," and denominations deriving from it became known as "**Peace Churches**." Examples are the Mennonites, the Amish, and the Church of the Brethren. Although they were not Anabaptists and not part of the Radical Reformation, the Quakers (see below) also practiced pacifism.

Anabaptist Peace Churches

Among the positions held by the Anabaptist peace churches, three are directly relevant to justice and peace: (1) Christians should separate from the world and from the state, and therefore not be involved in politics; (2) Christians should not resist evil violently, but instead should practice nonviolence and pacifism (which could be understood as a form of separation from the state); and (3) Christians should share their goods, or should even own goods and property in common, as the Hutterites did. Diverging from the beliefs and practices of Catholics and Protestants, Anabaptists were persecuted by both.[36]

Following the Mennonites into modern history, a Mennonite relief agency was established in Holland in the early eighteenth century. In 1920 North American Mennonites established the Mennonite Central Committee, which in 2003 administered relief projects in more than sixty countries with a budget exceeding $62 million. Most Mennonites today seek to alleviate world poverty by means of social and economic justice. They oppose war—especially nuclear weapons—as incompatible with achieving justice.[37]

Quakers

The Religious Society of Friends (nicknamed Quakers by their critics) was founded in seventeenth-century England by George Fox (1624–1691), who wanted to end religious wars and prevent church conflicts. His quest led to his experience of inner peace and his "doctrine of the Inner Light." Fox held a positive view of human nature in contrast to the negative views of Luther and Calvin; and his experience of *direct, inner* revelation offset their emphasis on *biblical* revelation.

Fox and the Quakers were strong advocates of pacifism.[38] They regarded violence as satanic. Early Quakers testifying to their inner religious experiences risked prison, exile, and execution. Socially egalitarian, they addressed others as "thou" and "thee" without honorific titles;[39] they also refused to pay taxes to state churches. Their own meetings were silent except when the Spirit moved one of them to speak. Since the sacraments were internalized, no outer Eucharist was necessary.

In England and North America, Quakers opposed slavery and "most capital punishment."[40] They went to prison and paid fines rather than participate in warfare. Toward the Indians, they practiced reconciliation and friendship. The American Friends Service Committee[41] was founded in 1917 to enable World War I conscientious objectors to serve refugees and war victims instead of fighting. The Depression crystallized Quaker commitment to labor issues and workers' rights. Since 1943 the Friends Committee on National Legislation has worked to implement Quaker principles in American public policy. It is the largest peace lobby in Washington, D.C.[42]

Protestant Responses to the Enlightenment

In the nineteenth century, many Protestant churches, under the influence of the new scientific theories of the Enlightenment, began downplaying traditional theology in favor of humanitarianism. This movement was called "Liberal Protestantism." More conservative Protestant churches insisted on maintaining the "fundamentals" of the Christian faith, for example, Jesus' sacrificial atonement for human sinfulness, the inerrancy of the biblical text, literal interpretation of the Bible, and the bodily resurrection of Jesus. These churches called themselves **Fundamentalist**,[43] to be distinguished from the broader category of **Evangelicals**.[44]

Later, as the twentieth century was drawing to a close, some politically conservative American Evangelical Protestants formed the "Christian Right," epitomized in the "Christian Coalition of America,"[45] which cooperated with similarly conservative Catholic, Jewish, Mormon, and secularist movements. Other Evangelicals did not share their political agenda. Grant Wacker, a professor at Duke University Divinity School, estimates that, while there are only about two hundred thousand core members of the Christian Right, millions more could be enlisted to promote a particular political issue. A recent Evangelical position paper on social issues claims that one-quarter of Americans are Evangelicals! Although they share the concerns of classical Evangelicals and Fundamentalists, the Christian Right can be traced to the 1960s, when civil rights, Vietnam, women's liberation, and sexual freedom were among key societal concerns. In response to what they perceived as the dangerous liberalization of American culture, conservatives such as Jerry Falwell and Pat Robertson "sought to defend traditional Christian values such as the authority of the Bible in all areas of life," catching mainline Protestants and the mainstream media by surprise.[46]

According to Wacker, the "four cornerstones" of the Christian Right are (1) an arsenal of "moral absolutes"; (2) a refusal to firmly separate "the public and private spheres of life"; (3) the conviction that the "proper role [of government] is to cultivate virtue, not to interfere with the . . . marketplace or the workplace"; and (4) the reaffirmation of Judeo-Christian values ("Christian civilization") as the proper foundation for life in the United States. Members of the Christian Right feel defensive in the face of hostile media, the public school system, and anti-family forces, including certain government policies. On its website, the Christian Coalition of America presents itself as a pro-family political organization, founded in 1989, whose mission is to "represent the pro-family point of view before local councils, school boards, state legislatures and Congress; speak out in the public arena and in the media; train leaders for effective social and political action; inform pro-family voters about timely issues and legislation; protest anti-Christianity bigotry; and defend the rights of people of faith.[47]

Progressive Evangelicals have promoted a different political vision. For specifics of their vision with respect to such issues as religious freedom, family life, human rights, war and peace, and ecology, see the program proposed by the National Association of Evangelicals in chapter 9 on religious social teaching.

ISSUES FOR JUSTICE AND PEACE

Women

Jesus' relations with women seem to have been more egalitarian than was typical of his society. The woman who anointed Jesus, the woman suffering from hemorrhages, the woman at the well, Martha and Mary, the woman caught in adultery, and Mary Magdalene are some who come to mind. Women were the first witnesses to the empty tomb and, in the final chapters of the Gospel of Mark, they are shown to be Jesus' "true disciples."[48]

Despite traditional views of Paul as a misogynist, he in fact expresses the same high regard for his female missionary colleagues as he does for his male colleagues (see Romans 16). In the early Christian era of house churches, women played prominent leadership roles, but institutionalization and adaptation to patriarchal Greco-Roman culture reduced women's influence. Nevertheless, the history of Christianity is unthinkable without the contributions of such women as the early Christian martyrs Perpetua and Felicitas; the great medieval mystics Julian of Norwich, Catherine of Siena, and Teresa of Avila; and countless other women (known and unknown) before and since. Today women may be ordained in the mainline Protestant churches, though not in the Catholic or Orthodox churches. Feminist scholars are engaged in important biblical and theological research, for example, regarding biblical "role models for women," biblical images of God, and women's liberation.[49]

War

Old Testament

The Old Testament takes war for granted. It does challenge common *attitudes* toward war: the Israelites are not to go to war unless God calls them to it; they are not to go to war to enrich themselves; they are not to build up impressive forces, weapons, alliances, or defenses, but rather to depend on God; and if they fail to act justly in their relationships with others and with each other, they should expect God to abandon them to their own (inadequate) resources, as God in fact did when Babylonia invaded Judah in 587 BCE. It also contains significant passages opposing war and advocating peace, especially in the prophetic writings.

New Testament

In contrast to the Hebrew Bible, the New Testament is almost exclusively pacifist. Commands to love enemies and *not* to retaliate violently against violent people are central. Passages that are sometimes quoted to justify war are marginal or are not primarily talking about war. The strongest pacifist argument in the New Testament is the example of Jesus. He resisted expectations that he should lead an armed revolt as a Davidic messiah. Instead he allowed himself to be betrayed and executed. The "cleansing of the temple," sometimes cited to show Jesus acting violently, was a symbolic act rather than a violent seizure of power; at the end of the incident, the temple police were still in control of the temple area. Jesus had caused considerable embarrassment, but he had not seized power.

Christianity in the Roman Empire

Especially since the Protestant Reformation, Christian churches have varied widely in their social and institutional practices. The Roman Catholic Church organizes itself worldwide with (usually) one pope in Rome, a bishop in each major city or geographic area, and one or more priests in charge of each sub-area under the bishop's charge. At the other extreme, some Protestant churches consist of little more than a minister, a store front, and a congregation. Churches also vary in their actions for justice and peace. It seems most helpful to consider all of the above through a brief historical survey, with primary attention given to actions for justice and peace.

In the first three centuries, before the emperor Constantine legalized Christianity, Christians were pacifist *with respect to persecutions*: they did not use arms to defend their religious rights. Yet their pacifism was active: they demanded their rights. In this early period, Christians *did not exercise state power*, so they didn't have to decide whether to use force to defend the political state. Most Christian *writers* were pacifist even in regard to *state* power: they explained why Christians could not serve in the army. Thus, the Christian "great tradition" was pacifist in its primary expression.

Some scholars have asked how well *ordinary Christians*—the "little tradition"— agreed with their writers. Others have pointed out that *even the writers* had *a variety of reasons* for keeping Christians out of the army, given that it was an environment permeated with pagan worship in which few soldiers were Christians. On those unusual occasions when a pagan soldier converted to Christianity, the Christian community was so happy to get a *soldier* convert that it didn't know quite what to do with him.

After Constantine legalized Christianity, and especially after Theodosius I made Christianity the state religion, the way was open for Christians to hold state power. How could or should a Christian official remain pacifist when he had the levers of police and army in his hands? Responding to the political context, Ambrose of Milan and Augustine of Hippo adapted classical just war traditions to Christian theology, transforming them in numerous ways (see chapter 12, "Just War Theory"). This was a very dangerous time for Roman power because barbarian migrations were threatening Roman civilization. But Rome lost control to the barbarians anyway—acceptance of just war didn't prevent the collapse of Rome's empire. And it wasn't all one-sided: Rome didn't act fairly toward the barbarian tribes, who were being driven out of their traditional territories by other tribes. Barbarians brought their own martial traditions; Roman Christianity had given them little reason to question these traditions. The Catholic Church would try to moderate barbarian ways in the following period.[50]

War and Peace in the Middle Ages

In the Middle Ages, power was much more localized than it had been in the Roman Empire. Feudal culture valued loyalty to the local lord. Wars tended to be small, local or regional, and fought by professional knights who were so wrapped up in armor that casualties among the knights were light.

The church tried to reduce warfare by instituting the "**Peace of God**" and the "**Truce of God**." The "*Peace* of God" tried to reduce the number of *people* who could take part in war by putting certain categories off limits (not monks, not priests, not peasants, etc.);[51] the *"Truce* of God" tried to limit the number of *days* on which war could be fought (not Advent, not Lent, not Sundays, not feast days, not Saturdays, not Fridays, not Thursdays, etc.).[52]

The pope tried to end petty wars *between Christians* by sending warriors off against a "worthy" enemy—the Muslims. A major factor in the origin of the *Crusades* was the Muslim military defeat of the Byzantine Christian army in Asia Minor (modern Turkey) in 1071, which opened the remaining Byzantine Empire to Muslim conquest.[53] Byzantine emperors asked the pope for military aid in 1074 and again in 1095. In the latter year, Pope Urban II responded by calling for a crusade to restore access for Christian pilgrims to Jerusalem and the holy sites that had been disrupted by the Seljuk Turks. The actual course of the Crusades revealed other economic and political motives. Despite widespread Christian support at first, including that of St. Bernard, sensitive Christians had second thoughts as the Crusades progressed. Ultimately the Crusades (which ended in 1453 when Turkish Muslims conquered Constantinople) did not achieve their purpose, but they did have a profoundly negative impact on Muslim-Christian relations, an impact that has continued to reverberate in our time with U.S. wars on various Muslim countries in the Middle East and beyond.

Various popes also called for intra-Christian crusades against "heretical" Christians in Europe. And during the Protestant Reformation, intra-Christian persecution led to wars among different denominations.

The Catholic Inquisition

The **Inquisition** was a campaign instituted by the Roman Catholic Church to quell internal religious dissent using special church courts. If the church court found people guilty of heresy (religious beliefs that were false according to the Roman Catholic leadership), they were handed over to civil authorities for punishment. The Inquisition was also used in Spain against Jews and Muslims who had falsely pretended to convert to Christianity in order to avoid sanctions, such as the 1492 edict expelling Jews from Spain.

The Inquisition used torture to force confessions, and it often burned its victims at the stake. A seventeenth-century Anabaptist (see *peace churches* above) gathered historical examples of persecutions from the first century through the fifteenth (thus, up to the Radical Reformation) and published them in 1660 (in Dutch) in a large book called *Het Bloedig Tooneel* (English translation: *The Bloody Theater: or, Martyrs Mirror*), evidently to encourage those who were being persecuted in his own day. Here is a sample account:

A. D. 1417 . . . M. Raymond Cabasse, D.D. . . . declared . . . that the aforesaid Catharine Saube . . . was a heretic, and that she had disseminated, taught and believed divers damnable heresies against the Catholic faith, namely, "That the Catholic (or true) church is composed only of men and women who follow and observe the life of the apostles." . . . Again, "That she did not worship the host or wafer consecrated by the priest; because she did not believe that the body of Christ was present in it." Again, "That it is not necessary to confess one's self to the priest; because it is sufficient to confess one's sins to God; and that it counts just as much to confess one's sins to a discreet, pious layman, as to any chaplain or priest." Again, "That there will be no purgatory after this life."

Said town-book . . . contained also four other articles with which Catharine was charged, . . . (1) "That there never has been a true pope, cardinal, bishop, or priest, after the election of the pope (or bishop) ceased to be done through miracles of faith or verity." (2) "That wicked priests or chaplains neither can nor may consecrate the body of Christ, though they pronounce the sacramental words over it." (3) "That the baptism which is administered by wicked priests is of no avail to salvation." (4) "That infants which die after baptism, before they have faith, are not saved; for they do not believe but through the faith of their godfathers, godmothers, parents, or friends."

Having pronounced this sentence upon her, the vicar . . . delivered her into the hands of the bailiff. . . . The people entreated him much in her behalf, that he would deal mercifully with her; but he executed the sentence the same day, causing her to be . . . burnt as a heretic, according to law.[54]

Colonialism

European powers had mixed motives for colonizing the New World of the Americas: the spread of Christianity, national glory, and personal enrichment. Some Christian leaders, like Bartholomé de Las Casas, resisted the corruption involved. Theologians argued seriously about whether the "natives" were really human beings who had souls, illustrating how theology can be distorted by desire for personal gain and can serve special privilege. By the twentieth century, European colonies in the Americas had broken their connections with their mother countries, but for the most part it was descendants of the colonizers who remained in power.

Also outside of the Americas, European colonialism was multifaceted: military, economic, political, and cultural. Napoleon's occupation of Egypt at the end of the eighteenth century marks the beginning of European colonization of the Muslim world, which for the most part did not reverse until the mid-twentieth century. Britain also ruled India from 1857 to 1947. France occupied Algeria for more than one hundred thirty years, and other North African countries experienced occupation by Britain, France, or Italy. After World War I, Britain and France divided up the defeated Muslim Ottoman Empire into discrete nations, over which they assumed control. The British Mandate over Palestine proved especially disastrous for the indigenous population (see chapter 8).

Economically, the colonial powers sought raw materials and new markets at the expense of local economies. Politically and militarily, they exercised power at the expense of local self-government. Culturally, their presence, evident, for example, in the architectural reshaping of cities, was experienced by the native inhabitants as "invasive, disturbing, and alien."[55] The colonizers' mentality conflicted with the Islamic worldview of Muslim countries, often reflecting the view that Christian civilization was superior to Islamic cultures, and showing a racist contempt for the colonized. In *The Wretched of the Earth*, Frantz Fanon writes that the French colonizers dehumanized Algerians to justify their oppression. Despite the decolonization process that occurred mostly after World War II, many would argue that today a type of Western neocolonialism in the form of "neoliberalism" operates in the Muslim world and elsewhere with devastating global and local effects.

The Prosperity Gospel

Some Evangelical writers and television evangelists have developed a "**Prosperity Gospel**" based on the premise that God wants Christians to prosper. As preacher and proponent Kenneth Copeland explains its message, Christians are to short-circuit worldly means of financing by investing in God and trusting God to provide what they need. God then meets their needs not grudgingly but abundantly. Christians "invest" resources generously and in faith through "tithing, giving to the poor, investing in the Gospel, and giving as a praise to God." Then they "draw out" on what they have "invested" spiritually through the following steps: (1) Decide how much money you need. (2) Get your family or local Christian group to pray with you for that intention, relying on Matthew 18:19: "[Amen], I say to you, if two of you agree on earth about anything for which they are to pray, it shall be granted to them by my heavenly Father." (3) Trust in faith that God will give you the money. (4) Pray in the name of Jesus to "bind" the devil and his forces so that they cannot interfere. (5) Pray that the forces of heaven [angels] will be "loosed" to produce the desired effect. (6) Praise God in advance for answering your prayer.[56] Critics point out that it is important to keep priorities straight and values clear. If the "laws" of the Prosperity Gospel are interpreted as a way to "get ahead of others," there is something un-Christian in that goal. If material wealth is valued for itself, human values are distorted.

The Catholic Church and Mainline Protestant Churches on Justice and Peace

Roman Catholic teaching on justice and peace for the past century has been dominated by strong papal leadership, recently reinforced by national groups of bishops. These sympathies are shared with several politically active liberal Protestant denominations. (See chapter 9, "Religious Social Teachings.") In recent years there have been important attempts to apply just war principles to conditions of modern warfare. Some question whether such discussions have ever been beneficial, or whether they have served as an excuse to do what those in power wanted to do in any case. Others claim that just war arguments have helped to limit the savagery of war and to mobilize opposition to war, for example in the United States during the Vietnam War. (See chapter 12, "Just War Theory.")

Christian Zionism[57]

In chapter 3 we discussed *Jewish* Zionism, which dates in its modern form to the end of the nineteenth century. **Christian Zionism** (originally called "restorationism") actually began earlier, in the early part of the nineteenth century. It is exemplified today in *The Late Great Planet Earth*, by Hal Lindsey, describing the end of the world, and in the Left Behind series of books describing the **rapture**.

Many Evangelical and Fundamentalist Christians are convinced that such beliefs are well founded. Scholars and most members of the Catholic Church and of mainstream Protestant churches disagree.

Christian Zionism began with speculation on the end of the world, which gave rise to scriptural interpretation called **dispensationalism**: the view that God deals with different historical ages according to different rules. In itself there is nothing objectionable about this idea—it depends on what one thinks the rules are for different ages. Classical dispensationalists, as represented by the notes in the *Scofield Reference Bible*,[58] think that the Sermon on the Mount was intended by God for Jews who recognized Jesus as the messiah because the Sermon centers on keeping the Law of Moses with its full implications, which dispensationalists see as "justification by works." When Jews failed to recognize the messiah, God set up an altogether different set of rules, represented by Paul's preaching on justification by faith. Thus the Sermon on the Mount does not apply to today's Christians, but it will apply to the Jews when they come to accept Jesus as messiah. Not all dispensationalists today follow this interpretation.

According to the Christian Zionist interpretation, when Jesus returns, all those Christians who truly believe in Jesus will be snatched out of this world, *raptured* into the air with Jesus. Everyone else, those "left behind," will have to go through seven years of severe **tribulation** leading to the Battle of **Armageddon**, when Jesus will defeat the *Anti-Christ*. After that battle, Jesus will rule on earth for a thousand years (the **millennium**). During the millennium, Satan will be chained so that he cannot cause any trouble. At the end of the millennium, Satan will reappear for one final battle with God. Satan and his followers will be thrown into hell, and all the saved will join God in heaven.

What makes such dispensational interpretations "Zionist"? Christian Zionists take their descriptions of the end of the world from Hebrew prophets (especially Ezekiel, chapters 40–48), who anticipated the future as they could understand it. Their prophecies describe the messiah coming to an Israel ruled by Jews who are sacrificing in the temple. If such prophecies are believed to depict end-time events literally, then the end cannot come until (1) the Jews are back in Israel and in control of the government, and (2) there is a Jewish temple in Jerusalem where animal and vegetable sacrifices are being conducted. But there is no Jewish temple in Jerusalem. Furthermore, the parts of the ancient "holy land" that comprised the ancient northern and southern kingdoms of Israel and Judah are mostly in the West Bank, assigned to the Palestinians by United Nations resolutions and international law. The most likely way to "set the stage" for the second coming of Jesus, if his coming has to look literally like the biblical prophecies, is to kick the Palestinians out of the West Bank, fill it with Jews, and erect a "third temple" in Jerusalem. Since it is widely believed that the Muslim Dome of the Rock sits on the spot where the temple stood (although recent research suggests that the so-called Temple Mount was a Roman military fortress, and the temple was farther south over the Gihon spring),[59] erecting a third temple is likely to involve tearing down the Dome of the Rock. Christian Zionists think that this is exactly what should happen.

Jewish Zionists are not so happy about the Christian Zionists' plans for *them*: when Jesus returns, about a third of the Jews in Israel will recognize him as their messiah; the other two-thirds will be destroyed in the Battle of Armageddon. Zionist Jews do not take Christian Zionists' *theology* seriously, but they do take their *political* support seriously. In 2002, when President George Bush objected publicly to Israel's invasion and devastation of the Jenin refugee camp on the West Bank, he received about one hundred thousand angry e-mails, mostly from Christian Zionists, telling him to quit interfering with God's plan for Israel. There are some militant Zionist Jews who believe that God wants them to rebuild the temple.[60]

Palestinian Christians wonder what they have done to deserve this treatment from their Christian brothers and sisters. They are proud of their ancestry, which in many cases goes back to the apostles and other first-century Jewish converts to Christianity. For their part, Christian Zionists insist that God gave Israel to the Jews millennia ago, thus in effect endorsing the ongoing Israeli ethnic cleansing of the Palestinians from their own land.

Relations with Other Religions

Christianity has always been a missionary religion, like Islam, and historically has seen itself as the only universally valid religion for human salvation, hence the difficult history between Christianity and Islam. But this perception is far less prevalent in today's pluralistic world. One of the documents from the Second Vatican Council (1962–1965), *Nostra Aetate*, articulates a much more tolerant view of other religions, especially Judaism, Islam, Hinduism, and Buddhism, by acknowledging some common ground with each of them.[61] Indeed Vatican II fostered the growth of both Jewish-Christian and Christian-Muslim dialogue.[62] Liberal Protestant churches would echo or surpass the tolerance of Vatican II, whereas some conservative Protestant denominations would fall far short of it. Orthodox Christianity has a "longstanding tradition of respect and tolerance for other faiths."[63]

SPOKESPERSONS FOR JUSTICE AND PEACE

Jane Addams (1860–1935, United States, Protestant Christian) founded Hull House in Chicago, an early settlement house for immigrants. Working both to meet *immediate* needs and to uproot the *causes* of poverty, she engaged in political action against child labor and on behalf of immigrants, industrial safety, labor unions, limited working hours, and women's right to vote. Arguing that war destroys social reform, she helped found the Women's International League for Peace and Freedom (WILPF), of which she was the first president, the National Association for the Advancement of Colored People (NAACP), and the American Civil Liberties Union (ACLU). She received the Nobel Peace Prize in 1931.

Dorothy Day (1897–1980, United States, Catholic Christian)[64] experienced poverty in her childhood when her father, a professional journalist, lost his job. Her connection with poverty never left her—she "had a gift for finding beauty in the midst of urban desolation."[65] After studying journalism at the University of Illinois for two years, she wrote for a socialist newspaper. Always a vehement opponent of injustice, she picketed the White House in 1917 on behalf of women's right to vote and, when jailed, went on a hunger strike for ten days. While working as a communist to achieve "revolutionary [social] change," she bore a child to her common-law husband. In 1928 she became a Roman Catholic, breaking with her daughter's father, who objected to her conversion to Catholicism. She then struggled to reconcile her Catholic identity with her passion for justice.

A major turning point in her life came in 1932 when she met Peter Maurin,[66] a wandering French radical anarchist and former Christian Brother, at the settlement house she had founded in New York City. He encouraged her to publish a newspaper, which appeared a few months later as *The Catholic Worker*.[67] The name also designated Day's settlement house in New York City, and eventually a cooperative farm for the poor that she and Maurin established in upstate New York. They emphasized disengagement from the power structures of our society and direct mutual aid. Within its first year, the Catholic Worker movement began to open more "houses of hospitality" for homeless persons; by 1936, thirty-three Catholic Worker houses, urban and rural, were functioning across the country.[68]

Day and the Catholic Worker movement maintained a strictly pacifist position during World War I and all subsequent wars. During the Cold War, she and the Catholic Workers refused to take shelter during New York City's annual civil defense drill, inaugurated in 1955. By 1961, when the protesters numbered about two thousand, the drills were discontinued. She traveled twice to Rome during the Second Vatican Council (1962–1965) in the cause of peace, once to express appreciation for Pope John XXIII's encyclical *Pacem in Terris*, and once to join a fast until the council issued an explicit statement against war, which they did in the document *Gaudium et Spes*. In 1972 she was awarded the Laetare Medal by Notre Dame University, which commended her for "comforting the afflicted and afflicting the comfortable."

Martin Luther King Jr. (1929–1968, United States, Baptist minister) was born in Atlanta, Georgia, and earned a doctoral degree from Boston University. As pastor of the Dexter Avenue Baptist Church in Montgomery, Alabama, he was selected to lead the Montgomery Bus Boycott. Strongly influenced by Mohandas Gandhi, he developed and implemented the nonviolent strategies of the civil rights movement in the United States. In addition to being persecuted by the FBI under J. Edgar Hoover, King was jailed, he was stabbed, his home was fire-bombed, and after he began to connect race relations with economic injustice and the war in Vietnam, he was assassinated.[69] He helped found the Southern Christian Leadership Conference and the Student Nonviolent Coordinating Committee, and ran a training school for nonviolence. He received the Nobel Peace Prize in 1964.

Daniel Berrigan (1921–, United States, Catholic priest) and **Philip Berrigan** (1923–2002, United States, Catholic priest, married in 1970) were brothers born in Minnesota who became instrumental in the Christian nonviolent antiwar movement before, during, and after the Vietnam War. Both were also teachers and writers. Both served time in prison; Phil was incarcerated for a total of eleven years. Two famous acts of civil disobedience in which they both participated took place in Catonsville, Maryland, in May 1968, and in King of Prussia, Pennsylvania, in September 1980. In the first action, nine Catholic priests burned 378 draft records in a parking lot outside the draft board office. In the second, a group of eight Plowshares antiwar activists gained entrance to a General Electric plant that produced nuclear missiles, where they hammered on two "nuclear warhead cones," poured blood on plant documents, and prayed for peace.[70]

Both Phil and Dan faced opposition from the Catholic hierarchy for their peace activism. Phil accused "the religious bureaucracy" of racism, complicity regarding the war, and hostility to the poor. After the King of Prussia action, Phil and others opened Jonah House in Baltimore as a community of resistance. Dan and Phil fought nonviolently against Martin Luther King Jr.'s three evils: capitalism, militarism, and racism. Phil, who had married Elizabeth McAlister in 1970, died in 2002. Standing with members of the Occupy movement in New York City in June 2012, Dan said that faith

> means an overriding sense of responsibility for the universe, making sure that universe is left in good hands, and the belief that things will finally turn out right if we remain faithful. But I underscore the word "faithful." This faith was embodied in the Occupy movement from the first day. The official churches remained slow. It is up to us to take the initiative and hope the churches catch up.[71]

SUMMARY

Christians believe that God united God's self with a human nature in Jesus of Nazareth, who invited his listeners to welcome *God's* kingdom in preference to the addictive and violent power structures of their world, confronted the power elites of his day, refused to back down when—under the influence of evil spirits—they threatened to kill him, but also refused to organize violence in his own defense, was killed, and rose or was raised from the dead. Alive today, Christians believe, he joins himself to his followers, who, transformed by baptism and the Eucharist and acting in his power through the Holy Spirit, continue his mission to save humans and their societies from the results of "original sin." Believing they will be raised from the dead as Jesus was, faithful Christians are freed to love their enemies and do good to those who hate them; they refuse to defend themselves by means of violence, but they will not be deterred from speaking truth to the powerful.

Christian Zionists expect Jesus to return momentarily, first snatching them out of this world and saving them from the tribulation that will then occur as Jesus battles the Anti-Christ. These Christians support Israel's project to return all Jews to Israel, even at the expense of Christian and Muslim Palestinians, since they believe that is a precondition for Jesus' return. Other Christians oppose the dispossession of Palestinians just as they oppose all oppression and injustice. Numerous courageous Christians have taken great risks to work for justice and peace on behalf of all humans, whatever their worldviews.

KEY TERMS

Anabaptists	Inquisition
Armageddon	interim ethic
baptism	Jesus Seminar
Christian Zionism	kerygma
Christmas	messiah
conversion of the head	millennium
conversion of the heart	original sin
Crusades	Peace Churches
dispensationalism	Peace of God
Easter	Pentecost
Enlightenment	Prosperity Gospel
Epistle	Radical Reformation
Eucharist	rapture
Evangelicals	resurrection
Fundamentalists	Sermon on the Mount
Gospel	social (structural) sin
historical Jesus	Son of God
Holy Spirit	tribulation
incarnation	Truce of God
indwelling	

DISCUSSION QUESTIONS

1. How does this chapter's description of "original sin" compare with your previous understanding of it? If any of these ideas are new, do you find them helpful or disturbing? Do you think the concept of "original sin" in some form is true and therefore beneficial, or false and therefore harmful?
2. Which of the interpretations of the Sermon on the Mount comes closest to your own view? If none of the interpretations seems to reflect your view, how would you explain the Sermon on the Mount? Do you think any of the interpretations could produce *bad* effects?
3. What experiences have you had with mainline Christian churches (Catholic and Protestant), Evangelical and Fundamentalist churches, peace churches,

Christian Zionists, and/or the Prosperity Gospel? Would you describe any of these groups differently than this chapter has described them?

4. Which of the churches described here, if any, do you think are contributing positively to justice and peace? Which, if any, are contributing negatively? What could be done about the latter?

5. This chapter introduces five Christian workers for peace. Which of them would you be most interested in reading about further? What details caught your attention and interest? With which of their ideas or actions did you particularly agree or disagree, and why?

SUGGESTIONS FOR FURTHER READING

Barr. *New Testament Story*, 3rd ed.
Ciszek. *He Leadeth Me.*
Copeland. *The Laws of Prosperity.*
Cory and Hollerich, eds. *The Christian Theological Tradition*, 3rd ed.
Curle. *True Justice: Quaker Peacemakers and Peacemaking.*
Dart. *Marjorie Sykes, Quaker Gandhian.*
Day. *The Long Loneliness: The Autobiography of Dorothy Day.*
Doherty. *The Gospel without Compromise.*
Douglass. *JFK and the Unspeakable.*
Ehrman. *The New Testament*, 4th ed.
Eliade, ed. *The Encyclopedia of Religion.*
Fanon. *The Wretched of the Earth.*
Fisher. *Living Religions*, 5th ed.
Funk. *The Acts of Jesus.*
——— et al. *The Five Gospels.*
Gorospe. *Forming the Filipino Social Conscience: Social Theology from a Filipino Christian Perspective.*
Halley. *Halley's Bible Handbook: An Abbreviated Bible Commentary.*
King. *A Testament of Hope: The Essential Writings and Speeches of Martin Luther King Jr.*
Lindsey. *The Late Great Planet Earth.*
Matthews. *World Religions*, 4th ed.
Merton. *The Nonviolent Alternative.*
Newsom et al., eds. *Women's Bible Commentary*, 3rd ed.
Peterson. *Martyrdom and the Politics of Religion: Progressive Catholicism in El Salvador's Civil War.*
Sanford. *The Healing Light.*
Schüssler Fiorenza. *In Memory of Her.*
Scofield and Weston, eds. *The Scofield Reference Bible. The Holy Bible, Containing the Old and New Testaments. Authorized King James Version.*
van Braght, ed. *The Bloody Theater: Or, Martyrs Mirror.*
Weaver, Brakke, and Bivins. *Introduction to Christianity*, 3rd ed.
Weber. *The Protestant Ethic and the Spirit of Capitalism.*
Wink. *Engaging the Powers: Discernment and Resistance in a World of Domination.*
Yarrow. *Quaker Experiences in International Conciliation.*
Zahn. *In Solitary Witness: The Life and Death of Franz Jägerstätter.*

5

Muslim Worldviews

God! There is no god but He—
the Living, the Self-subsisting, Eternal.
No slumber can seize Him nor sleep.
His are all things in the heavens and on earth.
Who is there can intercede in His presence
except as He permitteth? . . .
His throne doth extend over the heavens and the earth,
and He feeleth no fatigue in guarding, and preserving them
For He is the Most High, the Supreme (in glory).

—Quran 2:255

We ordained for the Children of Israel that if any one slew a person—unless it
be for murder or for spreading mischief in the land—
it would be as if he slew the whole people:
and if any one saved a life,
it would be as if he saved the life of the whole people.

—Quran 5:32

And dispute ye not with the People of the Book,
except with means better (than mere disputation),
unless it be with those of them who inflict wrong (and injury):
but say, "We believe in the Revelation which has come down to us
and in that which came down to you;
our God and your God is One; and it is to Him we bow."

—Quran 29: 46

O mankind!
We created you from a single (pair) of a male and a female,
and made you into nations and tribes,
that ye may know each other.

Verily the most honored of you in the sight of God
is (he who is) the most righteous of you.
And God has full knowledge and is well acquainted
(with all things).

—Quran 49:13[1]

EXPERIENTIAL AND EMOTIONAL DIMENSION

Although it traces its existence back to Adam, the first human, historical Islam originated with Muhammad's experience. While meditating in a mountain cave near **Mecca** in early-seventh-century Arabia, he had a powerful encounter with the angel **Jibril** (Gabriel), who commanded him to "recite," or "read." He objected that he could not because he was illiterate,[2] but Jibril insisted until he finally *submitted*. This voluntary submission (*islam* in Arabic) to the will of **Allah** (Arabic for "the God") is the central value of Islam and the reason the religion is called *Islam*. Until his death twenty-three years later, Muhammad continued to have similar encounters, during each of which he received verbal revelations from God in Arabic, which he was commissioned to recite to others. Like most seventh-century Arabians, the Arabs of Mecca prized poetic skills highly. When Muhammad recited the revelations he was receiving from God, the Meccans were in awe at the beauty and power of their language, which no human being could duplicate. Muslims consider the **Quran** to be the greatest miracle given by God to Muhammad.

While he was still living in Mecca, ca. 620, in what came to be called his **night journey and ascension**, Muhammad was transported to Jerusalem on a heavenly winged steed and then taken to heaven, where he encountered prophets, angels, and finally the presence of God. This experience revealed religious truths to Muhammad, confirmed his faith, and demonstrated that his stature was equal to that of the prior prophets. It was "a miracle that no one (except Muhammad) saw."[3]

Muhammad's followers, who had previously worshiped multiple gods, became convinced that there is only one God, and this one God was calling them to the straight path of submission to God's will. Muhammad challenged all Meccans, including the wealthy and elite religious-economic establishment, members of his own Quraysh tribe, to give up their pride and arrogance, submit to Allah, and give to others, especially the poor, out of whatever wealth God had blessed them with (see Quran 2:3; 8:3). The Quran repeatedly insists (e.g., 34:3–5) that Allah will judge all humans justly after their death, rewarding the good and punishing the wicked.

A major turning point for Muhammad and the first Muslims of Mecca was the **hijra**, or migration, from Mecca to **Medina** in 622; Muslims begin their calendar from this event. The new religious consciousness of Muslims found expression in such common sayings as: *La ilaha illa Allah* ("There is no other deity except God"), *Alhamdulillah* ("Praise God!"), *Allahu akbar* ("God is greater [than anything or anyone else]"), and *Hasbuna Allah* ("God is sufficient for us").

HISTORICAL PERIODS

Spread of Islam

After Muhammad's death in 632, Islamic rule spread rapidly as Arab Muslim armies conquered territory in the Byzantine and Sassanian (Persian) empires. By the Middle Ages Islam had moved north through Turkey to Constantinople and across Eastern Europe to just short of Vienna, west across North Africa, across the Mediterranean Sea to Sicily, across the Strait of Gibraltar and north into Spain, east into India and beyond, reaching eventually as far as Indonesia (which today is the world's most populous Muslim-majority nation) and China.

Dynastic and Medieval Periods

The first four ("rightly guided") **caliphs** ("successors") to Muhammad (632–661) were companions of Muhammad who lived simple lives as he had. The origins of the Sunni-Shia divergence go back to this period, which also saw the initial extension of Muslim rule beyond Arabia. The Umayyad dynasty (with its capital in Damascus, 661–750) and the Abbasid dynasty (with its capital in Baghdad, 750–1258) developed after the first four caliphs. The Umayyads further expanded and Islamized their empire. The Abbasids sponsored a phenomenal multicultural, Islamic civilizational renaissance, encompassing theology, philosophy, science, medicine, literature, art, and architecture. Muslim and non-Muslim scholars translated ancient philosophical, scientific, medical, and other texts from Greek (among other languages), complementing these with major contributions of their own. Thomas Aquinas came to know Aristotle first through Latin translations from Arabic. Starting in the sixteenth century, three politically and culturally outstanding imperial sultanates flourished: the Ottomans based in Turkey, the Shia Safavids in Iran, and the Moghuls (Mughals) in India. The Moghul sultan Akbar created a House of Worship for inter-religious dialogue.

Decline

Once the caliphate had become dynastic and Islam intercontinental, uniting the entire Islamic world under one caliph became less and less possible. The last dynasty with a functioning caliphate was the Ottoman Empire (1281–1922) centered in Istanbul (Constantinople). After World War I, when Turkey was going through an explosive process of Westernization and secularization under Mustafa Kemal (Ataturk), the caliphate was abolished. Since that time there has been no generally recognized caliphate.

Modern Reform

The modern period of Islam was marked by the emergence of three broad "reform movements," one mostly before and two after the onslaught of European colonization, which lasted into the post–World War II period of the twentieth century. These movements can be labeled "early revivalism," "**modernism**," and "neorevivalism," the last represented by the Muslim Brotherhood and the Jamaat-i-Islami.[4] Early revivalism, focusing on internal reformation, began with the eighteenth-century, militant "political-religious" **Wahhabi** movement. There were also early revivalist movements in nineteenth-century Africa and eighteenth- and nineteenth-century India, all seeking to install or restore Islamic government. Modernism is described later in this chapter, as is the Muslim Brotherhood. For European colonialism in the Muslim world, see the relevant section in this chapter and the section on colonialism in chapter 4. Relations with the West, where millions of Muslims now live—making Islam a global religion of East and West—have been an important concern of Muslim countries in the postcolonial period as their people seek democracy and representative government in an Islamic context.

SACRED WRITINGS

Muslims believe that historically their faith is a continuation, purification, and completion of the Jewish and Christian revelations; on a deeper level, Islam represents the original monotheism of Abraham. They accept the Jewish and Christian prophets without distinction, but believe that the core message of the Bible was changed over time: the Jewish people were *conditionally* chosen, and the Christian doctrines of incarnation and Trinity deviate from the original divine message. The Quran, understood to be God's actual words in Arabic, restores the true content of the prior revelations, restating Allah's message to the Jewish and Christian prophets. However, neither Judaism and Christianity nor their scriptures are seen as abrogated or illegitimate.

The Quran

The *Quran* (literally "recitation") is the miraculously received sacred revelation from God to Muslims. It is believed that the Archangel Jibril (Gabriel), in a series of spiritual encounters over a twenty-three-year period, recited the verses of the Quran in Arabic to Muhammad, indicating also where each verse belonged in relation to those earlier revealed.[5] Muhammad in turn recited the verses to his companions, who repeated them, memorized them, and wrote them down. Because the Arabic language is intrinsic to the Quranic revelations, no translation is regarded as adequately representing the Quran—translations are only "interpretations."

After Muhammad died, Abu Bakr, the first caliph, assigned Zayed Ibn Thabit, a former secretary to the Prophet, the job of assembling a complete, authentic copy of the Quran based on the oral and written materials. The verses of the Quran are arranged in 114 sections of varying length, called **suras**. The order of suras, and of the verses within the suras, is believed to be based on previous instructions by Jibril to Muhammad.[6] The resulting text was further standardized under Uthman, the third caliph, by an official commission also headed by Ibn Thabit. Copies of this

"Uthmanic Codex" were then widely distributed, while earlier partial copies and variant readings were destroyed to ensure the use of a uniform, authentic text. Nevertheless, the traditional practice of memorization remains to this day the primary means of transmission of the original text.

Muslims refer to each sura by a keyword that reflects something of its content. After the first sura, which introduces the whole revelation, the second sura is the longest. The remaining 112 suras are approximately in order of declining length; their arrangement also makes use of connections between keywords and ideas. The suras are divided into two categories: (1) those received earlier, in Mecca, which are generally shorter than the second group, and so appear later in the Quran; and (2) those received after the hijra (migration) in 622 of Muhammad and the first Muslims from Mecca to Medina, which are generally longer and appear earlier in the Quran. Since Muhammad and the Muslims established the first organized Muslim community (**umma**) in Medina, these later suras contain rules and regulations for the Muslim community that are not found in the earlier suras.

The Sunna: Recorded in the Hadith

Besides the Quran, Muslims refer to the **Hadith**—written reports of the **Sunna**, traditions that are believed to record the words and actions of Muhammad as remembered and passed on by his followers. Each individual hadith has an *isnad*, or chain of transmission, on which the tradition is said to rest. The value of a particular hadith (its claim to authenticity) depends on the trustworthiness of the witnesses cited in the isnad.[7] The substance of the hadith is called the *matn*. These texts are considered authoritative, but are subject to criticism in a way that the Quran is not, since the Quran is believed to consist entirely of divine revelation.

Here are five examples of hadith, words attributed to Muhammad, minus the isnad:

> "None of you [truly] believes until he wishes for his brother what he wishes for himself." (13)
> "Fear Allah wherever you are, and follow up a bad deed with a good one and it will wipe it out, and behave well towards people." (18)
> "Whosoever of you sees an evil action, let him change it with his hand; and if he is not able to do so, then with his tongue; and if he is not able to do so, then with his heart; and that is the weakest of faith." (34)[8]
> "You will not enter paradise until you have faith; and you will not complete your faith, until you love one another."
> "Faith is a restraint against all violence; let no [believer] commit violence."[9]

NARRATIVE OR MYTHIC DIMENSION

Islam took root in an Arabian society that was mostly pagan, although Jewish and Christian communities were also present, in addition to indigenous monotheists called *hanifs*. Some biblical figures, stories, and themes were known in Arabia largely through oral tradition. Muhammad would also have encountered Jews and Christians in his itinerant work as a caravan manager.[10] The fact that the Quranic text overlaps with the Bible suggests that its original audience was familiar with various biblical contents in some form. Muslims explain that Islam on the one hand, and Judaism and Christianity on the other, are similar, especially in material shared by the two scriptures, because their common source is God. Muslims trace themselves back to Abraham through his older son, Ismail (Ishmael), and so Jews, Christians, and Muslims can all be regarded as "children of Abraham."

Muhammad was born in 570 CE. His father died before his birth. Since his mother was very poor, he was raised at first by his foster mother Halima. When he was six, his natural mother died and his foster mother gave him to his grandfather Abd al Muttalib. Two years later his grandfather died, and he was entrusted to an uncle, Abu Talib. Muhammad grew up fairly poor in the trading center of Mecca, a place of much socioeconomic injustice, where the gap between rich and poor was growing.

As a young adult, Muhammad worked for a wealthy widow named Khadija managing her caravans. Impressed by his success and his integrity, Khadija proposed marriage to Muhammad. He accepted gratefully, and lived with her as his only wife until she died twenty-four years later in 619, when he was about forty-nine. After her death he took other wives, according to the customs of the time. Some of these marriages were political, that is, intended to strengthen relations with neighboring tribes; some were to widows of companions who had died in battle. With Khadija he had four daughters and two sons; but only one daughter, Fatima, had children who lived into adulthood.

By the time he was forty, Muhammad meditated frequently alone in a mountain cave. There, during the month of **Ramadan**, he received the first divine revelation through Jibril (Gabriel). Khadija encouraged Muhammad to trust his auditions and share them publicly. When he did so, the wealthy religious-economic establishment of Mecca, members of his own tribe, became concerned that the new way of life preached by Muhammad would produce radical changes in the status quo from which they benefited, so they tried unsuccessfully to bribe Muhammad to keep quiet.

Like Jesus, Muhammad the prophet was also a social reformer. The revelations he received became the Quran, which expresses God's will for the community and teaches people how to live out the will of God, to fulfill the "Quranic mandate."[11] Here are some of the reasons that Meccan elites opposed Muhammad's Islamic reforms:

1. Replacing tribal loyalty with loyalty to the whole community (*umma*) under one God would bring an end to retaliatory, tribal warfare as well as to polytheistic belief and practice. The Meccan elites profited from the annual pilgrimage of polytheists to a shrine called the **Kaaba** and its idols. Muslims believe that

the Kaaba was originally built by Abraham and Ismail as a house of monotheistic worship, and that Muhammad was restoring its original purpose when he destroyed its 360 pagan idols. The Kaaba consists of a sacred black stone within a cubical building. The building is covered with a black cloth and surrounded by a huge courtyard.

2. As God's prophet, Muhammad was disturbed that older values of caring and sharing were eroding in Mecca as trade and urban life grew. But the elite establishment gained its wealth from that trade. Muhammad and the Quran spoke against usury (lending at interest), false contracts, and the accumulation of wealth without reference to need. Two of the **five pillars** of Muslim faith, alms and fasting (zakat and saum) relate directly to economic justice.

3. As God's prophet, Muhammad opposed female infanticide and introduced reforms that improved the position of women with respect to marriage, divorce, and inheritance. These changes challenged the traditional patriarchal social order, which the elites wanted to maintain.

The Hijra to Medina

Opposition to Muhammad in Mecca developed into persecution, including an economic and social boycott that lasted several years. In 619, he lost both his wife Khadija and his uncle Abu Talib; without his uncle's protection, Muhammad's life was at risk. He realized that the Muslim community would have to relocate. In 621, a delegation from Yathrib (also called Medina: "the city"), about two hundred miles north of Mecca, invited Muhammad to mediate between two warring tribes there. The delegation pledged "to become Muslims and to obey the Prophet."[12] They were aware of Muhammad's reputation for fairness and reliability, which had gained him authority and respect. In 622, Muhammad and his followers fled from Mecca to Medina, where he was accepted as city leader. This *hijra* (*hegira*), or emigration, began his role as head of state, and the date, July 16, 622 CE, stands at the beginning of the Muslim calendar: as Christians measure dates with AD—*Anno Domini* ("in the year of the Lord [Jesus Christ]"), so Muslims measure dates with AH—**Anno Hegirae** ("in the year of the hijra"). More recently, scholars have begun to use the designation CE (the "common era") in place of AD in an attempt to de-link this most widely used dating system from a particular religion, although its origin was religious.

Muhammad in Medina

In Medina, Muhammad established a new constitution for the umma, or community, which included people of all religious faiths. This document granted the Jewish tribes religious and cultural autonomy as long as they agreed to live under Muhammad's political authority. His diplomatic skills in Medina and new defensive military tactics against his Meccan opponents increased the esteem in which he was held. Between 624 and 627 the Meccans engaged in three major battles with the

Muslims, but ultimately failed to thwart the growth of Muhammad's following and so of the nascent religion.

Having dealt with the Meccans diplomatically in 628–629, in 630 Muhammad and the Muslims of Medina returned in force to Mecca, which surrendered with almost no resistance. Proclaiming an amnesty toward his opponents, Muhammad entered the city and purged the Kaaba of its 360 idols, thus confirming Mecca's conversion to Islam. This ultimate Muslim victory and incorporation of Mecca into the umma was understood to be the fulfillment of God's will.

In 632 Muhammad made his final pilgrimage to Mecca and delivered his farewell sermon. By then most of Arabia was united under Islamic rule. In his sermon, Muhammad said:

> All mankind is from Adam and Eve: An Arab has no superiority over a non-Arab, nor does a non-Arab have any superiority over an Arab; also a white has no superiority over a black, nor a black . . . over a white except by piety *and good action. Learn that* every Muslim is a brother to every other Muslim and that the Muslims constitute one brotherhood.[13]

The Death and Legacy of Muhammad

Muhammad died in June 632. He was highly regarded as a mediator and adjudicator of tribal disputes. In early adulthood, before his call to prophethood, he was given the name *al-Amin* ("the trustworthy one"), indicating the confidence that his contemporaries placed in him. After his call to prophethood, he became known as "the living Quran," one whose words and actions revealed God's will. Muhammad lived simply and did not want a marker to be placed over his burial site, so that no one would worship him as more than an ordinary human being after he died.

DOCTRINAL AND PHILOSOPHICAL DIMENSION[14]

Basic Beliefs

1. *Allah. There is only one God*, both transcendent (totally unlike everything else, which he has created) and immanent. ("It was We who created man, and We know what dark suggestions his soul makes to him: for We are nearer to him than [his] jugular vein" [Quran 50:16]). The fundamental human sin (called **shirk**) is to associate any created being with God the creator. God is completely self-sufficient, all-powerful, and all-knowing, and needs no "help." Muslims are told not to make images of God (which might become objects of idolatry), who is far beyond anything we can imagine.[15] God's will governs every aspect of human life, so that religion, state, law, and society compose one reality; hence Islam is a way of life. God is merciful and just. God's justice is in dialogue with human accountability, but God forgives those who repent when they have erred.

2. *Angels.* Angels are superhuman beings created out of light by God; without bodies, they are powerful, intelligent, and good. They help humans surrender to God and so attain salvation. One such angel is Jibril (Gabriel), who transmits divine revelations to prophets. Iblis (Satan) is the one bad angel. Jinn are lesser superhuman beings who are made of fire and subject to final judgment.

3. *Prophets.* In addition to Muhammad, Islam accepts as prophets those whom Jews and Christians accept, with some omissions and additions. Noah, Abraham, Moses, Isaiah, and Jesus were all prophets in that they spoke God's word. They were also muslims because they surrendered to God. Muhammad is the last prophet—no future prophets are to be expected.

4. *Scriptures (revealed books).* Some prophets, like Moses, Jesus, and Muhammad, are also messengers, those who bring "a message for a community in book form."[16] God has revealed his truth verbally to humans through the messenger prophets, through Moses (in the *Torah*—the Law), through Jesus (in the **Injil**—the Gospel), and most perfectly through Muhammad in the Quran. Over time, distortions have crept into the Torah and Injil. The Quran, in contrast, was revealed word-for-word in Arabic by God through Jibril to Muhammad and preserved free from error. The purpose of the Quran is to guide those who worship Allah on the straight path through life leading to final judgment and (if the Quran is followed) paradise in the afterlife.

5. *The day of judgment.* According to the Quran, all humans will rise from the dead and assemble before God at the end of time. Then God will judge each person on the basis of his or her actions in life, all of which have been recorded in a "book of deeds." The good and compassionate will go to heaven, visualized as an oasis: a beautiful garden with underground sources of water. The evil and hardhearted will go to hell, visualized as a place of torment and everlasting fire. It is essential to take this life seriously, as it is the one testing ground that will determine our final destiny.

6. *The divine decree: predestination and free will.* God creates and sustains the universe, so he knows everything that has happened or will happen, and everything that happens is his will. Nevertheless, humans exercise free will and will be judged for their actions. The Quran seems to balance divine sovereignty and human freedom equally, whereas the Hadith seem to emphasize divine predestination more than human free will.

Additional Beliefs

7. *Dignity of humans.* Humans have a special status in God's creation as God's representatives on earth. Their collective purpose is to realize God's will in history by creating a just society. The Adam and Eve story as told in the Quran does not include "original sin" in the Christian sense. But the reality of Satan does stand behind humans' ongoing moral struggle ("the greater jihad") between their good and evil inclinations. Supporting them in this struggle are

the teachings of the Quran and the Hadith, including observance of the Five Pillars (see below).

8. *Role of the community.* Muslims live out their response of submission to God both as individuals and as members of the umma, or Islamic community, which is based on faith, not on ties of blood, tribe, race, ethnicity, or nation. It is open to all, and serves as an example to the nations (Quran 2:43). The umma has the moral mission of creating an ethical social order. The individual and collective struggle for social justice requires political-social activism. Muslims are called "to transform the world itself through action in the world."[17]

PRACTICAL AND RITUAL DIMENSION

The Quran refers to the ritual pillars of prayer, almsgiving, fasting, and pilgrimage. Repeatedly in the Hadith, Muhammad also mentions these basic practices required of Muslims.

The Five Pillars

1. **Shahada** is the profession of Islamic faith. You become a Muslim the first time you recite it sincerely; Muslims generally repeat it each day. Here is what they say: *La ilaha illa Allah, Muhammadan rasul Allah* ("There is no God but Allah, and Muhammad is his messenger"). *Allah* is a special form of *al-ilah* = the God, implying "the only God" (al-ilah has a plural; Allah does not). This profession of faith is part of the public "call to prayer" that the Muslim **muezzin** proclaims from the **minaret** (proclamation tower) of the **mosque** five times a day.

2. **Salat** is prayer: remembrance of and devotion to Allah, which every practicing adult Muslim does five times a day in a clean place, often on a carpet or small prayer rug (whether in a mosque or elsewhere), facing Mecca.[18] Salat keeps the believer in contact with God throughout the day and makes the Muslim less likely to act contrary to God's will. Men are required to attend the congregational noontime prayer on Friday, which includes a sermon by the imam (prayer leader). The prayer incorporates Sura 1 of the Quran:

> In the name of God, Most Gracious, Most Merciful.
> Praise be to God, the Cherisher and Sustainer of the worlds;
> Most Gracious, Most Merciful;
> Master of the Day of Judgment.
> Thee do we worship, and Thine aid we seek.
> Show us the straight way,
> The way of those on whom Thou hast bestowed Thy Grace,
> those whose (portion) is not wrath, and who go not astray.

3. **Zakat** ("that which purifies") is almsgiving: sharing one's possessions with those in greater need, for example, widows, orphans, the desperately poor, travelers,

and slaves needing ransom. Understood as an act of worship rather than a "tax," zakat is a fixed annual contribution, obligatory for Muslims, but usually privately handled. In a few countries, it is administered by the government.[19] Muslims are also encouraged to give *sadaqa*, an individual, spontaneous almsgiving. In general, zakat amounts to 2.5 percent of one's assets over and above basic living expenses and subsistence needs like food, clothing, housing, tools, and so on.[20] Zakat illustrates the convergence of worship and service in Islam. It serves to redistribute wealth and reduce somewhat the disparity between rich and poor. In addition to helping the poor, zakat "purifies" or legitimizes wealth that one has gained *honestly*, especially by one's own labor—one cannot use zakat to purify ill-gotten gains. Since all wealth is a gift from God, zakat is based on the right that poor people have to share in God's creation; the wealth of the rich is considered impure unless it is shared with the needy. In addition to purifying the *property itself*, zakat also purifies the *heart of the giver* from selfishness and greed. At the same time, it purifies the *heart of the receiver* from envy, jealousy, and anxiety; and it builds good will in the community.

4. **Saum**, or *sawm*, is fasting during daylight hours of the month of Ramadan.[21] One abstains completely from all sensory pleasures: food, drink (even water), tobacco, and sex. Muslims awaken before dawn to eat a meal before the sun rises and do not eat again until after sundown in the evening. Saum enables one to share the experiences of hunger and thirst, and to express solidarity with those who are actually so poor that they cannot afford sufficient food and drink. It reminds Muslims that they all belong to one umma; they care about and depend on each other. It also reminds them that they depend on God for the goods of the earth that sustain them, so it has a joyful character. Since the Muslim year is about eleven days shorter than the Western year because it consists of twelve lunar months, the calendar drifts backward about eleven days a year, and the month of Ramadan occurs in every season of the year over the normal lifetime of a Muslim. When Ramadan occurs in the summer in northern latitudes, the period of fasting from sunup to sundown can be very long.

5. **Hajj** is pilgrimage to Mecca, required at least once in a lifetime.[22] The hajj is required, provided that one can afford the trip from one's own resources; no one is obliged to borrow or depend on others to pay the costs. The hajj offers a dramatic experience of Muslim unity and equality before God. The male pilgrims wear a plain white gown. The pilgrims participate in common ceremonies with up to two million other pilgrims at one time. Malcolm X, who had been a leading member of the Nation of Islam (which at that time preached that blacks were superior to other races), made the hajj in 1964. His experience of unity and equality in Mecca was so overpowering that he converted to mainstream (Sunni) Islam, which upholds the equal value and dignity of every human regardless of race or ethnicity. Muslims make the hajj to Mecca because the events that took place there in the time of Muhammad are central to the Muslim worldview. Pilgrims circle around the Kaaba and perform a series of prescribed rituals over a number of days. They also visit Medina after the pilgrimage to Mecca to see where the prophet lived. They venerate Jerusalem because Muhammad prayed in Jerusalem and then ascended to heaven

from that city after his "night journey." Through pilgrimage, worshipers seek to connect with the power of those events.

Festivals

The two major feasts of the Islamic year are the three-day **Eid al-Fitr** (Feast of Breaking the Fast) celebrated at the end of Ramadan, and the three- or four-day **Eid al-Adha** (Feast of the Sacrifice) celebrated at the end of the annual pilgrimage, or hajj, in Mecca.

The Eid al-Fitr begins on the first day after Ramadan. In addition to feasting and visiting with family and friends, Muslims give food to the poor for their feast (Zakat al-Fitr) and gifts to children and others. The Eid begins with an Eid sermon and congregational prayer service.

The Eid al-Adha closing the hajj commemorates the story of Abraham's near-sacrifice of his son Ishmael (not his second son, Isaac, as in the Genesis 22 account). The animal sacrifice of cattle, goats, and sheep that precedes the feast alludes to God's substitution of a ram for the boy. The meat that is left over from the feast is given to poor people, who probably eat meat very infrequently. Note how this feast celebrates the key Muslim virtue of trusting surrender to God (Islam). Both Abraham and Ismail (Ishmael) trusted God: Abraham proved willing to sacrifice his dream of living on in his descendants, the essence of the promises he had received from God. Ismail offered his very life.

There are additional Shia religious practices, such as the celebration of the birth and death days of the Shia Imams, pilgrimage to tomb shrines including those of the "holy family," and commemoration of the martyrdom of Ali's son Husayn at **Karbala** (in Iraq) in the year 680 through annual and daily Muharram processions, the recital of sacred stories, and the performance of passion plays. Veneration of martyrs and saints draws attention to their virtues and encourages Muslims to imitate them. Commemorating the martyrdom of Husayn reminds Shia Muslims that trusting confidence in Allah is the core of Islam, and that such trust requires sacrifice. It also cautions them against putting trust in those who hold political power, who are often corrupt.

Sufism

Islam evolved out of Muhammad's revelatory experiences. Like all great religions, it has produced mystics throughout the centuries. Because of their special closeness to the spiritual world, which may challenge political authorities and may raise questions with religious authorities about traditional theological or doctrinal explanations, mystics are esteemed by some but mistrusted and feared by others.

Muslim mystics are called **Sufis**. They get their name from the woolen ("suf") garments that they traditionally wore. The Sufi movement began sometime in the seventh century CE, when various groups, including Shia, scholars, and mystics were reacting against the un-Islamic focus on power, wealth, and luxury apparent in the Umayyad court. For Sufis, Muhammad served as the key model of simplicity. Since he was married, Sufi asceticism did not necessarily include celibacy, as did Christian monasticism.

The early Sufis sought to avoid hell in the afterlife by renouncing worldliness, following the inner path of self-discipline and purification, and practicing repentance, prayer, meditation on the Quran, and imitation of the Sunna (the customary practice of Muhammad). While all Muslims emphasize the unity of Allah (*tawhid*), some Sufis claim a mystical experience of personal unity with Allah involving a loss of ego or sense of separate existence (similar to the pan-en-henic experience), and they interpret the shahada (profession of faith) to mean, "There is no reality but the Reality." They seek to know this Reality through perfect surrender to God and through spiritual methods which concentrate attention on the Real.[23] Sufis practice *dhikr*, or remembrance of the divine names, through recitation, song, and/or dance. In prayer and meditation they pass through a series of stations and states, leading to the final state of "yearning to be constantly with God."[24]

Faqir is the Arabic term for "poor person," especially one who is religiously (voluntarily) poor, in other words, those who detach themselves from material things in order to seek God; *dervish* is the Turkish and Persian equivalent. In thirteenth-century Turkey, the Sufi poet and sheikh Rumi (see below) founded the Mevlevi Sufi order, the members of which were sometimes referred to as "whirling dervishes" because of their slow spinning, spiritual dance, which produced a trance-like effect. Faqirs and dervishes are similar to Hindu *sramanas* and *sannyasin*. Mustafa Kemal (Ataturk) suppressed the Mevlevi order in the 1920s, but it is reviving today. Another common practice among Sufis is the veneration of saints, enacted especially by visiting their tombs to receive blessings. Reflecting the view of more conservative Muslims today, a Muslim colleague remarked that Sufis are a "fringe part of Islam." Sufis and less conservative Muslims would not agree with that judgment.

For some famous Sufis and their teachings, Rabia of Basra, al-Ghazali, and al-Rumi, see our supporting website.[25]

SOCIAL AND INSTITUTIONAL DIMENSION

Islam has been particularly well organized socially. Its worldview gives central importance to the umma. Umma (*umm* = mother) *in general* means a community or nation. In its *special* use it means a *religious* community in *submission* (*Islam*) to Allah and to Allah's **rasul** (messenger). Sometimes Muslims say the rasul for the Islamic umma is Muhammad, the rasul for the Christian umma is Jesus, and so on for other groups. But Christians and Jews could also be thought of as related to the Islamic umma if they paid two special taxes, partly in lieu of military service. From a universalist Muslim perspective, Islam is intended for all of humanity; all are called to accept Islam, which seeks common ground with prior revelations. Note also that the Quran states, and Muslims believe, that Jesus was a prophet and messiah with a special destiny.

The Islamic doctrine of *tawhid* connects all of existence. Thus every aspect of life should be marked by submission to Allah, so Muslims see no reason for a separation of religion and state. Muhammad functioned as both a religious and a civil leader, setting a pattern that some Islamic societies have tried to follow. Many modern countries with Muslim majorities organize themselves as Western-style, quasi-secular states with some Islamic regulations. Egypt and pre-invasion Iraq would be examples. Some, like Saudi Arabia, Iran, and Sudan have attempted to create officially Islamic governments, with mixed results.

Sunni and Shia Muslims

Those who became **Shia** Muslims divided from the main body of Muslims (later called **Sunni**) over the question of who should be the "successor" (*caliph: khalifa*) to Muhammad as leader of the umma.

The Shia Muslims believe that Muhammad's legitimate successor should have come from Muhammad's family. Thus, in their view, the first true successor to Muhammad was Ali, the fourth caliph after Muhammad. *Shiatu Ali* means "partisans of Ali." Tragically, Ali was killed at prayer by a Kharijite Muslim on the grounds that he had failed to punish the assassins of Uthman, the third caliph, and that he had illegitimately yielded to his Umayyad opponents on the battlefield. The Umayyad Muawiya became widely but not universally recognized as the next (fifth) caliph; in effect, he prevailed and inaugurated the Umayyad dynasty.

In 680, when Muawiya died, Ali's son Husayn attempted to claim the caliphate, but he was killed in battle at Karbala in modern Iraq by forces loyal to Yazid, Muawiya's son. Thus for Shia, the themes of persecution, suffering, and the quest for justice became paramount. Shia Muslims saw themselves as the "righteous remnant" struggling to restore God's rule through the rightful authority of their religious and political leader—the Imam—in opposition to the corrupt rule of one or another Sunni caliph. Shia commemorate Husayn's tragic death at Karbala each year on the tenth day (Ashurah) of the month of Muharram with passion play performances reenacting his martyrdom.

In contrast, the Sunni Muslims accept the three caliphs before Ali as true successors to Muhammad, as well as the caliphs since Ali. In addition to the succession issue, over time other religious, political, and social differences have developed between Shia and Sunni Muslims. However, there is a perception among some Muslims that Western interests have sought to exaggerate those differences in order to "divide and conquer" Muslims particularly in oil-rich areas. Shia Muslims add to the shahada the phrase, "Ali is the friend of Allah." Today about 85 percent of the world's Muslims are Sunni, and about 15 percent are Shia or members of other smaller groups. Iran is officially Shia; Shia Muslims are also found in Iraq (60 percent Shia), Lebanon, Pakistan, eastern Saudi Arabia, India, and Yemen.

ETHICAL AND LEGAL DIMENSION

The core of Islamic faith is surrender to Allah. Therefore, Islam emphasizes "orthopraxy," the ethical and legal implications of God's revelation in the Quran. **Sharia** (literally "the straight path") is the term for Islamic law as derived from Allah's will, which is articulated as **fiqh**. **Iman** means right *faith* or *belief* in Allah (similar to Christian ortho*doxy*). *Amal* means just *action* (similar to Christian ortho*praxy*).

There is an important distinction between **'adl** and **'ihsan**. *'Adl* is Allah's justice; it puts everything in its right place fairly according to its potential, situation, and status, maintaining a fair balance. It avoids all bias or favoritism in judging. *Ihsan* (literally "perfection" or "excellence") is justice (mercy, charity) that *restores* balance by making up for a loss or deficiency.

> [Ihsan] suggests doing more than that which a person is obligated to do and giving more to others than what they are entitled to. Thus, while *'adl* ensures the peace and security of human society, *ihsan* makes it loving and caring and adds beauty to it (emphasis in original).[26]

Thus, ihsan fulfills adl as love fulfills the law.

Islamic Law

Islamic law encompasses both (1) sharia (divine legislation) and (2) fiqh (human legislation), that is, both (1) the direct evidence for God's will as "law" in the Quran and (2) "the human effort to understand [sharia] and the results of this effort [fiqh]."[27] During the early Abbasid period, from about 750 to 900 CE, the ulama worked to systematize Islamic law, grounding it in the Quran; the Sunna; a restricted type of reasoning; and the consensus of the community. The content of Islamic law is divided between obligations to God (the five pillars) and social obligations (family law, regarding marriage, divorce, and inheritance). Actions are also assigned to one of five ethical categories ranging from *required* to *prohibited*; for example, adultery is prohibited. The five goals of Islamic law are to protect and promote faith, life, family, intellect, and property. Its overall purpose is to uphold justice and human well-being. Islamic law as fiqh is subject to revision and further development.

ISSUES FOR JUSTICE AND PEACE

Women

Like Jesus, despite his very different cultural context, Muhammad seems to have had congenial, open relationships with women that transcended societal norms; various hadith indicate that he opposed violence against women and urged kindness by men toward women. Islamic reforms gave women the right to keep their dowries and to inherit (thus the right to ownership), to initiate divorce, and to make a will. Culturally contextual, polygyny in the Quran provided women widowed by war with male protection. It restricted the number of wives a man could marry to four, and required that all his wives be treated equally, implying that such an arrangement would be difficult to impossible to maintain (see Quran 4:3, 4:129).

In the early period of Islam, women and men mixed publicly in the market and in the mosque. At different times in the history of Islam, exemplary women served as orators and as political leaders, as transmitters of hadith and as Sufis. A recent female political leader was Benazir Bhutto of Pakistan. Muslim feminists seek to be independent of Western feminism, remaining within an Islamic framework and not subject to Western dominance. Today Muslim women are "returning to the mosque," and Muslim feminist scholars such as Amina Wadud are finding that the Quran supports gender justice. They distinguish between what the Quran itself says and how the Quran has been traditionally interpreted by male jurists and scholars living in patriarchal societies. Wadud made waves when she assumed the role of imam (prayer leader) in a New York City mosque in 2005 for a mixed group of men and women worshipers.[28]

War

The early Muslim wars of expansion were relatively civilized. Conquered Christians and Jews were offered protection and toleration by payment of a poll tax. This tax took the place of the military and civil obligations which Muslims owed to the umma. In the late Ottoman period, Jews and Christians were required to pay an "exemption tax" instead. They were allowed to continue their religious practices because they were monotheists and "People of the Book" (adherents of scriptural religions). They did experience "social restrictions" in comparison with Muslims, which in some periods were lenient, in others oppressive.

The Lesser Jihad

In the current U.S. "war on terrorism," news reports speak of Islamic mujahideen waging jihad against democratic nations. To keep our terms straight, it is useful to notice the similarity between (a) an Arabic term for an *actor* and (b) the related term for the corresponding *action*. The term for the *actor* begins with the letter *m*; otherwise the *consonants* of the two words are identical. A change of *vowels* distinguishes actor from action. For example, a *Muslim* is a person who practices Islam; *Islam* is self-surrender to Allah. A *mumin* is a person who practices iman; *iman* is right faith or belief in Allah (*iman* in Arabic is related to *amen* in Hebrew). A **mujahid** is a person who practices jihad; *jihad* is the act of striving for justice in Allah's cause (including but not exclusively or even primarily by means of war). That may mean striving to defend Muslims' freedom to practice their faith. Or it may mean striving *to establish justice* in the world. Note also that one can strive *nonviolently*.

Outsiders associate *jihad* with wars of conquest to spread the Islamic faith. Muslims respond that they are not forcing anyone to change their faith. They are merely seeking to provide *conditions* in which people can *hear* the call to faith. To declare war in order to *force* a nonbeliever to believe is a violation of the Islamic principle "Let there be no compulsion in religion" (Quran 2:256). Force *is* legitimate to *keep others from oppressing Muslims or preventing them from choosing to believe* (2:190–193). Although *political* leaders have often maintained that one or another of the wars they were conducting should be considered a "jihad," Islamic *religious* leaders have rarely considered any of these wars to be a genuine jihad since the original struggle with Mecca in the 620s.

No one should be forced to *become* Muslim. However, once one has become a Muslim (either by conversion or through birth), a *rejection* of Islam is seen by conservatives as a rejection of Allah and a disgrace to family and community. Some Islamic legal scholars hold that one who *abandons* Islam should be executed. In March 2006, Abdul Rahman, a Pakistani citizen, was in court in Afghanistan seeking custody of his children from his former wife. He was denounced as a convert to Christianity, arrested, and threatened with execution. Western governments put immense pressure on the Afghan government to free Rahman. The Islamic court objected to political pressure, but offered to free Rahman if he would profess faith in Islam. An Afghan Muslim cleric declared, "Rejecting Islam is insulting God. We will not allow God to be humiliated. This man must die."[29] Popular opinion in Afghanistan, where there is much resentment over Christian missionary activity, supported his execution. The compromise reached was to drop the case on the grounds that Rahman was mentally unfit for trial. He was released and quickly flown to Italy, which granted him asylum.

Many Muslims would regard such a response as extreme and unacceptable. Although an Iraqi Muslim man with whom I (David) spoke in Baghdad asserted that he would kill his sister if she became a Christian, another Iraqi Muslim man whom we both know fully accepted his son's conversion to Christianity. The Muslim scholar Riffat Hassan (a woman; one of the "spokespersons for justice and peace" profiled below) argues that, from an Islamic perspective, "plurality of religions is part of God's plan for humanity" (Quran 49:13 and 2:256). While admitting that "according to *traditional* Islam, the punishment for apostasy is death," she counters that "nothing in the Quran . . . suggests any punishment at all, let alone the punishment of death," for apostasy. Religious freedom, she maintains, is a core component of Islam.[30]

Historically, Muhammad modeled and counseled patient endurance to the first Muslims in response to persecution by their powerful opponents in Mecca. When he gained community leadership in Medina, he developed *defensive* tactics against aggression from Mecca. His later acceptance of *offensive* military action may have been in part a concession to the desires of his followers, but would also have been prompted by the "fragile and trying circumstances" of the Muslims in Medina, who sometimes "had to resort to violence and warfare . . . in order to guarantee their own survival."³¹ Only after Muhammad died did his followers think of using offensive jihad to make Islam available to all humans throughout the world. Many people of other faiths preserved these faiths under Islamic rule, although the gradual conversion to Islam of non-Muslims in the Muslim world eventually turned the other faiths into minority religions.³²

Rules for Just War

Islam has rules for just war.³³ According to the Quran, wars to defend the umma from aggressors who threatened the survival of Islam were allowed. But women, children, the elderly, monks, and rabbis who were not engaged in fighting were to be protected, and fruit trees were not to be cut down nor wells poisoned. Later, in regard to wars to *extend* Islam, the following rules were formulated:

1. The jihad must be declared by the *khalifa* (caliph)—the head of the umma. Shia, who rejected the legitimacy of the caliphs after Ali and his son Husayn, held that their Imam would be required to lead a jihad. Since the twelfth Imam is in occultation (alive but hidden) and the caliphate has been abolished, there is currently no one qualified to lead a jihad (until the Imam returns or the caliphate is reestablished). Some claim that the ulama, or community of religious scholars, can act on behalf of the caliph or Imam.
2. The jihad must be for a *just cause*: to overcome injustice or oppression by polytheists or secularists and the barriers they raised, which prevented people from receiving the call to *islam*.
3. The *intention* must be right: not jealousy, envy, or desire for gain, but zeal for God or zeal for Islamic political control in order to guarantee a just social order according to the sharia.
4. War must be a *last resort*. The caliph or Imam must first call on the enemy to submit to Allah or, if People of the Book such as Jews and Christians, to yield to Islamic political control and pay the jizya (poll tax) in place of military service and the zakat, which Muslims paid. If these demands were met, then war was not justified.
5. There must be a good chance of *success*.
6. The war should target only those who were threatening the spread of Islam and the justice that it established, not women, children, or other *noncombatants*, as above.
7. The war should cause the *least harm* necessary to achieve its objectives.³⁴

Most Islamic scholars conclude that terrorism violates these conditions and so is forbidden to Muslims. As Professor Timothy J. Winter of Cambridge University says, "Terrorism is to jihad what adultery is to marriage."³⁵

The Greater Jihad

All of these meanings above deal with the world *outside* the believer, and are collectively called the **lesser jihad**. The **greater jihad** is the *inner* spiritual struggle. Sufis, and many modern writers, assert that jihad refers *primarily* to the *inner struggle against sin*—the inner religious striving that believers go through in their own spiritual quest.[36]

Travelers in the Sri Lankan jungles in the early 1900s reported meeting a holy man there who seemed to have a deep, sympathetic grasp of the core spiritualities of world religions and an ability to express himself in their terms. M. R. *Bawa Muhaiyaddeen* (died in the United States in 1986) emerged to author twenty books, although he himself was illiterate. (As in the New Testament, "authorship" means source of the words and ideas, not the scribal process of putting them into writing.) Especially important for our study is his book *Islam and World Peace: Explanations of a Sufi.*[37] He explains the "laws of holy war" as a concession that Allah made to the Arabs when they professed their inability to forgive as Muhammad forgave. He goes on to report that Allah said:

> To convert without force is the way of Islam; to destroy and kill and slaughter people is not. Therefore, tell your followers that the holy war they must wage is one of lifting up those who have fallen into the state of disbelief [*kufr*]. Tell them to use My actions, My words, and My behavior in order to release those who are hidden in Satan and buried in illusion. That is the true holy war. That is Islam. Reveal this to your followers.[38]

The Crusades[39]

See the earlier treatment of the **Crusades** in chapter 4. Even in the face of crusader cruelty, the Muslim general Salah al-Din demonstrated chivalry and generosity toward the crusaders he was defeating when he recaptured Jerusalem in 1187.

Arab memories of crusader cruelties and injustice continue to affect Middle Eastern politics, a fact that was quickly explained to President George W. Bush when he proposed a "crusade against terrorism" in response to the attacks of September 11, 2001, on the World Trade Center and the Pentagon.

Colonization

See the section on "colonialism" in chapter 4. Modernization and Westernization appeared to be synonymous to those on whom they had been foisted. Economically annexed to Europe, the Muslim world was also subjected to the colonizers' racist ideology of cultural superiority. Europe's initial colonization of the Muslim world—in Egypt, North Africa, India (including later Pakistan), and the Far East—took place in the nineteenth century. World War I extended European control to one of the last areas to resist colonization: the Ottoman Empire. Liberation from colonial rule came mostly after World War II.

Modernism

Before the Islamic world was subjected to European colonialism, Muslim revivalist movements had already sought to address the internal decline of some Muslim societies; this decline was broadly attributed to lack of submission to the will of God

(Allah). Western colonial domination throughout much of the Islamic world compounded existing internal problems. Muslim responses to its arrival and entrenchment varied; a centrist position called *modernism* rejected both secularist wholesale adaptation to the West and conservative wholesale rejection of the West. Modernists pursued internal social and other reforms based on their reinterpretation of the Quran and Sunna in light of modern conditions.[40] They tried to adopt ideas and technology from the West selectively within an Islamic framework. For the most part and sometimes vehemently, they rejected Western colonialist intervention in their countries. Nevertheless, more conservative Muslims still considered them to be pro-Western. As an alternative response to Western colonialism, secularism, and materialism, *neo-revivalist* (now called *Islamist*) groups such as the **Muslim Brotherhood** arose. Modernists presented Islam as dynamic, progressive, and rational in both the past and the present; they were confident that Islam could meet the challenges of colonialism and modernity on its own terms. They also supported family law reforms that improved the status of women.[41]

Two prominent modernist intellectuals and activists were Muhammad Abduh (Egyptian, d. 1905) and Muhammad Iqbal (Indian, d. 1938). Abduh sought to reform and transform society by reinterpreting Islamic sources. For example, he reinterpreted the Quran as advocating monogamy.[42] There was room for change because Islam divided into two spheres: the essential religious sphere and the variable social sphere. With Muslim thinkers of many ideologies, he shared the view that Islam firmly supports social justice and the sharing of resources by the rich with the poor.[43] Abduh served as Mufti of Egypt and Rector of al-Azhar University in Cairo.

Muhammad Iqbal studied philosophy and law at the Universities of Cambridge (UK) and Munich (Germany). Like Abduh, Iqbal opposed the dominance of traditional religious authorities at the expense of free thought. He saw the Islamic state as "an effort to realize the spiritual in a human organization." For Iqbal, freedom and equality were key Islamic values.[44] European democracies, by contrast, were "exploiting the poor in the interest of the rich," and "Europe [was] the greatest hindrance [to] the ethical advancement" of humanity. The answer lay with Islam, whose "ultimate aim" was "spiritual democracy."[45]

The Muslim Brotherhood

There are religious-social-political movements in the Islamic world challenging Western-style governments as un-Islamic. The *Muslim Brotherhood* in Egypt ("Al-Ikhwan Al-Muslimun"), founded in Cairo in 1928 by Hassan al-Banna, is a leading example. It objects to the 1924 suppression of the caliphate by Turkey and the fragmentation of what had been the Ottoman Empire into competing countries. It also maintains that the governments of these separate countries have abandoned Islamic principles for corrupt Western alternatives. Influenced by Saudi Arabian Wahhabi theology, it seeks to apply its interpretation of Islamic law to all areas of life, including government, with special attention to the role of women, promotion of social justice and political freedoms, elimination of poverty and corruption, and an end to colonialism. To further these aims, it supports schools, hospitals, pharmacies, and social services. Its theoretical foundations are found especially in the writings of Sayyid Qutb (see below).

The Brotherhood has supported some Muslim governments and challenged others. Most of these governments have been authoritarian with limited democratic institutions. When members of the Brotherhood tried to assassinate Gamal Abdel Nasser of Egypt in 1954, six were executed, four thousand were arrested, and thousands fled. Since then, the Brotherhood in Egypt has concentrated on nonviolent, reformist politics and grassroots community development.

Barred from running candidates in its own name in Egypt, Brotherhood candidates ran as independents in 2005 and, despite the fact that "government-friendly thugs roughed up Brotherhood supporters, killing one,"[46] they gained about 20 percent of the seats in the legislature, forming by far the largest opposition party. "In Egypt, the risk from the Muslim Brotherhood is that if it gained enough power, some fear it could do away with the secular state, as happened in Iran. Although the Brotherhood long ago renounced violence, defines itself as moderate, and says it respects the ballot box, it also supports the establishment of Islamic law, or sharia."[47]

In January 2011, a widespread popular revolution in Egypt toppled the government of secularist dictator Hosni Mubarak. An election widely judged to be free and fair elected Mohammed Morsi of the Muslim Brotherhood as president in June 2012. In the struggle between entrenched elites from both the previous administration and the newly installed administration, Morsi consolidated power in some questionable ways, which led to major new street demonstrations against his rule. A military coup then deposed and arrested him. The military rulers also killed and imprisoned hundreds of Muslim Brotherhood members. By the end of 2013, the new leaders declared the Brotherhood to be a "terrorist organization," potentially criminalizing and outlawing Brotherhood members and their social services. As of early 2014, Morsi was being detained and tried on various charges including conspiring with Hamas and Hezbollah to spread violence and chaos throughout Egypt.

A Theorist for the Muslim Brotherhood

Sayyid Qutb (1906[48]–1966) was an Egyptian teacher, writer, and eventually theorist for the Muslim Brotherhood who received a Quranic education in his home village and studied Arabic literature in Cairo. Early in his career he wrote fiction and was employed first as a teacher and then as a bureaucrat in the Ministry of Education. From 1948 to 1950, he earned a master's degree at Colorado State College of Education.

Originally Qutb was not anti-Western, but he changed his mind when he saw "what [the West] had done to the world of Islam through colonialist imperialism and [the] export of secularism, sexual immorality, and materialism."[49] While studying at Colorado State, he published *Social Justice in Islam*, calling on Muslims "to return to their true mission on earth as a just and balanced system of social life, governance, economy, and worship."[50] Disillusioned by what he had witnessed in the United States, he left the civil service when he returned to Egypt and became a major spokesman for the Muslim Brotherhood. He originally supported Gamal Abd al-Nasser's coup against King Farouk, but eventually became equally disillusioned with the Nasser regime. With other members of the Muslim Brotherhood, he was imprisoned in 1954 after a failed assassination attempt against Nasser. He wrote:

> The real struggle is between Islam on the one hand and the two camps of East and West on the other. Islam is the true power which opposes the strength of the materialistic philosophy professed by Europe, America, and Russia alike. . . . It is Islam which gives to life a spiritual doctrine to link it with the Creator in his heaven, and to govern its direction on earth; and it is Islam which is not content to allow life to be limited to the achievement of purely material aims, even though material and productive activity is one of the Islamic modes of worship.[51]

Except for eight months in 1965, Qutb spent his remaining years in prison. Witnessing the torture and murder of prisoners radicalized him as a firm opponent of the regime. From prison he wrote *In the Shade of the Quran* (1954), a thirty-volume commentary on the Quran,[52] and *Milestones*, which decries Muslim societies that are no longer guided by Islamic principles of social justice and outlines the way to establish truly Islamic societies (1964):[53]

> This movement uses the methods of preaching and persuasion for reforming ideas and beliefs and *it uses physical power and Jihad for abolishing the organizations and authorities of the Jahili system which prevents people from reforming their ideas and beliefs*. . . . [Islam] does not confine itself to mere preaching to confront physical power, as *it also does not use compulsion for changing the ideas of people.* . . . *Islam does not force people to accept its belief, but it wants to provide a free environment in which they will have the choice of beliefs* . . . to abolish those oppressive political systems under which people are prevented from expressing their freedom to choose whatever beliefs they want, and after that it gives them complete freedom to decide whether they will accept Islam or not. . . . No political system or material power should put hindrances in the way of preaching Islam. If someone does this, then it is the duty of Islam to fight him until either he is killed or . . . he declares his submission. (emphases added)[54]

After a brief reprieve from detention, Qutb was arrested again, accused of treason on the basis of statements in his book *Milestones*, and executed in 1966.[55]

Islamophobia

Islamophobia has been defined as the "close-minded prejudice" of "people who have decided that Islam has no place in [U.S.] society."[56] Some of its components include a view of Islam as "inferior to the West . . . barbaric, irrational, primitive, and sexist"; as "violent, aggressive, threatening, supportive of terrorism, and engaged in a 'clash of civilizations'" with the West; and as a "political ideology" in the form of "political Islam," sometimes with a military edge.[57]

Newer in the United States than in Europe, Islamophobia is a flourishing industry. Washington Post–ABC polls conducted between October 2001 and 2010 found that the percentage of Americans with a negative view of Muslims increased over this period from 39 percent to 49 percent. Another 2010 poll indicated that 62 percent of non-Muslim Americans (well over half) had "never met a Muslim."[58]

Author and researcher Jack Shaheen asserts that (1) the post-9/11 media stereotyping of Muslims as terrorists has enabled their "profiling, imprisonment, extradition, torture, and even death" with no significant public backlash; and (2) similarly, the media representation of Islam as the new global menace after Communism "primes American audiences [public opinion] for U.S. military aggression" in the Muslim world.[59] In other words, on both the individual and collective levels, Islamophobia serves to legitimate criminal action against Muslims. Laila Lalami concludes, "We have in America today two systems of citizenship: one for Muslims and one for non-Muslims."[60] If this is true, it sounds like an updating of American apartheid.

Two reports available online[61] provide an overview of the "Islamophobic network," including individuals and their organizations such as Pamela Geller and Stop the Islamization of America; former and current members of Congress such as Newt Gingrich; and "the grandfather of Islamophobia in America," Daniel Pipes, head of the Middle East Forum, a "right-wing think tank." The authors of "Fear, Inc." write that "a small group of foundations and wealthy donors are the lifeblood of the Islamophobia network in America."[62] The proponents and supporters of Islamophobia can be classified for the most part as right-wing Christians (the majority) or right-wing Jews, obviously not all members of either category.[63]

There is a Zionist connection to U.S. Islamophobia, which is relevant to chapter 8 of this book. In the fall of 2012 public advertisements in mass transit locations in New York City, San Francisco, and Washington, D.C., read: "In any war between the civilized man and the savage, support the civilized man. Support Israel. Defeat Jihad."[64]

You will find further treatment of Islamophobia on our supporting website.[65]

Islam and Other Religions

Historically Islam originated in a pluralistic environment, to which it naturally adapted. A number of modern scholars point to Quranic passages that express a tolerant attitude toward Judaism, Christianity, and other monotheisms, for example Quran 2:62, which reads: "Those who believe [the Muslims], and those who follow the Jewish (scriptures), and the Christians and the Sabians—any who believe in God and the Last Day and work righteousness, shall have their reward with their Lord: on them shall be no fear, nor shall they grieve."

As Muslims came into contact with adherents of non-monotheistic religions, such as Hinduism in India, they accepted them also as People of the Book, that is, those whose religion was scriptural. Nevertheless, Islam has always been a universalist missionary religion like Christianity. Yet historically in general, Islam has been more tolerant of non-Muslims than Christianity has been of non-Christians. Thus the Shia Islamic scholar Seyyed Hossein Nasr writes of "the harmony and peace that dominated most of the life of Jews and Christians within the Islamic world before modern times."[66] In the same essay, Nasr reflects that Muslim theological acceptance of Christianity (minus "the Trinity and Incarnation") occurs more readily than Christian theological acceptance of Islam: "Few Christians accept Islam as an authentic religion or revelation."[67] In addition to accepting Christianity, Islam also accepts "the revelations of Judaism," the enemy of authentic religiosity across faiths is Western secularism. Leaders from the three monotheisms must "reach a profound accord [based on] the certitude that the followers of these religions are all the children of Abraham and pray to the same God."[68]

Christian-Muslim Relations

Since 1965, there has been ongoing dialogue between Roman Catholics and Muslims. In 2001, Pope John Paul II visited Syria, where Christians form a significant religious minority, and spoke of how much we grow in understanding when we live side by side. Summarizing twenty years of U.S. Muslim-Catholic dialogue, John Borelli noted that what

> [Muslims] are truly looking for in religious individuals is God-consciousness. . . . Muslims are particularly eager to tell Christians about their respect for Jesus. They have difficulty understanding why Christians might not like them, or distrust them, or feel that they are out to get them, or why Christians say what they do about Muslim beliefs when Muslims know they themselves have such a wonderful respect for Jesus. . . . Christians and Muslims often judge one another by the extremists . . . they each make the mistake of judging the other's worst by their own best.[69]

In 2007, 138 eminent Muslims signed a document called "A Common Word between You and Us," addressed to Christian church leaders, which maintained that "the future of the world depends on peace between Muslims and Christians," and that the two shared principles on which this peace can be built are love of God and love of neighbor. The positive Christian response was "immediate and global."[70]

There are several active centers for Muslim-Christian Dialogue, some in universities, others free-standing. The Muslim-Christian Dialogue Center at the University of St. Thomas in St. Paul, Minnesota, is in active, ongoing conversation with the faculty of Dokuz Eylul University (Izmir, Turkey) and with theologians from Qom, Iran.[71]

SPOKESPERSONS FOR JUSTICE AND PEACE

Khan Abdul Ghaffar Khan (d. 1988, Afghanistan). One of Mohandas Gandhi's closest associates, named by Hindus the "Frontier Gandhi," was a Muslim leader from the Northwest Province of India, Khan Abdul Ghaffar Khan. As Gandhi was called

Figure 5.1. **Muslim Dome of the Rock, Part of Al-Aqsa Mosque complex, marking the spot in Jerusalem where Muhammad ascended to heaven after his night journey. Courtesy David Whitten Smith, April 2004.**

"Mahatma" (great soul) in recognition of his greatness, so Ghaffar Khan was called "Badshah Khan" (King of Khans). He enthusiastically adopted Gandhi's ideas of *ahimsa* and *satyagraha*, explaining them in terms of *Islam* or submission to God's will.

As a native of the Northwest Province of India, which the British had annexed from Afghanistan to provide an easily defended border for India, Ghaffar Khan grew up resentful of British power. His tribe, the proud Pathan, noted for their fearless fighting, had been split in two by the annexation. They had already given the British reason to regret having annexed them. More recently it was the Soviet Union that had reason to regret its invasion of Pathan territory, and today perhaps the United States—Ghaffar Khan's Pathan tribe is the same tribe that later embraced the Taliban.

But Ghaffar Khan discovered the power of Gandhi's ideas. He not only applied them in his own life, but he also founded a Pathan army without arms. Called the **Khudai Khidmatgars**, they swore themselves to fearless and provocative nonviolence in the face of oppression. For decades in the Northwest Province they supported Gandhi's campaign against the British. Their efforts were strikingly successful and played a major role in freeing India from British rule.

After India was independent, other Islamic leaders committed to a Muslim Pakistan imprisoned Ghaffar Khan and his followers, and the population was less supportive of his ideas of nonviolence now that local Muslim leaders controlled police and army. Yet a recent researcher has found that, a half-century later, many Afghans who took part in the struggle are still deeply influenced by Ghaffar Khan's example and consider their participation in his nonviolent campaign to have been a high point of their lives.[72] Ghaffar Khan died in 1988 at the age of 95.

Riffat Hassan (1943–, Pakistan, U.S.) did her undergraduate and graduate work in England. She is a leading Muslim feminist scholar and activist, with a "progressive understanding" of Islam. In 2009 she retired from thirty-three years of teaching at the University of Louisville, where she served as chair of the Religious Studies Program. Her interest and activity have focused on women's rights and human rights in the Muslim world, the work of the Indian Muslim philosopher Muhammad Iqbal (see above in the section on "modernism"), and interreligious dialogue especially with Jews and Christians. After September 11, 2001, Hassan created and ran two "peace-building exchange programs" between the United States and Muslims in the Muslim world.[73] Two of Hassan's many outstanding essays are "What Does It Mean to Be a Muslim Today?"[74] and "Peace Education: A Muslim Perspective."[75]

Fatima Mernissi (1940–, Morocco)[76] grew up in Fez, Morocco, in a progressive, middle-class family. Educated in Morocco, France, and the United States, she has taught sociology at Mohammad V University and advised UNESCO on issues affecting Muslim women. In her view as a major Muslim feminist scholar and prolific author, the veil has become a device to silence women and make them invisible. She criticizes the West for suppressing democracy by supporting autocratic Arab governments. Mernissi believes that, through repressive interventions, the West has reinforced North African and Middle Eastern tendencies to limit the freedom of Muslim women and of Muslims generally. Distinguishing between the authentic, liberating Islamic sources (the Quran and the Hadith, the latter revealing Muhammad as a proponent of gender equality) and later patriarchal misinterpretation of those sources by traditional scholars, she seeks to deconstruct the patriarchal "Islamic sexual ideology" of the political-religious establishment, and she studies Islam as a source for both individual freedom and social stability in modern Muslim societies.[77] In 2012 she published a book on the role of satellite TV in the "Arab Spring."[78]

Chandra Muzaffar (1947–, Malaysia) was born a Hindu. Professor of political science at the University of Malaysia from 1970 to 1983, he has written or edited a number of books and hundreds of articles. He was arrested briefly in 1987 while helping to direct the Asian Commission on Human Rights. Human Rights Watch nominated him as a monitor in 1988. Since 1991, he has been president of the International Movement for a Just World (JUST), the website of which describes its purpose as follows:

> For the first time in history, a global empire has emerged. This has had an adverse impact upon humankind. It is an empire that allows a privileged minority to dominate

and control the world. Its dominant power is perpetuated through war and violence. It is an empire in which the vast majority of humankind remains poor and powerless. It panders to the unbridled greed of a few but fails to provide for the basic needs of the many. An empire which encourages greed to grow and selfishness to spread is a threat to humanity. It undermines the spiritual and moral basis of civilization. It would be a tragedy if such an empire becomes the inheritance of our children. This is why all of us . . . must do all we can to help create a just world. . . . Today, more than at any other time in the past, human civilization possesses the knowledge and technology to create a just world. . . . This is what makes the present situation conducive for inter-faith, inter-civilizational dialogue. . . . The spiritual and moral worldviews and values embodied in all religious and cultural philosophies can offer the human race much needed guidance in our common quest for a just world.[79]

In an October 2001 interview, Muzaffar discussed the past impact of Western colonization and the present impact of Western globalization on the Muslim world as reasons for tension between Islam and the West. He identified Muslim women, Western Muslims, and middle-class and professional Muslims as three resources for a recommended progressive reinterpretation of Islam. He concluded the interview as follows:

The essence of Islam's mission . . . is to elevate our humanity, to make us more conscious of justice, to make us more conscious of the unity and the brotherhood and sisterhood of the human family . . . [to] restore to humanity that principle that is repeated over and over again in the Quran, to believe in God and to do good. . . . All the other schisms and divisions that we see . . . are the products of the human being's own failing, his or her own fallacies. But the strength of Islam lies in this—in making us more human.[80]

SUMMARY

When Arabian society was in tension between traditional Bedouin mores and the values of urban merchants and traders, Allah sent Jibril to reveal his will to Muhammad through his eternal word. Rejecting the revelation preached by Muhammad, the Meccan elite persecuted Muhammad and his followers. Fleeing to Medina, Muhammad and his followers developed a strong community, defended themselves against Meccan attacks, and eventually returned in triumph to Mecca, where the Prophet dealt generously with his former opponents. After Muhammad's death, Islam spread rapidly around the Mediterranean world and eastward as far as Indonesia and China.

The core of Islam is surrender to Allah, who guides and protects all humans, calls them to justice, and judges them individually at the end of their lives. Surrender involves an internal *jihad* against one's evil tendencies, which resist Allah. It also gives Muslims the courage to engage in external *jihad* as may be necessary to overcome injustice and to free people from political and religious oppression. Thus,

Islam affects every aspect of one's life, including politics. Some Muslims experience a deep mystical spirituality, but all that is truly necessary is submission to God's will and generous living on the basis of the five pillars and Islamic tradition.

KEY TERMS

'adl	Medina
Allah	minaret
Anno Hegirae	modernism
caliph	mosque
Crusades	muezzin
Eid al-Adha	mujahid
Eid al-Fitr	Muslim Brotherhood
faqir	night journey and ascension
fiqh	Quran
five pillars	Ramadan
Hadith	rasul
hajj	salat
hijra	saum
ihsan	shahada
iman	Sharia
Injil	Shia
islam	shirk
Islamophobia	Sufism
Jibril	Sunna
jihad, greater; jihad, lesser	Sunni
Kaaba	suras
Karbala	umma
Khudai Khidmatgars	Wahhabi
Mecca	zakat

DISCUSSION QUESTIONS

1. How did Muhammad seek to reform the society in which he lived? What are some measures that he advocated to create a more just society? What obstacles did he face?
2. Many Muslims believe that one's faith ought to influence one's politics, and that a Muslim-majority nation ought to have a government based on Islamic law. They maintain that such a government would allow other faiths to practice their beliefs without interference. Do you know of examples that support this statement? Alternatively, on what principles *should* the laws of nations be

based? Should a nation that is primarily Christian have a government based on Christian principles? What about a nation that is primarily Jewish?

3. After he joined the Muslim Brotherhood, Sayyid Qutb articulated the position of the organization in its struggle against what it regarded as destructive Western ideas and practices. Do his views sound reasonable to you? Which views would you agree with, and which would you disagree with? To what extent are Muslims who resist what they consider to be Western imperialism following Qutb's ideas?

4. This chapter introduces several Muslim peace workers. Which would you be most interested in reading about further? What caught your attention and interest? With which of their ideas did you particularly agree or disagree?

SUGGESTIONS FOR FURTHER READING

Abdel Haleem. *The Qur'an: A New Translation.*
Abduh. *The Theology of Unity.*
Abou El Fadl. "Islam and Violence: Our Forgotten Legacy."
Ali. *The Holy Qur'an* (translation).
Armstrong. *Islam: A Short History.*
Banerjee. *The Pathan Unarmed.*
Berndt. *Non-Violence in the World Religions: Vision and Reality.*
Borelli. "Christian-Muslim Relations in the United States."
Denny. *An Introduction to Islam,* 3rd ed.
Donohue and Esposito, eds. *Islam in Transition,* 2nd ed.
Easwaran. *Nonviolent Soldier of Islam: Badshah Khan.*
Esack. *Quran, Liberation and Pluralism.*
Esposito. *Islam: The Straight Path,* 4th ed.
Esposito and Voll. *Islam and Democracy.*
Fadiman and Frager, eds. *Essential Sufism.*
Glasse. *The Concise Encyclopedia of Islam.*
Griffith. *The Church in the Shadow of the Mosque.*
Hassan. "Peace Education: A Muslim Perspective."
Hodgson. *The Venture of Islam.* 3 vols.
Hovannisian, ed. *The Armenian Genocide in Perspective.*
Iqbal. *The Reconstruction of Religious Thought in Islam.*
Kaltner. *Introducing the Qur'an.*
Kelsay. *Islam and War.*
Khadduri. *War and Peace in the Law of Islam.*
Lalami. "Islamophobia and Its Discontents."
Lings. *What Is Sufism?*
Maalouf. *The Crusades through Arab Eyes.*
Macdonald. *The Religious Attitude and Life in Islam.*
Mahfouz. *Midaq Alley* (and many other novels).
Muhaiyaddeen. *Islam and World Peace: Explanations of a Sufi.*
Munif. *Cities of Salt.*
Nicholson. *The Mystics of Islam.*
Paige, Satha-Anand, and Gilliatt, eds. *Islam and Nonviolence.*
Qutb. *Milestones.*
———. *Social Justice in Islam.*

Rahman. *Major Themes of the Qur'an.*

Robinson. *Islam: A Concise Introduction.*

Saadawi. *A Daughter of Isis* [Autobiography].

———. *The Hidden Face of Eve: Women in the Arab World.*

———. *Memoirs from the Women's Prison.*

Shaheen. "Islamophobia: Anatomy of an American Panic."

Shepard. *Introducing Islam.*

Wadud. *Qur'an and Woman.*

6

Native American Worldviews

Two men were coming from the clouds, head-first like arrows slanting down.
. . . Each . . . carried a long spear, and from the points of these a jagged lightning
flashed. They came clear down to the ground . . . and stood a little way off and
looked at me and said: "Hurry! Come! Your Grandfathers are calling you!"

Then they turned and left the ground like arrows slanting upward from the
bow. When I got up to follow, my legs did not hurt me anymore and I was very
light. I went outside the tepee, and yonder where the men with flaming spears
were going, a little cloud was coming very fast. It came and stooped and took
me and turned back to where it came from, flying fast. And when I looked down
I could see my mother and father yonder, and I felt sorry to be leaving them.

Then there was nothing but the air and the swiftness of the little cloud that
bore me.

—The Great Vision of Black Elk[1]

Indigenous groups and their worldviews are highly diverse. In this chapter indigenous worldviews will be mostly represented by Native American tribes, in part
because they are more familiar to American readers. There will be brief mention of
the Yoruba of West Africa, for purposes of comparison, and also because British
colonizers of North America kidnapped West Africans and transported them to
North America as slaves, deliberately destroying their languages and cultures in
order to keep them from creating a united opposition to their enslavement.

EXPERIENTIAL AND EMOTIONAL DIMENSION

The core experience for Native American tribes is the struggle for survival and well-
being in a culture that is very close to nature. Mutual cooperation and interdepen-
dence are essential, as is an intimate awareness of natural processes and resources—
both material and spiritual.

Natives see spirit present in everything—a view called **animism**. Animals are our
"brothers and sisters." Plants, rocks, and earth all have spirit. Before hunting, many

tribes ritually ask the animals for permission to kill them, explaining that they will kill only what they need, use all parts of the animal, and leave a tobacco offering to the spirit of the animal. If animals are our brothers and sisters, we should be able to talk with them. The author of the book *Rolling Thunder* describes how her modern Indian host taught her to talk with bees.[2] It would be interesting to compare her description with the results of modern laboratory experiments concerning the effects of talking to flowers and other plants.

HISTORICAL PERIODS

Origins

The traditional explanation for how Native Americans got to the New World is that various Oriental tribes crossed the Bering Strait on dry land when the ocean level was low because glaciers had locked up so much water in ice. Some scholars have challenged this hypothesis, pointing out that there is no clear evidence for it whereas there is considerable evidence that human groups moved around the world's oceans in boats of various sorts.

Native American tribes belong to very diverse groups, speak diverse languages, and have diverse histories, but there are some frequently observed common features. We will illustrate some of those features, using especially the **Dakota** (or *Lakota* or *Wakota*) tribes as an example. But first, here are brief historical descriptions of some leading Native American tribes.

Some Imperial Tribes

The Aztecs and Our Lady of Guadalupe

The **Aztecs** in Mexico (fourteenth–fifteenth centuries) had a centralized government and a rich material culture. Their leading deity was both sun god and god of war. Depending on agriculture with uncertain rainfall, they believed that human sacrifice was required to keep the sun rising; so each morning they tore the heart out of a living human victim and offered it to the gods. At its height, the sacrificial system claimed thousands of victims a year, acquired by war with neighboring tribes. As a result, those neighboring tribes tended to support the Spanish invaders against the Aztecs. Apocalyptic expectation led the Aztecs themselves to imagine that Cortez, when he arrived with his soldiers, could be a returning hero-god; consequently, they did not resist the Spanish conquerors as vigorously as they otherwise would have.[3]

Christian missions in Central America made little headway until an Indian, *Juan Diego,* experienced a vision of the Virgin Mary—an example of the role played by mystical experience in religion. As a sign to the local bishop, in midwinter Mary produced flowers native to the bishop's Spanish homeland and imprinted on Juan Diego's cloak an image of herself as an Indian woman. This image also made use of native symbols, which convinced the Aztecs and others that the new religion could free them from oppressive features of their indigenous religions. Within a few decades, massive numbers of natives embraced Catholic Christianity. The cloak with its image is displayed today in the shrine to **Our Lady of Guadalupe** in Mexico City.[4]

The Mayans

Predating the Aztecs, **Mayan** tribes (third–eighth centuries CE) in Mexico and Guatemala had a less centralized government than the Aztecs did, yet they built sophisticated cities and developed astronomy, mathematics, and writing. Like the Aztecs, the Mayans also experienced agricultural instability and also practiced human sacrifice on a large scale.[5] The collapse of their urban culture, which left impressive structures such as the pyramids of the Yucatan Peninsula often overgrown by jungle, has been one of the puzzles of archaeology and ethnology—it now appears that they exploited their resource base of jungle soil and water unsustainably until their population crashed for lack of resources.[6] There are still many indigenous Mayans living in southern Mexico and the mountains of Guatemala, although they have mostly adopted a type of Catholicism with Mayan features. *Chiapas*, in southern Mexico, is the center of a nonviolent rebellion against the Mexican government and local landowners that began on January 1, 1994—the day that the North American Free Trade Agreement went into effect. The leader of that rebellion, who calls himself (or herself) *Subcomandante Marcos*, makes liberal use of the Internet to explain his or her policies.[7] Currently the Zapatistas control about one-third of the southeastern Mexican state of Chiapas, where they have established five decentralized regional governments, with community education, health care, and justice systems, in addition to producers' cooperatives.[8]

The Incan Empire

The **Incas** (thirteenth–fifteenth centuries) in Peru, Bolivia, and Chile developed agricultural expertise as well as impressive construction techniques using tightly fitted stones without mortar for walls, buildings, city streets, and extensive highways. Their polytheistic religion shared some features with that of the Aztecs and Mayans. The sun god, the earth mother (worshiped at Machu Picchu), and the moon goddess were all prominent. One of the priests' functions was to hear confessions and prescribe penance.[9] The Incas created a large empire that flourished until the Spanish conquerors destroyed their political power. Like the Mayans, there remain many ethnic Incans in Bolivia and Peru who speak tribal languages such as *Aymara*, spoken by over one million people in the area around Lake Titicaca,[10] and **Quechua**, the original language of the Incan empire, spoken today by more than eight million people.[11]

Five countries of Latin America have a majority or near majority of indigenous populations, in many cases speaking their native languages rather than, or in addition to, Spanish: Mexico and Guatemala (Mayan, Aztec, and others); Peru, Bolivia, and Ecuador (Incan: Aymara and Quechua).

The "Five Civilized Tribes" and the "Trail of Tears"

In the southeastern United States, five tribes (Chickasaw, Choctaw, Creek, **Cherokee**, and Seminole) came to be known as the **five civilized tribes** because they adopted many of the laws, politics, customs, and clothing of the European settlers. Before 1820, the *Cherokee* silversmith Sequoya developed an eighty-five-character "syllabary" with which to write the Cherokee language. (An "alphabet" represents each sound by one symbol; a "syllabary" represents each syllable, a more complex sound, by one symbol.) In 1821 that syllabary was used to print the Laws of the Cherokee Nation, and in 1828 to print the *Cherokee Phoenix*: the first Native American newspaper. The Cherokee set up a European-style government with legislative, executive, and judicial branches.

Unfortunately, these adaptations to the new immigrants were not sufficient to protect the Cherokee. When gold was discovered in the Cherokee territories in Georgia, whites found a small minority of Cherokee willing to sign a treaty—the Treaty of New Echota—which sold all the Cherokee territory east of the Mississippi River to whites for five million dollars. At forty-three thousand square miles, that would have amounted to about $116 per square mile (18 cents per acre) for well-developed farmland and potential gold mines. Most Cherokee disavowed the treaty and *John Ross*, the Cherokee chief, took the case to the U.S. Supreme Court, which ruled in favor of the Cherokee. Georgia officials ignored the Supreme Court's ruling, and President *Andrew Jackson*, on whose side the Cherokee had fought against the Creek fifteen years earlier, claimed that he had no right to intervene in a matter pertaining to one of the states. The Indian Removal Act of 1830 evicted the Cherokee by force, on foot under military escort, and sent them to Oklahoma. The journey took almost four months and was badly organized; about four thousand of the fifteen thousand Cherokee died on the way. This removal came to be called the **Trail of Tears.**

Another of the five tribes, the Choctaw, was actually the first to be removed, and it was an article by one of their chiefs, published in the *Arkansas Gazette* in the midst of the removal, that gave rise to the phrase "trail of tears." Sixteen years after their arrival at their new territory in Oklahoma, they heard news of the potato famine in Ireland. They were so moved by the suffering of the Irish that they collected $710 as a donation for Irish relief.[12]

Southwestern Indians

In the southwestern United States, important tribes included the **Apache**, **Pueblo**, and **Hopi** Indians. The Hopi are still noted for their relative success in preserving their traditional way of life. The following story illustrates their vigilance in maintaining the secrecy of their traditions. A graduate school friend of mine (David) reported that when he was a seminary student one of his classmates, a Hopi Indian, didn't return from a holiday. When the seminary investigated, they found out that his tribe had killed him because they believed that he had revealed some of their tribal secrets. *Kachinas*, or ritual dancing figures wearing masks and costumes and representing a spirit, ancestor, or animal, also helped Hopi parents teach their children proper tribal behavior, thus contributing to social order and stability.[13]

Indians around the Arctic

Tribes such as the **Inuit** (*Eskimo*) and **Aleuts** live in the far north. The Inuit are noted for their gentle, pacifist traditions. Their view of the world is animistic: all is alive, despite the environment of cold, snow, and ice (except for the brief summer season), which makes "opportunities to express kindness and friendliness . . . all the more precious." Children are taught to subordinate their wishes to the needs of the group. The main deities are the goddess Sedna and the god Sila; **shamans**, who have endured "death-resurrection" initiation rites, play a mediating role. A dark side of the culture is or was the unequal status of men and women, especially in marriage, with female infanticide reducing the number of women.[14]

New England Indians: the Pilgrims, the Pequot War

Our Thanksgiving traditions introduce us to Indian tribes of what became New England. The *Wampanoag* tribe, which inhabited the area around Plymouth Rock where the Pilgrims settled in the early seventeenth century, had been decimated by diseases caught from European traders sailing along the coast. In the three years before the Pilgrims first arrived, as high a proportion as 90 percent of the Indians along the Massachusetts coast died of disease,[15] leaving much idle land available to the Pilgrims and inclining the Wampanoag to view Pilgrims as allies who could strengthen them against their native enemies. They taught the Pilgrims local survival skills, such as how to grow corn, and so helped them to survive the first, difficult winter. But as the settlers increased in numbers, available land and resources became scarce. Indians did not understand the settlers' concept of landownership: Indians believed that land purchases became null and void if the land was not used. Also, later settlers treated Indians with disdain and dealt with them unjustly.

The first northeastern tribe to resist European settlers was the **Pequot**. A contemporary account of the **Pequot War** illustrates how the settlers' religious convictions contributed to the savagery of their combat with the Pequot:

> And indeed such a dreadful Terror did the Almighty let fall upon their Spirits, that they would fly from us and run into the very Flames, where many of them perished. . . . Thus were they now at their Wits End, who not many Hours before exalted themselves in their great Pride, threatning and resolving the utter Ruin and Destruction of all the English, Exulting and Rejoycing with Songs and Dances: But God was above them, who laughed his Enemies and the Enemies of his People to Scorn, making them as a fiery Oven: Thus were the Stout Hearted spoiled, having slept their last Sleep, and none of their Men could find their Hands: Thus did the Lord judge among the Heathen, filling the place with dead Bodies![16]

Blessed be the Lord God of Israel, who only doth wondrous Things; and blessed be his holy Name for ever: Let the whole Earth be filled with his Glory! Thus the Lord was pleased to smite our Enemies in the hinder Parts, and to give us their Land for an Inheritance: Who remembred us in our low Estate, and redeemed us out of our Enemies' Hands: Let us therefore praise the Lord for his Goodness and his wonderful Works to the Children of Men![17]

The Wampanoag Indians who had initially aided the Pilgrims also turned against them after several decades of abuse and were defeated, but not easily, in the war called King Philip's War.[18]

Forest and Plains Indians

The Iroquois Confederation

In the northeastern area of North America, there were also forest Indians. Especially notable were the **Iroquois**, a confederation of five nations. Their constitution influenced the content of the U.S. Constitution.[19]

Anishinaabeg (Ojibwa)

As white settlers took over the eastern United States and southern Canada, **Anishinaabeg (Ojibwa)** tribes were pushed west from the Lake Ontario region, where they had been (not always peaceful) neighbors to the Iroquois. The Ojibwa had guns and gunpowder, and used these innovative weapons to defeat the Dakota tribes in Minnesota. These two tribal groups were still competing for territory in Minnesota in the middle of the nineteenth century, at the time the state of Minnesota was admitted to the Union.

The Ojibwa agenda for the cycle of seasons for northern climates ran as follows: *winter:* trap, stay warm; *spring:* make maple sugar; *summer:* fish; *fall:* gather and process wild rice.

The Dakota Uprising

By 1862 in Minnesota, the **Dakota** had ceded all but about 2,800 square miles (a bit less than two million acres) of their land to the U.S. government in the Treaty of Travers des Sioux. In exchange for twenty-one million acres of Dakota territory, the U.S. government promised to pay the Dakota an annual annuity. But the annuity was often late, forcing the Dakota to purchase on credit from white traders. By the time the annuity arrived, the Dakota would find virtually all of it going to the traders.

In the summer of 1862, four years after Minnesota was admitted to statehood, the annuity arrived so late that the Dakota were starving. The white traders also refused credit. Several young Indians searching for food attacked some settlers, igniting an uprising that resulted in the death of over five hundred settlers or their supporters and sixty Dakota. Once the white government had regained control, it carried out quick trials which resulted in over three hundred Dakota being condemned to death. President Lincoln, on the urging of moderates including the Episcopal bishop Henry Whipple, asked for the trial records and pardoned all but thirty-nine Dakota. One more was later acquitted. The thirty-eight remaining condemned were hanged on December 26, 1862, at New Ulm, Minnesota, in a single public spectacle: the largest mass execution in United States history. The Dakota community was then removed from the state, mostly to South Dakota.[20]

Reservation lands in South Dakota were violated by white settlers and their armies as their population grew and gold was discovered in the Black Hills, which were regarded by the local Indians as the "heart of everything that exists."[21] An army expedition led by General George Custer was annihilated when it grossly underestimated the size of an Indian settlement it planned to attack. Retaliatory raids shattered Dakota and other communities, with some attempting to escape to Canada. A deliberate government policy of wanton slaughter had reduced the bison herds—the tribes' main source of food, clothing, and bone for tools—from tens of millions in 1800 to less than one hundred in the 1880s.

While the Plains Indians were reeling from these defeats, a Paiute Indian named Wovoka claimed to have had a vision designating him as the messiah who would restore the Indians to their former prosperity and independence by teaching them a "**ghost dance**"; the dance would miraculously bury the whites and revive dead warriors, filling the prairies again with buffalo. Indians who wore the special ghost dance shirt, marked with secret symbols, would be protected from the white man's bullets. Whites saw this as a rebellious movement that called for a strong response and decided to arrest *Chief Sitting Bull*, who refused to condemn the dance. The Indian police who were sent to arrest him accidentally shot him dead.

Some of Chief Sitting Bull's people decided to seek the protection of *Chief Red Cloud* because they thought he was at peace with the whites. As they were on their way to join him and his people, the U.S. Army caught up with them and forced them to surrender. The army led them to **Wounded Knee** Creek and helped them to set up camp. As the army went through the camp to collect weapons, a gun went off. Since tensions were already high, the surrounding soldiers began to open fire on the Indians with Hotchkiss guns, a sort of primitive machine gun. About three hundred Dakota men, women, and children died, as well as twenty-five U.S. soldiers. The date was December 29, 1890. The Wounded Knee massacre was the last large-scale encounter between the U.S. Army and Native Americans.[22]

SACRED WRITINGS

Most Native American tribes have no sacred *writings*, since their traditions are oral. An exception would be the Mayan classics, the *Popol Vuh* and the *Chilam Balam*. Spanish missionaries destroyed most Mayan writings in the sixteenth century.[23]

There are, however, compilations of native oral tales written by non-native scholars.[24]

NARRATIVE OR MYTHIC DIMENSION

Native American oral traditions contain numerous stories about the origins of the world, of human beings, and of their own tribe. The stories frequently involve multiple gods, spirits, and animals. For example, Mayan creation stories say that the gods tried unsuccessfully to create humans from mud (they fell apart) and from wood (they were "block-headed" and so unable to learn how to worship the gods); finally, they succeeded by creating them from corn. The Cherokee creation story begins with the animals crowded on a stone arch above water needing a solid surface to live on.[25] These stories make more sense to natives than they might to settlers, since natives believe that animals have souls and that each individual animal relates to the animal spirit of its type, such as Bear Spirit or Beaver Spirit.

DOCTRINAL AND PHILOSOPHICAL DIMENSION

Native traditions remain close to their original narrative forms, with very little doctrinal or philosophical elaboration. But they do have ritual, ethical, and social elaboration, as described below.

PRACTICAL AND RITUAL DIMENSION

Vision Quest

Indians are keenly aware of the sacred, or sacred energy, and they treasure spiritual experiences. The purpose of the **vision quest** is to connect with the sacred. The adolescent male Indian goes on a vision quest seeking relationship with a guardian animal spirit that will share some of its spiritual power, revitalizing his spiritual resources. Individual animals are thought to represent an underlying spirit symbolizing that species of animal; an individual bear, for example, is the visible representative of the spirit of bear. The vision quest usually involves fasting and keeping a vigil (staying awake outdoors wearing minimal clothing) for two to four days. This experience of "symbolic death and rebirth"[26] is supervised by a holy man. When the quest is successful, some animal approaches the quester with a message. Thereafter that animal (or, what is the same, its spirit) becomes the Indian's protector and guide.

Shamans and Spirits

The *shaman* is a human who has mysteriously been to the spirit world and back again through an initiation, often an episode of apparent illness or death. The shaman on his return forms a human link with the spirit world through visions. He (or occasionally she) has gained healing and exorcising powers. See Black Elk, whose vision is quoted at the head of this chapter, as an example. Young Indians may seek the advice of a shaman to understand the meaning of a dream or of their quest experience. Spirits of the dead live in the spirit world and can transmigrate.

Sun Dance

This major renewal festival of song, dance, drums, and whistles is held every summer for four to eight days by Plains Indians. The dancers fast for the duration of the festival, suffering for the sake of the people, to renew the community's strength. The sacrificial aspect of the **sun dance** is the enactment of a vow made by male "pledgers," who endure severe physical pain, symbolically crossing the boundary between life and death for the sake of their tribe's well-being. The pledgers pass skewers of wood through the skin of their breast and under part of the breast muscle; they then attach these skewers to thongs which are tied to the central pole. As they dance, these lines pull on the skin and muscle until, eventually, they tear loose. Until recently, whites forbade the practice of the sun dance, considering it "barbaric." Today it is again legal.

Other Practices: The Sweat Lodge, Peyote Religion

In a sweat lodge, the heat is provided by hot stones set at the center of the lodge interior. Water poured on the stones creates steam. The purpose of this collective ritual is spiritual purification.

Peyote is a medicinal and "hallucinatory cactus" that Indians began to combine with ceremonial actions such as praying, singing, and drumming to create "peyote religion" after the demise of the ghost dance in the late nineteenth century. Peyote ceremonies were physically and spiritually healing for the participants. Out of the peyote religion, to which some Christian elements had been added, evolved the Native American Church.[27]

ETHICAL AND LEGAL DIMENSION

Probably the most common image of Indians among whites is a Plains Indian on horseback. There were many Plains Indian tribes. One example is the Dakota, who developed their plains way of life as they were pushed out of Minnesota by the Ojibwa. The Dakota and other Plains Indians adopted a way of life based on the horse, which was originally brought to the New World by the Spanish.

Five Characteristics of the Dakota Worldview

In 1971 in South Dakota, a Jesuit priest, John F. Bryde, published *Modern Indian Psychology* based on his years of working with the Dakota. He wanted to help

Dakota schoolchildren understand and maintain their valuable cultural traditions. His discussion illustrates some of the characteristics that are widely shared among Native American tribes. Five specifically Dakota virtues or values that Bryde lists are bravery, individual freedom, generosity and sharing, adjustment to nature, and good advice from Indian wisdom.[28]

Bravery

Bryde defines bravery as "doing a hard thing without showing fear or running from it."[29] One could show bravery by stealing a horse or killing a buffalo. One could also show bravery by the particular way one engaged in warfare.

Dakota warfare emphasized bravery over effective killing. For example, "**counting coup**" (to gallop up through a hail of arrows, touch your enemy with a stick, and then get safely away) was considered more glorious and more courageous than killing from a distance, but no one was hurt (if you got away). If you were skilled at counting coup, you were considered to have "**strong medicine**" (in this case, strong spiritual power that protected you from harm). Another characteristic practice showing bravery was to stake yourself down in battle (attaching yourself to the stake by a cord) as a sign that you would not retreat. Warriors who did this were called "**dog strap soldiers.**"

Whites observed that Dakota males spent a lot of time sitting around letting the females wait on them, only "working" when hunger drove them to hunt or danger drove them to fight. Bryde points out an important reason for this. Hunting and warring were both very dangerous. If the men spent all their time hunting and warring, not enough of them would survive to continue the tribe.

Individual Freedom

As Bryde explains this characteristic, "You yourself decide to do the *right thing* in order to survive"—that is, in order that the *tribe* will survive and the *people* will remain strong. ("To survive" means "to go on living in the best way possible.") No one has the right to force his or her own will on anyone else. But one should allow those who refuse good advice to get hurt by their choices. One should "respect advice" by "listening all over" (to the elders). Those who ignore commonly respected advice are ridiculed by the whole group.[30]

It is important for the community that its members be able to stand alone, an essential component of the previous characteristic—bravery. Emphasis on individual combat produced superb individual warriors but less effective group action. Indians loved to set ambushes, but often failed with them because one of the warriors sprang the trap too soon. On the other hand, one white general is said to have welcomed his successor with the caution, "When fighting Indians, beware of three things: surprise, surprise, and surprise."

Generosity and Sharing

This characteristic is expressed especially with regard to (a) *food and shelter:* seven hunters can support one hundred people, and material goods, like captured animals, belong to everyone—the hunter is just the instrument; and (b) *praise and blame:* praise is shared with the whole group, which means that Dakota do not try to stand out from the group; rather the special talents of any one person and what he or she accomplishes raise the whole group, so there is no need for jealousy.[31]

The concept of the "**Indian giver**," properly understood, is admirable. It means that one gives freely to anyone who is in need without fear of not having enough for oneself, expecting that if one is later in need oneself someone else will provide what is needed. Thus it is not a question of giving something and later taking it back (as whites often misrepresent it) but rather of a free circulation of necessary goods, an unlimited giving and getting, which ensures that goods will end up at any moment where they are most needed. Dakota thus gain honor by giving things away; their center of attention is group wealth rather than individual wealth.

Adjustment to Nature

Bryde describes this characteristic as "getting along with all things, including humans." First, getting along with things: Dakota revere the earth that all things grow from. (This characteristic makes them suddenly "politically correct" in relation to the relatively recent white American concern for the environment.) Second, getting along with people: the Dakota word *oyate*, translated as "people," includes both humans and animals. So the contrast between "things" and "people" is not so strong as it is among white Americans. Attention focuses on survival for today, on the present. Enjoy what you have today. To "get along with someone" includes (a) *loving* that person, (b) *relying on* that person for your needs, and (c) *being responsible* to that person for his or her needs. The Dakota kinship system emphasizes the extended family: the Dakota have eleven different words for "cousin." They "adopt" close friends as brothers or sisters.[32]

In the late nineteenth and early twentieth century, white reformers thought that the Indians' sense of communal responsibility was keeping them in poverty, and that they would benefit from some competition and selfish individualism, which would push them to work hard to "get ahead." The reformers complained that the Indians would rather starve together than abandon the rest of their community to launch out on their own. So they proposed that the reservations be parceled out to individual Indian families in hopes that this would motivate them to work hard. Unfortunately, the lands "parceled out" were too infertile and small to support individual families, and the process of distribution left many families in such debt that they either sold their land or saw it foreclosed to pay taxes or other debts. As a result, large parts of the original reservations have passed into the hands of whites. In recent years, the White Earth tribe of Ojibwa in Minnesota, under the leadership of Winona LaDuke, has begun a program to re-purchase those parts of its original reservation that were lost through such sales and foreclosures.

Good Advice from Indian Wisdom

Natives judge each other by what they are, not by what they have. Before the whites came, they neither had nor used money. Everything is considered to be part of one body: *wakan* (the holy, or mysterious) is contained in (1) living things and (2) things that exhibit power, including (a) active power (such as wind) and (b) passive power (such as a rock). One is invited to listen to things, think about them, and learn from their power. Things "talk." One prays, then uses these powers—lets them flow through one—for human good.[33]

The visible world is a shadow of the real world. Some of the sacred traditions include the pipe and purification through the sweat lodge, the vision quest, and the sun dance (for most of these, see above). Speaking the truth and being happy with one another are both highly valued. Good people eventually come out ahead.

Comparing Native American and White Values

The following Native American values stand in tension with common white American values:

1. Bravery stands in tension with the white emphasis on material achievement and financial success. The Dakota learned to hunt or wage war *when necessary*, whereas white Americans value working every day.
2. Individual freedom stands in tension with material achievement. Material achievement requires daily discipline that may threaten individual freedom.
3. Generosity and sharing stands in tension with material achievement. Dakota acquire things to give them away, first to their own extended families. White Americans acquire things to keep them, and to express their sense of self-worth. Dakota value generosity highly; whites value possessions highly.
4. Adjustment to nature stands in tension with scientific progress. Dakota value getting along with nature and with other people. White Americans value conquering nature and competing with each other.
5. Good advice from Indian wisdom stands in tension with white American efficiency and practicality. Dakota seek to live in harmony with people and things. White Americans value making things and money to gain power and possessions.

SOCIAL AND INSTITUTIONAL DIMENSION

Land

Land belongs to God. A human can't "own" it, although one group can give others permission to hunt there. Whoever makes use of any piece of land should use it responsibly in a way that will sustain its resources.

If this seems strange to us, we might compare it with white attitudes toward water and air. Individuals do not buy and sell lakes, portions of the ocean, or rivers. We consider these to be "common property." We might well object to a group that claimed to buy Lake Michigan and to prevent anyone else from sailing on it or fishing in it. While we don't speak of God as the owner of the lakes, we do say they are common or state property: it is, for example, the state of Minnesota or the U.S. government that regulates their use. In some states, like Colorado, the water of the rivers is allocated in complex ways so that there is enough water for various users at various locations along the river: if someone upstream uses so much water that the stream dries up farther down (as could well happen in drier years), the government will come and shut off their access so that the water will be fairly shared. As to air, we have not thought to buy or sell its rights—until air pollution recently brought the problem to our attention.

Our current struggles with air and water pollution, indicating that one person's use may prejudice another person's use or cause significant harm to people in the area, parallel Native American attitudes toward land. White uses of the land, especially their fencing off of, and restricting access to, certain areas (by both hunters and grazing wild animals), in addition to their decimation of the buffalo herds, disastrously affected Native American users of the land.

Authority and Freedom

Individual freedom is treasured. Followers agree to accept a leader, normally for a particular purpose and limited time (ad hoc). This practice confused whites, who wanted to know who was in charge. So whites settled on someone as "chief" and tended to negotiate with that person alone. This procedure suited white purposes, not native ones. Worse, whites often deliberately chose a native who would agree with what the whites wanted and then dealt with that person as the "chief," even if the tribe did not recognize his leadership. The Treaty of New Echota between white settlers and a small group of Cherokee, mentioned above, is an example of this process. Indians tend to drift from one leader to another if they don't approve of the first one or trust his abilities. As a result, bad tribal leaders end up with small tribes, good ones with larger tribes.

ISSUES FOR JUSTICE AND PEACE

War among Plains Indians

Historically, Plains Indians went to war for two main reasons: (1) to gain territory to live on—if pushed out by others, the tribe tried to annihilate or frighten away an enemy tribe to make space for itself (Michael Steltenkamp quotes Black Elk as saying that "the Lakota customarily fought people whose language they did not understand")[34]; and (2) to gain glory by displaying manhood—this kind of warfare was mostly carried on by the young.

As already mentioned, Plains Indian warfare emphasized bravery over actual killing, for example, in the practice of counting coup. Also mentioned was the characteristic practice of the dog strap soldier—showing bravery by staking yourself down in battle as a sign that you would not retreat. Finally we noted that emphasis on individual combat reduced the success rate of Indian ambushes; nevertheless, Indians were remembered as masters of ambushes, and they excelled at surprising the enemy.

White settlers kept pushing into Indian territory, violated treaties, and finally "concentrated" the remaining Indians on reservations. The Red Lake Ojibwa reservation in northwest Minnesota is an example of land never ceded to the U.S. government and never parceled out to individual Indian families—this tribe was a holdout. Other tribes ceded land for money and what seemed at the time to be valuable promises. Later experience showed that the promises were mostly broken.

Twentieth-Century Revival

For years, many Indian ceremonies were illegal: not only the ghost dance, but even the sun dance. Indians were corralled onto reservations. Then in 1934 the U.S. Indian Reorganization Act established tribal councils. These councils did not follow Indian traditions of authority. Many Indians viewed these tribal governments as working the will of the U.S. government, not of the Indians. Sometimes the U.S. government would even "buy out" a tribal council; for example, the Menominee Tribal Council in Wisconsin accepted cash payment to dissolve itself in 1958.[35]

That same year, a Haudenosaunee Indian named Mad Bear led a nonviolent stand against the government of New York State and inspired a resistance movement called the **American Indian Movement (AIM)**. AIM leaders, including *Dennis Banks* and *Russell Means*, established a "Trail of Broken Treaties." Their goal was to expose broken treaties from West to East, ending in Washington, D.C. They organized various resistance activities to support Indian land claims. The secret FBI surveillance and disruption program called **COINTELPRO** began to target the movement. Many AIM leaders were arrested, and many Indians were killed.[36]

Wounded Knee Occupation

In February of 1973 the Oglala Sioux Civil Rights Organization was established on the Pine Ridge Reservation in South Dakota. The Oglala leaders asked AIM to help them make a statement by seizing the town of Wounded Knee. They demanded that a Presidential Treaty Commission be established to conduct hearings on Indian treaty rights, to investigate the practices and procedures of the Bureau of Indian Affairs (BIA), and to inspect all Sioux reservations in South Dakota.[37] U.S. agents surrounded the reservation and a sixty-nine-day siege resulted.

The Indians had been promised a meeting with a government official to discuss the Fort Laramie Treaty of 1868, which the Oglala maintained the U.S. government was violating. That treaty had set out the conditions and guarantees under which the Sioux would cede most of their land to the United States and end attacks on settlers.[38] A few years later, gold was discovered in the Black Hills, which were part of the territory allotted to the Sioux by the treaty, and gold prospectors repeatedly broke the treaty by invading the territory. The Sioux attacked the prospectors, also in violation of the treaty, and in 1877 the United States seized the Black Hills.

In 1973 the government official met with Frank Fools Crow, chief of the Oglala, who wanted one question answered: "Will the 1868 treaty be reinstated, yes or no?" He didn't get a direct answer because the official claimed that the Oglala fell under the Indian Reorganization Act of 1934.[39] Then in 1980, the United States Supreme Court agreed that the Lakota should be paid for the 1877 value of the land plus 5 percent interest for 103 years, totaling over $120 million, but the Lakota refused the money and insisted they wanted the land instead. Later courts have noted that some of the money has been spent; some thousands of Lakota are still litigating to get their share.[40]

This exchange illustrates two different understandings of law: (1) laws are historical, written, and built up on the basis of precedent (white British-American); (2) law is situational, spiritual, and based on the available human wisdom (Indian). Frank Fools Crow said through his interpreter: "They say they can't give us our land back because it was so long ago that they took it, and now so many white people live there, but the Indian doesn't believe that. One hundred years is not so long for us."[41]

Fishing Rights

There have been fishing disputes between whites and natives in Minnesota and Wisconsin, with resort owners and sports fishermen challenging treaty rights that authorize natives to hunt and fish in certain territories in return for their having ceded territory to settlers. Natives net or spear all fish indiscriminately, both game fish and rough fish (fish like carp, which are unpopular with sports fishermen). For the most part, natives preserve and eat what they catch; sometimes they sell part of the catch. Some of the reservations also stock lakes in their area with game fish. The Minnesota Department of Natural Resources (DNR) has stated that Indian fishing practices improve the availability of game fish. White resort owners claim that those practices threaten game fishing for others.

What would "game fish" mean to an Indian who takes only enough to eat and asks the animal's permission because he needs to eat? The Indian might well wonder about the white practice of "catch and release." Although to the whites this seems humane to the fish, the Indian might question why whites find pleasure in annoying fish that they don't need for food.

Evangelization, Conversion, and Syncretism

The Colonial Spread of Christianity and Islam

As noted above in the brief historical survey of Native American tribes, some of the European colonizers tried consciously to convert the natives to Christianity. Others were content to oppress, enslave, disperse, or slaughter them. In Africa, Muslims also converted natives to Islam, although more by invitation than by force. While the missionary religions experienced significant success, the natives often continued to practice their traditional faiths even after their "conversion," resulting in some syncretism between the indigenous and the colonial religions.

Spanish-dominated areas made use of a concept called "discovery," under which newly colonized areas were considered to fall by right under the authority of the pope and the Spanish king. The colonizing force would read a formal declaration to the natives explaining this right, inviting the natives to accept Christianity and the authority that the pope had granted to the king of Spain, and warning them that, if they were to reject the offer, they would be subject to war and slavery.

Unfortunately the text of the declaration, written in 1513 for repeated use, was read in Castilian Spanish, sometimes but not always with a translation into the native language, to natives who were incapable of understanding it. Its main function was to provide a specious justification for the actions of the Spanish conquerors, and it was criticized by many of the Catholic missioners, such as Bartholomé de Las Casas, whose life and work is described below in the section on spokespersons for justice and peace. In effect, it is an example of the "counterfeit tradition" hiding the real motive: the "hidden tradition" of theft, conquest, and enslavement.[42]

The discovery doctrine was also appealed to by British colonists with respect to the king of England and, later, the U.S. government. An 1823 U.S. Supreme Court case led to the following ruling:

> The tribes of Indians inhabiting this country were fierce savages, whose occupation was war, and whose subsistence was drawn chiefly from the forest. To leave them in possession of their country, was to leave the country a wilderness.[43]

When the local natives proved inadequate to meet the labor needs of the colonizers, either because of death by disease and slaughter, or because of resistance and flight, colonizers, especially on the plantations of the Caribbean and the two Americas, began to import slaves from Africa, such as **Yoruba** people from West Africa. Despite the efforts of the colonizers to destroy the language, culture, and history of their slaves, the large Yoruba populations in Brazil and the Caribbean managed to maintain their religious practices by combining them with Catholicism, producing Umbanda and Candomblé in Brazil, Santería in Cuba, and the related Vodou (Voodoo) in Haiti. Many have practiced similar syncretism in their African homelands such as Nigeria, where today half of the population officially professes Islam and half Christianity.

The survival of the indigenous Yoruba religion offers an interesting case study.

Survival of Indigenous Faiths: The Yoruba of West Africa

The Yoruba of West Africa believe in one overarching god called Olorun or Olodumare, who is too distant to be normally approached, and they worship deities, or spirits, called *orishas*, who provide help for their day-to-day needs. It is misleading to be too precise about their beliefs because the specifics vary greatly from one village to another. Although one can identify hundreds of orishas, any given group relates regularly with only a few dozen. According to one of their myths, the orishas were once united in a single deity, and they seek to regain that unity. Humans connect with the orishas through their myths and rituals; rituals also mediate between the Yoruba and their ancestors. The living, the dead, and the gods or spirits comprise the cosmos of the Yoruba.

The orishas, like the ancient Greek and Roman gods, combine good and bad qualities, engage among themselves in human types of activities like marriage and divorce, and sometimes quarrel or struggle with each other. In certain rituals, orishas can possess the bodies of Yoruba priests and speak or act through them. Humans are subject to attack by malevolent orishas, by evil spirits called ajogun, and by spells cast by witches and sorcerers. Yoruba make use of divination to determine which spirits are causing their troubles, and of sacrifice and devotion to gain the aid of one or more cooperative orishas in meeting their day-to-day needs, including protection from spiritual attack through curses and evil spells from their enemies. Their attention is focused on the concerns of this life; they give little attention to the next life except to hope that they will be reincarnated.

Social relations are a major Yoruba concern, especially the question of gender balance or imbalance. In actuality men are more dominant in contemporary Yoruba culture, whereas Yoruba mythology promotes gender equality. Their astounding oral tradition consists of more than 200,000 verses, which are chanted by Yoruba storytellers.

Preserving their oral tradition has become a major priority in the face of the destruction of indigenous cultures in the modern world. Yoruba slaves imported to the New World managed to maintain their religious practice, for example, creating Cuban Santería by identifying their particular orishas (which varied a lot from area to area) with appropriate Catholic saints—members practice both religions concurrently. Others, in contrast, converted fully and sincerely to Catholicism (or, in Africa, to Islam). It is not always easy for Christian churches and Muslim mosques to distinguish syncretists from full converts, and so to count numbers of adherents accurately.

Thus "justice and peace" issues among the Yoruba and their descendants include gender balance, cultural survival, syncretism, and full conversion. Presuming that forced conversion should be condemned, the question arises whether evangelization and conversion are themselves to be avoided as disrespectful. Who should decide?[44]

Interfaith Sharing and Conversion

Within North American native religion, the case of Black Elk is particularly compelling. The description of his great vision, with which this chapter begins, is quoted from the book *Black Elk Speaks* by John Neihardt. Critics point out that Neihardt took significant liberties with what Black Elk said, as can be seen by comparing his book with the original interview notes.[45] Most significantly, Neihardt chose to present Black Elk as a Lakota holy man nostalgically mourning the death of his people's culture and religion without mentioning that Black Elk spent the last fifty years of his life as a Roman Catholic catechist. Black Elk himself had urged Neihardt to include the Catholic period of his life.

Born into a family of medicine men in 1863, Black Elk had his great vision at the age of nine during a severe illness. He did not share it with anyone for eight years. At age twelve, he took part in the 1876 Battle of Little Big Horn (called Greasy Grass by the Lakota), the battle in which General Custer was killed. Around 1880 he revealed his great vision to a tribal medicine man. The tribe then dramatized the vision, and initiated Black Elk into the role of medicine man, a role that he practiced for over twenty years.

In 1887, he joined Buffalo Bill's Wild West show as an actor, drumming and dancing, which took him to England to perform before Queen Victoria. About to return in 1888, he literally missed the boat and was stuck in Europe for a year. He joined another Wild West show in Paris until he was able, in 1889, to return to Pine Ridge in South Dakota. A year later, in 1890, he was injured in the Wounded Knee massacre. That experience showed him that the ghost dance and its protective shirt covered with sacred symbols would not protect the Lakota as had been promised. Still, he continued as a practicing medicine man. In 1892, he married Katherine War Bonnet, who became Catholic and had their three children baptized. She died in 1903; the next year Black Elk was baptized Catholic. See Michael Steltenkamp for conflicting explanations of his conversion—which in any case did not mean that he rejected all of his Lakota spirituality.[46]

A year after Katherine's death, he married Anna Brings White, a widow with two daughters, and had three more children by her. He became very active as a Catholic catechist, working with the Jesuit priests of the Pine Ridge reservation and traveling to other reservations to promote Catholicism. Steltenkamp emphasizes Black Elk's admiration for the Jesuit priests of the Holy Rosary Mission. In 1930, Black Elk met and was interviewed by John Neihardt for the book *Black Elk Speaks*. In 1934, he instituted a new Wild West show in the Black Hills, but emphasizing Lakota culture rather than warfare. His second wife died in 1941, and he died in 1950.

Was Black Elk's conversion genuine? Or was he simply *pretending* to convert out of convenience? Did he believe that each of the two spiritualities had something positive to offer the other? These questions with regard to Christian missionary efforts directed to Native Americans have been raised by many, such as the Osage-Cherokee George Tinker, a professor at the Iliff School of Theology in Denver.[47] Tinker's position is that Christian missionaries, with the best of intentions, were unable to separate their religious convictions from their cultural biases. Thus even while resisting the worst abuses of colonialism, they in fact promoted the destruction of Native American cultures in what he calls "cultural genocide." For example, Bartholomé de Las Casas helped to design the "reductions" (defensive communities) to protect the Indians from slave raiders (kidnappers), but the "reductions" also Europeanized the natives; and Bishop Whipple cooperated in shrinking the Dakota land area so that the Dakota would be forced to become farmers on a European pattern.

In recent years, there has been a lively academic discussion questioning whether Black Elk's conversion was genuine, or instead a way to survive given the new political and religious realities. *The Black Elk Reader*[48] provides chapters by various authors discussing these issues. In his *Nicholas Black Elk*, Michael Steltenkamp concludes from detailed interviews with Black Elk's family and others who knew him and his ministry that his vocation as a Catholic catechist was genuine.[49]

Damian Costello offers a postcolonial analysis of Black Elk's Catholicism and how he used that tradition to challenge Christianity itself. He argues that Black Elk was applying Lakota and Catholic spiritualities in creative ways, accepting what was true and abandoning what, like the ghost dance, didn't work. The dispute between those who think that Black Elk's conversion to Catholicism was sincere and those who think it was just a practical means of survival is resolved, according to Costello, by realizing that his conversion was not to the Western Christianity of his time as it was being practiced to control the world, but rather to the true, original Catholic Christianity that was judging the greedy, violent Christians who were destroying the lives and cultures of other people. **Wakan Tanka** was the same God for everyone; he came to rescue the poor from the greed, violence, and oppression of the rich. Christians have forgotten the command to love their neighbor (including other nations) like themselves, and so have fallen away from Jesus. But God calls all to return.[50]

In considering how to judge the interactions of religions, especially between communities with great power differences, it is worth considering how those interactions unfold. The examples of the Yoruba and Black Elk suggest that oppressed peoples can find creative ways to continue some aspects of their faith, while even turning the oppressors' faith back against them (as black slaves did with their Christian spirituals). Perhaps the choices people make between elements that they find to be ineffective (like the ghost dance) or effective (like a reverence for nature), oppressive (like Aztec and Mayan human sacrifice, and the Christian "discovery" doctrine) or liberating, should not be limited. Is it worth asking whether some forms of spirituality are positive and some (like certain occult arts) malign? Under the latter category, is it acceptable, for example, to cast destructive spells? Would we all be better off if early Christians had decided not to interfere with Greco-Roman spiritualities by preaching what they thought was "good news"? Note, however, that early Christians *invited* conversion, working from a vulnerable position—those who died (who were "martyred") as a result of Christian evangelizing in the first three centuries were the Christians who were bringing the new message and those who accepted it, not the Greco-Romans (or others) who were being invited to embrace the new faith. No one was converted by force or fear.

SPOKESPERSONS FOR JUSTICE AND PEACE

Bartholomé de Las Casas (1484–1566)

The first Catholic bishop of **Chiapas** in what is now Mexico was *Bartholomé de Las Casas*, a personal friend of Christopher Columbus who was instrumental in preserving Columbus's journal. His famous book *The Tears of the Indians* is a moving protest against the cruelty of Spanish conquistadores, for example, their practice of cutting off Indians' hands, stringing the severed hands around their necks, and sending them off to "carry the message" to other Indians.[51] The book was quickly translated into English and distributed in England and its colonies as anti-Spanish propaganda. Therefore, some scholars have doubted its accuracy.

It is also de Las Casas who records for us the famous sermon of Friar Antonio de Montesinos on the Caribbean island of Hispaniola in 1511, nineteen years after Columbus's first voyage, in which he told his Spanish congregation that they were all in mortal sin because of the way they were treating the Indians, and that the Dominican monks would not hear their confessions or give them communion until they repented. Rather than repent, they protested to the Spanish king and to the Dominican superior in Spain, both of whom told the local preachers to stop upsetting their congregations.[52]

Winona LaDuke (1959–)

Born of an Anishinaabe (Ojibwa) father from Minnesota and a Jewish mother, Winona LaDuke was raised in Oregon. She studied at Harvard University and Antioch University, earning a graduate degree in community economic development. An environmentalist and economist, she lives with her family on the White Earth (Ojibwa) Reservation in Minnesota. In order to help the reservation buy back thousands of acres of the land that its 1867 treaty with the U.S. government should have guaranteed it, she founded the White Earth Land Recovery Project in 1989.[53] With others she also founded the Indigenous Women's Network in 1993,[54] and Honor the Earth in 1985.[55] She was Ralph Nader's vice-presidential running mate in the 1996 and 2000 presidential elections, representing the Green Party. The recipient of various awards, LaDuke has written a number of books, including *Recovering the Sacred: The Power of Naming and Claiming* (2005) and *The Militarization of Indian Country* (2012).

SUMMARY

Inspired by a worldview that sees spiritual power animating the whole natural world, and treats plants and animals as "people" like ourselves, Native American tribes developed sophisticated ways of surviving and thriving in their environment. European settlers, working from very different worldviews and with more advanced military technology, took control of most of the resources of the Americas, forcing

Native Americans onto small, infertile, and resource-poor reservations in North America, or exploiting them as poverty-level laborers in Central and South America. With renewed awareness of the injustices involved, descendants of the natives and of the settlers have taken some steps to compensate for the injustices, but there remains a wide gap in power and wealth between the two groups. Some settlers resisted the injustices; some natives are working to restore appropriate native culture and regain land and resources. As the industrialized U.S. culture draws down nonrenewable resources and increases unsustainable pollution, native traditions may have more and more wisdom to offer.[56]

KEY TERMS

Aleuts	"Indian giver"
American Indian Movement	Inuit
(AIM)	Iroquois
animism	Mayan
Anishinaabeg	Ojibwa
Apache	Our Lady of Guadalupe
Aztecs	Pequot, Pequot War
Cherokee	Pueblo
Chiapas	Quechua
COINTELPRO	shaman
counting coup	strong medicine
Dakota	sun dance
dog strap soldier	Trail of Tears
five civilized tribes	vision quest
ghost dance	Wakan Tanka
Hopi	Wounded Knee
Incas	Yoruba

DISCUSSION QUESTIONS

1. Was the removal of Indian tribes to reservations in the late nineteenth century an example of "ethnic cleansing"? Was it justified? Is it an appropriate model for Israel to follow in dealing with the Palestinians?

2. If the best model of human justice is for people to share the earth's resources fairly and in the process to redistribute resources that past injustice has distributed unfairly—land, money, education, etc.—how should the U.S. government and society compensate Native Americans for the injustices done to them?

3. When should land be individually owned, and when communally owned? What limitations should there be on what an owner can do to the land? For

example, should an owner be free to destroy productive farmland when people are starving?

4. When should water be individually owned, and when communally owned? What limitations should there be on what an owner can do to the water? For example, should drinking water supplies like city water systems be privately owned and managed? Should companies that bottle water be allowed to monopolize valuable water sources?[57] What if safe water becomes too expensive for the poor?

5. When should air be individually owned, and when communally owned? What limitations should there be on what an owner can do to the air, for example in a public building he or she owns? Should factory owners be required to pay for expensive pollution controls if the result will be that their product or service will become too expensive to compete in the free market? If so, should they choose not to produce that product or service? If not, who *should* pay for the damage?

6. Do you find some Native American attitudes and practices attractive? If so, which ones, and how might you integrate them into your own life?

SUGGESTIONS FOR FURTHER READING

Boyd. *Rolling Thunder.*
Brown. *Bury My Heart at Wounded Knee.*
Bryde. *Modern Indian Psychology.*
Carmody and Brink. *Ways to the Center.*
Churchill. *The COINTELPRO Papers.*
Costello. *Black Elk.*
Deloria. *God Is Red.*
Diamond. *Collapse.*
Ebbott. *Indians in Minnesota.*
Falola and Genova, eds. *Orisa: Yoruba Gods and Spiritual Identity in Africa and the Diaspora.*
Fisher. *Living Religions,* 5th ed.
Gill. "Native American Religions."
Heinberg. *The Party's Over.*
———. *Power Down.*
Holler, ed. *The Black Elk Reader.*
Las Casas. *Tears of the Indians.*
Mason. *A Brief History of the Pequot War.*
Matthews. *World Religions,* 4th ed.
Neihardt, ed. *Black Elk Speaks.*
Olupona and Rey, eds. *Òrìṣà Devotion as World Religion.*
Restall. *Seven Myths of the Spanish Conquest.*
Steltenkamp. *Black Elk: Holy Man of the Oglala.*
———. *Nicholas Black Elk.*
Tinker. *Missionary Conquest.*
Van Voorst. *RELG.*
Weyler. *Blood of the Land.*

7

Marxist Worldviews

You are horrified at our intending to do away with private property. But in your existing society private property is already done away with for nine-tenths of the population; its existence for the few is solely due to its nonexistence in the hands of those nine tenths. You reproach us, therefore, with intending to do away with a form of property the necessary condition for whose existence is the nonexistence of any property for the immense majority of society. . . .

Communism deprives no [one] of the power to appropriate the products of society; all that it does is to deprive [one] of the power to subjugate the labor of others by means of such appropriation.

—Karl Marx, *The Communist Manifesto*[1]

EXPERIENTIAL AND EMOTIONAL DIMENSION

The experiential basis of the Marxist worldview combines the secularizing tendencies of the Enlightenment, which raised doubts about God and the spiritual realm, with the sufferings produced by the Industrial Revolution: destruction of pre-industrial economies, long hours of boring or dangerous work, wages too low to support decent lives for workers and their families, squalid homes in crowded slums close to polluting factories. The gap between those realities and the luxurious lives of industrialists was giving rise to agitation and violence that threatened social stability. Various socialist thinkers, writers, and activists had sought solutions with limited success. Karl Marx thought his analysis showed "scientifically" what was really going on and where it was all headed.

HISTORICAL PERIODS

1. *Theoretical Beginnings (1842–1917).* As socialist ideas became popular in Europe, Karl Marx and Friedrich Engels published their theories about **communism**, based on industrial workers taking control of capitalist society. In

1891, Pope Leo XIII wrote the encyclical *Rerum Novarum* as an alternative to their ideas.

2. *Beginning in Russia (1917–1924)*. Vladimir Lenin (1870–1924) took advantage of a popular revolution in Russia to set up a pre-communist system in a peasant society, with the help of worker councils called *soviets*. He joined Russia to several smaller neighbors to create the Union of Soviet Socialist Republics.

3. *Russian Industrialization (1924–1939)*. When Lenin died, Josef Stalin (1879–1953) recast Russia as an industrial society through draconian reorganization and purges.

4. *The Second World War (1939–1945)*. Taking advantage of its industrialization, Stalin led Russia to defeat the Nazi German invasion.

5. *Postwar Expansions (1945–1953)*. Communist governments seized power in Eastern Europe, China, Indochina, and North Korea. Strong communist parties appeared in Western Europe, Latin America, and elsewhere.

6. *The Cold War (1953–1991)*. Nikita Khrushchev (1894–1971) moved to "de-Stalinize" the Soviet Union. Communist and capitalist nations carried on a power struggle through proxy Third World nations, involving wars in Korea, Indochina, and the Middle East. Cuba and Nicaragua chose communism through revolution, while other Latin American countries wavered.

7. *Decline (1991–present)*. Mikhail Gorbachev (1931–) tried and failed to modernize communism in the Soviet Union, leading to its total collapse there and in Eastern European satellites. China began to introduce a market economy; Vietnam and Cuba moved cautiously in the same direction.

CLASSIC WRITINGS

Karl Marx (1818–1883) was a German philosopher who became interested in social and economic issues. He was aghast at the sufferings produced by the Industrial Revolution. Banned from teaching because of his radical ideas, he entered a career as a journalist, traveling all over Europe in an attempt to enlighten the workers. He and his family suffered both from the circumstances of the Industrial Revolution itself and from reactions to his ideas that appeared in the press. Why would he take such risks for himself and his family? In his *Theses on Feuerbach* (1845) Marx writes, "The philosophers have only *interpreted* the world in various ways; the point however is to *change* it."[2] Whether or not we ultimately agree with his ideas—or the use to which they have been put—Marx was in his own way seeking to create justice.

In his study of economics, Marx was influenced by *Friedrich Engels* (1820–1895): it is their collaboration that produced many of the classic "Marxist" writings, especially **The Communist Manifesto** (1848) and the essential but incomplete **Das Kapital** (1867). Engels is also responsible for the wide dissemination of Marxist ideas, for he later supported Marx and his family in England so that Marx could continue his prolific writing.

In his writings, Lenin adapted Marxist ideas to the new and different situation in Russia. The writings of Lenin's successor, Josef Stalin, have proved to be less enduring. Other important authors include Antonio Gramsci, Peter Kropotkin, Rosa Luxemburg, and Leon Trotsky. Among more recent communist writers are Mao Zedong and Che Guevara.[3]

NARRATIVE OR MYTHIC DIMENSION

Marx wrote as a philosopher and economist. He described many *types* of oppression in his doctrinal explanations, but did not give much *concrete narrative* of the problems that energized his campaign. Some of Charles Dickens's novels help to fill in this gap, providing narrative descriptions of the acute sufferings caused by industrialization in nineteenth-century England.

DOCTRINAL AND PHILOSOPHICAL DIMENSION

In order to understand those worldviews that claim to be "Marxist" or "communist," it is necessary to understand some of Marx's own major ideas. Key concepts for understanding Marxism, derived from Marx's early philosophy, include *alienation*, **class struggle**, **dialectical materialism**, and **ideology**.

The German philosophers *Hegel* and *Feuerbach* were an early inspiration for Marx. To "alienate" means to "make alien or foreign." Feuerbach argued that we *alienate* ourselves from the human qualities that we should develop in ourselves by projecting them onto an external idea of God. This concept enabled Marx to understand modern working people's profound isolation (see below). Marx came to disagree with both Feuerbach and Hegel about both *why* this alienation existed and *how to remedy* it.

Marx accepted Hegel's conviction that a process of *dialectic* moves history itself through three basic stages capable of repetition—**thesis**, **antithesis**, and **synthesis**. A status-quo situation provides the *thesis*. As society begins to change, forces and ideas that challenge the status quo constitute an *antithesis*. As these two do battle with each other, the tension between thesis and antithesis ultimately results in something new, the *synthesis* (and a new status quo). But no status quo is stable forever. The synthesis itself becomes a new thesis. Repeating the process, this new thesis generates a new antithesis, and the continuing struggle produces a new synthesis.

Hegel believed that a dialectic of *ideas* moves all of history. Behind these ideas was something he called "Absolute Spirit." (His work could be interpreted religiously or not, as he himself is not clear as to what "Spirit" actually means.) For Hegel, the key example was Christianity: the Jewish Christianity of Jesus was the thesis, the Greek Christianity of Paul was the antithesis, and out of the struggle between these two was born the synthesis of Roman Catholicism. Marx saw dialectic in a very different way, however.

Dialectical Materialism

Marx rejected Hegel's assumption that history is moved by *ideas*—it is far more practical than that. History is moved by *materialism*—there is a recurring tension, struggle, and resolution in the *physical, material* world, not in the world of immaterial ideas. He described this theory as **dialectical materialism**. Thus Marx interpreted Hegel's dialectic in *socioeconomic* terms, whereas Hegel had been thinking in terms of *ideas* and religion. Concretely the (socioeconomic) *thesis*, a particular form of society at one historical period, develops inner tensions when new forms of economic production are badly directed by old forms of political and economic power. In reaction to these tensions, another vision of society is proposed, distributing power differently, which is called the *antithesis* because it stands opposed to the earlier form. These two forms struggle against one another. In actuality people who dominate the old forms of power (such as rural landholders) struggle for ascendancy over people who dominate the new forms of power (such as factory owners and managers). The result of these power struggles is a new form of society, the *synthesis* (industrial capitalism) that mediates both sets of power-holders and interests. For Marx, the struggle between the thesis of feudalism and the antithesis of industrial capitalism was in the process of producing the synthesis of **communism**.

Alienation

Alienation for Marx, unlike Feuerbach and Hegel, was not only about the individual self or ideas; it was also about the social and economic structure of nineteenth-century life. To understand the Marxist notion of alienation, we have to look first at the social and economic situation of nineteenth-century Europe.

Capital (the centralized ownership of costly productive resources like factories) causes the alienation of the working class. Modern conditions of production like the assembly line make abundant product possible, but at the same time they alienate workers from the products they produce, from themselves, and from other workers.

Workers are alienated from *the product*, which disappears down the assembly line. Part of the worker's self is in it, but the worker can't keep it and has no say over what becomes of it. Workers are alienated from *themselves*: they cannot express themselves adequately through dull, repetitive work; the worker becomes "just a machine." Workers are alienated from *other workers*: despite the fact that they have to cooperate on the job to build the product, workers are set in competition with each other for *scarce jobs and low wages*, when they should be cooperating with each other. Competition for low wages leads the worker to see *other workers* as an enemy rather than to see *the system and the managers* as the enemy.

Alienation, then, is the cause of *social and* **class struggle**, derisively called *class warfare* by the wealthy, who want to maintain their wealth and power without challenge. The interests of the capital-owning middle and upper classes (the bourgeoisie and aristocracy) and those of the wage-labor working class (the proletariat) are in tension with each other; their relationship is nearing a breaking point.[4]

Thus **capitalism** is the problem in society, the thesis that needs to be changed. What is the root of the problem that Marx and Engels saw with capitalism?

The Contradiction in Capitalism

Capitalism socializes *production* (humans have to act cooperatively to produce efficiently) *but not ownership* (one or a few people own the product and control what happens to it). This is a built-in contradiction that can't last. The few individuals who control production compete with each other for profit, producing a **boom-bust cycle** (overproduction leading to depression) because each individual wants to increase his production hoping that the others will limit theirs, and no one is doing overall planning. The solution, according to Marxism, is to socialize ownership as well as production and to institute centralized planning to avoid the boom-bust cycle.

Figure 7.1. São Paulo, Brazil. On right, Ford Motor Company assembly plant; on left, favela, where some of the Ford workers live. Courtesy David Whitten Smith, 1 December 1988.

Exploitation and Oppression

Capitalization (gathering enough resources to build machines and factories) is based on exploitation and oppression. Workers would not put so much of the profit from their labor back into a factory that someone else owned if they had anything to say about it. They do not get a fair share of the return from the product they make. According to Marx, an owner does not give a worker the full value that she produced, but steals part of it to pay for expansion—which the capitalist or shareholder, not the worker, then owns.

Consider for example a modern leveraged buyout. The new owner, who borrowed money to buy the company, will need to pay off the loan. Where will he get the money to do that? Was the company's profit big enough before his purchase to add up in a few years to the value of the company? If so, was that a fair profit? If not, how is the profit made big enough? By reducing wages and increasing prices? Then workers and consumers pay for the owner to buy the company. Are workers and consumers paying for ownership to be concentrated in fewer and fewer hands?

Marx expected the problems of capitalism to keep getting worse until the whole system collapsed and the workers took over. Historically, rather than what Marx predicted, a sort of mixed economy developed that prevented the worst effects of capitalism—at least in the most developed countries. Now this mixed economy is being challenged by a new wave of overproduction caused by the expansion of manufacturing into previously nonindustrialized societies. These newly industrializing societies are producing not so much for themselves (since their wages are too low to allow their workers to purchase their own products) as for citizens of the old industrialized societies, whose wages have been historically high enough to sustain a mass market. However, the old industrialized societies are being "de-industrialized" as their factories are moved to low-wage countries. As a result, workers' wages in industrialized societies are also going down, threatening the market on which all the production depends. It is too soon to predict how the world economy will respond to this new situation.

Theory of Value

Many people before Marx, such as Adam Smith, had accepted a **theory of value** based on worker hours, although few made it as central and controversial as Marx and Engels did. This theory is one of the least accepted of Marx's key ideas. It states that the value of a product is based on the worker-hours used to produce it. Before dismissing the theory out of hand, one has to be reminded that in the late nineteenth century, with fewer options to choose from, it may have been more plausible than it seems today.

This definition makes sense until you ask about the value of the product *for you*. Three electric typewriters may take more human hours of labor to produce than one computer, but are they of more value to you? A lot of expensive typewriters found no buyers once personal computers became available. An ornate horse-drawn carriage may take more hours to produce than a small automobile, but who would trade the car for the carriage?

It might be more appropriate today to speak of the labor theory of *costs*. The human work used to produce it *does* affect the *cost* of the typewriter or carriage even if that may not determine its value to you or a prospective buyer. A movie studio might be willing to pay the cost of the carriage for a historical movie, while no one would want one for transportation. If something costs more than its value to *anyone*, the logical choice is not to produce it at all.

The roles of management and inventiveness also need to be included in a valid theory of value. Badly managed companies waste a lot of worker energy making or doing things that people don't need or want, or doing them inefficiently. So management deserves return, too. In that sense, as we will see in chapter 9: "Religious Social Thought," Pope John Paul II was correct to insist that *management* is *labor, not capital*.[5] But how much return does management deserve? In the United States in 2003, chief executives made twenty-four times as much as the average production worker (with production workers being among our most highly paid laborers). In Germany, chief executives made eight times as much as the average production worker.[6] Nine years later, in 2012 in the United States, CEOs of companies on the Standard and Poor 500 Index averaged a pay rate that was 354 times the wage earned by the average worker in those companies.[7]

Pope John Paul II, in his 1987 encyclical *Sollicitudo Rei Socialis*, criticized what he perceived to be dangerous ideologies: *communism* (as Americans would expect) and *capitalism* (which upset lots of Americans). It is worth reading his clear, personalist, and pithy account of the failings of the two worldviews, both of which base themselves solely on an *economic* understanding of the human person.[8]

Apparently less concerned about communism by November 2013, Pope Francis issued an "apostolic exhortation" (*Evangelii Gaudium*) in which he referred to global capitalism as "a new tyranny." He wrote:

> Today everything comes under the laws of competition and the survival of the fittest, where the powerful feed upon the powerless. As a consequence, masses of people find themselves excluded and marginalized: without work, without possibilities, without any means of escape.[9]

Less than a year earlier, in his New Year's Day message, Pope Benedict XVI had decried the increasing economic inequality caused by "unregulated financial capitalism."[10]

Ideologies

According to Marxism, the widely accepted "common sense" of a particular society—the key ideas of that era—are based on the economic and social conditions of industry, and are the ideas of those in power promoting their own selfish interests over the interests of others. Those with less power and influence tend to accept these assumptions without questioning them adequately. For example, the ideas of God and rewards in heaven keep the poor from complaining about their misery in the present, since their future reward will be great. Marx himself did not entirely blame the poor for taking this attitude. When he wrote that "religion is the opiate of the people," he meant both that people are being drugged by the powerful and that they drug themselves so as to hide from themselves the extent of their misery.

Marx called concepts such as God, heaven, and hell *ideologies*. (Note that **ideology** is a negative term here.) He and many other thinkers considered religion to be the worst deception, but not the only one. In fact, Marx's writings, especially *The German Ideology*, support the notion of a "hierarchy of ideologies" that people need to see through. Thus religious ideology is only one ideology within a hierarchy of ideologies (distorted representations of reality in human consciousness). In order of increasing "density," they are science, art, politics, law, morality, philosophy, and religion.

Dialectical Stages of History

Marx taught that the stages of history produced by dialectic are necessary. We cannot proceed from one to another without passing through the intermediate stages. Therefore the stage of capitalism cannot be avoided; it has to be passed through. It produces the economic efficiencies that alone make an abundant material product possible. This abundant product offers the material basis for communism, or the ideal state, in which everything is based on equality. Moreover, dialectical tensions expose the falsity of many of the ideologies that Marx lists above, especially by revealing the way they are used to alienate and disempower the worker.

Thus Marx reversed Hegel's belief that Spirit is the most important reality. Rather, Marx asserted that material things are the basis of all reality. Everything is determined by the state of economic production in a particular period. These are the five key stages that Marx thought society had passed through or was in the process of passing through: primitive communism, ancient slavery, feudalism, capitalism, **socialism**. The fifth stage—socialism—had not yet been reached, but society was on the verge of reaching it through an inevitable historical evolution from modern modes of production. Eventually socialism would give way to communism, which would be the final synthesis. After communism, there would be no further need for dialectic, since there would be no more structural tension. Within these stages, the prevailing mode of production produced characteristic results in seven areas (see table 7.1 for details).

Note in conclusion that, according to Marx, the capitalist organization of society alienates workers from themselves, their product, and fellow workers. Once the workers seize control, these problems will solve themselves. Unfortunately, almost a century of experience fails to support that optimistic claim, as we will now see.

Table 7.1.

	Primitive Communism	Ancient Slavery	Feudalism	Capitalism	Socialism
Prevailing mode of production	Hunting, gathering, fishing	Slave labor to increase private property (growth of agriculture and irrigation)	Peasant labor and use of animals for farming	Commerce and small-scale manufacturing	Mass production
Measure of wealth	Group welfare	Number of slaves and amount of land	Amount of land	Amount of money	Satisfaction of human needs
Ruling class	None	Slave-owners and emperor	Landholders and king	Entrepreneurs and capitalists (bourgeoisie)	Workers (proletariat)
Oppressed class	None	Slaves	Peasants	Factory workers and unemployed persons	None
Government	Communal rule	Emperor and open coercion	King and court of lords with personal loyalty to immediate superior	Capitalistic democracy or fascism	People's state governed by workers' party
Prevailing philosophy	Collectivism (What is good for the group?)	Pragmatic obedience to those with power (What is commanded?)	Loyalty to immediate superior in exchange for protection (What is expected by my overseer?)	Individualism or totalitarianism (What is good for me?)	Collectivism (What is good for the group?)
Prevailing religion	Tribal gods and personified natural forces	Worship of God, who is powerful and demanding	God works through the Church, His intermediary (Catholicism)	God deals directly with individuals (Protestantism)	No divine master (atheism)
Prevailing art form	Decoration of everyday objects	Palaces and monuments for emperors	Art for worship and for the pleasure of the king and court	Snobbish art for those with money and leisure	Art to advance collectivist attitudes and for edifying the life of the masses

Source: Ronald J. Glossop, *Confronting War: An Examination of Humanity's Most Pressing Problem*, 4th ed. (Jefferson, NC: McFarland & Company, 2001). Used by permission of McFarland & Company, Inc., Box 611, Jefferson, NC 28640.

SOCIAL AND INSTITUTIONAL DIMENSION

Marxist Societies and Applications

Other than control by the working class, Karl Marx laid out no plans for the structuring of a communist society or of the socialist society that the working class would build on the way to communism. He assumed the working class could do that for themselves, and that it would be a productive society able to meet the needs of the people and much more. The political parties that adopted his theories followed Marx in his optimistic approach, so that detailed plans for the structuring of socialist society were not put forth or developed by them either.

Historically, Marxism was appropriated by many different revolutionary movements. The best known was the attempt to apply his principles made by Russian revolutionaries, led by Vladimir Lenin.

First Application: Russia

Vladimir Lenin (1870–1924)

Marx and Engels had expected that their ideas would be implemented first in one of the advanced industrial countries like England or Germany. But after Marx's death, *Vladimir Lenin* took advantage of the Russian Revolution, much of whose early direction was in the hands of local workers' councils called *soviets*, to create a communist society in Russia, which at the time was a feudal society that had not reached the developed capitalist stage that Marx thought would be a necessary precursor to socialism and communism. Marx had insisted that you cannot "skip" any phase of history. Lenin countered that the movement of history, though inexorable, was too slow—power had to be seized through revolution by those who knew what needed to be done. He coined the phrase "**dictatorship of the proletariat**," signifying that a small group, or "vanguard," would lead the revolution of the masses, organize and educate them, and eventually become obsolete as socialism and then communism were fully realized.

Faced with a Russian civil war for the first five years (1917–1922), Lenin nationalized all enterprises and requisitioned all food produced in the countryside, giving priority to the government and army in its distribution. A famine ensued. When the "White Russian" opposition to the new government was finally defeated in 1922, Lenin united several republics to form the Union of Soviet Socialist Republics (Soviet Union).

Lenin and his comrade Leon Trotsky initially tried to bolster Russian communism by encouraging a *worldwide* revolution, especially in advanced capitalistic societies, founding the Third Communist International (Comintern) with the slogan, "Workers of the world, unite"; this project met with little success. Later in his life, Lenin would come to prefer a *one-state* socialism on the grounds that, since the rest of the world wasn't coming around, efforts should be focused on the country where the revolution had succeeded.

Lenin had to explain why the economic collapse that Marx expected had been delayed. He concluded that England and other European countries had been enabled to offer decent wages at home by exploiting their colonies overseas, in other words by exporting their exploitation. According to the Marxist lexicon, these countries were practicing **imperialism**. They had bribed their workers at home to cooperate with them at the expense of foreign workers. If you are stealing millions, you can afford to use thousands to buy a few lieutenants!

Imperialism

The modern Norwegian peace theoretician Johan Galtung[11] explains that every country has a "center" and a "periphery." Moreover, some countries are "central" countries and others are "peripheral" countries. Thus the elites at the "center" of a "central" country, say Britain, strike a deal with the elites at the "center" of a "peripheral" country, say India, to exploit Indian peasants and working class Indians (at the "periphery of the periphery") for the benefit of British elites. Indian elites get permission to skim off some of the wealth as it leaves India for Britain, and Britain promises to provide these local elites with military support so they can stay in power. (This strategy works well when you prop up local leaders who couldn't maintain power without your support.) The British elites then convince the British workers that this arrangement is in their interest by bribing them with better wages. Of course, they also expect British commoners to fight in wars designed to maintain this arrangement. Indian common people—the "periphery of the periphery"—are just out of luck.

The whole system begins to unravel when the common people in the central country (Britain) realize that they have more in common with the common people in the peripheral country (India) than with their own elites. British textile workers came to this conclusion when Gandhi visited England. Many American citizens came to this conclusion when President Reagan seemed poised to invade Nicaragua in the mid-1980s, in the lead-up to the U.S. invasion of Iraq in 2003, and with the threatened attack on Syria by the Obama administration in 2013.

Josef Stalin (1879–1953)

After Lenin died in 1924, a brief period of collective leadership ended when *Josef Stalin* seized control of the (Russian) Soviet Communist Party and held it until his death in 1953. Shifting attention decisively from *international* communism to the development of communism *in Russia*, Stalin created a totalitarian, centralized bureaucracy and suppressed alternative voices with merciless purges and draconian policies, executing or exiling many of his opponents and finally even assassinating Trotsky in Mexico because he dared to challenge Stalin's rise to power. His policies resulted in millions of deaths, but they quickly turned the Soviet Union into an industrial power in the years preceding World War II.

Stalin oppressed religions—until World War II moderated his domestic savagery. Once that war started and German troops were threatening Moscow, he needed all the help he could get.

> Joseph Stalin revived the Russian Orthodox Church to intensify patriotic support for the war effort and presented Russia as a defender of Christian civilization, because he saw the church had an ability to arouse the people in a way that the party could not and because he wanted western help.[12]

After World War II, the Soviet Union under Stalin consolidated communist control over much of Eastern Europe by treachery or force. Although several Eastern European communist governments then tried to gain freedom from Soviet control, only Yugoslavia succeeded. This experience of aggression made many people suspicious of Russian intentions in other cases. From the Russian standpoint, the satellite countries served as protection against a new invasion from the West.

By the end of Stalin's rule, critics concluded that the "communism" of the Soviet Union bore little resemblance to Marx's dream, having become, rather, either "**state capitalism**" or "bureaucratic socialism." The Polish psychiatrist Andrew Lobaczewski, who lived through the Stalinist era in Poland, characterized Stalin as a "spellbinder," the result of damage to the frontal areas of his brain at birth. Consequently, Stalin promoted Marxism as a counterfeit tradition, concealing the hidden tradition or agenda created by his own lust for power.

> Literature and news about him abounds in indications: brutal, charismatic, snake-charming; issuing of irrevocable decisions; inhuman ruthlessness, pathological revengefulness directed at anyone who got in his way; and egotistical belief in his own genius on the part of a person whose mind was, in fact, only average.[13]

Nikita Khrushchev (1894–1971)

After another brief period of collective rule, *Nikita Khrushchev* led Russia's program of "de-Stalinization" (1956). Khrushchev was "liberal" in many areas. He worked for peaceful coexistence with Western democracies. But he *increased* internal attacks on Christian *churches*, which had grown significantly stronger during World War II. During his presidency, Russia developed intercontinental ballistic missiles with nuclear warheads, launched Sputnik, the world's first artificial satellite, put the first human in orbit, established the first manned space station, and landed the first unmanned spacecraft on the moon. A panicked United States poured resources into space technology and raced to put a human on the moon, a race they won in the summer of 1969—Russia never did put humans on the moon.

Khrushchev's decision to send nuclear missiles to Cuba to defend against U.S. threats produced the **Cuban missile crisis** in late October 1962. After he and President Kennedy worked together, with concessions on both sides, to avoid a nuclear war, Soviet hard-liners forced his resignation.[14] The world can be grateful that he accepted his own demotion rather than yielding to Soviet generals who were pressing to launch a devastating nuclear war.

After his replacement, the high costs of the Cold War military created economic stress that none of his successors was able to manage.

Collapse of the Soviet Union

Mikhail Gorbachev (1931–) had the courage to say publicly what many Russian people believed privately: that the system wasn't working well and could not continue without radical reforms. He tried to develop a freer society and a more market-based economy in the Soviet Union, promoting *glasnost* (openness, literally "publicity") and *perestroika* (restructuring) and hoping to make needed reforms gradually while maintaining a communist government, but once he opened the door to change, he couldn't close it again—the Soviet Union lost control over most of Eastern Europe, the **Berlin Wall** was demolished in 1989, and the Soviet government (USSR) collapsed in 1991. Proponents of capitalism claimed that capitalism had won, but time will tell whether capitalism itself will eventually suffer a similar fate.

Ironically, the collapse of the Soviet Union does echo one of the key predictions of Marxism-Leninism: that the state would gradually "wither away." Even in the capitalist West, the traditional institutions of nineteenth- and twentieth-century republican government have been declining in importance—in favor of multinational corporations! Thus, in a new historical dialectic, the decline of traditional state institutions has tended to increase the power of capitalists and decrease the democratic power of common people. In the United States this became all the more evident in January 2010, when the Supreme Court ruled that corporations (and labor unions) could spend unlimited amounts of money to influence the outcome of elections.

The political repression and economic problems of several historical communist states have done much to destroy Marx's reputation in the Western world, as the Soviet bureaucracy often invoked Marx in their propaganda. Yet the post-communist changes in Russia have not brought the widespread prosperity that many had hoped for. Those who held power in the old system have found ways to hold power in the new system.

Second Application: China

Mao Zedong (1893–1976) led the Chinese Communist Party from 1937 until his death, defeating Chiang Kai-shek's non-communist government in 1949. Emphasizing a *rural-based* communism, his party broke with the Soviet Union. Without idealizing Chinese communism, it did move somewhat closer to Marxist ideals. There had been some burgeoning capitalism in China prior to the communist takeover, although not much. What may have been a key difference was the attitude of the population.

First, a society influenced by Confucian ideas tended toward the practical. This fit Marxist concerns better. The purpose of traditional Confucian education had been to produce dedicated and disinterested civil servants motivated by justice and compassion to govern a hierarchical society. The curriculum was based on classical texts and rituals. Mao rejected the rituals, texts, and hierarchical worldview of Confucianism while retaining the ideal of public service; he sought to improve the condition of the Chinese lower classes and women.[15] Second, it is often overlooked that, before communists took control in China, workers and peasants had no real standing at all as members of society. They were not even regarded as people, let alone as workers. Membership in the Communist Party gave many of them an identity and a common cause that they had been lacking. Paradoxically, this new worker-peasant identity and dignity caused problems for Mao's government. He wanted a communist society, but on his terms, and not too fast!

When China's **"great leap forward"** toward industrialization failed, resulting in widespread famine, Mao launched the **Cultural Revolution** (1966–1976) to reestablish his authority. He organized a "Red Guard," or militia of activist youth, to purge "counter-revolutionaries." Intense struggles produced a disastrous purge of leadership; the "moderate" Deng Xiaoping, who later became Mao's successor, was sent to work in a factory for "re-education."

Maoism targeted traditional Chinese religions, including their temples, personnel, and texts. In recent years hundreds of temples and churches have been closed, the Chinese Muslim Uighurs have been subjected to government repression, and Tibetan Buddhists have experienced severe persecution along with members of groups such as the Falun Gong.[16] For a fuller treatment of China's persecution of religions, see the section below: "Issues for Justice and Peace."

Deng Xiaoping (1904–1997) gained power when Mao died and gradually moved China toward a more capitalist economy. When students demonstrated nonviolently for broader human rights and more rapid liberation from government surveillance and repression, the government responded with a violent attack in June 1989 on the students gathered in Tiananmen Square, followed by countrywide repression.

China has weathered many changes in the post-Soviet world because it appropriated Lenin's openness to markets. With the influx of Western influence in the late 1970s after the death of Mao, the conflict between Western materialism and Confucian values became more apparent. As a result, there has been a revival of Confucianism in public education and the civil service system. The emphasis in China today on "making money" in a "free market" environment, along with the devaluing of scholars, is at serious odds with traditional Confucianism and Taoism[17] as well as with Chinese Marxist communism. Many question whether the Communist Party in China today is truly a Marxist party and a party of the people.

According to the party constitution the [Communist Party of China] adheres to Marxism–Leninism, Mao Zedong Thought, socialism with Chinese characteristics, Deng Xiaoping Theory, Three Represents [sic], and the Scientific Outlook on Development.[18]

Other Applications

North Korea

North Korea represents an extreme ideological form of Marxism patterned in many ways after Stalinism. It has even spawned a religion of its own called **Juche**, which inculcates absolute loyalty to the leader of North Korea and the official Party. Juche also emphasizes Korean military and economic *self-reliance*. Although Westerners may consider this a *cult* of the leader, those who follow it closely claim that it is not religious at all, but embodies the spirit of North Koreans. It does, however, follow the pattern of "one-state" socialism and is highly intolerant of outsiders as well as any perceived internal disloyalty: In December 2013 the seemingly highly placed uncle of head of state Kim Jong Un was executed on suspicion of planning a coup. North Korea's recent economic growth has been offset by its nuclear program and missile tests, which have brought international isolation and condemnation. The country is officially atheist, with more than 64 percent of the population classified as not religious. From 1945 through the Korean War (ending in 1953), many Christians fled to South Korea, and the North Korean government associated Christians with the United States, which was attacking them. Little can be known about the religious situation in North Korea today, but there are some signs of a religious revival despite government repression.[19]

Vietnam

Ho Chi Minh (1890–1969) led *Vietnam*'s struggle for national liberation from French, Japanese, and U.S. colonialism. Final victory came in 1975 after his death. Vietnam maintains a communist government, but with significant openness to a free-market economy.

Cuba

Fidel Castro (1927–) led the Cuban Revolution against the corrupt, pro-U.S. government of Fulgencio Batista, seizing control in 1959 and closing down Mafia-controlled gambling and prostitution. Faced with a boycott by international oil corporations, he nationalized the oil refineries to keep them running. Soon after, he nationalized all private enterprises, including private educational institutions, without compensating their owners, distributed large landholdings in small plots to individual farmers, and established a centrally planned agricultural and industrial economy. Most people became employees of the state. Most of the dispossessed rich fled to the United States, where they formed strong lobbies against Castro's government, which meanwhile introduced universal free education and health care, virtually eliminating Cuban illiteracy. The U.S. quickly responded with sanctions. In 1965 Cuba officially declared itself a communist state and developed an advanced centrally planned economy (in the face of rigid U.S. embargos and other pressures) that has given Cuba some of the best vital statistics of any country in the Americas—

better than those of the United States—though at the cost of limited freedoms and a low average standard of living.

Castro closed the schools for one year in 1961 in order to send urban school-children into the rural areas to teach the population to read and write, in one stroke virtually eliminating illiteracy and helping urban children learn about the hard life of rural Cuba. Education became free at all levels, including universities and professional schools. When the new system began to produce more physicians than the health system needed, Castro established a block health program that assigned a physician and nurse to each block in Havana and other cities. He also began to send physicians to volunteer in other Third World countries.

The planned economy tries to minimize the use of money by providing essentials either for free or at highly subsidized rates. Education and health care are free. Housing costs 10 percent of one's monetary income. There is a ration book for basic food, adequate for perhaps two weeks of food each month at a cost of about $2. For a time, there was also a clothes ration. The government traded sugar to the Soviet Union for petroleum and other needs. U.S. sanctions made other trade difficult, but Cuba managed fairly well until the Soviet Union fell. For the rest of the story, see the case study below: "Will Marxism or Communism Survive?"

MARXIST THEORY TODAY

There is still today an active interest in both socialism and Marxism in Western Europe—despite the collapse of East European communist governments—although necessarily modified in light of the socioeconomic climate and realities of the twenty-first century. Many countries practice a modified form of socialism in terms of benefits for the poor and the elderly. Some question whether these programs can remain effective and sustainable, but they have for many years been a success story supporting a socialist outlook, if not a Marxist one. For example, parts of Europe and Scandinavia have adopted more moderate forms of Marx's views leading to a socialist state, although they have rejected Lenin's dictatorship of the proletariat.

Criticisms of Marxism

Critics from the ruling class in capitalist societies and from elites who dominate the global market reject any form of socialism, whether liberal, democratic socialist, or Marxist. These criticisms come from the Right, and most often from those with power and privilege. Some aspects of Marxism have also been criticized from the Left. In particular, democratic socialists and social democrats reject the idea that socialism can be accomplished only through class conflict and violent revolution.

Today some critics question the theoretical and historical validity of "class" as an analytic construct or as a political actor. Similarly, the Marxist stages of history and theory of social evolution have been critiqued. Some argue that class is not the most fundamental inequality in history and call attention to patriarchy (gender) or race.

Marxists respond that these inequalities are linked to class and therefore will largely cease to exist after the formation of a classless society. Political "realists" retort that, since human nature is naturally self-seeking, it will reproduce a class society no matter how thoroughgoing a revolution has been; the best we can do is to manage conflict using the societies and the human nature that we have.

Will Marxism or Communism Survive?

While there are functioning communist parties in over one hundred countries, those parties are part of the ruling coalition in only about twelve countries, and only four countries—China, Vietnam, Cambodia, and Cuba—currently claim to be Marxist. North Korea says it is inspired by Juche rather than by Marxism. China and Vietnam have moved toward joining the global free market. Cuba describes itself as influenced both by Marxism and by "Fidelism."

Case Study: Cuba

When I (David) visited Cuba for the third time, in the fall of 2013, I remarked to a host that nothing in Cuba looked anything like the slum housing I had seen in Central America and South Africa: flimsy structures of scrap wood, mud brick, and cardboard. He responded that the government destroys such housing and replaces it with substantial homes. The ones I saw appeared to be made of cement blocks and stucco. These homes may be crowded, however, and they do not always survive Cuban hurricanes.

When the Soviet Union failed, Cuba handled its economic crisis by declaring a "special period" and used rationing to be sure that everyone's most basic needs were met. Cubans lost weight together. Unable to afford petroleum-based agricultural inputs like artificial fertilizers, herbicides, and pesticides, Cuba switched to organic agriculture. To earn foreign exchange, Cuba reinstated the tourist industry, which had been allowed to lapse. To manage tourism, Cuba introduced a dual currency: Cuban pesos for Cubans, dollars—later "convertible" pesos—for foreigners. One U.S. dollar is valued at about 25 Cuban pesos, but it trades approximately one-to-one with convertible pesos. Convertible pesos are necessary to shop in the special stores carrying imported goods for tourists. Unfortunately, the result of the dual currency was to "invert the social pyramid": physicians and teachers earn the cash equivalent of about $30 a month, and the average Cuban earns about $20—plus free education, free health care, half of their month's food for $2, and subsidized housing for about $2 to $3 (10 percent of their monetary income). But people who work for the tourist trade earn much more in tips: a bellhop might get a $1 tip—a day's wage for a physician—for carrying one tourist's bags to the hotel room. Some teachers were choosing to drive taxicabs, causing teacher shortages. (The physicians, I was told, tended to be more committed.) At the end of 2013, Raul Castro committed Cuba to eliminating the dual currency, but it remains to be seen how he will manage to do that while maintaining Cuba's free education and health care: as fewer

Cubans are employed by the government, some form of taxation of the privately employed will be necessary to maintain these social services.

During my visit I (David) became aware of Cubans' considerable dissatisfaction with their daily lives. If one's salary and benefits are fixed without regard to one's output, there is not much incentive to perform well. When I asked my hosts whether Cubans appreciated their free education and health care, I was told, "The three greatest successes of the revolution are universal free education, universal free health care, and sports. The three greatest failures of the revolution are breakfast, lunch, and dinner." People aren't sick or studying every day, but they do have to eat every day, so food has a higher priority for them. Many Cubans depend on dollars sent by relatives overseas, while others engage in some modest private enterprise; some steal what they have produced above their daily quota and sell it on the black market.

One informant maintained that the current government is most strongly supported by the rural poor, since it has substantially improved their lives. But Cuba's centralized planning leaves many others feeling disempowered, and there is a striking lack of consumer goods along with stores to sell them. Cubans may expect change to make their country like Miami, but it could equally well make it like Haiti.

New Socialism in Latin America

Many Latin Americans still believe Marxist criticisms of capitalism. Globalization and structural adjustment policies of the International Monetary Fund have put pressure on Third World governments. A new wave of resistance to U.S.-controlled capitalism and "free trade" has led a number of Latin American countries to elect socialist leaders and governments—a movement that the late Hugo Chávez of Venezuela (1954–2013) called a "**Bolivarian Revolution.**"

Chávez used Venezuelan oil money to build housing for the poor. He brought in teams from Cuba for a major literacy campaign. When the United States helped sponsor a coup to overthrow his rule in 2002, a massive demonstration by Venezuelans brought him back to power.[20] Then in 2004, when U.S. and Venezuelan elites forced a referendum seeking to end his term in office, Chávez triumphed easily. Until his death in 2013, he worked to form networks with other socialist-leaning leaders in Argentina, Brazil, Bolivia, Chile, Cuba, and Nicaragua.

Will Capitalism Survive?

Those who support free-market capitalism, with as few regulations as possible, claim that the collapse of old-style communism has proved that capitalism is "right." But the world economic system shows major signs of strain. The cheap hydrocarbons, especially petroleum and natural gas, which have fueled an unprecedented expansion of human power are at or near their peak production, while global industrialization is rapidly increasing demand for energy.[21] Pollution resulting from their use in addition to unsustainable depletion of other resources, including forests, soils, fresh water, and natural food stocks, threaten potentially disastrous global changes in climate and habitat that could lead to major social collapse.[22] Competition for the control of energy resources has already spawned war by the United States against Iraq, and has generated intense hatred of the United States, leading to terrorist attacks.

The U.S. economy and the international financial system depend on foreign countries enabling huge U.S. deficits in its balance of payments by buying U.S. Treasury Bonds—a sort of Ponzi or pyramid scheme. American consumers have been financing their spending spree by withdrawing equity from an inflated housing bubble under the lure of low interest rates. Many of these loans have been short-term; refinancing at much higher interest rates could bring down the house of cards. (Note that we first wrote these sentences in the spring of 2007, just before the housing crash. Other "bubbles" are credit card debt and student loan debt.) As cheap, exploited global labor and widespread technology multiply product and weaken markets, the "boom and bust" cycle that Marx saw as the Achilles' heel of capitalism looks increasingly dangerous. Only time will tell whether one of the two classical systems was "right," or whether they both contained fatal flaws.

ISSUES FOR JUSTICE AND PEACE

Religious Persecution

Marx did not plan to attack churches: he believed that, as the workers realized their power and took over the state, the "opium" of religion would no longer be needed because there would be no more misery. But leaders who were trying to introduce Marxism into their respective countries soon found that religion was more tenacious than their theories had led them to believe. In the previous chapter, we considered how indigenous groups responded to colonial efforts to convert them to Christianity. Here we will consider how major religions in Marxist-oriented nation-states responded to Marxist efforts to close them down and enforce atheism.

The Soviet Union

Lenin was actively hostile to religion, not only because the dominant Orthodox Church initially supported his adversaries in Tsarist Russia, but also because his experience led him to consider all religions to be "organs of bourgeois reaction, used for the protection of the exploitation and the stupefaction of the working class."[23] According to Marx's thought, the Russian society of the time was not yet ripe for socialism, to a large extent because of the endurance of religious institutions. Therefore, when the new revolutionary leaders in Russia bypassed the capitalist stage and forced the country directly into socialism on the way to communism, they also attacked the Orthodox Church, other churches, and Islam for resisting this radical change. Severe persecution followed, with large numbers of bishops, priests, and lay leaders executed, churches and mosques closed, restrictions placed on those which remained open, properties and lands confiscated, charitable works taken over by the government, and widespread atheistic propaganda disseminated.[24]

When Nazi Germany invaded the Soviet Union, Stalin realized that Christianity and other religions strongly influenced their followers, so he relaxed his attack on the churches and allowed some that he had closed to reopen in order to rally his people behind Soviet resistance to Germany. After Stalin died, Khrushchev (premier from 1958 to 1964) led a campaign to denounce Stalin's crimes. Noting that the churches had taken advantage of the wartime relaxation of persecution to grow in numbers and influence, Khrushchev resumed the campaign against religion, closing churches, monasteries, and religious schools and increasing antireligious propaganda. Foreign criticism caused the campaign to wax and wane until the final fall of communism in Russia, at which time religion strikingly revived.[25]

China

Communist China is officially committed to atheism. Fenggang Yang, a professor of sociology at Purdue University, divides Communist China's campaigns against religion into four periods. His study helps us understand how religions can survive major state persecution aimed at destroying them.

1. 1949 to 1957—the period of "co-optation and control." The Communist Party established "patriotic religious associations" for the five major religions: Buddhism, Taoism, Islam, Catholicism, and Protestantism. (The party treated Catholics and Protestants as two distinct groups, and created an association for each.) Other religions were suppressed; Confucianism was not treated as a religion. The government tried to enforce a "three-self movement": self-rule, self-support, and self-propagation, deporting foreign religious leaders and breaking ties to foreign bodies such as the Vatican and U.S. mission bodies. Many native Chinese religious leaders were prosecuted on the pretext that they were landlords or dangers to the revolution.[26]
2. 1957 to 1966—the period of "socialist transformation." Central planning tried to increase economic productivity. Clergy were seen as parasites: worship and scripture reading wasted what could be productive time. Protestant denominations were eliminated in favor of a single Protestant patriotic association. Many churches and mosques were closed or destroyed and church properties confiscated.[27]
3. 1966 to 1979—the period of "eradication." Mao unleashed the Red Guards (zealous young communists) on a campaign of destruction called the Great Proletarian Cultural Revolution. Red Guards destroyed churches, religious objects, and sacred books; all religious venues were forced to close, and religion was totally banned. Mao and his Little Red Book of sayings became quasi objects of worship. But in fact real religion went underground.[28] In theory, the 1975 constitution granted religious freedom to all, but this was not observed in practice; quite the contrary.

4. 1979 to 2009—the period of "strengthening the regulation." When Mao died and Deng Xiaoping gained control, he abandoned efforts to eradicate the five major religious groups, realizing that these efforts had failed; nevertheless, he subjected religions to highly restrictive regulations. The Falun Gong movement was proscribed.[29]

Recently, alarmed by rapid Christian growth, the government has cautiously favored Buddhism, Taoism, folk religions, and Confucianism.[30]

Examining how the churches have reacted to these conditions, Yang imagines that churches are seeking adherents in a marketplace. He distinguishes three "markets of religion" from which consumers can choose:

> A *red market* of religion consists of all legal (officially permitted) religious organizations, believers, and religious activities.[31] . . . A *black market* of religion consists of all illegal (officially banned) religious organizations, believers, and religious activities. . . . A *gray market* of religion consists of all religious and spiritual organizations, practitioners, and activities with ambiguous legal status.[32]

The gray market includes "folk religion, popular religion, primal religion, quasi religion, New Age, occults, magic, yoga, client and audience cults, and/or new spiritualities."[33] It also includes illegal activities quietly carried on by the red market churches. The Chinese government attempted to destroy the black market and to control the red market in ways that would constantly weaken it, but found the gray market harder to deal with. The more China restricted the red market, the more the black market grew, despite its high cost to adherents. Beyond the very committed willing to risk these costs, the rest of the population couldn't do without religion entirely—they found substitutes in the gray market, which became so amorphous and widespread that it was impossible to destroy or control. Yang concludes:

> The social reality is the emerging market economy in the increasingly globalized society, yet the religious policy was initiated around 1957–58, when China was just beginning to experiment with the central-planning economy in a totalitarian society. To apply Marxist terms, the superstructure, which includes ideology, has become incompatible with the economic basis today. The result is that the outdated religious policy has rendered itself ineffective in controlling religion, all the while antagonizing the Chinese populace and the world community. The religious policy has become one of the liabilities in China's stride for modernization and for entering the global stage. If the restrictive regulation persists in the current form of constraints and suppression, I would not be surprised if the religious policy becomes the last straw that breaks the camel's back.[34]

Marxist Wars and Violence

Traditionally, Marxists believed that war was necessary for workers to seize power from the owner class. "You can't make an omelet without breaking eggs," they said. But some see war now as much too dangerous in a nuclear world, which gives them second thoughts.

In the early 1980s, the Solidarity labor union movement in Poland used nonviolence successfully until the government cracked down with martial law. Then, many people said that nonviolence was impractical: the Poles had tried it and it "didn't work." As it turned out, they spoke too soon. By 1991, not only Polish but also East European communism had been overcome, mostly nonviolently.

Beginning in 1979, the Soviet Union supplied troops and equipment to support a pro-Soviet government in Afghanistan, which was threatened by civil war. Various internal and external groups violently attacked this Afghan government and its Soviet supporters. The U.S. secretly supplied Osama bin Laden and other resistance fighters. Over time Soviet violence and technology proved inadequate to maintain control. After the Soviets left in 1989, the Afghans continued fighting each other, until order was restored by Islamic extremists called Taliban ("students").

U.S. Supported Violence against Marxists

In Latin America, wealthy elites tend to call anyone who threatens their privileges a "communist" or "Marxist." Working with the poor, as advocated, for example, by Christian liberation theologians, is considered threatening. But Christian liberation theologies are very different from Marxism. Sometimes liberation theologians and Marxists appreciate each others' passion for justice. Sometimes in Latin America, communists undermine the work of liberation theology because they perceive it as competing with them for power. They also argue that partial alleviation of misery prevents people from carrying out the full revolution that is necessary to create a socialist government and society.

Nicaragua

U.S. pressure in Nicaragua, especially terrorist attacks by U.S.-financed "Contras," led to an electoral defeat for the Marxist **Sandinista Party** in 1990. But the Sandinista Party remained a major political force in Nicaragua, despite the fact that Sandinistas held a minority of seats in the legislature and lost several presidential elections. In 2007, as a result of a split between conservative parties, Daniel Ortega, the former president of communist Nicaragua, was reelected president, a position which he still holds as of early 2014. From his first to his second administration, he moderated his position from Marxism-Leninism to democratic socialism, while allying himself with Hugo Chávez of Venezuela and the Bolivarian movement.

Cuba

The U.S. has been trying to isolate Cuba's Marxist government by maintaining an economic embargo against Cuba that has been in place since the time of President Kennedy (1960). The embargo is not supported by other countries, however, which resent what they consider to be interference in their foreign affairs. Several groups of Cuban refugees strongly support the embargo, but other Cuban refugees believe it is time for the U.S. to accept Cuba's right to decide its own form of government. Pope John Paul II visited Cuba in 1998 against the desires of the U.S. government, seeking to promote a Catholic religious revival on the island.

A number of groups in the United States challenge the Cuba boycott, notably the Pastors for Peace, who since 1992 have been organizing and leading illegal trips to Cuba by pastors and other interested people bringing supplies and labor to help Cuba cope with the effects of the U.S. embargo. Pastors for Peace publicize and explain the embargo so that Americans understand its impact and will pressure their government to end it. In late 2013, when a one-hundred-ton shipment of humanitarian aid had just reached Cuba, a codirector of the organization said, "By not seeking or accepting a license from the U.S. government to collect and deliver aid to our brothers and sisters in Cuba, we prove that the U.S. blockade is not merely unjust and immoral, as the United Nations has affirmed overwhelmingly year after year, but it is also genocidal and an economic war against the people of Cuba."[35] The U.S. government is indicting a number of those who have traveled to Cuba on such missions—among them people bringing relief supplies, including medicines— and threatens to punish them with large fines and up to ten years in prison.

U.S. Attacks on Socialism

There is growing suspicion that American interventions worldwide have been specifically designed to counter—that is, destroy—socialist economies and governments. U.S. sanctions on Cuba are a prime example. Our relations with North Korea are another.

Yugoslavia

During the Cold War, Yugoslavia had one of the most successful economies of Eastern Europe. When the Berlin Wall fell in 1989, the United States canceled its foreign aid to Yugoslavia. U.S. policies then helped to destabilize the Yugoslav society; these policies included the sponsorship of "democratic" leaders, which in practice meant secessionist leaders, resulting in the country's dismemberment. The U.S. bombing of Serbia compounded the destruction. If one includes Kosovo, whose 2008 declaration of independence is rejected by Serbia and controversial internationally, the former Socialist Federal Republic of Yugoslavia has divided into seven separate countries.

Iraq

The U.S. invasion and occupation of Iraq from 2003 until 2011[36] was in practice a huge experiment in dismantling a socialist economy. The first American appointed to administer the U.S. occupation after the 2003 invasion, General Jay Garner, was dismissed after a month on the job because he "wanted free elections and rejected an imposed program of privatization."[37] His successor, Paul Bremer, put nearly all the government-owned businesses up for sale. Before Iraqi leader Saddam Hussein invaded Iran in 1980, Iraq had benefited from one of the most successful Arab economies anywhere, with widespread high-quality health care, education, affordable housing, and food. Eight years of war with Iran followed by thirteen years of crippling U.S. sanctions left the country devastated. The 2003 U.S. invasion and subsequent occupation have had even more disastrous effects.

Iran

Iran, with its substantial nationalized oil reserves, is another case in point. Motivated by its own geopolitical considerations plus heavy pressure from the Israel lobby, which also pushed hard for the war on Iraq, the U.S. has been exerting tremendous pressure on Iran over its alleged "nuclear program," on the assumption that Iran intends to produce nuclear weapons, which Iran denies, maintaining that its nuclear program is entirely peaceful. Since 1979, the U.S. has imposed heavy economic sanctions on Iran, recently intensified, which are known to be imperiling the middle class (for example, by dramatically devaluing the Iranian currency), to say nothing of the poor.

The election in 2013 of the liberal Hassan Rouhani as president helped to strengthen the call by many Americans for diplomacy with Iran rather than war. Showcasing the nuclear issue with Iran seems disingenuous to those who are aware of Israel's sizable nuclear arsenal, estimated by journalist Seymour Hersh in November 2006 to consist of about 600 weapons.[38] It is worth noting that Iran is on the list of seven countries deemed to be legitimate targets of the United States that was drawn up by the neoconservative Project for a New American Century after September 11: Iraq, Syria, Lebanon, Libya, Somalia, Sudan, and Iran.

Economic Coercion

In addition to military coercion, modern forms of imperialism make use of economic pressures. John Perkins introduces us to "**economic hit men**":

> Economic hit men (EHMs) are highly paid professionals who cheat countries around the globe out of trillions of dollars. They funnel money from the World Bank, the U.S. Agency for International Development (USAID), and other foreign "aid" organizations into the coffers of huge corporations and the pockets of a few wealthy families who control the planet's natural resources. Their tools include fraudulent financial reports, rigged elections, payoffs, extortion, sex, and murder. They play a game as old as empire, but one that has taken on new and terrifying dimensions during this time of globalization.
>
> I should know; I was an EHM.[39]
>
> There were two primary objectives of my work. First, I was to justify huge international loans that would funnel money back to MAIN and other U.S. companies (such as Bechtel, Halliburton, Stone & Webster, and Brown & Root) through massive engineering and construction projects. Second, I would work to bankrupt the countries that

received those loans (after they had paid MAIN and the other U.S. contractors, of course) so that they would be forever beholden to their creditors, and so they would present easy targets when we needed favors, including military bases, UN votes, or access to oil and other natural resources.[40]

A condition of such loans is that engineering and construction companies from our own country must build all these projects.[41]

According to Perkins, when economic hit men failed to convince local elites to cooperate, "jackals" came behind them to assassinate the troublesome leaders; he mentions specifically Jaime Roldós of Ecuador and Omar Torrijos of Panama. When the troublesome leaders proved impossible to assassinate, as did Saddam Hussein with his multiple doubles, U.S. elites found pretexts to send in the Marines, as in Panama, or the entire military, as in Iraq. The most spectacular failure has been Cuba, where Fidel Castro has survived numerous U.S. attempts to assassinate him, and the resolution to the Cuban missile crisis included a U.S. pledge not to invade Cuba. But Cuba has been neutralized by U.S. sanctions, which have made it impossible for Cuba to create an economy prosperous enough to tempt other nations to follow its example.

SUMMARY

Outraged at the sufferings caused by nineteenth-century industrial capitalism, Karl Marx identified such serious problems as the alienation of workers from themselves, their product or service, and their fellow workers, together with the instability of the system's anarchic planning, which leads to periodic crises and the eventual pauperization of all but a few mega-industrialists. He predicted that the system was unsustainable and would collapse, ushering in a new stage of society directed by workers.

Marxism as it was *practiced* in the Soviet Union and Eastern Europe proved to be an inadequate answer to the problems Marx raised. Whether global capitalism as practiced under the leadership of the United States will be more successful in the long run remains to be seen. But Marx's *criticisms* retain their force for people in many parts of the world. In chapter 9: "Religious Social Teachings" and chapter 10: "Liberation Theologies," we will offer for comparison with Marx's criticisms other criticisms of global capitalism, along with alternative proposals for solutions.

KEY TERMS

alienation	capitalism
Berlin Wall	capitalization
Bolivarian Revolution	class struggle
boom-bust cycle	communism

The Communist Manifesto   ideology
Cuban missile crisis   imperialism
Cultural Revolution   Juche
Das Kapital   Sandinista Party
dialectical materialism   socialism
dictatorship of the proletariat state capitalism
economic hit men   theory of value
great leap forward   thesis, antithesis, synthesis

DISCUSSION QUESTIONS

1. Which of the figures in this chapter would you describe as a spokesperson or actor for justice and peace? On what grounds?
2. Is Marxism still a significant force in the world? What do you think is good about Marxism and socialism? What do you think is bad about them?
3. Do you think that worldwide capitalism is facing serious trouble, or can it overcome its problems and prosper in the long term? Can it do so in a way which increases justice and reduces poverty?

SUGGESTIONS FOR FURTHER READING

A Marx Bibliography, www.sussex.ac.uk/Users/sefd0/bib/marx.htm (accessed 17 March 2014). *There is an enormous and reliable set of documents on the World Wide Web about all forms of Marxism (as long as you stick to the original thinkers!). This website has everything you could want online, and then refers you to the other academic Marx sites. It is helpful in its diversity, its use of online materials (though one should check the translators), and its listing of contemporary debates and issues.*
Bottomore, ed. *A Dictionary of Marxist Thought.*
Brecht. *The Caucasian Chalk Circle.*
Clark and Holquist. *Mikhail Bakhtin.*
Domhoff. *Changing the Powers That Be: How the Left Can Stop Losing and Win.*
———. *Who Rules America?*
Gramsci. *Prison Notebooks,* 3 vols.
Kropotkin. *Memoirs of a Revolutionist.*
Lash. *A Matter of Hope: A Theologian's Reflections on the Thought of Karl Marx.*
Leigh. "General Sacked by Bush Says He Wanted Early Elections."
Lenin. *The Lenin Anthology.*
———. *What Is to Be Done?*
Luxemburg. *Reflections and Writings.*
Marx and Engels. *The Communist Manifesto.*
———. *Karl Marx: Selected Writings.*
———. *Karl Marx, Frederick Engels: Collected Works.*
———. *The Marx-Engels Reader.*
McLellan. *Karl Marx: His Life and Thought.*
———. *Marx before Marxism.*
Perkins. *Confessions of an Economic Hit Man.*
Solzhenitsyn. *The Gulag Archipelago 1918–1956.*
———. *One Day in the Life of Ivan Denisovich.*
Trotsky. *The Revolution Betrayed.*

8

The Israeli-Palestinian Conflict

Then Moses went up from the plains of Moab to Mount Nebo, the headland of Pisgah which faces Jericho, and the LORD showed him all the land. . . . The LORD then said to him, "This is the land which I swore to Abraham, Isaac and Jacob that I would give to their descendants."

—Deuteronomy 34:1–4

Glory to (Allah) Who did take His servant for a journey by night from the Sacred Mosque to the farthest Mosque [Masjid Al-Aqsa in Jerusalem], whose precincts We did bless.[1]

—Quran 17:11

"Our ancestors worshiped on this mountain; but you people say that the place to worship is in Jerusalem." Jesus said to her, "Believe me, woman, the hour is coming when you will worship the Father neither on this mountain nor in Jerusalem. . . . The hour is coming, and is now here, when true worshipers will worship the Father in Spirit and truth. . . . God is Spirit, and those who worship him must worship in Spirit and truth."

—John 4:20–24

You will know the truth, and the truth will make you free.

—John 8:32

PURPOSE OF THIS CHAPTER

Now that we have looked at Muslim, Jewish, Christian, and Marxist worldviews, we can consider a current struggle involving all four: the Israeli-Palestinian conflict. This chapter is intended as a case study to determine whether understanding various worldviews helps us to understand and resolve conflicts. As you read the following account, consider which of the points would be most significant to each of the following groups. (These descriptions are an attempt to present their positions as they themselves might state them. Endnotes suggest who might hold each position, and in some cases point out problems with their descriptions.)

1. A *Political Zionist Jew* whose main concern is to create, with the support of foreign world powers, a Jewish state where the indigenous non-Jewish population has been transferred out so that the Jews of the world can be separate and safe;[2]
2. A *Socialist Zionist Jew* whose main concern is to create a Marxist-style classless society where Jews can labor together, as on a kibbutz, until eventually they form the critical mass needed to establish a worker-controlled Jewish state and society;[3]
3. A *Cultural Zionist Jew* who doesn't care who runs the state so long as they can live their Jewish life fully in the land where their religious tradition originated, in peaceful cooperation with non-Jewish citizens of the same state;[4]
4. A *Religious Zionist Jew* (seeking a single state for Jews only) who believes that G-d wants Jews to "redeem" every square inch of the land that G-d gave them, driving out the non-Jewish inhabitants, who shouldn't be there anyway;[5]
5. A *Religious Anti-Zionist Jew* (opposed to a Jewish State of Israel) who believes that forming a Jewish state anywhere before the messiah comes is an act of rebellion against G-d who, in his inscrutable designs, has assigned the Jewish nation to dispersal ("the Diaspora") until the end times, and who will Himself establish such a "state" if and when he chooses to;[6]
6. A *Zionist Jewish peace activist* (seeking a two-state solution) who fears that Judaism is losing its soul and violating its prophetic heritage by illegally occupying Palestinian land and oppressing Christian and Muslim Palestinians;[7]
7. An *anti-Zionist Jewish peace activist* (seeking a single, secular state for all of its citizens) who sees **Zionism** as a Western colonialist, imperialist power and land grabber, which uses the Holocaust as justification for ethnic cleansing and, by oppressing Palestinians, impoverishes diverse Jewish traditions, betrays Jewish principles of justice and peace, and endangers the future ethical survival of Judaism;[8]
8. An *unaffiliated Israeli Jew* who just wants to raise a family in peace;[9]
9. An *ideological Islamist Palestinian* who believes that Palestine is an Islamic waqf (religious endowment) which no human can "give away" to "infidels" and which, by rights, ought to have an Islamic government based on Islamic law;[10]
10. A *non-ideological Palestinian supporter of Hamas* who doesn't care whether Palestine has an Islamic government based on Islamic law, but is disgusted by the corruption in the Palestinian Authority and observes that Hamas has worked harder to meet the basic needs of Palestinians.[11]

11. A *Palestinian supporter of the Palestinian Authority* who would prefer a secular, bi-national state offering full citizenship and freedom to Muslims, Jews, and Christians, but would accept a two-state solution in the pre-1967 **Occupied Palestinian Territories** if that were the only option;[12]

12. A *Palestinian supporter of Al Mubadara*, the Palestinian National Initiative, a pro-democracy, nonviolent grassroots movement, who would support two states or one state with equal rights for all;[13]

13. An *unaffiliated Palestinian* who grieves and resents the loss of his or her ancestral land and home, but above all just wants to raise a family in peace as a citizen with equal standing;[14]

14. An *American Christian Zionist* who is eager to create the circumstances required for the return of Jesus, and who either doesn't notice the Palestinians or considers them an obstacle to the fulfillment of God's plan;[15]

15. An *American peace activist, Jewish or non-Jewish,* who feels outraged by Israeli oppression of Palestinians;[16]

16. An *average non-Jewish American* who has Jewish friends but no Palestinian friends and who knows little about the situation largely because the mainstream media have failed to provide accurate information;[17]

17. An *American politician* who wants the United States to control the oil-rich Middle East and, wanting to be elected, fears the political power of the American Israel Public Affairs Committee (AIPAC);[18]

18. An *Israeli politician* who seeks election in a society marked by deep fears for survival and safety with a broad range of contradictory, deeply held convictions, with numerous settlements in occupied Palestinian territory that are heavily populated by religious Zionist Jews;[19]

19. A *Palestinian politician* who, given the political divisions between Hamas and the Palestinian Authority, has had almost nothing positive to offer his people in return for their support;[20]

20. A *psychopath* seeking an appropriate counterfeit tradition in support of his or her quest for political or economic power.[21]

Despite the basic *scholarly* agreement on the main historical facts, there is *popular* ignorance or confusion about those same facts. The American mainstream media have not reported the facts accurately or completely. There is also widespread disagreement about which facts are *significant* for understanding the problem and *why* they are significant. And we often don't know the *motivation* of the actors: *why* they did what they did. Since the issue makes a great deal of difference for the people involved, there is a strong temptation to lie, exaggerate, and omit or obscure inconvenient facts. Some people are poorly informed or confused. Even eyewitness accounts, documents, and memoirs of leaders can be misleading. In addition to *deliberate* distortion, people's *unconscious* presuppositions lead them to notice, remember, and emphasize certain realities and ignore, forget, or discount others. People *trust* reports that favor their interests and disbelieve reports that do not. History is a mystery puzzle inviting us to test whether the purported data are true, whether they adequately represent the whole reality, and whether the conclusions drawn from them are justified. Understanding the actors' worldviews helps us to discern their motivations and to anticipate their actions.

PALESTINE-ISRAEL: GEOGRAPHY AND HISTORY
TO 1967

Historical Palestine

Humans have lived in Canaan, the area now called Israel-Palestine, for about five hundred thousand years.[22] Some four thousand years ago, wandering Hebrew tribes and, a half-millennium later (around 1300 BCE), their Israelite descendants, moved into Canaan, sharing the territory with several other groups who had long inhabited it, and settling in poorer areas between strong Canaanite city-states which were often allied to Egypt.

For about four and a half centuries, from about 1000 BCE, the Israelites (divided for most of that period into two rival kingdoms) exercised primary political control over the highlands to the west of the Jordan River, while contesting the highlands to the east of the Jordan with other tribal groups. Then they came under the rule of foreign empires. At the beginning of the Common Era, they were living under Roman rule and hoping for a leader to be anointed by God—a "messiah"—who would defeat foreign rule and restore their independence. Romans called these people "Jews" after **Judea**, their main province.

A Galilean Jew named Jesus made a deep impression on his contemporaries with his teaching and healing. After the Roman occupiers crucified him, his followers claimed that they had seen him risen from the dead and that he was the awaited "messiah," but that destroying Roman rule and restoring Jewish independence was not his role. Their energetic preaching and growth produced a reformed Judaism that came to be called Christianity. Their Arab descendants in Palestine form one of the three main religious groups in the current struggle.

When the Jewish community revolted against Roman rule in 66 CE and again in 132 CE, their limited political power was destroyed, they were forbidden to live in their capital, Jerusalem, and many of their leading citizens were scattered outside their homeland. However, large numbers of Jews, especially farmers, remained in Palestine along with pagans, Samaritans, and Christians.[23] When the Roman Empire embraced Christianity, Palestine came under Christian control centered in Constantinople—the capital of the Byzantine Empire—and much of the population converted to Christianity.

Arab Muslims gained political sovereignty in the early seventh century. Over the course of several centuries, Arabic replaced Aramaic as the common language, and many inhabitants converted to Islam. From the late seventh century until the mid-twentieth century (almost thirteen centuries), the people and culture of the country were predominantly Arabic-speaking and Islamic, although local farmers referred to themselves as Muslims and "fellahin" (farmers), reserving the term "Arab" for the Bedouin of the desert.[24] Generally an Arab is someone whose first language is Arabic.

From 1516 until the end of World War I, Palestine was a province of the Muslim **Ottoman Empire** with its capital in Istanbul (formerly Constantinople), Turkey. By the later Ottoman period, the indigenous Palestinians, who traced themselves back to the original inhabitants of the land (first Canaanites, then Hebrews) as well as to the seventh-century Muslim conquerors, were "deeply entrenched in their country." The population was concentrated in about twenty "cities and towns" as well as "some eight hundred villages and hamlets, built of stone." The majority of the people were farmers, with urban dwellers "engaged in commerce and . . . crafts"; others worked as civil servants or in the professions. Both Christian and Muslim, Palestinians "formed a proud and vibrant community that had [entered] an intellectual and national renaissance."[25]

At the start of the twentieth century, most of the inhabitants of modern Palestine (Palestinians) were Muslim, with Christian and Jewish minorities of between 5 percent and 10 percent. Demographic numbers are hard to determine. Ottoman census data were used to collect taxes, draft (Muslim) soldiers, and identify illegal immigrants, so many people found ways to avoid being counted or to let someone else hold title to their land.[26] Arabic was the common language. After the formation of the state of Israel in 1948, Jews—even those who would earlier have been called "Palestinians"—generally preferred to be called "Israelis." In this chapter the term "Palestinian" will refer to the indigenous, *non-Jewish* Arab inhabitants of the land, Muslim and Christian. Palestinian *Muslims* form the second main religious group in the current struggle.

Jews had developed communities in the **Diaspora** (outside Palestine) well before the Romans crushed the 67–73 and 132–135 CE Jewish revolts. From about 300 BCE to 300 CE, Judaism expanded greatly through the conversion of pagans. The Maccabees and Hasmoneans forcibly converted and circumcised neighboring groups, especially the Idumeans. Other Jewish communities in Babylonia, Syria, Egypt, North Africa, Asia Minor, Greece, Rome, and as far as Spain grew through voluntary conversion.[27] In a later period, beginning in the eighth century CE, the king and nobility of the Khazars in Eastern Europe north of the Caucasus converted to Judaism; their subjects gradually followed suit. The suggestion that the Khazars may be a major source of Ashkenazi Jews is maintained by some, though contested by others.[28] Over time, these Diaspora Jews came to center their lives on study of the Torah and observance of its laws, developing the way of life we call "Jewish." Once their growth through conversion faltered under the pressure of Christian and, later, Muslim rule, a strong sense of community helped maintain their distinctive way of life. Mainly under Christian rule, they suffered frequent persecution, and some dreamed of moving to the land of their religious origins, joining those who had never left and establishing a communal life there; but few made serious attempts to do so. Most believed that God did not want them to do so until the messiah returned.[29]

Modern Palestine: Historical Overview to 1930

As we saw in chapter 4, around the 1840s some Western Christians began to believe that Jesus would soon return to a Jewish Jerusalem with a functioning Jewish temple. But this could not happen until the Jewish community and the temple were restored in Jerusalem. Some of these Christians moved to Jerusalem and worked to encourage a Jewish restoration.

A few decades later, as we saw in chapter 3, some Jews also began thinking of an expanded Jewish presence in Palestine. Baron Edmond de Rothschild financed the first Zionist agricultural settlements at Petah Tikva and Rishon LeZion in Ottoman Palestine in 1882–1883 for about twenty-five thousand mostly Eastern European Jews, and helped finance about thirty more settlements over the next several decades.[30] These Zionist Jews were not coming to a "land without a people"—the indigenous Arab population of Palestine in the 1880s (Muslim and Christian) was about half a million people.[31] In this early period, Wikipedia asserts that "Jews and Arabs lived amicably on Rothschild's land, with no Arab grievances, even in the worst periods of disturbance." This was not the case in the settlements, which dispossessed Arab farmers and refused to hire Arab labor. In a 1934 letter to the League of Nations, Edmond de Rothschild urged that "the struggle to put an end to the Wandering Jew could not have as its result, the creation of the Wandering Arab."[32]

A modern, revived form of Hebrew was beginning to be spoken and used in schools by the Jewish immigrants. The descendants of these Zionist Jews who were immigrating to Palestine, along with successive waves of Zionist Jewish immigrants, form the third main group in the current struggle.

Renewed persecution in Europe accelerated Jewish efforts to colonize Palestine. The question arises whether Jewish Zionist leaders were simply looking for a safe place for Jews to live within Palestine (a Jewish "home"), or whether they intended from the beginning to gain Jewish political control over all of Palestine, with a majority Jewish population (a Jewish "state"). According to Rashid Khalidi, "The Jewish national home . . . for most Zionists . . . always meant . . . transforming all of Palestine into a Jewish state."[33] Rabbi Chaim Simons has written a book studying proposals from 1895 (Theodor Herzl) to 1947 (Anthony Eden) to transfer Arabs out of Palestine. He was surprised to find how widespread the plans were and how knowledge of their existence has been suppressed. But, far from being disturbed, he himself supports transfer.[34] Intentions varied and leaders did not always express their aims clearly—even to their supporters. In 1899, the leading early political Zionist Theodor Herzl wrote to the Arab mayor of Jerusalem: "You see another difficulty, Excellency, in the existence of the non-Jewish population in Palestine. But who would think of sending them away? It is their well-being, their individual wealth which we increase by bringing in our own."[35] But he was freer to consider other plans in his diary. There, Herzl proposed to form a company or association which suddenly, within a week, would purchase massive amounts of land in Palestine through intermediate agents not known to be Jews, then help European Jews sell their property in Europe, move them to Palestine, organize their life there, and act as the precursor to an eventual **Jewish state.** In an entry for 1895, he wrote:

We shall try to spirit the penniless [indigenous] population across the border by procuring employment for it in the transit countries whilst denying it any employment in our own country. The property-owners [many of whom were absentee landowners] will come over to our side. Both the process of expropriation and the removal of the poor must be carried out discreetly and circumspectly. Let the owners of immovable property believe that they are cheating us, selling us things for more than they are worth. But we are not going to sell them anything back.

For Palestinian property owners who might not want to sell out and move away, he added an extra inducement: "[Those reluctant to part with their properties for sentimental reasons] will be offered a complete transportation to any place they wish. . . . This offer will be made only when all others have been rejected."[36] This offer was a subsidized relocation plan. Zionist leaders occasionally considered subsidizing Palestinian relocation, but they never put such plans into practice. If even this offer failed, Herzl proposed leaving the recalcitrant locals in place and organizing Jewish life and commerce without them.[37] Although early Jewish properties in Palestine were purchased by wealthy European Jews, often from absentee landowners, most displaced Palestinians were forced to leave their homes and property after 1947 unwillingly and without compensation. The one consistent feature was this: once property transferred to Jewish ownership, it did not return to non-Jewish ownership.[38]

From 1904 to the start of World War I, about forty thousand Russian Jewish immigrants came to Palestine, but only about half stayed. Many were socialists or communists disappointed by the failure of the 1905 Russian Revolution. They came as laborers in the *moshavim* or as *urban* laborers, formed strong labor unions and political parties, founded the first *kibbutz*, founded the new city of Tel Aviv, formed the first Jewish self-defense organization, and expanded the use of modern Hebrew.[39]

Except for a brief period of European Christian control during the Crusades (barely over one hundred years for Jerusalem; another hundred years for parts of the seacoast), Palestine had been under Muslim control from 638 CE until World War I—a period of nearly 1,300 years. The Muslims had been mostly tolerant of other faiths; the Crusaders, in contrast, slaughtered thousands of Jews and Muslims when they captured Jerusalem in 1099.

At the time of World War I, many peoples in the world, including Arab Muslims and Christians under the Turkish Ottoman Empire, sought national self-determination. Arab independence conflicted with the secular Zionist movement to build a Jewish homeland in Palestine.

Germany and Turkey were allies in World War I. Because England wanted to protect its access to India through the Suez Canal, to gain control of the territory along those access routes, to ensure access to Middle Eastern oil, and to limit German control in the Middle East, it courted Arab leaders. The war was not going well for England in 1915. So when Sharif Husayn ibn Ali, the ruler of Mecca and Medina (in Arabia) and descendant of Muhammad (but not a Palestinian), asked the British whether Britain would support him if he declared himself to be "King of the Arabs" and independent from the Ottomans, the British agreed with qualifications. Husayn specified for his Arab state everything from the Mediterranean Sea to Iran and from southern Turkey to the Persian Gulf.[40] The British tried to avoid specifying borders. When Husayn objected, they agreed to his area with certain exceptions along the Mediterranean coast which they left vague. Arabs insisted that Palestine was to be part of Husayn's state; Zionists insisted that it was excluded by the vague British qualifications. In June 1916, reassured by Britain's ambiguous promises and aided by the British army intelligence officer T. E. Lawrence ("Lawrence of Arabia"), Husayn revolted against Turkey. The following year, Britain also invaded from Egypt to capture Palestine.

Meanwhile, other British negotiators had been talking with the French. In May 1916, in the **Sykes-Picot Agreement**, the British had offered to give Syria and Lebanon to France and to put Palestine under international control, keeping for itself what became Transjordan (later known as Jordan), Iraq, and the United Arab Emirates.[41]

The war continued to go badly. By 1917 Britain feared that Russia, whose tsar had just been overthrown by the Bolshevik Revolution, might withdraw from combat against Germany. Russian Jewish socialists and communists were prominent in the new government. Britain also wanted the United States, which had a large Jewish community, to declare war on Germany. To avoid Russian withdrawal from the war and to achieve American entry into the war, in November 1917 Arthur James Balfour of the British Foreign Office sent to Lord Rothschild, a leader of the British Jewish community, a statement approved by the British Cabinet (the **Balfour Declaration**), which read in part:

> His Majesty's Government views with favour the establishment in Palestine of a national home for the Jewish people, and will use their best endeavors to facilitate the achievement of this object, it being clearly understood that nothing shall be done which may prejudice the civil and religious rights of existing non-Jewish communities in Palestine, or the rights and political status enjoyed by Jews in any other country.[42]

Note that nothing was said about the *political* rights of the "non-Jewish communities" in Palestine, the vast majority of the population.

Unfortunately, these British promises to Sharif Husayn, to the French, and to Lord Rothschild, were incompatible. After the war, the French and British ignored the Sharif's claims. Britain assumed sole control of Palestine, freezing out "internationals"—specifically the French—against the terms of the Sykes-Picot Agreement. The League of Nations granted "mandates" to govern the former Ottoman territories. Britain was given mandates over Palestine, Transjordan, and Iraq, and France was given mandates over Lebanon and Syria. Meanwhile, the Saud family had chased Sharif Husayn out of Mecca and Medina and set up their kingdom of "Saudi Arabia." Britain installed one of the Sharif's sons, Amir Abdullah, as king of Transjordan, which they separated from their mandate for Palestine, to the annoyance of

Zionists who wanted Transjordan included in their Jewish homeland. The Arabs elected Husayn's other son, Faysal, to be king of Syria (including Palestine), but the French drove him out of Damascus; Britain then installed Faysal as king of Iraq—minus Kuwait, which they established as a separate kingdom, denying Iraq its natural seaport. All of these countries were newly carved out of the Arab areas of the former Ottoman Empire—the territory promised to the Sharif—with the European powers determining the lines of division. England's mandate for Palestine included the following provisions:

> ART. 2. The Mandatory shall be responsible for placing the country under such political, administrative and economic conditions as will secure the establishment of the Jewish national home, . . . and also for safeguarding the civil and religious [*not political*] rights of all the inhabitants of Palestine, irrespective of race and religion. . . . ART. 6. The Administration of Palestine, while ensuring that the rights and position of other sections of the population are not prejudiced, shall facilitate Jewish immigration under suitable conditions and shall encourage . . . close settlement by Jews on the land.[43]

After World War I, about thirty-five thousand committed Zionist Jews immigrated, mostly from Russia and Eastern Europe. New kibbutzim and moshavim were established, mostly secular and socialist in orientation, although there were a few religious kibbutzim. The **Histadrut** labor organization was founded in 1920 with the following resolution:

> It is the aim of the United Federation of all the [*implied* Jewish] workers and laborers of Palestine who live by the sweat of their brows without exploiting the toil of others [meaning, without sharing the work with Arabs], to promote land settlement, to involve itself in all economic and cultural issues effecting [*sic*] labor in Palestine, and to build a Jewish workers society there.[44]

The Palestinian Arabs objected vigorously to the **British Mandate**, insisting that, since the British had promised them self-government, they should be able to control immigration into their own country. Instead, the British allowed open immigration and land sales to Jews. In 1920 and 1921, when Arab demonstrations led to riots, Ze'ev Jabotinsky created an armed Jewish defense force. The local British administration convicted him of creating an unauthorized police force and sentenced him to fifteen years in prison, but he was soon released on orders from London. He went on to organize the **Haganah**—an unofficial (illegal) Jewish army.

The Arabs sent a delegation to London in late 1921 demanding that the British repudiate the Balfour Declaration and support a democratic government elected by all the inhabitants of Palestine: Muslim, Christian, and Jewish. A British White Paper declared that Britain did "not contemplate that Palestine *as a whole* should be converted into a Jewish National Home, but that such a Home should be founded *in* Palestine" (emphases added).[45] Britain also promised to limit immigration to what the country's economy could absorb, and to work toward setting up a "legislative council." Palestinians responded that immigration quotas should be a political decision, not an economic one, and should be set democratically by the population affected. The 1922 census showed that the Jewish community had grown to be 11 percent of the population of Palestine.

In place of traditional family and tribal leaders, the British appointed weak Palestinian leaders who would depend on the British for their power. As Grand Mufti of Jerusalem, they appointed Hajj Amin al Husayni, also naming him head of the newly created Supreme Muslim Council (SMC), which provided him with substantial revenue from various fees and religious endowments to distribute to his favorites.

Mandatory Britain enabled *Jewish* "national self-determination" while preventing the same for *Palestinian Arabs*. Thus the Zionists were permitted to operate a "parastate within . . . the mandatory state," whereas the Palestinians were granted no such "access to a state" of their own. The text of the British Mandate explicitly included the Balfour Declaration, resulting in a biased and skewed "constitutional structure" in relation to the two populations. Therefore when the Palestinian leadership demanded "national and political rights" from the British colonial government, the British authorities counter-demanded that the Palestinians first accept the terms of the Mandate, which denied those very rights! The framework thus imposed by Britain on the Palestinians functioned as a "fiendish iron cage," from which the Palestinian leadership ultimately proved unable to extricate itself and its people.[46]

In 1924, persecution of middle-class Jews in Poland brought a new wave of shopkeepers, artisans, and small industrialists to Palestinian cities. The new settlers were attracted to the **Revisionist Zionism** promoted by Ze'ev Jabotinsky, who preferred liberal capitalism to the earlier labor union socialism. He rejected the dominant Zionist view that the Jewish community should quietly build up its population, along with its economic and political strength, until it had a majority before proposing a Jewish state. Believing that the British were committed to Jewish colonization, he urged the Jewish community to capture Palestine and Jordan by force of arms, maintain control by means of a political and military "iron wall," and declare a Jewish state on both sides of the Jordan River.

In 1929, Muslim Palestinians complained that Jewish worship at the **Western Wall** was interfering with Muslim worship at the **al-Aqsa Mosque**. Muslims feared that Jews would destroy the Dome of the Rock to rebuild the temple, a position advocated by some right-wing Revisionist Jews although, according to mainstream Jewish tradition, the temple should not be rebuilt until the messiah comes. Tensions and provocations mounted on both sides. False rumors of a Jewish attack on the al-Aqsa Mosque circulated. Arabs burned Jewish prayer books at the Western Wall, pillaged Jewish neighborhoods, and killed seventeen Jews in Jerusalem. Some Arab families protected their Jewish neighbors by hiding them. Rioters from Jerusalem traveled to Hebron, site of the tomb of Abraham and Sarah, revered ancestors of Jews, Christians, and Muslims. Within a few hours, rioting had killed sixty-seven Jews and wounded hundreds. Britain evacuated Jewish survivors from Hebron to Jerusalem. Overall, the riots killed 133 Jews and 116 Arabs. Most of the Jews were killed by rioters, most of the Arabs by British police. The armed Jewish settlers in

Hebron today, who moved into the city center illegally after 1967, refer to this incident to justify their demand for special protection by the Israel Defense Forces (IDF).

An official study by the British Shaw Commission reported in 1930 that 30 percent of the Palestinian population, which had been mostly farmers, had lost their land, so that there was not enough land left to the Arabs for their children to inherit. They were not necessarily unemployed, since industrial development directed by the British was creating many new jobs and the Arab population was actually increasing. The Passfield White Paper (also 1930) recommended that Jewish immigration be stopped and land sales be restricted. The British Parliament repudiated the White Paper, and the League of Nations pointed out that stopping Jewish immigration would violate terms of the mandate. This exchange was characteristic: local British administrators tended to sympathize with Arab concerns, while the government in London tended to favor the Jewish community, often reversing decisions made locally.

Beginning in 1929 and increasing rapidly as Nazis gained power, Jewish professionals from Germany and Austria flooded into Palestine. Jewish land purchases drove up prices, tempting absentee Palestinian landholders to sell for profit, just as Herzl had predicted. The purchaser was the Jewish National Fund,[47] which held the land for Jewish use and leased it to Jews, displacing its former Arab laborers. In addition, during the depression of the 1930s, many small Arab farmers lost their land when they couldn't pay taxes to the government or rent to the landowner.

The Arab Revolt of 1936–1939

In 1935, alarmed by the growing Zionist community, the Arabs demanded an end to Jewish immigration, an end to land sales to Jews, and the creation of a Palestinian national government. The local British administration offered to form a legislative council on which the Palestinians, though not proportionally represented, would have a majority. The Jewish community strongly objected, fearing that the council would cripple development of their national home, and London killed the proposal. A full-scale Arab revolt (1936–1939) resulted. The "Arab High Command," led by the Grand Mufti, called a general strike of Arab workers and a boycott of Jewish products. England was approaching war with Germany and needed Middle Eastern oil. In 1937, the British Peel Commission recommended that Palestine be divided between Arabs and Jews. About 20 percent would go to the Jews; Britain would retain control of Jerusalem, Bethlehem, and Nazareth. Jews would be moved out of the Arab section and Arabs out of the Jewish section, preferably by agreement with compensation, but by compulsion if necessary.[48] As precedent, the commission pointed to the forced transfer of Greek and Turkish populations after World War I.[49] Although they objected to the proposed boundaries, Jewish leaders considered the project seriously, arguing among themselves that it was only a first step which could later be expanded, eventually giving them control of the whole of Palestine. They discussed how to transfer Palestinians to Jordan or Iraq.[50]

The Arabs rejected the plan and declared that if the British did not limit Jewish immigration, the Arabs would side with their enemies in the impending European war. A new commission trashed the Peel proposal, proposing a much smaller Jewish state; now the plan was unacceptable to *both* sides. The Arab revolt resumed. The British suppressed it harshly, exiling many of its leaders. They also allowed the Jews to arm the *Haganah*, and they trained its *Special Night Squads*, which attacked Arab villages. Jabotinsky broke away from the *Haganah* to form the **Irgun**. Two years later, another breakaway group formed the **Stern Gang**, also known as **Lehi**. Believing that the *Haganah* was too restrained, these two groups committed themselves to attacking Arab civilians:

> The Irgun established the pattern of terrorism adopted 30 years later by [the Palestinian party] Al-Fatah. Among its actions were the wheeling of a vegetable barrow containing a bomb into an Arab market in Jerusalem, firing at a bus and throwing bombs into market places (Jerusalem, Haifa). The perpetrators of these acts were declared national heroes and martyrs.[51]

Overall, the Arab revolt of 1936–1939 killed 415 Jews and about 5,000 Arabs. The Arabs also suffered 15,000 wounded, 5,600 imprisoned, and most of their leadership exiled. Putting down the revolt required 20,000 British troops.[52] The failure of the revolt crippled Arab political and military strength, which would be sorely needed in 1947–1948. In contrast, the *Jewish* military posture was enhanced, since Britain had armed many Jews to help put down the revolt. In addition, the Arab boycott encouraged the Jewish economy to become more self-sufficient.

Although Britain had brutally suppressed the Arab revolt, some British officials realized they could not entirely ignore Arab grievances. In 1939 Britain issued a White Paper that announced a policy of seriously limiting Jewish immigration over the following five years to no more than seventy-five thousand, thereafter immigration only with Arab approval, and the promise of an inclusive, independent Palestinian-Jewish state within ten years, if feasible. For different reasons, neither the Palestinians nor the Zionists welcomed the document.

As Nazi persecution of Jews intensified and Jews urgently needed to emigrate, most countries severely restricted their immigration. In 1938, the World Zionist Organization boycotted a multinational conference in France convened to deal with the resettlement of Jewish refugees from Nazism *in countries other than Palestine*, fearing it would reduce immigration to Palestine.[53] A poll taken in November 1938, immediately after the destructive German anti-Jewish riots called Kristallnacht ("Night of Broken Glass"), showed that 94 percent of Americans opposed the Nazi treatment of Jews, but 72 percent opposed letting more German Jews immigrate to the United States, and two-thirds even opposed accepting twenty thousand German Jewish *children* as emergency refugees.[54] With nearly all countries closed to their immigration by restrictive quotas, many European Jews headed for Palestine. Some managed to enter illegally; others were arrested or deported. Zionist groups organized illegal shipments of refugees on whatever rickety ships they could acquire; many were turned back by the British or sank.

The Biltmore Program

In 1942, a conference declaration signed at the Biltmore Hotel in New York City signaled a major shift in the Zionist position. The British White Paper of 1939 had effectively ended British support for the Balfour Declaration. The Biltmore Declaration condemned the White Paper, promised Jewish military participation in the war against Nazism, and implicitly demanded a Jewish *state* covering *all* of Palestine: "The Conference calls for the fulfillment of the original purpose of the Balfour Declaration and the Mandate which recognizing the historical connection of the Jewish people with Palestine, was to afford them the opportunity, . . . that *Palestine* be established as a Jewish Commonwealth integrated in the structure of the new democratic world" (emphasis added).[55] Note that "commonwealth" has a very different connotation than "national home," and that it was not the *original purpose* of Balfour to transform *the whole of Palestine* into a Jewish state.

While the Haganah, the largest Jewish underground army, chose to support Britain's war effort against Nazi Germany, the Irgun and the Stern Gang (Lehi) attacked the British occupying authority. In Cairo in 1944, two Lehi members murdered Lord Moyne, the British minister of state for the Middle East. He had been a personal friend of Winston Churchill, and his assassination turned Churchill against the Zionists. The Haganah began to see the Irgun and Lehi as liabilities and acted for several months to reduce their influence, even helping British police to capture some of their members.[56]

As World War II ended and it became clear that the British would not support a Jewish state, both the Irgun and Lehi launched terrorist attacks against British forces in Palestine, bombing trains, railroad stations, and the British government headquarters at the King David Hotel in Jerusalem, killing ninety-one people there. A weakened, exhausted, and seriously compromised Britain decided to withdraw from both India and Palestine.

The United Nations Plan and the War of 1948

England announced its withdrawal date and asked the United Nations to work out a settlement. In November 1947, the United Nations recommended that the land be divided into a Jewish area and an Arab area based on the majority population in each area. After more than a half century of Jewish land purchases, Jews or the Jewish Agency owned about 7 percent of Palestine, Arab individuals owned slightly less than half, and the state (the British administration) claimed slightly less than half.[57] Much of the state-owned land was desert or unproductive. Under the UN plan, the Arab city of Jaffa, assigned to the Arab state, would be completely surrounded by the Jewish state. The Jerusalem-Bethlehem district, split almost equally between Jewish and Arab inhabitants, would be wholly surrounded by the Arab area with no Jewish land access; it was to be an international area controlled by neither group.[58] The UN intended the two states to form an economic union with open borders.

The partition plan heavily favored the Jews. Although Jews represented only 33 percent of the population, the Jewish state was allotted 55 percent of the land area, the Palestinian state 42 percent. The final 3 percent—mainly Jerusalem and Bethlehem—would be under international control. *Within* the proposed, disproportionately large Jewish area, Jews made up a slim majority of 55 percent. If wandering Bedouin herders were included in the count, the population of the Jewish area was almost evenly split between Jews and Arabs. In contrast, the proposed *Arab* area was 99 percent Arab![59] The lines as drawn gave the Jewish area as much land as possible while maintaining a (slight) Jewish majority; supporters said the extra territory would provide space to settle Jewish refugees—but as a result the Jewish majority was very slight and Jewish control fragile.[60] Once the Jewish leaders decided to conquer even *more* territory than the UN plan allotted them, they *had* to drive out non-Jews if they were to maintain Jewish majority control.

The partition plan was passed by the General Assembly as a *recommendation* (Resolution 181), since only the Security Council had the authority to pass a binding resolution. The UN charter in Article 11 no. 2 specifies:

> The General Assembly may discuss any questions relating to the maintenance of international peace and security brought before it by any Member of the United Nations, or by the Security Council, or by a state which is not a Member of the United Nations . . . and, except as provided in Article 12, may make recommendations with regard to any such questions to the state or states concerned or to the Security Council or to both. *Any such question on which action is necessary shall be referred to the Security Council by the General Assembly either before or after discussion.* (emphasis added)[61]

The majority of the Jewish community accepted the recommendation with reservations and with the intention to expand its allotted territory. The Palestinian community rejected the plan and promised to resist it by force of arms. Violence from both sides started almost at once, as a natural intensification of the agitation and terrorism which had induced the British to end their Mandate. Realizing that the plan was unworkable, the UN General Assembly never submitted it to the Security Council for action. Instead, the UN sent the Swedish diplomat Count Folke Bernadotte to Palestine to negotiate an alternative. He negotiated a cease-fire, proposed two plans, and was assassinated in September 1948 by members of the Jewish group Lehi (the Stern Gang). Neither of his plans was adopted by the UN, and fighting between Zionists and Palestinians resumed.

Based on recently released Israeli archives, Israeli Jewish historian Benny Morris shows that Jewish attacks on Arab villages in 1948 were much more extensive and deliberate than previously thought.[62] According to Morris, as the Zionist assault in April 1948 produced a flood of Palestinian refugees, Zionist leaders recognized the advantage of reducing the Arab population in what would become the Jewish state and began to provoke the flight deliberately.[63] "Ultimately the atmosphere of transfer . . . prevailed through April–June: Most communities attacked were evacuated and, where no spontaneous evacuation occurred, communities more often than not were expelled. Throughout, Arabs who had fled were prevented from returning to their homes."[64] Morris judges that those attacks were *necessary* to assure Jewish control of the new Jewish-majority state. "Ben-Gurion was a transferist. He understood that there could be no Jewish state with a large and hostile Arab minority in its midst.... Without the uprooting of the Palestinians, a Jewish state would not have arisen here."[65]

Another Israeli historian, Ilan Pappe, critiques his colleague Morris for relying exclusively and literally on "Israeli military reports." Pappe supplements Morris's findings with "Palestinian sources" and "oral history" accounts. Thus he adds to the record, "such atrocities as the poisoning of the water supply into Acre with typhoid, numerous cases of rape and the dozens of massacres the Jews perpetrated."[66] "Before 15 May," he writes, the number of refugees already amounted to around three hundred fifty thousand, "if one adds all of the population from . . . 200 [destroyed] towns and villages."[67] Pappe also traces the planning by Zionist leaders for a possible "enforced transfer of the entire indigenous population" back to the late 1930s.[68] He concludes that the events of 1947–1949 should be described not as a war, but rather as **ethnic cleansing.**[69]

Zionist spokespersons have contended that Arab radio broadcasts encouraged the Arab flight so that civilian Arabs would be out of the way when Arab armies pushed the Jews into the sea. This contention is not supported by the relevant records of radio broadcasts, and Arab historians have long denied it. In 1961, the Irish journalist Erskine Childers published the results of his thorough investigation of all possible evidence (statements, documents, broadcasts) for Arab, that is, Palestinian, "promotion" of a Palestinian exodus and found it to be either nonexistent or not credible.[70] Morris agrees that there was no such generalized appeal. He concludes: "The prime movers throughout were the Yishuv [the Jewish community] and its military organizations. It was their operations that were to prove the major precipitants to flight."[71]

A prime example was an Irgun attack on the village of **Deir Yassin**, located just west of Jerusalem near the highway from Tel Aviv.[72] Deir Yassin had negotiated nonbelligerency status with the Haganah and had resisted infiltration by Arab fighters. Given its nonaggression pact with Deir Yassin, and therefore to avoid "official accountability," the Haganah "decided to send the Irgun and Stern Gang troops" to "wipe out" the village.[73] In their attack on the village, the Irgun killed over one hundred Palestinians, all of them civilians. Early reports numbered the dead at 254. A careful study conducted in the 1980s at Bir Zeit University (Palestinian) reduced the number to 110–120.[74] Pappe comments that "the victims of the massacre itself" numbered 93 (rather than 170), but "dozens of others were killed in the fighting, and hence were not included in the official list of victims." He adds, "The Jewish leadership proudly announced a high number of victims" with the purpose of provoking a greater Palestinian exodus.[75] Zionist leaders realized that the story was causing Arabs from other villages to flee in panic. The Jewish Agency, which controlled the Haganah, publicly and disingenuously denounced the attack, but other Zionist leaders helped spread the panic. Menachem Begin (head of the Irgun and, later, prime minister of Israel) wrote in his memoirs that the flight of the Arabs was a welcome result of the attack.[76]

Both sides knew at the time that the number was exaggerated but found it preferred to accept it. Palestinians hoped that news of the massacre would induce neighboring Arab nations to send troops to their support.

The State of Israel

The Jewish community unilaterally declared the existence of the state of Israel on May 14, 1948. U.S. president Harry Truman, concerned about Jewish war refugees, impressed by recent Zionist advances in the Palestine war, annoyed by Zionist lobbying but grateful for crucial Jewish financial and political support in a desperate election campaign, recognized the new state eleven minutes after its declaration;[77] the Soviet Union followed almost at once. Britain withdrew from Palestine the next day. Jordan's Arab Legion and armies from Egypt, Syria, and Iraq entered Palestine. The invading armies were crippled by conflicting objectives: King Abdullah of Jordan wanted to annex to Jordan the area of Palestine along his border (the **West Bank**), President Quwatly of Syria feared that Abdullah intended to grab part of the territory he coveted to create and control a "Greater Syria," and King Farouq of Egypt sought control over southern Palestine plus as much of the West Bank as he could capture, in order to limit Abdullah's power. None of the invaders wanted a new Arab state in Palestine ruled by Hajj Amin al Husayni. There was little coordination among the Arab parties and no central command.

The Zionists had better arms, motivation, organization, and leadership than the Arabs, along with significant numbers of veteran soldiers from the World War. Israel ended up controlling 42 percent more territory than had been designated for the Jewish state in the original partition plan—from 55 percent of the territory to 78 percent—including all of Galilee, most of which had been designated for the Palestinian state. That left the Palestinians with only 22 percent of the land. The war was disastrous for the Palestinians; they named it **al-Nakba**—"The Catastrophe." As Pappe summarizes the consequences, "Half of the indigenous people living in Palestine were driven out, half of their villages and towns were destroyed, and . . . very few among them ever managed to return." Furthermore, he expresses astonishment that this "crime . . . perpetrated in modern times . . . [has] been . . . totally ignored." He writes, "The ethnic cleansing of 1948 has been eradicated . . . from the collective global memory and erased from the world's conscience." As a historian, Pappe has found no comparable, post–World War II "case of this nature."[78] See the section in chapter 12 titled "Genocide and Ethnic Cleansing" for discussion of the Armenian genocide, which occurred during World War I.

When the fighting ended with an armistice, Palestinians who had been driven out of their homes or had fled to save their lives tried to come home, but the Israeli army blocked their way. Israel speciously argued that the returning refugees might be spies or subversive, but in reality sealed its borders to guarantee an overwhelming Jewish majority in the new state. The Israeli decision not to let the refugees return home was a key turning point in Israeli-Palestinian relations. Addressing the issue in December 1948 with Resolution 194, the UN General Assembly declared: "The General Assembly . . . resolves that the refugees wishing to return to their homes and live at peace with their neighbors should be permitted to do so at the earliest practicable date, and that compensation should be paid for the property of those choosing not to return and for loss of or damage to property."[79] Israel has never complied.

Other Arab countries did not want 750,000–800,000 instant, involuntary immigrants. The Palestinian refugees wanted to return to their homes, orchards, and fields. Caught in between, they struggled to survive near the borders, occasionally crossing over to harvest crops or rescue items from their homes. Not until late 1949 did the United Nations begin to administer refugee camps with tents for the refugees to live in. After a short time, Israel confiscated the lands and homes of the Palestinians whose reentry they were blocking and either gave them to new Jewish immigrants, who were flooding into the new state of Israel, or bulldozed the Arab villages and planted new villages or forests in their place. Israel argued that it was resettling thousands of Jews—the neighboring Arab countries could resettle the refugee Palestinian Arabs. The Arab League urged Arab countries not to grant citizenship to the refugees; except for Jordan, most complied. Millions of Palestinian refugees, including their descendants, remain stateless today; many of them have no citizenship in any country.[80]

The 1956 Suez War

The surrounding Arab nations were shaken by their defeats in 1948—within four years, Abdullah of Jordan was assassinated and the governments of both Syria and Egypt fell to revolutions. In 1952, Gamal Abdel Nasser seized control of Egypt from King Farouq. In 1956 he nationalized the Suez Canal Company's assets. In collusion with an Israeli attack across the Sinai Desert, English and French military forces captured the canal. But U.S. president Dwight D. Eisenhower, angry that he had not been consulted and wishing to use U.S. power for peace, pressed the United Nations to condemn the aggression, and the armies retreated.[81]

The 1967 Six-Day War

In 1967 Israel and Syria were in conflict over Israeli military patrols and land cultivation in the demilitarized zone between them, and over use of water from the sources of the Jordan River. General Moshe Dayan states that Israel deliberately provoked Syrian shelling from the **Golan Heights** so that Israel could seize more Syrian land.[82] Egypt moved about 100,000 troops and 600–700 tanks into defensive positions facing the Israeli border in the Sinai, ordered the UN to withdraw its observers, and blockaded shipping lanes to the Israeli port of Eilat. Nasser probably hoped that this threatening behavior alone, without war, would make Israel ease up on Syria and deal fairly with Palestinian refugees, since Israel's reserve army could not remain mobilized for very long without devastating its economy. But Israel brought matters to a head by attacking Egyptian airfields in a move widely portrayed in the West as defensive, although this has been disproved.

Recently declassified discussions between the Israeli army general staff and the Israeli cabinet reveal that neither believed the Egyptian threat was real. Egypt had received new weapons from Russia, but the Israeli army argued that it would take eighteen months to two years for the Egyptians to learn how to use them properly. Nasser had foolishly moved the Egyptian army right next to the Israeli army, making it easy for Israel to destroy the former. So, said the Israeli army, let's do it. The Israeli cabinet gave their army permission to attack the Egyptian army. Once they had destroyed the Egyptian army, resenting the fact that Ben-Gurion had not allowed them to capture the entire West Bank in 1948, the army officers kept right on going to "finish the job" without formal authorization.[83] In a few days Israel captured the rest of the areas of Palestine allotted to the Palestinians by the 1947 UN Partition Plan—Gaza and the West Bank, including **East Jerusalem**—plus the entire Sinai peninsula between Israel and Egypt and the strategic Golan Heights of Syria. At least three hundred twenty-five thousand Palestinian refugees were again displaced. UN Security Council Resolution 242[84] declared that the acquisition of territory by war was invalid. Israel's continued military control over the conquered territories is known as "the occupation" and is illegal under international law.

Before the 1967 war, France was Israel's prime source of weapons. But after ending its occupation of Algeria, France withdrew its support for Israel. Impressed by the military might that Israel demonstrated in the war, and seeking a counterbalance to Soviet influence in the Middle East, the United States greatly increased its financial and military aid to Israel.

The USS *Liberty*

The **USS *Liberty*** was a U.S. "spy ship" sent to the Eastern Mediterranean in late May 1967 to gather intelligence regarding Israel's intention to attack Syria in order to take the Golan Heights, which the U.S. government wanted to prevent; they feared that such a move might provoke the USSR and trigger a world war. On June 7 the CIA learned that Israel planned to sink the *Liberty* if it did not retreat, and the Navy sent messages to the *Liberty* ordering it to do so, but bureaucratic confusion prevented the messages from being received. On June 8 beginning early in the morning, Israeli aircraft flew over the *Liberty* eight times, securely identifying it as American. The Israeli leadership, especially Moshe Dayan, did not want the U.S. to know that Israel was moving its tank force from the Sinai to the Golan Heights in order to attack Syria. So for well over an hour from about 2:00 PM, Israeli aircraft followed by torpedo boats attacked the *Liberty* with rockets, napalm, and torpedoes. The three lifeboats that were still intact after this assault were hit with machine gun fire. The Israeli intention was to destroy and sink the ship, along with every member of its crew, so that nobody would survive to tell the truth. The attack killed 34 crewmembers and wounded 171 out of a total of 294. Soon afterward a U.S.-Israeli cover-up was launched; crewmembers were told to be silent. But eventually they began to speak out. James Ennes Jr., the lieutenant on deck when the attack occurred, published *Assault on the Liberty* in 1980.[85]

Former CIA Director Richard Helms observed:

> Israeli authorities subsequently apologized for the accident, but few in Washington could believe that the ship had not been identified as an American naval vessel. . . . When additional evidence was available, more doubt was raised. . . . I had no role in . . . the board's finding that there could be no doubt that the Israelis knew exactly what they were doing in attacking the Liberty.[86]

THE ISRAELI OCCUPATION SINCE 1967

Israeli Colonies in the Occupied Territories

Shortly after the 1967 war, Israel began building **Jewish-only settlements (colonies)** inside the newly captured territories—a policy Israeli leaders called creating "**facts on the ground**": promise whatever you like, but create physical realities which make those promises impossible to keep, thus consolidating Israeli control. Over time, Israel reserved half of the West Bank and nearly a third of the **Gaza Strip** either for military use or for Jewish-only colonies (the Gaza colonies were dismantled in 2005). By 2013 about 125 Jewish-only settlements plus 100 outposts dotted the West Bank, monopolizing the productive land and water rights around them. Under international law, all settlements in occupied territory are illegal. With an estimated three hundred fifty thousand settlers living in "officially recognized" settlements on the occupied West Bank (not including settlement and military outposts), three hundred thousand in illegally annexed East Jerusalem, and twenty thousand in the occupied Golan Heights, the total comes to at least six hundred seventy thousand.[87] The settler population is increasing twice as fast as the Israeli population in Israel, and the rate of settlement construction in 2013 was 130 percent higher than in 2012.[88]

The West Bank has also been cut into isolated blocks by "access roads," which only Jews are allowed to use, thus creating an apartheid road system. Israel closes off those isolated blocks arbitrarily at will, not allowing Palestinians to cross the access roads. In addition, roads open to Palestinians are beset with **checkpoints** and roadblocks. Some numbers: in September 2013, there were 99 fixed checkpoints and 174 "flying [temporary] checkpoints" per month; at the end of 2012 over five hundred physical obstructions (concrete blocks, trenches, earth mounds) per month.[89]

Palestinians (but not illegal Israeli settlers) in the occupied territories are governed not by Israeli civil law but by Israeli military decrees. They have experienced frequent arrest, imprisonment and detention without trial, torture (95 percent or more of Palestinian prisoners are tortured, according to a December 2013 report by the Palestinian Prisoners Club),[90] deportation, destruction of homes (from 1967 to early 2012, Israel demolished around 27,000 Palestinian homes and other structures in the occupied territories),[91] loss of land and livelihood, severe injury, and death.

In sum, they are treated as stateless noncitizens without rights.[92] West Bank Palestinians are also subject to lawless settler violence, which has been on the rise especially since 2006 and appears to be tolerated by Israeli authorities, who may see it as a means of gradual ethnic cleansing. Such violence, occurring almost daily, ranges from physical attacks to property damage to agricultural injury and more.[93]

Under international law, specifically Article 49 of the Fourth Geneva Convention, an occupying power is not allowed to move its own population into the occupied area. Israel has argued that the Territories should not be considered "occupied" because they were not independent before Israel captured them but were governed by Jordan and Egypt. The United Nations and the International Court of Justice have rejected those arguments and ordered Israel not to colonize the territories,[94] but the ICJ has no enforcement mechanism.

The Palestine Liberation Organization (PLO)

Palestinians felt betrayed by their Arab neighbors, who had failed to defend their rights. Some decided to take matters into their own hands. In 1968, Yasser Arafat assumed leadership of the **Palestine Liberation Organization** (PLO), which had been founded four years earlier in Egypt. In addition to its administrative, social service, and diplomatic functions, the PLO began to use terrorist attacks against civilian targets to harass the Israeli leadership and gain world attention. Some Palestinian exiles turned to *international* terrorism, killing Jewish athletes at the 1972 Olympic Games in Munich and seizing airliners and a cruise ship in order to take hostages.

The 1973 Yom Kippur or Ramadan War

In 1973 Egypt and Syria, supplied with Soviet weapons, simultaneously attacked Israeli forces in the Sinai and the Golan Heights on the Jewish high holy day of Yom Kippur. Egypt especially had surprising success at first. Israeli casualties were very high, both in soldiers and equipment. Israel made an emergency appeal for a U.S. resupply of weapons. When Kissinger delayed, there is strong evidence that Israel armed missiles and aircraft with nuclear warheads and threatened to use them against Egypt and Syria. The U.S. then airlifted the requested weapons.[95] Reassured by the resupply, Israel regained much of the invaded territory, though not the Suez Canal. After a UN cease-fire that had been accepted by Israel and Egypt went into effect (UN Resolution 338),[96] Israeli general Ariel Sharon broke the cease-fire to cut off the Egyptian Third Army in the desert and threatened to starve it out, giving Israel a bargaining advantage and the appearance of victory in the war. But Israel had lost confidence, and Egypt and Syria regained their dignity.

Furious at the U.S. resupply of weapons to Israel, the Arab states mounted an oil boycott that escalated fuel prices in the United States, causing a price inflation and an economic recession. When Jimmy Carter was elected president, he pursued a comprehensive settlement resulting in the 1978 Camp David Accords,[97] which mandated the return of the Sinai to Egypt; a self-governing authority in the West Bank and Gaza; the withdrawal of Israeli forces from those areas; and normalized relations between Israel, Egypt, and Jordan within five years, based on UN resolutions 242 and 338. Withdrawing from the Sinai in accordance with the agreement, Israel contravened the rest of the agreement by annexing the Golan Heights and continuing to expand settlements in the West Bank and Gaza. With Egypt no longer a threat, Israel felt less constrained in its military occupation of the West Bank. Religious Zionists founded the group **Gush Emunim** ("Block of the Faithful") to promote the settlement and "redemption" of Gazan and West Bank land. Jordan and the other Arab states, accusing Egypt of weakening the Arab position, refused to negotiate with Israel.[98]

The 1982 Lebanon Invasion

In 1982, the Israeli army invaded Lebanon. Although Israel claimed it was trying to eliminate guerrilla attacks launched from Lebanon, its invasion violated a truce negotiated by the United States that had eliminated such attacks throughout the previous year. Israel took advantage of a minor violation by an anti-PLO Palestinian splinter group to justify its pre-planned attack. After the invasion killed an estimated seventeen thousand civilians, the PLO leadership agreed to abandon Lebanon and move to Tunisia. Still, Israel's military success was limited: the invasion took much longer than expected, costs were high, and many Israeli politicians, generals, and soldiers began to resist government policies. A group of soldiers founded the organization **Yesh Gevul** ("there is a border [limit]") for military personnel who refused to serve in Lebanon, later extended to the West Bank.[99] Especially damaging to Israel's reputation was the September massacre of Palestinians in the **Sabra and Shatila** refugee camps in Beirut. Surrounding the camps, the Israeli army allowed soldiers of the Lebanese Phalange (a Christian Fascist political group) to enter the camps and massacre "between 2,000 and 3,000" Palestinian refugees.[100] An Israeli investigation blamed the Israeli commanding officer, Ariel Sharon, for failing to prevent the massacre when he could and should have done so.

The First "Intifada" (1987–1993)

In the fall of 1987, a spontaneous Palestinian uprising began in a refugee camp in Gaza and continued throughout the Territories until 1993. The Arabic term for uprising is *intifada*—literally "shaking off." The intifada utilized many nonviolent tactics, although their effectiveness was weakened (see chapter 11) by Palestinian demonstrators who threw rocks, burned tires, and murdered unrepentant collaborators. According to international law, armed resistance to foreign occupation is legitimate, as long as it does not target civilians.[101] Whether it is wise or effective against overwhelming force is another question.

Gene Sharp, a scholar of nonviolent movements, has estimated that the first intifada was 85 percent nonviolent; the 15 percent violence was mostly youth throwing stones. But perception is often as important as reality, and the U.S. media concentrated attention on *Palestinian* violence—the Israel Defense Forces (IDF) were far more violent—giving a distorted impression which muted the impact of Palestinian nonviolence. Still, the sight of violent Israeli military responses to Palestinian nonviolence began to change world opinion. In the first four years of the intifada, 1,100 Palestinians (among them children) were killed by the Israeli military; "tens of thousands" were wounded.[102]

Palestinians within the occupied territories began the intifada to express their frustration both with the illegal, oppressive Israeli occupation and with the failure of the exiled PLO leadership in Tunisia to end it. Leaders of Arab states and the PLO leadership in Tunisia quickly adjusted to this new movement and supported it verbally, but when—after Oslo—Arafat and the Tunisia PLO gained political control in Palestine, they shut down the popularly organized nonviolent resistance to Israeli occupation, seeing it as a challenge to their own authority.

Hamas

The Muslim Brotherhood has been active in Palestine since 1948, when they provided fighters to oppose Zionist forces fighting to expand and establish the new state of Israel. More recently, in Gaza, they have provided schools, libraries, health facilities, and youth activities. In 1987, Sheikh Ahmed Yassin, a Gazan member of the Brotherhood, created a local chapter which he named **Hamas**. Their 1988 covenant refused to accept the state of Israel: "'Israel will exist . . . until Islam will obliterate it, just as it obliterated others before it' (The Martyr, Imam Hassan al-Banna, of blessed memory)."[103] Yet, before his assassination by Israel in 2004, Sheikh Yassin stated publicly that he would "consider a long-term cease-fire" in exchange for Israel's withdrawal from the occupied territories.[104] Moreover, Hamas leaders have publicly stated that they will abide by a two-state solution negotiated by the Palestinian Authority if it is supported by a referendum of the Palestinian people, including international refugees.

Palestine National Congress Recognizes Israel

Early in the first intifada, in 1988, the **Palestine National Congress** voted to accept Israel's right to exist within internationally recognized secure borders *if Israel accepted the right of a Palestinian state to exist.* Israel refused to accept the offer, arguing that the written constitution of the Palestine Liberation Organization (PLO) still called for the destruction of Israel. Palestinians felt that neither Israel nor the United States responded fairly to the PNC vote, which involved a major concession on their side—they relinquished any claim to sovereignty over 78 percent of Palestinian land, including areas conquered by Israel in 1948 that the 1947 UN Partition Plan (General Assembly Resolution 181) had allotted to the Palestinian state. In return they asked Israel to recognize that Palestinians had an equal right to a state and a normal life with self-determination and justice.

The Israeli government at first thought it could quash the intifada quickly. Brutal responses included arbitrary arrest, beating, destruction of houses of suspects and their relatives, and the use of "rubber bullets" (rubber-coated metal) for crowd control—sometimes at point-blank range resulting in serious injury and death. An Israeli colonel, on trial for ordering soldiers to break the arm and leg bones of Arab children and teenagers, swore under oath that the tactic had been authorized by Yitzhak Rabin, the defense minister.[105]

After the First Gulf War in 1991, renewed pressures from the United States, including restrictions on financial aid, pushed Israel toward negotiations. When Yitzhak Rabin of the **Labor Party** defeated the incumbent **Likud** president Yitzhak Shamir in 1992, Israeli voters anticipated sincere efforts to come to an agreement with the Palestinians.

The Oslo Accords

Hope was high in September 1993 as Yitzhak Rabin and Yasser Arafat signed a preliminary peace agreement called the "Declaration of Principles" (DOP), or **Oslo Accords**, on the White House lawn under the eye of President Bill Clinton.[106] The agreement established "a Palestinian Interim Self-Government Authority . . . in the West Bank and the Gaza Strip, for a transitional period not exceeding five years, leading to a permanent settlement based on Security Council Resolutions 242 and 338."[107] Yasser Arafat returned triumphantly from Tunisia to inaugurate the Palestinian Authority. The most difficult questions still needed to be decided: Israeli withdrawal from the rest of the West Bank, arrangements to share land and water resources, the status of Jerusalem, final borders, Israeli settlements in the occupied territories, and the rights of refugees from the 78 percent of pre-1948 Palestine which had become the state of Israel.

Many *Palestinians* thought that the agreement offered them far too little. *Israeli* settlers in the West Bank intended to maintain control of all the occupied territories; they harassed Palestinians and attacked whatever they thought threatened the permanence of their settlements. In February 1994, a Jewish settler physician entered the Ibrahimi Mosque in Hebron on the Jewish feast of Purim and killed twenty-nine Muslim worshipers with a hand grenade and an automatic rifle; thirty more people died in the riots that ensued. Settlers inscribed his gravestone as follows: "Here lies the saint, Dr. Baruch Kappel Goldstein, blessed be the memory of the righteous and holy man, may the Lord avenge his blood, who devoted his soul to the Jews, Jewish religion and Jewish land. His hands are innocent and his heart is pure. He was killed as a martyr of God." It was after the massacre that Palestinians began to attack Israeli military targets and civilians with suicide bombers.[108] In 1995, Yitzhak Rabin was assassinated by a right-wing Jewish law student. In 1996, the Israeli secret service assassinated Yahya Ayyash, a Hamas bomb maker, with an exploding telephone. Five Palestinian suicide bombings followed, killing seventy-two Israelis in two months. Rabin's successor, Shimon Peres, then lost the elections to the right-wing Binyamin Netanyahu.

Netanyahu had promised to continue the "peace process" but never to allow a Palestinian state—an impossible combination that repudiated the Oslo Accords. He stalled Israeli withdrawals for six months, using suicide attacks as justification, finally withdrawing from about 80 percent of Hebron in January 1997 but continuing to occupy its central market with about 400–800 extremist Jewish settlers protected by 1,500 Israeli soldiers in a city of over 150,000 Palestinians.[109] Arafat wanted Netanyahu to withdraw further from rural areas, but Netanyahu's political base expected him to stop or even reverse the withdrawals.

Israeli leaders complained that they had traded land for peace (withdrawn from occupied territory) but terrorism continued. Furthermore, the agreements were signed with the *Palestinian Authority* headed by Yasser Arafat, but the rival organization *Hamas*, which had been gaining support did not recognize the agreement or the state of Israel. *Palestinian* leaders complained that Israeli attacks and expansion of illegal settlements continued, creating disconnected Palestinian areas which left them worse off under Oslo than before.

Wye River Memorandum

In 1998, U.S. President Bill Clinton convened another peace conference at the Wye River plantation in Maryland. Netanyahu agreed to withdraw from more of the West Bank, to allow the Gaza Airport to open, to develop an industrial park on the Israel-Gaza border, to arrange a safe-passage route for Palestinians between Gaza and the West Bank, and to develop an eventual Gaza seaport. Arafat agreed to demobilize terrorist groups. Both sides agreed to work toward a final settlement in 1999. Criticized by right-wing Israelis, Netanyahu explained that Israel wouldn't have to carry out the agreements because Arafat wouldn't be able to end all acts of terrorism. He began the withdrawals, but suspended them part way through, and left most of the other points of the agreement unfulfilled.[110]

The process of regaining occupied land for a Palestinian state stalled. The Palestinian economy grew worse as Israel periodically closed the borders to trade, ostensibly in retaliation for terrorist attacks. Only individual cities of the West Bank without their surrounding rural areas had been granted to Palestinian control, producing a series of isolated pockets that made travel difficult—travelers had to pass through multiple checkpoints that were frequently closed. Furthermore, as Yasser Arafat tried to rein in terrorist groups, some Palestinians alleged that he had "sold out" to Israel in return for power—that he was simply implementing Israeli oppression under the guise of a Palestinian authority. Finally a vote of "no confidence" in the Israeli legislature, the **Knesset**, forced an early election in 1999, in which the Labor Party won back power from the right-wing Likud.

Ehud Barak and Camp David

The new premier, Ehud Barak, promised to restore the movement toward peace. In May 2000, Barak withdrew the Israeli army from southern Lebanon, which it had been occupying since 1982. But he also accelerated the illegal construction of Jewish settlements in occupied Palestinian territory. Barak wanted a peace agreement with Syria in order to neutralize Syria along with Jordan and Egypt and so to further weaken Arafat's position, but not at the price of returning the Israeli-occupied Syrian Golan Heights. Fearful of likely Israeli reactions to a real rapprochement with the Palestinians, he attended the summit at Camp David with President Clinton and Chairman Arafat without a serious commitment to peace.[111]

Barak's "Generous Offer" at Camp David

In the summer of 2000, under pressure from President Bill Clinton, Barak is often said to have extended to the Palestinians a "generous offer" that would have given them possession of 95 percent of the West Bank. However, his definition of "West Bank" omitted the greatly expanded East Jerusalem, which Israel had illegally incorporated; 10 percent of the total allegedly offered (the fertile Jordan Valley) was to remain under "temporary" Israeli control—duration unspecified—as was a network of access roads that only Israeli settlers could use; 80 percent of the Israeli settlers in the West Bank were to remain; and there would be no sharing of Jerusalem, no right of return for Palestinian refugees, and no viable water policy.[112] In fact, Barak's position was rejectionist, and his offer was an oral ultimatum, which Arafat rejected; subsequently Arafat was blamed for the failure of Camp David.[113]

Ariel Sharon's Temple Mount Visit

Then in late September 2000, Barak allowed Ariel Sharon to visit the Muslim **Haram al-Sharif** (the Noble Sanctuary) in Jerusalem accompanied by over one thousand armed Israeli police. The **Temple Mount** carries special religious significance for both groups, and sovereignty over it was one of the issues that Barak and Arafat had contested. Sharon had designed the 1982 Israeli invasion of Lebanon and had been judged by an Israeli commission of inquiry to be personally responsible for the Sabra and Shatila massacres in September 1982. (The inquiry had been demanded by 400,000 Israelis who demonstrated in Tel Aviv.) His visit to the Temple Mount triggered a Palestinian protest followed by Israeli suppression. On the next day, a Friday (the day of special community prayer for Muslims), crowds of Muslims gathered at the al-Aqsa Mosque to demonstrate their displeasure. As they left the mosque, some threw stones at Israeli police, who responded with "withering fire": four Palestinians were killed and hundreds were injured.[114] Thus began the second intifada (see below).

Figure 8.1. Palestinian home dynamited by Israel to clear an area through Rafah near the wall dividing Gaza from Egypt. Courtesy David Whitten Smith, July 2005.

The Second (Al-Aqsa) Intifada (2000–2005)

In the judgment of seasoned British journalist Alan Hart, Sharon's "real purpose" with his visitation to the Temple Mount, or Haram al-Sharif, "was to provoke Palestinian violence" in order to win election as Israel's next prime minister. Until then, in the wake of the Israeli failure to implement Oslo, Arafat had managed to contain "Palestinian violence."[115] However, once unleashed, the second intifada had a much more violent character than the first, largely nonviolent intifada. Palestinian suicide bombings increased greatly for several years. From 1993 to 2000, there were from one to five a year. Then there were 40 in 2001, 47 in 2002, 23 in 2003, 17 in 2004, and 9 in 2005. Over the next three years there were from one to three a year.[116] These suicide bombings were "repeatedly condemned" by Arafat and his Palestinian Authority, as well as by "Palestinian intellectuals and activists." In 2003, American analyst Phyllis Bennis wrote that the suicide bombings at the time expressed "the anger and hopelessness that has become endemic among the . . . Palestinians living under military occupation. . . . People become willing to use their own body as a weapon when other means are unavailable."[117] Israel regularly fired on Palestinian homes from helicopter gunships and tanks, dropped bombs, and launched rockets into Palestinian neighborhoods.

Taba Talks

Threatened with a vote of no confidence, Barak called early elections. At Taba, an Egyptian resort town, President Clinton made one last effort in January 2001 to negotiate peace. These discussions significantly narrowed the gaps between the parties,[118] especially regarding the return of Palestinian refugees and the administration of holy places in Jerusalem, but Barak ended the talks without making any offers on the pretext that the date of the Israeli election was too close.[119] He lost the election to Ariel Sharon.

Ariel Sharon as Prime Minister and the Reinvasion of Palestinian Towns and Cities

If Israelis expected Sharon to re-establish peace with a show of force, they got half of what they had voted for: a show of force, but no peace. As the situation spiraled downward, Palestinian violence continued and Israel assassinated selected Palestinian leaders—especially, but not exclusively, leaders of Hamas and of guerrilla groups that had carried out terrorist attacks; such extrajudicial murders violate international law. Early in 2002, Israel "re-invaded" Palestinian areas, killing more than two hundred Palestinians, wounding more than four hundred, and detaining more than four thousand; in addition, Israeli forces bulldozed more homes and buildings, cut trenches across highways, and uprooted fruit trees for what they claimed were security reasons. They closed down major areas of the West Bank and Gaza with twenty-three- or twenty-four-hour "curfews," forcing inhabitants to stay indoors for days at a time unable to buy food or medicines, and destroying the Palestinian economy.

The Road Map

In 2002, following the Israeli "reinvasion" of the West Bank, the so-called Quartet, consisting of the United States, Russia, the EU, and the UN, proposed a resolution to the conflict called the "Road Map," which was not publicized until the summer of 2003 after the U.S. invasion of Iraq. The Road Map had three goals: to end the occupation, to create some sort of Palestinian state, and to ensure Israeli security. It laid out three phases of activity, beginning in phase one with a set of obligations for each of the two sides, including a settlement freeze by Israel and the imposition of Mahmoud Abbas as Palestinian leader in place of Arafat. In phase two, a "provisional" Palestinian state was supposed to be created; and in phase three, final status issues were to be addressed. In fact, the proposal was seriously flawed, omitting crucial elements such as the right of return and the overall framework of international law. In effect, it enabled Israel to substitute ending the conflict for ending the occupation, whereas Mahmoud Abbas was told to call off the "armed intifada." One result of the Road Map was the inauguration of Israel's construction of the Wall.[120]

Israel's Separation Barrier, or Apartheid Wall[121]

In June 2002, Israel began to build a "**separation barrier**" allegedly to separate the West Bank from Israel as protection against terrorist infiltration. It consists of a wall or fence sandwiched between patrol roads, trenches, raked gravel, and electronic sensors, and guarded by watchtowers and firing posts every two hundred meters. In rural areas, the main "fence" is chain link and razor wire. In urban areas, it is a concrete wall eight meters high. It is constructed almost entirely within the West Bank (as much as twelve miles inside) in order to locate major Jewish settlements on the Israeli side of the barrier. About 10 percent of the West Bank, where over five thousand Palestinians live, lies on the Israeli side of the barrier. In 2003, these areas to the west of the barrier were declared "**closed military zones.**" Palestinians need special permits to enter, exit, or live in them; Israeli settlers do not require these permits.[122] The main barrier with its subsidiary barriers and checkpoints to its east (inside the West Bank) cuts off Palestinian villages from their fields and often from their water supplies, schools, hospitals, and resources in other Palestinian villages. Construction of the wall has destroyed significant amounts of Palestinian farmland and uprooted thousands of productive olive trees. The Israeli government says it is protecting Israel from terrorists. Palestinians and international observers say it is confiscating West Bank land and water. They call it Israel's "**apartheid wall.**"

International Law on the Wall

In July 2004, the International Court of Justice ruled overwhelmingly that the Israeli separation barrier, or wall, was illegal under international law wherever it intruded on Palestinian land, including East Jerusalem, which Israel had illegally annexed and incorporated into "greater Jerusalem"—an action which the ICJ and the UN rejected. The wall would be legal if it were built on the Israeli side of the 1948 cease-fire line between Israel and the occupied territories, but most of it is built on the Palestinian side of the border. The court ordered Israel to cease building the intrusive sections, dismantle them where they existed, and make reparations for the damage caused; it also ordered other UN member countries to ensure that Israel complied with the ruling.[123]

The Geneva Accord

In late 2003 and early 2004 an unofficial group of Israeli and Palestinian leaders engaged in a "Geneva Initiative" leading to a "Geneva Accord," which proposed a detailed solution to the conflict and distributed it widely to both populations. The document follows closely the understandings reached at the Taba negotiations. For the first time, a publicly available document offered concrete solutions to most of the outstanding issues, although its proposals for normalizing the status of refugees (to resettle them in Israel, in Palestine, in the countries where they currently reside, or in other countries willing to accept them) depended on the preferences of the refugees themselves and on the willingness of various countries to absorb them (with compensation). Also it said nothing about Palestinian citizens of the state of Israel. Hard-liners on both sides denounced the document and its signers, but it showed that there were partners on both sides willing to make compromises for peace. It also provided a benchmark against which other proposals could be measured.[124]

The Withdrawal of Israeli Settlers from Gaza and the Death of Arafat

Also in 2004, Prime Minister Sharon announced his intention to close the Jewish settlements in Gaza and remove all Israelis—settlers and soldiers—relocating the settlers primarily in West Bank settlements. Religious Zionist settler groups strongly protested Israel's abandonment of any occupied territory. Israeli public opinion surveys showed a majority even of Israeli *settlers* supporting the plan, but Sharon's Likud Party was opposed, so he formed a new coalition government less dependent on Likud. A leading advisor to Sharon declared publicly that the purpose of the Gaza withdrawal was to kill the "peace process," providing "just enough formaldehyde" to prevent the formation of a Palestinian state. Sharon disavowed the statement.[125]

In late 2004, Chairman Arafat died of an unexplained, and suspicious, illness. Mahmoud Abbas (Abu Mazen), elected to succeed him, had campaigned on a platform of using only nonviolent resistance to the Israeli occupation. He convinced militant groups to cease their rocket and bomb attacks, sending Palestinian police to patrol the areas from which such attacks had most often been launched. For a time Israel then ended proactive assassinations of militants and relaxed some major checkpoint controls. In late 2013, Arafat's body was exhumed and examined to try to determine the cause of death; the discovery of radioactive polonium in his remains raised the possibility of deliberate polonium poisoning.

In August 2005, the Israeli army moved all the Jewish settlers and soldiers out of Gaza. The Palestinians of Gaza were concerned whether Israel would supply them with electricity and would allow them to use their own water resources, to cross their border for travel and trade, to open and operate their airport (Israel had bombed and destroyed the airport's radar and control tower in 2001 and bulldozed trenches across its runways), and to construct a seaport. Their fears were well placed. Israel continued to control the border of Gaza and therefore the land crossings (except the Rafah crossing, controlled by Egypt), the airspace, and access to Gaza by sea; Israel did not allow the airport to be repaired or reopened. Alleging danger from terrorists, Israel kept the border closed for most of the harvest season, causing the Gazan export crop to spoil. Gaza is in effect a huge open-air prison.

Palestinian Elections and the Siege of Gaza

Israel's hard line in Gaza came just as the Palestinians were campaigning for elections to their parliament, leaving Mahmoud Abbas with no success to show for his policy of nonviolence and conciliation. In democratic elections held in January 2006, Hamas captured a majority of the seats in Parliament and the right to create the new Palestinian government. Israel attempted to cripple the Hamas government by refusing to turn over the border duties which it collects on behalf of the Palestinian Authority. The U.S. Congress and the European Union also cut off funding to the Palestinians. As a result, Palestinian public school teachers and thousands of other civil servants went for months without salaries. In addition, Israel closed the crossings into Gaza for extended periods, causing severe shortages of food and medicine.

The Israeli siege on Gaza, supported by the U.S., Egypt, and other powers, was still in place eight years later in 2014. Aside from extreme restrictions on the import of such necessities as food, water, medicine, and energy, another aspect of the siege is the heavy surveillance of Gaza fishermen, who may only take their boats a few miles out into the Mediterranean, where pollution from raw sewage is prevalent and fish are scarce.[126]

Israeli Elections, Invasions of Gaza and Lebanon

After the Gaza disengagement, Prime Minister Ariel Sharon proposed withdrawing from a few West Bank settlements, while strengthening the major settlements and the separation wall. When his Likud Party objected, he formed a new party, **Kadima** (the Hebrew word means "Forward"—it also means "Eastward"). Then Sharon suffered a massive stroke (from which he died in January 2014) and was succeeded by Ehud Olmert. In the elections of 2006, Kadima gained the largest number of seats in the Knesset and formed a government. Sharon had insisted that the "separation barrier" would not constitute the border with Palestine and could be moved or removed, but Olmert, his successor, announced that the barrier would become the border; this policy is called "convergence." Palestinians, in line with international law, maintain that borders cannot be set unilaterally.

In 2006, Gazans fired primitive Qassam rockets into Israel, which Israel used to justify attacking Gaza with shells, bombs, and helicopter gunships. When Gazan militants captured an Israeli soldier who was guarding the siege border, Israel reinvaded Gaza, destroying the electric-generation plant on which its water and sewage systems depend. Soon after, **Hezbollah** fighters in Lebanon captured two more Israeli soldiers, triggering an Israeli reinvasion of Lebanon that had long been planned. The operation went badly—although Israel caused massive damage with its bombing and land invasion, it suffered heavy casualties, failed to defeat Hezbollah, and finally withdrew its forces from southern Lebanon.

Reporting on the physical and psychological state of Gazans after Israel's aggression, the Israeli journalist Gideon Levy wrote in the leading Israeli newspaper, *Haaretz*, "There are thousands of wounded, disabled and shell-shocked people in Gaza, unable to receive any treatment. . . . Tens of thousands of children suffer from existential anxiety, while their parents are unable to provide help."[127]

Two years later, after breaking a cease-fire with Hamas on November 4, 2008—election day in the U.S., Israel launched a three-week assault on Gaza in late December, killing more than fourteen hundred (including eight hundred fifty civilians and three hundred fifty children) and wounding more than five thousand; destroying more than four thousand homes and damaging more than forty thousand; and damaging or destroying 215 factories and some seven hundred businesses, in addition to hospitals, government buildings, police stations, mosques, schools, universities, and UN properties. An organization of IDF veterans called "Breaking the Silence" published a book of testimonies describing what they saw and did: *Operation Cast Lead Gaza 2009*. The 113-page book is available for free download.[128] When he saw the devastation, Jimmy Carter commented feelingly on the "deliberate destruction" inflicted by Israel on the people of Gaza and their infrastructure. A 574-page United Nations report, "Human Rights in Palestine and Other Occupied Arab Territories," by the UN Fact Finding Mission on the Gaza Conflict, chaired by Justice Richard Goldstone (15 September 2009) stated:

> It is clear from evidence gathered by the Mission that the destruction of food supply installations, water sanitation systems, concrete factories and residential houses was the result of a deliberate and systematic policy by the Israeli armed forces. It was not carried out because those objects presented a military threat or opportunity but to make the daily process of living, and dignified living, more difficult for the civilian population (par. 1688).
>
> The operations were carefully planned in all their phases. . . . There were almost no mistakes made according to the Government of Israel. It is in these circumstances that the Mission concludes that what occurred in just over three weeks at the end of 2008 and the beginning of 2009 was a deliberately disproportionate attack designed to punish, humiliate, and terrorize a civilian population, radically diminish its local economic capacity both to work and to provide for itself, and force upon it an ever-increasing sense of dependency and vulnerability. (par. 1690)[129]

Because of the Israeli siege, imposed in 2006, it became difficult to impossible to bring building materials into Gaza for reconstruction; the supply of food, water, fuel, electricity, humanitarian relief, and medicines was also imperiled due to the siege. In November 2012, Israel broke another truce with Hamas and again attacked Gaza with warships, F-16s, and tanks for a week.

In an attempt to challenge Israel's blockade of Gaza's coast, several flotillas of small ships have brought humanitarian supplies to Gaza. Israel permitted five such flotillas to reach Gaza before **Operation Cast Lead**, but it intercepted and seized the ships of later flotillas. In its 2010 attack, Israeli soldiers killed nine activists on the Turkish ship Mavi Marmara. Relations between Israel and the government of Turkey, one of Israel's few allies in the region, were seriously strained by the incident.[130]

Avi Shlaim, an Israeli professor at Oxford University, has described Israel as a rogue state whose "entire record is one of unbridled and unremitting brutality towards the inhabitants of Gaza."[131] Likewise, British journalist Alan Hart views Israel as "a brutal occupying power," and Israel's occupation and blockade of Gaza as "the cause of the . . . rockets" fired from Gaza. In his judgment, "Israel's leaders have no interest in peace on terms the Palestinians could accept."[132]

Hard-Line Religious Positions

The Israeli government refuses to negotiate with the Hamas government because Hamas does not acknowledge the legitimacy of the state of Israel *as a state for all Jews of the world.* But neither does the Israeli government acknowledge as legitimate a Palestinian state with internationally recognized borders within the pre-1967 territories. Since early 2013, it has been reported that Khaled Mashaal, the leader of Hamas, would accept a two-state solution to the conflict with Israel, the state of Palestine being located in the West Bank and Gaza, with East Jerusalem as its capital.[133]

Platforms and charters are frequently referred to, but just as frequently ignored in practice. Also, political parties in Israel form, merge, divide, and collapse recurrently. For example, Kadima was formed in 2005, became the largest party in the Knesset with twenty-nine seats in 2006, slipped to twenty-eight and lost its leadership role in 2009, and crashed to become the smallest party in 2013 with only two seats. In 2014 the largest Knesset parties are Likud Yisrael Beitenu (a merger of two parties) with thirty-one seats, Yesh Atid (a brand new party) with nineteen, Labor (which dominated the Knesset until 1977) with fifteen, Jewish Home with twelve, and Shas with eleven. The Likud leader Binyamin Netanyahu is prime minister.[134]

Here are some quotations from the Hamas Charter (1988):

> The Islamic Resistance Movement is a distinguished Palestinian movement, whose allegiance is to Allah, and whose way of life is Islam. It strives to raise the banner of Allah over every inch of Palestine, for under the wing of Islam followers of all religions can coexist in security and safety where their lives, possessions and rights are concerned (Article 6).
>   The Islamic Resistance Movement believes that the land of Palestine is an Islamic Waqf [religious endowment] consecrated for future Moslem generations until Judgment Day. It, or any part of it, . . . should not be given up. Neither a single Arab country nor all Arab countries, neither any king or president, . . . neither any organization . . . possess the right to do that. (Article 11)[135]

Compare those statements with this excerpt from the recent Likud Constitution (2006):

> Article 2, 1b. Safeguarding the right of the Jewish people to the Land of Israel as an eternal, inalienable right, working diligently to settle and develop all parts of the land of Israel, and extending national sovereignty to them.

And with these statements from the Likud platform (as of February 2007), which seems not to have been changed:

Article 2. 1b. The Jewish communities in Judea, Samaria [that is, the West Bank] and Gaza are the realization of Zionist values. Settlement of the land is a clear expression of the unassailable right of the Jewish people to the Land of Israel and constitutes an important asset in the defense of the vital interests of the State of Israel. The Likud will continue to strengthen and develop these communities and will prevent their uprooting. . . . The Government of Israel flatly rejects the establishment of a Palestinian Arab state west of the Jordan river. . . . The Palestinians can run their lives freely in the framework of self-rule, but not as an independent and sovereign state. . . . The Jordan Valley and the territories that dominate it shall be under Israeli sovereignty. The Jordan river will be the permanent eastern border of the State of Israel.[136]

The new Kadima Party, founded by Ariel Sharon, realized that claiming the whole of the West Bank and Gaza for Israel would lead to an Arab majority and produce a state that would be either non-Jewish or nondemocratic. Therefore it concluded:

The Israeli nation has a national and historic right to the whole of Israel. However, in order to maintain a Jewish majority, part of the Land of Israel must be given up to maintain a Jewish and democratic state. Israel shall remain a Jewish state and homeland. Jewish majority in Israel will be preserved by territorial concessions to Palestinians. Jerusalem and large settlement blocks in the West Bank will be kept under Israeli control.[137]

At the present time, official Israeli positions on the Palestinian question are hard to determine. Netanyahu, in a 2009 speech at Bar-Ilan University, approved of a "Demilitarized Palestinian State," but other indications suggest that such a "state" would not include any part of Jerusalem, the Jordan Valley, the major Jewish settlements in the West Bank, an army, or control over border access, water, air space, electronic communication, or foreign affairs. In other words, it would be similar to the South African Bantustans. Palestinians call the results "Palestans."

A Palestinian Christian Appeal and an American Response

Kairos Palestine[138]

Kairos Palestine is a statement issued in December 2009 from Bethlehem, Palestine, by Palestinian Christians representing various churches, which names itself "a prayerful call to end the occupation" and "a moment of truth: a word of faith, hope, and love from the heart of Palestinian suffering." Its title echoes that of the Kairos Document, issued in 1985 from apartheid South Africa by black Christian theologians.

The Kairos Palestine statement highlights the crucial importance of Jerusalem as a city for "two peoples of three religions," the sinfulness of the Israeli occupation, and the validity of the BDS movement (boycott, divestment, sanctions) "as a means of nonviolent resistance" to the Israeli occupation; nonviolent resistance is described as "a right and duty for all Palestinians." The document expresses gratitude to "the churches of the world" for their solidarity; it invites them to "come and see" the situation of Palestinians under Israeli domination, and then to "tell the truth publicly for the sake of justice, peace, and reconciliation." Appealing to the authority of international law, it seeks "an independent Palestinian state with Al-Quds [Jerusalem] as its capital."

After describing the "reality on the ground," the statement voices strong opposition to the practice of using the Bible to justify injustice, as for example, by fundamentalist Christians, and speaks of how to apply hope and love to a situation that seems to lack both. The concluding sections of the statement address Christians, Muslims, Jews, Palestinians, and Israelis, respectively, condemning "all forms of racism, whether religious or ethnic, including anti-Semitism and Islamophobia"; and explaining (among other issues) why a Jewish or Islamic state is untenable, given the diverse demography of Palestine and Israel. In the final paragraph, the belief is confirmed "that God's goodness will finally triumph over the evil of hate and of death that still persists in our land."

Kairos USA: The Moment of Grace and Opportunity[139]

Kairos USA is a movement of U.S. Christians in support of the Kairos Palestine call for nonviolent resistance to the Israeli occupation of Palestine. The movement has published the document "Call to Action: U.S. Response to the Kairos Palestine Document—A word of confession and faith from the churches in the United States."[140] The document opens with a church confession of repentance for Christian persecution of Jews, and a statement to the effect that "the 'peace process' has continued to be no more than a cover for the continuing colonization of the West Bank and East Jerusalem, the imprisonment of Gaza and the intensification of the structures of oppression." Part one of the document, "the signs of the times," speaks of justice and offers a church confession of repentance for having failed to seek justice in Palestine. Part two, "theological reflections," rejects both the Christian Zionist view that biblical Israel is identical with the modern state of Israel, and the "supersessionist" view that "the Church has taken the place of Israel in God's purposes, and . . . the Jews have been condemned to suffering as punishment for rejecting the Gospel." Part three, "interfaith relationships," condemns anti-Semitism and Islamophobia, claiming that the underlying struggle in Israel-Palestine is not between religions, but is about human rights and equality. Part four, "call to action," discusses various responses such as education, support of civil society, an invitation to come and see for oneself, worship and spiritual disciplines, the role of boycott, divestment, and sanctions (BDS), and political advocacy.

International Responses, Including BDS

In 2005, 170 Palestinian civil organizations issued a call for **BDS** against Israel until it (1) deals fairly with Palestinian citizens of Israel, (2) withdraws its occupation of Palestinian lands, and (3) allows refugees to return.[141] The Palestinian Authority applied successfully to the UN General Assembly in late 2012 to receive the status of "non-member observer *state*"—the same category as the Vatican—which enables them to join UN agencies, to speak at the General Assembly, and to bring cases before the International Criminal Court. U.S. Secretary of State John Kerry (spring 2014) is pressing strongly for a two-state solution based on borders close to the 1949–1967 lines, engaging in "shuttle diplomacy" between the two parties, and setting deadlines for a final settlement. While maintaining that it supports a two-state solution, Israel has increased construction of Jewish-only housing in illegal West Bank settlements, making a separate Palestinian state less and less possible.[142] Those who sincerely seek two states are losing hope that a two-state solution is still politically viable: were Netanyahu to make a serious proposal, his government, which is heavily dependent on the vote of ideological settlers, would instantly fall. Yet Kerry is warning Israel that the status quo is not sustainable.

In this quagmire, voices on several sides are reconsidering a single state. Ideological settlers are pressing the government to incorporate the entire West Bank—usually with the proviso that the Palestinians would not be citizens, sometimes with the suggestion that they be transferred out of the state (ethnically cleansed). Miko Peled, son of the late General Matti Peled, notes that a single state in fact exists—but a single state with laws that differ for three classes of people: (1) for Jews in Israel *and in the settlements*, Israeli civil law; (2) for non-Jews in Israel, an alternate Israeli civil law (Adala: the Legal Center for Arab Minority Rights in Israel lists over fifty laws that explicitly discriminate);[143] (3) for West Bank Palestinians, military orders. Were all these people to live under the same laws, the eventual result would be a single state with a non-Jewish majority. Peled recommends a single, secular state with truly equal rights for all its citizens.[144]

The initial Zionist dream was of a Jewish and democratic state that would encompass all the territory which ancient Israel under David and Solomon controlled at its zenith. The problem was that this territory was already occupied. With the colonial mentality of 1900, Zionists hoped that a world power would deliver the wished-for territory into their hands and enforce their control of it, preferably cleansing it of its native population. Such thinking is no longer acceptable under international law. Self-determination means that a population—the entire population—directs its own politics. Within a post-colonial framework, encompassing the territory that Zionists desire requires them to choose between a Jewish or a democratic state and, if the choice is for a Jewish state, to engage in ethnic cleansing.

If Israel were to flagrantly (rather than covertly) engage in ethnic cleansing, it should expect to be confronted with a massive international campaign of boycott, divestment, and sanctions. With a modern economy highly dependent on trade, such consequences would be crippling. Perhaps it is time to revisit the vision promoted by cultural Zionists like Ahad Ha'am and Martin Buber: a single state of all its citizens which honors and supports all worldviews, especially those born in or near this land: Judaism, Christianity, and Islam.

SPOKESPERSONS FOR JUSTICE AND PEACE

There are many more remarkable spokespersons than we have space for in this book. For others, check our website.[145]

Although mainstream media highlight violent Palestinian resistance to Israeli colonization, by far the most frequent, widespread, and effective resistance has been nonviolent. Mazin Qumsiyeh has written an extensive survey of Palestinian nonviolent struggles from Ottoman times to about 2010,[146] and Maxine Kaufman-Lacusta describes the attitudes of current nonviolent activists in Palestine based on interviews, with special attention to the Beit Sahour tax strike of the first intifada, resistance to the Wall, and current resistance by the village of Bil'in near Ramallah to Israeli land appropriation. She includes essays by Ghassan Andoni of Beit Sahour, cofounder of the **International Solidarity Movement**; Jeff Halper of the Israeli Committee against House Demolitions; the lawyer Jonathan Kuttab; and the Jewish-American activist Starhawk.[147] All of the following spokespersons have been committed to nonviolent resistance.

Uri Avnery

Uri Avnery, an atheist Israeli Jew, former member of the Knesset, and author of the book *My Friend, the Enemy*, risked his life and reputation by traveling to Beirut to meet with Yasser Arafat when such contacts were illegal and considered treasonous. He founded the Israeli Council for Israeli-Palestinian Peace with the weekly newsletter *The Other Israel*, and helped found **Gush Shalom**,[148] which carries out nonviolent resistance to Israeli settlements in the occupied territories.[149]

Mustafa Barghouthi

Mustafa Barghouthi is a Palestinian Muslim physician, politician, and advocate of nonviolent resistance to the Israeli occupation. A former Communist, he is married to a Christian Palestinian woman. Since its founding in 2002, he has been the head of Al Mubadara,[150] the Palestinian National Initiative, a pro-democracy, nonviolent grassroots movement. In 2004–2005 (after the death of Arafat), Barghouthi ran as a reformist candidate in the presidential elections against Fatah's Mahmoud Abbas. He saw himself as representing the "silent majority" of Palestinians who wanted a third alternative apart from either **Fatah** or Hamas. Supporting the Arab League's Arab Peace Initiative in favor of a two-state solution, Barghouthi called for an international peace conference with the proviso that, if Israel would not participate in such a conference, he would then organize "nonviolent resistance and an international campaign of 'boycotts and sanctions' against the Israeli government."

Barghouthi has suffered violence at the hands of the Israeli military numerous times. During the presidential campaign, he experienced Israeli "harassment and intimidation," for example, being beaten by Israeli soldiers at a checkpoint south of Jenin on the West Bank. Nonetheless, he persisted with his message that, in the absence of negotiations conducted in good faith, "the way to peace and justice was through nonviolent resistance." Barghouthi's candidacy was mostly ignored by local media, despite his stature as "the first serious democratic opposition candidate in Palestinian history." Yet on election day Barghouthi came in second, winning 19.5 percent of the vote in contrast to Abbas's 62.5 percent. Given the constraints that he suffered under, this was a surprisingly positive result.[151] In 2010, Mairhead Maguire nominated Barghouthi for the Nobel Peace Prize. In September 2011, he predicted that Palestinians would eventually "give up on the two-state solution and pursue equal rights for all" in one state.[152]

Abuna Elias Chacour

Many Jews, Muslims, and Christians—religious, political, and educational leaders— have cooperated with the Palestinian Arab Christian priest Elias Chacour, who built an interfaith Christian-Muslim-Jewish grade school, high school, and college in Ibillin, Galilee.[153] In February 2006 he was elected Bishop of Akko, Haifa, Nazareth, and All of Galilee (approximating a territory equivalent to Palestine and Israel) for the Melkite (Greek Catholic) Church.[154] He is the first Israeli citizen to be named a Catholic bishop. See his fascinating, moving, and mind-expanding books *Blood Brothers* (1984, 2003) and *We Belong to This Land* (1990).

International Peace Teams

Inspired by Gandhi's dream of nonviolent peace teams, several groups have organized teams of Israeli, Palestinian, and international nonviolence activists. From a largely secular perspective, the *International Solidarity Movement* (ISM)[155] was founded by Palestinians. Their website explains: "Internationals with the ISM are not in Palestine to teach nonviolent resistance. Palestinians resist nonviolently every day. The ISM lends support to the Palestinian resistance to the occupation and their demand for freedom through Direct Action . . . [and] Documentation."[156] A U.S. college student named Rachel Corrie was serving as an ISM volunteer when she was killed in March 2003 by an Israeli bulldozer about to demolish a home in Rafah (Gaza Strip) that she was trying to protect. Similar groups active in Israel-Palestine include the (mostly Protestant) *Christian Peacemaker Teams* (CPT) and the largely Roman Catholic Michigan Peace Team (MPT), now called the *Meta Peace Team*.[157] The CPT website asks, "What would happen if Christians devoted the same discipline and self-sacrifice to nonviolent peacemaking that armies devote to war?"[158]

Refuseniks, Resisters, and Others

Israel Defense Forces (IDF) officers and troops who in conscience refused their assignment to fight in Lebanon formed the group Yesh Gevul, which means, "There is a border [limit]." That is, there is a border with Lebanon (or the occupied territories) that should be respected, and there is a limit to what Israel may do. Once the

first intifada started, the movement also resisted assignment to the occupied territories. Recently, high school age draft resisters (the *Shministim*)[159] have formed *Ometz
Le'sarev* (Courage to Refuse) and New Profile.[160] Resisters can be imprisoned for
up to twelve months, then released, reassigned to the occupied territories, and re-
imprisoned—effectively being kept in jail without limit. More commonly, resisters
are given punitive assignments, sent home after a brief jail term, or reassigned outside the problem areas—the government does not want to draw attention to the
issue. One refusenik applying for conscientious objector status said: "When I try to
consider in what kind of a world I would like to live, I know that such a world does
not include violence. . . . My refusal is one expression of my belief in . . . the power
of nonviolent resistance."[161]

"Combatants for Peace" consists of former *Israeli and Palestinian* fighters who,
having renounced their former violence, now cooperate nonviolently for a just and
peaceful two-state resolution. They say, "Only by joining forces, will we be able to
end the cycle of violence, the bloodshed and the occupation and oppression of the
Palestinian people."[162]

"Breaking the Silence" is an organization of IDF veterans who describe their disturbing experiences in the occupied territories. They have a database of testimonies
on their website,[163] a series of electronic books of testimonies that can be down-
loaded, and the published book *Our Harsh Logic* in hard copy or electronic
format.[164]

SUMMARY

For millennia, various peoples together lived in the area that is now Israel/Palestine.
In the second millennium BCE one of these peoples were the Hebrews, whose story
is told in the Tanakh from the arrival of Abraham to the early common era, including the parallel origins in the first century CE of rabbinic Judaism and the Jewish
messianic Jesus movement that became Christianity. The people who remained in
the land, and became known as Palestinians, sometimes changed their religion, for
example, from Judaism to Christianity in the Byzantine period, and from Christianity to Islam after the arrival of Arab Muslims in the seventh century CE. From that
time until the twentieth century, the vast majority of the population consisted of
Arab Muslims, although some were Christians and a smaller number were Jews.

After two millennia of Diaspora, the Jewish world community was split between
those who recommended assimilation or patience in exile, and those who wished to
establish an explicitly Jewish nation in Palestine despite the fact that another people
(Palestinians) had been living there for centuries. The Holocaust and U.S. political
pressure tilted the scale decisively toward a Jewish state, even though the majority
of Jews still live outside of Israel. The Zionist goal has been to establish (a) an explicitly Jewish state, (b) with a Western-style democracy, (c) in the territory controlled
for less than five hundred years during the first millennium BCE by the ancient
kingdoms of Judah and Israel. Some Jews believe that this territory was promised

to them by God and so they have an obligation to "redeem" it by settling there and dominating it—this belief requires major dispossession of its non-Jewish inhabitants. Even today, a border encompassing (c) would result in a Jewish minority, allowing at best either (a) a Jewish state, or (b) a democratic state, but not both. All three could be realized only by further dispossession.

A minority of Muslim Palestinians believe that Palestine is an Islamic waqf—a religious endowment given to them by God—which they are required to preserve as such. Most Palestinians have not traditionally been committed to an Islamic government; rather they have sought a secular state with freedom and justice for all faiths. All Palestinians suffer under the injustice of dispossession and illegal occupation. Efforts by Israel to motivate Palestinian emigration by making life in Palestine unlivable, and to prevent refugees from exercising their internationally recognized right of return, have failed to solve the problem. Israeli leaders dispute whether to accept less territory than 100 percent of historic Palestine (Israel plus the occupied territories), at least temporarily, or to "transfer" the remaining Palestinians by force. To date, no Israeli government has been willing to propose a sovereign Palestinian state in all of the West Bank, including East Jerusalem, and Gaza, although the Palestinian Authority has said that it would accept such a solution, thus forfeiting 78 percent of historic Palestine. In 2002 the Arab League offered to normalize relations with Israel in exchange for such an arrangement.

Within Israeli society attitudes vary greatly, from settlers determined to retain control over all the land to peace activists nonviolently resisting their government's illegal military occupation of the West Bank and Gaza. A few Muslim Palestinians and some Israeli Jews believe that their religion requires them to exercise political control over all the land—incompatible positions that cannot both prevail. Others appeal to religious prophets who spoke for justice and compassion—suggesting some kind of sharing. Similar splits divide Christians between Zionists who support complete Jewish control and progressives who advocate religiously based justice and compassionate nonviolence for all inhabitants of the land whether in one or two states.

Local and international political leaders have various reasons for supporting one party or another, combining religious convictions, commitment to peace with justice, and self-interest. Currently, the United States massively funds the state of Israel and supports it politically at the UN. How long Israel can count on support from a declining imperial power is a serious question.

FOR MORE INFORMATION

Check the reading list below and at the end of this book for works by Ateek, Avnery, Chacour, Ellis, Hart, Rashid Khalidi, Walid Khalidi, Pappe, Peled, Qumsiyeh, Ruether, Said, and others. For up-to-date references to many more groups and individuals, see the website for this book at http://courseweb.stthomas.edu/justpeace/rowman.html.

KEY TERMS

al-Aqsa Mosque

apartheid wall

Balfour Declaration

BDS

British Mandate

checkpoints

closed military zone

Deir Yassin

Diaspora

East Jerusalem

ethnic cleansing

"facts on the ground"

Fatah

Gaza Strip

Golan Heights

Gush Emunim

Gush Shalom

Haganah

Hamas

Haram al-Sharif

Hezbollah

Histadrut

International Solidarity Movement

intifada

Irgun

Jewish settlements (colonies)

Jewish state

Judea

Kadima Party

Knesset

Labor Party

Lehi/Stern Gang

Likud Party

al-Nakba

Occupied Palestinian Territories

Operation Cast Lead

Oslo Accords

Ottoman Empire

Palestine Liberation Organization

Palestine National Congress

Refuseniks

Revisionist Zionism

Sabra and Shatila

Samaria

separation barrier

Sykes-Picot Agreement

Temple Mount

USS *Liberty*

West Bank

Western Wall

Yesh Gevul

Zionism

DISCUSSION QUESTIONS

1. Which of the twenty character-types mentioned at the beginning of the chapter would come closest to representing your own approach to this conflict?

2. How much of the history presented here were you aware of from previous reading and from the media? How much of what you were *not* aware of is important for understanding the conflict?

3. Let each student role-play one of the character types or actual persons mentioned in the chapter by entering into conversation with other students over the history presented here: its accuracy and completeness, its biases, the significance of the various events, and appropriate responses.

4. Within the context of the conflict, discuss the relevance of the following terms and of the controversial realities they signify: apartheid, collective punishment, colonization, ethnic cleansing, facts on the ground, Holocaust, international

law, intifada, martyrs, military necessity, nonviolent action, occupation, occupied territories, racism, redeeming the land, self-defense, state terrorism, suicide bombing, targeted assassination, terrorism, transfer, Zionism.

5. How would you resolve the Israel-Palestinian conflict? What steps would you take to bring about justice and peace for both peoples?

SUGGESTIONS FOR FURTHER READING

Ateek. *Justice, and Only Justice.*
——. *A Palestinian Christian Cry for Reconciliation.*
——, ed. *Faith and the Intifada.*
Avishai. *The Tragedy of Zionism.*
Avnery. *Israel and the Palestinians.*
——. *My Friend, the Enemy.*
Begin. *The Revolt: Story of the Irgun.*
Beit-Hallahmi. *The Israeli Connection.*
——. *Original Sins.*
Bennis. *Understanding the Palestinian-Israeli Conflict.*
Carter. *Palestine: Peace Not Apartheid.*
Chacour. *Blood Brothers.*
Chomsky and Herman. *Middle East Illusions.*
Ellis. *Beyond Innocence and Redemption.*
Farber. *Radicals, Rabbis and Peacemakers.*
Flapan. *The Birth of Israel: Myths and Realities.*
——. *Zionism and the Palestinians.*
Hart. *Zionism: The Real Enemy of the Jews*, 3 vols.
Herzl. *The Complete Diaries of Theodor Herzl.*
Jews for Justice in the Middle East. *The Origin of the Palestine-Israel Conflict.*
Katz. *Days of Fire.*
Khalidi, R. *The Iron Cage.*
Khalidi, W., ed. *All That Remains.*
——. *Before Their Diaspora.*
——, ed. *From Haven to Conquest.*
London Sunday Times. *The Yom Kippur War.*
Lucas. *The Modern History of Israel.*
Morris. *The Birth of the Palestinian Refugee Problem Revisited.*
——. *Righteous Victims.*
Olson. *Fast Times in Palestine.*
Pappe. *The Ethnic Cleansing of Palestine.*
Peled. *The General's Son.*
Qumsiyeh. *Popular Resistance in Palestine.*
Ruether and Ellis, eds. *Beyond Occupation.*
Ruether and Ruether. *The Wrath of Jonah.*
Said. *The Question of Palestine.*
Schiff and Ya'ari. *Intifada.*
Shahak. *Jewish History, Jewish Religion.*
Shahak and Mezvinsky. *Jewish Fundamentalism in Israel.*
Tessler. *A History of the Israeli-Palestinian Conflict.*

9

Religious Social Teachings
Christian and Beyond

Towards the end of the last [nineteenth] century the Church found herself facing . . . a critical point. A traditional society was passing away and another was
beginning to be formed—one which brought the hope of new freedoms but also
the threat of new forms of injustice and servitude . . .

In the sphere of economics, . . . new structures for the production of consumer goods had progressively taken shape. A new form of property had
appeared—capital; and a new form of labor—labor for wages, characterized by
high rates of production which lacked due regard for sex, age or family situation, and were determined solely by efficiency, with a view to increasing profits.

Labor became a commodity to be freely bought and sold on the market, its
price determined by the law of supply and demand, without taking into account
the bare minimum required for the support of the individual and his family.
Moreover, the worker was not even sure of being able to sell "his own commodity," continually threatened as he was by unemployment, which, in the absence
of any kind of social security, meant the specter of death by starvation.

The result . . . was a society "divided into two classes, separated by a deep
chasm". . .

At the height of this clash, when people finally began to realize fully the very
grave injustice of social realities . . . and the danger of a revolution . . . Pope Leo
XIII . . . dealt in a systematic way with the "condition of the workers."

—Pope John Paul II, *Centesimus Annus*, par. 4[1]

Christian social teaching is not a recent phenomenon. We have the example of
Jesus himself, followed by the earliest Christian communities, hermits and
monks and nuns, begging orders of preachers (Dominicans and Franciscans),
"peace churches" (Mennonites, Quakers), prophetic condemnations of those in
power (John Chrysostom, Martin Luther, Bartholomé de Las Casas), and social services to the poor and disadvantaged (hospitals, organized relief). But the industrial

revolution of the nineteenth century raised new social issues that challenged people of faith to seek and formulate new responses.

This chapter concentrates on *Christian* social teaching as an example. A short section at the end illustrates how similar studies could be carried out for other major worldviews.

In order to introduce many of the key concepts of Christian social teaching, we begin with the Roman Catholic Church, whose social teaching has been particularly well developed. Then we will expand the treatment to Protestant churches and, briefly, to other religions.

ROMAN CATHOLIC SOCIAL TEACHING

In the nineteenth century, industrialization was radically altering society in Europe and North America, creating great tensions. Feudal landlords and their peasant farmers were losing power to the owners of great manufacturing enterprises utilizing wage labor. Capitalist owners were setting wages as low as possible in order to increase their profits, and paying inadequate attention to worker health and safety. Karl Marx was urging workers to rise up and take power from the rich. In this explosive situation, Pope Leo XIII wrote a revolutionary encyclical.

Pope Leo XIII (1810–1903; Pope from 1878)

Leo XIII published as an **encyclical** the first of the modern papal documents on social teaching. An encyclical is a papal circular letter sent to all bishops of the world dealing with some problem of common interest to the church. Leo's encyclical *Rerum Novarum*[2] (1891) dealt with the problems raised by recent social changes. He listed injustices connected with the changes, some matching those earlier decried by Karl Marx, but he rejected Marx's analysis and proposals partly because of Marx's atheistic worldview. Leo challenged the rich to accept responsibility for the common good, and proposed a new system of *guilds* to organize workers and managers. He wanted workers and managers to cooperate for the common good rather than fight each other in a class struggle.

Private Property

Leo supported *private ownership* of property, but what his arguments actually supported was *widely distributed* ownership of *modest amounts* of property. He did not want a few people to own so much property that most people could own nothing. He argued that people care for property better when they own it, they have more incentive to work well, and they have the security of being able to pass something on to their children. Notice that he was talking primarily about *workers* owning property.

If a workman's wages be sufficient to enable him comfortably to support himself, his wife, and his children, he will find it easy . . . to practice thrift, and he will not fail, by cutting down expenses, to put by some little savings and thus secure a modest source of income. . . . The law, therefore, should . . . induce as many as possible of the people to become owners (par. 46).

Many excellent results will follow from this; and, first of all, property will certainly become more equitably divided. (par. 47)

Leo encouraged employers and workers to cooperate in negotiating a fair day's work for a fair wage. He suggested new social forms for such cooperation, proposing a **corporative state** where the political and economic structures of the society itself would promote worker-management cooperation: different classes in society could be represented *as classes* and thus feel that they were part of a cooperative venture. "The great mistake is to [think] that class is naturally hostile to class. . . . The direct contrary is the truth. . . . Capital cannot do without labor, nor labor without capital" (par. 19).

Pope Pius XI (1857–1939; Pope from 1922)

In 1931, Pope Pius XI wrote the encyclical *Quadragesimo Anno* (Forty Years Ago), confirming but also updating Leo's ideas. Fascist and Nazi thinkers had claimed to be developing Leo's idea of a corporative state. Rather than having the legislature represent *territorial districts*, as is the case in most democracies (local precincts and wards drawn without regard to what type of people lived in them), they designed it to represent different *economic groups*: industrialists, labor unions, farmers, universities, and so on. Their system sounded good in theory, but in practice the government ended up controlling all the institutions of society. Pius responded that their system was not what Leo had in mind.

Subsidiarity

Pius XI introduced the principle of **subsidiarity**: "It is an injustice and . . . a grave evil and disturbance of right order to assign to a greater and higher association what lesser and subordinate organizations can do. For every social activity ought of its very nature to furnish *help* to the members of the body social, and never *destroy and absorb* them" (par. 79, emphases added).

Note the *two* characteristics of subsidiarity: (1) higher levels of political (and economic) organization should not take over responsibilities that lower levels can accomplish (that is, we should push control and decision making to the lowest level at which it can be effectively done), but (2) higher levels should give aid (Latin: *subsidium*) to the lower levels to enable them to do what they can. The aid (subsidium) is what gives subsidiarity its name. Notice its relation to our word "subsidy," although we tend to connect subsidies solely with money, whereas the word *subsidium* actually refers to any kind of aid.

For example, (1) local school boards control the schools, but (2) they get state and federal *subsidies* to help even out inequality between wealthy neighborhoods and poor ones. State and federal departments of education also provide *expert advice, required standards,* and programs to local schools. Private publishing firms offer *textbooks* that teachers and schools can adopt.

Pius objected to injustices against workers even more strongly than Leo had. Leo had proposed workers' organizations, but he had in mind something like the medieval guilds. Pius more clearly supported the new *manufacturing unions* that were coming into being: "Dead matter comes forth from the factory ennobled, while men³ there are corrupted and degraded" (par. 135). Given the mixed record of communism in Russia, Pius warned Christians against the kind of *socialism* that had developed there. Note also that the Nazi Party in Germany called itself the *National Socialist* Party.

World War II broke out around the end of Pius XI's papacy and overshadowed other concerns for the next decade.

Pope John XXIII (1881–1963; Pope from 1958)

On the seventieth anniversary of *Rerum Novarum,* shortly before the Second Vatican Council opened, Pope John XXIII published the encyclical *Mater et Magistra* (Mother and Teacher). To the previous concerns, he added agriculture and aid to developing countries. He was much more open to socialist ideas than earlier popes had been, leading some elite Catholics to respond, "Mater, si; Magistra, no." In his encyclical the pope wrote:

> Probably the most difficult problem today concerns the relationship between political communities that are economically advanced and those in the process of development. ... The solidarity which binds all men together as members of a common family makes it impossible for wealthy nations to look with indifference upon the hunger, misery and poverty of other nations whose citizens are unable to enjoy even elementary human rights. (par. 157)

Two years later, during the church council, Pope John published another encyclical, *Pacem in Terris* (1963). It was the first papal encyclical addressed not only to Catholics through their bishops but significantly to "all people of good will." Published shortly after the resolution of the Cuban missile crisis and the building of the Berlin Wall, it dealt mainly with human rights and a better organization of international society. Among the new topics was the right of people to emigrate from one country to another:

> Every human being has the right to freedom of movement and of residence within the confines of his own State. When there are just reasons in favor of it, he must be permitted to emigrate to other countries and take up residence there. [22] The fact that he is a citizen of a particular State does not deprive him of membership in the human family,

nor of citizenship in that universal society, the common, worldwide fellowship of men. (par. 25)

Second Vatican Council (1962–1965)

The Second Vatican Council produced sixteen documents, including *Gaudium et Spes* (Pastoral Constitution on the Church in the Modern World), which speaks of recognizing the "signs of the times"—the special circumstances, opportunities, and responsibilities of each historical period. There has been much controversy over what these signs are and what they mean:

> The Church has always had the duty of scrutinizing the signs of the times and of interpreting them in the light of the Gospel. Thus, in language intelligible to each generation, she can respond to the perennial questions which men ask about this present life and the life to come, and about the relationship of the one to the other. We must therefore recognize and understand the world in which we live, its explanations, its longings, and its often dramatic characteristics. (par. 4)

Pope Paul VI (1897–1978; Pope from 1963)

In 1967 Pope Paul VI published the encyclical *Populorum Progressio*, moving from the struggle between rich and poor *classes* to that between rich and poor *nations*. The letter came out during the "**decade of development**," which was supposed to bring the developing countries closer to the rich countries. (See the following chapter on liberation theologies.) Paul VI challenged the church (dioceses and religious orders) to share 10 percent of their resources—both money and personnel—with Latin America. Proposing a world fund financed with money saved by reducing the arms race, he criticized major aspects of capitalism:

> Certain concepts have somehow arisen out of these new conditions and insinuated themselves into the fabric of human society: . . . profit as the chief spur to economic progress, free competition as the guiding norm of economics, and private ownership of the means of production as an absolute right, having no limits nor concomitant social obligations. This unbridled liberalism paves the way for a particular type of tyranny . . . the "international imperialism of money." . . . But if it is true that a type of capitalism . . . has given rise to hardships, unjust practices, and fratricidal conflicts that persist to this day, it would be a mistake to attribute these evils to the rise of industrialization itself, for they really derive from the pernicious economic concepts that grew up along with it. We must . . . acknowledge the vital role played by labor systemization and industrial organization in the task of development. (par. 26)

Paul VI observed the eightieth anniversary of *Rerum Novarum* by writing *Octogesima Adveniens* (1971)—not an encyclical but an "apostolic letter" to the president of the Pontifical Commission on Justice and Peace. In it he discussed the problems of urbanization and considered how Christians and local churches could respond

Figure 9.1. American Catholic priest, Charlie Hardy, with neighbors in Nueva Tacagua, Venezuela, a *barrio* outside Caracas, Venezuela. Courtesy David Whitten Smith, October 1988.

to injustice: "Man is experiencing a new loneliness; it is not in the face of a hostile nature which it has taken him centuries to subdue, but in an anonymous crowd which surrounds him and in which he feels himself a stranger. Urbanization, undoubtedly an irreversible stage in the development of human societies, confronts man with difficult problems" (par. 10).

The 1971 worldwide Roman Synod of Catholic Bishops produced a document entitled *Justice in the World:*

> We have . . . been able to perceive the serious injustices which are building around the world of men a network of domination, oppression and abuses which stifle freedom and which keep the greater part of humanity from sharing in the building up and enjoyment of a more just and more fraternal world. [par. 3] . . . Action on behalf of justice

and participation in the transformation of the world fully appear to us as *a constitutive dimension of the preaching of the gospel*, or, in other words, of the Church's mission for the redemption of the human race and its liberation from every oppressive situation. (par. 6, emphasis added)

Paul VI also published the apostolic exhortation *Evangelii Nuntiandi* on "evangelization in the modern world"—sharing the good news of the Gospel—in which he claimed that you can't preach the gospel without combating injustice:

> Evangelization would not be complete if it did not take account of the unceasing interplay of the Gospel and of man's concrete life, both personal and social. This is why evangelization involves an explicit message . . . about the rights and duties of every human being, about family life without which personal growth and development is hardly possible, about life in society, about international life, peace, justice and development—a message especially energetic today about liberation. (par. 29)

Pope John Paul II (1920–2005; Pope from 1978)

Pope John Paul II commemorated the ninetieth anniversary of *Rerum Novarum* with the encyclical *Laborem Exercens* (On Human Work). It presented a powerful and novel treatment of human work (labor), criticized both capitalism and Marxism, and emphasized that labor is always more important than capital. The following paragraph illustrates the Catholic Church's support for labor unions:

> There is a need for ever new *movements of solidarity of* the workers and *with* the workers . . . whenever it is called for by the social degrading of the subject of work, by exploitation of the workers, and by the growing areas of poverty and even hunger. The Church is firmly committed to this cause, for she considers it her mission, her service, a proof of her fidelity to Christ, so that she can truly be the "Church of the poor." (par. 8; emphases are in original)

The encyclical emphasized how important work is for humans. It enables them to (a) express themselves creatively, (b) support their own families, and (c) make a contribution to the larger society.

It also defined capital and labor in a new way. For John Paul, management is not capital; all human activity is labor. Capital is the tools of production that humans make and use. Managers are doing one form of labor; workers on the line are doing another. The assembly line itself is one form of capital; the books in the manager's library are another. In this sense, labor always has priority over capital because people have priority over things:

> [W]e must first of all recall . . . *the priority of labor over capital* . . . labor is always a primary *efficient cause*, while capital, the whole collection of means of production, remains a mere *instrument* or instrumental cause. . . . Everything that comes from man throughout the whole process of economic production, whether labor or the whole collection of means of production and the technology connected with these means (meaning the capability to use them in work), presupposes these riches and resources of the

visible world, riches and resources *that man finds* and does not create. . . . At the beginning of man's work is the mystery of creation. . . . All the means of production . . .
everything that is at the service of work, everything that in the present state of technology
constitutes its ever more highly perfected "instrument," *is the result of work.* . . . Everything contained in the concept of capital . . . is only a collection of things. Man, as the
subject of work, and independently of the work that he does—man alone is a person.
(par. 12, emphases in original)

In 1987, on the twentieth anniversary of *Populorum Progressio,* John Paul II published the encyclical *Sollicitudo Rei Socialis* (On Social Concern). This letter is noteworthy for its strong emphasis on the reality of **structural sin.**

Structural Sin

"Structural sin" refers to unjust laws, customs, situations, and habitual ways of
doing things. Slavery is an example of structural sin—it was held in place by laws,
but also by custom and habit. Racial segregation is a structural sin. Gender injustice
is a structural sin. So is U.S. urban homelessness, although in that case the structures
that hold it in place are less obvious.

In *Sollicitudo Rei Socialis* Pope John Paul points out the relationship between personal sin and structural sin: those who cause, intensify, protect, or share in the
unjust fruits of—or fail to combat—unjust social, political, economic, and other
structures are guilty of personal sin. We may fail to combat these structures because
we or our friends are benefiting from them, because we are too apathetic to be both-
ered, or because we are afraid we may get hurt or lose friends if we object:

It is not out of place to speak of "structures of sin," which . . . are rooted in personal
sin, and thus always linked to the concrete acts of individuals who introduce these
structures, consolidate them and make them difficult to remove.[65] And thus they
grow stronger, spread, and become the source of other sins, and so influence people's
behavior. (par. 36)

Here is the "[note] 65" referred to in par. 36 above:

Whenever the Church speaks of situations of sin, or when she condemns as social sins
certain situations or the collective behavior of certain social groups, . . . she knows . . .
that such cases of social sin are the result of the accumulation and concentration of
many personal sins . . . of those who cause or support evil or who exploit it; of those
who are in a position to avoid, eliminate or at least limit certain social evils but who
fail to do so out of laziness, fear or the conspiracy of silence, through secret complicity
or indifference; of those who take refuge in the supposed impossibility of changing the
world; and also of those who sidestep the effort and sacrifice required. . . . The real
responsibility, then, lies with individuals. A situation—or likewise an institution, a
structure, society itself—is not in itself the subject of moral acts.

ıundredth Year

ıally in 1991, John Paul published the encyclical *Centesimus Annus*. In it he "re-
.ead" *Rerum Novarum* in the light of the human person as uniquely valuable—
made in God's image and destined to spend eternity with God. He re-emphasized
the importance of human solidarity, both affirmed and criticized key concepts of
capitalism, and called for a new economic system now that communism had collapsed and capitalism in its current forms had proved inadequate. He affirmed the
value of free markets, but only when wealth is well enough distributed to give all
humans significant buying power to "vote" in the market:

It would appear that . . . the *free market* is the most efficient instrument for utilizing
resources and effectively responding to needs. But this is true only for those needs
which are "solvent," insofar as they are endowed with purchasing power, and for those
resources which are "marketable," insofar as they are capable of obtaining a satisfactory
price. But there are many human needs which find no place on the market. It is a strict
duty of justice and truth not to allow fundamental human needs to remain unsatisfied,
and not to allow those burdened by such needs to perish. (par. 34)
   [I]t is right to speak of a struggle against an economic system, if the latter is understood as a method of upholding the absolute predominance of capital, the possession
of the means of production and of the land, in contrast to the free and personal nature
of human work.[73] In the struggle against such a system, what is being proposed as an
alternative is not the socialist system, which in fact turns out to be State capitalism, but
rather *a society of free work, of enterprise and of participation.* Such a society is not
directed against the market, but demands that the market be appropriately controlled
by the forces of society and by the State, so as to guarantee that the basic needs of the
whole of society are satisfied . . . profitability is not the only indicator of a firm's condition. It is possible for the financial accounts to be in order, and yet for the people—who
make up the firm's most valuable asset—to be humiliated and their dignity offended.
. . . The purpose of a business firm is not simply to make a profit, but is to be found in
its very existence as a *community of persons* who in various ways are endeavoring to
satisfy their basic needs, and who form a particular group at the service of the whole of
society. Profit is a regulator of the life of a business, but it is not the only one; *other
human and moral factors* must also be considered which, in the long term, are at least
equally important for the life of a business. (par. 35, emphases in original)
   It is not wrong to want to live better; what is wrong is a style of life which is presumed to be better when it is directed towards "having" rather than "being," and which
wants to have more, not in order to be more but in order to spend life in enjoyment as
an end in itself.[75] . . . *Even the decision to invest in one place rather than another, in
one productive sector rather than another, is always a moral and cultural choice.* . . . The
decision to invest, that is, to offer people an opportunity to make good use of their own
labor, is also determined by an attitude of human sympathy and trust in Providence,
which reveal the human quality of the person making such decisions. (par. 36, last two
emphases added)

Centesimus Annus also gives significant new attention to problems of the environment:

At the root of the senseless destruction of the natural environment lies an anthropological error. . . . Man, who discovers his capacity to transform and in a certain sense create the world through his own work, forgets that this is always based on God's prior and original gift of the things that are. Man thinks that he can make arbitrary use of the earth, subjecting it without restraint to his will, as though it did not have its own requisites and a prior God-given purpose, which man can indeed develop but must not betray. Instead of carrying out his role as a co-operator with God in the work of creation, man sets himself up in place of God. . . .

One notes first the poverty or narrowness of man's outlook, motivated as he is by a desire to possess things . . . and lacking that disinterested, unselfish and aesthetic attitude that is born of wonder in the presence of being and of the beauty which enables one to see in visible things the message of the invisible God who created them. (par. 37)

Pope Francis (1936–; Pope from 2013)

Early in Pope Francis's pontificate, it became clear that he would set a new pattern for papal life. He chose his papal name in honor of Francis of Assisi because he wished his pontificate to give special attention to poverty in the world. He chose to live not in the elegant papal apartments but in the guest house which had been home to the cardinals during the papal election. His speeches began to give major attention to poverty. In the following example he is speaking of financial reform to an audience of ambassadors:

While the income of a minority is increasing exponentially, that of the majority is crumbling. This imbalance results from ideologies which uphold the absolute autonomy of markets and financial speculation, and thus deny the right of control to States, which are themselves charged with providing for the common good. A new, invisible and at times virtual, tyranny is established, one which unilaterally and irremediably imposes its own laws and rules. Moreover, indebtedness and credit distance countries from their real economy and citizens from their real buying power. Added to this, as if it were needed, is widespread corruption and selfish fiscal evasion which have taken on worldwide dimensions. The will to power and of possession has become limitless. . . .

Dear Ambassadors, there is a need for financial reform along ethical lines that would produce in its turn an economic reform to benefit everyone. This would nevertheless require a courageous change of attitude on the part of political leaders.[4]

Catholic Relief Services has collected quotations from many of his speeches, which give a good sense of his views.[5]

Social Teaching of Groups of Catholic Bishops

National and regional groups of Catholic bishops were also studying social justice. The United States Catholic bishops produced pastoral letters on nuclear war (1983) and on economic issues (1986). Here are some key passages from the bishops' pastoral letter on nuclear war, *The Challenge of Peace: God's Promise and Our Response:*[6]

Under no circumstances may nuclear weapons or other instruments of mass slaughter be used for the purpose of destroying population centers or other predominantly civilian targets (par. 147).

Retaliatory action whether nuclear or conventional which would indiscriminately take many wholly innocent lives, lives of people who are in no way responsible for reckless actions of their government, must also be condemned. This condemnation, in our judgment, applies even to the retaliatory use of weapons striking enemy cities after our own have already been struck. *No Christian can rightfully carry out orders or policies deliberately aimed at killing noncombatants* (par. 148, emphasis added).

We do not perceive any situation in which the deliberate initiation of nuclear warfare, on however restricted a scale, can be morally justified (par. 150).

These considerations . . . lead us to a strictly conditioned moral acceptance of nuclear deterrence. We cannot consider it adequate as a long-term basis for peace. (par. 186)

And from *Economic Justice for All: Pastoral Letter on Catholic Social Teaching and the U.S. Economy*:[7]

Every perspective on economic life that is human, moral, and Christian must be shaped by three questions: What does the economy do *for* people? What does it do *to* people? And how do people *participate* in it? (par. 1, emphases in original).

The dignity of the human person, realized in community with others, is the criterion against which all aspects of economic life must be measured (par. 28).

The obligation to provide justice for all means that the poor have the single most urgent economic claim on the conscience of the nation (par. 86).

(a) The fulfillment of the basic needs of the poor is of the highest priority . . . (b) Increasing active participation in economic life by those who are presently excluded or vulnerable is a high social priority . . . (c) The investment of wealth, talent, and human energy should be specially directed to benefit those who are poor or economically insecure . . . (d) Economic and social policies as well as the organization of the work world should be continually evaluated in light of their impact on the strength and stability of family life. (par. 90–93)

An especially important feature of these two letters is the process by which they were written. They were published in three drafts, with comments invited on the first two drafts from anyone who cared to offer them. This process gave rise to extensive comments, so that the final product was the result of much more democratic sharing than is usual for Roman Catholic church documents. For this reason among others, the documents have had a much wider influence than is usual for bishops' pastoral letters.

Latin American Bishops

In Latin America, after the Second Vatican Council, the bishops moved quickly to establish the Conferencia Episcopal Latino-Americana, abbreviated **CELAM**. Their second and third meetings, in *Medellín*, Colombia, in 1968, and in *Puebla*, Mexico, in 1979, were most significant. In Medellín the bishops committed themselves to a "preferential option for the poor"—meaning that, when resources are limited, the poor deserve help first. They applied the principle quite radically:

> A business, in an authentically human economy, does not identify itself with the owners of capital, because it is fundamentally a community of persons and a unit of work, which is in need of capital to produce goods. A person or a group of persons cannot be the property of an individual, or a society, or of the state.
>
> The system of liberal capitalism and the temptation of the Marxist system would appear to exhaust the possibilities of transforming the economic structures of our continent. Both systems militate against the dignity of the human person. One takes for granted the primacy of capital . . . in the function of profit-making. The other, although it ideologically supports a kind of humanism, is more concerned with collective man, and in practice becomes a totalitarian concentration of state power. We must denounce the fact that Latin America sees itself caught between these two options and remains dependent on one or other of the [foreign] centers of power which control its economy. (Document on Justice, par. 10)[8]

Summary of Catholic Social Teaching

The great wealth of Catholic social teaching is frequently summarized in the following nine principles[9] (paragraph references are to the National Conference of Catholic Bishops, *Economic Justice for All*):

1. *Dignity of the human person.* Every human person is sacred because God makes humans in God's own image and likeness and gives them an eternal destiny. People do not lose dignity because of their race, sex, nationality, age, disability, poverty, or lack of success. People are more important than things; what we *are* is more important than what we *have* (intro. par. 13; body par. 25, 28, 32).
2. *Realized in community.* This "human dignity can be realized and protected only in community" (par. 14). The human person is both sacred and social.
3. *Involving rights, responsibilities, and the common good.* This dignity in community implies that people have rights (civil, political, and economic) and responsibilities. People have a fundamental right to "life, food, clothing, shelter, rest, medical care, education and employment" (par. 17). Society as a whole has the responsibility to organize itself in such a way that these rights will be provided for all (par. 15). Corresponding to these rights are duties and responsibilities to respect the rights of others and to work for the common good.
4. *Not just given, but participated in.* All people also have the right to *participate* in economic life and in the decisions and activities that affect their lives (intro. par. 15; body par. 15).
5. *Through dignified and productive work.* The right to participate in society includes the right to meaningful work which enables people (a) to express themselves through their talents and initiative, (b) to support their families through fair wages, and (c) to contribute to the larger society (intro.).

6. *Marked by subsidiarity.* Humans carry on their work in association with other people. As we saw above, subsidiarity involves two principles:

   a. What individuals can accomplish by their own initiative and industry should not be taken from them and given to the community; what lesser and subordinate organizations can accomplish should not be taken over by larger or higher associations.

   b. If individuals or lesser organizations need help (financial, technical, organizational) to accomplish these tasks, the higher associations should provide that aid (*subsidium*) (intro. par. 99).

7. *Solidarity and the universal destination of the earth's goods.* We are all related as members of one human family that is only superficially divided by race, sex, nation, ideology, and class. The riches of the earth are intended for all humans. We may or may not be responsible for *causing* injustice, but we are all responsible for working to *end* it (intro. par. 12, 13, 28, 34, 40).

8. *With special attention to the poor.* Because we are all related, and because much poverty is a result of injustice, not simply of misfortune, the poor have the most urgent moral claim on the conscience of the world. A society is judged by how it treats its most vulnerable members. Decisions on public policy should be judged especially in terms of how they affect the poor (intro. par. 16, 19, 35, 36, 38–40).

9. *Maintaining care for God's creation.* The goods of the earth—animal, plant, and mineral—are gifts from God. We have a responsibility to care for these goods as stewards and trustees, not as mere consumers and users, both because we recognize our solidarity with future generations and because we revere God's creation for its own sake (intro. par. 25, 31).

In their document *Economic Justice for All*, the U.S. Catholic bishops explain how its treatment of justice differs from philosophical treatments of justice that deal with individual human rights: "Biblical justice is more comprehensive than subsequent philosophical definitions. It is not concerned with a strict definition of rights and duties, but with the rightness of the human condition before God and within society. Nor is justice opposed to love; rather, it is both a manifestation of love and a condition for love to grow" (intro. par. 39).

Five Key Concepts (The Five S's)

Five concepts can encapsulate and help us remember key points of Catholic social teaching: solidarity, sharing fairly, subsidiarity, structural and cultural change, and simple living. The numbers in parentheses refer to the nine principles explained above.

Solidarity. "Love your neighbor as yourself" (including even "love your enemy") presumes that our neighbor, whether now alive or yet to be born (principle 9), is, like us, a human being with an eternal destiny (1) with needs like our own, dependent on the goods of God's creation (7). So our brother or sister should be treated with dignity (1), in community with ourselves (2), with rights as well as responsibilities (3) that require him or her to be accepted as a participant (4). Each one needs dignified and productive work (5) that calls on all or most of her or his skills, including skills of planning and decision making (6). No one is to be left out, so the poor need special help (7).

Sharing Fairly. If we truly love our brother and sister as ourselves, we will share goods and burdens fairly with each other. Goods include natural resources (7), the fruits of human labor (5), and access to basic human institutions (2) such as health care and education. Goods also include the opportunity to participate in decisions that affect one's life (4, 6). Burdens include work (4), compromise for the sake of common effort (2), and risks such as crime and pollution (9). Positive externalities of economic life (benefits that corporate balance sheets do not take into account), such as the human development that comes from having responsibility and making decisions (4–6), need to be shared fairly, as do negative externalities (burdens that corporate balance sheets do not take into account) such as depletion and pollution (9).

Subsidiarity. Community (2) involves division of labor, but in such a way that work challenges the full humanity of the worker and allows workers to express themselves (5), and in such a way that decision making is shared as widely and democratically as possible (6).

Structural and Cultural Change. Solidarity and fair sharing of both resources and decision making (subsidiarity) require changes in the structures which organize our society. An example would be unfair laws and rules for international trade. We also need to change the cultural practices and explanations that attempt to justify unjust structures. (Johan Galtung calls such explanations "cultural violence.") An example would be arguments in favor of "free trade" that fail to point out how current trade rules allow for massive U.S. agricultural subsidies while insisting that Third World countries eliminate import tariffs that would protect their own poorly subsidized farmers. As a result Mexican farmers, unable to compete, lose their farms and immigrate (illegally) to the U.S. Such changes require courage (because those who benefit from the status quo will attack those who try to change the structures) and commitment of resources (time and money).

Simple Living. Sharing fairly (7, 8) presupposes that we have something to share. The consumer society, driven by advertising, threatens to devour all our resources, leaving us nothing to share. So an authentic Christian life calls us to resist the lure of possessions and to choose a simple life that will leave us with resources to share. Such a life may leave us poorer in material goods but richer in relationships with our brothers and sisters—and with God. Indeed, surrender to the consumer society can leave us constantly dissatisfied, since no one is able to buy all the goods one sees advertised, nor are most of these goods really satisfying. Choice of a simple life with abundant human relationships may be both more peaceful and more satisfying.

Johan Galtung observes that, in the modern capitalistic world economy, "the major conditions for economic growth are hard work, saving/investment, greed, and inconsiderateness."[10] He is thinking of inconsiderateness toward nature (9), toward national and international labor (5, and 2: how wide is our community?), and even toward oneself (1: one's noneconomic needs). Inconsiderateness implies exploitation of nature, labor, and ourselves without reflecting on what these factors need in order to be sustainable, to reproduce themselves, and to maintain a dignified existence according to their own natures.

PROTESTANT SOCIAL TEACHING

Protestant Christianity has also contributed significantly to Christian social teachings. In this section we focus particularly on the issues of (a) economic justice and (b) war and peace. The Protestant denominations surveyed below periodically issue statements on these and various other social issues, such as the environment, health care, politics, gender, race, and more. They also institute programs to help realize their social goals.

The Evangelical Lutheran Church in America (ELCA)[11]

Economics

The ELCA's 1999 social statement on economic life, "Sufficient, Sustainable Livelihood for All,"[12] begins by drawing attention to the extreme gap between rich and poor:

> Economic life pervades our lives—the work we do, the income we receive, how much we consume and save, what we value, and how we view one another.
>
> An economy . . . is meant to meet people's material needs. . . . many are prospering as never before. At the same time, others continue to lack what they need for basic subsistence. . . . We of the Evangelical Lutheran Church in America here assess economic life today in light of the moral imperative to seek sufficient, sustainable livelihood for all.

Noting that "outrage over the plight of people living in poverty is a theme throughout the Bible," it stresses the human dignity of workers and the imperative to provide adequate compensation (a living wage) for their labor, to defend their rights, and to enhance their well-being.

> Human impoverishment, excessive accumulation and consumerism driven by greed, gross economic disparities, and the degradation of nature are incompatible with this reign of God. . . . Because most of us in the United States have far more than we need, we can easily fall into bondage to what we have. . . . If judged by their multimillion dollar compensations, top corporate officers and sports superstars would seem to be the most highly valued in our society. Enormous disparities between their compensations and the average wages of workers are scandalous.

The statement also supports environmental protection, preserving agriculture as a "viable means of livelihood" for farmers, and developing low-income communities in a sustainable way.

War and Peace

The statement "For Peace in God's World,"[13] adopted by a church-wide ELCA assembly in 1995, recommends that the church be a "disturbing presence" during times of apparent peace "when there is no peace" (Jeremiah 6:14) by refusing "to be silent and instead speak[ing] the truth." "Because of the sin-filled reality of earthly life, [we affirm] just war teaching in the service of just peace." The "just war" criteria must be met if a military action is to be legitimate: "We begin with a strong presumption against all war; support for and participation in a war to restore peace is a tragic concession to a sinful world." Just war principles may obligate Christians to "say 'no' to wars in which their nation participates." Nuclear war is absolutely rejected, and "selective conscientious objection" is upheld. Just war principles must also be used to evaluate coercive political activities such as the imposition of sanctions [as, for example, currently on Iran and Cuba].

In support of pacifism, the document states:

> This church today needs the witness of its members who in the name of Jesus Christ refuse all participation in war, who commit themselves to establish peace and justice on earth by nonviolent power alone, and who may suffer and die in their discipleship. We support members who conscientiously object to bearing arms in military service. . . . We must continue the perennial discussion in the Church universal about whether Christian love and discipleship prohibit participation in war in all circumstances, or whether they may permit it in some circumstances.

The United Methodist Church[14]

Economics

In its statement on "The Economic Community," the United Methodist Church calls on governments to create and support policies that promote individual and corporate economic well-being, including "full employment" and minimal inflation. Businesses are accountable for the "social costs" they incur, for example, damage to the environment. Governments should take action to reduce unequal wealth distribution, including reforming the tax system and ending "programs that . . . benefit the wealthy." Government must fill in the jobs gap for "all who seek and need" employment; workers should have adequate, quality leisure time; "persons come before profits"; consumers should purchase Fair Trade products as much as possible; war increases and peace decreases poverty; workers must be paid a living wage; and poor people must be given ways to build wealth.

War and Peace

In this section of its statement on "The World Community," the UMC rejects "war as an instrument of national foreign policy." International disputes should be resolved peacefully; and "aggression, terrorism, and genocide" should be addressed by means other than war, including treaties and law-abiding institutions. "Military claims" must be subordinated to "human values"; "the militarization of society must be . . . stopped"; and the making, selling, and use of conventional weapons "must be reduced and controlled." Nuclear weapons are banned. "We endorse general and complete disarmament under strict and effective international control."

The Episcopal Church

Economics[15]

Similar to the ELCA and UMC above, the Episcopal Church provides rich resources on social justice. Appendix C[16] of its *Economic Justice How-To Manual*[17] quotes Walter Rauschenbusch: "Christianity makes the love of money the root of all evil. Capitalism cultivates the love of money for its own sake, and gives its largest wealth to those who use monopoly extortion." The manual provides advocacy issue papers on "Eleven Essentials of Justice," namely affordable food, employment, affordable quality child care, education, health care, a just immigration policy, cultural affirmation, equal protection under the law, economic opportunity, a healthy environment, and housing.

War and Peace[18]

Episcopal teachings on war and peace have varied over the past seven or so decades. A pastoral letter in 1934 defined war as mass murder, and a 1937 pastoral letter declared that "modern war could no longer be justified"; but by 1962 not only were "limited wars" considered acceptable under certain conditions, so was *nuclear deterrence*—though *not* "massive nuclear retaliation." Then a 1982 pastoral letter ruled out a policy of "nuclear first-strike deterrence." The 1982 General Convention recommended that Christians use nonviolent civil disobedience against government "military and defense policies," and called (*before* the collapse of the Soviet Union) for a bilateral freeze on the production of nuclear weapons.[19]

Since then additional "statements on peace and nonviolence" have been passed, for example, at the 2000 General Convention, to "develop specific plans . . . for the church to live into a culture of nonviolence"; and at the 2006 General Convention, to implement nonviolence training in each diocese. The 2006 GC also passed a resolution to "end the war in Iraq," asserting that the Iraq war had not met just war criteria, and that Iraq should be stabilized, U.S. troops withdrawn, and returning U.S. military personnel helped. The resolution further noted that "our government's participation in the war in Iraq has resulted in individual and global injustices including passive acceptance of the loss of our military personnel . . .

indifference to the loss of countless Iraqi citizens, silent response to atrocities, [to] illegal confinement without representation or formal charges, and [to] torture."[20]

National Association of Evangelicals

The NAE statement "For the Health of the Nation" (passed unanimously on October 7, 2004)[21] affirms that Evangelicals have "an awesome opportunity to shape public policy" since they make up "fully one-quarter of all [U.S.] voters." The statement's preamble notes that "the presence and role of religion in public life is attacked more fiercely now than ever, making the bias of aggressive secularism the last acceptable prejudice in America." The biblical roots of the positions taken are made evident throughout the document, which (under "the basis for Christian civic engagement") justifies Christian social action as follows:

> We engage in public life because God created our first parents in his image and gave them dominion over the earth (Gen. 1:27–28). The responsibilities that emerge from that mandate are many, and in a modern society those responsibilities rightly flow to many different institutions, including governments, families, churches, schools, businesses, and labor unions. Just governance is part of our calling in creation. . . . We also engage in public life because Jesus is Lord over every area of life. Through him all things were created (Col. 1:16–17), and by him all things will be brought to fullness (Rom. 8:19–21). To restrict our stewardship to the private sphere would be to deny an important part of his dominion and to functionally abandon it to the Evil One . . . to deny the all-encompassing Lordship of Jesus (Rev. 19:16).

Regarding "just government and fundamental liberty," it reads:

> As followers of Jesus, we obey government authorities when they act in accord with God's justice and his laws (Titus 3:1). But we also resist government when it exercises its power in an unjust manner (Acts 5:27–32) or tries to dominate other institutions in society. A good government preserves the God-ordained responsibilities of society's other institutions, such as churches, other faith-centered organizations, schools, families, labor unions, and businesses.

On "religious freedom and liberty of conscience":

> God has ordained the two co-existing institutions of church and state as distinct and independent of each other with each having its own areas of responsibility (Rom. 13:1–7; Mark 12:13–17; Eph. 4:15–16, 5:23–32). We affirm the principles of religious freedom and liberty of conscience. . . . As God allows the wheat and tares to grow together until the harvest, and as God sends the rain on the just and on the unjust, so those who obey and those who disobey God coexist in society and share in its blessings (Matt. 5:45, 13:24–30). . . . Participating in the public square does not require people to put aside their beliefs or suspend the practice of their religion. All persons should have equal access to public forums, regardless of the religious content or viewpoint of their speech.

On family life and the protection of children:

From Genesis onward, the Bible tells us that the family is central to God's vision for human society. God has revealed himself to us in the language of family, adopting us as his children (Rom. 8:23; Gal. 4:5) and teaching us by the Holy Spirit to call him *Abba Father* (Rom. 8:15; Gal. 4:6). Marriage, which is a lifetime relationship between one man and one woman, is the predominant biblical icon of God's relationship with his people (Isa. 54:5; Jer. 3:20, 31:32; Ezek. 16:32; Eph. 5:23, 31–32). In turn, family life reveals something to us about God, as human families mirror, however faintly, the inner life of the Trinity. . . . Many social evils—such as alcohol, drugs, gambling, or credit-card abuse, pornography, sexual libertinism, spousal or child sexual abuse, easy divorce, abortion on demand—represent the abandonment of responsibility or the violation of trust by family members, and they seriously impair the ability of family members to function in society. These evils must be viewed not only as matters of individual sin and dysfunction, but also as violations of family integrity. Because the family is so important to society, violations of its integrity threaten public order. Similarly, employment, labor, housing, health care, and educational policies concern not only individuals but seriously affect families. In order to strengthen the family, we must promote biblical moral principles, responsible personal choices, and good public policies on marriage and divorce law, shelter, food, health care, education, and a family wage (Jas. 5:1–6).

On the "sanctity of human life":

We believe that abortion, euthanasia, and unethical human experimentation violate the God-given dignity of human beings.

"On justice and compassion for the poor and vulnerable":

We further believe that care for the vulnerable should extend beyond our national borders. American foreign policy and trade policies often have an impact on the poor. We should try to persuade our leaders to change patterns of trade that harm the poor and to make the reduction of global poverty a central concern of American foreign policy. We must support policies that encourage honesty in government, correct unfair socio-economic structures, generously support effective programs that empower the poor, and foster economic development and prosperity.

On human rights:

As recipients of God's gift of embodied life, people need food, nurture, shelter, and care. In order to fulfill their God-given tasks, all people have a right to private property. God's design for human existence also implies a right to marry, enjoy family life, and raise and educate children. While it is not the primary role of government to provide everything that humans need for their well-being, governments are obligated to ensure that people are not unjustly deprived of them and to strengthen families, schools, businesses, hospitals, social-service organizations, and other institutions so they can contribute to human welfare. . . . American foreign policy should reward those countries that respect human rights and should not reward (and prudently employ certain sanctions against) those countries that abuse or deny such rights. We urge the United States to increase its commitments to developing democracy and civil society in former colonial lands, Muslim nations, and countries emerging from Communism.

On "peace and work to restrain violence":

Jesus and the prophets looked forward to the time when God's reign would bring about just and peaceful societies. . . . But from the beginning, Christians have recognized that God did not call them to bring in God's kingdom by force. . . . We have long differed on when governments may use force and whether we may participate in government-authorized force to defend our homelands, rescue others from attack, or liberate other people from oppression. . . . We urge governments to pursue thoroughly nonviolent paths to peace before resorting to military force. We believe that, if governments are going to use military force, they must use it in the service of peace and not merely in their national interest. Military force must be guided by the classical just-war principles. . . . In an age of nuclear and biological terrorism, such principles are more important than ever.

And finally on the environment:

We affirm that God-given dominion is a sacred responsibility to steward the earth and not a license to abuse the creation of which we are a part. We are not the owners of creation, but its stewards, summoned by God to "watch over and care for it" (Gen. 2:15). This implies the principle of sustainability: our uses of the Earth must be designed to conserve and renew the Earth rather than to deplete or destroy it. The Bible teaches us that God is not only redeeming his people, but is also restoring the whole creation (Rom. 8:18–23). . . . We show our love for the Creator by caring for his creation. Because clean air, pure water, and adequate resources are crucial to public health and civic order, government has an obligation to protect its citizens from the effects of environmental degradation. . . . Because natural systems are extremely complex, human actions can have unexpected side effects. We must therefore approach our stewardship of creation with humility and caution. . . . We urge Christians to shape their personal lives in creation-friendly ways: practicing effective recycling, conserving resources, and experiencing the joy of contact with nature. We urge government to encourage fuel efficiency, reduce pollution, encourage sustainable use of natural resources, and provide for the proper care of wildlife and their natural habitats.

Progressive Presbyterians

These Presbyterians are represented by Presbyterian Voices for Justice, with its News and Networking for Progressive Presbyterians. On the organization's website,[22] "2014 GA Overtures" refer to subjects such as drug policies, gun violence, the death penalty, and sexual misconduct. An "interim report" entitled, "Encountering the Gospel of Peace Anew: An Invitation to Discernment and Witness," presents nonviolence as the church's "fundamental response to . . . violence, terror, and war." Among the Overtures, particular attention is paid to the Israel/Palestine situation, with one presbytery recommending divestment from three corporations that profit from "illegal Israeli settlements, . . . walls and fences, . . . checkpoints, . . . [and] the relentless, five-decade-long military occupation of the Palestinian territories." A recent UN General Assembly Human Rights Council report is cited with respect to, among others, the "system of segregation" imposed by the settlements, settler violence against Palestinians, and official Israeli mistreatment of detained Palestinian children as well as interference with Palestinian children's access to education.

Peace Churches: The Quakers

Friends General Conference

On its website[23] under "FAQs" (frequently asked questions about Quakers), to the question, "Do I have to be a pacifist to be a Quaker?" the answer given is: "This determination is left to the individual and his or her conscience. For many, it has meant a commitment to nonviolence and conscientious objection to participating in war. Some Quakers, however, have served in the military."

Friends Committee on National Legislation

Established by Quakers in 1943, the FCNL is the largest lobby organization for peace in Washington, D.C. At the bottom of its home page[24] are situated the four areas of Peace, Justice, Communities, and Environment, with links to various topics under each, for example, to Afghanistan, Drones, Iran, Foreign Policy, and six others under Peace; to Campaign Finance, Gun Violence, Immigration, Torture, and two others under Justice; to Pentagon Spending, Poverty, and two others under Communities; and to Climate Change and Sustainable Energy under Environment. The Preamble to its latest Policy Statement (2013) declares that the "FCNL acts in faith to create a world free from war, a society with equity and justice for all, a community where every person's potential may be fulfilled, and an earth restored."

Peace Churches: The Mennonites

Established in 1920, the Mennonite Central Committee[25] (MCC) describes itself as "a worldwide ministry of Anabaptist churches [that] shares God's love and compassion for all in the name of Christ by responding to basic human needs and working for peace and justice." The organization is "committed to nonviolent peacemaking" and loving enemies.

The sixteenth-century Dirk Willems remains an indelible example of the Mennonite commitment to loving one's enemy:

> Dirk was caught, tried and convicted as an Anabaptist in those later years of harsh Spanish rule under the Duke of Alva in The Netherlands. He escaped from a residential palace turned into a prison by letting himself out of a window with a rope made of knotted rags, dropping onto the ice that covered the castle moat. Seeing him escape, a

palace guard pursued him as he fled. Dirk crossed the thin ice of a pond, the "Honde-gat," safely. His own weight had been reduced by short prison rations, but the heavier pursuer broke through. Hearing the guard's cries for help, Dirk turned back and rescued him. The . . . guard then seized Dirk and led him back to captivity. This time the authorities threw him into a more secure prison, a small, heavily barred room at the top of a very tall church tower. . . . Soon he was led out to be burned to death.[26]

BEYOND CHRISTIANITY: SOCIAL THOUGHT
IN OTHER RELIGIONS

Buddhist, Jewish, and Islamic Social Thought (A Selective Sample)

Buddhist: Important Buddhist positions on economics and on war and peace go back to the Buddha himself. Yet, writes Walpola Rahula, "Little is known, particularly in the West, about his teaching on social, economic, and political matters."[27] The Buddha considered economic prosperity, a moral life, and happiness to be causally connected, the foundation being "social and economic welfare."[28] Without economic security and "sufficient income" (i.e., a living wage), he regarded crime and social conflict as inevitable; at the same time, he spoke against hoarding and wrong livelihood (such as arms manufacture). Of the "four kinds of [ordinary] happiness" noted by the Buddha, three are economic.[29]

Regarding war and peace, the Buddha and Buddhism prohibit any and all violence, nor is "just war" recognized as a valid category; rather it is seen as a pretext for rationalizing the use of violence. The first of Buddhism's "five precepts" is "not to destroy life." Likewise, one of the "ten duties of the king," or principles of good government, is "to promote peace by avoiding and preventing war." In contrast to self-conquest, the conquest and subjugation of others destroy peace and happiness.[30]

For accounts of individual Buddhists who have given special attention to these questions, see our treatment of A. T. Ariyaratne and Thich Nhat Hanh, both in chapter 2.

Jewish and Islamic: According to Jewish social thought, Jews as human beings are called to contribute to the general social welfare, to support human rights and the poor. With its concept of *tikkun olam* (repairing the world), traditional Judaism opposes secularization and the privatizing of religion.[31]

Jewish economics is "neither socialist nor capitalist";[32] Muslim economists say the same about Islamic economics.[33] Judaism and Islam both are inclined to support government "intervention and legislation" on behalf of the disadvantaged.[34] Again both religions have traditionally opposed lending money at interest.[35] The sin of Sodom in Genesis 19 can be understood as failing to share wealth with the poor. Thus both regard a portion of a (non-poor) person's wealth as due to others; surplus wealth is to be shared. Poor people are to be helped globally, and society is collectively responsible for establishing and maintaining socioeconomic justice.[36]

For neither religion is the goal literal economic equality, which is viewed as unrealistic and undesirable; rather, the goal is to end poverty. Both religions oppose an economic system that favors the wealthy.[37] The "Islamic welfare state" allows free enterprise, private property, a free market, and profit, but within the framework of commitment to social welfare;[38] likewise, in Judaism "there is no such thing as unlimited private property."[39] In Jewish tradition, 20 percent of income is often considered the maximum allowable for charitable purposes. The figure for Islamic zakat is 2.5 percent of one's total assets above basic needs, but Taliqani also refers to "a fifth of [one's] income."[40]

The Jewish Peace Fellowship (since 1941) and the Muslim Peace Fellowship (since 1994) are both affiliated with the Fellowship of Reconciliation (FOR). Drawing on the Tanakh, the Talmud, and other texts, the JPF has supported conscientious objection to serving in the military by Jews as well as "Jewish resistance . . . to the arms race in the U.S. and Israel and the world." The JPF stands against "capital punishment, . . . the Israeli occupation, U.S. armed interventions (including a military strike on Iran), war, and all violence, advocating instead for peace with justice and reconciliation."[41]

The Muslim Peace Fellowship is much younger but already now extant for twenty years. It has recently stated that "all modern weapons are weapons of mass destruction" and that only "unarmed struggle" is a lawful form of fighting. The MPF identifies nonviolence as the "core social teaching of all the great religious traditions."[42]

PRELUDE TO LIBERATION THEOLOGIES

Most Christian social teaching, Catholic and Protestant, is optimistic that commitment to Gospel values will inspire participants in the American free-market system, tempered with democratic principles, to empower the poor and engage all levels of society in social justice. Some Christian thinkers doubt that a system motivated by power politics and self-interest is capable of promoting justice.

The next chapter will deal with liberation theologies, which represent above all a new way of doing theology, characterized by the "circle of praxis" described in that chapter. Because liberation theologians are less likely to trust elite leaders to accept the social teachings expressed in this chapter and to adopt its prescriptions, they seek more radical ways to influence public life.

SUMMARY

The various Christian churches have developed social teachings to help guide public life. The Roman Catholic Church, especially over the past century, has formulated the most extensive body of teaching, and perhaps holds the greatest confidence that its teaching can affect public policy through political, business, and other leaders of good will. Mainline Protestant churches like the Lutherans, Methodists, Episcopalians, and Presbyterians hold positions similar to Catholic ones. The historic peace churches have differed radically on the question of war and the extent to which Christians should be involved in public life. More recently, some Evangelical churches, forming a "Moral Majority," have offered their own distinctive policy positions. Buddhist, Jewish, and Muslim views either resemble or complement Christian ones.

Key issues have included poverty and wealth, private property, labor unions, socialism and capitalism, war and peace, and—more recently—the environmental carrying capacity of the planet; gender equality is another vital issue that has received less attention. Important principles for judgment have included human rights and dignity, solidarity, subsidiarity, and a preferential option for the poor. Some churches have seriously considered major structural changes that could help to achieve a better society.

KEY TERMS

CELAM
corporative state
decade of development
encyclical

solidarity
structural sin
subsidiarity

DISCUSSION QUESTIONS

1. Did any of the social principles of the various Christian churches or of other religions surprise you? If so, which ones and why?
2. Which of the Christian or other social principles do you agree with? Which do you disagree with? On what grounds?
3. Could a fully committed member of one of these groups follow its principles and still be a successful Chief Executive Officer (CEO) of a major multinational corporation?
4. Could a fully committed member of one of these groups follow its principles and still be a successful president of the United States? Could he or she get elected?

SUGGESTIONS FOR FURTHER READING

Curran. *Catholic Social Teaching, 1891–Present.*
Donohue and Esposito, eds. *Islam in Transition.*
Dwyer, ed. *The Catholic Bishops and Nuclear War: A Critique and Analysis of the Pastoral, The Challenge of Peace.*
———, ed. *The New Dictionary of Catholic Social Thought.*

Fernando and Sullivan. *Launching the Second Century: Catholic Social Thought in Asia.*
Flannery, ed. *Vatican Council II: More Postconciliar Documents.*
Galtung. *Peace by Peaceful Means.*
———. "A Structural Theory of Imperialism."
Gottlieb, ed. *Liberating Faith.*
Hiatt, ed. *A Game as Old as Empire.*
Hood. *Social Teachings in the Episcopal Church.*
Lebacqz. *Justice in an Unjust World.*
———. *Six Theories of Justice.*
Maas Weigert and Kelley, eds. *Living the Catholic Social Tradition.*
Massaro. *Living Justice: Catholic Social Teaching in Action.*
Maurin. *Easy Essays.*
Mich. *Catholic Social Teaching and Movements.*
National Conference of Catholic Bishops. *The Challenge of Peace: God's Promise and Our Response.*
———. *Economic Justice for All.*
Palackapilly and Felix. *Religion and Economics: A Worldview.*
Perkins. *Confessions of an Economic Hit Man.*
Pontifical Council for Justice and Peace. *Compendium of the Social Doctrine of the Church.*
Pope John XXIII. *Mater et Magistra.*
———. *Pacem in Terris.*
Pope John Paul II. *Centesimus Annus.*
———. *Laborem Exercens.*
Pope Leo XIII. *Rerum Novarum.*
Pope Paul VI. *Evangelii Nuntiandi.*
———. *Octogesima Adveniens.*
———. *Populorum Progressio.*
Pope Pius XI. *Quadragesimo Anno.*
Rahula. "The Social Teachings of the Buddha."
Roman Synod of Catholic Bishops. *Justice in the World.*
Second Vatican Council. *Gaudium et Spes.*
———. *Lumen Gentium.*
———. *Nostra Aetate.*
Shatz et al., eds. *Tikkun Olam.*
Strain, ed. *Prophetic Visions and Economic Realities: Protestants, Jews, and Catholics Confront the Bishops' Letter on the Economy.*
Walsh and Davies, eds. *Proclaiming Justice and Peace: Papal Documents from Rerum Novarum through Centesimus Annus.*
Wink. *Unmasking the Powers.*

10

Liberation Theologies

The evil inequities and oppression of every kind which afflict millions of men and women today openly contradict Christ's Gospel and cannot leave the conscience of any Christian indifferent.

—Vatican Instruction on Christian Freedom and Liberation[1]

A broad and deep aspiration for liberation inflames the history of humankind in our day, liberation from all that limits or keeps human beings from self-fulfillment, liberation from all impediments to the exercise of freedom. Proof of this is the awareness of new and subtle forms of oppression in the heart of advanced industrial societies, which often offer themselves as models to the underdeveloped countries. . . . We must beware of all kinds of imitations as well as new forms of imperialism—revolutionary this time—of the rich countries, which consider themselves central to the history of humankind.

—Gustavo Gutiérrez[2]

Christian liberation theologians share much with the social teachings of Christian churches described in the previous chapter. They also share with Marxists a sense of outrage over socioeconomic injustice and a suspicious attitude toward status quo structures. They illustrate how important it is to live the experience of oppressed people. This experience makes the existence of injustice so palpable that elaborate theories are not necessary to prove that it exists. Oppression turns people into "nonpersons." Their poverty is not just unfortunate; it is caused by the dominant structures themselves. As a result, it will not be resolved by "development" within the current world structures. Liberation theologians, therefore, do not seek a formula for distribution or exchange; they seek a restoration of right relationships in a fractured community. If they are Christians or Jews, they seek this restoration because they observe that this is what God sought in the exodus from Egypt, in the denunciations of social injustice by the prophets, and (for Christians) in the ministry of Jesus of Nazareth. If they are Muslims, they seek it because they believe it is mandated by God in the Quran.

HISTORICAL BACKGROUND

Liberation theologies first developed in Latin America, so it is helpful to know some Latin American history. Students should research the subject beyond what can be provided here.

European Colonization of the Americas and Its Long Shadow

Beginning in the late fifteenth century, Spanish warriors, having recaptured Spain from Muslim rule, came to the "newly discovered" lands of Latin America to win kingdoms for themselves; their mentality was feudal. In contrast, *North* America was not colonized for another hundred years or more, so the colonization of the North took place in the post-feudal era of developing trade and industry. A number of religious leaders, like Bartholomé de Las Casas (one of Gustavo Gutiérrez's heroes), were sincerely interested in sharing their faith with the natives on an equal footing, and resisted Spanish oppression. But the main goal of the "conquistadores," or conquerors, was to enrich themselves by exploiting natural and human resources in the "new" lands.

This pattern has continued to the present day in important ways. Many of the Latin American elites are not interested in developing their countries for the benefit of their fellow citizens. They establish industries to sell goods to the First World, invest much of their wealth in First World enterprises (buying stock in General Motors and Nestlé rather than investing in local companies), do their shopping in Miami and their vacationing in Nice, see themselves primarily as world citizens, and use their own country primarily as a resource for enhancing their own wealth and power.

For a sense of how separate the elites feel from the common people, the film *Romero* (1989), which dramatizes the situation in El Salvador in the 1970s, is especially revealing. A remarkable example of the early struggle between well-meaning evangelization and elitist oppression is dramatized in the film *The Mission* (1986), which deals with the Jesuit utopian communities, or "**reductions**," for indigenous people in Paraguay. Striking and provocative, *The Mission* raises important moral questions: the reductions were criticized for being patriarchal, treating the natives like children, and educating them into a European way of life. (Perhaps it is better to be treated like children than to be treated like slaves: the reductions protected their Indians from the slave raiders.)

Independence and Church-State Relations

"Independence" from Spain, which occurred for most Latin American countries in the early nineteenth century, was not so much a social revolution as it was a coup d'état by local elites against their absentee Spanish lords. It did not change local power realities significantly, since there was no real social change. One result of postcolonial independence in many places was to exile Spanish priests because of their loyalty to the crown. The result was to leave the people for as long as a century with virtually no priests. This did not improve Christian life and practice.

In the late nineteenth and early twentieth centuries, church leaders had a reputation for supporting corrupt political leaders. The Second Vatican Council began to change the attitude of church leaders, with the result that many elites now feel that the church, or at least certain elements within the church, have abandoned them. This process is dramatized in the film *Romero* (see above). Archbishop Romero was a conservative priest who enjoyed good relations with the elites in El Salvador until he was named archbishop. The film shows how he came to a deep conversion and what the consequences of his conversion were.

Catholic Action

In the 1930s, Cardinal Cardijn in Belgium promoted a movement called the Young Christian Workers (in French abbreviated JOC, in English YCW). The same movement developed Young Christian Students. Collectively, these movements were called "Catholic Action." Members of these movements met in small groups to carry out a three-part process: *observe, judge, act.* These **JOCists** were very influential in both North and South America until the 1960s.

The Decade of Development

In the early 1960s, President John Kennedy and the United Nations launched a "decade of development" for industrialized nations to help poor ones. There was a lot of hope at this time. Assassinated in 1963, John Kennedy is still widely regarded by Latin Americans as their favorite U.S. president. But at the end of the decade, the economic gap was worse than before. Developing nations had much higher debt and, because of the oil crisis brought on by the OPEC oil embargo, the United States and other industrial nations allowed interest rates to increase enormously. Progressive scholars began to think that the problem was not *underdevelopment* but rather stronger nations oppressing weaker ones.

Transition to Liberation Theology in Thought and Action

With "development" falling apart in the 1970s, some began to expand the JOCist idea. Theologians said, the dominant reality of our world is oppression and theology needs to address the situation. But as theologians we are not experiencing oppression directly. Therefore, if we are to engage in the process of observing, judging, and acting, we first have to get into the situation we are concerned about. We have to experience oppression along with our brothers and sisters. So they added a fourth step at the beginning of the process, and went deeper into the other three, coming up with the **"circle of praxis"**:

The Circle of Praxis in Four Steps

1. *Insert* yourself into the situation. Share the real *experiences* of the oppressed.
2. *Analyze* the situation carefully with the help of sociological, economic, historical, and cultural studies. Find out *what is* and *why* things are that way. This is a **descriptive analysis**; it does not yet evaluate the situation.
3. *Theologize* about the situation. What *should be* according to the Gospels and church teaching? What practical alternatives are there? This is a **normative analysis**; it asks what is good about the current situation, what is bad about it, and what might be a better situation.
4. Make a **pastoral plan** that will help us to move from what *is* toward what *should be*. This is an *action step*.

Insertion, or step 1, usually involved sharing the life of small groups of poor Christians formed in the immense parishes of Latin American cities, where the poor were often left to their own devices. As an outgrowth of the discussion groups previously encouraged by the JOCist movement, these small groups of ten to thirty people were the church in miniature. Functioning as places for discussion, mutual support, and common action, they were called **Base Christian Communities—** *Communidades Ecclesiales de Base*, abbreviated CEB.

In many areas where priests were scarce, the CEBs provided most of the effective ministry. More traditional clergy were sometimes alarmed by this development, both because they feared a transfer of power from clergy to laity, and because these small local groups often raised embarrassing political questions and engaged in activities that threatened the status quo. Laity, empowered by small-scale local action, began to form larger associations and networks and to hold regional and national meetings.

This four-step process is called a *circle* because, once you put step 4 into operation, you change the situation. For example, the poor may develop new means of organizing their economic life, certain elites may feel threatened and retaliate, you may end up in jail or dead. So then you will need to start the analysis, or circle of *praxis*, over again (if you are still alive). **Praxis** means activity that is reflected on and consciously chosen to produce a particular effect, a transformation of society. The activity and the reflection go together and influence each other.

Three Power Questions

Three questions to be posed in this analysis are the following:

1. Who is *making the effective decisions* in this situation?
2. Who is *benefiting* from the decisions made?
3. Who is *paying the cost* of those decisions?

Where is this kind of analysis done? Here are a few places in Latin America:

1. Some Latin American universities, but not many. Most Latin American universities cater to the elites and promote the status quo. (Would that be true of most North American universities, or not? of your school, or not?)
2. "Think tanks" (study centers), especially those in contact with the poor and with pastoral action.
3. Groups of church workers, ministers, priests, and sisters.
4. Base Christian Communities, usually on a fairly simple level.

Conscientization

This kind of analysis makes people aware of the power relations in their world, namely, who is controlling those relations and what they might do about it. It brings them into a new consciousness of reality and empowers them to make decisions consciously rather than passively following the path laid out for them by power brokers. This process of coming to awareness is called **conscientization**—you become "conscious" of the way things are and the causes that have made them that way. Conscientization involves learning how to ask questions and find answers. Most people have come to believe the way of seeing things promoted by the elites, which is usually a way of seeing things that maintains the privileges of the elites. (Even the elites are often not aware of how much this is true. It is largely an unconscious process.)

Gustavo Gutiérrez and CELAM

In 1971 Gustavo Gutiérrez, a Peruvian diocesan priest and theologian, put into writing new ideas that were developing in Latin America in his book *Teología de la Liberación: Perspectivas* (English translation: *A Theology of Liberation*). It is from the title of that book that the movement took its name. Gutiérrez has been one of the key thinkers in the development of liberation theology. For many years, he lived with the poor in Lima, Peru, and worked at a study center for pastoral action. Currently a professor of theology at the University of Notre Dame in Indiana, he has taught at a number of universities in the Americas and Europe.

Gutiérrez was also a key consultant for the second general meeting of the Latin American Bishops' Conference (abbreviated in Spanish as CELAM), organized as a result of the Second Vatican Council and held in 1968 at *Medellín* in Colombia. There CELAM announced a "preferential option for the poor," meaning that the poor deserve help first (see also chapter 9 on Medellín). More conservative leaders hoped that the third meeting, held at *Puebla* in Mexico in 1979, would reverse the direction that Medellín had set. But instead, it confirmed the direction of the earlier meeting and carried it further. Pope John Paul II also attended Puebla and approved the general direction of the conference. Both the Medellín and Puebla conferences produced documents that are very important for justice and peace.[3]

Gutiérrez's research, observation, and reflection led him to insist that:

- one must see the world as it is and resolve to change the world;
- the status quo is unjust in regard to race, class, culture, and gender;
- social conflict and class struggle are undeniable, and the elites are responsible for class struggle;
- the working class is engaged in a legitimate "struggle for justice";
- the goal of liberation theology praxis is a "society of equals" freed of racism and oppression;
- to have peace there must be real development and justice;
- the "absence of love" is what causes conflict; and
- the authentic church of the poor must lead the way to unity, love, and justice.[4]

The CEBs in Brazil

In Brazil by the 1970s, the bishops had approved of the Base Christian Communities, protecting them from hostile political pressures. Some of the other hierarchies were less encouraging or even overtly antagonistic to the CEBs. The bishops distributed study questions for the CEBs each Advent and Lent. In the 1980s, Brazil probably had the largest number of CEBs—about eighty thousand. But if you counted up all the members of these eighty thousand groups, the total still represented only between 1 and 3 percent of Brazilian Christians. (Another 1 to 3 percent of the Brazilian Christian population were Evangelical Protestant Christians who tended to support the status quo power structures.) It is important to realize that percentages do not have to be large to have a major social effect. We are used to thinking in terms of electoral majorities, but a group of truly committed people amounting to 1 to 3 percent of a society can have a major effect on that society.

Most CEB members were poorly educated and depended on theologians and other experts to get them started. Still they were encouraged to trust the value of their own understanding and not just accept the views of experts. In terms of their own experiences they knew much more than the experts did.

According to Andrew Dawson, "since the mid-1980s" the CEBs have been pushed toward "depoliticization and spiritualization" by "Vatican-orchestrated forces." Yet Brazil's economic context has continued to favor the few rich at the expense of the many poor, which means that the CEBs retain their "relevance and purpose."[5] Overall, the CEBs still play a "central role" for the Catholic Church in Brazil.[6]

The Question of Violence

A key concept of liberation theology is **structural violence**. If the laws and the way they are carried out result in half of the children in a country dying before the age of five, as is true in many Latin American countries, then the people who develop, support, and defend those laws and their implementation are guilty of violence against the poor, for example, by preventing adequate nutrition, even if they don't physically attack poor persons.

The question, then, is whether violent revolution is justified in response to unjust laws and structural violence. (See James Cone on this question in the section on Black Liberation Theology below.) Most liberation theologians are unwilling to renounce the validity of just war theory—as was even Pope Benedict XVI, who was head of the Vatican Congregation for the Teaching of the Faith at the time that liberation theology was developing. Whereas just war theory, following the specific teaching of St. Thomas Aquinas, allows for just revolution in extreme cases, most of the poor in Latin America prefer nonviolent methods and choose them whenever they can. This is especially true of indigenous peoples. Much active nonviolence is being practiced there, with great courage and at high cost.

Some of the liberation theologians I (David) talked with during my 1988 sabbatical in Latin America explained that, although they preferred nonviolent approaches, they were unwilling to condemn just war or just rebellion. They were afraid that unjust elites would use their condemnation to attack those who were resisting injustice by means of armed force. They didn't want their words, for example, to be used against their friends in Nicaragua who supported the Sandinista revolution and government.

Michael Novak and José Míguez Bonino

The North American philosopher and journalist Michael Novak wrote the book *Will It Liberate?* (1986), in which he raised critical questions about liberation theologies. When I (David) was in Argentina in 1988, I attended a small seminar at a Protestant seminary discussing the book under the leadership of *José Míguez Bonino* (d. 2012), then a prominent liberation theologian and a Methodist. (Most Latin American liberation theologians are Catholics because most Latin Americans are Catholics.) The clarity of Míguez Bonino's writing makes him an excellent resource for students. He agreed with Novak that a democratic-capitalistic society should have a mixture of economic, political, and moral forces; inventiveness is important; there is a need for small-scale enterprise; and U.S. prosperity is not essentially dependent on Latin American oppression, which is supported by the U.S. The United States would still be a prosperous country even if Latin America sank into the sea. Bananas would be more expensive, but even with its level of affluence considerably reduced, the U.S. standard of living would remain well above the current standard of living in Latin America. Most U.S. industry produces for an internal market; in other words, we use what we produce. Since the time of our conversation, this balance has been threatened by U.S. corporations moving factories into low-wage countries.

In Míguez Bonino's view, Novak's *weakness* was that he didn't take either the power question or the extent of corruption seriously enough; to follow his suggestions in Latin America could get you murdered. If Latin America sank into the sea, *its elites* would not continue to prosper. And some key North American elites would lose a large part of their economic power base.

When liberation theology was beginning in the late 1960s, its writers spoke of the United States oppressing Latin America. By 1988, they were speaking of Latin American *elites* colluding with North American *elites* against the interests of the common people in both places.[7]

Juan Luis Segundo

When I (David) spoke in 1988 with the Uruguayan Jesuit liberation theologian *Juan Luis Segundo* (d. 1996), he reflected on how he had come to appreciate the letters of the apostle Paul. Previously he had preferred Matthew's Gospel and thought that Paul had sold out to the establishment. But then his own experience of how resistant the establishment is, and how difficult it is to bring about change, made him appreciate Paul more.

In this light, Segundo wrote about the disparate positions (within liberation theology) of theologians and biblical scholars, on the one hand, and poor people, on the other. He urged the theologians and scholars to move their position closer to that of poor people, lest they become "an instrument of oppression"; they need to be theologians and scholars of and for the poor.[8]

Vatican Reactions

Many people have heard that "the Vatican is opposed to liberation theology." The reality is more complex. People who really are opposed to liberation theology will find little support from the Vatican's position. The Vatican Congregation for the Teaching of the Faith (directed from 1981 to 2005 by Cardinal Ratzinger) published two documents on liberation theology. The first expressed caution, especially with regard to Marxist methods of analysis. The second emphasized what was positive in the movement.

The First Vatican Document

In the 1984 *Instruction on Certain Aspects of the "Theology of Liberation,"* the Congregation warned that Marxist principles may be dangerous bases for a theology —especially if they draw our attention away from human sin to concentrate exclusively on earthly liberation. Yet it insisted that the struggle for justice, freedom, and human dignity is an important aspect of Christian faith and life:

> Faced with the urgency of certain problems, some are tempted to emphasize, unilaterally, the liberation from servitude of an earthly and temporal kind . . . they seem to put liberation from sin in second place, and so fail to give it the primary importance it is due. . . .
>
> The present Instruction has a . . . limited and precise purpose: to draw the attention of pastors, theologians, and all the faithful to the deviations, and risks of deviation . . .

that are brought about by certain forms of liberation theology which use, in an insufficiently critical manner, concepts borrowed from various currents of Marxist thought.

This warning should in no way be interpreted as a disavowal of all those who want to respond generously and with an authentic evangelical spirit to the "preferential option for the poor." It should not at all serve as an excuse for those who maintain an attitude of neutrality and indifference in the face of the tragic and pressing problems of human misery and injustice. It is, on the contrary, dictated by the certitude that the serious ideological deviations which it points out tends [*sic*] inevitably to betray the cause of the poor. More than ever, it is important that numerous Christians, whose faith is clear and who are committed to live the Christian life in its fullness, become involved in the struggle for justice, freedom and human dignity because of their love for their disinherited, oppressed and persecuted brothers and sisters. More than ever, the Church intends to condemn abuses, injustices and attacks against freedom, wherever they occur and whoever commits them. (Introduction)

The following passage of the document makes it clear that the Congregation is not speaking in a detached, "spiritualizing" sense, but is addressing concrete social problems of our day:

In certain parts of Latin America, the seizure of the vast majority of the wealth by an oligarchy of owners bereft of social consciousness, the practical absence or the shortcomings of a rule of law, military dictators making a mockery of elementary human rights, the corruption of certain powerful officials, the savage practices of some foreign capital interests constitute factors which nourish a passion for revolt among those who thus consider themselves the powerless victims of a new colonialism in the technological, financial, monetary or economic order. (VII,12)[9]

The Second Vatican Document

Here are some passages from the second, 1986 document, the *Instruction on Christian Freedom and Liberation*:

New relationships of inequality and oppression have been established between the nations endowed with power and those without it. The pursuit of one's own interest seems to be the rule for international relations, without the common good of humanity being taken into consideration. (par. 16)

When man wishes to free himself from the moral law and become independent of God, far from gaining his freedom he destroys it. Escaping the measuring rod of truth, he falls prey to the arbitrary; fraternal relations between people are abolished and give place to terror, hatred and fear. Because it has been contaminated by deadly errors about man's condition and his freedom, the deeply-rooted modern liberation movement remains ambiguous. It is laden both with promises of true freedom and threats of deadly forms of bondage (par. 19).

Man's sin, that is to say his breaking away from God, is the radical reason for the tragedies which mark the history of freedom. In order to understand this, many of our contemporaries must first rediscover a sense of sin. In man's desire for freedom there

Figure 10.1. Children living in a dump; their homes are in the background, near Dumaguete City, Philippines. Courtesy David Whitten Smith, 7 February 1998.

is hidden the temptation to deny his own nature. Insofar as he wishes to desire everything and to be able to do everything and thus forget that he is finite and a created being, he claims to be a god (par. 37).

Having become his own centre, sinful man tends to assert himself and to satisfy his desire for the infinite by the use of things: wealth, power and pleasure, despising other people and robbing them unjustly and treating them as objects or instruments. Thus he makes his own contribution to the creation of those very structures of exploitation and slavery which he claims to condemn (par. 42).

For the Beatitudes, by teaching trust which relies on God, hope of eternal life, love of justice, and mercy which goes as far as pardon and reconciliation, enable us to situate the temporal order in relation to a transcendent order which gives the temporal order its true measure but without taking away its own nature. . . .

The Beatitudes prevent us from worshipping earthly goods and from committing the injustices which their unbridled pursuit involves.[90] They also divert us from an unrealistic and ruinous search for a perfect world (par. 62).

Man is worth more for what he is than for what he has. [The Church] bears witness to the fact that this dignity cannot be destroyed, whatever the situation of poverty, scorn, rejection or powerlessness to which a human being has been reduced. (par. 68).

The recognized priority of freedom and of conversion of heart in no way eliminates the need for unjust structures to be changed. It is therefore perfectly legitimate that those who suffer oppression on the part of the wealthy or the politically powerful should take action, through morally licit means, in order to secure structures and institutions in which their rights will be truly respected. It remains true, however, that structures established for people's good are of themselves incapable of securing and guaranteeing that good. The corruption which in certain countries affects the leaders and the State bureaucracy, and which destroys all honest social life, is a proof of this. Moral integrity is a necessary condition for the health of society. It is therefore necessary to work simultaneously for the conversion of hearts and for the improvement of structures. (par. 75)[10]

Despite the fears of Pope John Paul II and Cardinal Ratzinger, one liberation theologian with whom I (David) talked on my Latin American trip emphasized that there is little or no Marxism in liberation theology. He said most students and practitioners of liberation theology wouldn't even know how to do Marxist analysis.

Leonardo Boff

In 1985 *Leonardo Boff,* a Franciscan priest, university professor, and leading Brazilian liberation theologian, published *Church, Charism, and Power,* in which he argued that, reflecting the Trinity, the church could only have a qualified hierarchy, and also that authority "could come from below."[11] He accused the church of violating human rights by virtue of its hierarchical structure. The Vatican Congregation responded by relegating Fr. Boff to a period of reconsideration and prayer. "Condemned to 'obsequious silence,'" he "was removed from his editorial functions and suspended from religious duties."[12] Fr. Boff cooperated with the discipline. Then the Brazilian bishops went to Rome in a body and spent a week talking with Pope John Paul II. They explained to the pope what Fr. Boff and other liberation theologians were trying to do, and how important for Brazil their efforts were. After the meeting, Fr. Boff was released from the discipline early by the Vatican Congregation. And Pope John Paul II wrote a letter to the Brazilian bishops in response to the meeting, affirming that liberation theology is *essential to the Church.*[13] Boff had also voiced his "indictment of capitalism," explaining that his use of "Marxist analysis" did not mean he was a Marxist.[14] In 1992, faced with a new censure, Boff left the priesthood. He described his treatment as "cruel harassment."

It should be noted that Pope John Paul II was especially concerned about Marxism because of his experience in Poland. He felt that many people had been betrayed by the implementation of Marxist visions, and he didn't want other parts of the world to fall into the same problems. Some Americans criticize this attitude, as if the pope's experience made him hypercritical and unfit to judge. But we should recognize the importance of respecting each other's insights, especially in those areas where they have more experience than we do. Out of a certain tension and dynamic of discussion comes a better understanding than any one person could reach alone. Also, just as the pope was influenced by his environment and early experience, so were we by ours. Of course, it takes a lot of courage to present your own experience and insight in dynamic tension with a pope! But that is what the Brazilian bishops did.

Appointments of Bishops

Appointments of bishops in Latin America by Pope John Paul II from 1978 through 2005 caused much concern to people who esteem liberation theologies. The character of the bishops in a particular area has a major effect on what is allowed, encouraged, and supported. The bishops John Paul appointed tended to be people who agreed with him on such questions as women's ordination and birth control, but supported the elites against liberation theologies—something which John Paul II didn't do: he was a strong advocate for social justice. But it seemed that, when he had to make a choice, the doctrinal questions of women's ordination and birth control were more important to the pope than the social justice questions were. So the effect of many (not all) of his bishops' appointments has been to reduce support for liberation theologies, and the pope must take some responsibility for that effect, even if it was not directly intended.

Examples of Pope John Paul's concern for social questions are found in his 1987 encyclical *Sollicitudo Rei Socialis*[15] and his 1991 encyclical *Centesimus Annus*.[16] Those letters introduce the concept of "structures of sin" that become the source of personal sins.[17] For a discussion of the two documents, see chapter 9 on religious social teaching.

Recent Developments

Responding to the Vatican censure of Leonardo Boff, younger priests in Brazil have taken traditional liberation theology in several new directions, focusing on environmental, racial, and gender issues, among others. But liberation theology is not dead. Two recent liberation theologians in action are Dorothy Stang, an American nun martyred in 2005, who struggled to help landless peasants regain land in rural Brazil;[18] and Julio Lancelotti, a priest who opened a homeless shelter for children suffering from AIDS in 1991 in São Paulo, and has worked with other vulnerable people there. When receiving an award in 2005, Lancelotti claimed that "the city is applying a 'cleanup' policy against those considered undesirable . . . [it] accuses the Churches of turning misery into a Cult and tries to hide the poor from the eyes of the elite, who cannot stand to see the results of the economic concentration. . . . São Paulo belongs to its residents."[19]

Pope Benedict XVI

Since Cardinal Ratzinger had spearheaded the investigations of liberation theologians, when he was elected pope, many expected the pressure to continue. Yet in his youth, and at the beginning of the Second Vatican Council, Ratzinger was known as a progressive. Recent writings have suggested that he was speaking not for himself but for John Paul II, whose views he actually tried to moderate. Joshua McElwee reported on a recent interview with Gustavo Gutiérrez:

> Gutiérrez said he thought Ratzinger "understood" liberation theology and had helped explain its concepts to John Paul II. Benedict . . . even played a key role in organizing a seminal meeting of the Latin American bishops that discussed the subject in Aparecida, Brazil, in 2007. . . . In Aparecida . . . [Benedict] spoke of the preferential option for the poor. "[This showed that liberation theology] is strictly connected to faith in Christ, which means it is at the center."
>
> Asked if he had more problems explaining himself to John Paul II or Ratzinger, the theologian responded: "I honestly can say that Ratzinger's understanding helped us . . . because being a theologian he knew what it was about from the beginning, . . . He knew it was never connected to Marxism."[20]

Gerhard Müller, whom Pope Benedict XVI appointed in 2012 to head the Vatican's Congregation for the Teaching of the Faith—the congregation that, under Ratzinger, had censured some liberation theologians—is coauthor with Gustavo Gutiérrez of the book *On the Side of the Poor: Liberation Theology, Theology of the Church*. The book "describes liberation theology as one of the 'most significant currents of Catholic theology of the 20th century' that helped the church bridge the divide between 'earthly happiness and ultra-earthly salvation.' "[21]

In a recent interview, Gutiérrez discusses how he maintained his balance during the period when liberation theology was under pressure from the Vatican:

> I learned that you don't need to lose your sense of humor, a virtue that helps us not to feel like the center of the world or a perpetual exile, not to take ourselves too seriously, and that keeps us from becoming bitter. I like to laugh a lot and I think this has helped me in difficult times. One should move forward, without feeling indispensable, because theological reflection would go on without me too. However, I was never the subject [of] a process [by the Vatican] but of a dialogue—even though I became aware of it after it had already started![22]

Pope Francis

In addition to setting a new papal example of simplicity and solidarity with the poor, Pope Francis has shown a new openness to liberation theology. Immediately after his election, he invited Fr. Gustavo Gutiérrez to concelebrate Mass with him and share a breakfast chat. His apostolic exhortation *Evangelii Gaudium*[23] expresses many attitudes common to liberation theology. He strongly critiques "trickle down" theories of economic growth

> which assume that economic growth, encouraged by a free market, will inevitably succeed in bringing about greater justice and inclusiveness in the world. This opinion, which has never been confirmed by the facts, expresses a crude and naïve trust in the goodness of those wielding economic power and in the sacralized workings of the prevailing economic system. Meanwhile, the excluded are still waiting . . . [and] a globalization of indifference has developed. (par. 54)

He also agrees with liberation theologians that structural changes need to be made:

> As long as the problems of the poor are not radically resolved by rejecting the absolute autonomy of markets and financial speculation and by attacking the structural causes of inequality, no solution will be found for the world's problems or, for that matter, [for] any problems. Inequality is the root of social ills. (par. 202)[24]

In a recent interview conducted by Antonio Spadaro, S.J., Pope Francis affirms the importance of "insertion," the first step of liberation theology's circle of praxis:

> When it comes to social issues, it is one thing to have a meeting to study the problem of drugs in a slum neighborhood and quite another thing to go there, live there and understand the problem from the inside and study it. . . . One cannot speak of poverty if one does not experience poverty, with a direct connection to the places in which there is poverty. . . . The word *insertion* is dangerous because some religious have taken it as a fad, and disasters have occurred because of a lack of discernment. *But it is truly important.*[25]

Pentecostals and Charismatics

"While Liberation Theology opted for the poor, the poor opted for Pentecostalism."[26] While liberation theology was at first strongly supported in Brazil by Catholic bishops and succeeded through its base Christian communities in energizing many poor in the favelas (slums) and rural areas of Brazil, it was seriously weakened by Vatican disapproval, the appointment of more conservative bishops, hostile U.S. government pressure, and the growing power of neighborhood drug gangs. Into that partial vacuum stepped Pentecostal churches.

When I (David) spent four months in 1988 in Latin America, I wanted to find out how four movements interacted: liberation theologies, active nonviolence, charismatic renewal, and Christian missions. I had personal experience with and commitment to all four of these movements. As I had expected, there was a fair amount of mutual misunderstanding and some antagonism among them.

Charismatic Christians—Pentecostal, mainline Protestant, and Roman Catholic—were gaining strength. Often charismatics emphasized evangelism and personal spirituality with less attention to social context, but not always. I found charismatic communities that were both serving the poor and empowering them, especially (1) "Our Lady's Youth Center" and "The Lord's Ranch," now collectively called "Las Alas" (The Wings), founded in El Paso, Texas, and Juarez, Mexico, by the late Fr. Rick Thomas, a Jesuit[27]; (2) the "Living Water Charismatic Community," founded in Trinidad, West Indies, by two women, Rhonda Maingot and Rose Jackman[28]; and (3) "El Minuto de Dios"—a community of homes given free to the poor, a Catholic charismatic parish, radio and TV stations, grade schools, a high school, and a university, founded in Bogotá, Colombia, by the late Fr. Rafael García Herreros.[29] The charismatics did tend to do less social analysis and to be less critical of economic and political structures, but most of them would still make a U.S. parish look conservative by comparison and would agitate typical North American elites.

The *missions* I (David) visited also tended to raise social issues and to have a real "option for the poor"—for example, Parroquia San Lucas Toliman, Guatemala.[30] That's probably because I searched for mission contacts at Maryknoll, New York. Active nonviolence was less often well understood, but Fr. Don Hassler in Mexico City was an exception. No one I contacted voiced support for violent revolution.

Richard Shaull, a U.S. Protestant theologian, and Waldo César, a Brazilian sociologist, have written a study, published in 2000, challenging the traditional churches, Protestant and Catholic, to pay attention to the experience of Brazilian Pentecostals.[31] The study also admits weaknesses in the Pentecostal churches, which are growing rapidly among the poor:

> Wherever we turned, we found what appeared to us as a strange mixture of diverse and frequently contradictory elements . . . : a mixture of deep insights into the message of the gospel and what we considered to be serious distortions of it; open-ended reflection on the movement of the Spirit and rigid fundamentalism; serious biblical study and theological naiveté; rich experiences of transforming spiritual power alongside exploitation of the desperate situation of lost souls; identification with the poorest and manipulation of them; participation in and support of the struggles of the poor and promotion of reactionary social and political programs; and support of powerful and even corrupt politicians in exchange for favors for the church and its leaders.[32]

Yet the authors also observe that

> whatever its limitations, the Pentecostal message and experience had radically transformed their understanding and experience of their world and enabled them to put together their broken lives and thus find new life and energy. Poor marginalized women and men had found the power they needed for physical, mental, and often material renewal and for a successful struggle to overcome the most destructive forces around them. They knew an ecstatic experience of the Spirit that filled their lives with joy and hope. Life in family and in community was being re-created. Some of those touched by the Spirit were responding dynamically to the most urgent needs of others and were involved in struggles for social transformation. And they enthusiastically witnessed to others about the new life they had found.[33]

The ideal outcome would be to unite the best insights of these four movements, including theological and social analysis of economic and political realities leading to effective action to transform structures (liberation theologies), analysis of spiritual realities that impact the lives of the poor—including physical, emotional, and spiritual healing by the power of the Holy Spirit (charismatic and Pentecostal movements), respectful ways of sharing these exciting possibilities with those who could benefit from them (missions that invite rather than compel), and the power of nonviolence to transform the hearts of oppressors—not necessarily the most psychopathic, but the many collaborators they depend on for their power. (See the next chapter on active nonviolence.)

OTHER FORMS OF LIBERATION THEOLOGY

Latin American liberation theologies have inspired and interacted with other important liberation movements. Gustavo Gutiérrez comments on the liberation of other groups beyond the "poor":

> It has always seemed important to me to have a comprehensive concept, which for me was "insignificance," because it is possible to be insignificant due to lack of money, but also due to skin color or the fact of not speaking the dominant language of a country well, [as] occurs in Peru with the indigenous half of the population. When I speak of "the poor," I'm not just referring to those who have a low income, but also to "those who don't count, who have no social weight," those who are marginalized or forgotten.[34]

Palestinian Liberation Theology

Naim Ateek (1937–), a Palestinian Israeli Anglican priest, inspired the founding in 1993 of the Palestinian liberation theology organization and peacemaking center known as *Sabeel*, which is based in Jerusalem and Nazareth. As a child in 1948, Ateek experienced dispossession first by the Zionist Haganah and then by the Israeli military, when he and his family were forced to leave their hometown, Beisan, and move to Nazareth. Ateek went on to attend college in Texas and did his ministerial training at San Francisco Theological Seminary, returning to Palestine to work as a priest.

In 1989 he published *Justice, and Only Justice: A Palestinian Theology of Liberation*, which includes a chapter on political-historical background. Most people forget that about one hundred fifty thousand Palestinian Arabs were left in the territory bordered by the "green line" (the cease-fire line), which became the state of Israel in May 1948. Ateek identified three stages experienced by these Palestinians between 1948 and 1988: shock, resignation, and awakening. The stage of "awakening" (1968–1988) included the Palestinians in the Occupied Territories (East Jerusalem, the West Bank, and the Gaza Strip); it produced the first intifada (1987–1993).[35]

Noting that the Palestinian churches were relatively silent for about twenty years (from the late 1960s to the late 1980s), Ateek encouraged them to speak out, following the courageous examples of people like the American Christian theologian *Rosemary Radford Ruether*, who investigated and publicized chemical warfare by Israel in 1988, and the American Jewish theologian *Marc Ellis*, who has led the way in creating a Jewish liberation theology, including confrontation with Israeli anti-Semitism toward Palestinians.[36] The churches must pursue both justice and peace, and shifting from a war mentality to a peace mentality takes work—it doesn't happen automatically.

Ateek himself had to struggle to accept Israel's existence. He came to believe that the land of Israel/Palestine is intended for both peoples. Two states are necessary as long as Israel refuses to accept one bi-national state. Palestinian self-determination and Israeli security go together. Peacemaking requires two equal states and new attitudes on both sides: Palestinians must acknowledge the trauma of the Holocaust, and Israelis must acknowledge the trauma of the catastrophe they have inflicted on the Palestinians. Israel must abolish its nuclear weapons, a shared Jerusalem is essential for peace, and the final solution is to love our enemies while insisting on justice.[37]

As he did in *Justice, and Only Justice,* in his second book, *A Palestinian Christian Cry for Reconciliation* (2008), nearly twenty years later, Ateek analyzes the even more critical situation of Christian Palestinians living under Israeli occupation in relation to the biblical roots of their faith. He has sought to heal Christian Palestinian alienation from the Hebrew Bible through a process of "de-Zionizing" the texts, helping Palestinian Christians to rediscover the biblical God as a God of justice, reconciliation, and forgiveness.[38]

Ateek defines the task of Palestinian liberation theology as one of offering a credible and effective response to the ongoing realities for Palestinians of ethnic cleansing and genocide, extremities that go beyond apartheid and oppression. Even though Palestinian "violence is the outcome of unbearable stress,"[39] the model for Palestinian liberation theology is the human Jesus, who chose the way of nonviolence in the face of imperial brutality. As a Palestinian Jew living under Roman occupation, while experiencing God as inclusive, universal, and liberating rather than exclusive, nationalist, and unjust, Jesus taught justice toward enemies.[40]

Ateek also discusses the origins of Sabeel, in the context of the first intifada, as a reflective and activist organization committed to nonviolence. An important priority of Sabeel is to strengthen interfaith relations with Palestinian Muslims, who account for the vast majority of Palestinians, especially given official Israeli efforts to divide Palestinians along religious lines.[41] When I (Elizabeth) interviewed Rev. Ateek at the offices of Sabeel in Jerusalem in 2009, he focused on the principle of nonviolence and the need for Palestinians in general to internalize nonviolence as the more effective weapon (which many do). "If Gazans committed to dying," he declared, "we would win."

Jewish Theology of Liberation

Rosemary Radford Ruether (1936–) promotes "a new theology of Jewish-Christian solidarity," encouraging a relationship between "peer communities." Both communities (a) are now empowered and have been oppressive, (b) must work to recover a "prophetic consciousness" along with their "prophetic traditions" so that they can practice mutual solidarity with the poor and oppressed, including Palestinians, and (c) need to help Israel normalize itself as a pluralistic country with equal rights for non-Jewish citizens.[42] About 25 percent of Israeli citizens are non-Jews. In her 2002 Postscript to *The Wrath of Jonah* (2nd edition), Ruether warns that Western and other Christians must not allow the "ethnocide of the Palestinian people" to continue as misguided payment for the genocidal Holocaust.[43]

Marc Ellis (1952–)[44] is the leading representative of Jewish liberation theology. As a Jew, Ellis remembers "growing up in 1950s America" before the Holocaust had been named and learning "little of contemporary Jewish history."[45] American Jews joined the Black struggle for civil rights, but mostly ignored Israel's repressive treatment of Palestinians. His first two visits to Israel, in 1973 and 1984, brought him into contact with Palestinians as well as Israelis.

Focusing on the Palestine issue, Ellis has become the foremost voice of Jewish liberation theology. He rejects a "Holocaust theology" that denies the ongoing injustice done to the Palestinians by the state of Israel. Rather he seeks a theology that would encompass *both* Jewish empowerment *and* Jewish solidarity with all suffering humans—especially the victims of modern Israel. Only in this way will Jews reconnect with their ethical, prophetic traditions. Jews of conscience must confront "Constantinian Judaism," and "Jews, Christians, and Muslims of conscience must come together." Christian Zionists he condemns as "participants in [the] crime against the Palestinian people. . . . I cannot embrace my own history or religion," Ellis writes, "without embracing the Palestinian people"[46]

Ellis maintains that (a) Christians must change their dialogue with Jews, which began after the Second Vatican Council, by helping Jews repent for the way they have treated the Palestinians, (b) so that Jews will no longer demand that Christians support the policies of the state of Israel as a condition for continuing the dialogue, which Ellis terms "the **ecumenical deal**." (c) Instead, Christians must demand that Jews criticize their own oppression of the Palestinians, just as Christians have rightly criticized their own anti-Semitism, and (d) religious communities who work to liberate the poor and oppressed must also resist the all-powerful state. Some Jewish thinkers have tended to regard Third World liberation struggles as anti-Jewish. Gutiérrez (see above) by contrast links liberation theology and the Holocaust, emphasizing that for Latin Americans the Holocaust is *now* and there is no contradiction between the two.[47]

In the third edition of his *Toward a Jewish Theology of Liberation*, Ellis describes "Holocaust theology" as originating on "the periphery of organized Jewish life." He calls for another "peripheral" Jewish theology to address Jewish empowerment through Israel's conquest of Palestine, which has inverted Jewish history. The new theology is Jewish liberation theology, which he sees as a means of saving the "Jewish ethical tradition." Classical anti-Semitism still exists, as does a campaign against Arabs and Muslims, notably since September 11. Although Ellis asks whether "the Jewish prophetic voice [will] survive Jewish empowerment," he also affirms Jewish liberation theology's will to empower both the Israeli people and the Palestinian people.[48]

Islamic, or Quranic, Theology of Liberation[49]

Farid Esack (1958–) grew up very poor in South Africa. For ten years in his youth, he belonged to the pacifist, apolitical Sunni Muslim movement *Tablighi Ja-ma'at*, which teaches "six principles" and is dedicated to "individual reformation" among

Muslims at the grassroots level.[50] For eight years he studied Islam in Pakistan, where he was influenced by Christian organizations working against poverty as he imagined "a radical Islam which is committed to social justice, personal freedom, and the search for the transcendent."[51] Back in South Africa, he founded "Call of Islam" in 1984, seeking "liberation from apartheid," gender equality, environmental preservation, and religious pluralism. Regarded as the foremost Muslim liberation theologian in the world today, Esack opposes silence in the face of injustice and personal morality divorced from any social context; in line with Islamic tradition, the individual must be socially responsible. To maintain our individual integrity while expressing solidarity with each other, it is necessary to renew our inner capacity to heal in solitude with God.[52]

Islamic liberation theology differs from both traditional and modern Islamic theology yet, like them, draws directly on the Quran and Hadith. In his *Quran, Liberation and Pluralism* (1997), Esack proposes a "hermeneutic of liberation" with attention to *taqwa, tawhid, al-nas,* the oppressed, balance and justice, and *jihad.*

Taqwa means *responsibility to God and to humans*. Its consequences include taking care (a) to remain in the conscious presence of Allah, to whom one has surrendered, so that one's interpretation of the Quran will not be biased by one's ideologies or popular enthusiasms, (b) to maintain aesthetic and spiritual balance when overwhelmed by one political crisis after another, and (c) to be aware that struggle for justice has to change *oneself* as well as *society* if the activist is not to become a tyrant.[53]

Tawhid refers to God's *oneness*. It rejects the dualism of sacred and secular, religion and politics, and insists that religion—theology and social analysis done together—is an appropriate means of struggling for justice. Similar to the Christian concept of "solidarity," it opposes racial, ethnic, and class divisions, especially when "money worship" leads one group to oppress others, and regards apartheid as apostasy or heresy.[54]

Al-nas signifies the *people* in contrast to the apartheid *state:* the people are sovereign because Allah has entrusted creation to *them* as stewards. The Quran sides with the marginalized and against the powerful elites, refusing to take a "neutral" position (see Quran 107:1–3, 104, and 22:45). The Quran echoes the Christian "option for the poor" in that Allah identifies with the *oppressed*: the prophets (whose message is revolutionary) were peasants and shepherds; Muhammad was well received by common people—the "weak and destitute"—and opposed by the powerful rich. The Quran teaches social equality and upholds "the principle of distributive justice," and in Mecca Muhammad challenged not only *shirk* (faithlessness) but also economic injustice (see Quran 28:4–8).[55]

Justice is a crucial theme in the Quran. For example, "God created the heavens and earth for a true purpose: to reward each soul according to its deeds" (Quran 45:22 on justice and creation). For Muslim liberation theologians, the Quran is a "force for justice" that is more than socioeconomic, and Islam is a religion of justice. Drawing on both the Quran and Islamic tradition, Esack defines *jihad* as the "struggle to transform both oneself and society."[56] Jihad is the Muslim's liberation "struggle and praxis" to achieve justice—not to impose "Islam as a religious system"—within a historical-social context.[57] Jihad means resistance in solidarity with the oppressed against the systems that dehumanize them.

Black Liberation Theology[58]

James Cone (1938–), author of *A Black Theology of Liberation* (2nd ed., 1986), among other works, is the foremost American black theologian. He maintains that black theology has always been a theology of liberation, and that gender and class are now part of its subject matter. (Notice the parallelism with Womanist theology.) Black theology refers back to the original black American experience of enslavement by white, self-identified Christians. Having salvaged Christianity from a racist misrepresentation, black theology operates between two polar realizations: that the world does not reflect God's will, and that the world does not have to remain as it is. For black theologians, Christ is identified with the black experience of oppression, and human nature is fulfilled only in liberation. "Jesus is the oppressed man *par excellence* and the liberator of all who suffer and are exploited."[59]

On the subject of violence, in 1997 Cone criticized the double standard of whites who tolerate systemic (structural) violence, including overt white violence for example by the police, while condemning violence by the oppressed, or revolutionary violence. Jesus' nonviolence in his view was not necessarily the model for oppressed blacks to follow. He concluded that, "if the system is evil, then revolutionary violence is both justified and necessary."[60] Black theology can be summarized as "the affirmation of black humanity that emancipates black people from white racism, thus providing authentic freedom for both white and black people."[61]

Feminist Liberation Theology

Feminist theologians seek justice for women and social transformation. Elizabeth Johnson (1941–) is an American feminist theologian, a Sister of St. Joseph, and past president of the Catholic Theological Society of America. Her best known book is *She Who Is: The Mystery of God in Feminist Theological Discourse* (1992). She has written a number of other books and edited a collection of essays entitled, *The Church Women Want: Catholic Women in Dialogue* (2002). Her own essay in that collection, "Imaging God, Embodying Christ: Women as a Sign of the Times," traces support for gender inequality in the Christian theological tradition, contrasting it with the gender equality expressed in such biblical passages as Genesis 1:26–28 and Galatians 3:27–28. Scrutinizing two ambiguities in recent papal teaching, she discusses the fallacy of determining social roles on the basis of gender, and being the image of Christ nonliterally.[62]

U.S. secular feminism has an equal rights agenda and is especially concerned to rectify the exclusion of women from power. According to one classification system, "romantic" feminists regard gender from an "essentialist" perspective, seeing gender as shaped primarily by nature (genetic determination) and proposing that women's superior qualities be transferred from the private to the public arena; "radical" feminists focus on oppressive patriarchy, seeking women's spaces liberated from "male-controlled spaces"; and "socialist" feminists consider class as well as gender in their analysis, which highlights ways that gender is shaped by nurture or culture.[63]

Christian feminist theologians work to expose unjust, sexist theologies and practices and to create a feminist liberation theology. Although the Second Vatican Council was a major turning point for Roman Catholic feminist theologians, it raised hopes that were not fulfilled. For Protestant feminist theologians, the World Council of Churches, established in 1948, played a supportive role in their pursuit of women's ordination and global justice for women.[64]

Today feminist theology is found in Europe, the global south (including Latin America and Africa), the Muslim world, and Asia. Thus Third World women have become integral to feminist theology. **Womanist theology** is the term for black feminist theology done by black women, who include race and class as well as gender in their analysis, which also draws on its roots in black church life. Hispanic feminist theology is called **Mujerista theology**, deriving from the "experience of being . . . a permanent underclass."[65]

Feminist biblical scholarship can take several forms, all of them attempting to establish the "full humanity of women in Christian community." Theologically, it is Christ's humanity rather than his maleness that is important; maleness does not constitute divinity. Doctrines that justify women's gratuitous suffering and that make the male more godlike than the female are discredited. God is imagined as relational, as suffering "with the pain of women," as Mother, as immanent.[66]

The *Women Church* spirituality movement began in the United States in 1983 with a membership of 1,400 Catholic women; now it is inter-religious and global. Women Church aspires to the early church's "discipleship of equals" freed from patriarchy in "justice-based communities." Other spirituality groups across religions engage in "the quest for the goddess."[67]

Asian Liberation Theology[68]

Although less prevalent in Asia than it has been in Latin America, liberation theology is notable in five Asian countries: India, Sri Lanka, South Korea, Taiwan, and the Philippines.[69] Two main sources of this theology are the Ecumenical Association of Third World Theologians (EATWOT) and the Conference of Churches in Asia (CCA). Asian liberation theology differs from Latin American in that most of Asia's poor are non-Christian, and so it is strongly interfaith. Because most repressive Asian governments do not use Christianity to justify their repression, the "establishment ideologies" that most Asian liberation theologians critique tend to be non-Christian.

Asian liberation theologians confront widespread postcolonial poverty, exemplifying the reality of suffering as recognized in Buddhism's first noble truth (see chapter 2). They also confront state sponsorship of global capitalism, which threatens democratic rights; the negative role of religion, for example, in relation to women; and ecological concerns in response to which the "little tradition" may correct and

improve on the "great tradition." Some Asian liberation theologians draw on sha-
manism and messianic (Maitreya) Buddhism as they turn grief and rage into revolutionary energy for justice, embodying the power of the resurrection.[70]

The Taiwanese liberation theologian and Methodist minister Choan-Seng Song,
who has taught Theology and Asian Cultures at the Pacific School of Religion in
Berkeley, California, talks about the meeting of the Christian cross and the Buddhist
lotus in relation to the suffering that must be faced by those who struggle for liberation. In India and South Korea the crucified Christ symbolizes "God's identification" with suffering "cruciform humanity." Indian liberation theology draws on the
egalitarian heritage of the Dalits and their experience of Christ as liberator (see
chapter 1 for more on the Dalits). **Dalit theology** expresses the Dalits' outrage at
their ongoing oppression and their yearning for equal status. The Indian Jesuit
priest Sebastian Kappen (d. 1993) saw Jesus as a countercultural prophet modeling
a "praxis of subversion" that was relevant to the Indian struggle between oppressive
theologies (the Vedas, Manu) and liberative theologies (Buddhism, Hindu Bhakti).
In his view, Indian society needed to be liberated from "both orthodox Hinduism
and modern capitalism."[71]

Korean **Minjung theology** is an outgrowth of the suffering of the Korean "common people" (translation of Minjung). In the late nineteenth century, Protestant
missionaries in Korea connected with poor people there by translating the Bible into
Korean instead of Chinese, giving them access to biblical symbols and stories that
they found meaningful in their quest for liberation from poverty and foreign domination. During its occupation of Korea from 1905 to 1945, Japan banned the exodus
story of God rescuing slaves from Egypt! Since the Korean War, North and South
Koreans have had to endure authoritarian government, whether communist or capitalist. Christ's suffering was symbolically linked to the people's suffering in the
poetry of the Korean Catholic writer Kim Chi-ha (1941–), who had his own experience of "torture and years of solitary confinement in prison."[72]

The Sri Lankan Jesuit Aloysius Pieris holds a doctorate in Buddhist studies, which
he has used to engage in dialogue with the Buddhist community. He identifies two
Asian forms of religious socialism: *monastic* and *peasant*—the simple, voluntarily
shared cooperative life chosen and lived by monks and members of ashrams; and
the dehumanizing, grinding, hopelessly shared poverty in which peasants are forced
to live. He calls *involuntary* poverty "enslaving religion," and *voluntary* poverty
lived in solidarity with the involuntarily poor "liberating religion."[73]

Philippine liberation theology[74] arose in the midst of armed struggle by the Muslim community on the southern island of Mindanao against the central (Christian)
government in Manila. Public perceptions of political power were transformed
when a popular movement (trained by the Goss-Mayers of the Netherlands and
supported by the Roman Catholic Cardinal Sin) used techniques of active nonviolence to install Corazon Aquino as president in 1986 after she had defeated Ferdinand Marcos in elections earlier that year, but was being denied the fruits of her
victory. Filipinos then began to speak of "people power."

THE VISION OF KAREN LEBACQZ

Theologian and ethicist Karen Lebacqz, ordained in the United Church of Christ, offers a compelling vision of justice, incorporating elements from Christian social teaching enriched by liberation theology:

1. Justice is not primarily a philosophical determination of rights. It is right relationships in community among humans who understand their need for each other, and between humans and God.
2. For this reason, it deals primarily with the duties necessary to create and maintain human community—duties appropriate to humans who care for each other. It is not dominated by individual human beings asserting their rights.
3. The primary injustice is exploitation, domination, and oppression, which break the community's covenant, violating the human dignity of the victim and destroying the humanity of the oppressor. Both the victim and the oppressor need to be liberated.
4. The move toward justice is then a move toward restoration of what has been damaged by injustice. This move involves God and humans acting together to *rescue* the oppressed, who themselves have engaged in *resistance*, refusing to accept their degradation. It also involves God and humans acting together to *rebuke* oppressors and to challenge them to make *reparations* to set things right. This move toward reparation involves both ending the oppression itself and acting to undo the damage caused by past injustice. In particular, those who benefit from the effects of past injustice, even if they were not responsible for the injustice in the first place, should be challenged to share their benefits with those who suffered from the effects of the injustice. The biblical concept of a periodic jubilee of redistribution is appropriate in this context.
5. All of these actions will be incomplete. One must continually return to the beginning of the circle of praxis to assess, from the standpoint of the most oppressed, what the actual effects have been of the actions taken. Then one must seek again to approximate the ideal. Work for justice is unending, and celebration of the jubilee redistribution of resources must recur time after time.[75]

SUMMARY

Beginning in Latin America, liberation theology felt impelled to ask what God had to say about situations of injustice—glaring disparities between wealth and poverty. They applied a "circle of praxis" (insertion, descriptive analysis, normative analysis, and action plans) and a series of power questions (who is making the effective decisions, who gains from the decisions, and who loses?). Because the analysis challenged status-quo structures and power relations—trying to rescue the oppressed, resist the oppression, rebuke oppressors, and demand reparations to restore Christian community—it became very controversial. While accepting much of the social criticism, the Catholic Church leadership warned against secular aspects of Marxist analysis; wealthy elites simply labeled the whole enterprise "communist," attacking its theologians and their communities with police, military, and paramilitary violence.

The Christian Latin American liberation theology movement gave rise to similar liberation theology movements in Judaism and Islam, among blacks and feminists, and in Asia and Palestine.

KEY TERMS

al-nas	Mujerista theology
Base Christian Communities	normative analysis
circle of praxis	pastoral plan
conscientization	praxis
Dalits, Dalit theology	reductions
descriptive analysis	structural violence
ecumenical deal	*taqwa*
insertion	*tawhid*
JOCists	Womanist theology
Minjung theology	

DISCUSSION QUESTIONS

1. This chapter has discussed several types of liberation theology. Which type is most likely to deal with situations that are important to you? Which of its insights do you find most convincing?

2. How might the circle of praxis apply to a situation that you think needs to be changed? What would you have to do to fulfill each of its four parts?

3. Apply the three power questions to a particular situation to help judge whether or not it is a situation of oppression. For example, how might the three power questions apply to a college or university system of grading? That is, who decided that your university would adopt its current system of grading (e.g., A–F; number rankings; pass-fail for certain courses or for all courses; faculty-written evaluations of students instead of grades; no grades at all)? What groups gain something from that system (faculty, staff, administration, students, boards of directors, employers, accrediting agencies, corporations producing standardized tests, the overall society)? What do they gain? What groups lose something from that system, and what do they lose? Did the groups that made the decision get all the gains, and did someone else pay all the costs?

SUGGESTIONS FOR FURTHER READING

Antonio. "Black Theology."

Ateek. *Justice, and Only Justice: A Palestinian Theology of Liberation.*

———. *A Palestinian Christian Cry for Reconciliation.*

Berndt. *Non-Violence in the World Religions.*

Berryman. *Liberation Theology.*

Boff. *Church, Charism and Power.*

Cone. "Black Theology and Black Power."

Dawson. "The Origins and Character of the Base Ecclesial Community."

Domhoff. *Who Rules America?*

Ellis. *Toward a Jewish Theology of Liberation*, 3rd ed.

Esack. *Quran, Liberation and Pluralism.*

Farber. *Radicals, Rabbis and Peacemakers.*

Ferm. *Profiles in Liberation.*

Fernandes, ed. *The Emerging Dalit Identity.*

Galtung. "A Structural Theory of Imperialism."

Gorospe. *Forming the Filipino Social Conscience.*

Gottlieb, ed. *Liberating Faith.*

Grey. "Feminist Theology: A Critical Theology of Liberation."

Gutiérrez. "Faith and Social Conflict."

———. *A Theology of Liberation.*

Hebblethwaite. "Liberation Theology and the Roman Catholic Church."

Johnson, ed. *The Church Women Want.*

———. "Imaging God, Embodying Christ: Women as a Sign of the Times."

———. *She Who Is: The Mystery of God in Feminist Theological Discourse.*

Lebacqz. *Justice in an Unjust World.*

———. *Six Theories of Justice.*

Maduro, ed. *Judaism, Christianity, and Liberation: An Agenda for Dialogue.*

McGovern. *Liberation Theology and Its Critics: Towards an Assessment.*

Míguez Bonino. *Christians and Marxists.*

Nelson-Pallmeyer. *Harvest of Cain.*

———. *Saving Christianity from Empire.*

Novak. *Will It Liberate?*

Pieris. *An Asian Theology of Liberation.*

Pope John Paul II. *Centesimus Annus.*

———. *Sollicitudo Rei Socialis.*

Ratzinger. *Instruction on Certain Aspects of the "Theology of Liberation."*

———. *Instruction on Christian Freedom and Liberation.*

Rowland. "Introduction: The Theology of Liberation."

———, ed. *The Cambridge Companion to Liberation Theology*, 2nd ed.

Ruether. *The Wrath of Jonah*, 2nd ed.

Segundo. *The Liberation of Theology.*

Shaull and César. *Pentecostalism and the Future of the Christian Churches.*

Topel. *The Way to Peace: Liberation through the Bible.*

Villa-Vicencio. "Liberation and Reconstruction."

West. "The Bible and the Poor."

Wielenga. "Liberation Theology in Asia."

Wink. *Engaging the Powers.*

11

∞

Active Nonviolence

Pursuit of truth [does] not admit of violence being inflicted on one's opponent, but . . . he must be weaned from error by patience and sympathy. For, what appears to be truth to the one may appear to be error to another.[1]

If you want something really important to be done you must not merely satisfy the reason, you must move the heart also. The appeal of reason is more to the head, but the penetration of the heart comes from suffering. It opens up the inner understanding in [humans]. Suffering is the badge of the human race, not the sword.[2]

It is the acid test of nonviolence that in a nonviolent conflict there is no rancor left behind, and in the end the enemies are converted into friends. That was my experience in South Africa with General Smuts. He started with being my bitterest opponent and critic. Today he is my warmest friend.[3]

Nonviolence is a power which can be wielded equally by all—children, young men and women or grown up people—provided they have a living faith in the God of Love and have therefore equal love for all [humanity].[4]

—Mohandas K. Gandhi

There is no way to peace; peace is the way.[5]

—A. J. Muste

WHAT IT IS AND HOW IT WORKS

Active nonviolence is an exercise of power for social and political change that courageously refuses to support evil but also refuses to cause harm to its opponents. The power exercised is spiritual, moral, and persuasive.

Unspiritual, immoral, and unpersuaded people experience this power when they discover that the people they depend on for their power no longer support them or their goals. Thus Philippine president Ferdinand Marcos experienced the power of active nonviolence in 1986, when he discovered that his army was no longer following his orders.

Many people stop supporting their leaders when they see those leaders unjustly attacking people who are causing no harm. In June 1989, when Chinese tanks ran over unarmed students and Chinese soldiers shot unarmed students in Tiananmen Square, Beijing, bystanders lost confidence in their army and government. In such a situation, people may still go along with the government for a while, but they will do so inefficiently and without enthusiasm. And if an opportunity arises to shift their support to a different government or to different leaders, they will be inclined to do so.

Power Depends on Cooperation

A key insight of active nonviolence is that power depends on widespread cooperation. The more powerful a leader is, the more people she depends on to maintain that power. An Amazon tribal chief may depend only on twenty picked warriors, but he has only modest power. The president of the United States has much more power, but that power depends on the cooperation of many more people. In the 1960s, when a significant number of U.S. citizens lost confidence in President Johnson's prosecution of the Vietnam War and began to cooperate halfheartedly, seek primarily their own safety, do no more than they absolutely had to, conscientiously protest the war, or actively interfere with it, the president found that his power was seriously weakened.

Modern leaders depend on generals, sergeants, privates, police, jailers, cabinet members, senators, congresspersons, judges, lawyers, editors, newspaper reporters, union leaders, industrial workers, transportation workers, farmers, construction workers, teachers, janitors, garbage collectors, and many other people. Senators who refuse to vote as lobbied to vote by the president can interfere with the president's power, but so can garbage collectors who deliver their gatherings to the front door of the White House just as a foreign diplomat arrives or, more realistically, secretaries who "forget" to transmit messages. Nuclear researchers in Nazi Germany quietly buried their research in their files to prevent the regime from developing nuclear weapons.

Why People Cooperate and Obey Authority[6]

Some people feel morally obliged to obey government authority. The rule of law seems fairer than naked personal power. Laws may be seen as God's will, or as legitimate, reasonable, and essential for a good society. But laws can also be arbitrary—enriching and protecting elites rather than common people.

Some obey authority because they identify themselves with their boss, ruler, or government. Rulers encourage this identification by appealing to a common nationality, tribe, religion, or other deeply held shared identity. Some obey out of habit—they don't realize they have a choice. Anyone who "empowers" common people to think for themselves and make choices threatens the power of authoritarian rulers.

Some obey because unjust laws benefit them personally. They support the corrupt system which has enriched them. They may not be conscious of the injustice their privilege is based on. When poverty is widespread, the privileged fear that any change of the power structure will throw *them* into poverty.

Some obey because they fear punishment. Almost all governments of the world torture prisoners, many routinely, not primarily to gain information but to intimidate and divide the population, making people mistrust each other, and to destroy any group that might challenge the government's authority.[7] More generally, some are just too timid to challenge authorities. When their empowerment and self-confidence increase, authoritarian rulers lose power over them.

Finally, many don't care about a particular law, especially if it doesn't affect *them*. We can't give serious attention to everything. We may just want to live our everyday lives without thinking about the needs of *strangers*.

The Decision to Resist Nonviolently

The starting point for a campaign of active nonviolence is the conviction of injustice. Usually it is a relatively small group that first notices the injustice and draws attention to it, or that comes to believe it is possible to do something about it. The *circle of praxis* described by liberation theologians is a process for confirming the suspicion of injustice. *Insertion* puts one into the experience where injustice is suspected, *descriptive analysis* clarifies its causes, *normative analysis* shows how things could and should be, and *pastoral action* moves the situation toward justice. If the injustice is deep, those who profit from it will usually resist the pastoral action and attack the campaigners. At that point, the hidden, structural violence that held the injustice in place will become visible through the violent counterattacks on nonviolent resisters.

Three Types of Nonviolent Action

Theorist Gene Sharp has identified 198 forms of nonviolent action, arranged into three main types in ascending order of intensity:[8]

1. **Protest and persuasion** involve moral appeals to those in power, including letters and e-mails to political leaders and editors, public appeals and demonstrations, and other attempts to influence public opinion.
2. **Noncooperation** involves refusing to do what one is normally expected to do. It includes strikes, boycotts, and other refusals to follow orders. Bulgarians who refused to hand over Jews to Nazis during World War II were practicing noncooperation. So were the politicians who refused to serve in General Kapp's cabinet after his 1920 putsch in Germany,[9] and the Catholic bishops in Chile who refused to give Pinochet's government the legitimation it expected.[10] So are U.S. citizens who become war tax resisters because they do not want to fund the Pentagon.

Figure 11.1. Nonviolent demonstration seeking to close the School of the Americas, also known as the Western Hemisphere Institute for Security Cooperation, at Fort Benning, Georgia. Each cross bears the name of someone killed by graduates of the school. Courtesy David Whitten Smith, November 2002.

3. **Intervention** involves "getting in the way" of injustice by doing what one is normally forbidden to do. Czechs intervened in 1968 by taking down all the street signs in Prague so that the Soviet invaders couldn't find the people they wanted to arrest.[11] Philippine civilians intervened in 1986 by standing between two factions of President Marcos's army.

Strategy and tactics require careful planning. Both nonviolence and war can be effective or ineffective. Some nonviolent campaigns have been unsuccessful; so have many wars—which is why modern nations have war colleges, such as West Point in the United States. If we spent as much energy studying and preparing for nonviolent action as we devote to war, our modern world would be revolutionized. In addition, the astronomical sums of money allocated to the military (injustice and war) would instead be dedicated to meeting human needs (justice and peace).

Find the Symbolic Action That Will Reveal the Injustice

Effective nonviolent actions symbolize the injustice being resisted. A few protesters at the government center don't carry much weight—they look inconsequential.

What is needed is a more powerfully symbolic action. When Gandhi led Indians on a march to the sea to make salt in violation of British tax laws, the British government of India couldn't ignore the action, nor could they counter it effectively, because it symbolized the issue too clearly. In a hot climate like India, people die without salt. The poor could make salt for themselves, but the colonial government wouldn't allow them to because it gained revenue by taxing its government-monopolized salt.[12]

In Sicily in the 1950s, Danilo Dolci led unemployed villagers to "strike in reverse" by repairing free of charge the road leading into the village. The government objected because repair of roads was *their* responsibility. The villagers were dramatizing government inaction in the face of severe unemployment. When Dolci and a number of villagers were arrested, the well-publicized trial made the government look ridiculous.[13]

In Brazil, two lawyers preparing a routine case were astonished to find that the legal archives of the oppressive military government held trial transcripts in which prisoners described their tortures in detail. From 1979 to 1982, Cardinal Arns of São Paulo helped the two lawyers copy thousands of pages of testimony, analyze and record the data, and write a twelve-volume report in 6,891 pages, based on the cases of seventeen thousand victims and describing almost three hundred forms of torture. As the study proceeded, microfiches of the findings were sent to the World Council of Churches in Geneva. Then a popular single-volume summary was prepared. Published in 1986 shortly after the transition to civilian government, with no advance publicity, and with only the Archdiocese of São Paulo identified on the title page, the summary was delivered to bookstores all across Brazil on a single day. Realizing that it had been widely distributed already, the government decided to ignore it. A few months later, the diocesan newspaper printed lists of the torturers with the number of times each had been named by defendants. Protected by a 1979 amnesty law, none of the perpetrators were brought to criminal trial, but two were sued in civil court and $1.5 billion was paid in reparations to 135 families.[14] For ongoing efforts to invalidate the amnesty, see our website at http://courseweb .stthomas.edu/justpeace/rowman.html.

Active Nonviolence Is Not Passive

Nonviolent leaders choose *provocative actions* that publicly reveal their *opponents'* violence. In Chile, when Augusto Pinochet (1973–1990) was torturing citizens in secret, nonviolent activists unfurled banners that read, "People are being tortured here." They did so during rush hour when a lot of people could see them. Those people also witnessed police clubbing and hosing the nonviolent demonstrators. They came to realize that Pinochet felt threatened because he had something to hide. They also felt respect for the demonstrators, who were willing to be beaten without retaliating.[15]

In the mid-1990s, the American organization Voices in the Wilderness (since replaced by Voices for Creative Nonviolence),[16] founded by Kathy Kelly in Chicago, began to dramatize the impact of U.S./UN sanctions against Iraq by bringing medicines and toys to Iraq. In 1998, the group and its leaders were given a "pre-penalty notice" by the Office of Foreign Assets Control (OFAC) of the U.S. Department of the Treasury saying that they could be fined $160,000 for delivering these donated medicines and toys without prior authorization. In response, they delivered to the Treasury Department, OFAC, and U.S. Attorney General Janet Reno declarations signed by numerous people stating that they supported and had taken part in the campaign to end the U.S./UN sanctions against Iraq. Those who had traveled to Iraq offered to assist investigators by bringing samples of the medical supplies and toys in question, along with enlarged photographs of Iraqi children they had met, most of whom had since died for lack of medicines to treat curable diseases.

On January 15, 1999, the birthday of Martin Luther King and eight years after the first Gulf War of 1991, Witness for Peace members began an eighteen-day walk from the Pentagon to the United Nations in New York City. Along the way, they campaigned for an end to the U.S./UN sanctions against Iraq and called on the United Nations to "walk away from the Pentagon": to stop allowing U.S. policy to pervert the UN into an instrument of warfare that brutalizes children.[17]

Imperative That Action Remain Nonviolent

Active nonviolence works to keep its followers nonviolent and to help the public see that they are nonviolent. If some of the activists start to throw bombs or to burn tanks, then the soldiers will take the position that they are only defending themselves, and bystanders will be sympathetic to that view. But if the activists can maintain the discipline of nonviolence, then the more the ruler orders a violent response, the more he or she will lose public respect and support.

At the same time that they maintain their own nonviolence (as noted earlier), activist leaders want the symbolic actions of nonviolent activists to reveal, through the repressive violence of the *establishment opponent*, the structural violence of the establishment, which is otherwise hidden. Some examples of such nonviolent public actions have just been given. Similarly, if a leader is supporting unjust wage laws that cause half of the laborers' children to die from malnutrition before the age of five, then the activists will seek a means of making that connection visible. For example, they might hold massive mock or real children's funerals with long processions around the government center to keep the issue before the eyes of the general public. Or workers in luxury industries could go on strike, offer their services to meet the basic needs of the poor, and then march in a body to city hall to present a bill for their labor.

Expect Violent Repression

It is a misunderstanding to think that a campaign of active nonviolence has failed if violence breaks out against the campaigners. The first response of unjust governments is *usually* violent repression. If the injustice is deep and the nonviolence effective, those who profit from the injustice will violently attack the campaigners.

Activist leaders will be arrested, detained, and perhaps tortured. Or they will be beaten up by thugs, as were opposition leaders in Panama in 1987–1989.[18] Or they will be murdered or made to disappear, as frequently happens in Central America. This repression brings out into the open the violence that was previously only threatened but has held the unjust situation in place through fear.

If the activists overcome their fear of pain and death and remain firm, the repression will further weaken the government's support. A kind of moral **ju-jitsu** begins to operate: instead of defending themselves from the opponent's violence by responding with violence of their own, the activists use his violence to throw the opponent off balance and to raise hesitations in his supporters' minds. The more repression the opponent uses, the worse he looks to his supporters and the weaker his position becomes. When enough supporters become hesitant, inefficient, or obstructive, the opponent's power dissolves.

Three Forms of Success

As the process of nonviolent resistance proceeds, success can come to the resisters in one of three ways: The opponent's leadership may actually be *converted* to see the justice of the resisters. This result is not as rare as is normally believed, but it tends to occur years *after* the issue has been resolved by the second form of success: **accommodation.**

In *accommodation*, leaders decide that maintaining their position is not worth what it is costing them. For example, the Southern white establishment in the United States *first* accepted integration as an accommodation. Much *later* they came to **conversion**—to see that segregation had been unjust.

The third possible form of success is by **coercion**. In this case, the leader seeks to maintain the status quo, but finds that the army, police, lawyers, judges, and others he depends on to do so refuse to carry out his orders. In the Philippines in 1986, President Marcos lost the power he exercised through *coercion* when both his army and the U.S. government refused to support his administration.

Even Monsters Are Vulnerable

Active nonviolence can work against the most oppressive governments, and even against psychopaths, if the activists are persistent and courageous enough. If enough people overcome their fear of death and pain, the process is very powerful. But it is a serious question whether a community is courageous enough to make it work.

Remember that these activities produce their effects from the bottom up, by influencing first, not the main leader, but those on whom the leader depends for support. It isn't Hitler who has to be convinced, but rather those who support him. Most of his supporters are not psychopaths—they do have functioning consciences. The contrast between the activists' nonviolence and the oppressors' violence affects various people in various ways. Uncommitted third parties are repelled by the oppressors' violence. Members of the oppressors' group begin to have doubts. And the activists' group gains encouragement and support.

Among Gene Sharp's vast array of historical examples (198 different types of active nonviolence)[19] are several successful actions taken against Hitler's "final solution" and against communist governments. The nonviolent actions all had a significant effect. They did not necessarily solve the problems being faced, but neither did the violent efforts made to solve the same problems.

For example, in Berlin in 1943 the Gestapo arrested the Jewish husbands of Gentile wives. The wives responded, some six thousand of them, by demonstrating at the gates of the center where their husbands were being detained. Although security police kept trying to disperse the crowd, they kept reassembling. Despite the fact that the Gestapo headquarters were a short distance away, the authorities negotiated with the women and eventually released their husbands.

In Norway under Nazi occupation in the early 1940s, the Norwegian leader installed by the Germans, Vidkun Quisling, attempted to promote fascist education with a new teachers' organization. Twelve thousand of the fourteen thousand Norwegian teachers wrote letters,[20] which they personally signed, refusing to have anything to do with fascist teaching or Quisling's organization. When the government closed the schools, teachers taught in homes. When Quisling arrested a thousand teachers and shipped them to concentration camps, schoolchildren gathered at the railroad stations that the trains passed through singing songs of support. The teachers who remained still refused to give in. Quisling raged at the teachers, "You teachers have destroyed everything for me!" Eight months after the original arrests, all the arrested teachers were sent home to heroes' welcomes.

The 1989–1991 collapse of communism in Eastern Europe and the Soviet Union shows how much power active nonviolence can have when the situation is right. But even under earlier, harsher Soviet rule, there were nonviolent campaigns that had a significant effect. Among these earlier campaigns were strikes in the slave labor camps, especially at Vorkuta after Stalin died. That strike involved thirty thousand prisoners. Some of the leaders were shot during the three-month strike, and the strike ended without an official victory, but considerable material improvements in the conditions of the prisoners did follow.

Better known is the resistance to Russia's 1968 invasion of Czechoslovakia. Russian leaders expected that the invasion of over a half million troops would eliminate resistance within a few days and allow them to replace President Alexander Dubcek with a conservative president who would follow the Moscow line. Instead, the invaders were met with massive noncooperation and concealed disruption. Czechs climbed onto tanks to ask their invaders why they had come. "No, we didn't ask for your help. We were doing fine." The night before massive arrests were to be made, citizens of Prague took down the street signs and piled them in large heaps so that the invading soldiers couldn't find the addresses they had been given. Engineers and mechanics cheerfully went out of their way to carry out long repairs on equipment that somehow broke down anew as soon as the repairs were completed. Secret radio transmitters broadcast new ideas for resistance and information on Soviet moves.

Political leaders refused to cooperate with the invaders despite the invaders' over-whelming military power. Invading troops hadn't brought enough food for such a long campaign—it was eight months before the Soviets were finally able to gain some of their objectives. And their final gains were a compromise, which is unusual given such overwhelming force—defeated countries aren't supposed to have bar-gaining power.

The Czech experience influenced the Poles, who in 1980 founded an independent labor union, *Solidarnosc* (Solidarity), rivaling the official communist union. That move seemed at first to be too weak to affect Poland; later events showed just how powerful it actually was. The Polish experience then paved the way for the stunning "house of cards" collapse of communist rule in Eastern Europe and the Soviet Union. When active nonviolence surfaced again in Czechoslovakia and led to full independence, who reappeared but Alexander Dubcek!

These examples are incomplete in the sense that the gains they achieved were limited. Still, they were mostly ad hoc efforts enacted without advance planning. A campaign that did benefit from such planning was the 1986 Philippine popular resistance to Ferdinand Marcos. A year before the election that led to his downfall, the Philippine Catholic Church under Cardinal Sin invited a Dutch couple noted for their nonviolence training programs, the Goss-Mayers, to run training sessions for the people. During the height of the crisis, the Goss-Mayers met daily with Cardinal Sin to plan what they would do under various potential circumstances. They had worked out in advance that if the army divided and seemed about to engage in civil war, they would ask civilians to turn out in force and crowd in between the two army units, making it difficult for them to attack each other. The situation occurred just as they had imagined it might, and their pre-planned strategy succeeded brilliantly.

This last example illustrates the fact that active nonviolence can be a lot more effective if it is carefully planned and prepared in advance. Gandhi's success in India and Martin Luther King Jr.'s in the United States are further illustrations of the value of such preparation.

All of these examples, and many which could be added, show that even the most brutal governments are vulnerable to campaigns of active nonviolence if the popula-tion is courageous enough to persist in the face of repression. Of course the popula-tion may not be courageous enough. But it may not be courageous or committed enough to make a *violent* campaign such as a revolution or armed resistance work either. It turned out that the United States was either not committed enough or not powerful enough to "win" in Vietnam. Most critics conclude that it was not committed enough, in part because American opponents of the war convinced enough people that the damage being caused was out of proportion to the possible good that could be gained (see just war principle 9 in chapter 12). It is probably also true that, with recruitment by means of a draft, most Americans were unwilling to lose their lives and fortunes in the war.

Overcoming Fear of Death

Attackers or oppressors expect their victims to fight or to run. They are prepared for either of those reactions. They are not prepared to face people who offer them no threat, but who also refuse to cower or shrink in fear. This unexpected reaction, exemplified by "Jesus' Third Way" (see the last section of this chapter), derails their attack and substitutes a human relationship for a master-victim relationship. Gordon Fellman speaks of "opening the frame of adversarialism."[21] James Aho studies how adversaries constitute each other as enemies and how that enemy-formation can be reversed, using the example of a Jewish cantor who converted a Ku Klux Klan grand dragon who was threatening him and his family.[22]

Because willingness to suffer and die is so important for successful social change to promote justice, either through armed resistance or through active nonviolence, activists would do well to call on the deepest energies and commitments available to humans. These energies and commitments usually flow from the core elements of a person's worldview. For religious people, their greatest courage derives from their religious convictions. For secular people, analogous aspects of their worldview carry a similar spirit.

As Fr. Emmanuel Charles McCarthy notes, "For the Christian, survival is not a problem. For the Christian, survival is guaranteed."[23] The same could be said of, at least, Hinduism and Islam. Aleksandr Solzhenitsyn points out that clinging to physical survival leads to disaster:

> And the conclusion is: . . . "Survive! At any price!" . . . And whoever takes that vow, whoever does not blink before its crimson burst—allows his own misfortune to overshadow both the entire common misfortune and the whole world. This is the great fork of camp life. . . . If you go to the right—you lose your life, and if you go to the left—you lose your conscience. . . . "At any price" means: at the price of someone else.[24]

SOME NONVIOLENT ACTIVISTS

Many proponents of active nonviolence have been deeply religious persons. See chapter 1 for discussion of Swami Agnivesh, Vinoba Bhave, and Mohandas Gandhi; chapter 2 for A. T. Ariyaratne, Aung San Suu Kyi, the Dalai Lama, Nagarjuna, and Thich Nhat Hanh; chapter 3 for Martin Buber, Ahad Ha'am, and Etty Hillesum; chapter 4 for Jane Addams, Daniel and Philip Berrigan, Dorothy Day, and Dr. Martin Luther King Jr.; chapter 5 for Khan Abdul Ghaffar Khan, Riffat Hassan, Fatima Mernissi, and Chandra Muzaffar; chapter 6 for Bartholomé de Las Casas and Winona LaDuke; chapter 8 for Uri Avnery, Mustafa Barghouthi, Abuna Elias Chacour, the Israeli Refuseniks, and various local and international peace teams; and chapter 10 for Naim Ateek, Marc Ellis, Farid Esack, and Rosemary Radford Ruether.

Here are twelve more examples from the past two centuries:

Adin Ballou (1803–1890), United States, Protestant minister. Ballou was an active member of the New England Non-Resistance Society, which promoted radical social change without violence, and a friend of William Lloyd Garrison, who campaigned against slavery. Ballou developed the principles of pacifism and nonviolence, influencing Thoreau, Tolstoy (with whom he corresponded), and Gandhi. His 1846 book *Christian Non-Resistance* exercises our imaginations with numerous accounts of people engaged in creative, compassionate, and effective nonviolence. Tolstoy translated Ballou's writings into Russian and circulated them there.

Henry David Thoreau (1817–1862), U.S., Transcendentalist. Thoreau was jailed overnight in 1846 when he refused to pay the Massachusetts poll tax because it was used to finance the Mexican-American War, which he believed was designed to extend slavery; he was a staunch opponent of both the war and slavery. When his friend Ralph Waldo Emerson saw him in prison, he said, "What are you doing in here?" Thoreau responded, "What are you doing out there?" As a result of this experience, Thoreau wrote his famous essay "On Civil Disobedience." In it he stated:

> The mass of men serve the state thus, not as men mainly, but as machines, with their bodies. They are the standing army, and the militia, jailers, constables, posse comitatus, etc. In most cases there is no free exercise whatever of the judgement or of the moral sense; but they put themselves on a level with wood and earth and stones; and wooden men can perhaps be manufactured that will serve the purpose as well.[25]

Count Leo von Tolstoy (1828–1910), Russia, disaffected Orthodox Christian. A renowned Russian novelist, author of *War and Peace* and other great works, Tolstoy was converted to radical pacifism late in his life, arguing that there would be no wars if soldiers would simply refuse to fight. His later, nonfiction writings such as *The Kingdom of God Is within You* (1894), in which he promoted Christian nonviolence, became very influential, giving rise to numerous Tolstoy Clubs for the study of his ideas. Strongly influenced by Ballou and Thoreau, he himself influenced Jane Addams (see chapter 4) and Mohandas Gandhi.

Eleanor Roosevelt (1884–1962), U.S., Christian.[26] Probably the best known First Lady (1933–1945) in the history of the United States, she was a feminist, a supporter of the civil rights movement, and a human rights advocate. She and her fifth cousin once removed, Franklin Delano Roosevelt, were married in 1905 and had six children. When the Daughters of the American Revolution (DAR), to which Eleanor belonged, would not allow the great black opera singer Marian Anderson to perform in their Constitution Hall in Washington, D.C., Eleanor dropped her membership in the organization and organized a performance by Anderson at the Lincoln Memorial before an audience of about seventy thousand people; the concert was broadcast live by radio to millions more. During World War II, Eleanor disagreed with Executive Order 9066, which authorized the confinement of 110,000 Japanese and Japanese-American citizens of the United States in internment camps. Among her most important achievements was her work as chair of the committee that wrote the United Nations Universal Declaration of Human Rights, approved by the UN General Assembly in December 1948.

A. J. Muste (1885–1967), U.S., Protestant Christian. Dutch by birth, Muste was a child when his family emigrated to the United States. He was raised in the Calvinistic Dutch Reformed Church and ordained as a Dutch Reformed minister in 1909. In addition to his undergraduate degree, he earned a Bachelor of Divinity degree from Union Theological Seminary in New York City. He voted for the Socialist presidential candidate Eugene Debs in 1912. Influenced by the Quakers, he responded to both world wars as a pacifist. Having left the Dutch Reformed Church for the Congregational Church, he was forced out of the latter because of his pacifism. He worked with the ACLU in Boston and with the Society of Friends (Quakers) in Providence, Rhode Island. In the 1920s he became head of Brookwood Labor College in upstate New York after supporting the textile workers' strike in Lawrence, Massachusetts. He also worked with the Fellowship of Reconciliation. He became involved with labor politics through the Conference for Progressive Labor Action, the American Workers Party, and the Trotskyist Workers Party of America. But after meeting Trotsky himself in Norway in 1936, Muste abandoned Marxism and resumed his core identity as a Christian pacifist. From 1940 to 1953, he served as FOR's executive secretary, contributing also to the establishment of the Congress on Racial Equality (CORE). From 1953 to 1967, he led the Committee for Nonviolent Action against nuclear installations, submarines, test zones, and the like, participating in a 1961 walk for unilateral disarmament from San Francisco to Moscow. Friend and mentor to Martin Luther King Jr. and his wife Coretta, Muste played a crucial organizing role for the antiwar movement during the Vietnam War. After a failed trip to Saigon in 1966 with other pacifists, he traveled with religious leaders toward the end of the same year to Hanoi, meeting there with Ho Chi Minh. He died early in 1967. Muste lived a life dedicated both to peace and nonviolence and to social and economic justice.[27]

Corrie Ten Boom (1892–1983), Netherlands, Dutch Reformed Christian. Working as a Dutch watchmaker in her family's jewelry store, Ten Boom was forty-eight when the Nazis occupied Holland. Once when a visiting pastor turned down her request to help a Jewish mother and her baby on the grounds that he and his family might die as a result, her father took the baby in his arms and said to the pastor, "You say we could lose our lives for this child. I would consider that the greatest honor that could come to my family."[28] Like her father, Ten Boom joined the Dutch underground (resistance), finding or offering shelter to homeless Jews and helping to feed them. She hid seven Jews in a secret room behind a false wall in her bedroom. After an informer betrayed her family to the Gestapo and they had been arrested, her father died. She and her sister were sent to various prisons and camps, the last being Ravensbruck in Germany, where her sister died. Two of her sister's visions came true: a home for recovering former detainees and a camp for survivors of the Third Reich. After giving a talk about forgiveness in a Munich church in 1947, Ten Boom was approached by a former guard from Ravensbruck whom she recognized. He thanked her for her talk and extended his hand. She found herself unable to move her arm; she had to ask God to share with her *God's* forgiveness of this guard. "As I took his hand, the most incredible thing happened. From my shoulder along my arm and through my hand a current seemed to pass from me to him, while into my heart sprang a love for this stranger that almost overwhelmed me. And so I discovered that it is not on our forgiveness any more than on our love that the world's healing hinges, but on His."[29]

Rosa Parks (1913–2005), United States, Baptist Christian. Rosa Parks is best known for her refusal to give up her seat on a Montgomery, Alabama, city bus in December 1955. As a child in Pine Level, Alabama, Parks walked to and from school because there was no school bus for black children there or anywhere else in the South with its Jim Crow segregation laws. She remembered seeing the white bus go by every day: "The bus was among the first ways I realized there was a black world and a white world."[30] She graduated from high school in 1933 with her husband's support, one of only 7 percent of African Americans to do so at the time. After two failed attempts, she registered to vote, and she became a member of the local NAACP chapter in 1943. Her activism was furthered by the friendship of a white couple named Durr, for whom she worked.

Before the famous 1955 incident, Parks had encountered the same hostile bus driver in 1943, when she sat in a "white" bus seat momentarily on her way out of the bus in order to retrieve her purse. The driver drove away before she could reenter the bus at the back, and she faced a rainy five-mile walk home. On December 1, 1955, the same driver asked her and three other black riders to move back to make room for more whites entering the bus. Parks was the only one of the four who would not stand up; committing civil disobedience, she said to the driver, "I don't think I should have to stand up." When he told her he would call the police and have her arrested, she responded, "You may do that." Later she commented that her reason was neither ordinary fatigue nor old age (she was forty-two), but rather that she was "tired of giving in." During her arrest, she realized, "It was the very last time that I would ever ride in humiliation of this kind." Parks's arrest and her subsequent trial precipitated the Montgomery bus boycott, which lasted for 382 days, forcing the city bus system to desegregate. Parks wrote two books: *Rosa Parks: My Story* (1992) and *Quiet Strength* (1995). Martin Luther King Jr. praised Parks as "one of the finest citizens of Montgomery."

Gene Sharp (1928–), U.S., Christian promoting universal active nonviolence. Sharp wrote *The Politics of Nonviolent Action* (1973) and numerous other books advancing the thesis that governments and nations can defend themselves from their enemies with exclusively nonviolent means if they educate and train their people appropriately. Nonviolent national self-defense has the advantage that one's enemies do not feel threatened by it, so it does not lead to an arms race. It also encourages people to act nonviolently in their everyday relations with others, whereas emphasizing armed resistance can easily encourage domestic violence.

When the government itself is the problem, Sharp shows how people can bring the government down. In 1993 he published *From Dictatorship to Democracy: A Conceptual Framework for Liberation* for Burmese dissidents, which has been applied to numerous successful nonviolent revolutions since, notably in Serbia, Tunisia, and

Egypt (although the Egyptian revolution was later reversed). He has published numerous other practical studies analyzing what works and what does not.[31]

Mubarak Awad (1943–), Palestinian born in Jerusalem, U.S. citizen, Greek Orthodox Christian. Awad founded the Center for the Study of Nonviolence in Jerusalem, which began to develop nonviolent strategies and tactics for Palestinians in their struggle for justice and equality under Israeli rule. He has taught Gandhi's methods of resistance effectively among Palestinians in Israel and the Occupied Territories (the West Bank, Gaza, and East Jerusalem). In 1988, the Israeli government refused to renew his visa, although he was born in Jerusalem and holds U.S. citizenship, suggesting that they find the promotion of nonviolence to be particularly dangerous. After he was expelled from Jerusalem, Awad founded Nonviolence International in the United States.[32] Inspired by Awad's ideas, during the first intifada, the Palestinian village of Beit Sahour (near Bethlehem) maintained a tax revolt against Israel from 1988 to 1989. They took as their motto "No taxation without representation," pointing out that they received no services for their taxes. In retaliation, the Israeli army entered the village and confiscated automobiles as well as appliances, furniture, clothing, and machinery used for small manufacturing such as sewing machines from people's homes. As part of their resistance, the villagers bought eighteen cows so that they would not have to buy Israeli milk. When the Israel army demanded that the dairy farm be closed down, they hid the cows in a cave. When that hiding place was discovered, they hid the cows in individual homes. For four years, the Israeli army was unable to find the cows, and milk was daily distributed.[33]

Shirin Ebadi (1947–), Iran, Muslim.[34] Winner of the 2003 Nobel Peace Prize, Shirin Ebadi is an Iranian lawyer who served for ten years in the Iranian Justice Department as a judge, until the revolution of 1979, when all women judges were demoted to clerical positions. After protests, they were promoted to the level of "expert." She retired early and was not able to engage in the practice of law again until 1992. While unemployed, she wrote articles and books, concurrently teaching "human rights training courses at Tehran University," where she had earned her law degree. Her cases have involved the assassination of liberal dissidents and other victims of murder, child abuse, banned periodicals, and similar issues. Her dedication to human rights and to democracy has become internationally known. After receiving the Nobel Peace Prize, she stated her opposition to foreign interference in Iranian affairs, including the Iranian struggle for human rights. More recently she has sought to end legalized gender discrimination in Iran.

Mother Agnes Mariam (1952–), Syria, Greek Catholic Christian. Mother Agnes is the foremost representative of the nonpartisan Syrian Mussalaha Reconciliation Initiative (MRI), which was inaugurated in January 2012 with a "peace congress" convened in Syria, and which seeks a nonviolent end to the conflict in Syria, including "all forms of sectarian violence and denominational strife." Mother Agnes is the mother superior at the Monastery of St. James in Qara, Syria. She has risen to international fame because of her words and actions on behalf of peace for all Syrians. In August 2013 she convincingly debunked the video footage allegedly proving that the Assad government had used chemical weapons against civilians in East Ghouta outside Damascus, thereby helping to prevent a U.S. attack on Syria. She has also accused the Western media and Western nations of turning a blind eye to the atrocities perpetrated by "U.S.-backed insurgents" against Syrian civilians by neither reporting nor censuring them. In addition, she mediated the evacuation of 6,600 women and children, and the surrender of 650 armed "young men," from the besieged Syrian town of Moadamiya near Damascus in late 2013. In the words of Mother Agnes, "We help to implement a nonviolent spirit; we work with everybody, all sides, to do this." The Irish 1976 Nobel Peace Prize winner Mairead Maguire has nominated Mother Agnes and the MRI for the 2014 Nobel Peace Prize.[35]

Chaiwat Satha-Anand (1955–), Thailand, Muslim. Satha-Anand is professor of political science at Thammasat University, Bangkok, and director of the Thai Peace Information Centre. In his essay "The Nonviolent Crescent," the scholar-activist lists "eight theses on Muslim nonviolent action." Note that these theses begin with four principles of *just war*. Since those principles prove incapable of being satisfied (1–4), he is led to four principles of *nonviolent action* (5–8).

1. For Islam, the problem of violence is an integral part of the Islamic moral sphere.
2. Violence, if any, used by Muslims must be governed by rules prescribed in the Quran and Hadith.
3. If the violence used cannot discriminate between combatants and noncombatants, then it is unacceptable in Islam.
4. [The] modern technology of destruction renders discrimination virtually impossible at present.
5. In the modern world, Muslims cannot use violence.
6. Islam teaches Muslims to fight for justice with the understanding that human lives—like all parts of God's creation—are purposive and sacred.
7. In order to be true to Islam, Muslims must utilize nonviolent action as a new mode of struggle.
8. Islam itself is fertile soil for nonviolence because of its potential for disobedience, strong discipline, sharing and social responsibility, perseverance and self-sacrifice, and its belief in the unity of the Muslim community and the oneness of [human]kind.[36]

WOMEN'S GROUPS

Much of women's peace work has been done by groups in which no single woman stands out. Because of social attitudes toward women, groups of women are harder for repressive governments to attack than are individual men or groups of men. We have already noted the Gentile wives of Jewish husbands who faced down the Gestapo in Berlin in 1943. Here are some other famous groups of peacemaking women who have courageously confronted repressive situations and governments:

Women Abolitionists against Slavery (U.S.)

In the 1860s in the United States, no blacks (male or female) and no white women had any legal rights. The Northern black women who began organizing usually had jobs; they tended to form mutual aid societies and established orphanages, settlement houses, schools, and cultural (e.g., literary) societies. A landmark was the series of four public lectures delivered over a seventeen-month period in 1832–1833 by a self-educated, middle-class Christian black woman named Maria Stewart in Boston; Stewart was the first woman to give a public speech in the United States. In her lectures she opposed slavery and decried the lack of opportunity for freed black persons; she also pressed black women to fight for their rights and black men to gain "distinction" in their work.[37]

Black and white women abolitionists (opponents of slavery) attended the Anti-Slavery Convention of American Women in New York City in 1837; attendees at the convention supported a women's abolitionist movement independent of the men's abolitionist movement. The Grimké sisters associated the issue of women's rights with abolitionism. There was widespread Northern opposition to the women's abolitionist movement and to any interracial women's antislavery movement; in one incident the newly constructed convention hall—Pennsylvania Hall—in Philadelphia was destroyed by fire shortly after the ACAW had met there in May 1838.[38]

Women used the practice of political petitioning frequently, since they could not vote. "More than half of the thousands of antislavery petitions sent to [Congress in the 1830s] had women's signatures on them."[39] The homes of black and white women served as stations along the Underground Railroad (by which southern slaves traveled north to freedom), despite a law passed in 1850 making this illegal. Abolitionist women in the North also rescued numerous runaway slaves who were about to be returned to the South.

Greenham Common (Britain)

In 1981 the Greenham Women's Peace Camp was established on Greenham Common in southern England as a protest site next to a military base where the United States had stationed some of its cruise missiles. Protest actions by the women peaked in 1983, with the participation of thirty thousand women. Partly as a result of this campaign, the United States and the Soviet Union ratified the INF (Intermediate-Range Nuclear Forces) Treaty in 1987. By 1991 the base had been emptied of all missiles.

The women who struggled nonviolently against these nuclear weapons were seen as unconventional by the British society around them; often they were banned from local businesses and subjected to police brutality. Yet they steadfastly adhered to the fundamentals of nonviolent resistance, refusing to retaliate or to be verbally abusive. "Hundreds of women learned the principles and practice of nonviolence at Greenham. It changed from a tactic to a way of life, a sustainable system of recognition of the other not based on religion or rules," writes Di McDonald in an article entitled "A Way of Life."[40]

A key action by the Greenham women was their piecemeal destruction, using wire cutters, of the barbed wire fence erected around the base, resulting in hundreds of arrests leading to charges and fines; many chose to serve prison terms rather than pay the fines. Developing legal expertise, the women were also able to demonstrate the illegality of the base in that it had been constructed on "common land," which was off limits to the military.

Mothers of the Disappeared (Argentina, Guatemala [GAM], Chile)

On April 13, 1977, fourteen mothers of "**disappeared**" children demonstrated for the first time at the Plaza de Mayo in Buenos Aires, Argentina. They continued demonstrating there every Thursday afternoon by walking around in a circle and holding pictures of their disappeared loved ones. Eventually they numbered between two hundred and three hundred. On October 5, 1977, they placed an advertisement in *La Prensa* showing pictures of 237 of the disappeared together with their mothers' names and the words, "We do not ask for anything more than the truth." On October 15, the women went to the congress building with a petition signed by twenty-four thousand Argentineans and demanded a government investigation into the disappearances.

Government repression followed, and the group was infiltrated by a young man whose activity led to the kidnapping and disappearance of twelve of the women. The demonstrations at the Plaza de Mayo died out for a while, but the women met silently in churches instead. In 1979 they formed a legal association with elections and a bank account, and in 1980 they began to rent office space and publish a bulletin; as a result, their membership increased from hundreds to thousands. They resumed demonstrations in the Plaza, despite police repression, gaining more popular support. In December 1983 the military regime was replaced with an elected democratic government.[41]

Women in Black (International)

Women in Black is an international peace movement founded in 1988 by a group of Israeli women. Its name was taken from the practice of wearing black at a weekly hourlong vigil held on Friday in cities and towns across Israel. At the vigils the women hold up signs reading "Stop the Occupation," meaning the illegal Israeli military occupation of the Palestinian West Bank, Gaza Strip, and Golan Heights. Among major actions organized by the Israeli Women in Black was a march of about five thousand Israeli and Palestinian women and men from Israeli West Jerusalem to Palestinian East Jerusalem in December 2001. Two banners leading the procession read, "The Occupation Is Killing Us All" and "We Refuse to Be Enemies."[42]

Women in Black exist around the world—in Italy, Germany, India, the former Yugoslavia, and many other countries. They seek justice and a world without violence. In Israel, Women in Black is a member organization of the Coalition of

Women for a Just Peace. A film entitled "Stuck with the Truth," made in 2003 by the Canadian Friends of Sabeel (a Palestinian nonviolent liberation theology organization referred to in chapter 10) shows these Women in Black at a vigil in Jerusalem. One of them talks about praying for peace so that the next generation will not live in fear as her generation has. Another woman affirms that "there is a peaceful way out of this conflict. . . . We can live together" in two nations side by side.

The international organization and the Israeli Women in Black have won various peace prizes; the movement was nominated for the Nobel Peace Prize in 2001. At the end of her address to the UN Security Council on October 23, 2002, Israeli peace activist Gila Svirsky asked, "Is it not preposterous that not a single Israeli woman, and only one Palestinian woman, have held leadership roles at a Middle East peace summit? . . . Is it any wonder that we are still locked in combat?" She concluded, "What we need now is leadership committed to swiftly concluding this era awash in blood. . . . What we need now is women."[43]

RAWA (the Revolutionary Association of the Women of Afghanistan)

Founded in 1977 (two years before the Soviet invasion of Afghanistan), this organization is dedicated to providing medical, educational, and economic assistance to Afghans in need, especially women and children, for example, Afghan refugee women and children in Pakistan. It has sought an Afghanistan independent of foreign occupation and interference, whether by the former Soviet Union or by the U.S. and NATO. It is equally opposed to religious fundamentalism, the warlords, the U.S. occupation, and the "puppet" Hamid Karzai regime. It sees the U.S. as allied with Afghan "enemies of human rights, democracy, and secularism." RAWA's work is both humanitarian (for which international funding has been scarce or nonexistent) and political, that is, directed against the "criminal policies and atrocities" of the Taliban and others visited on the Afghan people, especially on women and children. Since 1981 the organization has published a bilingual magazine with the English title, *Woman's Message*.[44] The most famous individual associated with RAWA is Malalai Joya.[45]

Women of Liberia Mass Action for Peace

During Liberia's second civil war (2000–2003) between the armed forces of President Charles Taylor, in power since 1989, and armed insurgent groups, a Liberian Christian social worker, Leymah Gbowee, began to organize Christian women to pray for peace. Soon this group of antiwar women expanded to include Muslim women too. In the Liberian capital of Monrovia, initially for seven days, these and other women "sat, danced, and sang for peace" in the fish market. While continuing this form of protest, their next tactic was a "sex strike" for the duration of the war, which was claiming hundreds of thousands of lives, as well as wreaking havoc by fire, looting, rape, and recruitment of child soldiers. Then the women marched to

Monrovia's city hall with the message, "Peace is our goal, peace is what matters, peace is what we need." This led to a meeting with President Taylor, followed by meetings with the rebels, rocky but conclusive peace negotiations conducted in Ghana, Taylor's resignation, the arrival of UN peacekeepers, a transitional government, disarmament, and democratic elections on November 23, 2005, which made Ellen Johnson Sirleaf the first woman president of Liberia. Both she and Gbowee won the Nobel Peace Prize in 2011.[46]

NONVIOLENCE AS A TACTIC, OR AS A WAY OF LIFE

Some advocates, like Gene Sharp, promote active **nonviolence as a tactic** suited to the twentieth- and twenty-first-century nuclear stalemate. They believe that, if we can just teach people how to *fight differently, wielding nonviolent force*, we may be able to prevent nuclear devastation. To insist that people commit to nonviolence in *every situation* would, in their view, weaken its power by reducing the total number of people who would use it. Others, like Gandhi, promote active **nonviolence as a way of life** to be used in all situations and independent of its success in achieving the goals of the activists. Gandhi distinguishes the *satyagraha* ("truth force"—his word for active nonviolence that emphasizes its spiritual power) of the *strong* from that of the *weak*. *The weak* choose satyagraha when they feel they don't have the power to use force. If later they get that power, they prefer to use force. *The strong* choose satyagraha even when they have the power and opportunity to use force. They do so because they are committed to active nonviolence as a way of life.

Satyagraha as a way of life implies that no human being can be sure that she is right. Therefore she should struggle in a way which respects the opponent, who sees things differently. She accepts unavoidable suffering at the opponent's hands because she believes that innocent suffering has the power to touch and transform hearts. She trusts that most humans cannot long attack those who do not threaten them with harm, and that those who do continue to attack the nonviolent, especially those who are psychopaths, will find themselves more and more isolated.

Each of the worldviews presented in chapters 1–7 seeks to foster the courage and energy that a person needs in order to realize satyagraha. See our supporting website[47] for some suggestions on how they might do this.

WALTER WINK, *ENGAGING THE POWERS*

To illuminate the specific Christian view of active nonviolence developed by the American biblical scholar Walter Wink, activist, professor, and writer Jack Nelson-Pallmeyer explains some of the insights contained in Walter Wink's three-volume study of the New Testament language for "principalities and powers," titled *Naming the Powers* (vol. 1, 1984), *Unmasking the Powers* (vol. 2, 1986), and *Engaging the Powers* (vol. 3, 1992).

"Active Nonviolence: Jesus' Third Way," by Jack Nelson-Pallmeyer (May 1994)

The persistence of evil and the pervasiveness of violence serve to legitimate violence and make it difficult for Christians and others to take nonviolence seriously, including the nonviolence of Jesus. Television shows and movies, nightly news programs, and daily living surround us with images of violence. From battered women, crime, urban riots, and Bosnia we are nearly overwhelmed with violence.

In most instances the solution to the problem of pervasive evil and violence is projected to be the exercise of more creative, and oftentimes more lethal, forms of violence. Violence saves, or in the words of New Testament scholar Walter Wink, we believe in "the myth of redemptive violence." According to Wink, in his provocative book *Engaging the Powers*,[48] violence and not Christianity is the real religion of America. The myth of redemptive violence "undergirds American popular culture, civil religion, nationalism, and foreign policy" (p. 13). Wink writes that "one of the most pressing questions facing the world today is, How can we oppose evil without creating new evils and being made evil ourselves?" The answer, he says, involves taking the nonviolence of Jesus seriously.

Wink describes the traditional responses to danger and evil as flight or fight:

- Flight = submission; passivity; withdrawal; surrender.
- Fight = armed revolt; violent rebellion; direct retaliation; revenge.

Wink says Jesus offers a third alternative or way: creative, active nonviolence. Drawing out the wisdom and tactics of Jesus as described in the Matthew text (turn the other cheek, give your cloak, walk an extra mile), Wink shows how Jesus' Third Way empowers oppressed people to take the initiative and respond with dignity to a situation of oppression, to put the oppressor in an awkward position while offering the possibility of repentance and transformation.

Wink summarizes Jesus' Third Way as follows:[49]

- Seize the moral initiative.
- Find a creative alternative to violence.
- Assert your own humanity and dignity as a person.
- Meet force with ridicule or humor.
- Break the cycle of humiliation.
- Refuse to submit to or to accept the inferior position.
- Expose the injustice of the system.
- Take control of the power dynamic.
- Shame the oppressor into repentance.
- Stand your ground.
- Make the Powers make decisions for which they are not prepared.
- Recognize your own power.
- Be willing to suffer rather than retaliate.

- Force the oppressor to see you in a new light.
- Deprive the oppressor of a situation where a show of force is effective.
- Be willing to undergo the penalty of breaking unjust laws.
- Die to the fear of the old order and its rules.
- Seek the oppressor's transformation.

Wink notes that in the Matthew passage we see Jesus as a tactician of nonviolence and that these tactics need to be adapted to our own time. However, Jesus' commitment to nonviolence goes beyond tactics. It is reflected in his death on a cross. Jesus was committed to nonviolent resistance because nonviolence reflects and reveals the character of God.

Before dismissing the nonviolence of Jesus as somehow utopian, we would do well to remember that Jesus also lived during very violent times. Rome routinely crucified those it considered agitators, and it sent in its legions to destroy entire cities when necessary; some Jewish groups assassinated Jews who collaborated with Rome, and eventually there was an armed rebellion against Rome, led by the Zealots. There were also many Jews waiting for a violent coming of God, a messiah who would come and throw out the hated Romans, cleanse the temple, and reestablish Israel as an independent nation ruled by a Davidic-type king. In other words, Jesus' nonviolence was as strikingly countercultural in his time as active nonviolence is in our own.

SUMMARY

Active nonviolence is based on the realization that political power depends on the cooperation of the ruled. When they withdraw consent—by protesting, refusing to cooperate with, or even interfering with, an unjust situation—an oppressive leader's power can collapse. Oppressive leaders can be expected to respond with violent repression, which reveals the threatened, clandestine violence that has maintained the unjust situation. If the nonviolent campaigners can overcome their fear and maintain their resistance in the face of suffering and death, they can destroy the political power even of tyrants. This is because the effect works from the bottom up, not by making the tyrant change his or her mind, but by causing those whom the tyrant depends on to change their minds. Occasionally an oppressor is led to see the injustice he is perpetrating. More commonly, the oppressor gives in because maintaining the unjust situation costs more than it is worth. In extreme cases, an oppressor may lose political control entirely, despite every effort to maintain the unjust situation. Numerous examples show that active nonviolence has been effective even against regimes such as Nazi Germany and systems such as Soviet Communism. If it were studied as intently as military force is studied, active nonviolence could be even more effective than it has been.

KEY TERMS

accommodation
coercion
conversion
the disappeared
intervention

ju-jitsu
noncooperation
nonviolence as a tactic
nonviolence as a way of life
protest and persuasion

DISCUSSION QUESTIONS

1. This chapter refers back to twenty-nine individual leaders of active nonviolence discussed in previous chapters and introduces twelve more plus six women's groups. Which of them would you be most interested in reading about further? What caught your attention and interest? Which of their ideas did you particularly agree or disagree with?

2. Do you believe that active nonviolence can be a practical and effective way to struggle for justice and peace? If so, would you be committed to it as a tactic to be used in particular circumstances, or as a way of life to be used in all circumstances? If as a tactic, under what circumstances would you set nonviolence aside in favor of violence or war? (This leads to the next chapter. But first, see the special study questions proposed below by Jack Nelson-Pallmeyer.)

Special Study Questions

3. Watch several Saturday morning cartoons. In what ways is the message of redemptive violence conveyed to children?

4. Read Matthew 5:38–42. You might also want to read pp. 175–82 of Wink's *Engaging the Powers*. Why do you think the nonviolence of Jesus is often not taken seriously? What are some examples from recent history of people and movements that have rooted their commitment to nonviolence in the example of Jesus?

5. Choose a recent or current situation where violence is or was pervasive—for example, Afghanistan, Bosnia, Darfur, Iraq, Israel-Palestine, Rwanda, Syria, or the U.S. urban crisis. What might a strategy of nonviolent action based on Jesus' Third Way look like in one of these situations?

SUGGESTIONS FOR FURTHER READING

Ackerman. *A Force More Powerful.*
Aho. *This Thing of Darkness.*
Ballou. *Christian Non-Resistance.*

Berndt. *Non-Violence in the World Religions.*

Bhave. *Shanti Sena.*

Bondurant. *Conquest of Violence.*

Burrowes. *The Strategy of Nonviolent Defense.*

Catholic Church, Archdiocese of São Paulo (Brazil). *Torture in Brazil.*

Cavanaugh. *Torture and Eucharist: Theology, Politics, and the Body of Christ.*

Cooney and Michalowsk, eds. *The Power of the People: Active Nonviolence in the United States.*

Dellinger. *From Yale to Jail: The Life Story of a Moral Dissenter.*

Dolci. *A New World in the Making.*

———. *Outlaws.*

Fellman. *Rambo and the Dalai Lama.*

Gandhi. *All Men Are Brothers: Life and Thoughts of Mahatma Gandhi.*

———. *Non-Violent Resistance (Satyagraha).*

Gregg. *The Power of Nonviolence.*

Hallie. *Lest Innocent Blood Be Shed.*

Hasek. *The Good Soldier Schweik.*

Holmes and Gan. *Nonviolence in Theory and Practice.*

King. *A Testament of Hope: The Essential Writings and Speeches of Martin Luther King Jr.*

Masters and Davidov. *You Can't Do That: Marv Davidov, Non-violent Revolutionary.*

McAllister. *You Can't Kill the Spirit.*

McDonald. "A Way of Life."

McManus and Schlabach, eds. *Relentless Persistence: Nonviolent Action in Latin America.*

Muste. *The Essays of A. J. Muste.*

Olson. *Freedom's Daughters: The Unsung Heroines of the Civil Rights Movement from 1830 to 1970.*

Paige, Satha-Anand, and Gilliatt, eds. *Islam and Nonviolence.*

Rosenberg. *Nonviolent Communication: A Language of Compassion.*

Samuel. *Safe Passage on City Streets.*

Satha-Anand et al., eds. *The Frontiers of Nonviolence.*

Sharp. *Gandhi as a Political Strategist.*

———. *The Politics of Nonviolent Action.*

———. *Waging Nonviolent Struggle: 20th Century Practice and 21st Century Potential.*

Suttner. *Lay Down Your Arms: The Autobiography of Martha von Tilling.*

Ten Boom, Sherrill, and Sherrill. *The Hiding Place.*

Tolstoy. *Writings on Civil Disobedience and Nonviolence.*

Watterson. *Not by the Sword: How the Love of a Cantor and His Family Transformed a Klansman.*

Wink. *Engaging the Powers: Discernment and Resistance in a World of Domination.*

Yoder. *What Would You Do? A Serious Answer to a Standard Question.*

Zahn. *In Solitary Witness: The Life and Death of Franz Jägerstätter.*

Zunes, Kurtz, and Asher, eds. *Nonviolent Social Movements: A Geographical Perspective.*

12

Just War Theory

We must take sides. Neutrality helps the oppressor, never the victim. Silence encourages the tormentor, never the tormented. Sometimes we must interfere. When human lives are endangered, when human dignity is in jeopardy, national borders and sensitivities become irrelevant. Wherever men and women are persecuted because of their race, religion, or political views, that place must—at that moment—become the center of the universe.

—Elie Wiesel[1]

In order for a war to be just, three things are necessary. First, the authority of the sovereign by whose command the war is to be waged. . . . Secondly, a just cause . . . namely that those who are attacked should be attacked because they deserve it on account of some fault. . . . Thirdly, it is necessary that the belligerents should have a rightful intention, so that they intend the advancement of good, or the avoidance of evil.

—Thomas Aquinas[2]

The Islamic historical experience was primarily concerned not with war-making, but with civilization-building. Islamic theology instructs that an integral part of the divine covenant given to human beings is to occupy themselves with building and creating, not destroying life. The Qur'an teaches that the act of destroying or spreading ruin on this earth is one of the gravest sins possible. *Fasad fi al-ard,* which means to corrupt the earth by destroying the beauty of creation, is considered an ultimate act of blasphemy against God. Those who corrupt the earth by destroying lives, property, and nature are designated as *mufsidun* who, in effect, wage war against God by dismantling the very fabric of existence.

—Abou El Fadl[3]

GENERAL BACKGROUND[4]

Christianity

For the first three centuries, the Christian church refused to engage in warfare, although it occasionally accepted soldier converts without requiring them to renounce their profession. Soon after Constantine (280–337 CE) converted to Christianity in the early fourth century, and Christianity was established as the official religion of the Roman Empire under Theodosius I in the late fourth century, the bishop Augustine of Hippo (354–430 CE) developed a Christian justification for the use of armed force in limited circumstances. Later Thomas Aquinas, Martin Luther, Franciscus de Vitoria, and the legal scholar Hugo Grotius made important contributions to just war theory.[5]

Foremost among the pre-Christian sources for just war theory are the Book of Joshua in the Hebrew Bible, Aristotle, and Cicero. The Crusades (1095–1453) exemplified the category of "holy war," which is "a different form of just war"; this distinction was further clarified by the work of Erasmus (d. 1536) and Machiavelli (d. 1527) on just war criteria. The sixteenth-century Protestant Reformation had the overall effect of making war more acceptable by elevating the status of rulers and the state above that of the churches and Protestant ministers, eliminating moral accountability for rulers, secularizing "times and places" so that war could happen anywhere anytime, and placing fewer restraints on war in the context of a fragmented Christendom.[6]

Buddhism, Judaism, Islam

Buddhism normally rejects the legitimacy of so-called just war, which "is only a false term coined and put into circulation to justify and excuse hatred, cruelty, violence, and massacre."[7]

Jewish and Muslim attitudes toward war are covered in chapters 3 and 5. Their attitudes toward the ten principles we are studying will be noted under each principle.

Presumption against War and Violence

In the rest of this chapter, we concentrate on the moral questions, not the legal ones. Just war theory is based on two general principles: the presumption against war and violence, and the duty to resist evil. These two principles are then applied by the ten specific principles that will follow.

As just war principles are usually presented *academically*, the presumption is against violence and killing. It requires a strong case to override that presumption and to justify violence and killing in a particular instance.

As just war principles are often argued *in an actual case*, the presumption seems to be in favor of one's own government. Thus in the 1991 Gulf War, the U.S. Catholic bishops concluded that war in the Persian Gulf "might well" violate just war principles, but that they did not have sufficient certitude in the matter to ask Catholics to disobey their government and *refuse* to go to war. If the bishops had intended the presumption to be against war and violence, they could have concluded rather that they did not have sufficient certitude in the matter to *allow* Catholics to obey their government and go to war.

Duty to Resist Evil

In tension with the presumption against violence is the duty to resist evil. It is presumed that individuals have a duty to resist evil, and governments have a duty to protect people in their charge. Note that this duty does *not necessarily imply a duty to use lethal or damaging force*, though the use of lethal force is not in principle excluded. If individuals can resist evil and governments can protect people in their charge by nonviolent means, the duty would be adequately fulfilled.

Possible Responses to Injustice

In the face of injustice, humans have several choices, not all good. (a) They can cooperate with the injustice or benefit from it. (b) They can do nothing, avoiding trouble. (c) They can resist with lethal violence. (d) They can resist with provocative nonviolence. Gandhi used to say that the fourth choice was the best, and the third was the second best. Doing nothing or cooperating were not acceptable choices to him.

The ten just war principles that follow can help a *sincere* person judge whether and how to resist injustice with lethal violence. Basic to this judgment is the presumption that an unjust attacker forfeits his or her right to have his or her life protected. But note that one should threaten another's life only to stop an unjust attack on oneself or on innocent others.

Christian theology may challenge the notion that an aggressor forfeits his right to life. Jesus did not resist those who took his life, nor did he protect his followers from being killed. He did instruct them *not to cooperate* with evil, to *confront* it prophetically, and to practice *alternatives* that sometimes *interfere* with evil. The early Christian communities also accepted death as witness to a greater spiritual reality, while challenging their persecutors to accept the kingdom of God that they were already exemplifying in the alternative communities they were forming.

How can we tell whether a person is sincere in his or her use of these principles? They are frequently appealed to in an insincere way by psychopaths seeking popular support. The best judge of sincerity is *consistent use of the principles across a range of situations*. If a leader uses the principles one way when discussing his own interventions and differently when discussing interventions of others, we have reason to presume insincerity. Other criteria of sincerity include the character of the leader, the character of the government the leader heads, the circumstances, and the leader's actions before, during, and after a war.

The Impact of Demonstrations

Proponents of war frequently object that public demonstrations against government policy and discussions questioning the government's decisions regarding war weaken a nation. They argue, for example, that demonstrations against the Vietnam War weakened the United States and encouraged the communists to continue their resistance. According to this view, demonstrations suggest to an adversary that we are not united in our position. They may, then, encourage the adversary to continue their fight (or their actions which threaten war), and discourage our own soldiers from fighting. But this only weakens a nation if war truly is the right choice. If war is the wrong choice, then denying or restricting discussions and demonstrations of concern weakens the nation by making a wrong choice more likely. Unfortunately, we can't know what the true situation is unless there is a genuine public discussion. So in general, *restricting* debate *weakens* a nation.

Universality of Just War Discussion

The "just war principles" that we will be discussing have roots in varied traditions: pagan, Jewish, Christian, Muslim, chivalric, crusader, and so forth.

See above for brief reference to Buddhist, Jewish, and Muslim just war theory. Everyone who chooses or considers war makes use of *some* principles to judge whether or not war is appropriate.[8] No one would be upset by atrocities if they really thought that "all's fair in love and war."

Just war principles in general act to the advantage of warriors. While they may make some aspects of war more difficult or more dangerous, they also protect soldiers from especially cruel or inhumane practices. An example would be principles for the treatment of prisoners of war. Recent efforts to re-categorize Taliban or al-Qaeda fighters by the ambiguous term "enemy combatants"[9] evade these principles.

Wider Application of Principles

The ten moral principles that are appealed to in an argument for or against war can be applied more broadly. They can be used with modest changes for almost any communal action that harms or inconveniences people in some way. Examples would include economic or other kinds of boycotts, strikes, and third-party electoral politics. That is why we name them "principles for a just use of communal force." To judge these unintended but foreseeable side effects, we need the **principle of double effect.**

The Principle of Double Effect

When an action has several foreseen effects, not all of which are willed by the actor, the action can be morally chosen *if* (a) the agent *intends only* the effects that are morally good or indifferent, *not* those that are morally evil, *and* (b) the good effects are *not the result* of the evil effects (that is, the good does not come about *because of the evil*; if, for example, the evil effects do not happen, the good can still be attained), *and* (c) the good effects *outweigh* the evil effects, since *all are foreseen*, even if the evil is *not willed or wanted*. *Note that all three conditions must be met.*

Example: A factory that is manufacturing tanks is bombed at night. Some workers may be injured or killed. If the workers are all asleep at home, the raid is still a success since the factory can no longer make tanks.

Example: A police sharpshooter fires into a room where a terrorist is holding captives and threatening to kill them all. The sharpshooter aims carefully at the terrorist, although the bullet may also injure one or more of the hostages. The terrorist (by just war principles) has forfeited his right to life by his unjust intention to kill the hostages. If a hostage is injured by a wayward bullet or ricocheting fragment, the injury is not intended, and it is worth the risk. If no hostages are killed, the mission is even more of a success.

Example: The residential area of a city in which a tank factory is located is bombed, hoping that the terrorized survivors will pressure their government to end the war. The raid is *not* considered just, because the good effect (the end of the war) comes about through the terror caused by the deaths of uninvolved civilians. This is an example of state-sponsored terrorism.

Example: The room where a terrorist is holding captives is blown up so that future terrorists will know that they had better not fool around with us. While the aim would be attained even if all the captives miraculously escaped, the action would still be immoral because the *likely result clearly foreseen* would be damage (deaths of innocent captives) disproportionate to the good attained.

Example: A guest caught in a burning hotel jumps from the ninth-story window as the flames surround her. She is terribly afraid of death by fire, but knows that the fall will probably kill her anyway. Her action is justified because, although she is moving from one deadly risk to another, it is not her death from the fall that would save her from death by fire: if by some chance she landed on a new shipment of pillows and survived the fall, she would be delighted. Note, however, that she endangers the pedestrians she might land on.

Example: Another guest in a nearby hotel jumps from the ninth-story window because life has become too much for her. Her action is not justified because it is the death itself that she seeks: if she by chance were caught by a protruding awning and softly deposited on the terrace, she would be disappointed.

TEN PRINCIPLES OF JUST WAR

The ten principles are rarely listed all together. When a number is given, it is most often seven—but different authors include different principles in their list of seven. Thomas Aquinas listed three, the Catechism of the Catholic Church four, and the U.S. Catholic bishops seven in their 1983 pastoral letter. We have simply assembled and arranged all the principles we have found people using that seem appropriate to us. The principles are listed in table 12.1.

Table 12.1. Principles for a Just Use of Communal Force (War, Revolution, Strike, Boycott)

Principle	OK	Disputed	No Good
1. Just Cause	*Defense against unjust aggression: a real and certain danger.* "The damage inflicted by the aggressor on the nation or community of nations must be lasting, grave, and certain." (Catholic Catechism 2309)	Protect innocent in someone else's charge. Correct injustice other authority ignores. (Re)establish order necessary for decent human existence, basic human rights. Other side crossed border first. Punish evildoers. Correct wrong ideology.	Empire building, glory, selfish advantage.
2. Comparative Cause	*Compare grievances both sides. No one has absolute justice, but the war is justified only if there is a preponderance of justice on one side over the other.*		No effort made to consider justice of other side. Major injustice on both sides, no clear preponderance. Values at stake not significant enough to justify damage/killing.
3. Attitude	Love weak, enemy. Sorrow and regret for damage and killing caused. See opponent as human like oneself.		Revenge, cruelty, love of violence, wild resistance, the lust of power, delight in killing and destruction, pride and self-seeking.

4. Intention	Establish justice and peace. Incapacitate combatant: (a) capture, (b) wound, (c) kill.	Help rebuild conquered enemy. "Convert" enemy.	Unreasonable demands, e.g., unconditional surrender.
5. Last Resort	Tried all other steps had reasonable time for.	Preemptive strike in face of imminent unjust threat.	Other options not seriously considered.
6. Likely Success	Reasonably likely to achieve goals.	Defend key values against great odds as proportionate witness.	Lost cause: no hope of winning. Destroy what fighting for. Both sides perhaps annihilated.
7. Authority	Those responsible for common good really supported by those they represent.	Revolutionary movements.	Unrepresentative despot or rebel seeking own advantage. Private citizen.
8. Declared	Publish reasons, including conditions for settlement, before attack.	Undeclared but not unexpected in broad sense.	"Sneak attack."
9. Proportionality	More good gained than damage caused for war as a whole, and for each strategy/step/weapon. Include all affected *on both sides*, especially poor, helpless.	Include spiritual dimensions in calculation.	More damage caused than good gained. Destroy all life to preserve some principle ("We had no choice").
10. Discrimination	Immune: noncombatants, prisoners, future citizens. Long-term effects.	"Defense workers"—how broadly conceived? Guerrilla war.	Harm hostages, uninvolved; guerrillas "hugging the people."

To illustrate these principles, we will consider the conflict between the United States and Iraq, which began with war in 1991; it then continued for twelve more years through ruinous sanctions combined with frequent bombing campaigns, followed by another U.S. invasion of Iraq ("shock and awe") in 2003, and concluded with a U.S. occupation of Iraq that has officially but not really ended. On our companion website,[10] we will apply the principles to the U.S. war in Afghanistan.

Classical discussions on just war distinguish two sets of questions: those relating to **jus ad bellum**—whether it is justified to *begin* a war (or to *continue* one); and those relating to **jus in bello**—how a war, once begun, can be justly carried out. This distinction dates from a time when people took it for granted that it was the sovereign who decided whether to go to war, and that all soldiers had to do was to fight it fairly. In that case, the leaders could be trusted to apply the *jus ad bellum* principles. Today, aware of the danger of being misled by psychopathic leaders, the whole population needs to consider whether or not to support its leaders' decisions and whether or not to cooperate with the war or sanctions. In general, all ten principles must be satisfied in order to begin a war, to continue a war, and to conduct a war justly. So we will not make use of this distinction.

Recent writers have added principles for **jus post bellum** discussing responsibilities that continue after a war is over. We will discuss these principles also on our companion website.[11]

Principle 1: Just Cause

Note that this first principle's key justification is "defense against *unjust* aggression: a real and certain danger." Defense of the Auschwitz extermination camp in World War II would fail to be justified by this principle because the aggression that was trying to close the camp down was not unjust. A preemptive nuclear attack by the U.S. against the Soviet Union in, say, 1983 would also fail to be justified by this principle because there was not a real and certain danger of invasion or attack by the Soviet Union.

For rabbinic Judaism,[12] optional or discretionary wars to expand territory beyond what God promised were declared invalid in the twelfth century. Wars to defend the national territory and citizens are mandatory, not optional. As we noted in chapter 8, Israel launched the six-day war when its leaders (but not its citizens) were aware that the danger was neither real nor certain.

Islam[13] accepts as legitimate war waged for justice and truth, to preserve the Islamic society or the community, and to end oppression. Historically there have been two streams of thought regarding whether war to extend Islamic sovereignty was justified in addition to defensive war; some approved of war to make Islam available to non-Muslims by establishing Islamic political control and requiring the payment of tribute. If the war is just, all Muslims who are able to fight are obliged to do so. Exempt from combat (and so classified as noncombatants) are women, the old and weak, the sick, the blind, and non-Muslims, although they too must resist when the umma is threatened.

"Protect the innocent in your own charge" refers primarily to the innocent in your own country. The United States has an obligation to preserve innocent Americans, but not a clear obligation to preserve innocent Kuwaitis or Iraqis. The morality of protecting the innocent in someone else's charge (so-called "humanitarian intervention," or the "doctrine of the responsibility to protect") is disputed because it has so often been used as an excuse for heinous actions.[14] Mussolini used it to justify his invasion of Ethiopia, and Hitler used it to justify his invasion of Czechoslovakia. President Obama used it in 2011 to justify the NATO bombing of Libya.

Few would dispute that someone should have done something about the slaughter of Jews and others in Nazi Germany during World War II. What *is* disputed is whether the Allied nations in World War II were greatly motivated by that slaughter to act. They didn't prosecute the war in a way designed to rescue the Jews and other victims quickly.

Many believed that someone should have done something about the slaughter of Muslims in Bosnia-Herzegovina in the 1990s. Just what one *could effectively* have done is another question. So few foreign troops were provided to keep the two sides apart and to enforce the Dayton Accords that their success depended on the warring factions' willingness to stop the fighting. To be effective, a much larger commitment would have been needed.

Most Americans feel that something should have been done about the slaughter in 1975–1979 of around two million Cambodians—about a quarter of the population—by Pol Pot's government, which leaves us wondering why our government continued to support that government after it was removed from power by a Vietnamese invasion.

For many years, most Americans were not aware of the slaughter in East Timor by Indonesian troops—a slaughter long ignored by the U.S. government and press. Perhaps "ignored" is not the right word. President Ford and Henry Kissinger visited the Indonesian president in Jakarta twenty-four hours before Indonesia invaded East Timor in 1975.

As you can see, the just war principle of **just cause** has been inconsistently applied in these examples. See the end of this chapter for discussion of genocide and ethnic cleansing, including suggested responses to these crimes.

In the Gulf Wars

We will be giving examples from Roman Catholic lobbying to illustrate how religious leaders can appeal to political leaders by referring to general moral principles. Naturally, leaders of other denominations and faiths can do and have done the same, but these examples are more publicly available.

Before the 1991 Gulf War, U.S. Catholic bishops, in testimony before Congress, commented that too many reasons were given for attacking Iraq: Iraq's invasion of Kuwait, protection of oil supplies, the need for jobs in the U.S. economy, the perceived regional threat of a strong Iraq, and Iraq's alleged weapons of mass destruction.

Inconsistent application of the just cause principle suggested that the U.S. administration was not sincere. President George H. W. Bush declared that the invasion of a sovereign nation could not go unchallenged, yet the United States under his leadership had invaded Panama in 1989, and the United States had done little to challenge the Israeli invasion of the Palestinian territories in 1967 (not to mention the "catastrophe" of 1948) and its continuing illegal occupation of those territories.

Little effort was made to justify the harsh sanctions that the U.S. imposed on Iraq from 1990 through 2003, some of which were explicit violations of the Geneva Conventions, which the U.S. had ratified. See the comments below on principle 10. It was argued that the sanctions were necessary to protect Kurds and Shia Muslims, and to prevent Iraq from developing nuclear weapons.

Just cause was even less clear in the 2003 Gulf War. President George W. Bush said he went to war to prevent Saddam Hussein from developing weapons of mass destruction and to fight the terrorism responsible for the attacks on the World Trade Center and the Pentagon. However, there is no credible evidence that Saddam Hussein was connected with the 9/11 attacks or with al-Qaeda, and no weapons of mass destruction have been found in Iraq. The 2003 Gulf War seems rather to have *increased* terrorist attacks on Americans: the U.S. soldiers in Iraq.

On February 26, 2003, before the invasion, Bishop Wilton Gregory released a statement on behalf of the U.S. Catholic bishops that read, in part, "With the Holy See and many religious leaders throughout the world, we believe that resort to war would not meet the strict conditions in Catholic teaching for the use of military force."[15] The Vatican's permanent observer at the United Nations told the Security Council, in part, "The Holy See is convinced that . . . to resort to force would not be . . . just."[16]

Earlier, the bishops had written to the president:

> We conclude, based on the facts that are known to us, that a preemptive, unilateral use of force is difficult to justify at this time. We fear that resort to force, under these circumstances, would not meet the strict conditions in Catholic teaching for overriding the strong presumption against the use of military force. Of particular concern are the traditional just war criteria of just cause, right authority, probability of success, proportionality and noncombatant immunity.[17]

With regard to just cause, they challenged the president with these questions:

> Is there clear and adequate evidence of a direct connection between Iraq and the attacks of September 11th, or clear and adequate evidence of an imminent attack of a grave nature? Is it wise to dramatically expand traditional moral and legal limits on just cause to include preventive or preemptive uses of military force to overthrow threatening regimes or to deal with the proliferation of weapons of mass destruction? Should not a distinction be made between efforts to change unacceptable behavior of a government and efforts to end that government's existence?[18]

Principle 2: Comparative Cause[19]

According to the second principle, **comparative cause**, it is not enough to show that an opponent has hurt us. We also need to investigate whether we have hurt the opponent, and then compare the two grievances to see whether there is a clear preponderance of just cause on one side or the other. "He hit me back first" is not a good justification for a fight.

In their 1983 pastoral letter, the U.S. Catholic bishops wrote, "No state should act on the basis that it has 'absolute justice' on its side. Every party to a conflict should acknowledge the limits of its 'just cause' and the consequent requirement to use only limited means in pursuit of its objectives." And in the following paragraph:

> Given techniques of propaganda and the ease with which nations and individuals either assume or delude themselves into believing that God or right is clearly on their side, the test of comparative justice may be extremely difficult to apply. Clearly, however, this is not the case in every instance of war. Blatant aggression from without and sub-version from within are often enough readily identifiable by all reasonably fair-minded people.[20]

After September 11, 2001, George Bush said that Osama bin Laden attacked the United States because he hated our freedoms. Before the 2003 U.S. invasion of Iraq, bin Laden himself named the following grievances against the U.S.: (a) the U.S. supported Israeli oppression of Palestinians; (b) the U.S. maintained sanctions against Iraq that resulted in the deaths of over five hundred thousand Iraqi children, not to mention elderly and others; (c) the U.S. had troops stationed in Saudi Arabia near the holy sites of Mecca and Medina; and (d) the U.S. propped up repressive Arab governments that denied Arabs the freedoms which Americans enjoy.

In the Gulf Wars

The Iraqi invasion of Kuwait in 1990 was generally judged unjust but not unprovoked. That is, Iraq was not justified in invading Kuwait, but there is suspicion that Kuwait and the United States, knowing Saddam Hussein's character, goaded him into taking rash action that would justify a harsh response. Kuwait took dangerous chances that would have been foolhardy if it had not been certain of American support. Both Kuwait and the United States may have been surprised by the *extent* of Hussein's response (invading and annexing Kuwait). Yet here are some of the actions that provoked Iraq: (a) Kuwait used American experts in oil drilling to slant wells from their side of the border with Iraq into oil fields under the Iraqi side of the border. (b) Kuwait had lent Iraq substantial sums to help finance its war against Iran in the 1980s. In 1990, Kuwait demanded that the loans be repaid *at once*. Iraq objected that it had fought on behalf of *all* modern Arabs, including Kuwait, against Iranian Islamic fundamentalism, and therefore the loans should be forgiven. (c) Iraq and Kuwait were arguing over the location of their border. Iraq wanted OPEC to limit oil production in order to keep prices up and enable Iraq to repay its loans, but Kuwait *increased* its oil production to drive prices down and so give it leverage over Iraq in its border dispute. (d) Historically Kuwait had been separated from Iraq and defended by the British, thereby cutting Iraq off from its natural harbor on the Persian Gulf.

Iraqi human rights violations in Kuwait were probably real but exaggerated: we now know that infants were not dumped out of hospital incubators by invading Iraqi soldiers and left to die, as was alleged by "Nayirah" (who turned out to be the daughter of the Kuwaiti ambassador to the U.S.) in testimony before the U.S. Congressional Human Rights Caucus. Iraqi violations were not unlike others in the region that go unchallenged by our government.

There are credible doubts about American sincerity in the case of Kuwait. The U.S. had helped to arm Iraq right up to the invasion of Kuwait itself; President Bush overrode efforts by Congress to cut off arms shipments. The U.S. called for Iraqis to rebel against Saddam Hussein after the U.S. booted him out of Kuwait, but it apparently wanted one or another *Sunni* army general to lead the rebellion. When the *Kurds* and southern *Shia* responded to the call, the U.S. allowed Saddam Hussein to use his helicopter gunships to slaughter the rebels. *After* the rebellion had been crushed, the U.S. instituted the "no-fly zones" ostensibly to protect the Kurds and Shia.

By 2003, Iraq had even more grievances against the United States. Thirteen years of economic sanctions had resulted in the death of some million and a half Iraqis, including a half million children. Theoretically, medical supplies and food were not included in the sanctions, but explicit permission was required for each shipment, and permission was frequently denied. Doctors were unable to give consistent treatment, since medications were inconsistently available. More important, the sanctions prevented Iraq from importing the machine parts it needed to repair the damage that U.S. bombing had caused to their electric grid, water purification system, and sewage disposal system—the last two being of critical importance since Iraq is basically a desert watered by two rivers. Sanctions also severely limited supplies of chlorine, needed to purify the water. Finally, the 1991 war had littered Iraq with depleted uranium shells, which were causing major cancers especially among children, including birth deformities, and also among U.S. soldiers.

Principle 3: Attitude

You won't find this principle appealed to very often, although it is prominent in Augustine's just war theory. Augustine was highly influential in developing Christian principles of just war. He insisted that an army at war should love the weak and the enemy, and fight with sorrow and regret for the damage and killing that it caused. Soldiers and their leaders may well object that it is impossible to sustain a war with these attitudes. Some will assert that this principle is unrealistic; they conclude that just war principles have been discredited. Alternatively, although this principle may be unrealistic in war, it is *war* that has been discredited rather than just war principles.

There is a Muslim tradition about Imam Ali when his enemy Amr, whom he had overcome, spit in his face. Ali, very angry, walked away for a few minutes, and then returned to kill Amr. He explained, "If I had killed you then I would have satisfied myself and not God's will."[21]

Two quotations from Augustine may shed more light on **attitude:**

> But, say they, the wise man will wage just wars. As if he would not all the rather lament the necessity of just wars, if he remembers that he is a human. . . . Let everyone, then, who thinks with pain on all these great evils, so horrible, so ruthless, acknowledge that this is misery. *And if anyone either endures or thinks of them without mental pain, this is a more miserable plight still, for he thinks himself happy because he has lost human feeling.*[22]

> What is the evil in war? Is it the death of some who will soon die in any case, that others may live in peaceful subjection? This is mere cowardly dislike, not any religious feeling. The real evils in war are love of violence, revengeful cruelty, fierce and implacable enmity, wild resistance, and the lust of power, and such like; and it is generally to punish these things, when force is required to inflict the punishment, that, in obedience to God or some lawful authority, good men undertake war.[23]

The peace theoretician Johan Galtung makes *attitude* one of the three key dynamics in conflict. The other two dynamics are *behavior* and *contradiction*. Contradiction is caused either by a *dilemma* (one actor wants two incompatible goals) or by a *dispute* (two or more actors want the same goal, which is in scarce supply and can't be shared). Frustrating contradiction leads to dangerous attitudes (emphasizing one's own humanity and importance while dehumanizing the opponent), which in turn cause destructive behaviors. His proposal for resolution is *creative, compassionate nonviolence* in search of innovative proposals that benefit all the disputants.[24]

In the Gulf Wars

Contrary to the principle of attitude, hatred and racism were encouraged. The enemy was demonized. Disrespectful language was used of Saddam Hussein (as a "Hitler-type character") and of Iraq (as part of an "Axis of Evil," thus playing on the World War II "Axis" composed of Nazi Germany, Fascist Italy, and Imperial Japan). Atrocity stories were invented or exaggerated. Connections with terrorism, most famously with the September 11 attacks, were implied but carefully not alleged, since they were false.

Principle 4: Intention

According to this principle, a just **intention** for war is to establish justice and peace. It is reasonable to wish to stop or prevent unjust invasion or violence. But one

Figure 12.1.   Children in Baghdad, January 2003, two months before the U.S. invasion, standing outside the Al-Amariya Shelter, which had been destroyed by U.S. bombing in 1991. Courtesy David Whitten Smith.

should use the lowest level of force that can be reasonably expected to accomplish that goal. If one can stop the injustice by capturing the enemy, that should be the first choice. If capture is not possible, then capture or destruction of the enemy's weapons, or wounding of enemy soldiers so that they cannot fight, is the second choice. Only if these are insufficient is it reasonable to kill the attacker.

In the actual heat of combat, such distinctions are extremely difficult to make, since combat is characterized by limited information and deliberately induced uncertainty. Dennis Carroll, an experienced army officer wrote, "I have been in combat and in heavy jungle and when the shooting starts it is next to impossible to decide if you are going to just wound someone, capture him or kill him."[25]

For rabbinic Judaism, survival of the Jewish nation is right intent. Expansion of borders is legitimate only if it is necessary for survival. Historically for some Muslims, right intent included extending Islamic rule and requiring the conquered to accept Islam or pay tribute as "protected people."

The intention to "convert" the enemy, for example from communism to capitalism (or vice versa), is a disputed intention because it is very likely to promote or continue a war that otherwise could be settled. It is likely as well to violate the rights of those one is converting.

The intention to help rebuild an enemy's country after the war, although admirable if sincere, is not generally considered to be essential, particularly if the conflict was initiated by the enemy. Americans remember the Marshall Plan after World War II without understanding that U.S. elites decided it was urgent to rebuild West Germany and Japan as bulwarks against communist Eastern Europe and the Soviet Union. It was also considered urgent to limit the appeal of communism in Western Europe.

Unconditional surrender is widely held to be an unreasonable demand except in very special circumstances, because it normally lengthens the war. Few people are willing to surrender with no conditions; most would give up much sooner if they knew the conditions of surrender would be tolerable. Because of the special nature of the Nazi government in Germany, some would support the Allied demand for unconditional German surrender in World War II. In particular, the demand for unconditional surrender signaled to German leaders that the Allied forces were committed to a unified position, and prevented Germany from trying to negotiate with its enemies one at a time to split the alliance. However, most moralists conclude that the demand for unconditional *Japanese* surrender was unjustified. Some argue that it lengthened the war with Japan and resulted in the unnecessary and tragic use of atomic bombs on Hiroshima and Nagasaki.

In the Gulf Wars

In 1991, President George H. W. Bush emphasized that all he wanted Iraq to do was to "get out of Kuwait," but when it was in fact doing so, UN forces destroyed the fleeing column. Other possible intentions for U.S. participation in the 1991 war have been suggested and have enough plausibility to be investigated and discussed. None of these intentions would be justifiable under just war principles: to test new weapons, new strategies, and personnel untried in battle; to control the Middle East; to control oil supplies; to weaken the Iraqi army so that it would be less of a factor in the region; and to intimidate other potential opponents of the United States by displaying frightening power: "Mess with us, and you will be in trouble."

The intensity of the bombing in 1991, for example, the targeting of the electric power stations, water purification system, and sewage disposal system, went beyond military necessity and suggest other intentions—probably to weaken Iraq well into the future. In 1991, a demand for unconditional surrender was considered. There does not seem to have been justification for it. In fact, the United States appeared to resist negotiations with Iraq.

The demand to depose an established leader such as Saddam Hussein ("regime change") is generally considered unjustified. Countries should determine their own leadership without interference from outside. At the same time, they are not free to follow or support their leaders in attacking their neighbors. If they do so, and if their neighbors then force them to change their leadership, they bear much of the responsibility for that change.

Likely intentions for the 2003 war included reassuring Americans frightened by the attacks of September 11, 2001; controlling oil supplies and the Middle East region to gain leverage over other industrialized nations; building permanent military bases in Iraq to replace threatened bases in Saudi Arabia; weakening the Iraqi army so that it could not compete with the state of Israel; destroying a successful Middle Eastern socialist economy and replacing it with an extreme free-market, capitalist economy; helping George W. Bush win election for a second term; and providing lucrative construction contracts for major U.S. corporations. The U.S. occupation force dismantled Iraqi socialism and tried to sell off its state assets to foreign private investors. U.S. construction companies received lucrative construction contracts in Iraq, but hundreds of millions of dollars remain unaccounted for.

Principle 5: Last Resort

This principle presumes that one has tried all other practical steps that one *reasonably had time for*. It does not rigidly demand that everything else be tried. The principle "justice delayed is justice denied" means that a prudential judgment has to be made about what is reasonable and practical.

If a threat is grave and imminent, some moralists would justify a preemptive strike to resist it. This new principle was proposed by the George W. Bush administration, but without the qualifier "imminent." However, the U.S. would probably not accept this justification if *other* countries were to claim it. An example often given is the Israeli attack on Egyptian and Syrian airfields in 1967. Historians have disputed whether Egypt intended to attack, or simply to "bleed," Israel by forcing an extended period of mobilization for war and consequent slowdown of the civilian economy. Recently declassified documents reveal that Israeli political and military leaders had no fear of an Egyptian attack. Rather, they welcomed the opportunity to extend the borders of Israel, to control more territory, and to establish military superiority over Egypt, Jordan, and Syria.[26] Thus, the Israeli leaders violated Judaism's insistence on **last resort**. The bombing of Iraq's Osirak reactor was morally questionable by rabbinic Judaism's principles. Historically Muslims interpreted "last resort" to mean that one must first demand surrender and either conversion or payment of tribute. If the opponent agreed, war was not allowed.

The principle of last resort is especially relevant now that we have concrete experience of how effective active nonviolence can be—it is the "other practical option" that is rarely considered seriously. Within the past one hundred years, active nonviolence has affected probably a third of humanity: Mohandas Gandhi in India and South Africa, Martin Luther King Jr. in the United States, Nelson Mandela at times in South Africa, Corazon Aquino in the Philippines, "Solidarity" in Poland, and similar movements elsewhere in Latin America, Africa, Eastern Europe, and Russia.

In the Gulf Wars

This principle received extensive discussion in both Gulf Wars. Economic sanctions were imposed early in the 1990–1991 crisis. Many people argued that they were having an effect and should be continued without military action; peace activists argued that the sanctions were a form of warfare and should be discontinued. The U.S. government argued that the sanctions were not and would not be effective. Sincerity was damaged by the awareness that previous U.S. support of Saddam Hussein, despite his bad human rights record, had helped to "set up" the crisis, as had long inattention to the Palestinian problem. Published estimates that the boycott had reduced the Iraqi GNP by 50 percent suggested that the economic sanctions were effective. The insistence of the U.S. government that such sanctions are generally ineffective seems inconsistent with its historic or ongoing use of such sanctions against Cuba, Iran, Nicaragua, South Africa, and North Korea. In fact, the U.S. maintained its sanctions against Iraq for twelve years *after* the 1991 war—sanctions that wreaked havoc on civilian health and survival, violating the just war principles we are studying.

Officially the 1991–2003 sanctions did not include food and drugs, but there was good evidence that in practice it did. Such a boycott is morally questionable. The FOR (Fellowship of Reconciliation) reported in its newsletter for 18 January 1991 that a shipment of medicines that the organization had collected for Iraq was being held up by regulation 31 CFR 575 of the U.S. Treasury Department—a regulation that required a license to ship medicines to Iraq. Penalties that the FOR was threatened with included $250,000 in civil fines, $1 million in criminal fines, and twelve years in prison. The FOR challenged the regulation by shipping the medicines anyway, but the U.S. government seized them in the warehouse and prevented their shipment. The FOR then publicized the situation in newspapers and on television, and within a few days the government reversed its position and granted the license.

In the 2003 war, George W. Bush proclaimed perhaps disingenuously that we "couldn't afford to wait for a mushroom cloud" before re-invading Iraq. There is much evidence, however, that U.S. war planners suppressed contrary data and exaggerated or fabricated data supporting their position. The UN inspection team insisted that Iraq had ended its nuclear weapons program, and eyewitness reports after the invasion supported that conclusion.

Principle 6: Likely Success

This principle states that a party should not go to war unless it is reasonably likely to achieve its goals. In almost every case, at least one side in a conflict fails to apply the principle of **likely success** correctly. Often both sides fail. In exceptional circumstances a party might be justified in fighting to defend key values against great odds as a witness to justice. For this reason, the Jewish tradition of defensive war does not require likely success: self-defense is obligatory even if hopeless. Nor is this principle relevant to Islam, since they believe that it is Allah who determines success, so one cannot determine in advance whether success is likely. However, such a witness could be given in other ways without using lethal resistance.

It is never justified to go to war when the result is to destroy what one is fighting for, much less when the result is to destroy human life on the planet. Yet the practice of nuclear deterrence may well threaten exactly that result. The study of "nuclear winter" in the mid-1980s finally made this danger salient to world leaders.

In the late fourth century CE, the early Christian "church father" John Chrysostom said, "War is the plaything of the rich." The Russian author Aleksandr Solzhenitsyn, in *The Gulag Archipelago*, wrote that *governments* need victories, but *people* need defeats. Victories strengthen governments and tend to launch them on to new adventures—adventures which eventually lead to disaster. Defeats weaken governments and enable people to insist on—and usually achieve—peace. An example of Solzhenitsyn's principle would be the 1982 Falklands-Malvinas war between Argentina and England. After the war, the Argentine military government was so discredited that it resigned and the country was restored to democracy.

In the Gulf Wars

Before the 1991 U.S. invasion and attempted regime change in Iraq, other Western nations had tried and failed in the same attempt. After World War I, England occupied Iraq and tried to establish a pro-British Iraqi government. "Ultimately, the British-created monarchy suffered from a chronic legitimacy crisis. . . . The continuing inability of the government to gain the confidence of the people fueled political instability well into the 1970s."[27] The U.S. Catholic bishops testified before Congress that the impact of the 1991 war on the whole Middle East was likely to be more negative than positive. At that time, objections to the principle of likely success included the following points: War will continue Western colonial control in the Middle East. It will isolate Arab government leaders who supported the war from their populations who did not. There may still be popular uprisings against unpopular leadership (which turned out to be true). The increase in "fundamentalist Islam" in the area suggests that we do not yet see the final results of these policies. War will poison U.S. relations with Iraq and with most Arab societies for a long time into the future.

What was gained overall by the 1991 war? Iraq was expelled from Kuwait. Iraq was seriously weakened. Its nuclear weapons program was dismantled. But that war also left Saddam Hussein in power.

Success in the 2003 war was even less likely, despite the execution of Saddam Hussein on December 30, 2006. The U.S. Catholic bishops warned Bush before the second war:

> War against Iraq could have unpredictable consequences not only for Iraq but for peace and stability elsewhere in the Middle East. Would preventive or preemptive force succeed in thwarting serious threats or, instead, provoke the very kind of attacks that it is intended to prevent? Would the use of military force lead to wider conflict and instability? Would war against Iraq detract from our responsibility to help build a just and stable order in Afghanistan and undermine the broader coalition against terrorism?[28]

U.S. troops became mired down in a costly, unpopular, and unwinnable invasion and occupation. Western-oriented Iraq lost power in contrast to conservative

Islamic Iran. Terrorists attracted recruits and gained valuable experience fighting against U.S. soldiers. North Korea and, arguably, Iran concluded that only nuclear weapons would protect them from U.S. invasion. The U.S. lost the sympathy it had received in the wake of the terrorist attacks of September 11, 2001. In Abu Ghraib, Guantanamo, and elsewhere, the U.S. began torturing and "disappearing" opponents—something that we thought only Third World governments did.

Principle 7: Authority

According to this principle, war should be undertaken under the **authority** of leaders who are responsible for the common good and are really supported by those they represent. Unacceptable would be war ordered by unrepresentative despots or by rebels seeking only their own advantage or by a democratically elected president whose decision contravenes the will of the people as expressed in reliable opinion polls. For the Jewish community, the historically legitimate authorities for an optional war—a prophetic word from God, the king, and the Sanhedrin—are not available. In practice in Israel, the government is generally considered a legitimate authority for defensive war, and such a war is required. Sunni Muslims recognize the authority of the head of the state; Shia require a legitimate Imam, and since there hasn't been one for centuries, only defensive wars are legitimate, led by the head of state. Attacks by nonstate actors such as al-Qaeda are illegitimate.

A special problem arises in the case of a popular revolutionary uprising against a despotic government. The revolutionary leader is not legally recognized, but the "legally recognized" leader is not seeking the common good. Thomas Aquinas says that in such a case the legally constituted despot, who is seeking private advantage rather than the common good, is responsible for the outbreak of revolution. His or her leadership is not morally justified, whatever the law may say.

> A tyrannical government is not just, because it is directed, not to the common good, but to the private good of the ruler. . . . Consequently there is no sedition in disturbing a government of this kind, unless indeed the tyrant's rule be disturbed so inordinately, that his subjects suffer greater harm from the consequent disturbance than from the tyrant's government. Indeed it is the tyrant rather that is guilty of sedition.[29]

In such a case, we need to ask to what extent the leaders of the revolutionary movement truly represent the common good and the aspirations of most of the population.

In a democratic system, the leaders are supposed to seek out and reflect the common judgment. To the extent that they manipulate public opinion, they are interfering with the normal functioning of a healthy democracy and placing in question the extent to which they are really supported by those they represent. Good public discussion requires that honest and adequate information be provided to the citizens. Various forms of media control prevent people from knowing relevant facts, different points of view, and alternative options. It is important to involve the entire population in vital decisions through open public discussion, and to define "proper authority" broadly for purposes of just war.

In the Gulf Wars

The question of authority was more widely discussed before the wars of 1991 and 2003 than is usually the case. Although Congress was consulted both times, the U.S. Constitution is not satisfied with *consultation*—war is supposed to require a *declaration* by Congress. Congress chose to avoid responsibility for a declaration of war, and to allow the president to initiate both wars. In the case of the 2003 war, President Bush argued that earlier UN declarations gave him the authority to attack. But he refused to let the UN decide the issue, and the secretary general complained that the attack was not authorized. As a signatory to the UN Charter, the United States yields authority to authorize war to the UN except in the case of defense against invasion. International treaties carry constitutional authority in the United States. Unauthorized war making is considered a war crime.

Principle 8: Declared

The purpose of requiring a clear declaration of war, as does this principle, is to let an opponent know how the war can be avoided or ended. Opponents are more willing to avoid or end a war if they can do so without public humiliation. Demands should be clear and unchanging, as much as possible. "Creeping demands" are especially counterproductive, since they give the impression that the adversary is playing on sheer power rather than justice, and will take whatever he can regardless of any principles. They convince the other side that it would be dangerous to appear weak or to give in.

It is worth noting that very few of the wars in which the United States has been involved in the twentieth century have been **declared**. There is a lack of consistency in U.S. attitudes toward the declaration of war. While we often repeat that it was Japan's sneak attack on Pearl Harbor on December 7, 1941, that justified our war with Japan, and we refer to that attack as a "day of infamy," many of our own wars have started with similar undeclared attacks. This would be true of our wars on Libya, Grenada, and Panama among others.

In the Gulf Wars

The actions that both Presidents Bush took leading up to their acts of aggression against Iraq and the public statements that they made seemed designed to humiliate Saddam Hussein rather than to give him a "face-saving," ostensibly honorable way to retreat. Such an approach increased the likelihood of war and reduced the likelihood that the war would end quickly once it had begun.

The U.S. employed creeping demands in the 1991 war. Stages in the escalation of demands that were publicly announced included: get out of Kuwait; surrender unconditionally; change your government; face a war crimes trial. In the 2003 war, when Hussein suggested at the last minute that he was willing to leave Iraq, the U.S. declared that it would invade anyway. Clearly one or more of its demands had actually been pretexts.

Principle 9: Proportionality

This principle states that more good should be gained than damage caused (a) for the war as a whole, and (b) for each strategy, step, and weapon employed along the way. When measuring damage caused, one should include everyone who is affected, especially the poor and helpless, future citizens, and the environment the survivors will have to live in.

Incorporating a spiritual dimension may change the balance of judgment. For example, how valuable is freedom of speech, freedom of the press, religious freedom, the right to a decent standard of living? Is God calling us to respond beyond our own self-interest (often verbalized as "vital national interests")? Of what value to a country is integrity? For example, the U.S. "won" in its wars with Native American tribes, but what did that victory "cost" in terms of the national character that we developed in the process?

Proportionality is basic for Jewish thought—they reject total war. Nuclear arms are legitimate only as a deterrent. With regard to decisions to go to war, Muslims do not judge proportionality, except to say that Muslims should not war against other Muslims. Once one is engaged in a war, proportionality is required; mercy and forgiveness are encouraged. Some have labeled nuclear weapons un-Islamic.

The allegation that "we had no choice" usually indicates failure of thought, of imagination, or of honesty. There are always choices. What the allegation usually means is, "We didn't want to consider any other choices" or, "We didn't like the cost of other choices." The relative costs of various choices are rarely thought through adequately.

This principle appears in several different forms, which we might call the gold medal, silver medal, bronze medal, and lead medal forms. (a) The *gold medal form* is as stated above: more good must be gained than damage caused by the war. (b) The *silver medal form* is weaker: no more damage should be caused than necessary to achieve our objective. The principle is often presented this way in discussions of just war. The weakness here is that, in order to achieve our "objective," we might need to cause much more damage than the good eventually gained—something we are willing to do since it is *we* who will gain the good and *someone else* who will suffer the damage. In this form, the principle would not prevent war unless *our side* stood to lose more than it gained. By contrast, in the *gold medal form* of the principle, war is unjustified if the *sum total of damage on both sides* exceeds the sum total of good gained. (c) The *bronze medal form* states that we should cause no more evil than we ourselves have suffered. This might also be called the "eye for an eye" or the "Hatfield and McCoy"[30] form—it tends to produce permanent war, or in Gandhi's words, it leaves the whole world blind. (d) The *lead medal form*, which could be called "shock and awe," recommends that we cause far more evil than we could possibly suffer in hopes of so shocking our opponents that they will give up without resistance. This fourth version appears to be the form preferred by the U.S. leadership, as exemplified by the saturation bombing of German cities and the atomic bombing of Hiroshima followed by Nagasaki in World War II, and—explicitly—in Iraq.

In the Gulf Wars

The U.S. Catholic bishops testified before Congress that war against a successfully industrialized, populous nation like Iraq was likely to produce unacceptably high costs. They doubted that the gains anticipated by the United States in the 1991 war would be proportionate to the damage inflicted.

It is difficult to determine just what the costs of the 1991 war were. Estimates of Iraqi casualties vary wildly from a low of about 1,500 to highs between 250,000 and 300,000; the most common figures range between 100,000 and 200,000. Part of the problem with determining casualties is deciding whose deaths count: those of soldiers? civilians? What about deaths that occur after the war caused by unexploded landmines or cluster bombs, by depleted uranium, or by the destruction of the electric grid, of clean water and sewage disposal, of medical care?

Many interpreters conclude that there was excessive civilian destruction in Iraq, beyond what was necessary to achieve the publicly declared purposes of the war. The after-war report of the United Nations stated that Iraq had been returned to a pre-industrial condition. (Note that Iraq does not possess the pre-industrial social structures that are common in pre-industrial states. It is one thing to lose air conditioning in an Amazon hut, quite another to lose it in a high-rise building with windows that don't open—and summer temperatures in the range of 110–140 degrees Fahrenheit.)

Extensive destruction of Iraq's electric generation and distribution grid eliminated the refrigeration of medicines and vaccines along with water and sewage purification. Without water and sewage purification, cholera and other diseases easily spread, as the U.S. military was well aware they would. Moreover, the destruction of roads and bridges interfered with food transport. In the 1991 war, many of these transportation links were far away from Kuwait. Ecological damage was extensive, and the health effects of depleted uranium were permanent. The damage caused by burning oil wells could have reasonably been foreseen.

The 1991 death and destruction of columns retreating from Kuwait seemed excessive to many. Whereas soldiers are not required to risk their lives on the gamble that enemy soldiers who do not surrender are truly removed from the war (since soldiers driven out by military action rather than their own free will are liable to regroup and return once the pressure is off), American soldiers and pilots who described the situation as a "turkey shoot" in effect admitted that the use of force was excessive and therefore unjustified.

In the 2003 war, the U.S. bishops warned Bush:

> War against Iraq could have unpredictable consequences not only for Iraq but for peace and stability elsewhere in the Middle East. How would another war in Iraq impact the civilian population, in the short- and long-term? How many more innocent people would suffer and die, or be left without homes, without basic necessities, without work? Would the United States and the international community commit to the arduous, long-term task of ensuring a just peace or would a post-Saddam Iraq continue to be plagued by civil conflict and repression, and continue to serve as a destabilizing force in the region?[31]

Last but not least, one should include in the calculations the psychological damage to one's own soldiers. U.S. army psychologist David Grossman studied what militaries have to do to human beings to induce them to kill other humans.[32] J. Glenn Gray shares rare philosophical reflections on his experiences in World War II.[33] Rachel MacNair explains psychological research showing that by far the strongest cause of posttraumatic stress is not the danger of *being* killed, but rather the experience of *killing* another human being.[34] And Daniel Hallock has collected searing descriptions of combat veterans struggling with their psychological pain. He quotes a veteran sniper from the covert U.S. war in Latin America:

> In the military, everyone is expendable. . . . They will bring the primal beast out from everyone, and they will train you how to kill another human being. What they don't teach you, though, is how to deal with the emotions afterward. They just spit you out and find someone else to take your place. . . . My experience has left me a very lonely person. . . . The true hell of war doesn't start until you come home.[35]

In the end, it seems, U.S. success in overcoming its soldiers' natural resistance to killing other humans ensures that our combat veterans will suffer far more than has been conventionally calculated, and that our society will also suffer the consequences of their trauma.

Principle 10: Discrimination

This final principle requires that lethal violence be directed only at those who are threatening to do violence. Excluded are noncombatants, prisoners of war, children, and the unborn. Ecological damage affects the unborn as future citizens. While it is sometimes claimed that lethal violence is *directed* only at combatants, *excessive damage to noncombatants that can reasonably be anticipated* is also excluded by this principle. Damage that can be anticipated but is undesired, when honest attempts are made to avoid it, falls under the principle of double effect described above. Several problems have been made acute by modern warfare: nuclear weapons, defense workers, guerrilla warfare, and the well-being of future populations after a war.

Judaism, Christianity, and Islam generally interpret **discrimination** similarly. **Non-combatant immunity** and humane treatment of captives are explicitly included in Israel Defense Forces regulations, although regulations (as with other armies) are often not followed. Islam rejects terrorism which, by definition, targets non-combatants; it also regulates the treatment of captives.

Nuclear weapons, because of their wide range of destruction, are by nature indiscriminate on most foreseeable land targets. Presumably one could isolate an aircraft carrier task force at sea from civilian targets. In 1983, the U.S. Catholic bishops gave nuclear weapons a "strictly limited" temporary justification as deterrents in the face of a hostile enemy similarly armed, as long as serious efforts were made to achieve disarmament. Now that there is no credible hostile enemy similarly armed (since the demise of the Soviet Union), it is difficult to justify maintaining arsenals of nuclear weapons, especially in the numbers the U.S. currently holds. There may be a fleeting window of opportunity to reduce the number of actual nuclear weapons to zero (recognizing that humans will not "forget" how to make them), as a result making it far less likely that they would ever be used. They are far more likely to be used if they are in place, armed, and "combat ready" than if they have been dismantled and would have to be remanufactured before being used.

The dependence of militaries on complex arms has raised the question whether to consider defense workers as valid targets in war. Are workers in a factory making fighter aircraft or tanks truly noncombatants? Is it accurate to assert that they are not threatening violence to civilians? What about Caterpillar employees making armored bulldozers that will destroy Palestinian homes? What about steelworkers? What about railroad workers, if *part* of what they load onto cargo trains is ammunition? The tendency in this century has been toward "total war," giving rise to the argument that *everyone* in a modern industrial society is participating in the war. Just war theorists consider these justifications for nondiscrimination to be exaggerated.

In guerrilla warfare, soldiers try to hide amid the civilian population "as fish swim in the sea." Such activity makes it very difficult for their opponents to discriminate between combatants and civilians. Anyone might pick up a gun or explode a mine. In such a war, who is to blame for civilian deaths? Guerrilla warfare often catches in the middle those who truly are noncombatants. Both parties in the war try to enlist peasants on their side; guerrilla fighters hide deliberately in civilian areas in order to put the enemy in a bad light if it attacks. It becomes more difficult for civilians to remain neutral, and a civilian may be killed by one side or the other in any case.

Anti-personnel land mines are a prime example of weapons that kill long after the war has ended, kill more civilians than military, and are much more expensive to remove than they are to put in place. If armies cleaned up properly after themselves, they would remove the mines they had laid after the war was over. But they rarely do. Poor people and their children are the chief victims of the mines that remain active for decades afterward. Some areas in Europe are still unsafe from World War I mines. Large areas in Indochina are unsafe or unusable; the same is true of southern Lebanon. Since mines were invented that contain little or no metal, it has become much more difficult to detect and remove them. The most effective method is still to probe the soil diagonally with a rod while lying on one's stomach. Currently there is an international treaty to ban the production and use of land mines. Currently (2014) thirty-five nations, including the United States, have refused to signed the treaty. The ban is likely to be only partially successful, since land mines are low-tech, cheap, and much more useful to poor armies than to wealthy ones. Wealthy countries can afford tanks, and they like their tanks to be able to move around without being blown up by a $35 mine. One of the world's largest producers of land mines is Bosnia.

High-tech American companies, like Alliant Techsystems, argue that their mines are designed to disarm themselves after a certain number of weeks or months. But this does not mean that they are "safe" afterward. Machines are never 100 percent effective, as you may have noticed if you have used computers or automobiles. The most dangerous minefields are often those regarded as safe. And it is only the fuse or trigger that disarms; the mine is still full of explosive material.

In the Gulf Wars

In 1991, the U.S. Catholic bishops warned Congress that there were many military targets in civilian areas of Iraq, so that discrimination would be very difficult. Initial reports suggested that U.S. bombs were "smart," that is, well directed and successful in discriminating between civilian and military targets. After the war, it was admitted that most of the bombs that had been used were not "smart" but rather old-fashioned gravity bombs, which cannot be accurately aimed. It was also admitted that the targets at which the "smart" bombs were aimed were not always what the targeters thought they were. It doesn't do much good to discriminate if the target you are aiming at is not a poison gas factory, as you thought, but instead a baby milk factory. So targeting depends on correct information.

Sanctions applied to Iraq by the UN Security Council in August 1990, and continued with minor changes until 2003, violated the principle of discrimination. In particular, the UN forbade Iraq to import replacement parts for its water purification and sewage disposal systems. A declassified Defense Intelligence Agency document (January 22, 1991)[36] makes the following points:

> Iraq depends on importing specialized equipment and some chemicals to purify its water supply. . . . With no domestic sources of both water treatment replacement parts and some essential chemicals, Iraq will continue attempts to circumvent United Nations Sanctions to import these vital commodities. . . .
>
> Iraq's rivers also contain biological materials, pollutants, and are laden with bacteria. Unless the water is purified with chlorine, epidemics of such diseases as cholera, hepatitis, and typhoid could occur. Recent reports indicate the chlorine supply is critically low. Its importation has been embargoed. . . .
>
> Incidences of disease, including possible epidemics, will become probable unless the population were careful to boil water. . . . Although Iraq is already experiencing a loss of water treatment capability, it probably will take at least six months (to June 1991) before the system is fully degraded.

The Geneva Conventions specify:

It is prohibited to attack, destroy, remove, or render useless objects indispensable to the survival of the civilian population, such as foodstuffs, crops, livestock, drinking water installations and supplies, and irrigation works, for the specific purpose of denying them for their sustenance value to the civilian population or to the adverse party, whatever the motive, whether in order to starve out civilians, to cause them to move away, or for any other motive.[37]

In the 2003 war, the U.S. Catholic bishops warned Bush: "While we recognize improved capability and serious efforts to avoid directly targeting civilians in war, the use of massive military force to remove the current government of Iraq could have incalculable consequences for a civilian population that has suffered so much from war, repression, and a debilitating embargo."[38]

OVERALL APPLICATION OF THE PRINCIPLES TO THE GULF WARS WAGED BY THE UNITED STATES AGAINST IRAQ

The following table offers comments on the various criteria as applied to the 1991 war, the sanctions from 1991–2003, the 2003 war, and the subsequent U.S. occupation of Iraq.

GENOCIDE AND ETHNIC CLEANSING

The Polish Jewish lawyer Raphael Lemkin (1900–1959) coined the word "**genocide**" in 1944 as he pressed the United Nations to outlaw it formally. He had been seeking to expand international law to include such crimes since 1933, using as his prime example the 1915–1917 Armenian Genocide. The UN General Assembly adopted the Convention on the Prevention and Punishment of the Crime of Genocide in 1948, and it went into force in 1951. According to Article 2 of that convention, genocide consists of

any of the following acts committed with intent to destroy, in whole or in part, a national, ethnical, racial or religious group, such as: (a) killing members of the group; (b) causing serious bodily or mental harm to members of the group; (c) deliberately inflicting on the group conditions of life calculated to bring about its physical destruction in whole or in part; (d) imposing measures intended to prevent births within the group; (e) forcibly transferring children of the group to another group.[39]

Article 3 specifies:

The following acts shall be punishable: (a) genocide; (b) conspiracy to commit genocide; (c) direct and public incitement to commit genocide; (d) attempt to commit genocide; (e) complicity in genocide.[40]

The UN convention restricts itself to the *physical* effects of genocide. Lemkin himself urged the UN to include as well "non-physical, namely, psychological acts of genocide," which he personally defined as:

> a coordinated plan of different actions aiming at the destruction of essential foundations of the life of national groups, with the aim of annihilating the groups themselves. The objectives of such a plan would be disintegration of the political and social institutions, of culture, language, national feelings, religion, and the economic existence of national groups, and the destruction of the personal security, liberty, health, dignity, and even the lives of the individuals belonging to such groups. . . . Genocide has two phases: one, destruction of the national pattern of the oppressed group; the other, the imposition of the national pattern of the oppressor.[41]

Ethnic Cleansing

The term "**ethnic cleansing**" was coined by Serbian nationalists in 1992 to explain their policy of driving non-Serbs out of the areas of Bosnia that they wished to control. A 1994 UN commission defined it more specifically as

> a purposeful policy designed by one ethnic or religious group to remove by violent and terror-inspiring means the civilian population of another ethnic or religious group from certain geographic areas. To a large extent, it is carried out in the name of misguided nationalism, historic grievances and a powerful driving sense of revenge. This purpose appears to be the occupation of territory to the exclusion of the purged group or groups (par. 130).[42]

UN General Assembly resolutions condemn ethnic cleansing in Bosnia-Herzegovina without formally defining it, but they describe some of its defining acts.[43] Legal critics complain that ethnic cleansing is not well defined and that some of the acts associated with "violent and terror-inspiring means" that it commits are crimes under the rubric of genocide and should be prosecuted as such. Ethnic cleansing usually includes efforts to erase the memory of the target group by destroying its villages, shrines, monuments, place names, in sum, all evidence of its historical existence.

Ten Stages of Genocide

Dr. Gregory Stanton, the president of Genocide Watch, has described genocide as a process that passes through ten stages:[44]

1. Classification. People are divided into "us" and "them." This process needs to be resisted by stressing commonalities.
2. Symbolization. The oppressed group is forced to accept identifying symbols, such as the yellow star for Jews during the Holocaust or the identity card for

Table 12.2. The 2003 Persian Gulf War and Following Occupation in Relation to Just War Principles, (a) before the invasion, (b) after.

The War and Occupation Are Just	The War and Occupation Are Not Just
1. (a) Iraq has weapons of mass destruction (WMD) or soon will. Iraq could give those weapons to terrorists like al-Qaeda. Iraq supported al-Qaeda in its attack on the U.S. (b) Saddam Hussein destroyed weapons or moved them to Syria; he had capacity to produce them. Regime change was the main point: Saddam Hussein was captured and executed.	1. (a) No evidence Iraq has WMD, inspections guarantee it won't. Unlikely he would give such weapons to people who hate him and whom he does not control. No evidence that Iraq supported al-Qaeda in its attack on the U.S. (b) No weapons of mass destruction found. No evidence they were moved or destroyed. Capacity was not the original argument. Regime change was not the original argument, nor is it legal by international law.
2. Hussein oppressed his own people and used poison gas on them. So he might well use it on others, including us. Sanctions were necessary to keep Hussein from developing nuclear weapons.	2. The U.S. CIA helped Saddam Hussein overthrow the previous government, and helped keep him in power. U.S. companies provided chemicals and seed germs for WMD, and the U.S. administration refused to condemn his use of poison gas. After Iraq had eliminated its WMD, the U.S. and UN continued sanctions that killed a million and a half Iraqi civilians.
3. Principle not considered.	3. Hatred was evoked toward Iraq. Iraqis are daily dishonored and humiliated. Iraqi civilians are killed, arbitrarily arrested, tortured.
4. (a) Iraq must eliminate weapons of mass destruction; Iraq must eliminate Ba'ath party and disempower its former members; democratize, and renounce weapons of mass destruction.	4. (a) Regime change not acceptable intention under international law. (b) Protection of oil ministry while all else looted indicates that oil and regional control are intended; sale of state-owned enterprises indicates that privatization of socialized economy and foreign control of Iraq are intended.
5. Iraq did not cooperate with inspections. Hussein destroyed weapons or moved them to Syria; he had capacity to produce them.	5. Inspections and weapons control have contained Iraq. There were no WMDs, no evidence they were moved, no active program to produce them.

	6	7	8	9	10
Top	6. The U.S. has stepped into a quagmire that looks like Lebanon or the West Bank, involving guerrilla warfare that is impossible to control. Establishing a stable democratic government is very unlikely. Puppet government will be rejected by Iraqis. Our actions promote al-Qaeda recruitment.	7. There was little real debate. Information was incomplete or false. Congress wimped out. When the U.S. realized that the UN would refuse authority, it chose not to ask. The attack violated the UN charter, to which the U.S. is signatory, making the invasion a violation of U.S. law as well.	8. (a) Absolute disarmament is probably impossible ever to confirm. (b) It now appears there was nothing to disarm. Regime change is an unacceptable condition by international law.	9. There is no absolute security. Attempts to gain it by sanctions themselves caused mass death of Iraqis. Our invasion and occupation feed the very terrorism we seek to prevent.	10. (a) Sanctions before the attack killed a million and a half civilians. "Shock and awe" leaving "no safe place to hide in Baghdad" (as announced beforehand) would not be safe for civilians. The UN projected massive civilian deaths in an attack. (b) The initial attack did limit civilian deaths, but partly because the Iraqi army did not resist very vigorously—it was saving its resistance for later. Our response to later armed resistance (e.g., in Fallujah) has caused massive death, injury, and destruction. Our record in Afghanistan (and the Philippines in 1898), where we also promised democratization, is not encouraging. We seem more intent on privatizing than on democratizing.
Bottom	6. (a) There is little doubt the U.S. can defeat Iraq. Iraqis will welcome us and welcome democracy. (b) The U.S. defeated Iraq easily. Many Iraqis refused to fight; others welcomed U.S. with open arms—except for a small minority of Hussein supporters.	7. Bush is legally our president; he was reelected. Congress gave Bush authority to act. The UN gave implicit authority in the fall of 2002. The UN has become an irrelevant debating society.	8. (a) Demands for disarmament and regime change were clear. (b) Hussein hid his program so effectively that we have not yet found it, but we will. Regime change was worth it in any case.	9. Terrorist use of weapons of mass destruction is so horrible that almost any means is appropriate to prevent it. We can't wait for a mushroom cloud.	10. We made every effort, with use of smart bombs and missiles, to prevent civilian casualties. (b) Predictions of massive civilian deaths in the attack proved wrong. We are working to rebuild Iraqi civil society as a model of democracy for the region.

Palestinians under Israeli occupation. Such symbols, as well as hate speech, must be outlawed.

3. Discrimination. The oppressor group denies human rights to the oppressed group. Discrimination can be countered by insisting on full political and human rights for all groups regardless of race, ethnicity, religion, etc.

4. Dehumanization. The oppressed are described in inhuman terms: as cockroaches, rats, viruses, infections, cancers. Leaders need to condemn such speech, and those who incite genocide should have their foreign bank accounts frozen and be denied foreign travel.

5. Organization. Special militias or death squads are created. Arms embargoes need to be enforced and violations prosecuted. Leaders of these militia groups should be denied foreign travel.

6. Polarization. Propaganda and hate speech stir up hatred of the oppressed group. Intermarriage may be banned. Moderate leaders and human rights group may need security, such as by unarmed international accompaniment; coups d'état should be condemned.

7. Preparation. Plans for genocide are drawn up, weapons distributed, groups trained. Fear of the oppressed group is fostered: they are "terrorists," and FUD (fear, uncertainty, and doubt) fills the air. In response, leaders can be indicted for "incitement and conspiracy to commit genocide," which is a crime under the Genocide Convention.

8. Persecution. Property is seized, death lists prepared, the oppressed may be separated and concentrated into ghettos, and massacres occur. The international community must declare a genocide emergency.

9. Extermination. This is the term the killers use to deny the humanity of their victims and so to justify their murder. Armed intervention needs to create truly safe refuges and escape corridors from killing zones. An inadequately defended "safe refuge," such as Srebrenica in Bosnia, is worse than useless.

10. Denial. Perpetrators try to evade responsibility. International tribunals or local courts should prosecute those responsible.

Some Examples of Genocide

Religions and nations tend to be more tolerant when they are confident in their power than when they fear they are losing power. William Rubenstein claims that all the totalitarian genocides of the twentieth century arose out of a common circumstance: "the collapse of the elite structure and normal modes of government of much of central, eastern and southern Europe as a result of the First World War, without which surely neither Communism nor Fascism would have existed except in the minds of unknown agitators and crackpots."[45] Such collapse of elite structures gives psychopaths the opportunity to seize control. Recall that psychopaths distort the worldviews they appeal to in support of their projects. The following examples include genocides or ethnic cleansing in Buddhist, Christian, Islamic, and

Jewish countries or societies. We will indicate the perpetrator, the supportive population, the victim, and the trauma suffered by the perpetrators that helped set the conditions for each of the following cases.

Native American Genocide, 1492 to Present[46]

Perpetrators: colonial leaders, army, individual settlers. Supportive population: European Christian colonizers. Victims: Native American indigenous peoples. Trauma: religious wars in Europe, ambition, and greed.

Genocide and ethnic cleansing were carried out by war, seizure of land and resources, encouraging the spread of disease, destruction of food sources (plains bison), concentration of Indians in reservations, and re-education of native children with suppression of their languages and cultures. See chapter 6 on Native American worldviews for details.

Armenian Genocide, 1914–1923 (especially 1915–1917)[47]

Perpetrators: "Young Turks" (a new ruling group) seeking to unite all Turkish people under one religion and one language, and to expand the Turkish Empire. Supportive population: Turkish Muslims. Victims: 1.5 million Armenian Orthodox Christians, whose leaders were often European educated. Trauma: the breakup of the Ottoman Empire from the late nineteenth century until after World War I.

The Ottoman Empire, centered in Istanbul, had prided itself on its religious diversity and tolerance. During World War I, the empire had recently lost the territory of Greece and was in the process of losing to Western colonization or control what today is Iraq, Saudi Arabia, Syria, Lebanon, Jordan, Israel, Gaza, and the West Bank. A new ruling faction in Turkey decided that the (Christian) Armenians had the potential to support Turkey's enemies and dilute the "Turkish character" of the country. So they expelled or killed virtually all of their million and a half Armenians through murder and forced marches into the Syrian desert, in what became the first major genocide of the twentieth century. Hitler would later point to their success to support his "final solution" of the "Jewish problem." When Germany invaded Poland, he declared:

> I have issued the command . . . that our war aim does not consist in reaching certain lines, but in the physical destruction of the enemy. Accordingly, I have placed my death-head formation in readiness . . . with orders to them to send to death mercilessly and without compassion, men, women, and children of Polish derivation and language. Only thus shall we gain the living space (Lebensraum) which we need. Who, after all, speaks today of the annihilation of the Armenians?[48]

Turkey denies that what happened to Armenians was genocide. They describe it rather as "deportation" due to wartime conditions. They claim that the conflict was mutual, that Armenian groups attacked and killed Turkish neighbors, that all sides suffered in a time of warfare, that foreign witnesses were prejudiced against Turks, that there are no official documents establishing a deliberate campaign against Armenians, and that it is unfair to single out the Armenians as victims and accuse the Turkish government of deliberate genocide.

Most non-Turkish scholars argue that governments rarely describe their genocidal plans in official written documents, that the Turkish archives for that period are still sealed, that even prejudiced witnesses can give valid firsthand testimony, and that a comparison of population figures before and after the period do not support the notion that the suffering was of comparable degree. In addition, the Turkish government has applied significant pressure, for example, by threatening Microsoft with a lawsuit for including the "Armenian Genocide" in their online encyclopedia.[49]

Nazi Germany, 1933–1945[50]

Perpetrators: Nazi and Fascist leaders. Supportive population: Lutheran and Catholic Christian Germans, Poles, Italians, others. Victims: six million Jews in addition to Roma, homosexuals, opponents of the regime. Trauma: governmental and economic collapse from WWI reparations, national humiliation, and a world depression.

For details, see the sections on the Holocaust in chapters 3 and 4 (Jewish and Christian worldviews).

Cambodia, 1975–1978[51]

Perpetrators: Khmer Rouge Marxists and Pol Pot seeking to create a centralized Maoist society based on rural physical labor. Supportive population: Buddhist Cambodians. Victims: three million or more deaths, primarily of intellectuals, professionals, religious leaders, weak and elderly. Trauma: French decolonization, refugees and U.S. troops from the Vietnam War.

During the Vietnam War, Cambodian president Sihanouk tried to keep the country neutral. He was ousted in 1970 by the pro-Western Lon Nol, who himself fell in 1975 to the Maoist Marxist Pol Pot. The new government sought to transform Cambodia into a rural commune by killing or forcing into rural manual labor all the intellectuals and city dwellers. Pol Pot was deposed in 1978 by a Vietnamese invasion, after which the United States and Great Britain supported his efforts to drive the Vietnamese out of Cambodia, despite his genocidal actions.

Bosnia, 1992–1995[52]

Perpetrators: Bosnian Serbian militias supported by Slobodan Milošević. Supportive population: Orthodox Christian Bosnian Serbs. Victims: Croatian Catholics and Bosniak Muslims—100,000 deaths. Trauma: breakup of Yugoslavia into various ethnic nationalities after the death of Tito, which ensued after the United States withdrew financial aid from the central government and transferred it to separatist leaders.

Yugoslavia had been the most moderate of the East European communist countries, and had broken ties with the Soviet Union. With the help of U.S. financial aid, it developed a successful socialist economy. When Tito died and the Soviet Union broke up, the U.S. redirected its aid to regional, separatist leaders. Slovenia gained independence quickly, and Croatia did so with more difficulty, but Bosnia included significant communities of Catholic Croats, Orthodox Serbs, and Bosnian Muslims; Serbia began a process of ethnic cleansing in the eastern parts of Bosnia. The UN designated and attempted to defend several "safe areas" for the victims, but without adequate force. The city of Srebrenica (a UN safe area) was attacked by the Serb Ratko Mladić, who massacred seven thousand inhabitants in one action. Eventually the Croats and Bosniak Muslims joined forces to ethnically cleanse two hundred thousand Serbs from Krajina in the northwest corner of Bosnia, and finally the "Dayton Accords" provided sixty thousand NATO troops to maintain peace.

Rwanda, 1994[53]

Perpetrators: Hutu supremacists, the Rwandan government and army. Supportive population: the Hutu population (majority Catholic Christian, many charismatic), which consisted of 90 percent of the Rwandan population. Victims: five hundred thousand Tutsi, plus Hutu moderates and others killed, up to a total of one million in about a three-month period. Trauma: decolonization, tribal conflicts, poverty of arable land.

Rwanda was first a German and then a Belgian colony until 1961. The colonial leaders had supported members of the Tutsi tribe as a privileged group, including local leaders, although they represented only 9 percent of the population. When Belgium left, the Hutus were elected into power, and many Tutsis experienced discrimination or fled. A Rwandan Patriotic Front became active in 1985, and in 1990 it invaded Rwanda from Uganda. Meanwhile, population growth in Rwanda was putting great stress on land resources: in 1993, 45 percent of the Rwandan families in one sample owned less than 0.6 of an acre of farmland.

All these people who were about to be killed had land and at times cows. And somebody had to get those lands and those cows after their owners were dead. In a poor and increasingly overpopulated country, this was not a negligible incentive.[54]

An International Criminal Tribunal for Rwanda was established in Tanzania in 1996. By spring 2012, it had held thirty-five trials and convicted twenty-nine people of various crimes, including "the creation of hate media." Eight more trials are in progress. After watching the trial of a musician accused of writing and performing music that incited to genocide, Ina Ziegler, a University of Minnesota alumna, commented:

> The only justice that would be enough . . . would indict all of us . . . every person who has participated in or benefited from colonialism, which in many ways created this whole mess. Every person who killed another. Every person who supplied arms to combatants. Every person who remained silent when the genocide was happening. Every

person who remains silent now, when it is still going on. . . . The blood of our brothers and sisters is crying out, to whatever God can hear, from the ground where our apathy, our greed, our silence, has spilled it.[55]

Palestine, 1920s to the Present[56]

Perpetrators: Israeli Zionist leaders, army, and extremist settlers. Supportive population: Israeli Jewish citizens. Victims: seven hundred fifty to eight hundred thousand Muslim and Christian Palestinians ethnically cleansed in 1948, at least three hundred twenty-five thousand more in 1967, and more steadily since then; ongoing oppression with low-intensity killing. Trauma: the Nazi Holocaust, centuries of Christian persecutions in Europe and Russia.

For details, see chapter 8 on the Israeli-Palestinian conflict.

SUMMARY

From its pre-Christian beginnings, just war theory has been shaped first through religious moral reflection and then through secular legal reflection. Love for an innocent victim is said to justify a violent response to violence. Ten principles have been put forward to limit when and how a war can be morally undertaken and carried out: just cause, comparative cause, attitude, intention, last resort, likely success, authority, declaration, proportionality, and discrimination. The last principle allows for "collateral" damage or injury to people who are not involved in the conflict when the "principle of double effect" is satisfied. These principles can be appealed to sincerely or insincerely, leaving moralists undecided as to whether the principles are helpful or merely rationalizing pretexts for leaders to engage in power politics that are driven in reality by very different principles. The overwhelming destructiveness of modern warfare, together with the fruitful development of active nonviolence, prompts the question whether war should continue to be acceptable under any circumstances.

KEY TERMS

attitude	jus in bello
authority	jus post bellum
comparative cause	just cause
declared	last resort
discrimination	likely success
ethnic cleansing	noncombatant immunity
genocide	principle of double effect
intention	proportionality
jus ad bellum	

DISCUSSION QUESTIONS

1. How would you apply the ten principles of just war to a war that you know something about other than the Gulf Wars? How would you apply them to a nonviolent communal struggle with which you are familiar?
2. Do you think a presumption against violence is realistic and desirable? In other words, should a war be considered unjust a priori unless a strong case can be made to the contrary?
3. Would you allow the government of your own country, for example the United States, to determine when a war is just, and would you presume that your government is judging rightly unless you had strong evidence to the contrary? Would you do the same for the government of Iran, of Israel, of Nazi Germany, of North Korea, or of the former Soviet Union?
4. Do you respect individuals who have chosen to become conscientious objectors either to war in general or to particular wars, or do you regard them as unpatriotic cowards?
5. Do you think that the principles of just war are appropriate and practical in the real world today? If not, is there something wrong with the principles, or is there something wrong with the real world?

SUGGESTIONS FOR FURTHER READING

Cromartie. *Religion, Culture, and International Conflict.*
Dwyer, ed. *The Catholic Bishops and Nuclear War: A Critique and Analysis of the Pastoral Challenge of Peace.*
Galtung. *Peace by Peaceful Means.*
Gray. *The Warriors: Reflections on Men in Battle.*
Gregory. "Letter to President Bush on Iraq."
Grossman. *On Killing: The Psychological Cost of Learning to Kill in War and Society.*
Hallock. *Hell, Healing, and Resistance: Veterans Speak.*
Hashmi, ed. *Just Wars, Holy Wars, and Jihads: Christian, Jewish, and Muslim Encounters and Exchanges.*
Holmes. *On War and Morality.*
———, ed. *War and Christian Ethics.*
Johnson. *The Holy War Idea in Western and Islamic Traditions.*
———. *Just War Tradition and the Restraint of War.*
Kelsay. *Islam and War: A Study in Comparative Ethics.*
MacNair. *The Psychology of Peace.*
National Conference of Catholic Bishops. *The Challenge of Peace: God's Promise and Our Response.*
Rahula. "The Social Teachings of the Buddha."
Ramsey. *The Just War.*
Wakin. *War, Morality, and the Military Profession.*
Walzer. *Just and Unjust Wars.*
Yoder. "The Career of the Just War Theory."

Notes

PREFACE

1. Galtung, *Peace by Peaceful Means*, 1.

INTRODUCTION

1. Second Vatican Council, *Nostra Aetate*: Declaration on the Relationship of the Church to Non-Christian Religions, par. 1.

2. Cleckley, *The Mask of Sanity*. Available free in pdf form at http://www.cassiopaea.org/cass/sanity_1.PdF (accessed 4 December 2013); see also Hare, *Without Conscience*; Babiak and Hare, *Snakes in Suits*.

3. Lobaczewski, *Political Ponerology*, passim.

4. Ibid., chapter 5: "Pathocracy."

5. Ibid., Kindle locations 3696–3727.

6. Milgram, *Obedience to Authority*. See also Wikipedia, "Milgram Experiment," http://en.wikipedia.org/wiki/Milgram_experiment (accessed 16 November 2013).

7. Mayer, *They Thought They Were Free: The Germans, 1933–45*.

8. As recommended by the Norwegian peace theoretician Johan Galtung.

9. http://courseweb.stthomas.edu/justpeace/305pr01.html (accessed 3 November 2013). When teaching Theologies of Justice and Peace, we asked students to answer these questions for themselves at the start of the study (step 1), and again on behalf of the worldview they were studying toward the end of the study (step 8).

10. Smart, *The World's Religions*, 11–26. See also Smart, *Worldviews*.

11. For an alternative set of principles, see Cannon, *Six Ways of Being Religious*.

12. Christian mystical traditions are represented by people like Benedict of Nursia (the founder of Western monasticism), Symeon the New Theologian, Hildegard von Bingen, Catherine of Siena, Julian of Norwich, Teresa of Avila, John of the Cross, George Fox, and Thomas Merton.

13. You can read further details, including descriptions of the types of people having such experiences, some characteristics of the experiences themselves, and the effects on their lives, in Greeley, *Death and Beyond*, chapter 6: "Are We a Nation of Mystics?"

14. See Sanford, *Sealed Orders*, 32–34.

15. Black Elk, Neihardt, and DeMaillie, *Black Elk Speaks*. Note that Black Elk became a Catholic Christian catechist (lay teacher) for the second half of his life. See also Lindblom, *Prophecy in Ancient Israel*, chapter 1: "Religio-Historical Survey: Prophets Outside Israel."

16. Moody, *Life after Life*, 26.

17. Frossard, *I Have Met Him*, 119–20.

18. Smart, *Worldviews*, 79.

19. McKenzie, *Myths and Realities*, 182–200.

20. Wink, *Engaging the Powers*, 13–31.

21. Kohn, *Punished by Rewards*.

22. Gertner, "The Futile Pursuit of Happiness." Based on research by the psychologists Daniel Gilbert of Harvard University and Tim Wilson of the University of Virginia, the economist George Loewenstein of Carnegie-Mellon University, and the psychologist (and Nobel laureate in economics) Daniel Kahneman of Princeton University.

23. For several of the preceding points, I (David) am indebted to Joseph Schultz, one of my students.

24. Rawls, *Justice as Fairness*, 43.

25. United Nations General Assembly, "The Universal Declaration of Human Rights." The text is available at http://www.un.org/en/documents/udhr/ (accessed 4 December 2013).

26. United Nations, "International Covenant on Civil and Political Rights." The text is available at http://www.ohchr.org/EN/ProfessionalInterest/Pages/CCPR.aspx (accessed 4 December 2013).

27. United Nations, "International Covenant on Intellectual, Social, and Cultural Rights." The text is available at http://www.ohchr.org/EN/ProfessionalInterest/Pages/CESCR.aspx (accessed 4 December 2013).

28. Second Vatican Council, *Nostra Aetate*. The text is available at http://www.vatican.va/archive/hist_councils/ii_vatican_council/documents/vat-ii_decl_19651028_nostra-aetate_en.html (accessed 4 December 2013).

29. Second Vatican Council, *Lumen Gentium*. The text is available at http://www.vatican.va/archive/hist_councils/ii_vatican_council/documents/vat-ii_const19641121_lumen-gentium_en.html (accessed 4 December 2013). Note especially sections 13–17.

30. "From a homily written in the second century": cap. 13, 2–14, 5 (Funk 1, 159–61), which occurs in the second reading for Matins on Thursday of the thirty-second week of the year in the Roman Catholic Liturgy of the Hours. For the text, see http://test.ebreviary.com/ebreviary/usa2/ebusaprayer4dnav180.nsf/576f0c20d0d4344d852573f2000b9ba2/3d1c1520d1dcbaad8525775800774368/$FILE/1115Office_Thu.pdf (accessed 4 December 2013).

31. See, for example, chapter 6: "Why Religious Confrontations Are Violent," in Juergensmeyer, *The New Cold War?*

32. Groebel, "The Role of the Mass Media in Modern Wars": chapter 10 in Hinde and Watson, *War: A Cruel Necessity? The Bases of Institutionalized Violence*, 168. Used by permission of I. B. Tauris © 1995.

33. Ibid., 172. Used by permission of I. B. Tauris © 1995.

34. Ibid., 174. Used by permission of I. B. Tauris © 1995.

35. That book has become influential in the U.S. Foreign Service. Johnston founded the International Center for Religion and Diplomacy to develop and apply his ideas: http://icrd.org (accessed 10 December 2013). See also his book, *Faith-Based Diplomacy: Trumping Realpolitik*.

36. See also http://www.afr-iofc.org/Oxford_Research_Group.pdf (accessed 9 December 2013).

CHAPTER 1: HINDU WORLDVIEWS

1. www.sacred-texts.com/hin/gita/agsgita.htm (accessed 14 December 2013).

2. Yogananda, *Autobiography of a Yogi*, 166–67. Used by permission.

3. See *The Complete Works of Swami Vivekananda*, vols. 1–9. Kindle edition. Also available with other Ramakrishna and Vivekananda materials online at www.ramakrishnavivekananda.info (accessed 13 December 2013).

4. We are using the periodization from Smart, *The World's Religions*, 45.

5. Wikipedia, "Indo-Aryan Migration," http://en.wikipedia.org/wiki/Indo-Aryan_migration (accessed 15 December 2013).

6. See English translations of these texts at the Internet Sacred Text Archive: http://www.sacred-texts.com/index.htm (accessed 13 December 2013).

7. www.advaita-vedanta.org/avhp/ (accessed 13 December 2013).

8. See http://www.advaita-vedanta.org/avhp/dating-Sankara.html (accessed 13 December 2013); *Eastern Traditions*, 51–53.

9. *Eastern Traditions*, 69. See also note 3 above.

10. Prabhupada, *Bhagavad-Gita as It Is*, 35–36.

11. http://www.advaita-vedanta.org/avhp/mimved.html (accessed 13 December 2013).

12. "VI, 8. Charm to Secure the Love of a Woman." In *Hymns of the Atharva-Veda*.

13. Yogananda, *Autobiography of a Yogi*, 166.

14. Radhakrishnan, *The Bhagavadgita*, 59.

15. According to the 2011 census. See Wikipedia, "Scheduled Castes and Scheduled Tribes," http://en.wikipedia.org/wiki/Scheduled_Castes_and_Scheduled_Tribes (accessed 14 December 2013).

16. http://hinduism.iskcon.org/practice/703.htm.

17. Spiro, *Buddhism and Society: A Great Tradition and Its Burmese Vicissitudes*.

18. "Vedanta in its Application to Indian Life," in *The Complete Works of Swami Vivekananda*, Volume 3, Lecture 3.4.12. Kindle edition, location 19145. This quotation is also available at http://awakeningindia.org/Life/Teachings.aspx (accessed 14 December 2013).

19. www.ambedkar.org/ (accessed 9 March 2014). See also Coward, ed. *Indian Critiques of Gandhi*.

20. Look for a forthcoming book by Rambachan on Hindu liberation theology as the path to justice and structural transformation. For the notion that this openness to "development of doctrine" in Hinduism by people outside of official leadership positions can make Hinduism an "open source" religion—like some computer software—see Josh Schrei, "The God Project—Hinduism as Open-Source Faith," *Huffington Post*, 4 March 2010, http://www.huffingtonpost.com/josh-schrei/the-god-project-hinduism_b_486099.html (accessed 15 December 2013).

21. Oxtoby and Segal, eds., *A Concise Introduction to World Religions*, 268–69.

22. Ibid., 271–72.

23. Matthews, *World Religions*, 99.

24. Ibid., 101.

25. Ibid., 105.

26. Fisher, *Living Religions*, 105; see also Rambachan, "A Hindu Perspective."

27. Wikipedia, "Bride Burning," http://en.wikipedia.org/wiki/Bride_burning (accessed 15 December 2013).

28. Rambachan, "A Hindu Perspective," 26, 28–29.

29. http://www.yourarticlelibrary.com/communalism/problems-of-communalism-in-india-essay/4091/ (accessed 15 December 2013).

30. Varshney, "Understanding Gujarat Violence," http://conconflicts.ssrc.org/archives/gujarat/varshney/; Pankaj Mishra, "The Gujarat Massacre: New India's Blood Rite," *The Guardian*, 14 March 2012, http://www.theguardian.com/commentisfree/2012/mar/14/new-india-gujarat-massacre, both accessed 9 March 2014. See also Agnivesa and Thampu, *Harvest of Hate: Gujarat Under Siege*.

31. http://articles.timesofindia.indiatimes.com/2013-10-17/india/43142991_1_ysr-congress-seats-times-now-cvoter (accessed December 15, 2013).

32. See Nelson-Pallmeyer, *Is Religion Killing Us?*

33. Roy was studying a dispute that had taken place years earlier—before Bangladesh, the former East Pakistan, separated from West Pakistan in 1971.

34. Roy, *Some Trouble with Cows*, 168.

35. Gandhi, *Bhagvadgita* [sic], 15, 29–30.

36. Ibid., *Bhagvadgita*, 12.

37. Ibid., 18, 24–28. Radhakrishnan makes the same point in *The Bhagavadgita*, 68.

38. Quoted in Jordens, "Gandhi and the *Bhagavadgita*," 88–109. See 89, 91f, 97.

39. Jordens, "Gandhi and the *Bhagavadgita*," 97.

40. Wilson, "Vinoba Bhave's *Talks on the Gita*," 110–30.

41. http://swamiagnivesh.com. His books include _Vedic Socialism_ (1974; in Hindi), _Hinduism in the New Age_ (2005), and (spelled Agnivesa), _Religion, Spirituality, and Social Action._

CHAPTER 2: BUDDHIST WORLDVIEWS

1. Gautama, "The Sermon at Benares."
2. The periodization here is based on the article "Buddhism" in _The Encyclopedia of Eastern Philosophy and Religion_, 50.
3. Smart, _The World's Religions_, 59.
4. For example, Plum Village in France; http://plumvillage.org/ (accessed 26 December 2013).
5. Traditional dates for his life are 563–483 BCE. Smart, _The World's Religions_, suggests "possibly" the year 586 for his birth.
6. The first term given is the Sanskrit word; the term in parentheses is its Pali equivalent.
7. This Buddhist use of the word _dharma_ should not be confused with the Hindu use of the same word. For Hindus, _dharma_ means "duty based on the true nature of things and our place in that nature (caste)." For Buddhists, it means the "teaching of the Buddha."
8. Silouan and Sophrony, _Wisdom from Mount Athos_, 98.
9. Ciszek, _He Leadeth Me_, especially chap. 3.
10. Fischer-Schreiber et al., _Encyclopedia of Eastern Philosophy and Religion_, 249.
11. For a fuller discussion of various Buddhist views of nirvana, see Fischer-Schreiber et al., _Encyclopedia of Eastern Philosophy and Religion_, 249–50.
12. For a more extensive explanation of the five aggregates, see http://www.buddhanet.net/funbud 14.htm (accessed 15 March 2014). Some Buddhists deny the existence of God. Others hold that God might or might not exist, but the search to prove God's existence is a distraction from the search for enlightenment. Buddhism arose in dialogue with Hinduism and so denied the Hindu characterizations of God. The pamphlet _Twelve Principles of Buddhism_, by the Corporate Body of the Buddha Educational Foundation, says, "Reality is indescribable, and _a God with attributes_ is not the final Reality" (p. 8, emphasis added). You might think through the implications of this statement in view of Thomas Aquinas's conviction that no positive statement about God can be anything more than an analogy.
13. This connection between the Christian notion of the human creature and the Buddhist notion of _anatman_ is noted by Aloysius Pieris in _Love Meets Wisdom_ (based on a personal conversation between Pieris and David in Sri Lanka in the summer of 1998).
14. Spiro, _Buddhism and Society._
15. Spiro, _Anthropological Other_, 99. On pages 74–76, Spiro discusses Theravada Buddhism in terms of the three core doctrines of no self, no God, and impermanence.
16. See the description at http://www.teavana.com/tea-info/japanese-tea-ceremony (accessed 26 December 2013).
17. Spiro, _Anthropological Other_, 88.
18. Spiro, _Buddhism and Society_, chap. 6.
19. Ibid., 149.
20. Ibid., 70
21. Oxtoby, ed., _Eastern Traditions_, 221.
22. Fisher, _Living Religions_, 146.
23. Oxtoby, ed., _Eastern Traditions_, 291.
24. Matthews, _World Religions_, 155.
25. Fisher, _Living Religions_, 178.
26. Oxtoby, ed., _Eastern Traditions_, 293–94.
27. Ibid., 291.
28. Matthews, _World Religions_, 155.
29. Victoria, _Zen at War_, 137.

30. Ibid., 121. See also Victoria, *Zen War Stories*.

31. Note that the early chronicle says that the *first human inhabitants* entered Sri Lanka on the day the Buddha died. Earlier the Buddha himself had made several *visits* to the island. But Buddhism was not a major factor in Sri Lanka until about two centuries later, when the son of the emperor Ashoka of India, the Venerable Mahinda, brought Buddhism to the island. Soon after, the daughter of Asoka, Sanghamittaa, brought to Sri Lanka a cutting from the Bodhi Tree under which the Buddha had attained enlightenment. It took root and has survived to the present. See H. R. Perera, *Buddhism in Sri Lanka: A Short History*, for an account of these traditions at http://www.accesstoinsight.org/lib/authors/perera/wheel100.html#ssect-02 (accessed 26 December 2013).

32. Griffiths, ed., 136–40.

33. Matthews, *World Religions*, 164.

34. Oxtoby, ed., *Eastern Traditions*, 294–95.

35. Macy, *Despair and Personal Power in the Nuclear Age*.

36. Ibid., 155ff.

37. Ibid., 156–58.

38. Thurman, "Nagarjuna's Guidelines for Buddhist Social Action," 121–22.

39. Ibid., 125.

40. Ibid., 126.

41. Ibid., 138.

42. Ibid., 139.

43. Ibid., 127.

44. Ibid., 135.

45. Ibid., 137.

46. Ibid., 128.

47. Ibid., 128, 139.

48. Ibid., 139f.

49. Ibid., 130.

50. Ibid., 131.

51. Ibid., 132. For likely disasters caused by resource depletion, especially hydrocarbons, see Diamond, *Collapse*; Heinberg, *The Party's Over* and *Power Down*.

52. Nhat Hanh, *Interbeing*, 16.

53. Ibid., 8.

54. Ibid., 17.

55. For the current, updated version of these principles, now called "The Fourteen Mindfulness Trainings," see the publisher of the book *Interbeing*, now in its third (2005) edition, at www.parallax.org/about_oi.html (accessed July 9, 2006), or the website of Plum Village Meditation Center, founded by Thich Nhat Hanh, www.plumvillage.org (accessed July 9, 2006).

56. Nhat Hanh, *Interbeing*, 27–36.

57. Especially *Lotus in a Sea of Fire* and *Interbeing*. For Plum Village, see www.plumvillage.org/ (accessed 27 December 2013).

58. nobelprize.org/peace/laureates/1989/lama-bio.html (accessed 27 December 2013).

59. When a Dalai Lama dies, "high lamas of the Gelugpa tradition" begin a several-year-long, complex series of spiritual techniques to determine the child in whom Avalokitesvara, the Bodhisattva of compassion, has been reborn. See Wikipedia, "Dalai Lama," http://en.wikipedia.org/wiki/Dalai_Lama#Searching_for_the_reincarnation (accessed 27 December 2013). Meanwhile, the leaders of Communist China have announced that *they* will decide who the next Dalai Lama is. The current Dalai Lama says that his successor will not be born in China, and that this might even be the end of the rebirths of Avalokitesvara. For the politics involved, see "What Happens When the Dalai Lama Dies?" *USA Today*, 14 October 2010, http://usatoday30.usatoday.com/news/religion/2010-05-31-lama30_ST_N.htm (accessed 27 December 2013).

60. See www.dalailama.com/biography/ (accessed 27 December 2013); http://www.nobelprize.org/nobel_prizes/peace/laureates/1989/lama-bio.html (accessed February 17, 2014).

61. Ariyaratne, *Buddhism and Sarvodaya: Sri Lankan Experience.*

62. Ibid., 66.

63. Ibid., viii, 7–11.

64. Ibid., 74.

65. Ibid., 38f.

66. Ibid., 49ff.

67. Ibid., 126.

68. Smith, interview with A. T. Ariyaratne at his center in Colombo, Sri Lanka, summer 1998. See Sarvodaya Shramadana's own website at http://www.sarvodaya.org/ (accessed 24 March 2014).

69. See her website at www.dassk.org/index.php (accessed 27 December 2013).

70. Clements, *The Voice of Hope, Aung San Suu Kyi: Conversations with Alan Clements.* The first edition (1997) lists Suu Kyi as the author. The second edition, slightly expanded, notes on the frontispiece that "Alan Clements has asserted his right to be identified as the author of this Work in accordance with the Copyright, Designs, and Patents Act 1988."

71. http://gos.sbc.edu/k/kyi.html (accessed 27 December 2013).

CHAPTER 3: JEWISH WORLDVIEWS

1. Shahak and Mezvinksy, *Jewish Fundamentalism*, 2–4.

2. www.fordham.edu/halsall/source/rambam13.html (accessed 13 January 2014).

3. The Mishnah Tractate Shabbat (Sabbath) describes what one can or can't do on the Sabbath. See http://www.sacred-texts.com/jud/t01/t0109.htm or http://www.jewishvirtuallibrary.org/jsource/Talmud/ shabbattoc.html (both accessed 13 January 2014) for the Tractate Shabbat. (This is an English translation of the Talmud. The relevant Mishnah is given first, followed by the Gemara, or Talmudic expansion.)

4. For a sense of how this feast is often celebrated, see the website at www.holidays.net/purim/ (accessed 13 January 2014).

5. Ruth Meisels, "Purim Will Never Be the Same," a review of *Reckless Rites: Purim and the Legacy of Jewish Violence* by Elliott Horowitz, *Haaretz*, 9 June 2006, http://www.haaretz.com/purim-will-never-be-the-same-1.189873 (accessed 13 January 2014). Horowitz's book discusses how Purim has been used and abused throughout history. See also Marsha B. Cohen, "Purim: When Bad History Makes Bad Policy, *Lobe Log Foreign Policy*, 7 March 2012, http://www.lobelog.com/purim-when-bad-history -makes-bad-policy/ (accessed 13 January 2014).

6. Roetzel, e-mail communication with Elizabeth, 13 December 2013.

7. See the platforms of CCAR (Reform Judaism) at http://ccarnet.org/rabbis-speak/platforms/ (accessed 14 January 2014).

8. Wikipedia, "Conservative Judaism," http://en.wikipedia.org/wiki/Conservative_Judaism (accessed 14 January 2014).

9. For American Jewish groups, see "National Jewish Population Survey 2000–2001: Orthodox Jews—A United Jewish Communities Presentation of Findings. February 2004." Available at http://www .jewishfederations.org/local_includes/downloads/4983. pdf (accessed 22 January 2014). For Israeli Jewish groups, see the Central Bureau of Statistics (Israel) 2010 survey available at http://www.ynetnews.com/ articles/0,7340,L-3890330,00.html (accessed 22 January 2014). "Most Israelis don't belong to a synagogue, but the synagogue they don't belong to is Orthodox" http://www.jewfaq.org/movement.htm (accessed 22 January 2014). For Orthodox Jewish fears that American Conservative and Reform groups are dying out through assimilation, with disastrous long-term results even for the Orthodox, who will not survive without them, see "Op-Ed: American Jewry's Denominational Delusions," Arutz Sheva ("Channel 7"), http://www.israelnationalnews.com/Articles/Article.aspx/12864 (accessed 22 January 2014).

10. Fisher, *Living Religions*, 248–49; Schmidt et al., *Patterns of Religion*, 3rd ed., 175. See also Wegner, *Chattel or Person? The Status of Women in the Mishnah.*

11. Gordon and Grob, *Education for Peace*, chapter 3.

12. Talmud, Yevamot, 14b.

13. Wikipedia, "Mesha Stele, http://en.wikipedia.org/wiki/Mesha_Stele (accessed 9 March 2014).

14. Wikipedia, "Herem," http://en.wikipedia.org/wiki/Herem_%28war_or_property%29.

15. http://judaism.about.com/library/3_intro/level2/bl_war.htm.

16. Available at many websites. Quoted here from "Conclusion" of "The Evian Conference: Hitler's Green Light for Genocide" at the Google group soc.culture.jewish available at https://groups.google.com/forum/#!topic/soc.culture.jewish/vKFUM2mMhBQ (accessed 21 January 2014).

17. Wiesel, *Night*, 76.

18. The Yad Vashem Museum in Jerusalem, http://www.yadvashem.org/yv/en/museum/index.asp?WT.mc_id=200965WT.cg_n=g.en; the U.S. Holocaust Museum in Washington, D.C., http://www.ushmm.org/ (both accessed 29 December 2013).

19. Hajo Meyer, "The Blinding Effects of History," in *The End of Judaism*, 105–26.

20. For historical details on Jewish Zionism, see the article by Ami Isseroff at www.mideastweb.org/zionism.htm (accessed 14 January 2014).

21. Ellis, *Toward a Jewish Theology of Liberation*, 70–73.

22. Quoted in Wikipedia, "Religious Zionist Movement," en.wikipedia.org/wiki/Religious_Zionist_Movement (accessed June 15, 2006).

23. Benny Morris, *Righteous Victims*, 21.

24. http://en.wikipedia.org/wiki/Theodor_Herzl (accessed 29 December 2013).

25. www.jewishvirtuallibrary.org/jsource/Zionism/firstcong.html (accessed 29 December 2013).

26. http://www.jewishvirtuallibrary.org/jsource/Zionism/First_Cong_&_Basel_Program.html (accessed 29 December 2013).

27. Nahum Sokolow, *History of Zionism (1600–1918)*, Volume I (London: Longmans, Green, and Company, 1919), pp xxiv–xxv. (Available for free download from Google books: http://books.google.com/books?id=8rgpAQAAIAAJ&printsec=frontcover&dq=Sokolow+History+of+Zionism&hl=en&sa=X&ei=ZM3AUt1C49rIAbKKgdAL&ved=0CC8Q6AEwAA#v=onepage&q=Sokolow%20History%20of%20Zionism&f=false.

28. Steichen, Summer Chautauqua talk, August 8, 2013, St. Catherine University.

29. Wigoder, *Everyman's Judaica: An Encyclopedic Dictionary*, 338; Wikipedia, "Degania Aleph," http://en.wikipedia.org/wiki/Degania_Alef (accessed 21 January 2014).

30. Griffiths, ed., *Christianity through Non-Christian Eyes*, 14–15.

31. Matthews, *World Religions*, 4th ed., 319.

32. *Nostra Aetate*, paragraph 4; accessible at http://www.vatican.va/archive/hist_councils/ii_vatican_council/documents/vat-ii_decl_19651028_nostra-aetate_en.html (accessed 21 September 2014).

33. Ellis, *Toward a Jewish Theology of Liberation*, 210.

34. Adam Jacobs, "Jewish-American Gut-Check," *Huffington Post*, 15 December 2011, http://www.huffingtonpost.com/rabbi-adam-jacobs/jewish-american-gut-check_b_1142503.html (accessed 13 January 2014). But compare this with Gabriel Roth, "American Jews Are Secular, Intermarried, and Assimilated: Great News," *Slate*, http://www.slate.com/articles/life/family/2013/10/american_jews_embrace_your_secular_intermarried_selves.html (accessed 13 January 2014), which *approves* of Jews dissolving into the wider American community.

35. http://www.ccjr.us/dialogika-resources/themes-in-todays-dialogue/conversion/926-allen2011mar10 (accessed 21 January 2014) referring to *Jesus of Nazareth Part Two: Holy Week*. Kindle location 758. But note that he adds: "On the contrary, the Jews themselves are a living homily to which the Church must draw attention, since they call to mind the Lord's suffering (cf. Ep 363)."

36. Ellis, *Toward a Jewish Theology of Liberation*, 61–64.

37. Ibid., 187.

38. Ibid., 188.

39. Ibid., 181–87.

40. Wikipedia, "Etty Hillesum," http://en.wikipedia.org/wiki/Etty_Hillesum#The_Inner_Path (accessed 21 January 2014).

CHAPTER 4: CHRISTIAN WORLDVIEWS

1. Barr, *New Testament Story*, 3rd ed., 66; McKenzie, *Dictionary of the Bible*, 830; Meier, "Jesus," in *The New Jerome Biblical Commentary* 78:35 (p. 1324).

2. Wink, *Engaging the Powers*, 13–31.

3. http://www.30giorni.it/articoli_id_21194_l3.htm?id = 21194 (accessed 27 January 2014).

4. http://en.wikipedia.org/wiki/Ussher_chronology (accessed 2 February 2014).

5. Barth, *The Epistle to the Romans* and "The Barmen Declaration"; Niebuhr, *Moral Man and Immoral Society* and *Man's Nature and His Communities*; and Tillich, *The Courage to Be* and *Dynamics of Faith*.

6. Gorospe, *Forming the Filipino Social Conscience*, 58.

7. Ibid.

8. Ibid.

9. Ibid., 64–65.

10. See the discussion of caste in chapter 1 on Hindu Worldviews.

11. Gorospe, *Forming the Filipino Social Conscience*, 74–76.

12. Ibid., 83.

13. Ibid., 84.

14. http://www.gci.org/history/chalcedon (accessed 2 February 2014).

15. Cory and Hollerich, eds., *The Christian Theological Tradition*. God is so radically different from any creature that any positive statements about God are inadequate: our words are always (as Thomas Aquinas points out) mere analogies. In particular, God's way of knowing is completely different from the human's way of knowing. But using terms like "intellect" and "will" is the best we can do to approximate what we are trying to say.

16. See the helpful diagram at http://en.wikipedia.org/wiki/Christology#Post-Apostolic_contro versies (accessed 2 February 2014).

17. Borg, "The Palestinian Background for a Life of Jesus," Kindle locations 421–672 in Patterson, Borg, and Crossan, *The Search for Jesus*.

18. Borg, "Portraits of Jesus," Kindle locations 957–1255 in Patterson et al., *The Search for Jesus*. Note especially the "six portraits" beginning at Kindle location 1033.

19. Borg, *Meeting Jesus Again for the First Time*; Oakman, *The Political Aims of Jesus*; Crossan, *The Historical Jesus: The Life of a Mediterranean Jewish Peasant*.

20. Ehrman, *The New Testament*, 4th ed., 254–59.

21. Oakman, *The Political Aims of Jesus*, 111. For examples of the Jesus Seminar, see Funk et al., *The Five Gospels: What Did Jesus Really Say?*, Funk, *The Acts of Jesus: The Search for the Authentic Words of Jesus*, and Crossan, *The Historical Jesus*. For a nuanced application of "criteria of authenticity," see Meyer, "Jesus," section 78 in *The New Jerome Biblical Commentary*, 1316–28. For a contrary scholarly position, see Johnson, *The Real Jesus: The Misguided Quest for the Historical Jesus and the Truth of the Traditional Gospels*.

22. http://courseweb.stthomas.edu/justpeace/Rowman.html (accessed 15 March 2014).

23. See Wink, "Jesus' Third Way: Nonviolent Engagement," chap. 9 (pp. 175–93) in *Engaging the Powers*. See also Nelson-Pallmeyer's presentation of Wink's key points toward the end of chapter 11 (328–30) on active nonviolence.

24. Scofield, *The Scofield Reference Bible*, footnote 2 on pp. 999–1000 commenting on Matthew 5:2; footnote 3 on pages 1226–27 commenting on 1 Cor 15:24; http://www.middletownbiblechurch.org/dispen/sermon.htm (accessed 1 February 2014).

25. Wink also refutes this notion in "Jesus' Third Way: Nonviolent Engagement," chap. 9 (pp. 175–93) in *Engaging the Powers*.

26. Original sin makes it very hard to forgive really obnoxious or evil people. But God's unearned grace can make it possible. See our website (http://courseweb.stthomas.edu/justpeace/rowman.html) for a suggested exercise, based on the writings of Agnes Sanford (*The Healing Light* and other books) and on David's own experience praying with people for healing.

27. The theses are available online: "Disputation of Doctor Martin Luther on the Power and Efficacy of Indulgences, by Dr. Martin Luther (1517)," www.iclnet.org/pub/resources/text/wittenberg/luther/web/ninetyfive.html (accessed 4 February 2014).

28. See also 1 Corinthians 1:18; Philippians 3:9–14.

29. Anderson et al., *Justification by Faith: Lutherans and Catholics in Dialogue VII*.

30. Cory and Hollerich, eds., *The Christian Theological Tradition*, 325.

31. "Letter of 30 May 1525, from Wittenberg to Nicholas Amsdorf at Magdeburg," in Smith, *The Life and Letters of Martin Luther*, 164–65. Used by permission of Augsburg Fortress.

32. Based in Geneva, Switzerland, the LWF operates internationally with reference to five "focus areas": "theology and public witness," "holistic mission and member churches," "humanitarian and development assistance," "women and gender," and "youth." See www.lutheranworld.org (accessed December 27, 2013).

33. Weaver, Brakke and Bivens, *Introduction to Christianity*, 105.

34. Weber, *The Protestant Ethic and the Spirit of Capitalism*.

35. The Greek prefix *ana* means "again."

36. Weaver, Brakke, and Bivens, *Introduction to Christianity*, 107.

37. Dyck, "Mennonites."

38. Weaver, Brakke, and Bivens, *Introduction to Christianity*, 120.

39. Similar to the familiar French *tu* or German *du* used to address family members, close friends, and small children. The English "you" was equivalent to the formal *vous* or *Sie*—or "Sir"—used to address "people of importance."

40. Barbour, "Quakers."

41. www.afsc.org/ (accessed July 10, 2006).

42. See Barbour, "Quakers," and the website www.fcnl.org (accessed 4 February 2014).

43. The name "Fundamentalists" was taken from the title of a series of pamphlets published between 1910 and 1915, consisting of ninety essays in twelve volumes: *The Fundamentals: A Testimony to the Truth*. They are available online at http://fundamentalists.whybaptist.com/; for download at http://www.ntslibrary.com/New_Online_Book_Additions.htm; and, for the first seven of twelve volumes, in a very clear form, at https://archive.org/details/fundamentalstest17chic (New York Public Library).

44. Weaver, Brakke, and Bivens, *Introduction to Christianity*, 159, 176–77.

45. www.cc.org (accessed 4 February 2014).

46. For the article by Grant Wacker, see http://nationalhumanitiescenter.org/tserve/twenty/tkeyinfo/chr_rght.htm. For the Public Policy recommendations of the National Association of Evangelicals, see http://www.nae.net/government-relations (both accessed 4 February 2014).

47. http://www.cc.org/about_us (accessed 4 February 2014).

48. Schüssler Fiorenza, *In Memory of Her*, xiv.

49. Fisher, *Living Religions*, 5th ed., 354; see also the *Women's Bible Commentary*, 2nd ed.

50. Smith, "Inspired Authors and Saintly Interpreters in Conflict: The New Testament on War and Peace," chapter 7, pp. 152–78, in Tambasco, *Blessed Are the Peacemakers*. See especially pp. 169–70. For Augustine's attitudes, see Brown, *Augustine of Hippo*, 419–26.

51. "Medieval Sourcebook: Peace of God—Synod of Charroux, 989," http://cassian.memphis.edu/history/jmblythe/3370/PeaceOfGod989.htm (accessed 4 February 2014).

52. "Medieval Sourcebook: Truce of God—Bishopric of Terouanne, 1063," http://www.fordham.edu/halsall/source/t-of-god.html (accessed 4 February 2014).

53. Armstrong, *Islam: A Short History*, 95; Esposito, *Islam: The Straight Path*, 4th ed., 64.

54. van Braght, ed., *The Bloody Theater: Or, Martyrs Mirror*, 343–44.

55. Armstrong, *Islam: A Short History*, 144.

56. Copeland, *The Laws of Prosperity*, 76, 103.

57. See the discussions on Christian Zionism by Palestinian Christians and Mennonite biblical scholars available at "Christian Zionism and Peace in the Holy Land," http://www.mcc.org/system/files/PON_2005-03.pdf (accessed 4 February 2014). See Israel/Palestine Mission Network of the Presbyterian Church (USA), *Zionism Unsettled: A Congregational Study Guide*.

58. 1917, copyright renewed 1945. See also Halley, *Halley's Bible Handbook*.

59. Martin, *The Temples That Jerusalem Forgot*, http://askelm.com/temple/t001211.htm. For alternative views, see http://www.templemount.org/theories.html (accessed 4 February 2014).

60. http://www.templeinstitute.org/ and http://templemountfaithful.org/ (both accessed 2 February 2014).

61. http://www.vatican.va/archive/hist_councils/ii_vatican_council/documents/vat-ii_decl_19651 028_nostra-aetate_en.html (accessed 2 February 2014).

62. Matthews, *World Religions*, 4th ed., 371; Fisher, *Living Religions*, 5th ed., 331–32.

63. www.goarch.org/ourfaith/ourfaith8089 (accessed February 21, 2014).

64. Allaire and Broughton, "An Introduction to the Life and Spirituality of Dorothy Day," http://www.catholicworker.org/dorothyday/ddbiographytext.cfm?Number = 3. Her writings (721 articles from the *Catholic Worker* newspaper and four books) are available at http://dorothyday.catholicworker.org/ (both accessed 4 February 2014).

65. Jim Forest, "Servant of God Dorothy Day," available at http://www.catholicworker.org/dorothy day/ddbiographytext.cfm?Number = 72 (accessed 4 February 2014).

66. A collection of Dorothy Day's articles on Peter Maurin is available at http://www.catholicworker .org/roundtable/DDonPM.cfm (accessed 4 February 2014).

67. The main website is http://www.catholicworker.org/ The paper still costs a penny a copy. You can buy a year's subscription (seven issues), mailed to your home, for twenty-five cents. http://www .catholicworker.org/help/faq.cfm (both accessed 3 February 2014).

68. Tom Cornell, "A Brief Introduction to the Catholic Worker Movement," http://www.catholic worker.org/historytext.cfm?Number = 4 (accessed 4 February 2014).

69. The activist scholar James Douglass has done extensive research on King's assassination, which he associates with the assassinations of JFK (see his *JFK and the Unspeakable*), Malcolm X, and Robert Kennedy.

70. Chris Hedges, "America's Street Priest," posted June 10, 2012, on www.truthdig.com (accessed December 27, 2013).

71. Quoted in ibid.

CHAPTER 5: MUSLIM WORLDVIEWS

1. Our source for quotations from the Quran here and throughout this chapter is *The Holy Qur'an*, trans. Abdullah Yusuf Ali. Accessible at www.sacred-texts.com/isl/quran/00101.htm (accessed 15 February 2014). We have edited the capitalization and verse divisions to make the meaning more accessible to English speakers.

2. Shia Muslims usually believe that the Prophet was *literate*.

3. http://www.islamhinduism.com/prophet-muhammad/138-the-miracle-of-the-prophets-night -journey-al-isra-wa-l-miraj (accessed 14 February 2014).

4. For an expert overview, see Esposito, *Islam: The Straight Path*, 4th ed., chapter 4.

5. Personal communication from Adil Ozdemir of the Muslim-Christian Dialogue Center at the University of St. Thomas, St. Paul, Minnesota. See also http://www.missionislam.com/quran/revelation order.htm and http://www.islam-info.ch/en/Arrangement_of_the_Quran.htm (accessed 14 February 2014).

6. Personal communication from Adil Ozdemir of the Muslim-Christian Dialogue Center.

7. There are several websites that offer a hadith (and sometimes more) for each day of the year: http://hadithaday.org/ (with commentary); http://www.lessonsoftheday.com/ (ayah, hadith, wise quote, guidance, food for thought); http://www.hadithoftheday.com/hadith/ (with apps for iPhone and android); http://myhadithoftheday.com/hadiths/; http://www.dailyhadithonline.com/ (in Arabic and English); and, for twitter, https://twitter.com/DailyHadith, "A Hadith a day keeps Shaitan away" (all accessed 15 February 2014).

8. These first three examples are taken from "An-Nawawi's Forty Hadiths (Translation)"; http://sunnahfollowers.net/An-Nawawis-Forty-Hadiths/www.adly.net/deed/hadith/other/hadithnawawi.html (accessed 14 February 2014).

9. The last two examples are taken from http://www.theamericanmuslim.org/tam.php/features/articles/a_collection_of_sound_hadith_on_nonviolence_peace_and_justice (accessed January 1, 2014).

10. The dominant Christian communities within or on the edge of Arabia did not follow the Trinitarian or Christological formulas of the Council of Chalcedon and the Byzantine Empire. Thus in its polemic against the Trinity and incarnation, the Quran may be addressing these alternative doctrinal expressions. "Syriac-speaking dissenters from this policy [the decrees of Chalcedon] found refuge in the frontier zones of their homeland, the borderlands between Rome and Persia." Griffith, *The Church in the Shadow of the Mosque*, Kindle location 3762.

11. Esposito, *Islam: The Straight Path*, 4th ed., 36.

12. Denny, *An Introduction to Islam*, 3rd ed., 61.

13. http://www.ghazali.net/islam/ (accessed 14 February 2014). See also Esposito, *Islam: The Straight Path*, 4th ed., 11.

14. See Rahman, *Major Themes of the Qur'an*, 108, 120.

15. Some Muslims, like the Wahhabi Muslims of Saudi Arabia, claim that we should not even make images of Muhammad or other human beings. This latter belief is not shared by all Muslims.

16. Esposito, *Islam: The Straight Path*, 4th ed., 22.

17. Hodgson, *The Venture of Islam*, 1:185.

18. See for example Quran 2:3, 43, 177; 4:103.

19. See for example Quran 2:43, 110, 177, 277.

20. An Internet search for "zakat calculator" will turn up several sites that help to determine one's obligation. Some of them also accept and distribute the payment.

21. See for example Quran 2:183–87.

22. See for example Quran 2:158, 196–203.

23. Lings, *What Is Sufism?* 64–65; "Sufism," in Glasse, *The Concise Encyclopedia of Islam*, 375–80.

24. Quoted in Denny, *An Introduction to Islam*, 3rd ed., 232.

25. http://Courseweb.stthomas.edu/justpeace/Rowman.html (accessed 16 March 2014).

26. http://users.iafrica.com/n/ns/nsalie/concept_of_ihsaan.htm (accessed 14 February 2014).

27. Shepard, *Introducing Islam*, 137.

28. Esposito, *Islam: The Straight Path*, 4th ed., 271–72.

29. Wikipedia, "Abdul Rahman (Convert)," en.wikipedia.org/wiki/Abdul_Rahman_(convert) (accessed 14 February 2014).

30. Hassan, "Peace Education: A Muslim Perspective," in Gordon and Grob, *Education for Peace*, 102–4.

31. Kaltner, *Introducing the Qur'an*, 213.

32. Griffith, *The Church in the Shadow of the Mosque*, Kindle locations 409–16; 4730–40.

33. Kelsay, *Islam and War*.

34. Legenhausen, "Islam and Just War Theory." Available on www.academia.edu; http://mereorthodoxy.com/jihad-and-justice-islamic-just-war-theory-part-1/http://mereorthodoxy.com/jihad-and-justice-islamic-just-war-theory-part-2/http://ocw.nd.edu/peace-studies/islamic-ethics-of-war-and-peace/eduCommons/peace-studies/islamic-ethics-of-war-and-peace/lectures/islamic-just-war-theory-updated (all accessed 12 February 2014).

35. http://abidnyc.wordpress.com/2011/03/28/islam%E2%80%99s-view-on-war-and-terrorism-a-survey-of-the-quran-and-prophetic-traditions/ (accessed 12 February 2014).

36. This position is strongly challenged by some who claim that *jihad* in the Quran almost always refers to armed conflict. See http://wikiislam.net/wiki/Lesser_vs_Greater_Jihad (accessed 12 February 2014). See, however, Abou El Fadl, "Islam and Violence: Our Forgotten Legacy," who states that "the Quran does not use the word *jihad* to refer to warfare"; instead, it uses the word *qital*. His essay is found in Donohue and Esposito, *Islam in Transition*, 460–64.

37. Muhaiyaddeen, *Islam and World Peace: Explanations of a Sufi*. His followers maintain a website at www.bmf.org/ (accessed 15 February 2014). The entire book is available online at www.bmf.org/iswp/; click on the contents on the right-hand margin (accessed 15 February 2014).

38. Muhaiyaddeen, "Islam and Holy War," in Muhaiyaddeen, *Islam and World Peace*, www.bmf.org/iswp/laws-holy-war.html (accessed 14 February 2014).

39. See Esposito, *Islam: The Straight Path*, 4th ed., 58–59; en.wikipedia.org/wiki/Crusade (accessed 14 February 2014).

40. Esposito, *Islam: The Straight Path*, 4th ed, 153–54.

41. Ibid., 168–74.

42. Ibid., 158.

43. Abduh, *Theology of Unity*, 140; Esposito, *Islam: The Straight Path*, 4th ed., 157–58.

44. Iqbal, *Reconstruction*, 155–56.

45. Ibid., 179.

46. "Legalizing the Muslim Brotherhood," *Christian Science Monitor*, November 23, 2005, www.csmonitor.com/2005/1123/p08s02-comv.html (accessed 14 February 2014).

47. Ibid.

48. Most of our sources gave the year 1906 for his birth, but the Library of Congress classifications for his books give the year 1903.

49. Denny, *An Introduction to Islam*, 3rd ed., 344.

50. Ibid.

51. Qutb, *Social Justice in Islam*, 278.

52. His commentary on Suras 78–114 is available online at www.youngmuslims.ca/online_library/tafsir/syed_qutb/ (accessed 14 February 2014).

53. Qutb, *Milestones*. The entire book is available on the web at http://web.youngmuslims.ca/online_library/books/milestones/hold/index_2.htm (accessed 15 February 2014).

54. www.youngmuslims.ca/online_library/books/milestones/hold/chapter_4.htm (accessed 15 February 2014).

55. For an excellent summary of his life and work, see Denny, *An Introduction to Islam*, 3rd ed., 348–51.

56. The Council on American-Islamic Relations (CAIR). www.cair.com/islamophobia/our-vision.html (accessed February 22, 2014)

57. The Runnymede Trust (1997), a British think tank, included these among eight components of Islamophobia, www.runnymedetrust.org/uploads/publications/pdfs/islamophobia.pdf (accessed February 22, 2014).

58. Alex Altman, "TIME Poll: Majority Oppose Mosque, Many Distrust Muslims," *Time*, http://content.time.com/time/nation/article/0,8599,2011799,00.html

59. Jack Shaheen, "Islamophobia: Anatomy of an American Panic," *The Nation*, July 2–9, 2012. Also available at www.thenation.com/issue/july-2-9-2012 (accessed February 22, 2014).

60. Laila Lalami, "Islamophobia and Its Discontents," *The Nation*, July 2–9, 2012.

61. "Fear, Inc.," by the Center for American Progress, and "Same Hate, New Target," by CAIR. www.americanprogress.org/wp-content/uploads/issues/2011/08/pdf/ (accessed February 22, 2014); http://pa.cair.com/islamophobia/cair-report/ (accessed February 22, 2014).

62. "Fear, Inc.," by the Center for American Progress.

63. Ibid.

64. These ads were sponsored by a Zionist organization, the American Freedom Defense Initiative, http://freedomdefense.typepad.com/ (accessed 12 February 2014).

65. http://Courseweb.stthomas.edu/justpeace/Rowman.html (accessed 16 March 2014).

66. Nasr, "Reflections on Islam and the West," in *Islam in Transition*, 374.

67. Ibid., 376.

68. Ibid., 377.

69. Borelli, "Christian-Muslim Relations in the United States," 326–27.

70. Esposito, *Islam: The Straight Path*, 4th ed., 281. See also the article by Hans Küng, director of the Institute for Ecumenical Research at the University of Tübingen in Germany: http://www.religion-online.org/showarticle.asp?title = 1920 (accessed 14 February 2014).

71. https://www.stthomas.edu/mcdc/ (accessed 14 February 2014).

72. Banerjee, *The Pathan Unarmed*, for example 5–9, 193–205.

73. http://louisville.edu/artsandsciences/about/hallofhonor/inductees/riffat-hassan (accessed January 2, 2014)].

74. Published in *New Blackfriars* (February 1990).

75. Published in Gordon and Grob, *Education for Peace*.

76. Fatima Mernissi and Chandra Muzaffar are discussed in the "Islam" chapter in Berndt, *Non-Violence in the World Religions*.

77. Berndt, *Non-Violence*, 69–71. See also her website at http://www.mernissi.net/ (accessed 14 February 2014).

78. Fatima Mernissi, *Journalistes Marocaines: Generation dialogue* (Rabat, Morocco: Marsam, 2012). See Oxford Islamic Studies, "Mernissi, Fatema," www.oxfordislamicstudies.com/article/opr/t236/e0527 (accessed 14 February 2014).

79. http://www.just-international.org/about-us/ (accessed 12 February 2014). See also a number of Muzaffar's articles by doing a search for Chandra Muzaffar at https://www.transcend.org/tms/search/ (accessed 12 February 2014).

80. "Islamic Belief, Law, and Practice," PBS *Frontline*, http://www.pbs.org/wgbh/pages/frontline/shows/muslims/themes/beliefs.html (accessed 15 February 2014).

CHAPTER 6: NATIVE AMERICAN WORLDVIEWS

1. The Great Vision of Black Elk, from *Black Elk Speaks*, 22.

2. Boyd, *Rolling Thunder*.

3. Carmody and Brink, *Ways to the Center*, 82–83.

4. An official website can be seen at www.virgendeguadalupe.org.mx (accessed 19 February 2014).

5. Carmody and Brink, *Ways to the Center*, 81.

6. See "The Maya Collapses," chap. 5 in Diamond, *Collapse*, 157–77.

7. http://www.ezln.org/english/; http://enlacezapatista.ezln.org.mx/n; http://zeztainternazional.ezln.org.mx/ (all accessed 19 February 2014).

8. Zapatista Uprising 20 Years Later: How Indigenous Mexicans Stood Up against NAFTA "Death Sentence," http://www.youtube.com/watch?v = SllHjJjOx8A (accessed 19 March 2014).

9. Carmody and Brink, *Ways to the Center*, 84–85; Matthews, *World Religions*, 4th ed., 41–42.

10. www.aymara.org/ (accessed 19 February 2014).

11. www.zompist.com/quechua.html. If you would like to learn the Quechua language, check out www.ullanta.com/quechua/#about (both accessed 19 February 2014).

12. Many sources give the amount as $170, based apparently on "a misprint in Angi Debo's *The Rise and Fall of the Choctaw Nation*"; http://en.wikipedia.org/wiki/Choctaw#Pre-Civil_War_.281840. 29 (accessed 19 February 2014).

13. Matthews, *World Religions*, 4th ed., 29–30.

14. Carmody and Brink, *Ways to the Center*, 44–46.

15. Wikipedia, "Plymouth Colony," http://en.wikipedia.org/wiki/Plymouth_Colony#Early_relations_with_the_Native_Americans

16. Mason, *A Brief History of the Pequot War*, 29–30.

17. Ibid., 44.

18. http://www.pilgrimhallmuseum.org/ap_king_philip_war.htm (accessed 19 March 2014).

19. www.iroquoisdemocracy.pdx.edu/ (accessed 19 March 2014).

20. www.d.umn.edu/cla/faculty/tbacig/studproj/a1041/siouxup/ (accessed 19 February 2014).

21. Van Voorst, *RELG*, 44.

22. http://clio.missouristate.edu/lburt/Resources510/WoundedKnee_2.htm (accessed 19 March 2014).

23. Carmody and Brink, *Ways to the Center*, 81.

24. See, for example, http://www.sacred-texts.com/nam/index.htm (accessed 19 March 2014).

25. Matthews, *World Religions*, 27.

26. Van Voorst, *RELG*, 47.

27. Van Voorst, *RELG*, 48; Carmody and Brink, *Ways to the Center*, 50.

28. Bryde, *Modern Indian Psychology*, 26–30 (five characteristics). See a brief description of his life and character at http://www.lakotacountrytimes.com/news/2009-08-04/voices/012.html (accessed 16 March 2014).

29. Ibid., 31–38 (bravery).

30. Ibid., 39–51 (individual freedom).

31. Ibid., 52–61 (generosity and sharing).

32. Ibid., 62–75 (adjustment to nature).

33. Ibid., 76 and following (good advice from Indian wisdom).

34. Steltenkamp, *Nicholas Black Elk*, Kindle location 2727.

35. Weyler, *Blood of the Land*, 39.

36. Churchill, *The COINTELPRO Papers*.

37. Weyler, *Blood of the Land*, 78.

38. The text of the treaty is available at http://digital.library.okstate.edu/Kappler/Vol2/treaties/sio0998.htm (accessed 19 March 2014).

39. Weyler, *Blood of the Land*, 95.

40. Wikipedia, "Treaty of Fort Laramie," http://en.wikipedia.org/wiki/Treaty_of_Fort_Laramie_%281868%29

41. Weyler, *Blood of the Land*, 123.

42. "Christian Doctrine and Dehumanization," http://nativeamericannetroots.net/diary/491 (accessed 20 February 2014).

43. http://ftp.columbia.edu/itc/history/baker/w3630/edit/johnmintosh.html (accessed 19 March 2014).

44. Fisher, *Living Religions*, 5th ed., 54–55, 62; Eades, "Belief Systems and Religious Organizations," in chapter 6 of *The Yoruba Today*, http://lucy.ukc.ac.uk/yorubat/yt.html (accessed 17 February 2014).

45. The "Premier Edition" of 2008 has marginal notes comparing Neihardt's text of *Black Elk Speaks* with the oral interview notes.

46. Steltenkamp, *Black Elk: Holy Man of the Oglala*; Steltenkamp, *Nicholas Black Elk: Medicine Man, Missionary, Mystic*.

47. Tinker, *Missionary Conquest: The Gospel and Native American Cultural Genocide*, and *American Indian Liberation: A Theology of Sovereignty*.

48. Holler, *The Black Elk Reader*.

49. Steltenkamp, *Nicholas Black Elk: Medicine Man, Missionary, Mystic*.

50. Costello, *Black Elk: Colonialism and Lakota Catholicism*.

51. See, for example, sections from de Las Casas at "Bartholomé de Las Casas, Brief Account of the Devastation of the Indies (1542)," http://www.swarthmore.edu/SocSci/bdorsey1/41docs/02-las.html (accessed 19 March 2014). See also "The Man, The Issues," www.lascasas.org/manissues.htm (accessed 19 February 2014).

52. "Bartholomé de Las Casas," www.lascasas.org (accessed 19 February 2014).

53. "White Earth Land Recovery Project," www.nativeharvest.com/ (accessed 19 February 2014).

54. "Indigenous Women's Network," www.indigenouswomen.org/ (accessed 19 February 2014).

55. "Honor the Earth," www.honorearth.org/ (accessed 19 March 2014). For further information on LaDuke, see "Winona LaDuke," http://en.wikipedia.org/wiki/Winona_LaDuke (accessed 19 February 2014).

56. With regard to the radical transformations that our declining inexpensive energy will force on us, see Heinberg, *The Party's Over* and *Power Down*.

57. Royte, *Bottlemania*.

CHAPTER 7: MARXIST WORLDVIEWS

1. Marx, *The Communist Manifesto*, 69–70. Used by permission of W. W. Norton.

2. "Die Philosophen haben die Welt nur verschieden *interpretiert,* es kömmt drauf an, sie zu *verändern*," http://www.marxists.org/deutsch/archiv/marx-engels/1845/thesen/thesfeue-or.htm (accessed 17 March 2014).

3. For very extensive documentation, see "Marxists' Internet Archive," www.marxists.org/ and www.marx.org/ (accessed 17 March 2014). Note that this site was under periodic hostile attack in 2006 and 2007.

4. For a description of how a "power elite" consisting of perhaps a half of one percent of Americans effectively controls American politics, economy, and media, see Domhoff, *Who Rules America?*

5. Pope John Paul II, *Laborem Exercens* (*On Human Work*), par. 14.

6. Domhoff, *Changing the Powers That Be: How the Left Can Stop Losing and Win.*

7. www.aflcio.org/Corporate-Watch/ (accessed 17 March 2014).

8. Pope John Paul II, *Sollicitudo Rei Socialis*, par. 15, 20–21, 41.

9. Pope Francis, *Evangelii Gaudium*, par. 53.

10. Pope Benedict XVI, "Message for the Celebration of the World Day of Peace: 1 January 2013," par. 1. Accessible at http://www.vatican.va/holy_father/benedict_xvi/messages/peace/documents/hf_ben-xvi_mes_20121208_xlvi-world-day-peace_en.html (accessed 17 March 2014).

11. See his article "A Structural Theory of Imperialism," *Journal of Peace Research*, 8:2 (1971): 81–117; also available at http://www.jstor.org/stable/422946 (accessed 19 March 2014). See also his book *Peace by Peaceful Means*, Oslo/London: PRIO/SAGE, 1996, and the website *Transcend: Peace and Development Network*, http://www.transcend.org/ (accessed 19 March 2014).

12. Wikipedia, "Persecution of Christians in the Soviet Union," http://en.wikipedia.org/wiki/Persecution_of_Christians_in_the_Soviet_Union#World_War_II_rapprochement (accessed 24 February 2014).

13. Lobaczewski, *Political Ponerology*, Kindle locations 1868–70.

14. Douglass, *JFK and the Unspeakable*, 25–28.

15. Fisher, *Living Religions*, 205, 209; Carmody and Brink, *Ways to the Center*, 192.

16. Carmody and Brink, *Ways to the Center*, 192.

17. Fisher, *Living Religions*, 210, 213.

18. Wikipedia, "Communist Party of China," http://en.wikipedia.org/wiki/Communist_Party_of_China (accessed 21 February 2014).

19. Wikipedia, "Religion in North Korea," http://en.wikipedia.org/wiki/Religion_in_North_Korea (accessed January 6, 2014).

20. Documentary film *The Revolution Will Not Be Televised* (directed by Irish filmmakers Kim Bartley and Donnacha Ó Briain, 2003).

21. See Heinberg, *The Party's Over* and *Power Down*.

22. See Diamond, *Collapse*.

23. Wikipedia, "Marxism and Religion," http://en.wikipedia.org/wiki/Marxism_and_religion (accessed 24 February 2014).

24. Wikipedia, "Persecution of Christians in the Soviet Union," http://en.wikipedia.org/wiki/Persecution_of_Christians_in_the_Soviet_Union (accessed 24 February 2014).

25. Wikipedia, "Religion in Russia," http://en.wikipedia.org/wiki/Religion_in_Russia (accessed 24 Feb 2014).

26. Yang, *Religion in China*, Kindle locations 1047–49; 1059–1107; 1298–1300.

27. Ibid., Kindle locations 1049–50; 1108–50; 1300–1302.

28. Ibid., Kindle locations 1050; 1151–77; 1302–04.

29. Ibid., Kindle locations 1050–51; 1178–1225; 1304–30.

30. Ibid., Kindle locations 1214–15.

31. Ibid., Kindle locations 1344–45.

32. Ibid., Kindle locations 1357–61.

33. Ibid., Kindle locations 1376–77.

34. Ibid., Kindle locations 1322–30.

35. www.ifconews.org (accessed January 7, 2014).

36. According to Wikipedia, "The US embassy and consulates continue to maintain a staff of more than 20,000 including US Marine Embassy Guards and between 4,000 and 5,000 private military contractors." Wikipedia, "Iraq War," http://en.wikipedia.org/wiki/Iraq_War#cite_note-Denselow-331 (accessed 19 March 2014); the embassy covers an area roughly the size of Vatican City, and cost $750 million to build. See pictures at http://www.businessinsider.com/750-million-united-states-embassy-iraq-baghdad-2013-3?op=1 and their official website at http://iraq.usembassy.gov/ (the last two accessed 24 February 2014).

37. Leigh, "General Sacked by Bush Says He Wanted Early Elections."

38. *Democracy Now*, November 21, 2006, www.democracynow.org/2006/11/21/the_next_act_will _the_republicans.

39. Perkins, *Confessions of an Economic Hit Man*. See also Hiatt, ed., *A Game as Old as Empire*. Reprinted with permission of the publisher. All rights reserved. www.bookconnection.com (accessed 17 March 2014).

40. Perkins, *Economic Hit Man*, 6. Reprinted with permission.

41. Ibid., xvii. Reprinted with permission.

CHAPTER 8: THE ISRAELI-PALESTINIAN CONFLICT

1. *The Holy Qur'an*, trans. Yusuf Ali [1938; 1952], www.sacred-texts.com/isl/quran/index.htm (accessed 17 March 2014).

2. Theodor Herzl, Zev Jabotinsky. In contemporary international law, "transferred out" means "ethnically cleansed." See the end of chapter 12 for a definition and examples.

3. David Ben Gurion, many kibbutzniks. They also envisioned a state for Jews only.

4. Ahad Ha'am, Martin Buber.

5. Rabbi Avraham Kook, Gush Emunim, Women in Green. They model their "driving out," or ethnic cleansing, on Joshua's invasion of Canaan ca. 1300 BCE.

6. Neturei Kartai, the Jews of Mea Shearim. This position does presume that most modern Jews have lineal genetic ties to ancient Israel, which is highly disputed. These Jews are willing to live at peace with non-Jewish neighbors.

7. Uri Avneri, Gush Shalom, J-Street.

8. The International Jewish Anti-Zionist Network.

9. Many Israeli Jews.

10. The Hamas charter. Note that charters and political platforms tend to exaggerate their positions. It is likely that very few Palestinians hold a position this extreme.

11. The majority that gave Hamas a victory in the 2006 Palestinian elections.

12. Arafat, the PLO, Mahmoud Abbas.

13. Mustafa Barghouthi and many Palestinians who trust none of the current political leaders; http://www.almubadara.org/new/english.php (accessed 17 March 2014).

14. Many West Bank and Gaza Palestinians.

15. John Hagee, Hal Lindsay, *Left Behind* books.

16. Rachel Corrie, Nick and Mary Eoloff, U.S. Campaign to End the Occupation.

17. You probably know some.

18. Most U.S. federal legislators, neoconservatives.

19. Most Israeli premiers.

20. Most Palestinian politicians.

21. Ariel Sharon, some neoconservatives.

22. See the report of the UNESCO World Heritage Convention at http://whc.unesco.org/en/list/1393 (accessed 25 February 2014).

23. Sand, *The Invention of the Jewish People*, 183–85; Kindle locations 4542–88.

24. Ibid., 184; Kindle locations 4555f.

25. W. Khalidi, *Before Their Diaspora*, 32–33.

26. For a detailed description of the problem, see http://www.mideastweb.org/palpop.htm (accessed 25 February 2014).

27. "Chapter Three: The Invention of the Exile: Proselytism and Conversion," in Sand, *The Invention of the Jewish People*, 129–89.

28. "Chapter Four: Realms of Silence: In Search of Lost (Jewish) Time," in Sand, *The Invention of the Jewish People*, pp. 190–249. See also Hart, *Zionism*, 1:208–9.

29. See Shahak and Mezvinsky, *Jewish Fundamentalism*, 18–19.

30. http://www.jta.org/1931/08/20/archive/baron-edmond-de-rothschild-86 (accessed 25 February 2014).

31. Population estimates are notoriously difficult. See www.mideastweb.org/palpop.htm (accessed 10 March 2014).

32. Wikipedia, "Edmond James de Rothschild," http://en.wikipedia.org/wiki/Edmond_James _de_Rothschild#Zionism (accessed 26 February 2014).

33. R. Khalidi, *The Iron Cage*, 36.

34. His book, *A Historical Survey of Proposals to Transfer Arabs from Palestine 1895–1947*, is available on the internet at http://chaimsimons.net/transfer.html. See also his two imaginary scenarios if a two-state "solution" (1) is or (2) is not adopted, at http://www.freeman.org/m_online/jan04/simons .htm (both accessed 17 March 2014).

35. Quoted in http://chaimsimons.net/transfer03.html (accessed 10 March 2014), a section "Theodor Herzl," of Rabbi Dr. Chaim Simons, *A Historical Survey of Proposals to Transfer Arabs from Palestine, 1895–1947*. See footnote 55 in that work, namely "Theodor Herzl to Youssuf Zia Al-Khalidi, 19 March 1899 (CZA H iii D 13); Walid Khalidi, ed., *From Haven to Conquest* (Beirut, 1971), p. 92," which is available at http://chaimsimons.net/transfer32.html (accessed 10 March 2014). This article helped identify the following quotations as well.

36. All quotations are from Herzl, *The Complete Diaries of Theodor Herzl*, 90. Used by permission of Herzl Press.

37. Ibid.

38. The most influential of Herzl's writings, while going into great detail on the character of the "Jewish State" he envisioned, scarcely mentioned the indigenous population at all. See Herzl, *The Jewish State*.

39. www.jafi.org.il/education/100/concepts/aliyah3.html (accessed 17 March 2014); www.jewishvir tuallibrary.org/jsource/Immigration/Second_Aliyah. html (accessed 17 March 2014).

40. www.jewishvirtuallibrary.org/jsource/History/hussmac1.html#1 (accessed 17 March 2014).

41. www.lib.byu.edu/~rdh/wwi/1916/sykespicot.html (accessed 17 March 2014).

42. www.lib.byu.edu/~rdh/wwi/1917/balfour.html (accessed 17 March 2014).

43. www.mideastweb.org/mandate.htm (accessed 17 March 2014).

44. Quoted in "The Histadrut," in "A History of Israel: From Dream to Reality" at www.history central.com/Israel/1920HistadrutFounded.html (accessed 17 March 2014).

45. Quoted in "Palestine," *Encyclopædia Britannica*, from Encyclopædia Britannica 2006, Ultimate Reference Suite DVD (accessed June 8, 2006).

46. R. Khalidi, *The Iron Cage,* 31–33, 43–44, 47; www.wnyc.org/news/articles/898 (accessed 17 March 2014).

47. www.jnf.org/site/PageServer?pagename=history (accessed 17 March 2014).

48. Morris, *Righteous Victims*, 139.

49. The commission report is available at www.jewishvirtuallibrary.org/jsource/History/peel1.html (accessed 17 March 2014). See especially Section 10, "Exchange of Land and Population."

50. Morris, *Righteous Victims*, 139–44.

51. Flapan, *Zionism*, 116. He refers to Katz, *Days of Fire*, 31–37.

52. Wikipedia, "1936–39 Arab Revolt in Palestine," http://en.wikipedia.org/wiki/1936%E2%80% 9339_Arab_revolt_in_Palestine#Impact_on_the_British_Empire (accessed 28 February 2014); see also R. Khalidi, *The Iron Cage*, 107–8.

53. Quigley, *Palestine and Israel: A Challenge to Justice*, 26–27.

54. Quoted from the United States Holocaust Memorial Museum, www.ushmm.org/museum/ exhibit/online/stlouis//teach/supread2.htm (accessed 17 March 2014).

55. MidEast Web, "The Biltmore Program," http://www.mideastweb.org/biltmore_program.htm (accessed 17 March 2014).

56. Wikipedia, "The Hunting Season," http://en.wikipedia.org/wiki/The_Hunting_Season (accessed 28 February 2014).

57. MidEast Web, "Israel and Palestine, a Brief History, Part I," www.mideastweb.org/briefhistory .htm (accessed 17 March 2014). Most sources put Jewish ownership at 7 percent, not 8 percent as quoted here.

58. This is UN Resolution 181, available at www.yale.edu/lawweb/avalon/un/res181.htm (accessed 17 March 2014).

59. Report of UNSCOP—September 1, 1947. Available on MidEast Web at www.mideastweb.org/ unscop1947.htm (accessed 17 March 2014).

60. The full text of the majority report is available at https://www.jewishvirtuallibrary.org/jsource/ UN/UNSCOP.html. The minority report is available at http://en.wikisource.org/wiki/United_Nations _Special_Committee_on_Palestine_Report/Chapter_VII (both accessed 25 February 2014).

61. https://www.un.org/en/documents/charter/chapter4.shtml (accessed 25 February 2014).

62. Morris, *Birth of the Palestinian Refugee Problem Revisited*. See especially chapter 4: "The Second Wave: The Mass Exodus, April–June 1948," 163–308.

63. Ibid.

64. Ibid., 171.

65. Morris, quoted in "Survival of the Fittest," by Ari Shavit, *Haaretz*, January 26, 2004, http:// www.haaretz.com/survival-of-the-fittest-1.61345 (accessed 17 March 2014).

66. Pappe, *The Ethnic Cleansing of Palestine*, xv.

67. Ibid., xv, 263 n12.

68. Ibid., chap. 2; for quote, see p. 15.

69. Ibid., xvi.

70. Childers, "The Other Exodus," reprinted in *From Haven to Conquest*, 795–803.

71. Morris, *Birth of the Palestinian Refugee Problem Revisited*, 181. See the whole of chap. 4, 163–308.

72. Ibid., 237–40.

73. Pappe, *Ethnic Cleansing*, 90.

74. Morris, *Birth of the Palestinian Refugee Problem Revisited*, 238 and n566.

75. Pappe, *Ethnic Cleansing*, 91.

76. Begin, *The Revolt*, 164–65.

77. Truman's motives are highly controverted. See Cohen, *Truman and Israel*.

78. Pappe, *Ethnic Cleansing*, 9.

79. Wikipedia, "United Nations General Assembly Resolution 194," http://en.wikipedia.org/wiki/ United_Nations_General_Assembly_Resolution_194 (accessed 17 March 2014).

80. According to "Emirates News Agency," there are about six million Palestinians in Israel and the Occupied Territories, and another six million outside. About 44 percent of those in Gaza and the West Bank are refugees from homes in Israel. Most of the over five million in Arab countries are not citizens. Zawya, "Palestinian Refugees Make Up 44.2% of the Palestinian Population in Palestine, Says Statistics Bureau," http://www.zawya.com/story/Palestinian_refugees_make_up_442_of_the_Palestinian_popula tion_in_Palestine_says_Statistics_Bureau-WAM20131231190101729/ (accessed 17 March 2014).

81. "The Suez Crisis, an Affair to Remember," *Economist*, July 2006, http://www.economist.com/node/7218678 (accessed 17 March 2014).

82. Jews for Justice in the Middle East, *The Origin of the Palestine-Israel Conflict*, 14.

83. Peled, *The General's Son*, 43–47.

84. Available as appendix 1 (217–18) in Carter, *Palestine: Peace Not Apartheid*.

85. Ennes, "The USS *Liberty* Affair," in Mahoney et al., *Burning Issues*, 326–50; Hart, *Zionism: The Real Enemy of the Jews*, 3:79–112.

86. Quoted in Clifford, *Forging Swords into Plows*, Kindle locations 1788–93.

87. As of July 2012, according to the Israeli interior ministry. Wikipedia, "Israeli Settlement," http://en.wikipedia.org/wiki/Israeli_settlement (accessed 25 February 2014).

88. http://altahrir.wordpress.com/ (accessed January 9, 2014).

89. B'Tselem, "Restriction of Movement," http://www.btselem.org/freedom_of_movement/check points_and_forbidden_roads (accessed 25 February 2014).

90. https://www.middleeastmonitor.com/news/middle-east/8768-report-israeli-occupation-tortures -most-palestinian-prisoners (accessed January 9, 2014).

91. "The Israeli Committee against House Demolitions," http://icahd.org/the-facts (accessed January 9, 2014).

92. For a 641-page, heavily documented and illustrated book detailing Israel's techniques of control in the territories, see Ophir, Givoni, and Hanafi, *The Power of Inclusive Exclusion*.

93. See "When Settlers Attack," The Palestine Center, February 14, 2012.

94. See, for example, the 1980 UN Resolution 465, available as appendix 5 (pp. 235–36) in Carter, *Palestine: Peace Not Apartheid*.

95. Hersh, *The Samson Option*; Hart, *Zionism*, 3:194–95; Farr, *The Third Temple's Holy of Holies: Israel's Nuclear Weapons*, available at http://www.fas.org/nuke/guide/israel/nuke/farr.htm (accessed 25 February 2014).

96. Available as appendix 2 (219) in Carter, *Palestine: Peace Not Apartheid*.

97. Available as appendix 3 (221–30) in Carter, *Palestine: Peace Not Apartheid*.

98. Carter, *Palestine: Peace Not Apartheid*, ch. 3 (37–53).

99. http://www.yeshgvul.org.il/en/about-2/ (accessed 26 February 2014).

100. Bennis, *Understanding the Palestinian-Israeli Conflict*, 64. Israel Defense Forces estimate 700; Bayan Nuwayhed al-Hout names 1,300 victims; Robert Fisk and the Palestinian Red Cross estimate 2,000; Amnon Kapeliouk of *Le Monde Diplomatique* estimates 3,000–3,500. See Wikipedia, "Sabra and Shatila Massacre" at http://en.wikipedia.org/wiki/Sabra_and_Shatila_massacre (accessed 28 February 2014).

101. http://www.quora.com/International-Law-and-Legal-Institutions/Do-oppressed-people-have-a -right-to-resist-in-an-armed-fashion-according-to-international-law#; Dugard, John, "The Legal Status of Palestinian Political Prisoners" at http://www.un.org/depts/dpa/qpal/docs/2012%20Geneva/P2% 20John%20Dugard%20EN.pdf (both accessed 26 February 2014).

102. http://www.ifamericansknew.org/history/firstintifada.html (accessed January 10, 2014).

103. http://avalon.law.yale.edu/20th_century/hamas.asp (accessed 17 March 2014).

104. Interview with Khaled Mashaal in *Der Spiegel*, February 6, 2006.

105. Brilliant, "'Rabin Ordered Beatings,' Meir Tells Military Court," and "Officer Tells Court Villagers Were Bound, Gagged and Beaten. Not Guilty Plea at 'Break Bones' Trial." See also "General Assembly Security Council A/43/166 S/19537 25 February 1988 DOCUMENT S/19537* "Letter dated 24 February 1988 from the representative of Jordan to the Secretary-General," http://unispal.un.org/UNISPAL.NSF/0/CB4D8C6C519240EF852564050072199D (accessed 17 March 2014) and *New York Times*, "Israel Declines to Study Rabin Ties to Beatings," July 7, 1990, http://www.nytimes.com/1990/07/12/world/israel-declines-to-study-rabin-tie-to-beatings.html (accessed 17 March 2014).

106. Wikipedia, "Oslo Accords," http://en.wikipedia.org/wiki/Oslo_Accords (accessed 17 March 2014).

107. Text available at http://avalon.law.yale.edu/20th_century/isrplo.asp. Other important Mideast legal texts available at http://avalon.law.yale.edu/subject_menus/mideast.asp (accessed 17 March 2014).

108. A list of Palestinian suicide bombings is available at Wikipedia, "List of Hamas Suicide Attacks," http://en.wikipedia.org/wiki/List_of_Hamas_suicide_attacks (accessed 17 March 2014).

109. See https://www.jewishvirtuallibrary.org/jsource/History/hebron.html#3 (accessed 17 March 2014); Lazare, "Palestinians in Hebron."

110. Morris, *Righteous Victims*, 646–49.

111. Hart, *Zionism*, 3:282–85.

112. Bennis, *Palestinian-Israeli Conflict*, 53–54. For a projection of the Final Status Map showing what Barak was offering, see Foundation for Middle East Peace, http://fmep.org/maps/redeployment-final -status-options/projection-of-the-final-status-map-presented-by-israel-dec-2000/projection_final_status _map.gif/view (accessed July 2, 2006), and for maps in general on Israel-Palestine, http://www.fmep.org/ maps/all-maps (all accessed 17 March 2014).

113. Hart, *Zionism*, 3:285, 289.

114. Bennis, *Palestinian-Israeli Conflict*, 42. See also Morris, *Righteous Victims*, 660.

115. Hart, *Zionism*, 3:301–2.

116. Wikipedia, "List of Palestinian Suicide Attacks," http://en.wikipedia.org/wiki/List_of _Palestinian_suicide_attacks (accessed 27 February 2014).

117. Bennis, *Understanding the Palestinian-Israeli Conflict*, 5.

118. The following notes taken by Miguel Moratinos, the European representative to the talks, were leaked to the press. Israel said they were not accurate, and Israel was not bound to these views, www.jewish virtuallibrary.org/jsource/Peace/Taba.html (accessed 17 March 2014).

119. Carter, *Palestine: Peace Not Apartheid*, 152.

120. Bennis, *Understanding the Palestinian-Israeli Conflict*, 69–73.

121. Israel objects that the "barrier" is not a "wall" for the majority of its extent, but the Court used the term "wall," recognizing the disputed language and explaining it was "the term which the General Assembly has chosen to use and which is also used in the Opinion, since the other expressions sometimes employed are no more accurate if understood in the physical sense." http://www.icj-cij.org/docket/ index.php?pr = 71&code = mwp&p1 = 3&p2 = 4&p3 = 6 (accessed 27 February 2014). In this chapter, we will use several terms interchangeably. Note that the South African (Afrikaans) word "apartheid" means "separation."

122. "Israel's 'Separation Barrier' in the Occupied West Bank: Human Rights and International Humanitarian Law Consequences—A Human Rights Watch Briefing Paper," February 2004, hrw.org/ english/docs/2004/02/20/isrlpa7581.htm (accessed 17 March 2014).

123. http://www.icj-cij.org/docket/index.php?pr = 71&code = mwp&p1 = 3&p2 = 4&p3 = 6 (accessed 27 February 2014).

124. The official English-language website of the Geneva Initiative is http://www.geneva-accord.org/ (accessed 17 March 2014). The full text of the Accord is at http://www.geneva-accord.org/mainmenu/ english (accessed 17 March 2014). For results of various recent polls of Israeli and Palestinian attitudes toward this proposal in general and in detail, see http://www.geneva-accord.org/mainmenu/joint-polls/ (accessed 17 March 2014). In 2003, Phyllis Bennis regarded the Geneva Accord position on right of return to be ambiguous; see www.endtheoccupation.org/article.php?id = 306 (accessed 17 March 2014).

125. Mike Whitney, "Embalming the Peace Process," *Z-net*, October 15, 2004. See also Wikipedia, "Dov Weissglass," http://en.wikipedia.org/wiki/Dov_Weissglass (accessed 17 March 2014).

126. Oxfam, "Fishing under Fire in Gaza," http://blogs.oxfam.org/en/blogs/12-11-28-fishing-under -fire-gaza (accessed 27 February 2014).

127. Gideon Levy, "Bring Back Kfar Darom," *Haaretz* 19, November 2006, http://www.haaretz.com/ print-edition/opinion/bring-back-kfar-darom-1.205472.

128. http://www.breakingthesilence.org.il/testimonies/publications (accessed 28 February 2014).

129. Justice Goldstone came under fierce attack as a result of this report. A year or so later, he stated that he would have written the report differently if he had been aware of Israel's side of the story (Israel had refused to cooperate in the research for the report) and that Israel did not intentionally target civilians as a matter of policy. But the other authors of the report refused to change their conclusions. See Wikipedia, "United Nations Fact-Finding Mission on the Gaza Conflict," http://en.wikipedia.org/wiki/ United_Nations_Fact_Finding_Mission_on_the_Gaza_Conflict#Goldstone.27s_statement (accessed 28 February 2014).

130. Wikipedia, "Gaza Freedom Flotilla," http://en.wikipedia.org/wiki/Gaza_Freedom_Flotilla (accessed 28 February 2014).

131. *The Guardian*, 7 January 2009.

132. Alan Hart at www.AlanHart.net, 15 November 2012 (accessed 10 January 2014).

133. Zvi Bar'el, "Report: Meshal Says Hamas Accepts a Two-State Solution," http://www.haaretz .com/news/diplomacy-defense/report-meshal-says-hamas-accepts-a-two-state-solution.premium-1.5003 90 (accessed 27 February 2014).

134. Wikipedia, "List of Political Parties in Israel," http://en.wikipedia.org/wiki/List_of_politi cal_parties_in_Israel (accessed 28 February 2014). In the "parties with Knesset seats" diagram, click on a particular party for details of its electoral history.

135. http://avalon.law.yale.edu/20th_century/hamas.asp (accessed 18 March 2014).

136. Excerpts from the 'Peace & Security' chapter of the Likud Party platform, www.knesset.gov.il/ elections/knesset15/elikud_m.htm (accessed February 5, 2007, since taken down).

137. Wikipedia, "Kadima," en.wikipedia.org/wiki/Kadima (accessed 17 March 2014). See also the official Kadima website at www.kadimasharon.co.il/11-en/index.aspx (accessed February 25, 2007).

138. The Kairos Palestine website is http://www.kairospalestine.ps/. The document is available in pdf format at http://www.kairospalestine.ps/sites/default/Documents/English.pdf (both accessed 17 March 2014).

139. http://kairosusa.org/ (accessed 27 February 2014).

140. http://kairosusa.org/wp-content/uploads/2013/12/Kairos-USA-Call-to-Action.pdf (accessed 27 February 2014).

141. After a period of minimal progress toward a just peace, other countries are beginning to put pressure on the Israeli government. An energetic movement has developed promoting BDS: boycott, divestment, and sanctions, similar to the movement that helped end apartheid in South Africa.

142. Lustick, "Two-State Illusion."

143. http://adalah.org/eng/category/95/About/1/0/0/ (accessed 27 February 2014); Shahak, *Israeli Discrimination against Non-Jews*.

144. "One State, Two States, Three States," chapter 16 in Peled, *The General's Son*.

145. http://courseweb.stthomas.edu/justpeace/rowman.html (accessed 17 March 2014).

146. Qumsiyeh, *Popular Resistance in Palestine*.

147. Kaufman-Lacusta, *Refusing to Be Enemies*.

148. http://zope.gush-shalom.org/index_en.html (accessed 27 February 2014).

149. http://zope.gush-shalom.org/index_en.html (accessed 17 March 2014).

150. http://www.almubadara.org/new/english.php (accessed 27 February 2014).

151. Olson, *Fast Times in Palestine*, 175, 182–83, 195.

152. www.cnn.com/2011/09/21/opinion/opinion-mustafa-barghouthi/index.html (accessed January 10, 2014).

153. His Mar Elias Educational Institutions are supported by a U.S. organization called "Pilgrims of Ibillin," http://www.pilgrimsofibillin.org/ (accessed 18 March 2014).

154. See the website of the Melkite Greek Catholic Church Information Center at www.mliles.com/ melkite/abounaeliaschacour.shtml (accessed 17 March 2014).

155. http://palsolidarity.org/ (accessed 17 March 2014).

156. https://m.facebook.com/ismpalestine?v = info&expand = 1 (accessed 17 March 2014). This is the official Facebook page of ISM.

157. http://www.metapeaceteam.org/#!teams/c8k2 (accessed 17 March 2014).

158. www.cpt.org/ (accessed 17 March 2014).

159. http://www.whywerefuse.org/[2010web] (accessed 27 February 2014).

160. See their combined website (Refuser Solidarity Network) at http://www.refusersolidarity.net/ (accessed 27 February 2014).

161. http://www.refusingtokill.net/Israel/ShaulMograbiBerger.htm (accessed 27 February 2014).

162. https://www.facebook.com/c4peace. The quotation is from https://www.facebook.com/c4peace/ info (both accessed 17 March 2014). For news about conscientious objectors around the world, see http://www.refusingtokill.net/refusingtokillintro.htm (accessed 27 February 2014).

163. www.breakingthesilence.org.il (accessed 27 February 2014).

164. Breaking the Silence, *Our Harsh Logic: Israeli Soldiers' Testimonies from the Occupied Territories, 2000–2010.*

CHAPTER 9: RELIGIOUS SOCIAL TEACHINGS

1. The translations of papal and council documents are from the Vatican website at www.vatican.va (accessed 18 March 2014).

2. Texts of the Catholic Church documents mentioned in this chapter are available on the Vatican website at http://www.vatican.va/phome_en.htm. Click on "Supreme Pontiffs" on the upper right to access encyclicals organized under the pope's name (Encyclicals of the current pope, Francis, are posted separately at http://www.vatican.va/holy_father/francesco/encyclicals/index_en.htm). Click on "Resource Library" at the bottom of the circle to access connections to documents of the Second Vatican Council (http://www.vatican.va/archive/hist_councils/ii_vatican_council/index.htm), and the Compendium of the Social Doctrine of the Church (http://www.vatican.va/roman_curia/pontifical_councils/justpeace/documents/rc_pc_justpeace_doc_20060526_compendio-dott-soc_en.html), all accessed 1 March 2014. You can also find the web addresses of these documents in our index: look under the "author"—Pope John, Leo, Paul, Pius, "Roman Synod of Catholic Bishops," or "United States Catholic Conference," etc.

3. Most official Vatican documents use "man" in the allegedly generic sense of man and woman. The U.S. Catholic bishops have urged the Vatican to introduce nonsexist language, but to date with no success. Rather than inserting a multitude of "corrections" in square brackets or [*sic*], we invite readers to make the appropriate adjustments.

4. Audience with ambassadors regarding financial reform http://www.vatican.va/holy_father/francesco/speeches/2013/may/documents/papa-francesco_20130516_nuovi-ambasciatori_en.html (accessed 1 March 2014)).

5. http://globalfellows.crs.org/resources/selected-quotes-of-pope-francis/ (accessed 1 March 2014).

6. National Conference of Catholic Bishops, *The Challenge of Peace.*

7. National Conference of Catholic Bishops, *Economic Justice for All.*

8. Gremillion, ed., *The Gospel of Peace and Justice,* 449.

9. Material from Galtung and from *Principles of Catholic Social Teaching* (electronic document) in OSJ Catholic Social Teaching (Office for Social Justice; Archdiocese of St. Paul and Minneapolis), http://www.cctwincities.org/MajorThemesCatholicSocialTeaching (accessed 18 March 2014).

10. Galtung, *Peace by Peaceful Means,* 131.

11. www.elca.org/en/Faith/Faith-and-Society/Social-Statements/Economic-Life/ and www.elca.org/en/Faith/Faith-and-Society/Social-Statements/Peace (both accessed 19 January 2014).

12. http://download.elca.org/ELCApercent20Resourcepercent20Repository/Economic_LifeSS.pdf (accessed 1 March 2014).

13. http://download.elca.org/ELCA percent20Resource percent20Repository/PeaceSS.pdf (accessed 1 March 2014).

14. The United Methodist Church's Social Principles, which have been published in *The Book of Discipline of the United Methodist Church* (2012), are available at www.umc-gbcs.org/social-principles/Preface (accessed 19 January 2014); some of the topics dealt with are The Natural World, The Social Community, The Economic Community, The Political Community, and The World Community (including a section on War and Peace).

15. See the Episcopal Network for Economic Justice at http://www.enej.org/index.htm and www.enej.org/resources.htm (both accessed 2 March 2014).

16. Episcopal Network for Economic Justice, *How-To Manual,* App. C., http://www.enej.org/pdf/How-topercent20Manual/Appendixpercent20C.PDF (accessed 2 March 2014).

17. Episcopal Network for Economic Justice, *How-To Manual,* http://www.enej.org/howtomanual.htm (accessed 2 March 2014).

18. See the Episcopal Peace Fellowship at www.epfnational.org/ (accessed 19 January, 2014).

19. Hood, *Social Teachings in the Episcopal Church*, 83, 85–89.

20. See http://www.episcopalarchives.org/cgi-bin/acts/acts_resolution.pl?resolution; eq2006-D020 (accessed 19 March 2014).

21. "For the Health of the Nation: An Evangelical Call to Civic Responsibility," at http://www.nae.net/images/content/For_The_Health_Of_TheNation.pdf (accessed 2 March 2014). See also "Policy Resolutions and Documents," at http://www.nae.net/government-relations/policy-resolutions (accessed 2 March 2014). Used by permission. An associated book of essays edited by R. J. Sider and D. Knippers was published in 2005, entitled *Toward an Evangelical Public Policy: Political Strategies for the Health of the Nations.*

22. www.pv4j.org (accessed 19 January 2014). "2014 GA Overtures" is in small yellow type under the first two title lines on the page.

23. www.fgcquaker.org (accessed 25 January 2014).

24. www.fcnl.org (accessed 25 January 2014).

25. www.mcc.org (accessed 25 January 2014).

26. www.goshen.edu/mqr/Dirk_Willems.html (accessed 25 January 2014).

27. Rahula, "The Social Teachings of the Buddha," 145.

28. Ibid., 145.

29. Ibid., 146–47.

30. Ibid., 147–48.

31. Shatz et al., eds., *Tikkun Olam,* 4–5.

32. Tamari, "Social Responsibilities of the Jewish Individual," 240.

33. For example, Taliqani, "The Characteristics of Islamic Economics," 229–30.

34. Tamari, "Social Responsibilities," 242.

35. Biblical Judaism allowed Jews to loan money at interest to Gentiles, but not to fellow Jews (Deuteronomy 23:20–21). For a fuller discussion, see http://www.jewishvirtuallibrary.org/jsource/judaica/eju_0002_0014_0_14120.html (accessed 18 March 2014).

36. Tamari, "Social Responsibilities," 249.

37. Ibid., 252, 254.

38. Chapra, "The Islamic Welfare State," 246–47.

39. Tamari, "Social Responsibilities," 244.

40. Taliqani, "The Characteristics of Islamic Economics," 233.

41. www.jewishpeacefellowship.org (accessed January 25, 2014).

42. http://mpf21.wordpress.com (accessed January 25, 2014).

CHAPTER 10: LIBERATION THEOLOGIES

1. Ratzinger, *Instruction on Christian Freedom and Liberation*, par. 57.

2. Gutiérrez, *A Theology of Liberation*, rev. ed., 17–18. Used by permission.

3. Some of the Medellín documents are available in Gremillion, ed., *The Gospel of Peace and Justice*, 445–76.

4. Gutiérrez, "Faith and Social Conflict," in *Liberating Faith*, 196–200.

5. Dawson, "The Origins and Character of the Base Ecclesial Community," in *Cambridge Companion to Liberation Theology*, 152–53.

6. Rowland, "Introduction," in *Cambridge Companion*, 6.

7. The new understanding is well explained in Galtung, "A Structural Theory of Imperialism." See also Domhoff, *Who Rules America?*

8. West, "The Bible and the Poor," *Cambridge Companion*, 163–64; Villa-Vicencio, "Liberation and Reconstruction," *Cambridge Companion*, 185.

9. Ratzinger, *Instruction on Certain Aspects of the Theology of Liberation.*

10. Ratzinger, *Instruction on Christian Freedom and Liberation.*

11. Hebblethwaite, "Liberation Theology and the Roman Catholic Church," *Cambridge Companion*, 216.

12. The "Personal Information" link at Leonardo Boff's home page, www.leonardoboff.com/, takes one to http://www.leonardoboff.com/site-eng/lboff.htm (accessed 5 March 2014).

13. Pope John Paul II, Letter to the Episcopal Conference of Brazil (April 9, 1986), "*siamo convinti, noi e loro Signori, che la teologia della liberazione è non solo opportuna, ma utile e necessaria.*" http://www.vatican.va/holy_father/john_paul_ii/letters/1986/documents/hf_jp-ii_let_19860409_conf-episcopale-brasile_it.html (accessed 4 March 2014).

14. Ferm, *Profiles in Liberation*, 127.

15. http://www.vatican.va/holy_father/john_paul_ii/encyclicals/documents/hf_jp-ii_enc_30121987_sollicitudo-rei-socialis_en.html (accessed 4 March 2014).

16. http://www.vatican.va/holy_father/john_paul_ii/encyclicals/documents/hf_jp-ii_enc_01051991_centesimus-annus_en.html (accessed 4 March 2014).

17. See Pope John Paul II, *Sollicitudo Rei Socialis*, par. 36.

18. http://www.sndohio.org/sister-dorothy/; http://www.theguardian.com/world/2013/sep/20/brazlilan-rancher-jailed-dorothy-strang-murder (accessed 4 March 2014).

19. http://archive.wfn.org/2005/12/msg00102.html. See also www.washingtonpost.com/wp-dyn/articles/A51511-2005Apr13.html (all accessed 4 March 2014).

20. McElwee, "With Vatican Doctrinal Czar, Liberation Theology Pioneer Reflects on Troubles," http://ncronline.org/news/theology/vatican-doctrinal-czar-liberation-theology-pioneer-reflects-troubles (accessed 5 March 2014). See also the interview with one of Ratzinger's classmates reacting to his election as pope: Spalding, "A Humble Intellect," http://www.renewedpriesthood.org/ca/page.cfm?Web_ID = 579 (accessed 4 March 2014).

21. http://ncronline.org/news/theology/pope-meets-liberation-theology-pioneer (accessed 4 March 2014).

22. Castagnaro, "A Theological 'Giant': An Interview with Gustavo Gutierrez," 16 October 2013, http://iglesiadescalza.blogspot.com/2013/10/a-theological-giant-interview-with.html (accessed 4 March 2014).

23. *Evangelii Gaudium*: Apostolic Exhortation on the Proclamation of the Gospel in Today's World (24 November 2013), http://www.vatican.va/holy_father/francesco/apost_exhortations/index_en.htm (accessed 4 March 2014).

24. See Cox, "Is Pope Francis the New Champion of Liberation Theology?" http://www.thenation.com/article/177651/pope-francis-new-champion-liberation-theology?page = 0,1 (accessed 4 March 2014).

25. Spadaro, "A Big Heart Open to God: The Exclusive Interview with Pope Francis," http://www.americamagazine.org/pope-interview (accessed 4 March 2014).

26. Ormerod, "Catholics and Pentecostals—A Shared Mission in a Globalizing World," http://webjournals.ac.edu.au/journals/aps/issue-12/catholics-and-pentecostals-shared-mission-globalis/ (accessed 4 March 2014).

27. http://thelordsranchcommunity.com/las-alas/ (accessed 4 March 2014).

28. http://www.lwctt.org/index.php?option = com_content&view = article&id = 65&Itemid = 151 (accessed 4 March 2014).

29. Main link: http://www.uniminuto.edu/inicio; radio: http://minutodedios.fm/inicio; university: http://www.uniminuto.edu/sistema_universitario; home construction: http://www.elminutodedios.org/en/news.html (all accessed 4 March 2014).

30. www.dnu.org/service/sanlucas.html (accessed 4 March 2014).

31. Shaull and César, *Pentecostalism and the Future of the Christian Churches*.

32. Ibid. (Kindle locations 1280–86).

33. Ibid. (Kindle locations 1287–91).

34. Castagnaro, "A Theological 'Giant.'"

35. Ateek, *Justice, and Only Justice*, 32–49.

36. Ibid., 68–70.

37. Ibid., 165–73, 187.

38. Ateek, *A Palestinian Christian Cry*, 12, 187.

39. Ibid., 47, quoting American Jewish psychologist Mark Braverman.

40. Ibid., 20–21.

41. Ibid., 8–14.

42. Ruether, "False Messianism and Prophetic Consciousness," 91–93.

43. Ruether and Ruether, *The Wrath of Jonah*, 246.

44. Ellis, "Jews, Christians, and Liberation Theology." See also Ellis, *Toward a Jewish Theology of Liberation*.

45. Farber, *Radicals, Rabbis and Peacemakers*, 213.

46. Ibid., 217–20.

47. Ellis, "Jews, Christians, and Liberation Theology," 144–46.

48. Ellis, *Toward a Jewish Theology*, 204–11.

49. Esack, *Quran, Liberation, and Pluralism*, 82–113.

50. Wikipedia, "Tablighi Jamaat," en.wikipedia.org/wiki/Tablighi_Jamaat (accessed February 2, 2014).

51. Berndt, *Non-Violence in the World Religions*.

52. Ibid., 60–63.

53. Esack, *Quran, Liberation and Pluralism*, 87–90.

54. Ibid., 90–94.

55. Ibid., 97, 101.

56. Ibid., 107.

57. Ibid.

58. Antonio, "Black Theology," 79–104.

59. Ibid., 98.

60. Cone, *Black Theology and Black Power*, excerpted in *Liberating Faith*, 188–191.

61. Antonio, "Black Theology," 81 (quoting Cone).

62. Johnson, "Imaging God, Embodying Christ: Women as a Sign of the Times."

63. Grey, "Feminist Theology," 106–7.

64. Ibid., 108.

65. Ibid., 108–10.

66. Ibid., 111–13.

67. Ibid., 116–17.

68. Wielenga, "Liberation Theology in Asia," 55–78.

69. Ibid., 55.

70. Ibid., 56–60, 65.

71. Ibid., 62–63, 67–69.

72. Ibid., 63–64.

73. Ibid., 69–70.

74. Gorospe, *Filipino Social Conscience*.

75. Lebacqz, *Justice in an Unjust World*, 155–56.

CHAPTER 11: ACTIVE NONVIOLENCE

1. Gandhi, *Young India*, November 1919, quoted in *All Men Are Brothers*, 88; also in Fahey and Armstrong, *A Peace Reader*, 173. Reprinted by permission of UNESCO, © 1958.

2. Gandhi, *Young India*, November 4, 1931, quoted in *All Men Are Brothers*, 91; also in Fahey and Armstrong, *A Peace Reader*, 174. Reprinted by permission of UNESCO, © 1958.

3. Gandhi, quoted in *All Men Are Brothers*, 97. Reprinted by permission of UNESCO, © 1958.

4. Gandhi, *Harijan*, September 5, 1936, quoted in *All Men Are Brothers*, 91; also in Fahey and Armstrong, *A Peace Reader*, 174. Reprinted by permission of UNESCO, © 1958.

5. http://www.ajmuste.org/ (accessed 5 March 2014).

6. Sharp, *The Politics of Nonviolent Action*, 16–23.

7. http://en.wikipedia.org/wiki/Use_of_torture_since_1948#Torture_in_modern_society (accessed 5 March 2014).

8. Sharp, *The Politics of Nonviolent Action*, xii–xvi.

9. Ibid., 79–81.

10. Cavanaugh, *Torture and Eucharist*, 1998.

11. Sharp, *The Politics of Nonviolent Action*, 300–301.

12. Bondurant, *Conquest of Violence*, 88–102.

13. Sharp, *The Politics of Nonviolent Action*, 402; www.danilodolci.org/en/biografia/; "Danilo Dolci, Vivid Voice of Sicily's Poor Dies at 73," *New York Times*, http://www.nytimes.com/1997/12/31/world/danilo-dolci-vivid-voice-of-sicily-s-poor-dies-at-73.html (both accessed February 9, 2014).

14. Archdiocese of São Paulo, *Torture in Brazil*, 1986. See http://www.usip.org/publications/commission-of-inquiry-brazil and http://www.bradoretumbante.org.br/historia/brasil-nunca-mais (both accessed 5 March 2014).

15. We are describing the Sebastian Acevedo Movement Against Torture. See Cavanaugh, *Torture and Eucharist*, 273–77.

16. http://vcnv.org/ (accessed 5 March 2014).

17. http://www.cpt.org/news/sott/archives/winter1999#pentagon (accessed 5 March 2014).

18. http://news.google.com/newspapers?nid=1917&dat=19890511&id=nGIhAAAAIBAJ&sjid=cIgFAAAAIBAJ&pg=1642,3044797 (accessed 5 March 2014).

19. Sharp, *The Politics of Nonviolent Action; Gandhi as a Political Strategist; Waging Nonviolent Struggle: 20th-Century Practice and 21st-Century Potential.*

20. Joron Pihl, "The Teachers' Resistance against Nazification of Norwegian Youth and Education during World War II," www.atelierpopulaire.no/wp-content/uploads/2012/04/Pihl-The-teachers-resistance-against-nazification-of-Norwegian-education-during-World-War-II.pdf (accessed 5 March 2014).

21. Fellman, *Rambo and the Dalai Lama*, 220–23.

22. Aho, *This Thing of Darkness*. The Larry Trapp case is also mentioned in Fellman, *Violence to Nonviolence*, 222–23, where he refers to a book-length study of the case: Watterson, *Not by the Sword*.

23. http://www.centerforchristiannonviolence.org/. See also some of his articles at http://www.lewrockwell.com/author/fr-emmanuel-mccarthy/ (both accessed 5 March 2014).

24. Solzhenitsyn, *The Gulag Archipelago*, 602–3. Reprinted by permission of HarperCollins Publishers.

25. Thoreau, Henry David. *Civil Disobedience* (Kindle locations 41–44). Public Domain Books. Kindle Edition.

26. "Eleanor Roosevelt," en.wikipedia.org/wiki/Eleanor_Roosevelt (accessed 5 March 2014).

27. www.ajmuste.org/ajmbio.htm (accessed 8 February 2014).

28. Ten Boom et al., *The Hiding Place*, 99. Used by permission.

29. Ibid., 238. Used by permission.

30. Quoted from her autobiography in http://www.thehenryford.org/exhibits/rosaparks/story.asp (accessed 5 March 2014).

31. http://www.aeinstein.org/ (accessed 5 March 2014).

32. www.nonviolenceinternational.net/who.htm (accessed 5 March 2014).

33. For an extended study of the tax resistance in Beit Sahour, see http://issuu.com/georgen.rishmawi/docs/tax-boycott-beitsahour. For a short video of the terrorist cows, see http://electronicintifada.net/blogs/nora/watch-long-trailer-wanted-18-true-story-bovine-resistance (both accessed 5 March 2014). For a comparison of violent and nonviolent strategies in the Palestine struggle, with special attention to Mubarak Awad and Beit Sahour, see Baker, "How to Fight Back." For an extensive history of Palestinian nonviolence, see Qumsiyeh, *Popular Resistance in Palestine*. For contemporary interviews with Palestinian nonviolent activists, see Kaufman-Lacusta, *Refusing to be Enemies*.

34. Wikipedia, "Shirin Ebadi," en.wikipedia.org/wiki/Shirin_Ebadi (accessed 5 March 2014).

35. www.peacepeople.com/?p=453; www.mideastshuffle.com/2013/11/29/mother-agnes-mariam-in-her-own-words/; www.lewrockwell.com/lrc-blog/mother-agnes-mariam-footage-of-syria-chemical-attack-is-a-fraud/ (all accessed 7 February 2014).

36. Quoted from Paige and Satha-Anand, eds., *Islam and Nonviolence*, 23–24. Used by permission. See also Satha-Anand, "Three Prophets' Nonviolent Actions: Case Stories from the Lives of the Buddha, Jesus, and Muhammad," in *The Frontiers of Nonviolence*, ed. Satha-Anand et al.

37. Olson, *Freedom's Daughters*, 27; www.womenhistoryblog.com/%202013/02/maria-stewart.html (accessed 7 February 2014).

38. Ibid., 29.

39. www.humanities360.com/index.php/the-womens-rights-movement-of-the-mid-19th-century-2 -66949/ (accessed 7 February 2014).

40. McDonald, "A Way of Life"; available at www.sgiquarterly.org/feature2005Apr-7.html (accessed 7 February 2014).

41. McAllister, *You Can't Kill the Spirit*, 21–24.

42. http://www.womeninblack.org/es/history; http://www.wloe.org/WLOE-en/information/peace/ webarchive.html (both accessed 5 March 2014).

43. Svirsky, Gila, *What We Need Now Are Women*, http://www.genderacrossborders.com/2011/01/ 28/what_we_need_now_women_svirsky/ (accessed 5 March 2014).

44. www.rawa.org/rawa.html (accessed 8 February 2014).

45. See Suzanne Persard, "A Woman Among Warlords: An Interview with Malalai Joya," www.huf fingtonpost.com/suzanne-persard/malalai-joya_b_4160220.html (accessed 8 February 2014).

46. www.nvdatabase.swarthmore.edu/content/liberian-women-act-end-civil-war-2003 (accessed 8 February 2014). Women, of course, are not the only nonviolent activists who work in groups. See the website for the international Nonviolent Peace Force—a coalition of groups using active nonviolence to promote peace: http://www.nonviolentpeaceforce.org/ (accessed 18 March 2014).

47. http://Courseweb.stthomas.edu/justpeace/Rowman.html (accessed 18 March 2014).

48. Wink, *Engaging the Powers*.

49. Ibid., 186–87. Used by permission of Augsburg Fortress.

CHAPTER 12: JUST WAR THEORY

1. Nobel Prize Acceptance Speech, Oslo, Norway, 10 December 1986. Available at http://www .eliewieselfoundation.org/nobelprizespeech.aspx (accessed 6 March 2014).

2. Aquinas, *Summa Theologica*, 2–2 Q 40, trans. Fathers of English Dominican Province; quoted in Holmes, ed., *War and Christian Ethics*, 107f.

3. Abou El Fadl, "Islam and Violence," 460–61.

4. Walzer, *Just and Unjust Wars*, gives an excellent overview. James Turner Johnson has written prolifically on historical and modern developments of the principles. Ramsey, *The Just War*, is a classic twentieth-century study. In *The Challenge of Peace*, the U.S. Catholic bishops applied the principles to nuclear deterrence and introduced a new principle, *comparative cause.*

5. A convenient collection of texts is available in Holmes, ed., *War and Christian Ethics*. See also Yoder, "The Career of the Just War Theory," 107.

6. Yoder, "The Career of the Just War Theory," 105–6, 110, 113, 116–22.

7. Rahula, "The Social Teachings of the Buddha," 147.

8. Our local Air Science detachment (U.S. Air Force) lent David a copy of Wakin, ed., *War, Morality, and the Military Profession*, written from a military point of view.

9. Wikipedia, "Enemy Combatant," http://en.wikipedia.org/wiki/Enemy_combatant (accessed 6 March 2014).

10. http://Courseweb.stthomas.edu/justpeace/Rowman.html.

11. Ibid.

12. Jewish attitudes toward these ten principles are taken from Clifford, *Forging Swords into Plows*, Kindle locations 2747–3091.

13. Muslim attitudes toward these ten principles are taken from Clifford, *Forging Swords Into Plows*, Kindle locations 3295–656.

14. www.responsibilitytoprotect.org (accessed 7 March 2014).

15. United States Conference of Catholic Bishops, "Statement on Iraq" (February 26, 2003) available at http://www.usccb.org/issues-and-action/human-life-and-dignity/global-issues/middle-east/iraq/statement-by-bishop-gregory-on-iraq-2003-02-26.cfm (accessed 7 March 2014).

16. Migliore, *Intervention . . . on the Iraqi Issue.*

17. Gregory, "Letter to President Bush on Iraq" available at http://www.usccb.org/issues-and-action/human-life-and-dignity/global-issues/middle-east/iraq/letter-to-president-bush-from-bishop-gregory-on-iraq-2002-09-13.cfm (accessed 7 March 2014).

18. Ibid.

19. We first saw this principle in National Conference of Catholic Bishops, *The Challenge of Peace: God's Promise and Our Response.*

20. National Conference of Catholic Bishops, *The Challenge of Peace*, par. 93–94.

21. Wikipedia, "Military Career of Ali," http://en.wikipedia.org/wiki/Military_career_of_Ali (accessed 18 March 2014).

22. Augustine, *City of God*, 19:7; emphasis added.

23. Augustine, *Reply to Faustus the Manichean*, book XXII; quoted in Holmes, ed., *War and Christian Ethics*, 64.

24. Galtung, *Peace by Peaceful Means*, 70–76.

25. Dennis Carroll, personal letter to David Smith.

26. Peled, *The General's Son*, 43–47.

27. "A Country Study: Iraq—Chapter 1—Historical Setting (Mark Lewis)—World War I and the British Mandate" (Library of Congress Country Study on Iraq), http://lcweb2.loc.gov/cgi-bin/query/r?frd/cstdy:@field%28DOCID; pliq0019%29 (accessed 18 March 2014).

28. Gregory, "Letter to President Bush on Iraq."

29. Aquinas, *Summa Theologica*, 2–2 Q 42 A 2, reply to 3rd objection, quoted in Holmes, ed., *War and Christian Ethics*, 107f.

30. A long-running deadly feud (1863–1891) between two families in West Virginia and Kentucky. Wikipedia, "Hatfield-McCoy Feud," http://en.wikipedia.org/wiki/Hatfield%E2%80%93McCoy_feud#Hatfields_and_McCoys_in_the_modern_era (accessed 7 March 2014).

31. Gregory, "Letter to President Bush on Iraq."

32. Grossman, *On Killing.* See also http://www.killology.com/art_trained_killing.htm (accessed 7 March 2014).

33. Gray, *The Warriors: Reflections on Men in Battle.*

34. MacNair, *Psychology of Peace.*

35. Hallock, *Hell, Healing, and Resistance*, 90.

36. "Iraq Water Treatment Vulnerabilities," available at http://www.gulflink.osd.mil/declassdocs/dia/19950901/950901_511rept_91.html (accessed 7 March 2014).

37. Geneva Convention 1979 protocol "Protection of Victims of International Armed Conflicts" Article 54. Available at http://www3.nd.edu/~cpence/eewt/ICRC1977.pdf, p. 25 of 151 (accessed 7 March 2014).

38. Gregory, "Letter to President Bush on Iraq."

39. https://treaties.un.org/doc/Publication/UNTS/Volume%2078/volume-78-I-1021-English.pdf (accessed 6 March 2014).

40. Ibid.

41. Wikipedia, "Raphael Lemkin," http://en.wikipedia.org/wiki/Raphael_Lemkin#World_War_II (accessed 7 March 2014).

42. http://www.un.org/ga/search/view_doc.asp?symbol=S/1994/674 (accessed 7 March 2014).

43. UN General Assembly resolutions 46/242, http://www.un.org/documents/ga/res/46/a46r242.htm and 47/080 http://www.un.org/documents/ga/res/47/a47r080.htm (both accessed 7 March 2014).

44. Stanton, "The Ten Stages of Genocide" available at http://genocidewatch.org/genocide/tenstagesofgenocide.html (accessed 6 March 2014).

45. William Rubinstein, *Genocide: A History*, quoted in Wikipedia, "Genocide," http://en.wikipedia.org/wiki/Genocide#Genocide_in_history (accessed 6 March 2014).

46. Wikipedia, "Native American Genocide," http://en.wikipedia.org/wiki/Native_American _genocide. For a contrary view, see http://hnn.us/article/7302 (both accessed 7 March 2014).

47. http://worldwithoutgenocide.org/genocides-and-conflicts/armenian-genocide (accessed 7 March 2014).

48. http://www.unitedhumanrights.org/genocide/armenian_genocide.htm and http://worldwith outgenocide.org/genocides-and-conflicts/armenian-genocide (both accessed 6 March 2014).

49. See Akçam, *A Shameful Act.*

50. http://worldwithoutgenocide.org/genocides-and-conflicts/holocaust and http://www.chgs.umn .edu/ (both accessed 6 March 2014).

51. http://worldwithoutgenocide.org/genocides-and-conflicts/cambodian-genocide (accessed 6 March 2014).

52. http://worldwithoutgenocide.org/genocides-and-conflicts/bosnian-genocide (accessed 6 March 2014).

53. http://worldwithoutgenocide.org/genocides-and-conflicts/rwandan-genocide (accessed 6 March 2014).

54. Prunier, *The Rwanda Crisis 1959–1994—History of a Genocide,* quoted in Catherine André and Jean-Philippe Platteau, "Land Relations Under Unbearable Stress: Rwanda Caught in the Malthusian Trap," *Journal of Economic Behavior and Organization* 34 (1998): 1–47.

55. http://worldwithoutgenocide.org/genocides-and-conflicts/rwandan-genocide (accessed 6 March 2014).

56. http://www.unitedhumanrights.org/2010/11/the-palestinian-genocide (accessed 6 March 2014). In a return to our starting point, "The United Human Rights Council (UHRC) is a committee of the Armenian Youth Federation."

Glossary

access roads. Roads connecting Jewish-only settlements in the occupied territories of the West Bank (and formerly of Gaza) to each other and to the state of Israel. Palestinians are not allowed to use the roads.

accommodation. One of the possible outcomes of a nonviolent campaign. Opponents "accommodate" activists' demands when they remain convinced that they are right and just (and the activists are wrong) but decide that maintaining their position is costing them more than it is worth.

action possibilities. The final step in the circle of praxis outlined by liberation theologians. *See also* pastoral plan.

'adl. Justice as *maintaining* equal balance proportionate to a person's potential and situation. In Islam, *adl* is to *ihsan* more or less as justice is to charity in Christianity.

Advaita Vedanta. The nondual final meaning of the Hindu scriptures: my atman is Brahman. That is, there is no real distinction between the atman of an individual human and Brahman. It represents one interpretation in opposition to others.

ahimsa. Nonharm to all living beings in Hinduism.

al-Aqsa Mosque. The mosque located on the southern side of the Haram al-Sharif (Noble Sanctuary) in Jerusalem. Muslim tradition connects it with the "farthest mosque" mentioned in the Quran and identifies it as the site from which Muhammad ascended to heaven after his "night journey."

Aleuts. The indigenous people of the Aleutian Islands, which lie between Alaska and Russia. They are one of the far northern or circumpolar tribes.

Al-Fatah. A Palestinian political party; the largest component of the Palestine Liberation Organization. "Fatah" is a reverse acronym based on the Arabic phrase for "Palestine National Liberation Movement."

alienation. The state of being separated from someone or something that one should be closely related to. In Marxist thought, industrial capitalism alienates workers from nature, the productive activity of their work, their product, themselves, and other workers.

Allah. [The One] God, creator and judge of the universe, who has sent the prophets, including those also recognized by Jews and Christians.

Allah (hu) akbar. A common Islamic exclamation, meaning "God is greater [than anything or anyone else]."

al-Nakba. "The catastrophe"; Palestinian term for the 1948 war between the Jewish and Palestinian inhabitants of British Palestine that resulted in the forced displacement of more than 750,000 Palestinians and the destruction of more than 500 of their villages, both in the area allotted to the state of Israel by the UN partition plan and in additional areas conquered by Israel in 1948.

al-nas. An Islamic (Arabic) term denoting "the people" as contrasted with "the (apartheid) state." They are sovereign, because Allah has entrusted creation to them as stewards.

Amalek. An ancient desert tribe that opposed the Israelites as they fled from Egypt through the desert toward the "promised land" (Exodus 17: 8–16). Two centuries later, God ordered Saul to utterly destroy them—man, woman, and child—in punishment for this opposition (1 Samuel 15). Some militant modern Jews compare opponents of the state of Israel to Amalek and support radical policies of attack or expulsion. *See also* herem.

American Indian Movement (AIM). A modern North American Native movement advocating native rights and compensation by the U.S. government for broken treaties and other historic injustices. It was targeted by COINTELPRO.

Anabaptists. Christians who, in the Protestant Reformation, held that infant baptism is invalid, and so insisted on re-baptizing adults who had been baptized in infancy.

anatman. Buddhist belief that there is no "atman" or eternal spiritual reality (in the Hindu sense) which could be the subject of the experiences of an individual human being.

animism. The belief that all natural material things—humans, animals, plants, rocks, lakes, and rivers—have souls, or a conscious, underlying spiritual reality.

Anishinaabeg. The name that Ojibwa or Chippewa Natives of North America use of themselves. It means "original people."

Anno Hegirae (A.H.). The calendric year counting from Muhammad's "Hegira," or flight from Mecca to Medina in 622 CE. Because the Muslim year consists of twelve lunar months, and thus is ten or eleven days shorter than a solar year, one cannot match AH to the Common Era (CE) or a year expressed in Anno Domini (AD) by adding 621 or 622 to a year expressed in AH.

antithesis. The second stage of Marx's dialectical theory of history. As society begins to change under the influence of new forms of production, new forces and ideas challenge the status-quo *thesis.*

Apache. Group of native tribes of the southwest United States, including the Navajo, with a large reservation in Nevada and New Mexico, noted for their warrior skills exemplified by their famous leaders Geronimo and Cochise. Navajo speaking their native language were used by the U.S. Marines in World War II in place of code for secret messages.

apartheid wall. Palestinian designation for what Israelis call the "security barrier" or "separation barrier."

Armageddon. The anticipated final battle between Jesus and his forces against Satan and his forces, described in the New Testament Book of the Apocalypse (The Revelation to John).

Aryan. "Noble People"—the word that light-skinned Indians (who invaded from the northwest and took control in India) used to refer to themselves.

Ashkenazic. Adjective describing Jews (and their culture) who were strongly influenced by Germanic and Eastern European cultures.

atman. The Self, the imperishable part of each human.

attitude. The just war principle relating to one's beliefs about and images of one's enemies or opponents: one should love one's enemies, seek to do them good, and regret the damage and suffering one is causing them.

authority. The just war principle regarding who is a legitimate leader to declare and lead a just war.

avidya. The ignorance or delusion that (in Hinduism) keeps us from realizing the true nature of reality: the unity of all things; and (in Buddhism) keeps us from realizing the four noble truths.

Aztecs. Central American native tribe leading an empire centered around what became Mexico City. They captured neighbors so that on a daily basis they could tear beating hearts out of living humans to keep the sun rising.

Baal Shem Tov (abbreviated Besht). "Master of the Good Name"—the honorary title of Israel Ben Eliezer, the Polish founder (died 1760) of eighteenth-century Hasidism. In a time of persecution and despair, he taught that personal piety, as expressed in prayer and joyful, ecstatic worship of God, is more important than intellectual study of the Torah and literal Torah obedience.

Balfour Declaration. Official letter from Arthur James Balfour of the British Foreign Office to Lord Rothschild, written in November 1917, declaring that "His Majesty's Government views with favour the establishment in Palestine of a national home for the Jewish people . . . [providing that] nothing shall be done which may prejudice the civil and religious rights of existing non-Jewish communities in Palestine."

baptism. The Christian sacrament of initiation by which one's sins are forgiven, one receives the gift of the Holy Spirit, and one is incorporated into the "body of Christ," that is, the Christian community.

Base Christian Communities. Small groups of people within a large parish, originally in Latin America, who discuss how the church and Christian faith should influence current situations, offer mutual support, and promote common action.

BDS. Boycott, divestment, and sanctions: a grassroots, now global campaign of nonviolent resistance to exert economic pressure on Israel until it treats Palestinian citizens of Israel equally, ends its illegal occupation of Palestinian territory, and complies with the right of Palestinian refugees to return to their homeland.

Berlin Wall. Fortified barrier separating East Berlin from West Berlin—part of the "Iron Curtain"—designed to prevent East Berliners from fleeing to the West. Begun in 1961, it was demolished in 1989.

Besht. Abbreviation of the Baal Shem Tov. *See also* Baal Shem Tov.

Bhagavad Gita. Story of the god Krishna and warrior Arjuna on the eve of an epic battle; part of the epic poem the *Mahabharata*.

bhakti. In Hinduism, devotion or faith expressed in the fervent worship of a personal god.

Bhoodan. A land redistribution program, promoted by Vinoba Bhave, involving voluntary donations of land to heal the wealthy of their slavery to money and to help the poor stand on their own feet with productive resources of their own.

bi-national state. A modern nation-state embracing two "nations," preferably providing members of both nations with equal rights and responsibilities of citizenship. Palestinians have largely preferred a bi-national state in Palestine, giving equal rights to Jews, Muslims, and Christians, but many Palestinians have come to accept two unitary states dividing Palestine, since Israeli Jews have largely insisted on their state being Jewish.

bodhi. Enlightenment. Applied to the "bodhi tree" under which Siddhartha Gautama attained enlightenment, and to "Bodhisattvas" who delay entry into nirvana so that they can help others to attain enlightenment; also related to the Buddha—the "enlightened one."

Bodhisattva. A person destined to become a Buddha who delays his or her own progress toward Buddhahood out of compassion for other living beings.

Bolivarian Revolution. The recent pattern of socialist leaders winning office through elections in various Latin American countries, exemplified by Hugo Chávez in Venezuela.

boom-bust cycle. Alternation between economic growth and economic crisis caused by the over-production resulting from a lack of central planning in capitalism.

Brahma (capital B). Creator god, early period of Hinduism.

Brahman (capital B). Power (capital P); the one source or ground of being in the universe—unborn, uncreated, eternal, unchanging—that manifests itself in the many gods of Hindu tradition.

brahman (lowercase b). Spiritual power (lowercase p); for example, the ability of a Brahmin to make sacrifices and prayers that would effectively control spiritual reality on behalf of those who ask for his help.

Brahmana. (1) Brahmin, a Hindu priest; (2) part of the Shruti, inspired traditions used by the Brahmins to regulate their ritual.

Brahmin. A Hindu priest; a Western form for the term Brahmana in its first meaning, and an attempt by Westerners to avoid confusion. In the Hindu caste system, Brahmins constitute the first (twice-born) caste.

British Mandate. The quasi legal basis for British colonial rule over Palestine from 1922 to 1948; on the whole during this period Britain favored Jewish interests in Palestine. *See also* Balfour Declaration; Sykes-Picot Agreement.

Buddha. "Enlightened One." The most famous Enlightened One was Siddhartha Gautama.

caliph. Successor to Muhammad as leader of the *umma.*

capitalism. An economic system characterized by private ownership and control of the means of industrial production.

capitalization. Gathering enough resources to build machines and factories.

caste. A Western term reflecting two overlapping Indian systems that distinguish humans by birth into categories of work and social standing that affect whom one can marry, associate with, and eat with. The system of *varnas,* or "colors," divides society into four major categories (*brahman, kshatriya, vaishya, shudra*); that of *jatis* divides society into hundreds of occupational groups. The "outcastes" are outside the system and marginalized from society.

categorical imperative. According to Kant, moral principles for decision making that avoid religious doctrine: treat other humans as ends, never as means; and act so that what you do could be a general law.

CELAM. Conference of Latin American Bishops.

checkpoints. In the Israeli-occupied Palestinian territories, barriers to travel staffed by Israeli police or military personnel that restrict passage based on a traveler's documents or other characteristics. Palestinians complain that the principles used are often arbitrary.

Cherokee. Native American tribe that adopted European dress and created a syllabary with which it published a newspaper. When gold was discovered in its territories in Georgia, members were forced to relocate to Oklahoma in violation of a ruling of the U.S. Supreme Court that upheld their rights.

Chiapas. Largely Mayan city and rural region in southern Mexico. Bartholomé de Las Casas was its bishop in colonial times. When the North American Free Trade Agreement went into effect in January 1994, a movement called Zapatista began to resist the agreement.

Chilam Balam. A sacred book of the Maya.

Christian Zionism. The conviction that, for Jesus to return as promised, the Jewish community must first return to the historic holy land, reestablish its rule there, rebuild the temple, and resume offering sacrifices. When Jesus returns, he will convert a large portion of the Jewish population. The rest will be annihilated in the final battle of Armageddon.

Christmas. Christian celebration of the birth of Jesus, expressing the belief that God became human in Jesus of Nazareth, thus connecting humans to God in a new and permanent way.

circle of praxis. A four-step approach to understanding and affecting the world: *insert* oneself into conditions of poverty and injustice, make a *(descriptive) analysis* of the power relations that cause such conditions, make a *normative (or theological) analysis* of what is desirable and undesirable about the current situation, and make an *action plan* to change the situation toward a better, more just one.

class struggle. A Marxist conviction that economic classes are naturally antagonistic; the working class (proletariat) must seize control from the ownership class (bourgeoisie). Liberation theologians do not believe that this is a necessary state of affairs, but do point out that the bourgeoisie in fact often takes advantage of its power to oppress the proletariat.

closed military zone. An area in the occupied areas of Gaza, the West Bank, and East Jerusalem that has been declared closed to Palestinians by military decree, ostensibly for security needs, but often actually as the first stage in appropriating the land for use by Jews only.

coercion. One of the possible outcomes of a nonviolent campaign. Opponents are "coerced" when they remain convinced that they are right and just (and the activists are wrong) and make every effort to maintain their position and their power but find that they are unable to do so because the people on whom they depend for support no longer give that support.

COINTELPRO. "Counterintelligence Program": a 1956–1971 secret FBI program designed to study activist political organizations in the United States and disrupt their activities, often by spreading false information and promoting dissension within the group. Its targets ranged from violent groups like the Weathermen and the Ku Klux Klan to nonviolent groups like the Southern Christian Leadership Conference of Dr. Martin Luther King Jr.

communism. According to Karl Marx, the final stage of the historical evolution of society.

Communist Manifesto. A short, 1848 book by Karl Marx and Friedrich Engels, laying out the program of the Communist Party.

comparative cause. The just war principle insisting that one must balance one's own grievances against the grievances of one's opponent. Only if there is a preponderance of justice on one side is that side justified in waging war.

conscientization. Becoming aware of how political, economic, and social forces, structures, and convictions affect people's lives, and how things got to be that way.

Conservative Judaism. A twentieth-century form of U.S. Judaism seeking a middle position between Orthodox and Reform Judaism.

constructive program. Gandhi's plan to build strong, self-reliant local communities in India, ending dependence on British colonizers.

conversion. One of the possible outcomes of a nonviolent campaign. Opponents are "converted" to the activists' point of view when they come to believe that the activists' positions are right and just (and they themselves have been wrong) and, as a result, change their actions to meet the activists' demands.

conversion of the head. Coming to see (understand) people and things as God sees them.

conversion of the heart. Coming to love people and things as God loves them.

corporative state. Pope Leo XIII's proposal that the political and economic structures of society itself should promote worker-management cooperation. Rather than representing geographic areas, legislators would represent economic, agricultural, industrial, and professional sectors of society, such as the steel industry. Fascist Italy established twenty-two such groupings. Pope Pius XI objected that the Fascist form did not conform to Pope Leo's intention.

counterfeit tradition. The deceptive values and principles *falsely* claimed by some people, especially psychopaths, to justify their actions—those who claim to hold them don't actually believe in them or act on them. Although these values and principles resemble widely held worldviews, they are distorted to lead ordinary people to support the leaders' self-interest. *See also* hidden tradition.

counting coup. Native American practice of showing bravery in battle by riding through a hail of arrows, touching one's enemy with a "coup stick," and galloping safely away.

covenant. Ancient Near Eastern form of political association between two or more kings and their people, usually one dominant and the other subordinate, adopted by God in God's relationship with the Israelite people.

Crusades. Early second-millennium CE Christian campaigns to seize control of the holy land from its Muslim rulers.

Cuban missile crisis. Standoff between the U.S. and the Soviet Union in 1962, when the Soviet Union installed medium range missiles in Cuba aimed at U.S. targets. Khrushchev withdrew them in consultation with President Kennedy, both leaders resisting pressure by their militaries.

Cultural Revolution. Movement in Communist China initiated by Mao Zedong to reestablish his authority, which he believed was being threatened by younger and more liberal leaders. He organized a "Red Guard" or militia of activist youth to purge "counterrevolutionaries." Intense struggles produced a disastrous purge of leadership.

cultural Zionism. A movement seeking to bring Jews to Palestine, not to create a Jewish state, but rather to restore and renew Jewish cultural and religious life in Palestine, where history, geography, climate, and other natural factors were regarded as most suitable to that project.

Dakota. Minnesota tribe, thirty-eight of whose members were hanged in New Ulm, Minnesota, in 1862, after an uprising protesting unfulfilled treaty obligations.

Dalits. The name that "untouchables" or "outcastes" in India prefer to use in reference to themselves—it means "oppressed."

Dalit theology. A form of theology inspired by Latin American liberation theology, developed in India by Dalits.

Das Kapital. Classic 1867 book by Karl Marx and Friedrich Engels, giving a communist interpretation of political economy and a critique of capitalism.

Day of Atonement. Yom Kippur, a day of fasting and atonement for sins, the last day of the Jewish ten-day New Year celebration.

Days of Awe. The ten days of the Jewish New Year celebration, beginning with Rosh Hashanah and ending with Yom Kippur.

decade of development. President John F. Kennedy declared the decade 1960–1970 as a time to bring poor countries closer to rich countries in economic development.

declared. The just war principle that requires one initiating a war to state clearly the grievances that are giving rise to the war and what the opponent could do to avoid war.

Deir Yassin. Palestinian village on the edge of Jerusalem committed to neutrality where an informal Israeli army massacred more than 100 villagers in 1948.

dervish. Persian term for one who seeks spiritual poverty for the sake of Allah. One group (the "whirling dervishes") seeks to induce ecstatic trance through stylized dance.

descriptive analysis. The second step in the circle of praxis outlined by liberation theologians. It uses economics, political science, psychology, sociology, and similar disciplines to explain the power relations that shape the current situation, and history to explain how the current situation has come about.

deva. Hindu term for a god or a powerful and good supernatural being.

dharma. (Buddhist) The totality of the Buddha's teachings.

dharma. (Hindu) Responsibilities or duties that one has because of one's place in the caste system.

dialectic. Marxist (and Hegelian) term for the three-stage process that produces historical change: thesis, antithesis, and synthesis.

dialectical materialism. Marx's term distinguishing his form of dialectic from that of Hegel: whereas Hegel thought that dialectic was driven by Spirit, Marx insisted it was driven by the material conditions of production.

Diaspora. Jews living outside Israel/Palestine. The term is also applied to Palestinians.

dictatorship of the proletariat. The transition period between capitalism and communism when workers take over the governance of society.

dilemma. The conflict caused when a single actor wants to achieve two incompatible goals.

the disappeared. People who have been arrested, kidnapped, or killed for political reasons by police, army, or a paramilitary or guerilla group, and whose bodies have not been found. Those responsible refuse to reveal where they are or to give any information about their situation.

discrimination. The just war principle requiring that only those who are actually causing or threatening unjust violence can be attacked. Such uninvolved bystanders as captured soldiers, civilians, children, and future generations must not be harmed.

dispensationalism. The Christian theology holding that God deals with humans according to different rules in different periods of time, usually seven, the seventh and last being the millennium.

dispute. The conflict caused when two or more actors want to achieve a single goal that cannot be shared.

dog strap soldier. A Native American warrior who attaches himself to a stake driven into the ground as a sign that he will not retreat in battle.

Dome of the Rock. The Muslim shrine, built around 691 in the Noble Sanctuary in Jerusalem, enclosing the rock from which Muhammad is believed to have ascended to heaven after his night journey in 620.

dukkha. In Buddhism, suffering that arises from attachment to and craving for what is temporary and passing.

Easter. The Christian celebration of Jesus' rising from the dead to a new state of existence that includes life in the body. It includes the conviction that faithful Christians will share a similar experience.

East Jerusalem. The Palestinian sector of Jerusalem, designated as such after West Jerusalem (previously Palestinian as well) became part of the state of Israel in 1948. Since 1967, East Jerusalem, which is part of the West Bank, has been illegally occupied by Israel.

economic hit men. Advisors who project unrealistic economic growth as a result of major investments in infrastructure funded by loans that must be used to hire U.S. construction firms, intended to keep Third World nations perpetually in debt and thus forced to supply their raw materials to the United States at bargain prices, to allow U.S. military bases on their territory, to vote as the United States directs in the UN, and in general to follow U.S. directives.

ecumenical deal. The notion that Jewish-Christian dialogue requires Christians to support the policies of the state of Israel as a condition for continuing the dialogue.

Eid al-Adha. The Muslim feast that commemorates Ibrahim's willingness to sacrifice his son Ismail to God. It is celebrated toward the end of the annual hajj to Mecca.

Eid al-Fitr. The Muslim feast celebrated at the new moon that ends Ramadan.

encyclical. A circular papal letter sent to all Catholic bishops of the world dealing with some problem of common interest to the Catholic Church.

Engaged Buddhism. A movement that uses Buddhist principles to justify and empower social action on behalf of justice.

enlightenment (Buddhism). Awakening to the true nature of the universe; the experiential discovery that everything is impermanent and that the four noble truths show the way to end suffering.

Enlightenment. Eighteenth-century movement that gave authority to reason rather than religious faith as the basis for understanding reality.

Epistle. Letter written to a group rather than to an individual, or understood to have relevance beyond the individual to whom it was addressed; early Christian epistles make up about a third of the New Testament.

ethnic cleansing. A purposeful policy designed by one ethnic or religious group to remove by violent and terror-inspiring means the civilian population of another ethnic or religious group from certain geographic areas.

Eucharist. The Christian celebration of the Lord's Supper—the final meal Jesus shared with his disciples before he was crucified—in which the elements of bread and wine are variously understood to be, or to signify, the body and blood of Jesus and the loving sacrifice of his death.

Evangelicals. Protestant Christians who emphasize personal conversion, the Bible as the sole religious authority, salvation through the death and resurrection of Jesus, the reality of miracles, and active efforts to convert nonbelievers and affect the larger society. Sometimes used as a less pejorative term for Fundamentalists.

exaltation. The raising of Jesus of Nazareth to a position of power and authority "at the right hand of God."

exploitation. Unjust employment of other human beings for one's own enrichment without fair sharing of the wealth.

extrinsic motivation. Reasons for engaging in an activity other than the natural results of the activity itself, for example, to receive a reward or to avoid punishment.

"facts on the ground." Infrastructure, such as settlements, constructed so as to promote one political reality (Jewish control of the West Bank) and make another impossible (a viable Palestinian state).

faqir. Arabic term for one who seeks spiritual poverty for the sake of Allah.

Fatah. *See* al-Fatah.

fiqh. Islamic jurisprudence developed over centuries by legal-religious scholars on the basis of the Quran, the Sunna, consensus, and analogical reasoning; thus fiqh is derived from but not the same as Sharia, which is regarded as "divine legislation."

five civilized tribes. Five Native American tribes of the east coast of North America (Cherokee, Chickasaw, Choctaw, Creek, and Seminole) that adopted many customs of the European colonists. Except for part of the Seminole nation that was never conquered and still lives in Florida, they were moved west to "Indian territory," mostly Oklahoma. The most famous of these moves was the "trail of tears" transfer of the Cherokee.

five pillars. The five key requirements for Muslims: shahada (profession of faith), salat (prescribed daily prayer), saum (fasting during Ramadan), zakat (annual tax on surplus wealth), and hajj (pilgrimage to Mecca).

Fundamentalists. U.S. Protestant Christians who, in reaction to liberal Protestantism in the early twentieth century, committed themselves to traditional articles of faith: the five "fundamentals" of biblical inerrancy, the Virgin birth, the physical resurrection of Jesus, atonement by the sacrificial death of Christ, and the Second Coming of Jesus.

Gaza Strip. One of the Palestinian territories occupied by Israel since 1967, it borders Egypt and the Mediterranean Sea and, with a population of about 1.7 million, has one of the highest population densities in the world.

Gaza withdrawal. In 2005, without consulting the Palestinians, Israel removed Jewish settlers and their supporting Israeli soldiers from Gaza, an area considered of less importance than the West Bank, so as to strengthen their hold on the West Bank settlements, which were considered more important.

Gemara. The sections of commentary which, added to the Mishnah (and generally printed as a margin around it), make up the Talmud.

genocide. The intent to destroy, in whole or in part, a national, ethnic, racial, or religious group.

ghetto. An urban area reserved (sometimes voluntarily, sometimes by force, usually protected by walls) for members of one particular ethnic or racial group. Originally used with reference to Jewish areas, it is sometimes used more generally of any poor urban section.

ghost dance. A Native American dance, based on visions received by the Paiute Indian Wovoka, reputed to give miraculous power to bring dead native warriors back to life, protect them from bullets, bury the whites, and restore the prairies.

Golan Heights. The western plateau of Syria overlooking the Sea of Galilee from which Syrian guns could control the border with Israel. It was captured from Syria by Israel in 1967, fought over in 1973, and is currently illegally occupied by Israel.

Gospel. An account of Jesus' ministry, teaching, death, and resurrection written to proclaim their saving value. The New Testament contains four Gospels.

Gramdan. A land redistribution program promoted by Vinoba Bhave involving voluntary donations of villages to their poor inhabitants to heal the wealthy of their slavery to money, and to help the poor stand on their own feet with productive resources of their own.

great leap forward. A Chinese communist centrally planned program to promote industrialization. When it failed, resulting in widespread famine, Mao Zedong launched the Cultural Revolution to reestablish his authority.

great tradition. A term that applies to all world religions. It refers to the form in which a particular tradition is taught by its most enthusiastic leaders and practitioners, developed by its major writers and apologists (propagandists), and contained in its sacred and classic texts.

Gush Emunim. "Block of the Faithful"—a group of Israeli settlers seeking to "redeem the land," or establish Jewish control in all of historic Palestine, which they believe God promised to Jews, by building Jewish-only settlements throughout the occupied territories and then expanding the areas those settlements control.

Gush Shalom. "Block of Peace"—a group of Israeli Jews and other supporters seeking a just and nonviolent settlement to the Israeli-Palestinian dispute. It supports a two-state solution within the borders determined by the 1948 cease-fire line that prevailed until 1967 (except for small, mutually agreed land swaps), with both nations sharing Jerusalem as a capital, and makes use of strong nonviolent activism to further its cause.

Hadith. Collections of noninspired but highly revered written traditions about Muhammad and his companions highlighting his words and actions.

Haganah. The quasi-official underground Jewish army established to protect and promote Jewish settlers in Palestine when it was under British control.

haggadah. Parables, homilies, and other narrative materials found in the Talmud. It contrasts with Halakhah—the legal or prescriptive materials.

hajj. The once-in-a-lifetime pilgrimage to Mecca and Medina required of all Muslims who can afford it by their own resources.

halakhah. Legal materials in the Talmud (and in the Mishnah).

Hamas. Islamic Resistance Movement—a Palestinian political party founded in 1987 whose original purpose was to establish a Palestinian state in all of historic Palestine. Since winning the 2006 Palestinian elections, it has governed the Gaza Strip.

Hanukkah. Jewish holiday commemorating the recapture and rededication of the Jerusalem temple by the Maccabees in 165 BCE after it had been desecrated by Syrian Hellenists of the Seleucid Empire. It celebrates the miracle that one day's supply of oil burned for all eight days of the original dedication.

Haram al-Sharif. Noble Sanctuary: the Muslim designation in Arabic for the Jewish Temple Mount in Jerusalem; on it are situated the Islamic Dome of the Rock and the al-Aqsa Mosque.

Harijan. "Children of God"—the name that Gandhi coined for the "untouchables" or "outcastes."

Hasbuna Allah. A common Islamic exclamation meaning, "God is sufficient for us" (that is, God is all we need).

Hasidism. Now a particularly conservative form of Orthodox Judaism. Its eighteenth-century founder, the Baal Shem Tov, emphasized ecstatic piety.

herem. A dedication to destruction applied to certain groups whom God directed the ancient Israelites to kill: man, woman, and child.

Hezbollah. "Party of God"—a Lebanese Shia political and militant movement, founded during the 1982 Israeli invasion of Lebanon, it seeks to end Western colonization of Lebanon (including Israeli occupation), punish war criminals, and create an Islamic government for Lebanon. It carries on numerous social, health, and educational activities.

hidden tradition. The *actual* values, principles, and goals that motivate deceptive actors such as psychopaths who, in order to gain the support of others, *falsely* claim to hold and be motivated by quite different values, principles, and goals, especially by popular, widely held worldviews but in distorted form. *See also* counterfeit tradition.

hijra (Hegira). The flight of Muhammad and the first Muslims from Mecca to Yathrib, renamed Medina, in 622 CE. It marks year one of the Islamic calendar, *Anno Hegirae.*

Hinayana. "Little vehicle"—pejorative Mahayana term for Theravada Buddhism. *See also* Theravada.

Histadrut. The Israeli Jewish "General Federation of Labor," founded in 1921, which also fills numerous social support functions. It is a mainstay of the Labor Party, owns numerous businesses and the largest Israeli bank, and at its high point counted about 85 percent of Israeli workers as members. It began accepting Palestinian members in 1959.

historical Jesus. A term referring to the first-century, Palestinian Jewish Jesus of Nazareth (then a tiny village in Galilee) insofar as he can be retrieved as a historical figure.

Holocaust. Nazi Germany's program during World War II to kill everyone within Germany and the territories occupied by Germany who had at least one Jewish grandparent. For this purpose, Germany constructed labor and extermination camps that made use of Jewish labor, killed the Jews in gas chambers, and cremated their bodies.

Holy Spirit. The Third Person of the Blessed Trinity of God, who came in flames of fire to the disciples on Pentecost and to their converts through the "laying on of hands," empowering them to spread the "good news" of the death and resurrection of Jesus of Nazareth in the face of lethal opposition with the help of numerous supernatural charisms (gifts of power).

Hopi. Native American tribe of the southwest United States noted for having largely maintained its traditional way of life under the pressure of European settlement.

ideology (Marxist). Explanations developed to justify (unjust) existing power relations and economic/political/religious structures.

ihsan. Justice as restoring balance by making up for a loss or deficiency; *ihsan* is to *adl* in Islam more or less as charity is to justice in Christianity.

iman. Right faith or belief in Allah.

imperialism. Control of weaker nations by stronger nations. In the modern period, control of nonindustrialized societies by industrialized nations through colonization or other means of exploitation, typically in search of cheap raw materials and new markets for manufactured goods.

Incas. Native American tribe that controlled an empire around Lake Titicaca in what is today Peru, Bolivia, and Chile.

incarnation. The embodiment of a spiritual being in physical flesh, usually human. Christians celebrate the incarnation of the Second Person of the Blessed Trinity (God) in the human being Jesus of Nazareth, who was thus both divine and human.

"Indian giver." One who freely gives what another member of the community needs, without fear of the future, knowing that, if the giver later experiences need, someone else from the community will meet their need. European settlers distorted the phrase to mean "give something, then take it back."

indwelling. A good spiritual being other than the soul living within a human being without violating its freedom. Christians believe that God—Father, Son, and Spirit—indwells faithful Christians.

Injil. Arabic word for "Gospels," generally referring to the entire New Testament, which Muslims believe was inspired by God but has been altered in its current form.

Inquisition. An effort to deal with religious dissent through judicial examination, trial, and punishment of those unwilling to repent, including capital punishment. As was also true in regular secular courts, torture was sometimes used in the examination.

insertion. The first step in the circle of praxis outlined by liberation theologians: one seeks to experience, firsthand or vicariously, the problem one wishes to alleviate.

inspired. The conviction that God is in some sense the author of Sacred Scripture (the Jewish and Christian Bible and the Quran). There is wide variation among churches as to the extent and form of that authorship, from word-by-word dictation to various forms of divine-human cooperation.

intention. The just war principle regarding the aims and goals of a particular war: restoration of justice and peace is regarded as acceptable—plunder and domination are not.

interim ethic. The notion that Jesus expected God to end this world soon with a general judgment, so that extreme demands could be made for the short time left. If he had realized that the world would continue for thousands of years, he would not have made such difficult demands in the Sermon on the Mount.

International Solidarity Movement. Palestinian movement founded in 2001 to resist the illegal Israeli occupation through direct nonviolent action, supported by international observers whose presence should reduce Israeli violence and result in the situation being reported to a wider public.

intervention. Third of the three major forms of nonviolent action, the other two being (1) protest and persuasion and (2) noncooperation. One intervenes by getting in the way of another's unjust action—by doing something that interferes with it.

intifada. "Shaking off"—Palestinian resistance to the Israeli occupation of Gaza, East Jerusalem, and the West Bank. The first intifada, from 1987 to 1993, was largely nonviolent on the Palestinian side. The second, from 2000 to 2005, made use of violence as well. Israeli repression of both intifadas was very violent.

intrinsic motivation. Reasons for engaging in an activity based on the natural results of the activity itself, for example, satisfaction at producing a good result that is helpful for others.

Inuit. Arctic Native American tribes of Alaska, Canada, and Greenland noted for avoiding conflict; they have organized themselves into the Inuit Circumpolar Conference.

Irgun. Under the British Mandate, unofficial underground Jewish strike force established to attack British police and government installations and Palestinian resistance to Jewish expansion.

Iroquois. Confederation of five Native American nations, noted for its influence on the U.S. Constitution.

islam. Arabic word meaning self-surrender to Allah (God).

Islamophobia. unfounded hatred and fear of Muslims and Islam.

Israel Defense Forces. The Israeli army, navy, and air force.

Jataka Tales. Stories of the Buddha's previous lives, used to inspire good behavior in Buddhists.

Jesus Seminar. A group of North American scholars dedicated to the "quest of the historical Jesus"; attempting to identify words and actions in the Gospels that Jesus is most likely to have said and done, they have characterized his person and purpose in various ways.

Jewish home. What the Balfour Declaration promised to Lord Rothschild. Some Jews interpreted it to be a state under Jewish control encompassing all of Palestine, but Britain clarified that, while it intended the home to be a safe refuge for Jews, it did not intend it to be the sole authority in Palestine.

Jewish settlements. Colonies constructed in Gaza, East Jerusalem, and the West Bank since 1967 that only Jews can inhabit. Connected to each other and to Israel by roads that only Jews can use, they are illegal under international law.

Jewish state. Ideally, a Western-style democratic state dominated by Jews, Jewish traditions, and Jewish customs, where Jews can live securely and practice their traditions without interference. For such a modern state to embrace all the territory that the Tanakh designates as promised to the ancient Israelites, most non-Jews would have to be transferred out, voluntarily or involuntarily.

Jibril. Arabic form of the angelic name Gabriel, who revealed the Quran to Muhammad and revealed to Mary that she was to be the mother of Jesus..

jihad. Striving in Allah's cause; it can refer to inner struggle or to armed struggle to defend Islam or to spread the conditions that allow for its faith to be embraced.

jihad, greater. The inner struggle within an individual to overcome one's evil inclination and to develop one's good tendencies.

jihad, lesser. The external struggle to overcome injustice and unbelief, particularly to overcome structures and forces that prevent humans from surrendering to Allah according to the revelations of the Quran.

mendicant orders. Medieval Christian religious orders of "beggars" who owned nothing but lived and worked in the cities, challenging contemporary ideas about riches.

messiah. In Judaism and Christianity, God's anointed one sent to rescue or save oppressed humans. For Christians, the messiah was Jesus of Nazareth.

metta. Loving-kindness, a key Buddhist virtue.

metta bhavana. In Buddhism, "kindness meditation"—a five-stage meditation extending loving kindness to all beings throughout space and time.

midrashim. Expansions and explanations of the Tanakh serving as commentaries on the sacred text.

millennium. Among Fundamentalist and Zionist Christians, the thousand-year period during the end-time when Christ will reign. In the Book of Revelation, it precedes the final defeat of Satan, the last judgment, and the new heaven and earth.

minaret. In Islam, the proclamation tower from which the muezzin issues the call to prayer. It is a regular (usually detached) architectural feature of mosques in Muslim countries, analogous to the bell tower of a Christian church.

Minjung theology. A Korean form of liberation theology seeking social justice and human rights for the downtrodden common people—the "Minjung"—by interpreting the Bible (around the centenary of its first translation into Korean, the common language) with attention to Korean concepts like *han*: the indignation and grief of common people in the face of historic and current injustice.

Mishnah. The first written collection of the oral traditions of the Pharisees.

modernism. One of several modern Muslim reform movements; neither secularist nor conservative in its attitude toward the West, modernism has sought to demonstrate the dynamism and creativity of Islam in response to modernity.

moksha. In Hinduism, escape from the cycle of rebirth or reincarnation.

moshav. A semi-cooperative type of rural community originally set up in Palestine by socialist or Marxist Zionist immigrants. Present-day moshavim practice communal purchasing, marketing, and in some cases production. *See also* kibbutz.

mosque. The Muslim structure designed for communal worship; in the Muslim world a mosque usually has a dome, a courtyard for ablutions, and a minaret from which the call to prayer is sounded.

muezzin. In Islam, the one who calls Muslims to prayer five times each day from the minaret of the mosque.

mujahid. A person who strives in Allah's cause; one who practices jihad.

Mujerista theology. Hispanic feminist liberation theology.

mumin. In Islam, one who has *iman*, or right faith in Allah and in the basic teachings of Islam; a person of faith.

Muslim. A person of faith who surrenders himself or herself to the will of Allah.

Muslim Brotherhood. A prominent neo-revivalist movement founded in Egypt in 1928 by Hassan al-Banna. Although occasionally in the past it has used or approved of violence, it has espoused nonviolence since 1970, sponsors numerous social service projects, and seeks to participate in politics.

Nakba. *See* al-Nakba.

Nevi'im. In Judaism, the "Prophets," meaning the middle section of the Tanakh (Hebrew Bible), beginning with the book of Joshua and ending with the book of Malachi.

night journey and ascension. In Islamic tradition, Muhammad's miraculous transport to Jerusalem from Mecca in 620, followed by his ascension to the presence of God, where he conversed with other prophets.

nirvana. The blissful state of freedom from rebirth realized when we gain insight into the impermanence of our present existence and let go of our separate personality.

Noble Sanctuary. In Arabic, "al-Haram al-Sharif," the Muslim name for the great esplanade in Jerusalem that Jews call the Temple Mount, on which the Islamic Dome of the Rock and the Al-Aqsa Mosque are situated.

noncombatant immunity. Part of the just war principle of discrimination, it forbids attacks on those who are not threatening injustice or harm.

noncooperation. Second of the three major forms of nonviolent action, the other two being (1) protest and persuasion and (3) intervention. One withdraws cooperation by refusing to do something that one is normally expected to do and that is required for the injustice to continue. For example, one refuses to work by striking, or refuses to purchase through a boycott.

nonviolence as a tactic. Practice of nonviolence motivated by the fact that one is too weak to prevail violently. If one could prevail violently, one would do so.

nonviolence as a way of life. Practice of nonviolence based on the principle of respecting opponents and causing no harm. One practices nonviolence even if one could prevail through the use of violence.

normative analysis. The third step in the circle of praxis outlined by liberation theologians. It raises value questions, asking what is good about the current situation and what is bad about it, and then proposes a better or more just situation.

numinous. Something that is terrifying yet draws us toward itself: a dual experience.

Occupied Palestinian Territories. The West Bank, including East Jerusalem, and the Gaza Strip, all of which were conquered by Israel in the 1967 war; since then they have been subject to Israeli military occupation in violation of international law.

Ojibwa. Native American tribe pushed by European settlers west from the Lake Ontario region into Minnesota.

Occupied Palestinian Territories. The West Bank, including East Jerusalem, and the Gaza Strip, all of which were conquered by Israel in the 1967 war; since then they have been subject to Israeli military occupation in violation of international law.

Operation Cast Lead. Major Israeli military assault on Gaza (2008–2009) that killed more than 1,400 Palestinians.

oppression. The suffering of the poor in situations of structural violence, as a consequence of societal injustice; liberation theologians assert that both oppressor and oppressed need to be liberated.

original sin. A key doctrine of Christianity that attempts to express and explain what within human beings resists goodness, generosity, courage, and trust.

Orthodox Judaism. A major branch of modern Judaism that seeks to preserve all the historical Jewish traditions and beliefs, to be distinguished from Conservative Judaism, Reform Judaism, and Reconstructionist Judaism.

Oslo Accords. The Declaration of Principles negotiated in Norway and then signed in Washington, D.C., in 1993 by Yasser Arafat and Yitzhak Rabin, which established the Palestinian Authority and promised a permanent Israeli-Palestinian peace settlement within five years.

Ottoman Empire. One of the great medieval Muslim empires. Lasting through World War I, it was based in Turkey.

Our Lady of Guadalupe. A Catholic shrine in Mexico City dedicated to the Virgin Mary. Inside the shrine a cloak is displayed with an image of Mary as an Indian woman, which was miraculously imprinted on it in a 1531 appearance to the indigenous peasant Juan Diego.

outcastes. In the Hindu caste system, another term for the untouchables, or scheduled caste, or Dalits: those who fall below the three "twice-born" castes and the Shudra (fourth caste).

Palestine Liberation Organization (PLO). Secular Palestinian movement to return refugees to their former homes, led by Yasser Arafat, which at first made use of terror attacks to resist Israeli expansion and later evolved toward a Palestinian government willing to live alongside the state of Israel.

Palestine National Congress. The legislative branch of the Palestinian government, originally under the Palestine Liberation Organization and, since 1994, under the Palestinian National Authority.

pan-en-henic. The experience of unity with nature—of feeling lost to self but united to the cosmos around one.

parinirvana. In Buddhism, the mysterious state in which the Buddha ended his life, never to be reborn into this world, in which he neither exists nor does not exist. Thus, the final state of nirvana that an enlightened person reaches at death.

Passover. *See* Pesach.

pastoral plan. The fourth step of the circle of praxis, as developed by liberation theologians. It develops concrete policies and actions designed to transform the situation from what the descriptive analysis reveals toward the better or more just situation that the normative analysis recommends.

Peace Churches. Anabaptists who seek to follow the Sermon on the Mount literally—Mennonites, Amish, Church of the Brethren—plus (non-Anabaptist) Quakers with the same commitment.

Peace of God. A medieval attempt to reduce the savagery of war by exempting certain groups from warfare (for example, clergy and peasants).

peace teams. Attempts to realize Gandhi's dream of teams of nonviolent activists seeking positive social change. In the Israeli-Palestinian conflict, peace teams consist of Palestinians, Israelis, and internationals. They include the International Solidarity Movement, Christian Peacemaker Teams, Muslim Peacemaker Teams, and the Meta Peace Team.

Pentecost. For the Jewish festival, *see* Shavuot. The first *Christian* Pentecost is described in Acts of the Apostles, chapter 2, as the descent of the Holy Spirit on the first believers in Christ, empowering them to inaugurate the Christian mission. *See also* Holy Spirit.

Pequot. The Native American tribe, living in what is now southern Connecticut, which was the first to resist European settlers who had treated them unjustly.

Pequot War. A war waged in southern New England in 1637–1638 between the Pequot tribe and European settlers. The Pequot were defeated.

persuasion. With protest, the first of the three major forms of nonviolent action, the other two being (2) noncooperation and (3) intervention.

Pesach. The Hebrew word for Passover, the first of three pilgrimage feasts in the Jewish liturgical calendar. It takes place at the beginning of the spring grain harvest and commemorates God's rescue of the ancient Israelites from slavery in Egypt.

PLO. The Palestine Liberation Organization.

pogrom. An active Christian persecution of Jews; a Russian word.

political Zionism. A form of (modern) Zionism that pursued the goal of Jewish colonization outside of Europe by means of international support or the authorization of powerful states. Its goal was the eventual formation of a Jewish state in the colonized region.

praxis. Activity that is reflected on and consciously chosen to produce a particular effect—a transformation of society.

principle of double effect. The principle, basic to just war theory, that one can carry out an action that produces both good and bad effects provided that (1) the good effect is not caused by the bad effect, (2) one intends only the good effect, and (3) the good effect greatly outweighs the bad effect.

proportionality. The just war principle that requires the good results of a war or any part of a war to significantly outweigh the bad results, considering the effects on all sides, including future generations. Sometimes it is wrongly defined as producing no more harm than necessary to achieve one's objectives.

Prosperity Gospel. Invest generously in God and God's work, then trust God to meet your needs.

protest and persuasion. The first of the three major forms of nonviolent action, the other two being (2) noncooperation and (3) intervention.

Pueblo. Native American tribes living in communal, apartment-like stone or adobe structures in the southwestern United States that largely succeeded in maintaining their society, culture, and religion in the face of European settlers and missionaries. The Hopi are one of these tribes.

Purim. A Jewish festival commemorating the story told in the biblical Book of Esther, in which Jews take revenge on a royal Persian enemy, killing him and numerous other Gentiles.

Qassam rockets. Crude projectiles fired by Palestinians in the Israeli-occupied Gaza Strip across the border into Israel. In a recent two-year period, fourteen Israelis were killed by these rockets. The corresponding Israeli weapons include F-16s and Apache helicopters.

Quechua. Originally the language of the Incan Empire, it is spoken today by more than eight million people living in Bolivia, Peru, Ecuador, Colombia, and Argentina.

Quran. The holy scripture of Islam; the word means "recitation." Muslims traditionally regard the Quran as divinely inspired in every detail.

Radical Reformation. A movement within the Protestant Reformation that believed the Lutheran and Reformed movements did not go far enough. It condemned elite leadership, called for adult baptism (Anabaptists), taught that only fully committed believers were true members of the church, expected an imminent end of the world, and attacked the corruption of wealth and power. As the world and the more traditional churches continued to exist, the movement tended to create separatist communities of believers.

Ramadan. The ninth month of the Muslim lunar year, when observant Muslims fast from all food, drink, and sexual activity from dawn until dusk. Muhammad received his first revelation near the end of Ramadan.

Ramayana. One of Hinduism's two great national epics, it narrates the adventures of Prince Rama of Ayodhya after the demon king of Lanka abducts his wife. It is counted among the noninspired traditions known as the Smriti.

rapture. In the ideology of Fundamentalist and Zionist Christians, the first event of the end-time, the airlifting of believers in Jesus out of this world, thus rescuing them from the tribulation.

rasul. The Arabic word for "prophet." The Muslim profession of faith (sha-hada) refers to Muhammad as the (final) prophet of God.

Reconstructionist Judaism. An American form of Judaism, founded in 1983 as a progressive alternative to Conservative Judaism. In contrast to Reform Judaism, it holds that one should practice Jewish laws, traditions, and customs unless there is positive reason not to. But it considers halakhah to be "folk ways" rather than laws.

redemption of land. The idea, held by religious Zionists, that the biblical "land of Israel" must be returned in its entirety to exclusively Jewish ownership, and so individual seizures of land by Jews from non-Jews are encouraged.

reductions. Jesuit utopian communities for indigenous people in Paraguay early in the seventeenth century, designed to evangelize them and protect them from Spanish and Portuguese slave traders. They have been criticized by some as patriarchal, although they gave the natives far more freedom than the other colonial settlements did.

Reform Judaism. A nineteenth-century European movement attempting to bring Jewish life and belief more in line with modern thought.

refugees. Persons forced to flee from their homes and communities because of war or for other catastrophic reasons. *Internal* refugees remain in their native country, while *international* refugees flee from the country itself, especially to escape lethal political repression.

Refuseniks. Officers and soldiers in the Israel Defense Forces who refuse to serve in the Occupied Palestinian Territories (and when applicable, in Lebanon) and in doing so risk imprisonment for their stand.

reincarnation. In Hinduism, the rebirth of a human soul in another human body. Compare with the wider "transmigration of souls," which includes rebirth in animal or vegetable form. Some use the two terms as synonyms with this wider sense.

religious Zionism. A form of Zionism that asserts that God wants Jews to "redeem" all of the "land of Israel" for their exclusive possession, in effect ethnically cleansing it of its non-Jewish inhabitants.

resurrection. The raising of Jesus to life by God after his death and burial. Early Christians understood the resurrection to be God's vindication of Jesus and expected to experience a similar resurrection after their own deaths. They gained this confidence from the outward appearances of Jesus in his body to his disciples and from their inner experience of the risen Jesus alive within them.

Revisionist Zionism. A type of Zionism promoted by Ze'ev Jabotinsky, beginning in the 1920s, that urged the Jewish community to seize control on both sides of the Jordan River by force of arms and declare a Jewish state, which he expected would be backed by Britain, confining Arab resistance behind an "iron wall" of invincible force.

Rosh Hashanah. Hebrew for "head of the year"—in the Jewish liturgical calendar, this is the first day of the New Year celebration.

Sabbath. The weekly Jewish day of rest and religious celebration, which lasts from sundown on Friday to sundown on Saturday and may include synagogue attendance.

Sabeel. Palestinian Christian liberation theology organization with offices in Jerusalem and Nazareth.

Sabra and Shatila. Two Palestinian refugee camps located in southern Beirut, Lebanon, where in September 1982 as many as 3,000 Palestinians were massacred by the Lebanese Phalange under Israeli auspices during an Israeli invasion of Lebanon.

sadaqa (plural *sadaqat*). In contrast to the formal, annual tax of zakat, this is a more private, spontaneous form of almsgiving in Islam.

salaam. Arabic greeting meaning "peace," equivalent to the Hebrew shalom. *See also* shalom.

salat. The second pillar of Islam, obligating Muslims to observe a prescribed prayer ritual to Allah five times each day facing Mecca.

Samaria. In Roman Palestine, the area between Judea in the south and Galilee in the north where the group known as Samaritans lived and worshiped. Modern Jewish settlers use the term for that part of the West Bank to make the claim that it should be under Jewish control. *See also* Judea.

samsara. The cycle of rebirth or reincarnation, from which Hindus seek liberation (moksha).

Sandinista Party. The leftist Nicaraguan political party, headed by Daniel Ortega, that grew out of the Sandinista National Liberation Front after it defeated President Somoza in 1979. Although it lost majority control by election in 1990, it regained it in 2007.

sangha. The monastic community of the Buddha's disciples.

satyagraha. Truth-power, active nonviolence as developed by Mohandas Gandhi.

saum. The fourth pillar of Islam: fasting from food, drink, and sex during daylight hours of the month of Ramadan.

scheduled castes. The name that the government of India coined for "untouchables" or "outcastes." It indicates that they enjoy certain legal benefits.

scheduled tribes. A term used by the Indian government to refer to indigenous tribes in India that continue to follow an animist, hunter-gatherer way of life.

security/separation barrier/wall. In urban parts of the Palestinian West Bank, a concrete wall twenty-six feet high, and in rural parts of the West Bank, a razor-wire and electronic fence, flanked by patrol roads and equipped with gun towers. Under construction since 2002, it is projected to extend well over 400 miles (700 kilometers) upon completion. Despite its alleged purpose of protecting Israelis from Palestinian terrorists, this Israeli structure has been built mainly on Palestinian land, often leaving Palestinians on the Israeli side of the barrier, intruding up to ten kilometers into the West Bank to include Jewish-only settlements, reducing the land and water available to West Bank Palestinians, and hindering Palestinian movement within the West Bank.

Sephardic. Adjective describing Jews (and their culture) who were strongly influenced by Spanish and Arabic cultures.

Sermon on the Mount. The words of Jesus in the Gospel according to Matthew, chapters 5–7, including such challenging passages as the beatitudes, the antitheses demanding non-violence and love of enemies, and other core teachings. The parallel passage in the Gospel according to Luke is called the "Sermon on the Plain."

shahada. The first pillar of Islam. It is the Muslim profession of faith: "There is no god but God, and Muhammad is his prophet."

shalom. "Peace, victory, security, and prosperity" in the broad sense: what politicians promise to give their constituents. The Arabic form is salaam.

shaman. A person who, because of his or her special personality and initiation experience, can make contact with the supernatural world through a trance or other means, returning to the everyday world to help others.

Sharia. Literally, the "straight path"—the revealed law of God, of which there are traces in the Quran and Sunna, to be distinguished from *fiqh*, its application in jurisprudence.

Shavuot. The Hebrew name for Pentecost or the "Feast of Weeks," the second pilgrimage feast in the Jewish liturgical calendar. It occurs fifty days after Passover, at the end of the spring grain harvest. It commemorates God giving the Torah to Moses at Sinai.

Shia. Based on the Arabic word for "party," this designation refers to the approximately 15 percent of Muslims worldwide who believe that Muhammad chose his cousin Ali to succeed him, and that the office of caliph should not have gone to anyone unrelated to the Prophet.

shirk. In Islam, the only unforgivable sin—that of associating anyone or anything with God, equivalent to idolatry.

Shoah. The Hebrew word for Holocaust, referring to the Nazi program to exterminate European Jews that was attempted in the 1930s and 1940s.

Shruti. General name for the inspired Hindu scriptures, especially the Vedas, Brahmanas, and Upanishads.

Shudra. In the Hindu caste system, the fourth (servant) caste, situated below the three "twice-born" castes and above the untouchables, or scheduled caste.

Smriti. Noninspired traditions that complement the inspired scriptures of Hinduism.

social sin. *See* structural sin.

socialism. According to Karl Marx, the stage in the historical evolution of society coming after capitalism and before full communism. Since he believed that it would be realized through the automatic operations of dialectic, he thought that one could not predict what form it would take and so made no effort to describe it in detail.

socialist Zionism. A form of (modern) Zionism that advocated ongoing Jewish immigration into pre-1948 Palestine and socioeconomic development of the Jewish community, with the aim of eventually founding a Jewish state there.

solidarity. A word made famous by the Polish movement for an independent union. It emphasizes our need for each other and its spiritual implications: going beyond justice, we share with our brothers and sisters. There is only one form of human nature—we all have innate dignity and an eternal destiny; we depend on each other.

Son of God. A title found in the Hebrew Bible and applied by New Testament authors to Jesus. Christians believe that the humanity of Jesus is intimately and mysteriously united with the second "person" of the Trinity.

Special Night Squads. Divisions of the Zionist Haganah trained by British military personnel, which attacked Palestinian villages during the Arab Revolt of 1936–1939 in British Mandatory Palestine.

state capitalism. A term used by critics of the Russian Communist system who wished to make the point that the economic system that developed under Stalin and his successors in the Soviet Union was state-owned capitalism rather than Marxist communism.

Stern Gang (Lehi). Unofficial underground Jewish strike force established in 1940 to attack British police and government installations in the Middle East when the Irgun and Haganah chose to cooperate with Britain against Germany. Later, it attacked Palestinian resistance to Jewish expansion. Best known for assassinating Lord Moyne in 1944 in Cairo, bombing the Cairo-Haifa train, and participating in the attack on Deir Yassin.

strong medicine. Spiritual power. In Dakota Indian warfare, it effectively protected a warrior from harm in situations of danger.

structural sin. Unjust laws, customs, situations, and habitual ways of doing things that result in economic, political, social, or environmental harm, especially to marginalized people, in such a way that no individual person can be directly blamed for the specific harm. However, a range of people do carry responsibility for initiating, supporting, and failing to confront the unjust laws, customs, situations, and habits.

structural violence. *See* structural sin.

subsidiarity. Higher levels of political organization should not take over responsibilities that lower levels can accomplish. Higher levels should give aid to lower levels when needed.

Suffering Servant. A figure found in Second Isaiah (Hebrew Bible) who suffers for the sins of others. Early Christian interpreters used this figure to explain the ministry, death, and resurrection of Jesus the messiah.

sufficiency. A social norm proposed by the Evangelical Lutheran Church in America that confronts unjust disparities in income and wealth. It highlights the sharp contrast between those who do not have enough and those who have far more than they really need. God calls for mutual generosity, support of the common good, and release from the bondage of consumerism and endless accumulation.

Sufism. Islamic mysticism, which originated in the eighth century and remains a vibrant component of Islam. Sufi orders first arose in the twelfth century. Among the most famous Sufis were Rabia, Al-Ghazali, and Jalal al-Din al-Rumi.

sun dance. An important four- to eight-day-long ceremony celebrated by North American Plains Indians around the time of the summer solstice. Participants fast, pray, dance, and suffer (from self-inflicted pain) for the sake of the people, to purify themselves and the community, to gain insight through visions, and to renew the community's strength.

Sunna. "Trodden path"; in Islam, recommended behavior based on the reported teachings and actions of Muhammad, which are recorded in the Hadith.

Sunni. The shortened term for about 85 percent of Muslims taken from the longer phrase "the people of the custom and the community," as distinguished from Shia Muslims.

sura. A chapter-like unit of the Quran, which contains 114 suras. Each sura is in turn divided into *ayat* (verses), of which there are more than 6,000.

Sykes-Picot Agreement. A secret agreement between France and Britain signed in 1916, in which France was promised control over southeastern Turkey, Syria, Lebanon, and northern Iraq after the war, and Britain control over the rest of Iraq, Transjordan, and a corridor to Haifa. Palestine was to be internationally governed, but after the war Britain assumed complete control over it. Lenin caused an international outcry when he published the agreement.

synthesis. The third stage in the Marxist dialectic of history: the compromise that results from the tension between thesis and antithesis. As the synthesis is established and accepted, it is itself a new thesis.

Tabernacles. In Hebrew, Sukkot: the last of the three Jewish pilgrimage festivals. It comes at the time of the final fall harvest and commemorates the Israelite period of wandering in the desert.

Talmud. Expanded commentary on the Mishnah, existing in both a Palestinian and a Babylonian form.

Tanakh. The Hebrew sacred scripture, roughly equivalent to the Christian "Old Testament."

taqwa. An Islamic (Arabic) term denoting awareness of Allah, which is also prominent in Muslim liberation theology, where it means responsibility to God and to other human beings.

Targums. Free translations of the Tanakh into Aramaic, originally oral, for the benefit of common people who no longer understood Hebrew.

tawhid. An Islamic (Arabic) term meaning the unity of God. In Muslim liberation theology, it is used in opposition to the dualism of sacred and secular.

Temple Mount. The Jewish name for the artificially leveled hilltop in Jerusalem that Muslims call the Noble Sanctuary. On it the second Jewish temple stood until the first century CE. *See also* al-Aqsa Mosque; Haram al-Sharif.

terrorism. Killing or wounding civilians to advance a political agenda in the expectation that they will withdraw cooperation from their government (or some other group) or pressure it to yield. Often limited by government apologists to nonstate actors, the concept ought to apply equally to state-sponsored military or paramilitary action against civilians, often called "state-sponsored terrorism."

theory of value. The Marxist theory that the value of a product is based on the worker hours used to produce it.

Theravada. "The Doctrine of the Elders"—a school of thought in Buddhism that tries to hold to the original teaching without adding new elaborations and insists that each individual must accomplish his or her own enlightenment: no one can do it for another. This branch of Buddhism remains prevalent in Sri Lanka and Southeast Asia, except for Vietnam.

thesis. The first of three stages in Marx's dialectical theory of history, dominated by the status-quo forces and the ideas held by the privileged elites whom the productive processes of a particular moment in history have created.

tikkun. Hebrew word meaning "repair." The sixteenth-century Jewish mystic Isaac Luria used the term to describe the human task of restoring God's creation.

Torah. Also called the Pentateuch; the first five books of the Tanakh, sometimes inaccurately called "The Law."

Trail of Tears. The forcible removal by the State of Georgia, which violated a ruling of the U.S. Supreme Court, of the Cherokee Indian tribe in 1830 from its territories in Georgia (where gold had been discovered) to Oklahoma. About 4,000 of the 15,000 displaced Cherokee died on the four-month trek.

transfer. In the Israel-Palestine conflict, the illegal, forcible removal of the indigenous Palestinians from their historic homeland, which Zionists call the "land of Israel."

transmigration of souls. The widespread belief among Hindus that after death a person's soul is reborn in another body, whether vegetable, animal, human, or deva. The passage from one human body to another human body is normally called "reincarnation."

tribulation. According to Fundamentalist and Zionist Christians, an anticipated end-time period of seven years following the so-called rapture, during which those "left behind" will suffer. The tribulation will be followed by the battle of Armageddon.

Truce of God. A medieval attempt to reduce the savagery of war by limiting the number of days on which war could be fought (for example, forbidding war during Lent, Advent, Sundays, feast days, and so forth).

tzaddik. In Hasidic Judaism, a holy man or charismatic leader, as distinguished from an ordinary Hasid, whose values include humility and love.

umma. The global community of Muslims: those who submit to the will of Allah and the message of the prophet Muhammad.

universal destination of the earth's goods. The principle that we are all related members of one human family, so the riches of the earth are intended to be shared fairly among all humans.

untouchables. In the Hindu caste system, the category so low as to be outside the system entirely. The name alludes to fear by others of pollution from physical contact with them. Gandhi tried to raise their status by calling them "Harijan" or "children of God." The secular government of India calls them the "scheduled" caste. They prefer to call themselves "Dalits," meaning "oppressed."

Upanishads. Part of the Shruti that provide a philosophical reinterpretation of the Vedas. Each of the eleven Upanishads accepted as Shruti, or inspired, is associated with one of the four Vedas.

USS *Liberty*. U.S. spy ship heavily attacked by Israel during the 1967 Six-Day War.

utilitarianism. An ethical system developed by the British philosopher John Stuart Mill (1806–1873), it was based on the criterion that one should act according to what would produce the greatest good for the greatest number of people.

Vaishya. In the Hindu caste system, the third of the three "twice-born" castes, consisting of merchants, artisans, and farmers.

Vajrayana. A school of thought in Buddhism that uses mantras and ritual practices to put the worshiper into contact with spiritual powers. It is the dominant form of Buddhism in Tibet.

Vedanta. "End of the Vedas." In Hinduism, it refers to the contents and wisdom of the Upanishads. As a school of Hindu philosophy, it can take both nondualistic (Advaita) and dualistic (Dvaita) forms.

Vedas. The part of the Shruti that consists of inspired hymns used by the Brahmins in their ritual sacrifice and intercessory prayer.

vision quest. Among American Indians, an initiatory experience undergone by adolescent males. The seeker fasts and stays awake outdoors wearing minimal clothing, for two to four days, awaiting contact by a guardian animal spirit that will share some of its spiritual power, revealing the seeker's character and revitalizing his spiritual resources.

Wahhabi. The conservative form of Islam officially practiced in Saudi Arabia, it is named after Muhammad ibn Abd al-Wahhab (1703–1792), an early revivalist Muslim scholar. The Taliban of Afghanistan were strongly influenced by Wahhabi traditions.

Wakan Tanka. An expression referring to the spirit world of North American indigenous tribes such as the Dakota; it means "the sacred ones" and encompasses gods and spirits, the mysterious.

waqf. In Islam, an inalienable religious endowment designating a building or piece of land and its income for religious or charitable purposes. Income from the waqf might support a mosque, school, hospital, orphanage, or other institution of social service.

West Bank. One of the Palestinian territories occupied by Israel since 1967; it includes East Jerusalem, from which it extends in all directions. In addition to more than two million Palestinians, about 650,000 Israeli settlers live there.

Western Wall. The retaining wall supporting the west side of the artificially leveled hilltop of the (Jewish) Temple Mount or (Muslim) Noble Sanctuary in Jerusalem. The lower courses of stone date from the reconstruction by Herod. Since Orthodox Jews avoid the top of the mount for fear of accidentally walking on the site of the former Holy of Holies, they offer prayers and devotions at the Western Wall.

Womanist theology. Black feminist theology by black women theologians, who explore the theological implications of race and class as well as gender.

Women in Black. Now an international women's nonviolent peace movement, it was founded in 1988 by a group of Israeli women; they demonstrate against the Israeli occupation of Palestinian territory each Friday in Tel Aviv and Jerusalem.

Women in Green. "Women for Israel's Tomorrow." A conservative grassroots Israeli Jewish group convinced that Arabs intend to destroy the Jewish state. It wants Israel to annex the occupied territories and transfer Palestinians to Arab countries, asserting that the Israeli government is too weak in its policy toward the Palestinians.

Wounded Knee. The site in South Dakota where the last major confrontation between U.S. soldiers and American Indians took place in 1890. In 1973, the American Indian Movement occupied the site to force the government to observe its 1868 treaty and in protest against strip mining on the Pine Ridge reservation that was polluting their water sources. The occupation was broken up by federal forces after a few months.

Yesh Gevul. Organization of Israeli Refuseniks who, on moral grounds, refuse to serve in territories illegally occupied by Israel such as southern Lebanon, the West Bank, and the Gaza Strip, even though many of them are imprisoned for their refusal.

yetzer ha ra'. The evil inclination, and **yetzer ha tov**, the good inclination, represent two basic tendencies within human beings, according to Jewish ethical thought.

Yishuv. The Jewish community in Palestine before the establishment of the state of Israel in 1948.

yoga. The search for God and for union with God, in Hinduism.

yogi. One who searches for God and for union with God, in Hinduism.

Yom Kippur. The Day of Atonement—a day of fasting and repentance for sin. In the Jewish liturgical calendar, it is the last of the ten "high holy days."

Yoruba. West African tribe, many of whose members were transported to the Caribbean and South America, especially Cuba and Brazil, by the slave trade. Many of them preserved their native religion by syncretizing it with Catholicism, identifying their gods with Catholic saints, and thus producing such religions as Santería and Candomblé.

zakat. The third pillar of Islam, the obligatory almsgiving of 2.5 percent annually of one's assets over and above what is needed for daily living. The proceeds are used for community support, especially of the poor.

Zionism (Christian). *See* Christian Zionism.

Zionism (Jewish). A modern nationalist movement within Judaism that originated in nineteenth-century Europe and was largely secular until 1967. Originally conceived in colonial terms but in diverse forms (political, socialist, cultural, religious), its goal became the establishment of a Jewish state in most or all of Palestine.

Zohar. A Hebrew word meaning "way of splendor." It is the title of the foremost medieval text representing Jewish Kabbalah.

Bibliography

Abdel Haleem, M. A. *The Qur'an: A New Translation*. Oxford: Oxford University Press, 2008.

Abduh, Mohammad. *The Theology of Unity*. Translated by Kenneth Cragg. Kuala Lumpur, Malaysia: Islamic Book Trust, 2013.

Abou El Fadl, Khaled. "Islam and Violence: Our Forgotten Legacy." In *Islam in Transition: Muslim Perspectives*. 2nd ed. New York; Oxford: Oxford University Press, 2007.

Ackerman, Peter. *A Force More Powerful: A Century of Nonviolent Conflict*. New York: St. Martin's, 2000.

Agnivesa, Svami. *Religion, Spirituality, and Social Action: New Agenda for Humanity*. Gurgaon, Haryana: Hope India Publications, 2001.

Agnivesa, Svami, and Valson Thampu. *Harvest of Hate: Gujarat under Siege*. New Delhi: Rupa & Co., 2002.

Aho, James Alfred. *This Thing of Darkness: A Sociology of the Enemy*. Seattle: University of Washington Press, 1994.

Akçam, Taner. *A Shameful Act: The Armenian Genocide and the Question of Turkish Responsibility*. Translated by Paul Bessemer. New York: Henry Holt, 2006.

Ali, Abdullah Yussuf, ed. *The Holy Qur'an: Text, Translation, and Commentary*. Translated by Abdullah Yusuf Ali. Elmhurst, NY: Tahrike Tarsile Qur'an, Inc., 1987. Also available at www.sacred-texts.com/isl/quran/00101.htm. Accessed 13 February 2014.

Allaire, James, and Rosemary Broughton. "An Introduction to the Life and Spirituality of Dorothy Day." http://www.catholicworker.org/dorothyday/ddbiographytext.cfm?Number = 3. Accessed 4 February 2014.

Anderson, Hugh G. *Justification by Faith: Lutherans and Catholics in Dialogue VII*. Minneapolis: Augsburg, 1985.

Andre, Catherine, and Jean-Philippe Platteau. "Land Relations under Unbearable Stress: Rwanda Caught in the Malthusian Trap." *Journal of Economic Behavior and Organization*. September (forthcoming). http://www.foodnet.cgiar.org/scrip/docs%26databases/ifpriStudies_UG_nonScrip/pdfs/Southwestern_highlands/Land%20relations%20and%20the%20Malthusian%20trap%20in%20NW%20Rwanda,%20Andre%20a.pdf. Accessed 6 March 2014.

Antonio, Edward. "Black Theology." In *The Cambridge Companion to Liberation Theology*, edited by Christopher Rowland. 2nd ed., 79–104. Cambridge; New York: Cambridge University Press, 2007.

Aquinas, Thomas. *Summa Theologica* 2–2 Q 40 and 2–2 Q 42 A 2, reply to 3rd objection. Translated by Fathers of English Dominican Province. Numerous publishers. Second and revised edition, 1920. Available online at www.newadvent.org/summa/. Accessed 13 February 2014. Online edition © 2006, Kevin Knight.

Arendt, Hannah. *Eichmann in Jerusalem: A Report on the Banality of Evil.* New York: Viking Press, 1963.

Ariyaratne, A. T. *Buddhism and Sarvodaya: Sri Lankan Experience.* Edited by Nandasena Ratnapala. Bibliotheca Indo-Buddhica Series, vol. 168. Delhi: Sri Satguru Publications (Indian Books Centre), 1996.

Armstrong, Karen. *Islam: A Short History.* New York: Modern Library, 2000.

Ateek, Naim Stifan. *Justice, and Only Justice: A Palestinian Theology of Liberation.* Maryknoll, NY: Orbis, 1989.

———. *A Palestinian Christian Cry for Reconciliation.* Maryknoll, NY: Orbis Books, 2008.

Ateek, Naim Stifan, Marc H. Ellis, and Rosemary Radford Ruether, eds. *Faith and the Intifada: Palestinian Christian Voices.* Maryknoll, NY: Orbis, 1992.

Augustine of Hippo. *The City of God.* Available online at www.newadvent.org/fathers/1201 .htm. Accessed 13 February 2014.

———. *Reply to Faustus the Manichean.* Translated by R. Stothert in *The Nicene and Post-Nicene Fathers* (1st series) 4. Available online at www.new advent.org/fathers/1406.htm. Accessed 13 February 2014.

Aung San Suu Kyi. *Letters from Burma.* London: Penguin Books, 1997.

Aung San Suu Kyi: see also Clements.

Avishai, Bernard. *The Tragedy of Zionism: Revolution and Democracy in the Land of Israel.* New York: Farrar Straus Giroux, 1985.

Avnery, Uri. *Israel and the Palestinians: A Different Israeli View.* New York: Breira, 1975.

———. *My Friend, the Enemy.* Westport, CT: L. Hill, 1986.

Babiak, Paul, and Robert Hare. *Snakes in Suits.* Kindle. New York: HarperCollins e-books, 2009.

Baker, Joharah. "How to Fight Back." *Palestine Report* 8, no. 34 (2002). www.jmcc.org/media/reportonline/article4.htm. Accessed July 6, 2006. The journal's home address is www.palestinereport.org/. Accessed 13 February 2014.

Ballou, Adin. *Christian Non-Resistance in All Its Important Bearings, Illustrated and Defended.* (Reprint of: Philadelphia: J. Miller M'Kim, 1846.) The Peace Movement in America: A Facsimile Reprint Collection. New York: Jerome S. Ozer, 1972.

Banerjee, Mukulika. *The Pathan Unarmed: Opposition and Memory in the North West Frontier.* World Anthropology. Oxford: Oxford University Press, 2000.

Barbour, Hugh. "Quakers." *Encyclopedia of Religion.* Edited by Lindsay Jones. Vol. 11. 2nd ed., 7546–7550. Detroit: Macmillan Reference USA, 2005.

Barr, David L. *New Testament Story: An Introduction.* 3rd ed. Belmont, CA: Wadsworth/Thomson Learning, 2002.

Barth, Karl. "The Barmen Declaration" (1934). In *Radical Christian Writings: A Reader,* edited by Andrew Bradstock and Christopher Rowland. Oxford, UK, and Malden, MA: Blackwell, 2002. Also available at http://www.sacred-texts.com/chr/barmen.htm. Accessed 20 July 2014.

———. *The Epistle to the Romans.* 6th ed. Translated by Edwyn C. Hoskyns. London: Oxford University Press, 1968.

Begin, Menachem. *The Revolt: Story of the Irgun.* New York: Henry Schuman, 1951.

Beit-Hallahmi, Benjamin. *The Israeli Connection: Who Israel Arms and Why.* New York: Pantheon, 1987.

———. *Original Sins: Reflections on the History of Zionism and Israel.* New York: Olive Branch, 1993.

Bennis, Phyllis. *Understanding the Palestinian-Israeli Conflict.* 2nd ed. Lowell, MA: TARI, 2003.

Berndt, Hagen. *Non-Violence in the World Religions: Vision and Reality.* London: SCM Press, 2000.

Berryman, Phillip. *Liberation Theology: Essential Facts about the Revolutionary Movement in Latin America—and Beyond.* London: I. B. Tauris, 1987.

Bhave, Vinoba. *Revolutionary Sarvodaya: Philosophy for the Remaking of Man.* Bombay, India: Bhartiya Vidya Bhavan, 1964.

———. *Shanti Sena.* Varanasi: Sarva Seva Sangh Prakashan, 1963.

———. *Talks on the Gita.* New York: Macmillan, 1960.

Black Elk, John Gneisenau Neihardt, and Raymond J. DeMallie. *Black Elk Speaks: Being the Life Story of a Holy Man of the Oglala Sioux as Told Through John G. Neihardt (Flaming Rainbow).* Annotated by Raymond J. DeMallie with illustrations by Standing Bear. The Premier Edition. Albany: State University of New York Press, 2008 (c1932).

Bloomfield, Maurice, trans. *Hymns of the Atharva-Veda. Sacred Books of the East,* Vol. 42 [1897]. www.sacred-texts.com/hin/av/index.htm. Accessed 13 March 2014.

Boff, Leonardo. *Church, Charism and Power: Liberation Theology and the Institutional Church.* New York: Crossroad, 1985.

Bondurant, Joan V. *Conquest of Violence: The Gandhian Philosophy of Conflict.* New revised ed. Princeton, NJ: Princeton University Press, 1988.

Borelli, John. "Christian-Muslim Relations in the United States: Reflections for the Future after Two Decades of Experience." *The Muslim World* 94 (July 2004): 321–33. Also at http://onlinelibrary.wiley.com/doi/10.1111/j.1478-1913.2004.00056.x/full, with access restricted. Accessed 13 March 2014.

Borg, Marcus J. *Meeting Jesus Again for the First Time: The Historical Jesus and the Heart of Contemporary Faith.* [San Francisco]: HarperSanFrancisco, 1994.

———. "The Palestinian Background for a Life of Jesus." In *The Search for Jesus: Modern Scholarship Looks at the Gospels: Symposium at the Smithsonian Institution, September 11, 1993,* edited by Hershel Shanks et al. Kindle 2012, Kindle locations 421–672. Washington, DC: Biblical Archaeology Society, 1994, 2012.

———. "Portraits of Jesus." In *The Search for Jesus: Modern Scholarship Looks at the Gospels: Symposium at the Smithsonian Institution, September 11, 1993,* edited by Hershel Shanks et al. Kindle 2012, Kindle locations 957–1255. Washington, DC: Biblical Archaeology Society, 1994, 2012.

Bottomore, Tom, ed. *A Dictionary of Marxist Thought.* Cambridge, MA: Harvard University Press, 1983.

Boyd, Doug. *Rolling Thunder: A Personal Exploration into the Secret Healing Powers of an American Indian Medicine Man.* New York: Random House, 1974.

Breaking the Silence. *Our Harsh Logic: Israeli Soldiers' Testimonies from the Occupied Territories, 2000–2010.* New York: Metropolitan Books: Henry Holt, 2012.

Brecht, Bertolt. *The Caucasian Chalk Circle.* Rev. English version and introduction by Eric Bentley. New York: Grove Press, 1966.

Brilliant, Joshua. "Officer Tells Court Villagers Were Bound, Gagged and Beaten. Not Guilty Plea at 'Break Bones' Trial." *Jerusalem Post,* March 30, 1990.

———. "'Rabin Ordered Beatings,' Meir Tells Military Court," *Jerusalem Post,* June 22, 1990.

Brown, Dee Alexander. *Bury My Heart at Wounded Knee: An Indian History of the American West*. New York: Holt, Reinhart and Winston, 1971.

Brown, Peter. *Augustine of Hippo: A Biography*. Berkeley and Los Angeles: University of California Press, 1967.

Bryde, John F. *Modern Indian Psychology*. Rev. ed. Vermillion: Institute of Indian Studies, University of South Dakota, 1971.

Buber, Martin. *Between Man and Man*. With an afterword by the author on "The History of the Dialogical Principle." Introduction by Maurice Friedman. New York: Macmillan, 1965.

———. *I and Thou*. With a postscript by the author. Translated by Ronald Gregor Smith. 2nd ed. New York: Scribner, 1958.

Buddha Educational Foundation. *Twelve Principles of Buddhism*. Taipei, Taiwan: Buddha Educational Foundation, n.d.

Burr, Elizabeth. "Out of Palestine: Solidarity with a Displaced People." *America* 206, no. 6 (2012).

Burrowes, Robert J. *The Strategy of Nonviolent Defense: A Gandhian Approach*. Albany: State University of New York Press, 1996.

Cannon, Dale. *Six Ways of Being Religious: A Framework for Comparative Studies of Religion*. Belmont, CA: Wadsworth, 1996.

Carmody, Denise Lardner, and L. L. Brink. *Ways to the Center*. 6th ed. New York: Wadsworth, 2006.

Carter, Jimmy. *Palestine: Peace Not Apartheid*. New York: Simon and Schuster, 2006.

Castagnaro, Mauro. "A Theological 'Giant': An Interview with Gustavo Gutiérrez." *Iglesia Descalza: A Voice from the Margins of the Catholic Church*, no. 10 (16 October 2013). http:// iglesiadescalza.blogspot.com/2013/10/a-theological-giant-interview-with.html. Accessed 11 March 2014.

Catholic Church, Archdiocese of São Paulo (Brazil). *Torture in Brazil: A Report by the Archdiocese of São Paulo*. Translated by Jaime Wright. Edited by Joan Dassin. New York: Vintage, 1986.

Cavanaugh, William T. *Torture and Eucharist: Theology, Politics, and the Body of Christ*. Challenges in Contemporary Theology. Oxford: Blackwell, 1998.

Chacour, Elias. *Blood Brothers: A Palestinian Struggles for Reconciliation in the Middle East*. Grand Rapids, MI: Chosen Books, 1984.

Chappel, David W., ed. *Buddhist Peacework: Creating Cultures of Peace*. Somerville, MA: Wisdom Publications, 1999.

Chapra, M. 'Umar. "The Islamic Welfare State." In Donohue and Esposito, eds. *Islam in Transition: Muslim Perspectives*. 2nd ed. Oxford: Oxford University Press, 2007.

Chomsky, Noam, and Edward S. Herman. *Middle East Illusions: Including Peace in the Middle East? Reflections on Justice and Nationhood*. Lanham, MD: Rowman & Littlefield, 2003.

Churchill, Ward, and Jim VanderWall. *The COINTELPRO Papers: Documents from the FBI's Secret Wars against Domestic Dissent*. South End Press Classics Series, vol. 8. Boston: South End Press, 1990.

Ciszek, Walter J. *He Leadeth Me*. With Daniel Flaherty. Garden City, NY: Doubleday, 1975.

Clark, Katerina, and Michael Holquist. *Mikhail Bakhtin*. Cambridge, MA: The Belknap Press of Harvard University Press, 1984.

Cleckley, Hervey Milton. *The Mask of Sanity*. Edited by Emily S. Cleckley. 1941, 1950, 1955, 1964, 1976. Scanned Facsimile Produced for Non-Profit Educational Use. 5th ed. 1988. C. V. Mosby Co. Cassiopaea.Org. http://cassiopaea.org/cass/sanity_1.PdF. Accessed 11 March 2014.

Clements, Alan, and Aung San Suu Kyi. *The Voice of Hope, Aung San Suu Kyi: Conversations with Alan Clements.* EBook by EBooks by Design. Kindle revised and updated. [Vancouver, British Columbia, Canada]: World Dharma Publications, c1997, 2008, 2012.

Clifford, George M., III. *Forging Swords into Plows: A Twenty-First Century Christian Perspective on War.* Ethical Musings. Kindle Edition, 2012.

Cohen, Michael J. *Truman and Israel.* Berkeley: University of California Press, 1990.

Cone, James H. *Black Theology and Black Power.* New York: Seabury Press, 1969.

———. "From *Black Theology and Black Power.*" In *Liberating Faith: Religious Voices for Justice, Peace, and Ecological Wisdom,* edited by Roger S. Gottlieb, 188–95. Lanham, MD: Rowman & Littlefield, 2003.

Congregation for the Doctrine of the Faith. *Instruction on Certain Aspects of the "Theology of Liberation."* Vatican: Congregation for the Doctrine of the Faith, 1984.

Cooney, Robert, and Helen Michalowski, eds. *The Power of the People: Active Nonviolence in the United States.* Philadelphia: New Society, 1987.

Copeland, Kenneth. *The Laws of Prosperity.* Greensburgh, PA: Manna Christian Outreach, 1974.

Cory, Catherine A., and Michael J. Hollerich, eds. *The Christian Theological Tradition.* 3rd ed. Upper Saddle River, NJ: Pearson Prentice Hall, 2009.

Costello, Damian. *Black Elk: Colonialism and Lakota Catholicism.* Maryknoll, NY: Orbis Books, 2005.

Coward, Harold, ed. *Indian Critiques of Gandhi.* Albany: State University of New York Press, 2003.

Cox, Harvey. *Is Pope Francis the New Champion of Liberation Theology?* 6–13 January 2014. The Nation. http://www.thenation.com/article/177651/pope-francis-new-champion-liberation-theology?page=0,1. Accessed 4 March 2014.

Cromartie, Michael. *Religion, Culture, and International Conflict: A Conversation.* Lanham, MD: Rowman & Littlefield, 2005.

Crossan, John Dominic. *The Historical Jesus: The Life of a Mediterranean Jewish Peasant.* [San Francisco]: HarperSanFrancisco, 1991.

Curle, Adam. *True Justice: Quaker Peacemakers and Peacemaking.* London: Swarthmore, 1981.

Curran, Charles E. *Catholic Social Teaching, 1891–Present: A Historical, Theological, and Ethical Analysis.* Washington, DC: Georgetown University Press, 2002.

Dalai Lama, His Holiness the fourteenth (Tenzin Gyatso). *The Buddhism of Tibet.* Translated by Jeffrey Hopkins. The Wisdom of Tibet series. Ithaca, NY: Snow Lion, 1975.

Dart, Martha. *Marjorie Sykes, Quaker Gandhian.* Birmingham, UK: Sessions Book Trust in association with Woodbroak College, 1993.

Dawson, Andrew. "The Origins and Character of the Base Ecclesial Community: A Brazilian Perspective." In *The Cambridge Companion to Liberation Theology,* edited by Christopher Rowland. Kindle. 2nd ed., 139–58. Cambridge: Cambridge University Press, 2007.

Day, Dorothy. *The Long Loneliness: The Autobiography of Dorothy Day.* Illustrated by Fritz Eichenberg. Introduction by Daniel Berrigan. San Francisco: Harper & Row, 1952.

Dellinger, David. *From Yale to Jail: The Life Story of a Moral Dissenter.* New York: Pantheon Books, 1993.

Deloria, Vine. *God Is Red.* New York: Grosset & Dunlap, 1973.

Denny, Frederick Mathewson. *An Introduction to Islam.* 3d ed. New York: Macmillan, 2006.

Diamond, Jared. *Collapse: How Societies Choose to Fail or Succeed.* New York: Penguin Books, 2005.

Doherty, Catherine de Hueck. *The Gospel without Compromise*. Notre Dame, IN: Ave Maria Press, 1976.

Dolci, Danilo. *A New World in the Making*. Translated by R. Monroe. Westport, CT: Greenwood Press, 1965.

———. *Outlaws*. Translated by R. Monroe. New York: Orion, 1961.

Domhoff, G. William. *Changing the Powers That Be: How the Left Can Stop Losing and Win*. Lanham, MD: Rowman & Littlefield, 2003.

———. *Who Rules America? Power, Politics, and Social Change*. 5th ed. Boston: McGraw Hill, 2006.

Donohue, John J., and John L. Esposito, eds. *Islam in Transition: Muslim Perspectives*. 2nd ed. Oxford University Press, 2007.

Douglass, James W. *JFK and the Unspeakable: Why He Died and Why It Matters*. Maryknoll, NY: Orbis Books, 2008.

Dugard, John. "The Legal Status of Palestinian Political Prisoners with Special Reference to Prisoner of War Status." In *Plenary II*. United Nations International Meeting on the Question of Palestine: The Question of Palestinian Political Prisoners in Israeli Prisons and Detention Facilities: Legal and Political Implications. 3 and 4 April 2012. United Nations. http://www.un.org/depts/dpa/qpal/docs/2012%20Geneva/P2%20John%20Dugard%20EN .pdf. Accessed 12 March 2014.

Dwyer, Judith A., ed. *The Catholic Bishops and Nuclear War: A Critique and Analysis of the Pastoral, The Challenge of Peace*. Washington, DC: Georgetown University Press, 1984.

———. *The New Dictionary of Catholic Social Thought*. Collegeville, MN: Liturgical Press, 1994.

Dyck, Cornelius. "Mennonites." *Encyclopedia of Religion*. Edited by Lindsay Jones. Vol. 9. 2nd ed., 5860–5861. Detroit: Macmillan Reference USA, 2005.

Eades, J. S. *The Yoruba Today*. 1980. Especially chapter 6: "Belief Systems and Religious Organization." Cambridge University Press, 1980. Center for Social Anthropology and Computing of the University of Kent at Canterbury. http://lucy.ukc.ac.uk/yorubat/yt.html. Accessed 11 March 2014.

Easwaran, Eknath. *Nonviolent Soldier of Islam: Badshah Khan, a Man to Match His Mountains*. 2nd ed. Tomales, CA: Nilgiri, 1999.

Ebbott, Elizabeth. *Indians in Minnesota*. Edited by Judith Rosenblatt. 4th ed. Minneapolis: University of Minnesota Press, 1985.

Ehrman, Bart D. *The New Testament: A Historical Introduction to the Early Christian Writings*. 4th ed. New York: Oxford University Press, 2008.

Eliade, Mircea, et al., eds. *The Encyclopedia of Religion*. New York: Macmillan, 1987.

Ellis, Marc H. *Beyond Innocence and Redemption: Confronting the Holocaust and Israeli Power: Creating a Moral Future for the Jewish People*. San Francisco: Harper & Row, 1990.

———. "Jews, Christians, and Liberation Theology." In *Judaism, Christianity, and Liberation: An Agenda for Dialogue*. Edited by Otto Maduro. Maryknoll, NY: Orbis, 1991.

———. *Toward a Jewish Theology of Liberation: The Challenge of the 21st Century*. 3rd expanded edition. Waco, TX: Baylor University Press, 2004.

Ennes, James M. "The USS *Liberty* Affair." In *Burning Issues: Understanding and Misunderstanding the Middle East, A 40-Year Chronicle*, edited by Jane Adas, John Mahoney, and Robert Norberg. New York: Americans for Middle East Understanding, 2007.

Eppsteiner, Fred, ed. *The Path of Compassion: Writings on Socially Engaged Buddhism*. Revised 2nd ed. A Buddhist Peace Fellowship Book. Berkeley, CA: Parallax Press, 1988.

Erikson, Erik H. *Gandhi's Truth: On the Origins of Militant Nonviolence.* New York: W. W. Norton, 1993.

Esack, Farid. *Quran, Liberation and Pluralism: An Islamic Perspective of Interreligious Solidarity against Oppression.* Oxford, UK: Oneworld, 1997.

Esposito, John L. *Islam: The Straight Path.* 4th ed. New York: Oxford University Press, 2011.

Esposito, John L., and John O. Voll. *Islam and Democracy.* New York: Oxford University Press, 1996.

Fadiman, James, and Robert Frager, eds. *Essential Sufism.* San Francisco: HarperSanFrancisco, 1997.

Fahey, Joseph J., and Richard Armstrong, eds. *A Peace Reader: Essential Writings on War, Justice, Non-Violence and World Order.* Revised ed. New York: Paulist Press, 1992.

Falola, Toyin, and Ann Genova, eds. *Orisa: Yoruba Gods and Spiritual Identity in Africa and the Diaspora.* Perspectives on Yoruba History and Culture. Trenton, NJ: Africa World Press, 2005.

Fanon, Frantz. *The Wretched of the Earth.* Preface by Jean-Paul Sartre. Translated by Constance Farrington. New York: Grove Press, 1965.

Farber, Seth. *Radicals, Rabbis and Peacemakers: Conversations with Jewish Critics of Israel.* Monroe, ME: Common Courage, 2005.

Fellman, Gordon. *Rambo and the Dalai Lama: The Compulsion to Win and Its Threat to Human Survival.* With a foreword by the Dalai Lama. Global Conflict and Peace Education. Albany: State University of New York Press, 1998.

Ferguson, John. *War and Peace in the World's Religions.* New York: Oxford University Press, 1978.

Ferm, Dean William. *Profiles in Liberation: 36 Portraits of Third World Theologians.* Mystic, CT: 23rd Publications, 1988.

Fernandes, Walter, ed. *The Emerging Dalit Identity: The Re-Assertion of the Subalterns.* New Delhi: Indian Social Institute, 1996.

Fernando, Tarcisius, and Helene O'Sullivan. *Launching the Second Century: The Future of Catholic Social Thought in Asia.* Hong Kong: Asian Centre for the Progress of Peoples, 1993.

Fischer-Schreiber, Ingrid, et al. *Encyclopedia of Eastern Philosophy and Religion: Buddhism, Hinduism, Taoism, Zen.* Boston: Shambala, 1989.

Fisher, Mary Pat. *Living Religions.* 5th ed. Upper Saddle River, NJ: Prentice-Hall, 2002.

Flannery, Austin, ed. *Vatican Council II: More Postconciliar Documents.* Vatican Collection. Vol. 2. Collegeville, MN: The Liturgical Press, 1982.

Flapan, Simha. *The Birth of Israel: Myths and Realities.* New York: Pantheon Books, 1987.

———. *Zionism and the Palestinians.* London; New York: Croom Helm; Harper & Row, 1979.

Frossard, André. *I Have Met Him: God Exists.* New York: Herder and Herder, 1971.

Funk, Robert Walter. *The Acts of Jesus: The Search for the Authentic Deeds of Jesus.* [San Francisco]: HarperSanFrancisco, 1998.

Funk, Robert Walter, and Roy W. Hoover. *The Five Gospels: The Search for the Authentic Words of Jesus: New Translation and Commentary.* San Francisco: HarperSanFrancisco, 1997.

Galtung, Johan. *Buddhism: A Quest for Unity and Peace.* Colombo: Sarvodaya International, 1993.

———. *Peace by Peaceful Means: Peace and Conflict, Development and Civilization.* London: SAGE, 1996.

———. "A Structural Theory of Imperialism." *Journal of Peace Research* 8 (1971): 81–117. Reprinted in *Approaches to Peace: A Reader in Peace Studies*, edited by David P. Barash, 42–45. New York: Oxford University Press, 2000.

Gandhi, M. K. *All Men Are Brothers: Life and Thoughts of Mahatma Gandhi: As Told in His Own Words.* Paris: United Nations Educational, Scientific, and Cultural Organization, 1958.

———. *An Autobiography: The Story of My Experiments with Truth.* Translated by Mahadev Desai. Boston: Beacon Press, [1993], 1957.

———. *The Bhagvadgita.* New Delhi: Orient Paperbacks, 1980.

———. *Non-Violence in Peace and War.* Ahmedabad: Navajivan Publishing, 1942.

———. *Non-Violent Resistance (Satyagraha).* New York: Schocken, 1951.

Gautama, Siddhartha. "The Sermon at Benares." In *Buddha, the Gospel.* Edited by Paul Carus. Chicago: The Open Court Publishing Company, 1894. Available at www.sacred-texts.com/bud/btg/btg17.htm. Accessed 13 March 2014.

Gertner, Jon. "The Futile Pursuit of Happiness." *New York Times*, http://www.nytimes.com/2003/09/07/magazine/the-futile-pursuit-of-happiness.html. Accessed 12 March 2014.

Gill, Sam D. "Native American Religions: An Introduction." In *Religious Life in History.* 2nd ed. Belmont, CA: Wadsworth/Thompson Learning, 2005.

Glasse, Cyril. *The Concise Encyclopedia of Islam.* San Francisco: HarperSanFrancisco, 1991.

Glossop, Ronald J. *Confronting War: An Examination of Humanity's Most Pressing Problem*, 4th ed. Jefferson, NC, and London: McFarland, 2001.

Gopin, Marc. *How Religion Can Bring Peace to the Middle East.* New York: Oxford University Press, 2002.

Gordon, Haim, and Leonard Grob, eds. *Education for Peace: Testimonies from World Religions.* Maryknoll, NY: Orbis Books, c1987.

Gorospe, Vitaliano, S.J. *Forming the Filipino Social Conscience: Social Theology from a Filipino Christian Perspective.* 2nd ed. Makati City, Philippines: Bookmark, 2000.

Gottlieb, Roger S., ed. *Liberating Faith: Religious Voices for Justice, Peace, and Ecological Wisdom.* Lanham, MD: Rowman & Littlefield, 2003.

Gramsci, Antonio. *Prison Notebooks.* 3 vols. Translated by Joseph A. Buttigieg. New York: Columbia University Press, 2011.

Gray, J. Glenn. *The Warriors: Reflections on Men in Battle.* New York: Harper Colophon, 1970.

Greeley, Andrew. *Death and Beyond.* Chicago: Thomas More Press, 1976.

Gregg, Richard. *The Power of Nonviolence.* New York: Schocken, 1960.

Gregory, Bishop Wilton D. *Letter to President Bush on Iraq.* 13 September 2002. United States Conference of Catholic Bishops. http://www.usccb.org/issues-and-action/human-life-and-dignity/global-issues/mi ddle-east/iraq/letter-to-president-bush-from-bishop-gregory-on-iraq-2002-09-13.cfm. Accessed 7 March 2014.

Gremillion, Joseph, ed. *The Gospel of Peace and Justice: Catholic Social Teaching since Pope John.* Maryknoll, NY: Orbis, 1976.

Grey, Mary. "Feminist Theology: A Critical Theology of Liberation." In *The Cambridge Companion to Liberation Theology*, edited by Christopher Rowland. Kindle. 2nd ed., 105–22. New York: Cambridge University Press, 2007.

Griffith, Sidney H. *The Church in the Shadow of the Mosque: Christians and Muslims in the World of Islam.* Kindle. Princeton and Oxford: Princeton University Press, 2008.

Griffiths, Paul J., ed. *Christianity through Non-Christian Eyes.* Maryknoll, New York: Orbis Books, 1990.

Groebel, Jo. "The Role of the Mass Media in Modern Wars." In *War: A Cruel Necessity? The Bases of Institutionalized Violence*, edited by Robert A. Hinde and Helen E. Watson. London: I. B. Tauris, 1995.

Grossman, Dave, Lt. Col. *On Killing: The Psychological Cost of Learning to Kill in War and Society*. Boston: Little, Brown and Company, 1995.

Gutiérrez, Gustavo. "Faith and Social Conflict: From *A Theology of Liberation*." In *Liberating Faith: Religious Voices for Justice, Peace, and Ecological Wisdom*, edited by Roger S. Gottlieb, 196–202. Lanham, MD: Rowman & Littlefield, 2003.

———. *A Theology of Liberation: History, Politics, and Salvation*. Rev. ed. Maryknoll, NY: Orbis, 1988.

Halley, Henry Hampton. *Halley's Bible Handbook: An Abbreviated Bible Commentary*. 24th ed. Grand Rapids, MI: Zondervan, 1965.

Hallie, Philip Paul. *Lest Innocent Blood Be Shed: The Story of the Village of Le Chambon, and How Goodness Happened There*. New York: Harper Colophon Books, 1980.

Hallock, Daniel. *Hell, Healing, and Resistance: Veterans Speak*. Foreword by Thich Nhat Hanh. Preface by Philip Berrigan. Farmington, PA: Plough, 1998.

Hare, Robert D. *Without Conscience: The Disturbing World of the Psychopaths among Us*. Kindle. New York; London: The Guilford Press, 1993.

Hart, Alan. *Zionism: The Real Enemy of the Jews*. Vol. 1: *The False Messiah*. 2nd ed. Atlanta, GA: Clarity Press, Inc., 2009.

———. *Zionism: The Real Enemy of the Jews*. Vol. 2: *David Becomes Goliath*. 2nd ed. Atlanta, GA: Clarity Press, Inc., 2009.

———. *Zionism: The Real Enemy of the Jews*. Vol. 3: *Conflict without End?* 2nd ed. Atlanta, GA: Clarity Press, Inc., 2010.

Hasek, Jaroslav. *The Good Soldier Schweik*. Translated by Paul Selver. New York: Penguin, 1942.

Hashmi, Sohail H., ed. *Just Wars, Holy Wars, and Jihads: Christian, Jewish, and Muslim Encounters and Exchanges*. New York: Oxford University Press, 2012.

Hass, Amira. *Drinking the Sea at Gaza: Days and Nights in a Land under Siege*. Translated by Elana Wesley and Maxine Kaufman-Lacusta. 1st American ed. New York: Henry Holt, 1999.

Hassan, Riffat. "Are Human Rights Compatible with Islam? The Issue of the Rights of Women in Muslim Communities." The Religious Consultation on Population, Reproductive Health and Ethics. http://www.religiousconsultation.org/hassan2.htm. Accessed 12 March 2014.

———. "Peace Education: A Muslim Perspective." In *Education for Peace: Testimonies from World Religions*, edited by Haim Gordon and Leonard Grob. Maryknoll, NY: Orbis Books, c1987.

———. *Women's Rights and Islam: From the ICPD to Beijing*. Indiana University, 2010.

Hebblethwaite, Peter. "Liberation Theology and the Roman Catholic Church." In *The Cambridge Companion to Liberation Theology*, edited by Christopher Rowland. 2nd ed., 209–28. Cambridge: Cambridge University Press, 2007.

Heinberg, Richard. *The Party's Over: Oil, War, and the Fate of Industrial Societies*. Revised and updated. Gabriola Island, British Columbia: New Society Publishers, 2005.

———. *Power Down: Options and Actions for a Post-Carbon World*. Gabriola Island, British Columbia: New Society Publishers, 2004.

Hersh, Seymour M. *The Samson Option: Israel's Nuclear Arsenal and American Foreign Policy*. New York: Random House, 1991.

Herzl, Theodor. *The Complete Diaries of Theodor Herzl.* Translated by Harry Zohn. Edited by Raphael Patai. New York: Herzl Press and Thomas Yoseloff, 1960.

———. *The Jewish State.* eBook available for free download in various formats from Gutenberg at http://www.gutenberg.org/ebooks/25282. Accessed 13 March 2014.

Hiatt, Stephen, ed. *A Game As Old As Empire: The Secret World of Economic Hit Men and the Web of Global Corruption.* San Francisco: Barrett-Koehler, 2007.

Hillesum, Etty. *Etty: The Letters and Diaries of Etty Hillesum, 1941–1943.* Translated by Arnold J. Pomerans. Edited by Klaas A. D. Smelik. Grand Rapids, MI: William B. Eerdmans, 2002.

Hinde, Robert A., and Helen E. Watson, eds. *War: A Cruel Necessity? The Bases of Institutionalized Violence.* London: I. B. Tauris, 1995.

Hodgson, Marshall G. S. *The Venture of Islam: Consequence and History in a World Civilization.* 3 vols. Chicago: University of Chicago Press, 1974.

Holler, Clyde, ed. *The Black Elk Reader.* Syracuse, NY: Syracuse University Press, 2000.

Holmes, Arthur F., ed. *War and Christian Ethics.* 2nd ed. Grand Rapids, MI: Baker Academic, 2005.

Holmes, Robert L. *On War and Morality: Studies in Moral, Political, and Legal Philosophy.* Princeton, NJ: Princeton University Press, 1989.

Holmes, Robert L., and Barry L. Gan. *Nonviolence in Theory and Practice.* 2nd ed. Long Grove, IL: Waveland, 2005.

Hood, Robert E. *Social Teachings in the Episcopal Church: A Source Book.* Harrisburg, PA: Morehouse Publishing, 1990.

Horowitz, Elliott S. *Reckless Rites: Purim and the Legacy of Jewish Violence.* Princeton, NJ: Princeton University Press, 2006.

Hovannisian, Richard G., ed. *The Armenian Genocide in Perspective.* New Brunswick, NJ: Transaction Books, 1986.

Iqbal, Muhammad. *The Reconstruction of Religious Thought in Islam.* Lahore: Javid Iqbal, 1960.

Israel/Palestine Mission Network. *Zionism Unsettled: A Congregational Study Guide.* Booklet. Presbyterian Church (U.S.A.), 2014.

Israel/Palestine Mission Network of the Presbyterian Church (U.S.A.). *Zionism and the Quest for Justice in the Holy Land.* Eugene, OR: Pickwick Publications, Forthcoming 2014.

James, William. *The Varieties of Religious Experience: A Study in Human Nature.* New York: Collier, 1961.

Jews for Justice in the Middle East. *The Origin of the Palestine-Israel Conflict.* 3rd ed. San Rafael, CA: Jews for Justice in the Middle East, 2001.

Johnson, Elizabeth A., ed. *The Church Women Want: Catholic Women in Dialogue.* New York: Crossroad, 2002.

———. "Imaging God, Embodying Christ: Women as a Sign of the Times." In *The Church Women Want: Catholic Women in Dialogue,* edited by Elizabeth Johnson, 45–59. New York: Crossroad, 2002.

———. *She Who Is: The Mystery of God in Feminist Theological Discourse.* New York: Crossroad, 2002.

Johnson, James Turner. *The Holy War Idea in Western and Islamic Traditions.* University Park: Pennsylvania State University Press, 1997.

———. *Just War Tradition and the Restraint of War: A Moral and Historical Inquiry.* Princeton, NJ: Princeton University Press, 1981.

Johnson, Luke Timothy. *The Real Jesus: The Misguided Quest for the Historical Jesus and the Truth of the Traditional Gospels.* San Francisco: HarperSanFrancisco, 1996.

Johnston, Douglas, ed. *Faith-Based Diplomacy: Trumping Realpolitik.* Oxford: Oxford University Press, 2003.

Johnston, Douglas, and Cynthia Sampson, eds. *Religion, the Missing Dimension of Statecraft.* New York: Oxford University Press, 1994.

Jordens, J. T. F. "Gandhi and the *Bhagavadgita.*" In *Modern Indian Interpreters of the Bhagavadgita,* edited by Robert N. Minor, 88–105. Albany: State University of New York Press, 1986.

Juergensmeyer, Mark. *The New Cold War? Religious Nationalism Confronts the Secular State.* Comparative Studies in Religion and Society. Berkeley: University of California Press, 1993.

Kaltner, John. *Introducing the Qur'an for Today's Reader.* Minneapolis: Fortress Press, 2011.

Katz, Shmuel. *Days of Fire.* London: W. H. Allen, 1968.

Kaufman-Lacusta, Maxine. *Refusing to Be Enemies: Palestinian and Israeli Nonviolent Resistance to the Israel Occupation.* Reading, UK: Ithaca Press, 2010.

Kelsay, John. *Islam and War: A Study in Comparative Ethics.* Louisville, KY: Westminster/John Knox, 1993.

Khadduri, Majid. *War and Peace in the Law of Islam.* Baltimore: Johns Hopkins Press, 1955.

Khalidi, Rashid. *The Iron Cage: The Story of the Palestinian Struggle for Statehood.* Boston: Beacon Press, 2006.

Khalidi, Walid, ed. *All That Remains: The Palestinian Villages Occupied and Depopulated by Israel in 1948.* Washington, DC: Institute for Palestine Studies, 1992.

———. *Before Their Diaspora: A Photographic History of the Palestinians, 1876–1948.* Washington, DC: Institute for Palestine Studies, 1984, 1991.

———, ed. *From Haven to Conquest: Readings in Zionism and the Palestine Problem until 1948.* Beirut: The Institute for Palestine Studies, 1971.

King, Martin Luther Jr. *A Testament of Hope: The Essential Writings and Speeches of Martin Luther King Jr.* Edited by James M. Washington. San Francisco: HarperSanFrancisco, 1986.

Kohn, Alfie. *Punished by Rewards: The Trouble with Gold Stars, Incentive Plans, A's, Praise, and Other Bribes.* With a new afterword by the author. Boston: Houghton Mifflin, 1999.

Kotb, Sayed. *See* Qutb, Sayyid.

Kropotkin, Prince Peter. *Memoirs of a Revolutionist.* Montreal: Black Rose Books, 1989.

Lalami, Laila. "Islamophbia and Its Discontents." In "Islamophobia: Anatomy of an American Panic" (special issue). *The Nation,* 2/9 July 2012.

Las Casas, Bartholomé de. *Tears of the Indians.* Williamstown, MA: J. Lilburne, 1970 (originally published 1656).

Lash, Nicholas. *A Matter of Hope: A Theologian's Reflections on the Thought of Karl Marx.* Notre Dame, IN: University of Notre Dame Press, 1981.

Lazare, Sarah. "Palestinians in Hebron." *Truthout,* 17 April 2013. http://www.truth-out.org/news/item/15799-palestinians-in-hebron-to-be-here-is-a-form-of-resistance. Accessed 13 March 2014.

Lebacqz, Karen. *Justice in an Unjust World: Foundations for a Christian Approach to Justice.* Minneapolis: Augsburg Publishing House, 1987.

———. *Six Theories of Justice: Perspectives from Philosophical and Theological Ethics.* Minneapolis: Augsburg Publishing House, 1986.

Legenhausen, Hajj Muhammad. "Islam and Just War Theory." 7 February 2008. The Imam Khomeini Education and Research Institute. https://www.academia.edu/2522530/_Islam_and_Just_War_Theory. Accessed 13 March 2014.

Leigh, David. "General Sacked by Bush Says He Wanted Early Elections." *The Guardian/UK*, 18 March 2004. www.commondreams.org/headlines04/0318-01.htm. Accessed June 14, 2006.

Lenin, Vladimir Ilich. *The Lenin Anthology*. Edited by Robert C. Tucker. New York: Norton, 1975.

———. *What Is to Be Done? Burning Questions of Our Movement*. New York: International Publishers, 1969.

Lindblom, J. *Prophecy in Ancient Israel*. Philadelphia: Fortress Press, 1967.

Lindsey, Hal. *The Late, Great Planet Earth*. With the assistance of C. C. Carlson. Grand Rapids, MI: Zondervan, 1970.

Lings, Martin. *What Is Sufism?* Berkeley and Los Angeles: University of California Press, 1975.

Lobaczewski, Andrew M. *Political Ponerology: A Science on the Nature of Evil Adjusted for Political Purposes*. Translated by Alexandra Chciuk-Celt. Edited by Laura Knight-Jadczyk and Henry See. Grande Prairie, Alberta, Canada: Red Pill Press, 2012.

London Sunday Times. *The Yom Kippur War*, by the Insight Team of the London Sunday Times. Garden City, NY: Doubleday, 1974.

Lucas, Noah. *The Modern History of Israel*. London: Weidenfeld & Nicolson, 1974.

Lustick, Ian S. "Two-State Illusion." *New York Times*, 15 September 2013: Sunday Review Opinion Pages SR1. New York. http://www.nytimes.com/2013/09/15/opinion/sunday/two-state-illusion.html?pagewanted=all&_r=1&. Accessed 13 March 2014.

Luther, Martin. "Doctor Luther's Bull and Reformation." In *Against the Spiritual Estate of the Pope and the Bishops, Falsely So Called* (1522) in *Luther's Works*, vol. 39: Church and Ministry I. Edited by H. T. Lehmann and E. W. Gritsch. Philadelphia: Fortress Press, 1970.

Luxemburg, Rosa. *Reflections and Writings*. Amherst, NY: Humanity Books, 1999.

Maalouf, Amin. *The Crusades through Arab Eyes*. New York: Schocken, 1984.

Macdonald, Duncan Black. *The Religious Attitude and Life in Islam*. New York: AMS Press, 1970.

MacNair, Rachel. *The Psychology of Peace: An Introduction*. Westport, CT: Praeger, 2003.

Macy, Joanna Rogers. *Despair and Personal Power in the Nuclear Age*. Philadelphia: New Society Publishers, 1983.

Maduro, Otto, ed. *Judaism, Christianity, and Liberation: An Agenda for Dialogue*. Maryknoll, NY: Orbis, 1991.

Mahfouz, Naguib. *Midaq Alley*. Translated by Trevor Le Gassick. New York: Anchor Books, 1992.

Martin, Ernest L. *The Temples That Jerusalem Forgot*. Portland, OR: ASK Publications, 2000.

Marx, Karl, and Frederick Engels. *The Communist Manifesto: Annotated Text*. Edited by Frederic L. Bender. New York: W. W. Norton, 1988.

———. *Karl Marx: Selected Writings*. 2nd ed. Oxford: Oxford University Press, 2000.

———. *Karl Marx, Frederick Engels: Collected Works*. New York: International Publishers, 1975–2004.

———. *The Marx-Engels Reader*. Edited by Robert C. Tucker. 2nd ed. New York: W. W. Norton, 1978.

Mason, John. *A Brief History of the Pequot War*. Boston: S. Kneeland and T. Green in Queen Street, 1736. Available at http://digitalcommons.unl.edu/cgi/viewcontent.cgi?article=1042&context=etas. Accessed 13 March 2014.

Massaro, Thomas. *Living Justice: Catholic Social Teaching in Action*. Franklin, WI: Sheed & Ward, 2000.

Masters, Carol, and Marv Davidov. *You Can't Do That! Marv Davidov, Nonviolent Revolutionary.* Minneapolis: Nodin Press, 2009.

Matthews, Alfred Warren. *World Religions.* 4th ed. Belmont, CA: Wadsworth/Thomson Learning, 2004.

Maurin, Peter. *Easy Essays.* Chicago: Franciscan Herald Press, 1977.

Mayer, Milton. *They Thought They Were Free: The Germans 1933–1945.* Chicago: University of Chicago Press, 1955.

McAllister, Pam. *You Can't Kill the Spirit.* Philadelphia: New Society Publishers, 1988.

McDonald, Di. "A Way of Life." *SGI Quarterly* (April 2005). Available at http://www.sgi quarterly.org/feature2005Apr-7.html. Accessed 13 March 2014.

McElwee, Joshua J. *With Vatican Doctrinal Czar, Liberation Theology Pioneer Reflects on Troubles.* 28 February 2014. *National Catholic Reporter.* http://ncronline.org/news/theology/vati can-doctrinal-czar-liberation-theology-pioneer-reflects-troubles. Accessed 5 March 2014.

McGovern, Arthur F. *Liberation Theology and Its Critics: Towards an Assessment.* Maryknoll, NY: Orbis, 1994.

McKenzie, John L. *Dictionary of the Bible.* Milwaukee, WI: Bruce Publishing, 1965.

———. *Myths and Realities.* Milwaukee, WI: Bruce Publishing Co., 1963.

McLellan, David. *Karl Marx: His Life and Thought.* New York: Harper & Row, 1973.

———. *Marx before Marxism.* New York: Harper & Row, 1970.

McManus, Philip, and Gerald Schlabach, eds. *Relentless Persistence: Nonviolent Action in Latin America.* Philadelphia: New Society Publishers, 1991.

Mernissi, Fatima. *Journalistes Marocaines: Generation dialogue.* Rabat, Morocco: Marsam, 2012.

Merton, Thomas. *The Nonviolent Alternative.* New York: Farrar, Straus & Giroux, 1980.

Meyer, Hajo G. *The End of Judaism: An Ethical Tradition Betrayed.* G. Meyer Books, 2007.

Meyer, John. "Jesus." In *The New Jerome Biblical Commentary,* section 78, edited by Raymond E. Brown, Joseph A. Fitzmyer, and Roland E. Murphy, 1316–28. Englewood Cliffs, NJ: Prentice Hall, c 1990, 1968.

Mich, Marvin L. Krier. *Catholic Social Teaching and Movements.* Mystic, CT: Twenty-Third Publications, 1998.

Migliore. Msgr. Celestino. *Intervention at the Meeting in the Chamber of the Security Council of the United Nations on the Iraqi Issue.* 19 February 2003. Vatican. http://www.vatican.va/ roman_curia/secretariat_state/2003/documents/rc_seg-st_20030219_migliore-security-co uncil_en.html. Accessed 7 March 2014.

Míguez Bonino, José. *Christians and Marxists: The Mutual Challenge to Revolution.* Grand Rapids, MI: Eerdmans, 1976.

Milgram, Stanley. *Obedience to Authority: An Experimental View.* New York: Harper & Row, 1974.

Mill, John Stuart. *Utilitarianism.* London: Longmans, Green and Co., 1901.

Minor, Robert N., ed. *Modern Indian Interpreters of the Bhagavadgita.* SUNY Series in Religious Studies. Albany: State University of New York Press, 1986.

Moody, Raymond A. *Life after Life: The Investigation of a Phenomenon—Survival of Bodily Death.* New York: Bantam Books, 1976.

Morris, Benny. *The Birth of the Palestinian Refugee Problem Revisited.* Cambridge, UK: Cambridge University Press, 2004.

———. *Righteous Victims: A History of the Zionist-Arab Conflict, 1881–2001.* New York: Vintage, 2001.

Muhaiyaddeen, M. R. Bawa. *Islam and World Peace: Explanations of a Sufi.* Philadelphia: Fellowship Press, 1987.

Munif, Abd al-Rahman, and Peter Theroux. *Cities of Salt.* Translated by Peter Theroux. New York: Vintage, 1987.

Muste, Abraham John. *The Essays of A. J. Muste.* Edited by Nat Hentoff. Indianapolis, IN: Bobbs-Merrill, 1967.

Nanda, B. R. *Mahatma Gandhi: A Biography.* Abridged ed. London: Unwin, 1965.

Nasr, Seyyed Hossein. "Reflections on Islam and the West: Yesterday, Today and Tomorrow." Oxford Islamic Studies Online. http://www.oxfordislamicstudies.com/article/book/islam-97 80195174304/islam-9780195174304-chapter-59. Accessed 13 March 2014.

National Conference of Catholic Bishops. *The Challenge of Peace: God's Promise and Our Response: A Pastoral Letter on War and Peace.* Washington, DC: United States Catholic Conference, 1983. http://www.cctwincities.org/document.doc?id = 91. Accessed 14 March 2014.

National Conference of Catholic Bishops, United States Catholic Conference. *Economic Justice for All: Pastoral Letter on Catholic Social Teaching and the U.S. Economy.* Tenth anniversary. Washington, DC: National Conference of Catholic Bishops, 1997. www.usccb.org/upload/economic_justice_for_all.pdf. Accessed 12 March 2014.

Neihardt, John G. See Black Elk.

Nelson-Pallmeyer, Jack. *Harvest of Cain.* Washington, DC: Epica Task Force, 2001.

———. *Is Religion Killing Us? Violence in the Bible and the Quran.* Harrisburg, PA: Trinity Press International, c2003.

———. *Saving Christianity from Empire.* New York: Continuum, 2005.

Newsom, Carol A., Sharon H. Ringe, and Jacqueline E. Lapsley. *Women's Bible Commentary.* 3rd ed. Louisville, KY: Westminster John Knox Press, 2012.

Nhat Hanh, Thich. *Being Peace.* Edited by Arnold Kotler. Berkeley, CA: Parallax Press, 1987.

———. *Interbeing: Commentaries on the Tiep Hien Precepts.* Edited by Fred Eppsteiner. Berkeley, CA: Parallax Press, 1987.

———. *Vietnam: Lotus in a Sea of Fire.* New York: Hill and Wang, 1967.

Nicholson, Reynold A. *The Mystics of Islam.* London: Routledge and Kegan Paul, 1966 [1914]. Also available at www.sacred-texts.com/isl/moi/moi.htm. Accessed 14 March 2014.

Niebuhr, Reinhold. *Man's Nature and His Communities: Essays on the Dynamics and Enigmas of Man's Personal and Social Existence.* New York: Scribner, 1965.

———. *Moral Man and Immoral Society: A Study in Ethics and Politics.* New York and London: Scribner, 1932.

Novak, Michael. *Will It Liberate? Questions about Liberation Theology.* New York: Paulist Press, 1986.

Oakman, Douglas E. *The Political Aims of Jesus.* Minneapolis: Fortress Press, 2012.

Olson, Lynne. *Freedom's Daughters: The Unsung Heroines of the Civil Rights Movement from 1830 to 1970.* New York: Scribner, 2001.

Olson, Pamela J. *Fast Times in Palestine: A Love Affair with a Homeless Homeland.* Berkeley, CA: Seal Press, 2013.

Olupona, Jacob K., and Terry Rey, eds. *Òrìṣà Devotion as World Religion: The Globalization of Yorùbá Religious Culture.* Madison: University of Wisconsin Press, 2008.

Ophir, Adi, Michal Givoni, and Sari Hanafi. *The Power of Inclusive Exclusion: Anatomy of Israeli Rule in the Occupied Palestinian Territories.* New York: Zone Books, 2009.

Ormerod, Neil. *Catholics and Pentecostals: A Shared Mission in a Globalizing World.* http://webjournals.ac.edu.au/journals/aps/issue-12/catholics-and-pentecostals-shared-mission-globalis/. Accessed 4 March 2014.

Oxtoby, Willard Gurdon, ed. *World Religions: Eastern Traditions*. 2nd ed. Don Mills, ON: Oxford University Press, 2002.

Oxtoby, Willard Gurdon, and Alan F. Segal, Eds. *A Concise Introduction to World Religions*. Don Mills, ON: Oxford University Press, 2007.

Paige, Glenn D., Chaiwat Satha-Anand, and Sarah Gilliatt, eds. *Islam and Nonviolence*. Honolulu: University of Hawai'i, 1993.

Palackapilly, George, and T. D. Felix. *Religion and Economics: A Worldview*. New Delhi: AIDBES, 1996.

Pappe, Ilan. *The Ethnic Cleansing of Palestine*. Kindle 2011. Oxford: Oneworld, 2006.

Patterson, Stephen, Marcus Borg, and John Dominic Crossan. *The Search for Jesus: Modern Scholarship Looks at the Gospels: Symposium at the Smithsonian Institution, September 11, 1993*. Edited by Hershel Shanks. Kindle 2012. Washington, DC: Biblical Archaeology Society, 1994, 2012.

Peled, Miko. *The General's Son: Journey of an Israeli in Palestine*. Foreword by Alice Walker. Charlottesville, VA: Just World Books, 2012.

Perkins, John. *Confessions of an Economic Hit Man*. San Francisco: Berrett-Koehler, 2004.

Peterson, Anna L. *Martyrdom and the Politics of Religion: Progressive Catholicism in El Salvador's Civil War*. Albany: State University of New York Press, 1997.

Pieris, Aloysius. *An Asian Theology of Liberation*. Maryknoll, NY: Orbis, 1988.

———. *Love Meets Wisdom: A Christian Experience of Buddhism*. Faith Meets Faith. Maryknoll, NY: Orbis, 1988.

Pontifical Council for Justice and Peace. *Compendium of the Social Doctrine of the Church*. Città del Vaticano: Libreria Editrice Vaticana, 2004.

Pope Francis. *Evangelii Gaudium: To the Bishops, Clergy, Consecrated Persons, and the Lay Faithful on the Proclamation of the Gospel in Today's World*. Apostolic Exhortation. 24 November 2013. http://www.vatican.va/holy_father/francesco/apost_exhortations/docu ments/papa-francesco_esortazione-ap_20131124_evangelii-gaudium_en.html. Accessed 23 February 2014.

Pope John XXIII. *Mater et Magistra: On Christianity and Social Progress*. Libreria Editrice Vaticana: Vatican, 1961. Also available at http://www.vatican.va/holy_father/john_xxiii/ encyclicals/documents/hf_j-xxiii_enc_15051961_mater_en.html. Accessed 13 March 2014.

———. *Pacem in Terris: On Establishing Universal Peace in Truth, Justice, Charity, and Liberty*. Libreria Editrice Vaticana: Vatican, 1963. Also available at http://www.vatican.va/ holy_father/john_xxiii/encyclicals/documents/hf_j-xxiii_enc_11041963_pacem_en.html. Accessed 13 March 2014.

Pope John Paul II. *Centesimus Annus: On the Hundredth Anniversary of Rerum Novarum*. Libreria Editrice Vaticana: Vatican, 1991. Also available at http://www.vatican.va/holy _father/john_paul_ii/encyclicals/documents/hf_jp-ii_enc_01051991_centesimus-annus_ en.html. Accessed 13 March 2014.

———. *Laborem Exercens: On Human Work*. Libreria Editrice Vaticana: Vatican, 1981. Also available at http://www.vatican.va/holy_father/john_paul_ii/encyclicals/documents/hf_jp-ii _enc_14091981_laborem-exercens_en.html. Accessed 13 March 2014.

———. *Sollicitudo Rei Socialis: On the Twentieth Anniversary of Populorum Progressio*. Libreria Editrice Vaticana: Vatican, 1987. Also available at http://www.vatican.va/holy _father/john_paul_ii/encyclicals/documents/hf_jp-ii_enc_30121987_sollicitudo-rei-socialis _en.html. Accessed 13 March 2014.

Pope Leo XIII. *Rerum Novarum: On Capital and Labor*. Libreria Editrice Vaticana: Vatican, 1891. Also available at http://www.vatican.va/holy_father/leo_xiii/encyclicals/documents/ hf_l-xiii_enc_15051891_rerum-novarum_en.html. Accessed 13 March 2014.

Pope Paul VI. *Evangelii Nuntiandi: On Evangelization in the Modern World* Apostolic Exhortation. Libreria Editrice Vaticana: Vatican, 1975. Also available at http://www.vatican.va/holy _father/paul_vi/apost_exhortations/documents/hf_p-vi_exh_19751208_evangelii-nuntiandi _en.html. Accessed 13 March 2014.

———. *Octogesima Adveniens: Apostolic Letter to Cardinal Maurice Roy.* Libreria Editrice Vaticana: Vatican, 1971. Also available at http://www.vatican.va/holy_father/paul_vi/apost _letters/documents/hf_p-vi_apl_19710514_octogesima-adveniens_en.html. Accessed 13 March 2014.

———. *Populorum Progressio: On the Development of Peoples.* Libreria Editrice Vaticana: Vatican, 1967. Also available at http://www.vatican.va/holy_father/paul_vi/encyclicals/docu ments/hf_p-vi_enc_26031967_populorum_en.html. Accessed 13 March 2014.

Pope Pius XI. *Quadragesimo Anno: On Reconstruction of the Social Order.* Libreria Editrice Vaticana: Vatican, 1931. Also available at http://www.vatican.va/holy_father/pius_xi/en cyclicals/documents/hf_p-xi_enc_19310515_quadragesimo-anno_en.html. Accessed 13 March 2014.

Potok, Chaim. *The Chosen: A Novel.* New York: Simon and Schuster, 1967.

Prabhupada, A. C. Bhaktivedanta Swami. *Bhagavad-Gita As It Is.* Los Angeles: The Bhaktivedanta Book Trust, 1984.

Queen, Christopher S., ed. *Engaged Buddhism in the West.* Boston: Wisdom Publications, 2000.

Queen, Christopher S., and Sallie B. King, eds. *Engaged Buddhism: Buddhist Liberation Movements in Asia.* Albany: State University of New York Press, 1996.

Quigley, John. *Palestine and Israel: A Challenge to Justice.* Durham, NC: Duke University Press, 1990.

Qumsiyeh, Mazin. *Popular Resistance in Palestine: A History of Hope and Empowerment.* New York; London: Pluto Press, 2011.

Qutb, Sayyid [Sayed]. *Milestones.* India: Islamic Book Service, 2006. Also available at http:// www.izharudeen.com/uploads/4/1/2/2/4122615/milestones_www.izharudeen.com.pdf. Accessed 13 March 2014. [1964]

———. [Kotb, Sayed]. *Social Justice in Islam.* Translated by John B. Hardie. American Council of Learned Societies Near Eastern Translation Program, vol. 1. New York: Octagon, 1970. [1948]

Radhakrishnan, S. *Indian Philosophy.* 2nd ed. The Muirhead Library of Philosophy, vol. 1. New York; London: The Macmillan Company; George Allen & Unwin, 1929.

Radhakrishnan, S., ed. *The Bhagavadgita, with an Introductory Essay, Sanskrit Text [Transliterated], English Translation and Notes.* New York: Harper and Brothers, 1948.

Rahman, Fazlur. *Major Themes of the Qur'an.* 2nd ed. Minneapolis: Bibliotheca Islamica, 1994.

Rahula, Walpola. "The Social Teachings of the Buddha." In *Liberating Faith: Religious Voices for Justice, Peace, and Ecological Wisdom,* edited by Roger S. Gottlieb, 143–49. Lanham, MD: Rowman & Littlefield, 2003.

Rambachan, Anantanand. *The Advaita Worldview: God, World, and Humanity.* Albany: State University of New York Press, 2006.

———. "A Hindu Perspective." In *What Men Owe to Women: Men's Voices from World Religions,* edited by John C Raines and Daniel C. Maguire. Albany: State University of New York Press, 2001.

Ramsey, Paul. *The Just War: Force and Political Responsibility.* Reprint of 1968 edition. Lanham, MD: University Press of America, 1983.

Ratzinger, Cardinal Joseph. *Instruction on Certain Aspects of the "Theology of Liberation."* Sacred Congregation for the Doctrine of the Faith, 1984. Available at http://www.vatican .va/roman_curia/congregations/cfaith/documents/rc_con_cfaith_doc_19840806_theology -liberation_en.html. Accessed 14 March 2014.

———. *Instruction on Christian Freedom and Liberation.* Rome: Congregation for the Doctrine of the Faith, 1986. Also available at http://www.vatican.va/roman_curia/congrega tions/cfaith/documents/rc_con_cfaith_doc_19860322_freedom-liberation_en.html. Accessed 13 March 2014.

Rawls, John. *Justice as Fairness: A Restatement.* Edited by Erin Kelly. Cambridge, MA: Harvard University Press, 2001.

———. *A Theory of Justice.* Cambridge, MA: The Belknap Press of Harvard University Press, 1971.

Restall, Matthew. *Seven Myths of the Spanish Conquest.* Oxford: Oxford University Press, 2003.

Rinpoche, Samdhong. *Selected Writings and Speeches: A Collection of Selected Writings and Speeches on Buddhism and Tibetan Culture.* Jamtse Series. Alumni of Central Institute of Higher Tibetan Studies, 1999.

Robinson, Neal. *Islam: A Concise Introduction.* Washington, DC: Georgetown University Press, 1999.

Roman Synod of Catholic Bishops. "Justice in the World." In *Proclaiming Justice and Peace,* edited by Michael Walsh and Brian Davies, 268–83. Mystic, CT: Twenty-Third Publications, 1991.

Rosenberg, Marshall B. *Nonviolent Communication: A Language of Compassion.* Encinitas, CA: PuddleDancer Press, 1999.

Rowland, Christopher, ed. *The Cambridge Companion to Liberation Theology.* 2nd ed. Cambridge; New York: Cambridge University Press, 2007.

———. "Introduction: The Theology of Liberation." In *The Cambridge Companion to Liberation Theology,* edited by Christopher Rowland. Kindle. 2nd ed., 1–16. Cambridge; New York: Cambridge University Press, 2007.

Roy, Beth. *Some Trouble with Cows: Making Sense of Social Conflict.* Berkeley: University of California Press, 1994.

Royte, Elizabeth. *Bottlemania: Big Business, Local Springs, and the Battle Over America's Drinking Water.* Kindle. New York; Berlin; London: Bloomsbury, 2011.

Rubenstein, Richard L. *After Auschwitz: Radical Theology and Contemporary Judaism.* Indianapolis, IN: Bobbs-Merrill Company, 1966.

Rubenstein, Richard L., and John K. Roth. *Approaches to Auschwitz: The Holocaust and Its Legacy.* Atlanta, GA: John Knox Press, 1987.

Ruether, Rosemary Radford. "False Messianism and Prophetic Consciousness." In *Judaism, Christianity, and Liberation: An Agenda for Dialogue,* edited by Otto Maduro, 83–95. Maryknoll, NY: Orbis, 1991.

Ruether, Rosemary Radford, and Marc H. Ellis, eds. *Beyond Occupation: American Jewish, Christian, and Palestinian Voices for Peace.* Boston: Beacon Press, 1990.

Ruether, Rosemary Radford, and Herman J. Ruether. *The Wrath of Jonah: The Crisis of Religious Nationalism in the Israeli-Palestinian Conflict.* 2nd ed. Minneapolis: Fortress Press, 2002.

al-Rumi, Jalal al-Din. *Mathnawi.* Available at www.sacred-texts.com/isl/masnavi/index.htm. Accessed 14 March 2014.

Saadawi, Nawal. *A Daughter of Isis: The Autobiography of Nawal El Saadawi.* Translated by Sherif Hetata. London: Zed Books, 1999.

———. *The Hidden Face of Eve: Women in the Arab World.* Translated by Sherif Hetata. Boston, MA: Beacon Press, 1982.

———. *Memoirs from the Women's Prison.* Translated by Marilyn Booth. Berkeley: University of California Press, 1994.

Said, Edward W. *The Question of Palestine.* New York: Times Books, 1979.

Samuel, Dorothy T. *Safe Passage on City Streets.* Expanded ed. Richmond, IN: Liberty Literary Works, 1991.

Sand, Shlomo. *The Invention of the Jewish People.* Translated by Yael Lotan. Kindle. London; New York: Verso, 2010; c2009.

———. *The Invention of the Land of Israel: From Holy Land to Homeland.* Translated by Geremy Forman. Kindle. London; New York: Verso, 2013.

Sanford, Agnes Mary White. *The Healing Light.* 8th ed. St. Paul, MN: Macalester Park Publishing Co., 1949.

———. *Sealed Orders.* Gainesville, FL: Bridge-Logos, 1972.

Satha-Anand, Chaiwat, et al., eds. *The Frontiers of Nonviolence.* Honolulu: International Peace Research Association (IPRA)'s Nonviolence Commission, Center for Global Nonviolence, 1998.

Schall, James V., ed. *Out of Justice, Peace: Winning the Peace.* San Francisco: Ignatius Press, 1984.

Schiff, Ze'ev, and Ehud Ya'ari. *Intifada: The Palestinian Uprising: Israel's Third Front.* Translated by Ina Friedman. New York: Simon and Schuster, 1990.

Schmidt, Roger, et al. *Patterns of Religion.* Boston, MA: Wadsworth, Cengage Learning, 2014.

Schuhmacher, Stephan, Gert Woerner, and Kurt Friedrichs, eds. *The Encyclopedia of Eastern Philosophy and Religion: Buddhism, Hinduism, Taoism, Zen.* Boston: Shambhala, 1989.

Schüssler Fiorenza, Elisabeth. *In Memory of Her: A Feminist Theological Reconstruction of Christian Origins.* New York: Crossroad, 1983.

Scofield, C. I., and Henry G. Weston, eds. *The Scofield Reference Bible. The Holy Bible, Containing the Old and New Testaments. Authorized King James Version.* Scofield Facsimile Series, no. 2. New York: Oxford University Press, 1917.

Second Vatican Council. *Gaudium et Spes: Pastoral Constitution on the Church in the Modern World.* Libreria Editrice Vaticana: Vatican, 1965. Also available at http://www.vatican.va/archive/hist_councils/ii_vatican_council/documents/vat-ii_const_19651207_gaudium-et-spes_en.html. Accessed 14 March 2014.

———. *Lumen Gentium: Dogmatic Constitution on the Church.* Rome: Vatican, 1964. Also available at http://www.vatican.va/archive/hist_councils/ii_vatican_council/documents/vat-ii_const_19641121_lumen-gentium_en.html. Accessed 14 March 2014.

———. *Nostra Aetate: Declaration on the Relationship of the Church to Non-Christian Religions.* The Vatican: Rome, at St. Peter's, 28 October 1965. http://www.vatican.va/archive/hist_councils/ii_vatican_council/documents/vat-ii_decl_19651028_nostra-aetate_en.html. Accessed 8 July 2006.

Segundo, Juan Luis. *Liberation of Theology.* Maryknoll, NY: Orbis Books, 1976.

Shahak, Israel. "Israeli Discrimination against Non-Jews Is Carefully Codified in State of Israel's Laws." *Washington Report on Middle East Affairs* (January–February 1998). http://www.wrmea.org/wrmea-archives/191-washington-report-archives-1994-1999/january-february-1998/12037-other-voices-israeli-discrimination-against-non-jews-is-carefully-codified-in-state-of-israel-s-laws.html.

———. *Jewish History, Jewish Religion: The Weight of Three Thousand Years.* Forewords by Gore Vidal and Edward Said, with a new introduction by Norton Mezvinsky. London: Pluto Press, 2002.

Shahak, Israel, and Norton Mezvinsky. *Jewish Fundamentalism in Israel.* New ed. Pluto Middle Eastern Studies. London: Pluto Press, 2004.

Shaheen, Jack. "The Making of the 'Green Menace.'" In "Islamophobia: Anatomy of an American Panic" (special issue). *The Nation,* 2/9 July 2012.

Sharp, Gene. *From Dictatorship to Democracy: A Conceptual Framework for Liberation.* 4th U.S. edition. the Albert Einstein Institution: East Boston, MA: The New Press, 2010, 2012. http://www.aeinstein.org/wp-content/uploads/2013/09/FDTD.pdf. Accessed 13 March 2014.

———. *Gandhi as a Political Strategist: With Essays on Ethics and Politics.* Boston: Porter Sargent, 1979.

———. *The Politics of Nonviolent Action.* Boston: Porter Sargent, 1973.

———. *Waging Nonviolent Struggle: 20th Century Practice and 21st Century Potential.* Boston: Porter Sargent, 2005.

Shatz, David, Chaim I. Waxman, and Nathan J. Diament. *Tikkun Olam: Social Responsibility in Jewish Thought and Law.* Northvale, NJ and London: Jason Aronson, 1997.

Shaull, Richard, and Waldo César. *Pentecostalism and the Future of the Christian Churches.* Grand Rapids, MI; Cambridge, UK: William B. Eerdmans, 2000.

Shaw, William H. *Business Ethics.* 8th ed. Boston: Wadsworth, Cengage Learning, 2014.

Shepard, William. *Introducing Islam.* London and New York: Routledge, 2009.

Silouan, Staretz, and Archimandrite Sofronii. *Wisdom from Mount Athos: The Writings of Starets Silouan, 1866–1938.* Translated by Rosemary Edmonds. Edited by Archimandrite Sophrony. Revised ed. Crestwood, NY: St. Vladimir's Seminary Press, 1974.

Simons, Rabbi Dr. Chaim. *A Historical Survey of Proposals to Transfer Arabs from Palestine 1895–1947,* (c)2003. http://chaimsimons.net/transfer.html. Accessed 14 March 2014.

Sivaraksa, Sulak. *Conflict, Culture, Change: Engaged Buddhism in a Globalizing World.* Boston: Wisdom Publications, 2005.

———, ed. *Socially Engaged Buddhism for the New Millennium: Essays in Honor of the Venerable Phra Dhammapitaka (Bhikkhu P.A. Payutto) on His 60th Birthday Anniversary.* Bangkok: Parallax Press, 1999.

Smart, Ninian. *The World's Religions.* 2nd ed. Cambridge: Cambridge University Press, 1998.

———. *Worldviews: Crosscultural Explorations of Human Beliefs.* 3rd ed. Upper Saddle River, NJ: Prentice Hall, 2000.

Smith, David Whitten. "Inspired Authors and Saintly Interpreters in Conflict: The New Testament on War and Peace." In *Blessed Are the Peacemakers,* edited by Anthony J. Tambasco, 152–78. New York: Paulist Press, 1989.

Smith, Preserved. *The Life and Letters of Martin Luther.* London: John Murray, 1911.

Sokolow, Nahum. *History of Zionism (1600–1918),* vol. 1. London: Longmans, Green, 1919. Available for free download from Google books: http://books.google.com/books?id=8rgp AQAAIAAJ&printsec=frontcover&dq=Sokolow+History+of+Zionism&hl=en&sa=X &ei=ZM3AUt1C49rIAbKKgdAL&ved=0CC8Q6AEwAA#v=onepage&q=Sokolow% 20History%20of%20Zionism&f=false. Accessed 14 March 2013.

Solzhenitsyn, Aleksandr I. *The Gulag Archipelago 1918–1956: An Experiment in Literary Investigation.* Translated by Thomas P. Whitney. New York: Harper & Row, 1975.

———. *One Day in the Life of Ivan Denisovich.* Translated by Ralph Parker. Harmondsworth, UK: Penguin, 1963.

Spadaro, Antonio, S.J. "A Big Heart Open to God: The Exclusive Interview with Pope Francis." 30 September 2013. *America Magazine.* http://www.americamagazine.org/pope-interview. Accessed 4 March 2014.

Spalding, John D. *"A Humble Intellect."* Interview with Uta Ranke-Heinemann. Corpus—National Capital Region, Canada. http://www.renewedpriesthood.org/ca/page.cfm?Web_ID = 579. Accessed 4 March 2014.

Spiro, Melford E. *Anthropological Other or Burmese Brother? Studies in Cultural Analysis.* New Brunswick, NJ: Transaction Publishers, 1992.

———. *Buddhism and Society: A Great Tradition and Its Burmese Vicissitudes.* New York: Harper & Row, 1972.

Stanton, Gregory H. *The Ten Stages of Genocide.* Genocide Watch. http://genocidewatch.org/genocide/tenstagesofgenocide.html. Accessed 6 March 2014.

Steltenkamp, Michael F. *Black Elk: Holy Man of the Oglala.* Norman: University of Oklahoma Press, 1997.

———. *Nicholas Black Elk: Medicine Man, Missionary, Mystic.* Norman: University of Oklahoma Press, 2009.

Strain, Charles R., ed. *Prophetic Visions and Economic Realities: Protestants, Jews, and Catholics Confront the Bishops' Letter on the Economy.* Grand Rapids, MI: William B. Eerdmans, 1989.

Suttner, Bertha von. *Lay Down Your Arms: The Autobiography of Martha von Tilling.* Translated by T. Holmes. With a new introduction for the Garland ed. by Irwin Abrams. New York: Garland, 1972.

Suu Kyi, Aung San: see Aung San Suu Kyi; Clements.

Svirsky, Gila. "What We Need Now Are Women," 28 January 2011. http://www.genderacrossborders.com/2011/01/28/what_we_need_now_womenesvirsky/. Accessed 5 March 2014.

Taliqani, Ayatullah. "The Characteristics of Islamic Economics." In *Islam in Transition: Muslim Perspectives*, edited by Donohue and Esposito. 2nd ed. Oxford University Press, 2007.

Tamari, Ayatullah Mahmud. "Social Responsibilities of the Jewish Individual." In Shatz et al. *Tikkun Olam: Social Responsibility in Jewish Thought and Law.* Northvale, NJ, and London: Jason Aronson Inc., 1997.

Ten Boom, Corrie. *The Hiding Place.* With the assistance of John and Elizabeth Sherrill. Old Tappan, NJ: Fleming H. Revell, 1971.

Tessler, Mark A. *A History of the Israeli-Palestinian Conflict.* Bloomington: Indiana University Press, 1994.

Thurman, Robert. "Nagarjuna's Guidelines for Buddhist Social Action." In *The Path of Compassion: Writings on Socially Engaged Buddhism*, edited by Fred Eppsteiner. Revised 2nd ed., 120–44. Berkeley, CA: Parallax Press, 1988.

Tillich, Paul. *The Courage to Be.* New Haven, CT: Yale University Press, 1952.

———. *Dynamics of Faith.* New York: Harper, 1957.

Tinker, George E. *American Indian Liberation: A Theology of Sovereignty.* Maryknoll, NY: Orbis Books, 2008.

———. *Missionary Conquest: The Gospel and Native American Cultural Genocide.* Minneapolis: Fortress Press, 1993.

Tolstoy, Leo. *Writings on Civil Disobedience and Nonviolence.* Philadelphia: New Society, 1987.

Topel, L. John. *The Way to Peace: Liberation through the Bible.* Maryknoll, NY: Orbis, 1979.

Torrey, R. A., and A. C. Dixon. *The Fundamentals: A Testimony to the Truth.* Grand Rapids, MI: Baker Book House, 1972.

Trotsky, Leon. *The Revolution Betrayed: What Is the Soviet Union and Where Is It Going?* Garden City, NY: Doubleday, Doran, and Co., 1937.

United Nations. "International Covenant on Civil and Political Rights." http://www.ohchr.org/EN/ProfessionalInterest/Pages/CCPR.Aspx. United Nations, 23 March 1976.

———. "International Covenant on Economic, Social and Cultural Rights." http://www.Ohchr.Org/EN/ProfessionalInterest/Pages/CESCR.Aspx. United Nations, 3 January 1976.

United Nations General Assembly. *The Universal Declaration of Human Rights.* 10 December 1948. United Nations. http://www.un.org/en/documents/udhr/. Accessed 12 March 2014.

United States Catholic Conference: see National Conference of Catholic Bishops.

United States Conference of Catholic Bishops. *Statement on Iraq,* 26 February 2003. United States Conference of Catholic Bishops. http://www.usccb.org/issues-and-action/human-life-and-dignity/global-issues/middle-east/iraq/statement-by-bishop-gregory-on-iraq-2003-02-26.cfm. Accessed 7 March 2014.

van Braght, Thieleman J., ed. *The Bloody Theater: Or, Martyrs Mirror.* Scottdale, PA: Herald Press, 1992 [1660].

Van Voorst, Robert E. *RELG: World.* Boston, MA: Wadsworth, Cengage Learning, 2013.

Vasto, Lanza del. *Gandhi to Vinoba: The New Pilgrimage.* Translated by Philip Leon. New York: Schocken Books, 1956.

Victoria, Daizen. *Zen at War.* New York: Weatherhill, 1997.

———. *Zen War Stories.* London: Routledge, 2003.

Villa-Vicencio, Charles. "Liberation and Reconstruction: The Unfinished Agenda." In *The Cambridge Companion to Liberation Theology,* edited by Christopher Rowland. Kindle. 2nd ed., 183–206. New York: Cambridge University Press, 2007.

Vivekananda, Swami. *The Complete Works of Swami Vivekananda: Volumes 1–9.* 1989. Kindle. *Advait Ashram.* www.ramakrishnavivekananda.infohttp://www.ramakrishnavivekananda.info. Accessed 12 March 2014.

Vorspan, Albert, and David Saperstein. *Tough Choices: Jewish Perspectives on Social Justice.* New York: UAHC Press, 1992.

Wadud, Amina. *Qur'an and Woman: Rereading the Sacred Text from a Woman's Perspective.* New York: Oxford University Press, 1999.

Wakin, Malham M., ed. *War, Morality, and the Military Profession.* 2nd ed. Boulder, CO: Westview, 1986.

Walsh, Michael, and Michael Davies, eds. *Proclaiming Justice and Peace: Papal Documents from Rerum Novarum through Centesimus Annus.* Mystic, CT: Twenty-Third Publications, 1991.

Walzer, Michael. *Just and Unjust Wars: A Moral Argument with Historical Illustrations.* 3rd ed. New York: Basic Books, 2000.

Watterson, Kathryn. *Not by the Sword: How the Love of a Cantor and His Family Transformed a Klansman.* New York: Simon and Schuster, 1995.

Weaver, Mary Jo, David Brakke, and Jason Bivins. *Introduction to Christianity.* 3rd ed. Belmont, CA: Wadsworth, 1998.

Weber, Max. *The Protestant Ethic and the Spirit of Capitalism.* New York: Charles Scribner's, 1958.

Weber, Thomas. *Gandhi's Peace Army: The Shanti Sena and Unarmed Peacekeeping.* Syracuse, NY: Syracuse University Press, 1996.

Wegner, Judith Romney. *Chattel or Person?: The Status of Women in the Mishnah.* New York: Oxford University Press, 1988.

Weigert, Kathleen Maas, and Alexia K. Kelley, eds. *Living the Catholic Social Tradition: Cases and Commentary.* Lanham, MD: Rowman & Littlefield, 2005.

West, Gerald. "The Bible and the Poor: A New Way of Doing Theology." In *The Cambridge Companion to Liberation Theology,* edited by Christopher Rowland. 2nd ed., 159–82. Cambridge; New York: Cambridge University Press, 2007.

Weyler, Rex. *Blood of the Land: The Government and Corporate War against First Nations.* Revised ed. Philadelphia: New Society Publishers, 1992.

Wielenga, Bastiaan. "Liberation Theology in Asia." In *The Cambridge Companion to Liberation Theology,* edited by Christopher Rowland. Kindle. 2nd ed., 55–78. Cambridge; New York: Cambridge University Press, 2007.

Wiesel, Elie. *Night.* Translated by Stella Rodway. Toronto: Bantam Books, 1960.

Wigoder, Geoffrey. *Everyman's Judaica: An Encyclopedic Dictionary.* Jerusalem: Keter Publishing House, 1975.

Wilson, Boyd H. "Vinoba Bhave's Talks on the *Gita.*" In *Modern Indian Interpreters of the Bhagavadgita,* edited by Robert N. Minor, 110–30. Albany: State University of New York Press, 1986.

Wink, Walter. *Engaging the Powers: Discernment and Resistance in a World of Domination.* Minneapolis: Fortress Press, 1992.

———. "Jesus' Third Way: Nonviolent Engagement." In *Engaging the Powers: Discernment and Resistance in a World of Domination,* 175–93. Minneapolis: Fortress Press, 1992.

———. *Unmasking the Powers: The Invisible Forces That Determine Human Existence.* Philadelphia: Fortress Press, 1986.

Yang, Fenggang. *Religion in China: Survival and Revival under Communist Rule.* Kindle. Oxford; New York: Oxford University Press, 2012.

Yarrow, C. H. Mike. *Quaker Experiences in International Conciliation.* New Haven, CT: Yale University Press, 1978.

Yoder, John Howard. "The Career of the Just War Theory." In *Christian Attitudes to War, Peace, and Revolution,* edited by Ted Koontz and Andy Alexis-Baker. Grand Rapids, MI: Brazos Press, 2009.

———. *What Would You Do? A Serious Answer to a Standard Question.* Scottdale, PA: Herald Press, 1983.

Yogananda, Paramahansa. *Autobiography of a Yogi.* 12th ed. Los Angeles: Self-Realization Fellowship, 1993.

Zaehner, R. C. *Hinduism.* New York: Oxford University Press, 1966.

Zahn, Gordon Charles. *In Solitary Witness: The Life and Death of Franz Jägerstätter.* 3rd ed. Collegeville, MN: The Liturgical Press, 1964.

Zunes, Stephen, Lester R. Kurtz, and Sarah Beth Asher, eds. *Nonviolent Social Movements: A Geographical Perspective.* Malden, MA: Blackwell, 1999.

Index

Note: Page numbers followed by *f* indicate figures. Those followed by *t* indicate tables.